Guido Reni

Guido Reni

EDITED BY

David García Cueto

WITH TEXTS BY

Daniele Benati

Aoife Brady

Viviana Farina

David García Cueto

Rachel McGarry

Raffaella Morselli

Lorenzo Pericolo

Stefano Pierguidi

Javier Portús

Madrid, Museo Nacional del Prado, 2023

This catalogue was published on the occasion of the exhibition
Guido Reni, held at the Museo Nacional del Prado
from 28 March to 9 July 2023

Museo del Prado – Fundación BBVA

Organised by

MUSEO NACIONAL
DEL **PRADO**

With the collaboration of

STÄDEL
MUSEUM

With the exclusive sponsorship of

This exhibition was made possible through the generous loan of works by the following lenders:

Ascoli Piceno, Comune di Ascoli Piceno. Musei Civici
Bologna, Fondazione Bentivoglio
Bologna, Pinacoteca Nazionale di Bologna
Cambridge, The Fitzwilliam Museum
Chicago, The Art Institute of Chicago
Detroit, Detroit Institute of Arts
Dresden, Staatliche Kunstsammlungen, Gemäldegalerie Alte Meister
Dublin, National Gallery of Ireland
Edinburgh, National Galleries of Scotland
Florence, Biblioteca Nazionale Centrale
Florence, Fondazione di Studi di Storia dell'Arte Roberto Longhi
Florence, Gallerie degli Uffizi
Frankfurt, Städel Museum
Genoa, Gallerie Nazionali di Palazzo Spinola
Houston, The Museum of Fine Arts
London, Dulwich Picture Gallery
London, The National Gallery
London, The Royal Collection, Lent by His Majesty King Charles III
Madrid, Biblioteca Nacional de España
Madrid, Fundación Casa de Alba. Palacio de Liria
Madrid, Museo Arqueológico Nacional
Madrid, Museo de la Real Academia de Bellas Artes de San Fernando
Milan-Pesaro, Galleria Altomani & Sons
Modena, Gallerie Estensi
Naples, Museo e Real Bosco di Capodimonte
New York, The Metropolitan Museum of Art
New York, private collection
Orléans, Musée des Beaux-Arts
Osuna, Patronato de Arte de Osuna / Archidiócesis de Sevilla
Oxford, The Ashmolean Museum
Paris, Cathédrale Notre-Dame
Paris, Musée du Louvre
Patrimonio Nacional. Colecciones Reales
Pesaro, Palazzo Mosca. Musei Civici
Remagen, Arp Museum Bahnhof Rolandseck / Sammlung Rau für UNICEF
Rome, Galleria Colonna
Rome, Gallerie Nazionali d'Arte Antica di Roma
Rome, Musei Capitolini, Pinacoteca Capitolina
Salamanca, Madres Agustinas Recoletas. Convento de la Purísima
Sens, Musées de Sens
Siena, Arcidiocesi di Siena–Colle di Val d'Elsa–Montalcino
Toledo, Madres Clarisas Capuchinas. Federación Inmaculada Concepción. Convento de la Purísima
Toulouse, Musée des Augustins
Vaduz-Vienna, The Princely Collections of Liechtenstein
Valladolid, Museo Nacional de Escultura

As well as all those who have preferred to remain anonymous.

The Museo Nacional del Prado and the curator of the exhibition would like to express their gratitude to the following people, who have contributed significantly to the development of this exhibition and its catalogue:

Cristina Acidini, Marion Ackermann, Annamaria Ambrosini Massari, Alessandro Angelini, Andrea Bacchi, Martina Bagnoli, Francesca Banini, Sylvain Bellenger, Luca Bellingeri, Susanne Blöcker, Caroline Campbell, sor María José Cano Marín, Francesca Cappelletti, Andrés Carretero Pérez, Laurence des Cars, Stéphane Castelluccio, Patrizia Cavazzini, Dorothée Censier, Patrick Chauvet, Andrea Ciaroni, Stefano Cracolici, Katie Crawford Luber, Elizabeth Cropper, Ana de la Cueva, Teodora Danisi, Antonio Ernesto Denunzio, Anastasia Diaz della Vittoria Pallavicini, Marie-Hélène Didier, Laura Donati, Lily Dorment, Corentin Dury, Gabriele Finaldi, Carlos Fitz-James Stuart y Martínez de Irujo, sor Paz de la Fuente, Kate Ganz, Flaminia Gennari Santori, Véronique Gérard-Powell, Tomás Jesús Gil Rodrigo, Silvia Ginzburg, P. Enrico Grassini, Clément Guenebeaud, Alessandra Guerrini, Juliette Guez, Sante Guido, Axel Hémery, Max Hollein, Frédéric Jiméno, Marla J. Kinney, Tim Knox, Stephen Koja, Johann Kräftner, Francesco and Patrizia Lefebvre D'Ovidio, John Leighton, Madres Agustinas de la Purísima (Salamanca), Madres Capuchinas de San Miguel Arcángel (Puerto de Santa María), Tomás Marco Aragón, Gianni Luca Marco Galdenzi, P. Antonio Matilla Matilla, Carla Mazzarelli, Ilaria Miarelli Mariani, Isabel Morán García, Alejandro Nuevo Gómez, Maria Luisa Pacelli, Stefano Papetti, Federica Papi, Marialuisa Pappalardo, Claudio Parisi Presicce, Tommaso Pasquali, Patrizia Piergiovanni, Laura Ponticelli, Giuseppe Porzio, Nicolas Potier, Antoine-Marie Préaut, Yuri Primarosa, David Pullins, Sean Rainbird, Patricio Rodríguez-Buzón Calle, Roland Römer, Álvaro Romero Sánchez-Arjona, James Rondeau, Leticia Ruiz Gómez, Thomas Salomon, Salvador Salort-Pons, Ana Santos Aramburo, Eike Schmidt, Jennifer Scott, Petra Spielmann, Alexander Sturgis, María José Subiela, Luke Syson, Gary Tinterow, Letizia Treves, José Antonio de Urbina, Lucía Varela, Florent and Nikita de Vernejoul, Antonio Vignali, Daniele Vimini, Olivia Voisin, Clovis Whitfield, Francesca Whitlum-Cooper, Erica Witschey, Stephan Wolohojian, and Gianluca Zanelli.

Spanish Ministry of Culture and Sport

Museo Nacional del Prado

Miquel Iceta i Llorens
Spanish Minister of Culture and Sport

Taking a look at Guido Reni is tantamount to surveying the history of Spain in the sixteenth and seventeenth centuries. The exhibition the Museo Nacional del Prado has dedicated to one of the most highly acclaimed artists in Europe in his day, whose fame was comparable to that of figures such as Rubens, provides an insight into the continent's main courts, including that of Madrid, where his art was especially appreciated.

Examining Guido inevitably entails visiting, through his oeuvre, his place of origin, the cultured and prosperous Bologna. The city is home to the Alma Mater Studiorum, the oldest university in Europe, where the Spanish enjoyed a significant presence from the medieval period onwards, particularly following the founding of the Reale Collegio di Spagna in 1364. Evoking Bologna therefore involves speaking of Spanish life in the past, but also in the present, as these links have continued over time.

Thanks to the collecting of his paintings, Reni's reputation reached Golden Age Spain, where he became an important example for key Spanish artists such as Murillo. His prestige remained intact during the eighteenth century, but Romanticism unfairly brought him into disrepute on account of the academic nature of his art. Starting in the 1950s, however, a series of initiatives have restored him to well-deserved recognition.

This show, which has as its title the painter's name, is the latest of the exhibitions the Prado has been devoting to great Italian painters for more than twenty years. Together with the accompanying catalogue, it marks a new milestone in these initiatives, which have earned it such great scientific credit. The first monographic exhibition to be held on the great Bolognese painter in Spain, it offers visitors the chance to enjoy nearly a hundred outstanding artworks, mostly by Reni but also by other artists of his time, displayed together and in dialogue. Some of them have been restored specially for the occasion by the staff of the Prado and other institutions to enhance viewers' enjoyment.

I would like to congratulate the Museo Nacional del Prado on this extraordinary initiative, which helps strengthen its reputation as a leading international centre of Renaissance and Baroque Art, and to thank all the lenders who have made this show possible.

Javier Solana Madariaga

President, Museo Nacional del Prado Royal Board of Trustees

In these troubled times in which Europe is affected by an unjust war, recalling what has forged our common identity – largely underpinned by a shared culture – over the centuries is not only a source of intellectual and aesthetic delight but also a true invitation to peace. For several decades now, the Museo Nacional del Prado has been staging major exhibitions on some of the most important European artists whose work is represented in its rich collections, sometimes outstandingly. One such figure is the seventeenth-century Bolognese painter Guido Reni. As well as a sublime master – it is no coincidence that he was dubbed 'the divine' in his own century – he was, perhaps inadvertently, one of the figures who shaped the European identity both of that period and of the following centuries. Fascination for his art was not limited to the Italy of his time but extended to many other parts of the continent, even including some, such as England, that did not practise the Catholic faith and therefore had a somewhat different relationship with painting. Indeed, Reni's name is synonymous with one of the greatest contributions made by western art to the history of civilisation.

Despite the unquestionable importance of this artist, no retrospective had previously been devoted to him in Spain, though he was represented in the anthological exhibition on Italian art of his time entitled *Seventeenth-Century Italian Painting*, held at the Casón del Buen Retiro in 1970. Over these past two years, marked by challenging international circumstances, the Prado has intensified its efforts to bring to fruition this major project. An initiative of the Museum's director, Miguel Falomir, and deputy director for Conservation and Research, Andrés Úbeda de los Cobos, it is curated by David García Cueto, head of the department of Italian and French Painting up to 1800. The exhibition, restoration, publishing, and communication departments at the Prado have likewise done a commendable job in making the show and this catalogue possible. I would like to thank them all, as well as the national and international, public and private lenders who have generously allowed their works to be displayed in our Museum for a few months. A very special acknowledgement is due to Fundación BBVA, the exhibition's sponsor, with which we have enjoyed an enormously fruitful relationship for many years. With this initiative, the Prado has achieved its aim of raising awareness, through scientific dialogue and exchange, of the universally significant legacy in its care.

Carlos Torres Vila
President, Fundación BBVA

It is now two decades since Fundación BBVA became a benefactor member of the Museo Nacional del Prado with the aim of helping make possible major exhibitions and unique displays in this marvellous art museum. This year, 2023, we are delighted to have joined in the effort to bring people *Guido Reni*, the first large-scale show in Spain to survey this decisive Italian Baroque painter, his interactions with other artists of his time and his lingering influence on the visual arts.

In his early years Reni followed the tradition of the Bolognese school, influenced by artists such as Ludovico Carracci. His early works are characterised by the rigidity of his figures, but he gradually evolved towards freer, more naturalistic depictions. In the 1620s Reni joined the circle of Caravaggist artists, leading to a significant change in his paintings. From then onwards they were notable for their sharp contrasts of light and shade and the use of a darker palette.

Despite these influences, Reni remained faithful to his own unmistakable style. His work is characterised by technical perfection in the representation of the human body, the elegance and delicacy of his figures, and attention to detail in objects and landscapes, as well as by a pursuit of beauty that can be seen in his depictions of anatomies, his precision in the rendering of proportions and his desire to lend an overall harmony to the composition. This huge interest in, and attention to, the human figure allows him to be defined as a humanist in the broadest sense with a profound respect for facial features and their ability to express emotions and feelings.

In addition, his interest in classical culture and literature points to an extensive knowledge of the humanities and an awareness of the importance of education and knowledge. Reni was a keen reader of classical literature and philosophical texts, and this concern with ancient culture is reflected in many of his works, which are full of mythological and literary references.

Guido Reni was one of the most important Italian Baroque painters and his influence continued during the following centuries. The thorough work of David García Cueto, curator of the exhibition and head of the department of Italian and French Painting up to 1800 at the Museo Nacional del Prado, will enable visitors to appreciate all these subtleties, thanks also to the generosity of such important international lenders as the Musée du Louvre in Paris, the Metropolitan Museum of Art in New York, the National Gallery in London, the Pinacoteca Nazionale di Bologna and the Galleria Borghese in Rome.

We are grateful to the Museo Nacional del Prado and its director, Miguel Falomir, for giving shape to this extraordinary exhibition and making it available to the public.

Miguel Falomir Faus

Director, Museo Nacional del Prado

Anyone browsing through an art history reference book will inevitably come to a few pages on Guido Reni. They usually appear after those devoted to Annibale Carracci, his principal master, and close to those on Caravaggio, of whom he is often presented as the antithesis. The fact is that such was the genius of Guido, acclaimed in his own lifetime as 'the divine' – an adjective with deep implications that are both theological (for obvious reasons) and artistic (Vasari had judged Michelangelo, with his creative powers, to be the first artist capable of rivalling God and accordingly deserving of the adjective divine) – that he needs no endorsement to be hailed as one of the great painters in western art.

The huge fame and prestige Reni enjoyed when alive were associated with aesthetic and religious ideals that might seem remote to us today. This is true of any creator of the past, but great artists are precisely those who are capable of transcending their immediate circumstances in order to engage with viewers from any period. And our own time is – or at least so we would like to think – propitious for a re-reading of Guido's genius. The centrality of the human body in his oeuvre, and the aspiration to a beauty that combines the carnal and spiritual dimensions in equal measure, are yearnings that might be shared by any of our contemporaries. Our exhibition is aimed at them.

This show has been made possible by a close partnership with the Städel Museum in Frankfurt, where a version held months ago enjoyed great success. Our exhibition is very different from that hosted by the German museum because our respective collections of Reni are very different and so was the artist's reception in the two countries. Guido was highly appreciated by Spanish collectors, starting with Philip IV, and the mark he left on Spanish painting of the 1600s is visible everywhere; indeed, these are some of the novel subplots explored by the Madrid show. The person in charge of giving shape to these ideas was David García Cueto, curator of Italian and French painting up to 1800 at the Museo Nacional del Prado and a specialist in Bolognese painting, whom I would like to congratulate on this exhibition, his first at the Prado; I extend these congratulations to everyone at the Museum who has contributed to bringing the project to fruition.

This ambitious show features nearly a hundred works from a great many museums, institutions, and public and private collections in Europe and America. I wish to express my appreciation and thanks to all the lenders for their generosity and once again reiterate our most heartfelt gratitude to Fundación BBVA, without which an undertaking of this scale would be a chimera. Enjoy it.

CONTENTS

GUIDO RENI, A BOLOGNESE GENIUS FOR GOLDEN AGE SPAIN

David García Cueto

The epithet 'divine' denotes an exceptional status reserved for very few artists throughout the history of art. It was applied to Apelles for amazing his Greek contemporaries and subsequent generations with his lifelike creations; to Raphael (1483–1520) in the Renaissance for achieving supreme grace, charm, and sweetness in his paintings; and to the Bolognese Guido Reni (1575–1642) in the Baroque for being considered a genius capable of attaining an otherworldly beauty with his art [fig. 1].[1] Of the three, the disappearance of Apelles' entire oeuvre has relegated him to the role of a silent and learned historical reference, whereas Raphael's fame and prestige have remained intact to the present day. Reni, one of the most celebrated and admired European artists in his own time, enjoyed a long period of significant posthumous recognition. This fame began to wane at the dawn of the Romantic period, and he subsequently fell into almost complete disrepute until well into the twentieth century, along with the whole Bolognese school of his time. It was not until a bold exhibition devoted to him in his city of birth in 1954[2] that contemporary appreciation of Guido began to pick up again and was given decisive impetus by the successive shows held in the 1980s in Bologna, Los Angeles, Fort Worth, and Frankfurt.[3] Nevertheless, whether glorified as a sublime creator or criticised for his marked academicism, Reni has been powerfully present in the collective imaginary of the West since his own lifetime to the present day. For as Cesare Gnudi – one of the promoters of the abovementioned exhibition of 1954 – stated, 'every century has chosen its Reni. He has spoken in a different way in the Baroque 1600s, in the Arcadian 1700s, in Neoclassicism and in Romanticism. Each one has sought in his oeuvre a reaction to its own sentiment, a reflection of its own taste'.[4] As it is evident from recent art market trends and academic studies that he is being newly appreciated by collectors and scholars, it seems fitting to now examine, in accordance with Gnudi's words, what Reni means to our day. The exhibition at the Museo Nacional del Prado which this catalogue accompanies sets out to help answer that question.

Far from capricious, Reni's designation as a 'divine' artist reflected the extremely high esteem in which he was held by many of his contemporaries. The opinions of other great artists who had the chance to see his works for themselves are particularly significant in this connection, such as the Cavalier d'Arpino (1568–1640), his mentor during his first stay in Rome. Arpino referred to the frescoes executed by Reni in the Cappella Paolina of the basilica of Santa Maria Maggiore in Rome as made 'by an angel'.[5] Years later, after Guido's death, a *Penitent Magdalen* by his hand made an impression on Gian Lorenzo Bernini (1598–1680) no less, another of the foremost artists of the century, when he saw it in Paris in 1665: he is reported as calling this and the other pieces painted by Guido 'pictures of paradise'.[6] With their remarks, both artists acknowledged not only the outstanding beauty and masterful execution of Reni's works but above all their ability to engage with what according to Christian postulates constitutes the transcendental dimension.

The biographers of seventeenth-century Italian artists also refer to this 'otherworldly' nature of Reni's works, beginning with the main one, his fellow Bolognese Carlo Cesare Malvasia. Malvasia stated in his *Felsina pittrice* (1678) that Guido, like a 'generous eagle … took sublime flight to the spheres', from which he obtained his celestial ideas, bringing back to earth a 'heavenly craft'. As a result, according to Malvasia, the artist became 'father and promoter of the modern manner [and] made the entire world fall in love with it, art lovers desire it, and artists prosper from it.'[7] By acknowledging his 'fatherhood', Malvasia thus established Reni's leading role in the development of the arts in the city of Bologna. The death of Ludovico Carracci (1555–1619) had marked the end of what the theoretician called the 'third age of painting', ushering in a new stage: the 'fourth age', that of the new *maniera moderna*. The protagonists of this phase would be Ludovico's four main pupils: Domenichino (1581–1641), Guercino (1591–1666), Francesco Albani (1578–1660), and Reni, a generation responsible for attaining absolute perfection in painting, though Guido was the most outstanding of the four as he succeeded in taking this art beyond perfection.[8]

Undoubtedly less concerned than Malvasia with extolling Bologna's artistic glory, other biographers of Italian Seicento painters nonetheless praised Reni's qualities in a similar way, including Francesco Scannelli, who considered him to be blessed with *facilità* (effortlessness) and *gratia* (grace).[9] In Giovan Pietro Bellori's opinion, Guido possessed a mind uplifted to beauty and a heavenly idea.[10] For his part, Luigi Scaramuccia proclaimed that with his art Guido had marvelled nature itself, noting that some of the heads he painted were comparable to those of Raphael, which led the writer Claudio Achillini to praise him as the Apelles of his time.[11]

Yet Reni never acknowledged the 'divineness' of his painting to be an innate gift; rather, as Malvasia points out in a passage of his biography, he considered it to be solely the result of hard work and huge effort.[12] On his journey along that formative path and personal development towards the 'divine' Guido had, of course, had various guiding influences. The fact that his father Daniele was a musician by profession would necessarily have familiarised him with this art, even though he did not carve out a future in this field.[13] He began studying painting at a very early age in the workshop of the Bologna-based Flemish artist Denys Calvaert (c. 1540–1619). The elderly painter not only taught him the art itself but most likely also instilled in him much of his keen business sense, exemplified by his production of small devotional paintings on copper that enjoyed great success in the European market of the time.[14] Subsequently, beginning in around 1593–94, the Carracci's academy provided him with a demanding professional model based on a balance between pathos and classicism, achieved through perfect technical execution. A mastery of draughtsmanship and studying from life proved essential to learning those lessons, and he also practised

sculptural modelling – an experience that would help him establish the concepts of volume and chiaroscuro that were so useful in the training of a figurative painter.[15]

Throughout this process his admiration for Raphael and Correggio (c. 1489–1534), as well as for Francesco Francia (c. 1447–1517) and Paolo Veronese (1528–1588) – to whom he referred as 'his Paolino' – never waned. According to Malvasia, Reni 'used to say that whoever was able to combine the knowledge and exactness [*giustezza*] of Raphael, the liveliness and color of Correggio and the judiciousness and majesty of Veronese would surpass every other master, just as the Carracci had outshone all other painters by consistently applying this mixture'.[16] Guido rounded off his training in 1601 with a trip to Rome, whose art scene was then the most important in the western world. There he discovered the huge legacy of antiquity and was fascinated by the freest and most modern of the artists then living in the city, Caravaggio (1571–1610). Despite the fact that Caravaggio's suggestive influence marked a milestone in Reni's evolution, the effect he had on his art was limited to a very specific series of explorations.[17] Guido found Caravaggio's art to be 'too natural',[18] though he owned one of his paintings in his private collection and devoted part of his efforts to surpassing the force of Caravaggio's creations using a completely different language.[19] Reni's presence made such an impact on the Roman cultural scene that an art connoisseur even reformulated a commonly accepted paradigm. In a letter to the painter Pietro Marone (1548–1625) dated around 1595–1603, the learned Ottavio Rossi had spoken of the artistic triumvirate who prevailed in Rome in the early 1600s, namely Caravaggio, Annibale Carracci (1560–1609), and the Cavalier d'Arpino.[20] A few years later the nobleman and collector Vincenzo Giustiniani revised that metaphorical analysis and granted Arpino's place to Guido in his treatise on painting, *Discorso sopra la pittura* (c. 1620–30).[21] The beauty and novelty of the works he produced in the papal capital earned him this consideration.

With all these experiences under his belt, Guido shaped his own identity; in doing so he challenged his masters' precepts by asserting his conviction that studying from life should not be a goal but a starting point. He likewise took up Raphael's classical models and added a more firmly Christian devotional component in tune with Counter-Reformation ideas, establishing one of the ideological and stylistic keys of his art.[22] Malvasia even argued that Guido, having fully forged his identity, surpassed even the Carracci in 'nobility and celestial ideas'.[23]

Reni's evolution as an artist also involved adopting an intelligent approach to his large workshop and very many disciples; on

Fig. 1 Simone Cantarini, *Portrait of Guido Reni*, c. 1636. Oil on canvas, 37.5 cm diameter. Bologna, Pinacoteca Nazionale di Bologna, inv. 340

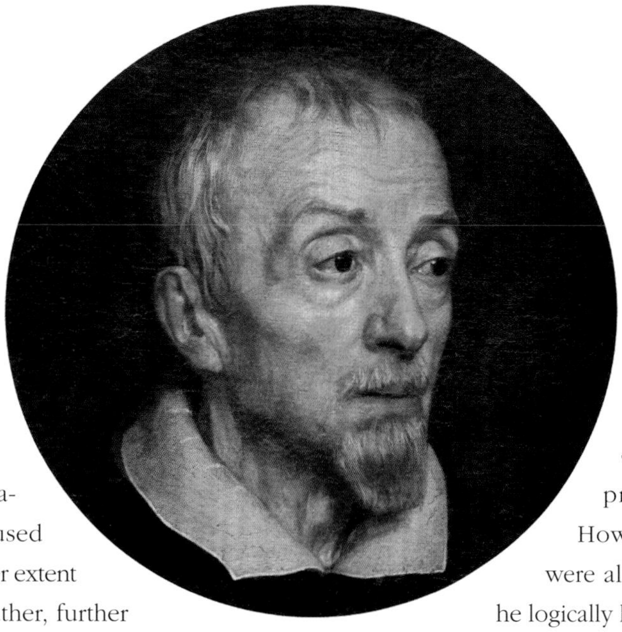

returning from Rome to Bologna permanently in 1613–14, he organised what would later become his 'scuola'.[24] This space, where he managed a huge group of assistants and apprentices, was designed as a complex machinery for artistic production focused primarily on creation, though to a lesser extent it was also a place of learning or, rather, further training. But Guido's art was so personal that it was not fully teachable, and many disciples therefore admired and imitated him but few truly assimilated his spirit.[25]

Another salient feature of his career entailed setting what were particularly high prices for the market in his time; far from being a hindrance, this further increased his fame. In a letter of 8 April 1628 to an unknown addressee, Guido stated that he had two types of prices:

> One as an ordinary painter, another as a painter who is a little special. The first is 15 scudi per life-sized figure …, when dealing, however, with paintings that can be gifted to great gentlemen, the second selling price can then be applied, depending on the occasion.[26]

A characteristic feature of Reni's art was the repetition, often many years apart, of certain prototypes of sacred, historical, or mythological figures, generally in formats close to half-length (Saint Sebastian, Saint Joseph, Mary Magdalene, Cleopatra, Lucretia…).[27] In his repetitions he sometimes modified the modelling of the anatomies by means of a new sense of materiality.[28] These autograph repetitions met the market demand and also helped Guido disseminate the image of some of his most celebrated creations. Some were largely studio products, to which he put the finishing touches (*ritocchi*) in a few cases. Reni's workshop also produced what could be called copies strictly speaking: that is, replicas of the master's creations in which he had no involvement. Copies could be made by members of the studio with a reputation of their own, such as Giovanni Andrea Sirani (1610–1670), or other members of the workshop who

specialised in copying, such as Ercole de Maria († 1640). What might be classed as 'authorised' copies naturally commanded different market prices depending on how prestigiously they were executed. However, copies of Guido's paintings were also made outside his workshop, and he logically had no control over them.[29] When he passed away in 1642, despite his huge number of assistants, he took the most genuine essence of his art with him to the grave. His paintings nevertheless remained and continued to fuel the thriving market for copies, which Guido himself had encouraged when alive. His creations were also widely disseminated through prints.[30]

Reni's fame was by no means limited to Italy in his own day; indeed, thanks to the interest his works aroused in foreigners visiting or based in Rome, Bologna, and Milan, among other cities, his reputation spread to various parts of Europe. The protection he enjoyed from several prelates and aristocrats, especially the Barberini family – relatives of Urban VIII, who was pope from 1623 to 1644, throughout much of Reni's life – fostered the international dissemination of his art and made it possible for him to receive significant commissions for the courts of Madrid, Paris, and London. Guido thus became a European phenomenon and, as we have seen, his fame grew until the end of the eighteenth century.

In fact, it was at the dawn of the Neoclassical period that his celebrity reached its peak thanks to the referential role assigned to him by the painter and theoretician Anton Raphael Mengs (1728–1779) in his writings and artistic practice. But the advent of the nineteenth century and the rise of Romanticism saw the appreciation of the artist wane rapidly owing to the delicacy and precision of his technique – qualities considered to hamper creativity – causing his works to be perceived in this new context merely as dispassionate exercises in painting.[31] Attempting to classify the schools of painting in 1845, John Ruskin devised four levels of perfection, assigning Reni to the fourth and last, which he called 'the school of errors and vices'.[32]

Fig. 2 J. Laurent y Cia, works by Guido Reni in the Museo del Prado's central gallery, in *Panoramic View of the Central Gallery of the Museo del Prado (Graphoscope)*, 1882–83. Albumen print on paper, 300 × 10415 mm. Madrid, Museo Nacional del Prado, HF-1

But even in that period an especially renowned intellectual, Jacob Burckhardt, judged Reni positively in the annotations he made in 1847 to Franz Kugler's handbook on the history of painting, *Handbuch der Geschichte der Malerei* (1837).[33] Despite Burckhardt's favourable opinion, the prevailing negative ideas made a deep impact throughout much of Europe, as illustrated, for example, by the testimony of the Catalan engraver Camilo Alabern (1825–1876), who stated in 1859 that 'Guido Reni truly began the feminisation of art'.[34] These judgements were not simply unfavourable opinions of the Bolognese artists but even led to significant changes in the layout [fig. 2] of some of the continent's leading cultural institutions, such as the Louvre. In 1875 the critic Augustin de Buisseret complained about the huge presence of Baroque Bolognese painters in the Parisian museum's Grande Galerie, referring to them as a 'detestable school infected with academic eclecticism'.[35] The institution's response to the discredit brought upon the Bolognese artists was to send them away: a policy of long-term loans to other institutions put into practice between 1872 and 1896 resulted in a drastic reduction in the number of works by painters of this school in its

galleries. The Bolognese painters disappeared from the Grande Galerie for good that same year, 1896, to make room for the important legacy of the painter Gustave Caillebotte (1848–1894), marking something of an end to the Bolognese influence on European art.[36]

In a sense the revival of the legacy of those Bolognese artists began some forty years later when the Italian art historian Roberto Longhi called for a critical reassessment of Bolognese painting in a famous article written in 1935.[37] Referring to Reni in his text, Longhi stressed 'the desire, very keen in his case, for a classical beauty but embodying a Christian soul', summing up with this sentence some of the key qualities on which the artist's seventeenth-century fame had been based.[38] Longhi was not alone in this affirmation: in the German-speaking world Otto Kurz shared the same desire to rescue the artist and proposed laying new foundations for the appreciation of Reni's art in an article written shortly afterwards, in 1937.[39]

Longhi's words, culturally and geographically closer to the Bolognese environment than those of Kurz, did have an evident effect, though it was not immediate: the abovementioned Reni

David García Cueto

exhibition in his native Bologna in 1954, which was part of a series of similar initiatives designed to save Bolognese Baroque art from critical condemnation.[40] The most prestigious art journal of the day, the British *Burlington Magazine*, mentioned it in its editorial of October 1954, where the chief editor, Benedict Nicolson, focused on the exhibition's rediscovery of the 'most unpopular of painters'.[41] The reasoning used in the exhibition catalogue shows how arbitrary the arguments used to criticise the Bolognese artists were.

The effects of that revival movement also extended to Spain, though they were more lukewarm and later occurring. The initial situation was comparable to that of Europe with respect to the negative prejudice against the painter, as attested by the annotation made by the eminent historian Elías Tormo on Reni's *Saint Sebastian* [cat. 19] in a copy of the Museo del Prado's 1900 catalogue following the visit of the leading specialist of the time in Italian painting, Bernard Berenson: 'it is a disagreeable painting, but very good in its kind'.[42] From a similarly negative perspective albeit aware of the historiographical advances being made in Italy, Alfonso E. Pérez Sánchez carried out a brilliant reassessment of Reni's works housed in Spain in his thesis of 1965, setting them in the context of the literary sources and inventories of the Crown and the aristocracy.[43] At the time Pérez Sánchez's sensibility seems to have been shared by Juan Antonio Gaya Nuño, who stated of *Hippomenes and Atalanta* [cat. 61], Reni's key work in the Prado collections on long-term loan in Granada: 'it is such a beautiful work so worthy of hanging in any select museum that it is inconceivable how men a century ago could have banished it to exile'.[44] Those efforts were reflected in the major exhibition on seventeenth-century Italian painting curated by Pérez Sánchez in 1970 to commemorate the 150th anniversary of the founding of the Prado, in which Reni enjoyed great prominence [fig. 3].[45]

Nevertheless, as the move to restore Reni's fame as an artist progressed, it was hampered to an extent by a circumstance shared by other great figures in art history: the existence of certain personality traits that are perceived from a modern-day perspective as somewhat controversial. Guido was a successful artist and a reserved person who was melancholic by nature and loathed public praise according to the testimony of Malvasia, to whom we owe the most detailed psychological description of the master.[46] He was fastidious about personal cleanliness, dressed elegantly in silk in the summer and in Spanish cloth in the winter, and kept his home decent, even though he lived without the service of women for fear of poisoning and witchcraft.[47] He was a very pious man, devoted in particular to the

Fig. 3 View of one of the rooms of the Casón del Buen Retiro during the exhibition *Seventeenth-Century Italian Painting* held in 1970

Virgin, and the first thing he instilled in his pupils was fear of God. 'He was commonly held to be a virgin … always appearing like marble in the presence and contemplation of the many beautiful girls who served him as models'.[48]

This characterisation of Guido's human qualities was subjected to a thorough psychoanalytic session in a book by Richard E. Spear published in 1997, which had certain repercussions.[49] Taking as a basis Malvasia's description and other contemporary testimonies, the author analysed Reni's oeuvre in the light of his supposed homosexuality, his relative misogyny, his tendency towards resentment, and also his confirmed addiction to gambling. When viewed from a more modern approach that takes into account the many sources of information not only on Guido but also on his period, these partial or prejudiced assessments of him fail to hold up in a more demanding theoretical framework. Indeed, Spear's ideas were challenged by Stephen Pepper, another major Reni specialist and the author of his first catalogue raisonné. According to Pepper, Spear's approach was inappropriate to understanding Guido's art as it 'acritically' took as a point of departure certain personal viewpoints on art and religion that hindered his appreciation of Guido's accomplishments as an artist. In the author's opinion, what was essential about these achievements was the artist's ability to combine divine and human components before the eyes of the beholders of his paintings, allowing them to appreciate at first sight the elements taken from reality in order to be transported from there to an experience of the celestial realm.[50]

Of all of Reni's purported 'pathological' traits, the one that most greatly influenced his work from an objective viewpoint was his addiction to gambling. It accentuated the unfinished (*non finito*) style of loose forms characteristic of his final period due to the haste with which he executed them, spurred by the desire for prompt payment of the proceeds from their sale.[51] This dependence was well known to his contemporaries and was even made fun of, as illustrated by a passage from Pietro Testa's *Trattato della pittura ideale* (1639–50), where the Graces jocularly comfort Guido on losing card games.[52] This last stage in his life sometimes led him to be misunderstood by his admirers and even by his friends.[53] Guido's addiction may have caused him particular torment during his final years, as apart from the dependence and lavish spending it entailed, gambling was especially frowned upon by certain Christian authorities of the period based on the actions of Jesus' executors when they threw dice for his clothes.[54]

In contrast to this shadier side of Reni's personality – albeit equally full of creative potential – a considerable number of aspects of his artistic practice were quite novel for the time, and appear more significant when viewed from a greater historical perspective.[55] One was Reni's use of silk as a support for paintings. Taking advantage of the fact that Bologna was an important centre for the production of this luxurious textile, he broadened the range of uses of silk, which had been employed since early times in battle flags but was unusual in easel paintings. The famous *Pallione del Voto* [fig. 30] – devised as a processional standard – and the *Assumption of the Virgin* in Munich's Alte Pinakothek[56] are both painted on silk, showing that Guido employed this material for some of his most important commissions.[57]

. . . . . .

From the time Guido achieved early recognition, various originals by his hand together with a considerable number of copies of his creations began to find their way into Spain, where they became valuable points of reference on the Baroque art scene.[58] Reni's relations with the Spain of his day took shape gradually, beginning in his youth. This circumstance was common to many inhabitants of the Italian peninsula during what was known as the period of *preponderanza spagnuola*, when the Spanish monarchy enjoyed a powerful political presence in Italy through the territories it ruled over directly and its networks of representation and influence in strategic enclaves such as Rome.[59] Indeed, Guido's own city, Bologna, had had a famous college for Spanish university students since the fourteenth century, and the particularities of this community would have helped the artist gain an idea about what the rest of their compatriots were like.

It is not yet known what marked the start of Reni's fame at the Spanish court, though a few works of his are documented as having arrived in Madrid during Philip III's reign [cat. 9 and 12]. It is quite likely that news of his brilliant art, of which the Crown and the courtly nobles would almost certainly have been aware, reached Madrid or Valladolid from Bologna and Rome in the early 1600s. Malvasia furthermore reports an unconfirmed episode of a certain quarrel Reni had in Bologna around 1613 with the cardinal legate. As a result the artist thought of fleeing to France or Spain, as 'already those monarchs had honored him with invitations to their courts'.[60] Guido felt appreciated by both nations and does not appear to have expressed a preference for either, as illustrated by another anecdote also reported by Malvasia: he was more inclined towards the one 'that would be the more useful, or at least less harmful' as a power dominant over Italy.[61]

During Philip IV's reign it was precisely the Crown that was the main collector of Reni's oeuvre in Spanish territory, as attested more widely by a certain preference for the Bolognese painter's creations among art lovers.[62] Philip IV's own taste was most likely conditioned by the lessons taught to him by his art master Juan Bautista Maíno (1581–1649) during his princely years from 1616 until his ascent to the throne in 1621. As the Aragonese painter Jusepe Martínez (1600–1682) recalls in his *Discursos practicables* (c. 1675), Maíno had been a pupil and friend of Annibale Carracci in Rome at the beginning of the century and a 'good companion to our great Guido Reni, who always followed his manner of painting'.[63]

Those years saw the arrival at the Spanish court of a Roman aristocrat, painter, and architect who would become an artistic advisor to the Crown: Giovanni Battista Crescenzi (1577–1635). A man of many talents, he began to serve Philip III in 1617, and his considerable experience included having known Guido in Rome.[64] It is therefore probable that Crescenzi contributed significantly to the painter's connection with Spain, as did the scholarly Cassiano dal Pozzo's express recognition of Reni's fame during his stay in Madrid as part of the retinue of Cardinal Francesco Barberini's papal legation in 1626. Cassiano's diary of his trip specifically notes the interest aroused in him by a *Virgin and Child with Saint Francis* that he had the chance to view in the Madrid residence of the Prince of Esquilache, Don Francisco de Borja y Aragón,[65] which must have been one of the first works by Reni to join the collections of the nobles of the court.

Possibly at the behest of Crescenzi, Reni was contacted from Madrid in 1627 through the Spanish ambassador in Rome, Íñigo

Fig. 4 Guido Reni, *Virgin and Child*, c. 1628–30. Oil on canvas, 114.3 × 91.4 cm. Raleigh, North Carolina Museum of Art, Gift of Mr and Mrs Robert Lee Humber in memory of their daughter, Eileen Genevieve, G.55.12.1

Vélez de Guevara, 5th Count of Oñate, to paint a large picture to decorate the most representative room in Philip IV's main residence, the Salón Nuevo or New Hall in the Alcázar in Madrid.[66] The painting in question was the celebrated *Abduction of Helen* [fig. 35], which never arrived in Spain owing to various disagreements between the painter and the Spanish king's representatives in Rome.[67] Despite this falling-out, Guido's fame had already spread among the courtly connoisseurs of painting, as attested by the fact that the two works by Domenichino that hung in the Hall of Mirrors were misattributed, as if by a stroke of poetic vengeance, to 'Guido Bolones' in the 1636 inventory of the room.[68]

Despite the failure to reach an understanding over the *Abduction of Helen*, another of Reni's commissions for the Spanish court did come to fruition: an *Immaculate Conception* for Philip IV's sister the Infanta Maria Ana, future

empress [cat. 55]. In addition, on an unspecified date during the regency of Philip's wife Elisabeth of France, queen consort of Spain from 1621 to 1644, the queen had her private oratory in the Alcázar in Madrid decorated with a *Virgin* which her husband had received as a gift.[69] It is currently not clear which painting this may have been, though the most plausible candidates are the *Virgin of the Chair* [cat. 52][70] or the *Virgin and Child* now in the North Carolina Museum of Art [fig. 4], both of which would have passed to the Royal Monastery of San Lorenzo de El Escorial after Philip IV's reign.

A work by Guido was also particularly highly regarded at a new royal site built to glorify the Spanish monarchy's territorial and military power: the Buen Retiro palace, a project in which Crescenzi played an essential role. The painting, a *Lucretia*, was mentioned in the laudatory poem Manoel de Galhegos addressed to the new palace in 1637 – a distinction similar to one granted earlier to a portrait, currently unlocated, of Don Pedro Girón, Duke of Osuna, painted by the Bolognese master and praised poetically by Francisco de Quevedo.[71]

Reni's progressive rise to fame at the Spanish court was also due to the presence in Madrid from 1636 of a distinguished compatriot of his, Marquis Virgilio Malvezzi (1595–1654), who was engaged by the Count-Duke of Olivares to write the history of the monarchy from the end of Philip III's reign. Malvezzi had already been in close contact with Guido: he had entrusted him with designing several title pages for his books and had written a letter praising the *Abduction of Helen*, which was included in *Il trionfo del pennello*, a compilation of poems published in 1633 [cat. 50].[72] His high opinion of the Bolognese artist is equally evident from some of his writings and gives an idea of how he would have spoken of Reni in the courtly circles of Madrid, which he frequented until his appointment as special ambassador to London in the spring of 1640. From there Malvezzi travelled to Flanders and returned to Spain in 1643 after learning of his mentor Olivares's fall from grace. Two years later he was granted leave to return to Bologna, from where he maintained correspondence with many Spaniards until his death. During those final years of his life he published a compilatory text on Philip IV's reign in which he alluded to the significant role played by Caravaggio with his 'strength in painting' and Guido with his 'nobility of air' in breathing new life into art.[73] He thus contributed to the concept of the two opposite approaches in Baroque pictorial language that was also advocated by Monsignor Giovanni Battista Agucchi, an idea that helped shape a negative reputation of the school of the Carracci from the Romantic period onwards.[74]

The attention paid to Reni by Italian artistic literature and even by Italian authors not strictly belonging to the art world – such as the briefly mentioned Malvezzi – contrasts with the relatively scarce references made to him by art theorists active in seventeenth-century Spain.[75] The abovementioned *Discursos practicables* by the Aragonese artist Jusepe Martínez, written around 1675 but not published until the nineteenth century, was the main exception to this norm and can be explained by this author's firsthand knowledge of Reni and the Italian art scene of the 1620s.[76] Martínez's accounts provided glowing descriptions of the painter, who is referred to as the 'celebrated' or 'illustrious Guido Reni'.[77] Vicente Carducho (c. 1576–1638), a painter and theoretician of Florentine origin who served the Crown, was tellingly silent about Guido in his treatise on painting, *Diálogos de la pintura* (1634), possibly because he was disdainful of his art.[78] For his part, Francisco Pacheco (1564–1644), the learned father-in-law of Diego Velázquez (1599–1660), named Reni only once in his own posthumous treatise, *El arte de la pintura* (1649), and even then only in connection with Jusepe de Ribera (1591–1652) to underline the latter's use of painting from life.[79]

Despite his discreet presence in Spanish art theory of his century, various events occurring after Guido's death in 1642 confirmed the express recognition of his impressive artistic legacy at the Madrid court and in other parts of the country. A significant example of the foregoing is the place granted to his works in the rehanging of the art collections in the most representative parts of the monastery area at El Escorial, an undertaking promoted by Philip IV's second *valido*, Luis Méndez de Haro y Guzmán, 6th Marquis of El Carpio, and carried out by Velázquez himself. This initiative, as the king's favourite acknowledged in 1654, was truly a matter of state, as El Escorial was very much a must-see for all distinguished foreigners who came to the court and needed to convey an image of magnificence that befitted the sovereign.[80] Velázquez began the revamp in 1656, increasing the number of works on view with an exquisite balance of sixteenth- and seventeenth-century paintings of the Italian, Flemish, and Spanish schools. Various pictures by Reni were used to decorate the royally founded building, and Father Francisco de los Santos gave a full account of them – sometimes with interesting critical appreciations – in the successive editions of his *Descripción* of the monastery (1657, 1667, 1681, and 1698).[81] In the prior's chapter room, the *Virgin of the Chair* [cat. 52] was displayed in an interesting dialogue with the *Immaculate Conception* by Peter Paul Rubens (1577–1640),[82] and between them were Guido's heads of *Saint Peter* and *Saint Paul* previously owned by the viceroy of Naples García de Haro Sotomayor y Guzmán, 2nd Count of Castrillo [cat. 33 and 34]. He decorated the sacristy with the abovementioned *Virgin and Child* now in North Carolina and the *Saint Joseph and the Child* that currently belongs to the Hermitage [fig. 5]. Both works attracted particular attention many years later from the 'intruder' king Joseph Bonaparte, who gifted them respectively to generals Horace Sebastiani and Jean-Joseph Dessolles.[83] A further testament to the fame enjoyed by all these Reni paintings during the years they hung in the royal monastery is the considerable number of copies made – no doubt with the blessing of the Hieronymite community – which are now scattered throughout Spain.

While El Escorial became the repository of those significant canvases by Reni, the number of original works by him in the Alcázar palace continued to increase. Guido's creations were commonly used as diplomatic gifts in the seventeenth century: a *Judith* was brought for Philip IV by Giulio Rospigliosi at the start of his term as nuncio in 1644 [fig. 92],[84] and in 1655 a *Cupid with a Bow* [cat. 64] was a present from another nuncio, Camillo Massimo, to the king, who placed it in his study in the ground-floor summer apartments, where it hung near *Girl with a Rose* [cat. 72], establishing a close dialogue with *Las Meninas* no less.[85] Despite such an intimate and prestigious location, the nuncio Massimo was under the impression that Reni and Guercino were 'not greatly esteemed' in the palace environment of the time.[86] Even so, the sovereign came to own further works by Guido during the following years through purchases, such as the most significant piece by the painter in the Museo del Prado: *Hippomenes and Atalanta* [cat. 61], acquired for Philip IV in 1664 from the Marquis Serra's heirs through the Count of Peñaranda, then viceroy of Naples. The *Risen Christ carrying the Cross* in the Real Academia de Bellas Artes de San Fernando, now considered a copy, was obtained in the same way.[87] In the last year of his life the king added a new picture to his collection of canvases by the Bolognese master through the bequest from Niccolò Ludovisi, Prince of Piombino († 1664), of one of the Reni works assembled in Rome by Ludovisi's relatives Pope Gregory XV and Cardinal Ludovico Ludovisi. The painting in question was the *Conversion of Saul* [cat. 40], which was sent to El Escorial after arriving in Spain.[88]

Philip IV's son and successor, King Charles II, was particularly zealous in his care of the picture collection inherited from his father and kept all the Reni paintings he had received from him. It is reported, for example, that the poor condition of the *Judith* gifted years earlier by the nuncio Rospigliosi prompted

Charles II to order a copy in order to preserve its memory in the royal collection; the task was entrusted to Juan Carreño de Miranda (1614–1685).[89] That royal commission may possibly explain the huge number of copies of that composition that are still found in many parts of Spain. A few new works by Guido may also have entered the Alcázar during Charles II's reign, such as the *Saint Jerome* now in the Prado.[90] As a result of that interest in the Bolognese master's art, as José Luis Colomer recalls, twelve originals by his hand and two copies of his creations hung in the Spanish king's principal residence in 1686, and further works were housed in the Buen Retiro and El Escorial.[91]

The importance attached to Reni's creations in the royal collection was echoed by several of the picture galleries of the upper nobility of seventeenth-century Madrid and even by those of a few officials in Crown service. But before this trend caught on in Madrid, it appears to have received its initial impetus from a few Spaniards based in Italy. For instance, as we have seen, Guido's connection – the details of which are still unknown – with the Duke of Osuna during his term as viceroy of Naples from 1616 to 1620 resulted in an important portrait whose whereabouts are now unknown.[92] As a centre of artistic production, Naples was hugely conducive to collecting for the Spaniards posted there as viceroys and sparked a similar interest among the high-ranking Crown officials who lived there, though this aspect has so far received less attention from scholars. The most paradigmatic case studied to date is that of the secretary Juan

Fig. 6 Guido Reni, *Christ embracing Saint John the Baptist*, c. 1640. Oil on canvas, 48.5 × 68.5 cm. London, The National Gallery, NG191

de Lezcano, the owner of an important picture gallery whose contents are documented in the inventory of his estate drawn up in Naples in 1631. Three works by Reni appear in it: a medium-sized *Assumption with Musical Angels* on copper, and a pair of larger canvases consisting of a *Saint Catherine* and a *Saint Susannah*.[93] The latter must be the one listed in Guido's Roman account books on 26 April 1610, suggesting a possible early link between the painter and the owner.[94]

As Guido's ties with Naples had been very specific and limited, it was somewhat easier for prospective buyers to acquire his creations in Rome, where he lived for much longer and worked on more important commissions. A very significant though relatively little-known case is the clergyman Luis de Oviedo, secretary to Cardinal Bernardo de Sandoval y Rojas, who lived in Rome from 1607 at least until his employer's death in 1618. There he assembled a large picture collection that was inherited by his brother Francisco, who later became secretary to Philip IV.[95] It may be inferred from the posthumous inventory of Francisco's estate drawn up much later, in 1663, that Luis de Oviedo purchased several major works by Reni in Rome, such as a *Saint Cecilia* that was paired with a *Saint Margaret*, a philosopher 'with his hand on his cheek and in the other a wooden bowl', a *Magdalen rising to Heaven*, and an intriguing ensemble consisting of 'two equal paintings of Venus and Eurydice naked, one in flames and the other bound'.[96]

The Spanish ambassadors to the pope also enjoyed an advantageous position with respect to acquiring works by Reni.

Don Fernando Afán Enríquez de Ribera, 3rd Duke of Alcalá de los Gazules, was living in the papal capital in 1626 as Philip IV's ambassador of obedience to Urban VIII. On ending his term, Alcalá received as a gift from the previous pope's cardinal-nephew, Ludovico Ludovisi, a *Virgin and Child* by the Bolognese master based on a model that enjoyed particular success on the Iberian Peninsula.[97] While in the post, he had commissioned an outstanding group of thirteen paintings, a series of Apostles that he sent to the family mausoleum in the charterhouse of Seville in 1629.[98] It included Guido's *Saint James the Greater* now in the Houston Museum of Fine Arts [cat. 39]. During his ensuing term as viceroy of Naples, Alcalá managed to add to his collection another piece by the Bolognese master, a *Cleopatra*.[99] One of the many duties of the 7th Duke of Infantado, Don Rodrigo Díaz de Vivar Mendoza y Sandoval, while serving as ambassador in Rome years later was to provide assistance to Diego Velázquez throughout his second trip to Italy. During his stint in Rome, Don Rodrigo acquired two equal-sized canvases of the *Incarnation* and a *Christ embracing Saint John the Baptist*, probably the one now in London's National Gallery [fig. 6].[100]

Nevertheless, the easiest place to come by Reni's paintings, as is only logical, was in his native Bologna. The 9th Admiral of Castile, Don Juan Alfonso Enríquez de Cabrera, was well aware of this and in 1641 wrote from Naples to the archbishop of Bologna, Cardinal Girolamo Colonna, to whom he was related on his mother's side. In his letter the admiral remarked to the archbishop:

> Your Eminence, being archbishop of Bologna, can judge how regretful I am that my gallery has no paintings by Guido, and I therefore beg Your Eminence to share with me those you may have or guard them from the lord Duke [of Corbara], who in order to do me a favour is determined to snatch them from Your Eminence.[101]

The aristocrat's plea must have been heeded, as by the time he died in Madrid in 1647 he owned one of the largest groups of works by Reni in the city, consisting of nine canvases, particularly half-length pictures of saints and heroines.[102] Among them were two of Saint Sebastian, one of which could be the painting now in the Museo del Prado [cat. 19].[103]

Another cultural and artistic hub where Spanish collectors of Guido's day could procure paintings by him was Milan, the capital of the duchy then under Spanish rule. One of its governors, the Marquis of Leganés, Diego Messía Felípez de Guzmán, managed to get hold of a few notable works by Reni during that

Fig. 7 Guido Reni, *The Abduction of Europa*, c. 1636. Oil on canvas, 157.5 × 115.3 cm. Ottawa, National Gallery of Canada, inv. 35939

stage of his career from 1635 to 1641, taking advantage of his political position and the closeness of Bologna. On his death in 1655, his huge picture gallery of more than 1,300 works included a few highly significant paintings by Guido. According to a testimony from Abbot Roberto Fontana, representative to the Duke of Modena in Milan, dated 26 February 1636, Leganés was especially interested in obtaining works by Reni and

Guercino at the time.[104] At the beginning of the following year Duke Francesco d'Este sent from Modena three paintings by these two masters: an unspecified *quadrone*, a *Saint Francis* by Guercino and a head of the *Saviour* by Guido.[105] Further gifts added to the number of works by the master in his possession, such as the superb *Abduction of Europa* now in the National Gallery of Canada in Ottawa [fig. 7], which was a present from

Ferrante Gonzaga, 3rd Duke of Guastalla.[106] The marquis came to own – though it is not known how – other important works by Reni, such as a repetition or copy of *Hippomenes and Atalanta* and a version of *Apollo and Marsyas* [fig. 84].[107]

When tracing the development of Spanish collecting over the course of the century it is necessary to recall the role of Manuel de Fonseca y Zúñiga, 6th Count of Monterrey, who as viceroy of Naples amassed a marvellous collection of Italian paintings to decorate the religious house he founded in Salamanca. The extraordinary *Saint John the Baptist in the Wilderness* on view in this exhibition [cat. 22] belonged to his holdings. In 1653 a *Saint Catherine kneeling with two Angels*,[108]

which must have been similar to the one now in the Pinacoteca Malaspina in Pavia, likewise hung in his sumptuous Madrid residence.

Although Italy was the natural source of paintings by Guido, an exceptional opportunity to obtain important pictures by the master arose in a different part of the world: the sale of the collection of King Charles I of England, who was executed in 1649 as a consequence of the English Civil War. Following the monarch's tragic fate, numerous buyers travelled to London with the hope of securing one or more of his paintings. Among them, as is well known, was Philip IV himself, represented by Alonso de Cárdenas, Spanish ambassador to the British government. In his

Fig. 8 Copy of Guido Reni, *The Crucifixion of Saint Peter*, mid-17th century. Madrid, parish church of San Pedro, high altar

David García Cueto

letters the diplomat progressively reported on the options to the king's favourite, Luis Méndez de Haro. Involved in those negotiations to acquire paintings for the royal holdings, the marquis also decided to buy a few for his own collection, including several major works by Reni. The main one was the *Toilet of Venus*, which originally hung in his Madrid home and, following a string of vicissitudes, is now in the National Gallery in London [cat. 74].[109] In the same sale Luis Méndez de Haro purchased a *Judith and Holofernes*, which was sent to him by the Count of Fuensaldaña,[110] along with a *Lucretia*[111] and a *Portia*,[112] attesting to the fascination Guido's female prototypes held for the potentate. His son and successor, Gaspar Méndez de Haro y Guzmán, 7th Marquis of El Carpio, an even keener collector than his father, kept them at his Madrid residence in the Jardín de San Joaquín before departing to take up his post as ambassador in Rome in 1677, displaying them in a highly unusual arrangement in its rooms.[113] Gaspar hung a few significant paintings in the form of ceiling panels, among them the abovementioned *Lucretia* and a *Sleeping Apollo with the nine Muses* – then attributed to Reni but actually by Orazio Gentileschi (1563–1639) – which had been purchased by his father in London.[114] During his ensuing stints as ambassador in Rome and viceroy in Naples, Gaspar assembled one of the largest picture galleries of his day, in which Guido was also represented.[115]

Aside from these major collections no other groups of works by Reni are currently known to have been owned by seventeenth-century courtly aristocrats and high-ranking officials, though a few sporadic mentions appear in Madrid inventories of the last third of the century. Although the hub of Guido collecting in Golden Age Spain was clearly the court, many other parts of the Spanish kingdoms were graced with the presence of works by the master or considered to be by his hand. The Duke of Alcalá's aforementioned pictures and the copies owned by the archbishop Fray Domingo Pimentel could be seen in Seville for a time,[116] as could a *Saint Jerome* by Reni's workshop in the convent of Santa Paula.[117] According to sources, an *Immaculate Conception* by Guido hung in pride of place in neighbouring Granada in the church of the no longer extant convent of the Ángel Custodio, accompanied in the nave by the famous cycle on the *Life of the Virgin* painted by Alonso Cano (1601–1667).[118] To this day the convent of the Conceptionist nuns of Ágreda (Soria) houses a *Virgin and Sleeping Child*, a studio product that was a gift to its charismatic founder, Sor María, from the nuncio Giulio Rospigliosi.[119] According to his will made in 1662, in Santiago de Compostela Archbishop Pedro Carrillo de Acuña y Bureba (1595–1664) owned a *Triumph of David* and an *Allegory of Painting and Sculpture*, which he bequeathed to Burgos cathedral.[120]

In the seventeenth century these sizeable holdings of original works coexisted with a number of copies that is impossible to quantify, including those brought from Italy and others produced in Spain after the originals preserved here or the prints then in circulation in Europe reproducing some of his creations. The fact that copies become unavoidably mixed with originals when following Reni's artistic trail in seventeenth-century Spain underlines how highly sought-after these products were even then, and attests to a process whereby Guido's models spread across Spanish territory in capillary fashion, spurred by the practice of copying.

The Reni works most widely copied in Spain were those owned by the Church, particularly those housed in El Escorial, where the Hieronymite friars who lived there must have been tolerant of copying. Indeed, as we have seen, there are numerous copies of the *Virgin of the Chair*, the *Virgin and Child*, and the *Conversion of Saul*, paintings formerly kept in the royal monastery. The prestige copies of Guido's works must have enjoyed in ecclesiastical environments may be inferred from the presence of one of his versions of the *Crucifixion of Saint Peter* in the seventeenth-century altarpiece decorating the main chapel in the church dedicated to that saint in Madrid, which was previously under the jurisdiction of the apostolic nuncio [fig. 8].[121]

Besides yielding economic benefits, the practice of copying Reni's works became established – at least in some Spanish circles – as a method of learning in the late seventeenth century, as indicated by the lines written by the painter and theoretician José García Hidalgo (1645–1717) in 1693–95 on how to improve colouring: 'if you wish to be a perfect Colourist, copy very beautiful originals, which elevate the senses through sight, like Corregio [sic], and Guido'.[122]

Reni continued to be increasingly highly regarded in Spain during the following century and studying and copying his oeuvre became part of the official training programmes of the Academia de San Fernando after it was founded in 1752. Until the start of the 1800s this appreciation was shared by most European nations and explains why, in their immense greed, the Napoleonic troops who invaded Spain stole a considerable number of the works by Guido they came across.[123] After a period of contempt followed by a progressive revival, it is now the turn of the twenty-first century – to paraphrase Cesare Gnudi – to choose its Reni. His ability to capture and construct the most sublime beauty would possibly be our own age's choice.

1 Dempsey 2008, XI.

2 See Cavalli 1954.

3 See Emiliani et al. 1988 and Ebert-Schifferer, Emiliani and Schleier 1988.

4 Gnudi 1954, 16.

5 Malvasia–Pericolo 2019, 1:62.

6 Fréart de Chantelou-Lalanne 1986, 90; Schmidt-Linsenhoff 1988, 63.

7 Malvasia–Pericolo 2019, 1:14 and 1:16: 'Aquila generosa, per così dire, prese un sublime volo alle sfere, e di là su ricavando quelle celesti idee, poté rapportarne alla terra un fare di paradiso. Padre e promotore della moderna maniera, seppe così innamorarne il mondo, invogliarne i curiosi ed arricchirne i professori che le fortune delle tavole greche siansi rese dimestiche e famigliari a' tempi nostri'. For the English translation, ibid., 1:15 and 1:17. See also Lorenzo Pericolo's essay, '*Novità*: Guido Reni and Modernity', in this catalogue.

8 Malvasia–Pericolo 2019, 2:1–132, in the section 'Beyond Perfection: Guido Reni and Malvasia's Fourth Age of Painting'.

9 Scannelli 1657, 85, 349–50.

10 Bellori–Wohl 2005, 347.

11 Scaramuccia–Giubbini 1965, 25.

12 Malvasia–Pericolo 2019, 1:70. On his youth, see Rachel McGarry's essay, '"Like a bee amongst the flowers": Young Guido Reni between Bologna and Rome', in this catalogue.

13 On his familiarity with organology, see Albini 1934.

14 Henning 2008.

15 Years later Maffeo Barberini noted this sculptural sense in Reni's frescoes in Santa Maria Maggiore, expressing it in a Latin verse he devoted to them; see Malvasia–Pericolo 2019, 1:50, and Cappelletti 2022b, 53. For Reni as draughtsman, see Viviana Farina's essay, '"A man who perpetually observes Nature": Guido Reni and Drawing', in this catalogue.

16 Malvasia–Pericolo 2019, 1:174: 'Stimò prima d'ogn'altro Rafaelle e 'l Coreggio, e dopo questi Paolo Veronese … dicendo che chi avesse potuto accoppiar insieme il sapere e la giustezza del primo, la vivezza e colorito del secondo, il giudizio e la maestà del terzo, avrebbe passato ogn'altro, come ogn'altro avean superato i Carracci per questa mistura così ben da loro praticata'. For the English translation, ibid., 1:175.

17 Toscano 2009.

18 Malvasia–Pericolo 2019, 1:176: 'troppo naturale'. Reni owned the *Denial of Saint Peter* now in the Metropolitan Museum of Art in New York (Gift of Herman and Lila Shickman, and Purchase, Lila Acheson Wallace Gift, 1997, 1997.167); see Nicolaci and Gandolfi 2011 and Barbieri 2012.

19 Malvasia–Pericolo 2019, 1:61–69 and 1:248, note 99.

20 Marzullo 2019, 351.

21 Cappelletti 2022b, 44.

22 Benati 2022, 18–19.

23 Malvasia–Pericolo 2019, 1:14: 'nella nobiltà e celesti idee'. For the English translation, ibid., 1:15. It is worth remembering, as Babette Bohn (2011) states, that in Bologna technical brilliance (*sprezzatura*), which Guido possessed in abundance, was then commonly valued more highly than iconographic inventiveness (*invenzione*).

24 Iseppi 2020, 32–37.

25 See the essays by Raffaella Morselli, 'The "most distinguished Compatriot Guido Reni", Glory of Bologna', and Daniele Benati, 'Guido Reni: A Master without a School?', in this catalogue.

26 Ciammitti 2000, 194. On the painter's finances, see Morselli 2007.

27 Pepper 1999b; Mazzarelli 2016.

28 Pepper 1999b, 32–33; Spear 2007.

29 Morselli 2012a; Pulini 2018.

30 Candi 2016.

31 Senkevitch 2008.

32 Evans 1970, 109. Reni was accompanied in this lowest category by the late Raphael, Correggio, the Carracci, Caravaggio, Carlo Dolci (1616–1686), and Bartolomé Esteban Murillo (1617–1682).

33 Kugler–Burckhardt 1847, 2:366–70, especially 366. Quoted in Emiliani 1988, XXXIV.

34 Alabern 1859, 53. Quoted in Úbeda de los Cobos 2006, 197–98. On his biography, see Ossorio y Bernard 1883–84, 14–15.

35 Buisseret 1875. Quoted in Loire 1996, 16–17, and Úbeda de los Cobos 2006, 203–5.

36 Úbeda de los Cobos 2006, 208.

37 Longhi 1935.

38 Ibid., 132.

39 Kurz 1937, 220.

40 Ferretti 2019.

41 Nicolson 1954, 301.

42 Úbeda de los Cobos 2006, 203–5.

43 Pérez Sánchez 1965a, 168–207.

44 Gaya Nuño 1969, 222–23.

45 Pérez Sánchez 1970.

46 Malvasia–Pericolo 2019, 1:134.

47 Ibid., 1:152–53.

48 Ibid., 1:164: 'Essendosi sempre mostrato un marmo alla presenza e contemplazione di tante belle giovane che gli servirono di modello'. For the English translation, ibid., 1:165.

49 Spear 1997.

50 Pepper 1998. This evocative power can be considered to be what Malvasia calls 'divinity humanised' (see Malvasia–Pericolo 2019, 1:71), a key concept in Reni's art which, according to Stephen Pepper, was misinterpreted by Richard Spear as 'divinity made flesh'.

51 Malvasia–Pericolo 2019, 1:105. See also Pericolo 2019.

52 Cropper 1984, 252, 20r: 'che ciò che per le tele avansò, le carte gli avevano tolto'.

53 Haskell 1988, 32.

54 Fidanza and Serafinelli 2022, 50–63.

55 On novelty in Reni, see the essay by Lorenzo Pericolo, '*Novità*: Guido Reni and Modernity', in this catalogue.

56 Munich, Bayerische Staatsgemäldesammlungen, Alte Pinakothek, inv. 446.

57 Brady 2019; Puglisi 2020, 266, and the essay by Aoife Brady, 'Painting for Posterity: Guido Reni's Materials and Technique', in this catalogue.

58 Pérez Sánchez 1988; Colomer 2006; García Cueto 2006, 192–212; Japón 2020b; Japón 2022b, as well as Javier Portús's essay, 'Guido Reni and Seventeenth-century Spanish Painting', in this catalogue.

59 Quazza 1950.

60 Malvasia–Pericolo 2019, 1:58: 'già che nell'una e nell'altra corte era onorevolmente stato invitato da quelle Maestà'. For the English translation, ibid., 1:59.

61 Ibid., 1:170: 'La più utile o almeno la men nociva alla nostra Italia'. For the English translation, ibid., 1:171.

62 Marías and De Carlos 2009, 63–65; García Cueto 2016c, 47.

63 Martínez–Carderera 1866, 120–21; Finaldi 2009.

64 Val Moreno 2016, 85, note 15. See also Pupillo 1996 and Bernstorff 2010.

65 Anselmi 2004, 248–49.

66 Val Moreno 2016, 424.

67 Pierguidi 2012b, and this author's essay, 'Viceroys, Ambassadors, Agents, Theologians: Thirty Years of (Stormy) Relations between Guido Reni and Spain', in this catalogue.

68 García Cueto 2016c, 51.

69 Malvasia–Pericolo 2019, 1:72–73.

70 Ibid., 1:288, note 197.

71 Ponce Cárdenas 2018, 111–12.

72 Colomer 1990; Malvasia–Pericolo 2019, 1:88.

73 Malvezzi 1651, n.p.; Colomer 1996; García Cueto 2006, 279–82.

74 Mahon 1947b.

75 See the reflections on this issue in Javier Portús's essay, 'Guido Reni and Seventeenth-century Spanish Painting', in this catalogue.

76 Manrique Ara 2001.

77 Martínez–Carderera 1866, 158 and 33, respectively.

78 Carducho 1634; Pérez Sánchez 1988, 690.

79 Pacheco–Bassegoda 1990, 443.

80 Berwick y Alba 1891, 492.

81 Vega Loeches 2016, 322–992.

82 Madrid, Museo Nacional del Prado, P-1627.

83 Madrazo 1884, 299.

84 Colomer 2006, 226. That *Judith* was one of the paintings Reni invited the anonymous addressee of his letter of 8 April 1628 to see at the home of the Rospigliosi in Rome (Ciammitti 2000, 196).

85 Madrid, Museo Nacional del Prado, P-1174. For somewhat different proposals, see Cruz Yábar 2017–18 and Greub 2019.

86 Beaven 2000; Colomer 2006, 220.

87 Madrid, Real Academia de Bellas Artes de San Fernando, inv. 291. Malvasia–Pericolo 2019, 1:428–29, note 636.

88 Redín Michaus 2013.

89 Madrid, Museo Nacional del Prado, P-226. García Cueto 2021b, 12.

90 Madrid, Museo Nacional del Prado, P-217. Colomer 2006, 227.

91 Ibid., 216.

92 The portrait must have been painted in 1619, when Reni visited Naples for a second time to discuss the possibility of decorating the Capella del Tesoro de San Gennaro.

93 Vannugli 2009, 352–53.

94 Ibid., 355.

95 Terzaghi 2021, 90.

96 Barrio Moya 1979, 168: 'con la mano en la mexilla y en la otra una ortera'; 'Dos quadros yguales de benus y euridize desnudas la una en las llamas y la otra atada'.

97 Brown and Kagan 1987, 235.

98 Japón 2022b, 91–98.

99 Brown and Kagan 1987, 245.

100 García Cueto 2010a, 121.

101 Subiaco, Archivio Colonna, Carteggio Girolamo I, Naples, 11 June 1641: 'Puede juzgar Vuestra Eminencia quanto sentiré que siendo Vuestra Eminencia arzobispo de Bolonia esté mi galería sin pinturas de Guido, y así supplico a Vuestra Eminencia parta conmigo de las que tuviere o

las guarde del señor duque [de Corbara], que por hacerme merced ba con firme resolución de urtarlas a Vuestra Eminencia'. Salort Pons 2002, 480, doc. b24C; García Cueto 2006, 354, doc. 80; Agüero Carnerero 2018, 71.

102 Pérez Sánchez 1965a, 191; Burke and Cherry 1997, 1:413–14, 1:416–17, and 1:432.

103 Burke and Cherry 1997, 1:432.

104 Pérez Preciado 2010, 379, note 1415.

105 Ibid., 382.

106 Zeri 1984; Pérez Preciado 2010, 384–85.

107 Pérez Preciado 2010, 643–45. Other works by Reni in the marquis's collection were a *Virgin and Child*, a *Virgin*, possibly by his school (no. 1046), and a *Saint Joseph*, also by his school and now in London, Apsley House.

108 Pérez Sánchez 1977, 437; Rivas Albaladejo 2015, 352–53. On the Pavia painting to which it is linked here, see https://www.lombardiabeniculturali.it/opere-arte/schede/F0200-00043/.

109 Brown and Elliott 2002, 291, no. 3, and 286, no. 4. On Luis Méndez de Haro as a collector, see Frutos Sastre 2016.

110 Brown and Elliott 2002, 295, no. 1.

111 Madrid, Museo Nacional del Prado, P-208. Ibid., 297, no. 1; R. Japón in Baños and Palacios 2022, 30–33.

112 Brown and Elliott 2002, 279, no. 1.

113 Burke and Cherry 1997, 2:1151; Frutos Sastre 2006.

114 Brown and Elliott 2002, 286, no. 4.

115 Frutos Sastre 2009.

116 Japón 2018b.

117 Japón 2022b, 118.

118 Madero López 2019.

119 Fernández Gracia 2002, 159–60.

120 Fernández Gasalla 1992.

121 Tormo 1985, 47.

122 García Hidalgo [1693] 1965, 5r: 'si quieres ser perfecto Colorista, copia de originales muy hermosos, que elevan los sentidos por la vista, como Corregio, y Guido'.

123 On the pillaging of foreign painting preserved in Spain, see Gaya Nuño 1964.

NOVITÀ: GUIDO RENI AND MODERNITY

Lorenzo Pericolo

The world of Guido Reni (1575–1642) moves fast. So fast that it cannot 'grow older in the state it was born because it cannot die in the age in which it lived and from which it has already emerged'. Paradoxical as it may sound, this sentence, excerpted from Carlo Cesare Malvasia's dismissed proem to his life of Guido published in his *Felsina pittrice* of 1678, deliberately conflates the past and future of art into an ever-changing present. Novelty – *novità* – rules the world: a force so disruptive that it 'disassembles orders' and 'alters protocols'. Novelty proves to be the opposite of tradition, the unaltered chain of orders and protocols that strives to maintain the world at a standstill.[1] For a professor of civil and canon law such as Malvasia, acknowledging the compelling superiority of novelty over tradition must have been a quandary. And yet, introducing the specificity of Guido's painting, he did not balk at describing the history of art as a sequence of novelties, the most recent of which was the one promoted by Guido.

Novelty, Malvasia remarks, does not happen to artists by accident. Quite the contrary, artists hunt novelty down 'with different strategies and through unusual routes'. Preying upon novelty, Michelangelo (1475–1564) came up with *terribilità*, Raphael (1483–1520) with 'precision' in draughtsmanship, and Titian (c. 1488–1576) with 'softness of impasto'. Jacopo Tintoretto (1519–1594) bet on the splashing effect of a new 'dynamism', Veronese (1528–1588) on that of 'composition', Correggio (c. 1489–1534) on the irresistible charm of 'purity', and Parmigianino (1503–1540) on the lure of 'grace'. More closely to Guido, the Carracci resolved to distinguish themselves through 'vigour'. Taking 'sublime flight to the spheres and deriving his

celestial ideas from there', Guido, a 'generous eagle', sought to excel in 'delicacy' and 'nobility'.[2]

It is no surprise that Malvasia came to discard this proem, composing a pristine one for the life of Guido where the 'divine' painter, cast this time as the promoter of modernity (or the fourth age of painting), remains nonetheless subjugated to the perfection achieved by his masters, the Carracci.[3] The notion that novelty and change are omnipotent, that, like Father Time, they devour whatever is freshly produced on earth by straight away making it dull and tasteless, clashes not only with the possibility of artistic perfection, but with the plausibility that any artistic canon may persist long enough to gain durable validity. In Malvasia's eyes, the Carracci, and in particular Ludovico (1555–1619), had instead reached a historical and conceptual artistic apogee: a 'synthesis of styles' that could not be superseded, but only elaborated upon by subsequent artists.[4] With such a yardstick planted deep into its course, history – the history of painting – is prevented from upending itself day after day through novelty: each new sun no longer brings about oblivion and thirst for the unseen, but a renewed reflection upon an authoritative past. To be sure, novelty does not cease to exist in a world ruled by canon, but it assuredly becomes enfeebled: it is no longer the force that modifies art radically and continually with each turning of the sun.

Which one was Guido's world, then? The one governed by novelty, as first evoked by Malvasia, or the one ruled by canonical tradition, as Malvasia proposes in the second version of his proem to Guido's life? In the early modern world, novelty never goes unbridled: this would just be inconceivable. Early modern societies are traditional by definition, and so were Guido's Bologna and Rome, Italy in its entirety, and Europe. Like any other painter of his time, Guido both struggled with and profited from the strictures that regulated painting, its practice and theoretical understanding. And yet, Malvasia's original intuition, his depiction of Guido's world as the realm of unrestricted novelty, may not be entirely off the mark, and indeed could be most helpful to a better comprehension of Guido's art and market strategies. Enthralled by the novelty of the Carracci academy, Guido quit the workshop of Denys Calvaert (c. 1540–1619), his first master, by abjuring 'his excessively mannered and highly licked northern style'.[5] What we might now condemn as Calvaert's benighted Mannerism was, when Guido joined the Carracci studio (most probably in 1594), an advanced, albeit conventional, conception of painting grounded in a solid pedagogical programme.[6] Scolding Guido for his infatuation with the Carracci, Calvaert accused his young disciple of renouncing the lesson of antiquity and the noble paradigm of Renaissance artistic luminaries by embracing the stubborn naturalism of his new idols. Calvaert's recourse to both casts of ancient bas reliefs and busts and to prints after exemplary artists in teaching drawing relied on a conviction antithetical to the one that had originally inspired Annibale's return to nature. For Annibale (1560–1609), Giorgio Vasari's notion that 'it is good to copy after the antiques … rather than from living things' was ridiculous since ancient sculpture is a 'secondary thing' by comparison to nature, which is the 'original and most primary' thing and therefore is always 'to be copied'.[7] When it was founded (most probably in 1582), the Carracci academy had espoused a then disfavoured artistic notion of nature – one radical enough to dethrone the supremacy of antiquity and Raphael, yet nimble enough not to reject history and tradition altogether. Correggio's sensuous treatment of flesh and Tintoretto's fury in energising the figure served as traditional stylistic platforms in exploring the human body through a brand-new immediacy.[8]

However, by the time Guido entered the Carracci workshop, that newness and directness had grown somewhat standardised. Whereas the Carracci disciples, Malvasia points out, 'followed a shorthand practice and a certain facility in the bold manner of Tintoretto … Guido on the contrary, already in possession of these qualities, delighted himself with a more accurate study of every minute part of the body, every muscle'. Focusing on distinct aspects of the nude in search of 'more grandeur', Guido drew 'in conformity with the practice of the Passerotti, but sweetening it all and endowing it with a certain effortless ease and marvelous *sprezzatura*'.[9] In other words, Guido was already attempting to outgrow the Carracci novelty by pursuing one of his own making: a trademark of consummate refinement in the depiction of the human body.

No early drawing by Guido survives that would confirm Malvasia's account. On the other hand, Guido's *Orpheus and Eurydice* of 1596–97[10] – one of his earliest great paintings – betrays the young painter's unease in adjusting to Agostino Carracci's (1557–1602) anatomical precision, especially in nudes destined for a monumental scale.[11] As late as 1601, Guido still had trouble defining the musculature of the semi-naked executioner in the *Martyrdom of Saint Cecilia* for Santa Cecilia in Trastevere, Rome [fig. 21].[12] Only around 1604 does Guido finally come to a confident proficiency in anatomy. The novelty embodied by the Carracci's unmediated and knowledgeable take on the human body proved initially impervious to Guido, and perhaps as a response to this hurdle he aspired to present himself not as a new Carracci but as a new Raphael. It is no coincidence that his copy of Raphael's *Ecstasy of Saint Cecilia*, then in San Giovanni in Monte, Bologna,[13] acted as his calling card in Rome, preceding his arrival in that city only by a few months.[14]

Executed, in my opinion, around 1601–2, Guido's half-figure *Saint Cecilia* [cat. 87] epitomises the kind of artistic novelty he aimed to display in the eyes of the prelates affiliated with the papal court. The quasi-frontal posture of the girl's slightly uptilted face and torso bespeaks the hallowed language of a late quattrocento devotional icon: an archaisation of a Raphael prototype retrofitted to the *maniera devota* of Pietro Perugino (c. 1450–1523) or Francesco Francia (c. 1447–1517). In its austere simplicity, Guido's *Saint Cecilia* not only outmodes Raphael's canonical *maniera moderna*, but equally competes in radicalism with the *maniera devota* developed by Counter-Reformation painters, such as Scipione Pulzone (1544–1598). A paradox, Guido's neo-Raphaelesque novelty was an unprecedented rebound into the fold of pre-Raphaelesque painting. No doubt, Guido's early protectors in Rome, like Cardinal Paolo Emilio Sfondrato (the rediscoverer of the martyred Cecilia's remains and the most zealous sponsor of her cult), Cardinal Antonio Maria Gallo, and most probably Cardinal Camillo Borghese (soon-to-be Pope Paul V) were charmed by Guido's reinvention of a premodern Raphael, revived with the substantial benefit of a softer impasto. It is noteworthy that Malvasia, who glosses over Guido's self-fashioning as a new Raphael upon his arrival in Rome, only notes that in his copy of Raphael's *Ecstasy of Saint Cecilia* the young painter was said to have 'achieved a painterly breadth of brushstroke and a softness' lacking in the original.[15] This point bears consideration. By 'softening' the 'dryness' associated with Vasari's *seconda maniera* (from Masaccio to Andrea Mantegna, including Perugino and the young Raphael in Malvasia's estimation), Guido demonstrated that he not only was aware of the risks involved in archaising Raphael, but had also managed to make his work compatible with the canon of the *maniera moderna* through additional softness.[16]

Guido's ability to produce small devotional paintings, especially in copper, assuredly afforded him financial survival and independence during his earlier years in Rome. But soon enough he must have realised that the Guido-as-the-new-Raphael novelty was utterly inadequate in his competition with the truly profound novelties of the Roman (and European) artistic scene: the consolidation of Annibale Carracci's synthesis of styles as the canon of a new modernity and the rise of Caravaggio's (1571–1610) radical naturalism. Guido's answer to these unfathomable challenges was to turn himself into a chameleon of stylistic experimentation. During his stay in Rome from 1601 to 1612, Guido never ceased to shed old skin adopting style upon style, transforming his painting to the point of unrecognisability. Some of these experimentations survive as the scant dead branches of a thwarted evolution. His *Landscape with a Country Dance* of about 1603–6 [fig. 23] and *Landscape with Cupids Playing* of about 1601–3 [cat. 63] attest to a serious engagement with a pictorial genre only recently set up by Agostino and Annibale Carracci, and later expanded upon by two of Guido's fellow students in both Calvaert's workshop and the Carracci academy: Domenichino (1581–1641) and Francesco Albani (1578–1660).[17] It is perhaps ironic that toward the end of his life Guido would mock Albani, who had made his fortune on mythological and allegorical landscapes, for being 'no painter, but a gentleman who attended to his little fancies, to small things as an amusement and in jest'.[18] Upon his arrival in Rome, Guido himself had nevertheless plied his hand in such 'little fancies' and 'small things', and, what is more, with such a brilliancy that he could have built a success as a first-rank landscapist. But Guido's bar was placed much higher. In a sense, he ought first to transform into a Carracci, then into Caravaggio in order to undermine these competitors' supremacy through the invention of new novelties.

In his 1604 *Saint Benedict receiving Gifts from the Peasants* [fig. 9] for the octagonal cloister of San Michele in Bosco, Bologna, Guido demonstrated his impeccable mastery of the Carracci synthesis of styles. In describing this mural picture, now completely faded, Malvasia cannot dissimulate his enthusiasm:

> A graceful young girl, girdled with the finest veils and carrying a basket of eggs, is in the style of Raphael; in the style of Correggio, an older girl, her companion, with a smiling face rests a hand upon her shoulder. Both look out toward the viewers with such liveliness and spirit they seem to breathe. In the style of Titian there is a little shepherd playing a flute with hands of a living and tender flesh; another shepherd, of not inferior beauty, listens intently to his music. In the style of Annibale is a woman with a nursing baby at her breast, and another older child whom she prods with her right hand into offering a basket of apples, on which he fixes greedy eyes. Passing over many other figures, I shall mention a full-length nude in the foreground who pulls forcefully at a donkey's reins, and who is so vigorously and furiously drawn that it would seem that Michelangelo himself had traced his contours, leaving to the school of Lombardy the task of covering his body with living flesh in a more tender manner.[19]

Although Annibale, and not Ludovico, was among the canonical masters whose lesson Guido had prodigiously synthesised in the painting, it was Ludovico, and not Annibale, who was the target of Guido's tour de force.[20] It was Ludovico who had been tasked with the decoration of the cloister in San Michele in Bosco; it was he, one of Guido's once revered masters, who directed the team of young artists responsible for the frescoes that composed this decorative scheme. According to Malvasia, Ludovico 'remained speechless' upon laying eyes on Guido's composition, 'the other painters' being 'brought to their knees'. They recognised that 'Guido had surpassed them', outshining even Ludovico 'with a certain softness, beauty, and grandeur never achieved before, even by the Carracci themselves'.[21] In San Michele in Bosco, Guido succeeded in eviscerating the charge of novelty inherent in the Carracci stylistic synthesis: he possessed it so thoroughly that it was no longer the exclusive prerogative of the Carracci, but a historical (and thus surmountable) pictorial device for him (and others) to bend at will in conformity with the dictates of the *istoria*.

It stands to reason that the turbaned girl with the basket of eggs in the picture should bear the likeness of the young Guido, as reported by Malvasia.[22] Guido's particular approach

Fig. 9 Giacomo Giovannini after Guido Reni, *Saint Benedict receiving Gifts from the Peasants*, late 17th–early 18th century. Etching, 557 × 372 mm. London, Victoria and Albert Museum, DYCE.1528

to the Carracci synthesis of styles was a feminine one as opposed to Annibale's male 'vigour'.[23] Majesty, nobility, softness, delicacy are the 'female' traits of Guido's vanguard in Raphael's name. His self-portrait as an androgyne could be construed in many ways, but it was first and foremost an audacious act of artistic pride. While working under Ludovico years earlier, one of his workshop companions, Lorenzo Garbieri (c. 1580–1654), would harass him by claiming that his style 'was feminine [*da donna*], weak, and washed-out', adding that Guido had 'plunged into the same faintness from which Ludovico had first

rescued painting after its decline'.[24] Garbieri may or may not have been referring to Guido's effeminacy (which is never mentioned in the sources), but he was certainly making an art historical statement. If, in Garbieri's opinion, the new direction of Guido's painting – his 'softness, beauty, and grandeur' – was not a novelty beyond the Carracci's pictorial zenith but a relapse into Calvaert's outdated Mannerism, Guido refuted this kind of criticism through his San Michele painting.

By inserting his effigy as a girl 'in Raphael's style', he put femininity in art under Raphael's protection. Riveting her eyes on the viewer, Guido-the-turbaned-girl stands out amid the figures, female and male, in which the master exerted his chameleon-like power of summoning Correggio, Titian, and Michelangelo, in addition (of course) to Raphael. Anchoring himself in the foreground, the nude man who pulls 'forcefully at a donkey's reins' is meant to exalt Guido's complementary dexterity in painting 'vigorously' and in a 'manly' fashion.[25] He heralds Guido's triumph by accomplishing the most paradoxical of all pictorial feats: channelling Michelangelo's *terribilità* in representing the male body through flawless contouring by dissolving it into Titian's *carne viva* (living flesh). Situated at mid-distance, Guido-the-turbaned-girl equally relativises Guido's affiliation with Raphael: if Guido had started his career in Rome as a new Raphael, this new Guido had gone beyond that artistic identity, and was now able to master the 'male' paradigm of Michelangelo. And Caravaggio's 'darkness' as well, should it come to that.

And it came in fact to that a few months after completing the San Michele picture. According to Malvasia, Guido obtained the commission for his famous *Crucifixion of Saint Peter* [fig. 10] through the intermediary of the Cavalier d'Arpino (1568–1640), who had promised 'Cardinal Borghese that Guido would transform himself into Caravaggio, making the painting in that dark and contrasted style'.[26] In reality, the patron was not Cardinal Scipione Borghese but Cardinal Pietro Aldobrandini, the nephew of the then reigning pope, Clement VIII. In November 1604, when Guido was contracted to execute the *Crucifixion*, Cardinal Antonio Maria Gallo was in all likelihood considering the possibility of having the Treasure of the Holy House in Loreto decorated by Guido and Caravaggio. When Guido, most likely on behalf of Cardinal Gallo, approached Caravaggio, offering the Loreto job to him, and even pledging to 'serve under him' had this been to his liking, Caravaggio assaulted Guido verbally, blaming him among other things for stealing 'his style and coloring in the *Crucifixion of Saint Peter*'.[27]

While Caravaggio is unlikely to have seen Guido's painting in late 1604, he must have known about the Aldobrandini commission – which apparently had first gone to him – and perhaps Guido's pledge to imitate his style. In Malvasia's opinion, Guido's enmity with Caravaggio mirrored his deep aversion toward his rival's 'dark style', the *Crucifixion of Saint Peter* being an isolated episode in Guido's career. Malvasia goes as far – reasonably enough, however – as to present Guido as a fully-fledged anti-Caravaggio. Recording an episode that supposedly took place in Bologna prior to 1595 (if it ever occurred, it plausibly unfolded in Rome in 1602), Malvasia describes Ludovico and Annibale's irritated reaction to Caravaggio's raging fame. In particular, Annibale allegedly cried out:

> Why all this marveling? Do you believe that this is a new effect of novelty? I tell you that whoever might come up with an unheard-of style, entirely invented by himself, will always encounter the same destiny and meet with not inferior praises.[28]

As an antidote against painting's decline at Caravaggio's hands, and as a means to become a successful painter in the tempestuous ocean of artistic novelty, Annibale added:

> I would certainly know another way of making a big splash, and even of defeating and mortifying this one. I would oppose an extreme tenderness to his fierceness of color. Does he use a compact and falling light? I would want it diffused and face-on. Does he conceal the difficulties of art amidst the shadows of night? I would like to uncover in the bright light of noonday the most learned and erudite researches. If he throws down on canvas whatever he sees in nature, without seizing the good and the best, I would choose the most perfect parts, the most correctly arranged, giving to the figures that nobility and harmony lacking in the originals.[29]

Albeit voiced as a provocation, Annibale's speech can be said to have turned into the manifesto of Guido's new art. Like Caravaggio, Guido would focus on the human figure, making it coextensive with the pictorial surface. Whether depicted as a bust, a half-figure, or a full-length figure, the body would inhabit Guido's canvas, the latter morphed into its material embodiment. Unlike Caravaggio, Guido would not systematically allow darkness to engulf the body, to dismember it visually, to negate its unity, or deny its right to thrive in its idealised glory. No longer would an exceedingly tight framing

Fig. 10 Guido Reni, *The Crucifixion of Saint Peter*, 1604–5. Oil on panel, 305 × 171 cm. Rome, Musei Vaticani, Pinacoteca Vaticana, MV.40387

crop and mutilate the body by depriving it of a congruous attitude. Rendering shadow as translucent penumbra, and reducing its extension, Guido would brighten the body up, displaying the beauty of lean and elongated limbs, the skilful build of hands and feet, the thrilling distortion of beautifully foreshortened heads. But the Guido prefigured in Annibale's statement was yet to come.

In 1604, Guido was not as much taken aback as spellbound by Caravaggio's novelty. Looking at the question from a different standpoint, Giovanni Battista Passeri stressed the significance of this fascination instead of disproving it as Malvasia would do. In his life of Guido (c. 1670), Passeri notes that Guido 'fell in love' with Caravaggio's 'vigorous style, adherent to nature, and [marked] by strong colouring'. As a result, he ended up painting 'half-figures and even whole figures in imitation of Caravaggio, with a nobler idea and invention, more graceful and exact in drawing, but inferior in terms of colouring and a certain strict adherence to the true'.[30] That Passeri did not err in assessing the young painter's intention is evidenced by Guido's *Martyrdom of Saint Catherine of Alexandria* of 1605–6.[31] There, the martyr's pyramidal posture, her stretched symmetrical arms echoing the triangular disposition of her expanding garment, acts as a reminder of Raphael's ingenuity in devising bodily triangulations with geometrical purity. The notable allusion to Raphael through the figure of Saint Catherine is intended to evince Guido's 'nobler idea and invention' along with the gracefulness and exactness of his drawing. Not surprisingly, the crepuscular setting of the martyrdom confirms that Guido's novelty incorporated Raphael only to challenge and defeat Caravaggio. But what exactly did Guido borrow from his feisty rival?

In the *Crucifixion of Saint Peter*, Guido understood for the first time that even without yielding to Caravaggio's strenuous chiaroscuro, he could enhance the relief and tactility of the human body through a contrasted chromatic calibration. Mitigating Caravaggio's darkness into indigo opalescence, he would cause the bright hues to vibrate, the flesh to curve forward, lighten up, and thicken as if palpable. By pushing the picture's frame close to the human figure, imbricating the body of the crucified within those of the crucifiers, he recreated a bodily machinery on the example of Caravaggio's *Crucifixion of Saint Peter* at the Cerasi Chapel in Santa Maria del Popolo, Rome, and most recent *Deposition* in Santa Maria in Vallicella, Rome.[32] The equation of figure and pictorial surface not only entailed that the human body operated as the focus of the composition and the pivot of the *istoria*, but also fostered the notion that the figure could count as a monetary unit in the purchase of a painting. In this regard, Passeri mentions an otherwise unknown tailor in Rome for whom Guido 'painted a few half-figures and even whole figures in imitation of Caravaggio'. 'In the beginning', Passeri adds, 'the tailor gave him six scudi for each of those paintings, then went up to twelve, and because he sold them with great profit, he progressively increased [the remuneration] up to thirty'. However, once Guido 'realised that the tailor was doing it for his own interests, he ceased to work for him'.[33]

Documentary evidence corroborates Passeri's account. In 1606, Guido received twenty-five scudi from Cardinal Sfondrato for a half-figure of *Saint Cecilia* [fig. 11].[34] But twenty-five or thirty scudi for a half-figure were not enough for Guido. Leaving Rome a few years later, Guido blamed the Borghese and their acolytes for exploiting him while complaining about his 'exorbitant fees'. Enraged, he would complain: 'Does a half-figure by Caravaggio come so promptly and easily? Does it cost less than mine, when he even asks twice its price?'[35] Having learned from experience, Guido came to charge two hundred scudi for each full-length figure by 1627. Demanding as much from the Spanish ambassador in Rome and the Constable of Navarre, Guido writes in a letter to his friend Antonio Galeazzo Fibbia that 'they found [it] strange at first, then accepted'.[36] That Guido deliberately overhauled the dynamics of the art market by, among other things, raising the price of paintings on the basis of the number of figures is acknowledged not only by Malvasia, but also by Passeri:

> There was neither prince nor sovereign … who did not seek works by his hand, acknowledging them with the reward of the highest remuneration. Therefore, as he became aware of this, he fixed the price of each of his figures at one hundred scudi, fifty for a half-figure, and twenty-five for a simple head. This did not squelch the desire of his admirers, who instead grew increasingly eager to purchase his works, and the more he raised his fees, the greater the passion of the *curiosi* waxed. In truth, the profession is much obliged to Guido's magnificence because, with his credit he put in high esteem through his own works those of other excellent painters, who, following his example, grew bolder and made themselves be treated and appraised honourably.[37]

In his own terminology, Passeri uncovers the deep relationship between desire, the human figure, and remuneration at the core of Guido's market strategies. On account of their novelty,

Guido's figures aroused passion, and viewers, who literally 'desire[d]' and 'f[e]ll in love' with them, yearned for nothing more than possession, no matter how stiff the price. Malvasia evokes the case of a most beautiful *Magdalen* by Guido that belonged to the Bolognese poet Cesare Rinaldi, who, jealous of *her*, was distraught when *she* was stolen – or abducted? – from his house. In this connection, Malvasia reports that Cardinal Bernardino Spada 'was downright enamored' of *her*. Every time he visited Rinaldi, he 'always wanted to be seated facing that beautiful penitent, being unable to take his eyes off her, enraptured as if in ecstasy by that celestial idea'. One day, when Guido's *Magdalen* was carried in procession, as it was customary for paintings on certain festive days in Bologna, *she* 'was almost touched and inadvertently damaged by the halberd of a Swiss guard'. Fearing for *her*, the prelate 'immediately left his position' in the procession 'and hurled himself toward the soldier in order to restrain him'.[38] What determined Rinaldi's jealousy and distress and rekindled Cardinal Spada's Pygmalion syndrome was a mix of carnal attraction, aesthetic pleasure, and, in the prelate's case, proclivity for religious contemplation.

Much is still to be written about how Guido's concept of beauty originated in and transcended the principles, practices, and reception of lyrical poetry and literature in Italy, an issue that has remained understudied. It is unknown whether Cardinal Sfondrato, like Cardinal Spada years later, became infatuated with and enraptured by Guido's *Saint Cecilia* when he first gazed upon *her* in 1606. He certainly did not remain unaffected in front of this adolescent girl whose ivory white skin, silky white turban, and foamy white sleeves paradoxically ignite the vermilion of her robe against the foil of the pitch-black background. Thanks to Caravaggio's 'dark and contrasted style' and 'fierceness of color', the Sfondrato *Saint Cecilia* is no longer a pre- and neo-Raphaelesque devotional icon, in keeping, for instance, with Guido's early *Saint Cecilia* [cat. 87], but a flesh-and-blood heavenly vision, celestial enough to lure the viewer into contemplation, yet human enough to impress the viewer's sight and touch through her chromatically and haptically magnified presence.

Counter to Malvasia's assumption, Guido never rid himself of Caravaggio. To be sure, after 1606, and especially in relation to his service under the Borghese between 1607 and 1612, Guido made a stylistic U-turn, reneging on Caravaggio, thereby briefly returning to the Carracci's lesson – his *Saint Andrew led to Martyrdom* of 1608 in San Gregorio al Celio, Rome, could also be interpreted as an acute reflection and elaboration upon the Carracci frescoes of 1589–92 in the Magnani Palace, Bologna –

Fig. 11 Guido Reni, *Saint Cecilia*, 1606. Oil on canvas, 95.9 × 74.9 cm. Pasadena, The Norton Simon Foundation, F.1973.23.P

and formulating a 'palatial' style inspired by two of the most successful painters in Rome at the time, the influential Cavalier d'Arpino and Giovanni Baglione (c. 1566–1643) – both sworn enemies of Caravaggio.[39] It is difficult to recognise Caravaggio's imprint in the frescoes produced by Guido in the Apostolic Palace in 1608–9 and, partly, in the Quirinal Palace in 1609–10, his most acclaimed *Virgin sewing in the Temple* (Quirinal) almost classifying as neo-Mannerist.[40] But soon enough Guido refocused on the potential of the human figure in the *istoria*, using the picture's margins as a dynamic boundary in contrast with the figures' bodies, now tightly entangled within the ongoing action like a clockwork mechanism. Reference is made here to Guido's *Massacre of the Innocents* of 1611–12 [cat. 20], the painting with which he was born as the herald of a new modernity.[41] Until then, Guido's originality had consisted in developing the Carracci synthesis of styles in light of a renewed study of Raphael or appropriating and revamping Caravaggio's subversive naturalism. Now Guido proceeds to modernise the principles of Leon Battista Alberti's (1404–1472) *istoria* by using the figures as structural units of action.

In doing so, he not surprisingly relied on two works traditionally associated with Raphael: the *Massacre of the Innocents* tapestry in three panels – executed possibly after designs by Giulio Romano (c. 1499–1546) – for Pope Clement VII, and the renowned engraving of the *Massacre of the Innocents* by Marcantonio Raimondi (c. 1470/82–1527/34) after a design by Raphael. Guido's allusion to these two compositions is not only deliberate, but deliberately conspicuous. At first glance, his painting looks like one of the Vatican tapestries, imitating in particular the set's central panel, where four overlapping rows of mothers, infants, and torturers appear enchained one to another in a condensed tangle of violence. While Giulio tends to overcharge, burdening the pictorial surface to the point of bodily saturation, Guido's figures disperse like clouds at sunrise, triangulating into a diamond of centrifugal motions that appears tipped downward with at its centre a triangular void pierced at its top by the menacing downthrust of a dagger. By structuring the composition in this manner, Guido enables the gaze to linger upon each of the figures, in particular the *Niobe*-like kneeling mother in the foreground, the epitome of beautiful sorrow.

Like Guido's mourning Virgin and Saint John in his 1619 *Christ on the Cross* painted for the main altar of Monte Calvario dei Cappuccini,[42] this mother's head, 'far from being disfigured, ha[s its] beauty increased in [its] grieving'.[43] Like the Magdalen in Correggio's *Lamentation* in San Giovanni Evangelista, Parma,[44] this mother's head stresses 'the great difficulty of representing a crying figure with propriety', proving 'an unmatched miracle of art for she [is] crying without inappropriately upsetting her face'.[45] As the poet Giovanni Battista Marino put it in a madrigal (initially composed for another picture, but subsequently and so felicitously dedicated to Guido's work), the *Massacre of the Innocents* demonstrates 'that even a tragic event is an endearing object / and that horror often goes with pleasure'.[46] As an antithetical dyad, horror and pleasure coexist through artifice: the diamond of figures in the painting is a crystalised structure on the brink of disintegration as a consequence of opposing fictive forces. It is this crystallisation that allows the gaze to safely approach the destructive vehemence of this compositional device, to single out each figure, to pause by progressively appreciating the artifice of Guido's craftsmanship. The

extreme beauty of the kneeling mother's gasping grief is artificially conveyed through the noble allusion to the antique *Niobe*.[47] Deemed paradigmatic of ancient perfection, most likely recognised as such by knowledgeable viewers despite Guido's deft elaboration upon it, this head becomes suddenly animated under Guido's hands. The plain relief of the antique statue softens into fluid form, swiftly blocked out from the priming through subtle glazing, her upper eyelids left almost at the stage of drawing/brushing. This animation of the antique is not only technically unprecedented; it also formally undermines the ancient canon by turning it into an empty shell, a locus of pictorial artifice – a form about to revert into the *non-finito* of the *sbozzo*.

Malvasia somehow intuited this when observing that in works executed after his return to Bologna in 1612, Guido 'painted with *sprezzatura* in bold strokes' in conformity with a technique that the historian had seen applied on occasion only by Titian and Tintoretto in Venice.[48] Unlike his Venetian predecessors, Guido was a master of 'delicacy', and by nature he would have refrained from imitating Titian's final style as described by Vasari in a memorable passage of his *Vite*: 'His late works are made up of frank and grand brushstrokes, sketched out summarily, and blurred, so as they cannot be taken in up close, whereas from a distance they appear to be perfect'.[49] Albeit dissimilar, Guido's technique nonetheless determines a 'bifocal' perception of the painting like that effected by Titian's works. At a distance, the forms appear fully rounded, while up close, the pictorial surface is enlivened by dint of subtle gradations in definition obtained through delicate hatching and quasi-ethereal strokes.

It is difficult to understand the intense marvel that Guido's neo-Venetian style instilled in early seventeenth-century beholders. As already mentioned, the layout of the *Massacre of the Innocents* is reminiscent of a Raphael composition enriched through some ancient borrowing (the *Niobe*). Contemporary beholders would therefore have perceived Guido's painting as a display of excellence in *disegno*. And yet, by nearing the picture, viewers were confronted with an exhibition of neo-Venetian bravura they would have recognised as pertaining to colour. Like horror and pleasure, *disegno* and colour coexist in the *Massacre of the Innocents*, and their coexistence is achieved – to paraphrase another passage by Malvasia – in a 'peculiar manner', regarded then as 'new because not used in the schools of Rome or Lombardy'.[50] Part and parcel of the aesthetic pleasure enjoyed upon seeing the *Massacre* derives from Guido's manipulation of the viewer's expectations and biases: what was considered irreconcilable, Rome and Venice, coalesces (without fusing together) into an artistic paradox.

Guido's enterprise was not without risks. His emphasis on the human figure as the armature of the *istoria* – on Caravaggio's example – dramatically reduces, if it does not annihilate, the importance of perspective and the role of the traditional accessories of the genre. The artistry infused in each figure admittedly leads to a neglect in the degree of coordination within the action, compromising the principle of verisimilitude. Celebrating the *Massacre of the Innocents*, Malvasia remarks, on the contrary, that in it, Guido 'sought to demonstrate to his detractors, who voiced abroad that he exceled only in depicting one or two figures, that he was capable of putting together many figures and composing a pictorial story'.[51] In Malvasia's eyes, the *Massacre of the Innocents* constituted a culminating point in Guido's art since the master had executed 'everything with a strength suffused with such tenderness, with a nonchalance thus reined in by precision, with movements regulated in such a manner by decorum, that no one has ever reached such a mark of distinction'.[52] Responding to an accusation otherwise levelled at Caravaggio – the inability to depict more than one or two figures – Guido not only created a *concordia discors* – a harmony of strength and tenderness, nonchalance and decorum, motion and stillness – but supposedly presented himself as a proto-academic master: one toeing the line of the *istoria* as a canonical pictorial genre. Of course, Malvasia knew that Guido's orthodoxy was to be short-lived. By 1630, when he completed his acclaimed *Pallione del Voto* or *Pala della Peste* [fig. 30], Guido had long been lacking 'that great invention, fertile composition, judicious modes of appropriately casting shadows and modulating light, that propriety in the figures and in the expression of the affections' that had distinguished his *Massacre of the Innocents*.[53] In short, Guido had disappointedly ceased to master the *istoria*.

At odds with Malvasia, it must be noted that as a multi-figural narrative the *Massacre of the Innocents* is a relative rarity in Guido's painting. More to the point, it could be argued that the painting was never the orthodox work described by Malvasia because Guido's interest lay primarily in the aesthetic effect of each figure separately, in the visual lure of the mothers' beautified agony, of the infants' tender horror, of the torturers' lithe and pensive cruelty. Furthermore, Guido's diamond of figures is also a feat of chromatism. A prism within the prism on account of her pyramidal posture, the kneeling mother towers over a socle of overflowing draperies, blue and yellow, articulated into quasi-polygonal, shallow folds: an overextension of her body

gracefully pervaded by an undercurrent of agitation. Soon, Guido would release the latent charge of his draperies, emancipating them from the body, stretching their reach beyond plausibility. In his monumental *Glory of Saint Dominic* of 1613–15 in San Domenico, Bologna, Guido, like Albrecht Dürer (1471–1528) before him, likely 'emptied all the warehouses' of his homeland 'for linens and cloths'. Excoriated by his former master, Ludovico, for 'overdressing' his figures 'in the style of Statius', Guido, as Malvasia implies, may have dismissed his former master's criticism as 'suspect', but in fact Ludovico's attack was all too grounded.[54]

In Guido's defence, Malvasia underscored the 'grandness' attached to 'supernatural objects':

> The breadth of the draperies in those celestial figures aims at exactly the same effect as the great trail of a mantle wrapped round a noble matron, or the great train of the cappa magna worn by cardinals, which adds so much external decorum and majesty to them.[55]

However, Christ's disproportionate white robe in the *Glory of Saint Dominic* is no matter of simple majesty: its bulk is such that, by comparison, the torso dwindles to almost one third of the figure, not to mention the huge discrepancy in perspective and foreshortening so blatantly introduced by that overhanging mass of drapery. In the seventeenth century, the Roman poet Statius was seen as the antithesis of Virgil, the latter incarnating the virtue of irreproachable measure in the highest genre of epic poetry.[56] Provocatively, Guido-the-new-Statius flaunts his entitlement to excess, to selectively transgressing proportion in order to evoke transcendence: a sublime sense of the human body, and its counterpart, the drapery, both of them exempt from the strictures of nature. It is notable that Guido, while often revindicating his indebtedness to antiquity and Raphael (specifically in the field of *disegno* and draughtsmanship), actively subverts the 'Roman' canon by pushing it toward and beyond the limits of extreme idealisation.

Guido's anticlassicism may be less manifest than Caravaggio's, but it proves no less corrosive since over time it dislocates the canon as if innocently, from within, under the pretext of a more acceptable poetics of the 'idea'. In the long run, Guido's subversion became unabashedly evident, and it was stigmatised as his 'second' or 'late manner'. In his *Microcosmo della pittura* (1657), Francesco Scannelli records the opinion of the nobleman and painter Fabio della Corgna (c. 1600–1643) about a later painting by Guido, which:

Fig. 12 Guido Reni, *Lucretia*, c. 1625–26. Oil on canvas, 108.6 × 98.1 cm. Providence, Rhode Island School of Design, inv. 56.102

was beautiful in and of itself, but chimerical, such as the work of contemporary writers, who usually in their romances summon up an analogue of a history or mythology, so to speak, so accurate and well adorned that, because the specific way of developing it brings the greatest pleasure, it causes the beholder to enjoy it accordingly, even though it is far from the truth.[57]

Tactfully and thoughtfully phrased, Della Corgna's assessment was no praise but a backhanded critique. In his view, Guido's work belonged to a successful, yet highly discredited, low genre of literature, the novel: a fantastic analogue of history and nature. Novels were made to 'bring pleasure'; in them, description was vivid and graphic so that the senses might revel in experiencing a pseudo-truth, an alluring chimera. In Della Corgna's view, Guido's late paintings were not substance, but sensual illusion. To understand what was considered chimerical in

Guido's 'second manner' it is useful to read Malvasia's objection to Della Corgna's statement, which appears in a broader reflection on Guido's novelty late in his life:

> He also wore himself out over his last paintings, never being satisfied … showing himself ever more erudite, with new effects and a thousand delightful refinements, blending subtle hues of violet-gray and pale blue mixed in amidst the half-tints and flesh colors … These tints can be observed on delicate skin, which reflects a diaphanous glow, more conspicuously when the light falls from above, in particular when passing through closed windows, especially those made of glass … These inventions of his are not chimerical, ideal, and without foundation, as was claimed by Don Fabio della Corgna.[58]

Meaningfully, Guido's utmost refinement, his final novelty, is identified by Malvasia with his way of rendering skin and flesh,

Lorenzo Pericolo

and it is thus made to reside specifically in the depiction of the body. Far from arbitrary – Malvasia argues – this unusual chromatism (the mixture of flesh tints with grey-violet and pale blue hues) results from empirical observation, namely, from close examination of the effects of light on skin almost at a microscopic level. For Malvasia, Guido's technique contrasted with Caravaggio's inasmuch as Guido,

> especially in his final years, refused to use those tremendous and contrived shadows that seem to fall from high up, from a window left ajar, motivated by the light of the sun or a burning torch, excessively artificial in any case, vehement and affected, and which are not to be seen ordinarily in nature unless one wants to represent a night scene, a fire, or similar things.[59]

While Caravaggio's dark manner, supposedly enslaved to nature, appears almost anti-naturalist to Malvasia, Guido's 'second manner' – a 'white' manner according to Malvasia – was the product of a ground-breaking empiricism, a discovery in keeping with the optical advances of Guido's age.[60] For Malvasia, Guido's apparent disregard for a more traditional rendition of the flesh was tantamount to a refusal of 'Aristotelian propositions' in natural philosophy, now 'at last overturned and submitted to the evidence of experimentation'.[61]

Malvasia, however, was of two minds about Guido's 'second manner'. In the end, he managed to dismiss his previous enthusiasm for it, agreeing that in the course of the years Guido's painting had declined: his modernity had not corresponded to empirical progress, but was a regression, a weakening caused by ageing and the demon of gambling.[62] At this point in his assessment of Guido, Malvasia did not see a continuity between the early and late Guido: the former was canonised as a champion of the fourth age of painting whereas the latter proved an unfortunate aberration. Informed by the French academic culture of his own time, this conclusion, a bitter one for Malvasia, stems from a notion of art centred on the authority of tradition, not on the upheavals of novelty.

But looking at Guido's evolution with novelty in mind as a criterion, the painter who then emerges from that standpoint is an unflinching pioneer, an indefatigable experimenter of the pictorial body as a catalyst for artistic innovation. With intelligence, Malvasia had pointed out in previous times that Guido's excessive 'delicacy', disliked as a feature of his 'second manner', was necessary insofar as 'he made only half-figures to enjoy in one's room and up close [*in camera e da presso*]'.[63]

Fig. 13 Guido Reni, *Cleopatra*, c. 1621–26. Oil on canvas, 124 × 94 cm. Potsdam, Schloß Sanssouci, Bildergalerie, GK I 5054

Needless to say, not all of Guido's late output was like this, but the idea that his paintings required intimacy and careful scrutiny may apply to his entire production, and perhaps explains why he seduced generations of viewers while painting 'simple' figures, with almost no accessories (symbolic or otherwise), with little to no architecture, and with some impressive, albeit limited, landscape views. Guido's world is made of skin and drapery, and with merely these two components he keeps devising quasi-infinite figural variations meant to impact on the audience once and again, each time for some unusual effect. It is time we leave behind the trite construct of Guido the Catholic image-maker, not because religion and devotion are absent from his art, but because it is urgent to wonder whether their presence may reflect religious and devotional tendencies that exceed those conventionally associated with the

Fig. 14 Guido Reni, *Samson Victorious*, c. 1617–19. Oil on canvas, 260 × 223 cm. Bologna, Pinacoteca Nazionale di Bologna, inv. 450

Counter-Reformation. It is time we acknowledge the crucial effect of attraction and desire sparked by Guido's figures, his boldness – so rare in his time – to provide us with life-size full-length nudity, both male and female, in competition with, but also capitalising on, the eroticised lure of the ancient nude in a culture uncomfortable with, if not plainly averse to nudity.

Studying and expounding on Guido's multiple novelties should be the task of a much longer essay. To grasp the extent of Guido's inventiveness in displaying the human body, it may be interesting to show side by side two of his half-figures, and two of his full-length figures. On the one hand, we could linger on his almost unknown Providence *Lucretia* [fig. 12] and his Potsdam *Cleopatra* [fig. 13].[64] In both paintings, multiple layers of drapery swirl around an unblemished expanse of flesh, suffused with bluish luminosity in the *Lucretia*, slightly tinged with green in the *Cleopatra*. In common, these two works propose a powerful dichotomy between bare skin and overbrimming drapery, the former almost translucent, the latter brushed in such a variety of hues and impasto to defy any attempt at technical description. On the other hand, we could briefly consider his magnificent Bologna *Samson Victorious* [fig. 14] and the Valletta *Risen Christ embracing the Cross* [fig. 15].[65] Only a few years pass between the execution of the former in about 1617–19 and that of the latter in 1621. In the *Samson* – a heroic nude – the body detaches itself from the background almost divested of shadows, in particular the elongated torso, densely built with incredibly subtle impasto. Dwelling on this figure, one seems to hear Annibale's fictive speech about a painting that would be antithetical to Caravaggio's. In the *Samson*, the light is 'diffused and face-on'; 'the most learned and erudite researches' come to the fore 'in the bright light of noonday';[66] and the limbs are endowed with the 'nobility and harmony' of a perfected, supernatural anatomy. A religious nude – something to scandalise Giovanni Andrea Gilio had he been alive – the *Risen Christ* models himself on Michelangelo's much-criticised *Christ* at Santa Maria sopra Minerva, Rome. With its feverish, corrosive light, the painting could pass for a Neapolitan or Sicilian Caravaggio – Guido had owned Caravaggio's late *Denial of Saint Peter*.[67] Examining these two works together, it would be easy to pit the 'white' Guido against the 'dark' Guido, the anti-Caravaggio against the Caravaggio 2.0. However, Guido is much more than this opposition. Earlier, we defined Guido as a chameleon of stylistic experimentation, and it is undeniable that he never quit experimenting throughout his career, even when his work was frowned upon as weak, chimerical, incongruous. Even when, unable or unwilling to finish his paintings, he gave free rein to invention by exploring the limits of the *non-finito*.[68] Guido's taste for novelty does not rely exclusively on a market strategy. Toward the end of his life, ever dissatisfied with his own work, Guido confessed that 'he was obliged to do even more than he knew and could do, if possible, since he was paid much more than any other paint- er before him'.[69] The desire he had embodied in his works and that had translated into his figures' irresistible enticement and his patrons' fever of possession was now introjected: it had become – although arguably it had always been – a desire for an art expression superior to and beyond his capabilities. An art never seen before; an art that can only be conceived and never fully materialises. Like Michelangelo before him, Guido gave the traits of divine beauty to that incommensurable thirst for art, aiming to attain novelty after novelty, ultimately resign- ing himself to the idea that only the unfinished work in its ven- turesome indefiniteness may reveal the unattainable quintessence of art. The multiple bodies of Guido's painting result from this trans-novelty, this ever-renewed quest for an embodiment that no body in painting could truly accomplish.

fig. 15 Guido Reni, *Risen Christ embracing the Cross*, 1621. Oil on canvas, 227 × 138 cm. Valletta, National Museum of Art MUŻA

1 Malvasia–Pericolo 2019, 1:459 and 2:27.

2 Ibid., 1:459 and 2:26–31.

3 On the fourth age of painting, see Malvasia–Pericolo 2019, 1:208–9, note 2; 1:215–16, notes 17–18; 2:50–56.

4 On the synthesis of styles, see Malvasia–Pericolo 2019, 2:45–53.

5 Malvasia–Pericolo 2019, 1:18–19 and 1:222–23, note 36: 'Quella maniera troppo manierosa appunto, leccata ed oltramontana'.

6 On Calvaert's pedagogy, see Malvasia–Pericolo 2019, 1:219–20, note 28; 1:221, note 31; 1:222, note 34; 1:223, note 37.

7 Perini Folesani 1990, 160.

8 See most recently Pericolo (in press).

9 Malvasia–Pericolo 2019, 1:24–25 and 1:229, note 55: 'Ove gli altri seguivano un'abbreviatura ed un certo facile tentoresco e risoluto … egli al contrario, trovandosi già di questa pratica possessore, dilettavasi di una più esatta ricercata d'ogni minutissima parte, d'ogni muscolo, all'uso quasi de' Passerotti, ma raddolcendo poi tutto e coprendolo d'una certa facilità e sprezzatura maravigliosa'.

10 New Haven, Yale University Art Gallery, inv. 2019.29.1.

11 Malvasia–Pericolo 2019, 1:28–29 and 1:235, note 69.

12 Ibid., 1:246–47, note 96.

13 Bologna, Pinacoteca Nazionale di Bologna, inv. 577.

14 Dublin, National Gallery of Ireland, NGI.70. Malvasia–Pericolo 2019, 1:36–37 and 1:245, note 94.

15 Ibid.

16 On Malvasia's concept of 'dryness' as specific of Vasari's *seconda maniera* and its association with Raphael, too, see Pericolo 2015.

17 On these two landscapes by Guido see most recently the catalogue entries by Francesco Gatta and Daniele Benati in Cappelletti 2022, 156–65, nos. 15–16. See also Malvasia–Pericolo 2019, 1:374, note 436.

18 Malvasia–Pericolo 2019, 1:176–77: 'L'Albani non esser pittore, ma un gentiluomo che attendeva a que' suoi pensieretti, a quelle cosarelle per trattenimento e per ischerzo'.

19 Ibid., 1:36–37: 'Sul gusto di Rafaelle una graziosa giovane ricinta di sottilissimi veli, con canestrello d'uvova, sovra la cui spalla una compagna più vecchia, sul gusto del Coreggio, posta la mano e la testa ridente, guardano ambidue gli spettatori con tanta vivacità e spirito che par che spirino. Sul gusto di Tiziano un pastorello che, sonando un flauto con certe mani di viva e tenera carne, viene attentamente da un altro, di non minor bellezza, ascoltato. Sul gusto di Annibale una donna con un bambino lattante in collo ed un altro adulto che con la destra ella spinge ad offerire una canestrella di pomi, da' quali non sa il golosello staccar gli occhi; e lasciandone tanti altri, sul principio un gran nudo intero, così terribile e risentito nel tirare per forza un asinello restio che pareva che Michelangelo l'avesse in tal forma contornato, perché più tenero poi e più ricoperto di vera carne ei venisse dalla scuola di Lombardia'.

20 Ibid., 1:242–45, notes 89–93, on the history of the commission and rivalry with Ludovico.

21 Ibid., 1:34–37: 'Poiché, finita che l'ebbe, fece stupire lo stesso Lodovico che prima d'iscoprirsi la vidde… Atterrì quegl'altri che si conobbero di gran lunga superati, e fece dire a tutti che passato egli avesse anche il maestro in certa morbidezza, venustà e grandezza, alla quale né anche fossero mai giunti gli stessi Carracci'.

22 Ibid., 1:365, note 410.

23 On Guido's 'delicacy' as opposed to Annibale's 'vigour', see Malvasia–Pericolo 2019, 2:18–23.

24 Ibid., 1:236–37, note 73.

25 The opposition between Michelangelo's *terribilità* (associated with the male muscular body) and Raphael's *dolcezza* and delicacy (more specific to the female body and evocation of tender flesh) is notoriously argued by Dolce 1557, 33r–35v, 44v, and 47v–48r.

26 Malvasia–Pericolo 2019, 1: 38–39 and 1:248, no. 99: 'Promettendo egli al cardinal Borghese che sarebbesi Guido trasformato nel Caravaggio, e l'avrebbe fatto di quella maniera cacciata e scura'.

27 Ibid., 1:38–41 and 1:248–50, notes 100–2.

28 Ibid., 1:26–29 and 1:233–34, note 66: 'Che tante maraviglie? … parvi egli questo un nuovo effetto della novità? Io vi dico che tutti quei che con non più veduta e da essi loro inventata maniera usciran fuore, incontreranno sempre la stessa sorte e non minore la loda'.

29 Ibid., 1:28–29: 'Saprei ben io, soggions'egli, un altro modo per far gran colpo, anzi da vincere e mortificare costui; a quel colorito fiero vorrei contrapporne uno affatto tenero; prende egli un lume serrato e cadente, ed io lo vorrei aperto e in faccia; cuopre quegli le difficoltà dell'arte fra l'ombre della notte, ed io a un chiaro lume di mezzo giorno vorrei scoprire i più dotti ed eruditi ricerchi; quanto ved'egli nella natura, senza isfiorarne il buono e 'l meglio, tanto mette giù, ed io vorrei scegliere il più perfetto delle parti, un più aggiustato, dando alle figure quella nobiltà ed armonia di che manca l'originale'. On the anti-Caravaggio, ibid., 2:61–69.

30 Hess 1934b, 80–81.

31 Albenga (Italy), Museo Diocesano. See most recently the catalogue entry by Antonio Iommelli in Cappelletti 2022, 112–15, no. 5.

32 The latter now in Rome, Pinacoteca Vaticana, inv. 40386.

33 Hess 1934b, 81.

34 Malvasia–Pericolo 2019, 1:246, note 96.

35 Ibid., 1:52–53 and 1:267, note 137: 'Si ha così presto e così facilmente una mezza figura dal Caravaggio? Si paga ella meno di una mia, quando ben il doppio ne vuole?'.

36 Ibid., 1:295–97, note 218.

37 Hess 1934b, 95. See Malvasia–Pericolo 2019, 2:116.

38 Malvasia–Pericolo 2019, 1:98–99 and 1:324, note 289.

39 On Guido's *Saint Andrew led to Martyrdom*, see Malvasia–Pericolo 2019, 1:42–45 and 1:253–54, note 109.

40 On these works, ibid., 1:46–51 and 1:251–52, note 106.

41 On the painting, ibid., 1:54–57 and 1:257–58, note 121.

42 Bologna, Pinacoteca Nazionale di Bologna, inv. 441.

43 Malvasia–Pericolo 2019, 1:70–73 and 1:283, note 187: 'Che nulla si difformano, anzi si abbelliscono nel pianto'.

44 Parma, Galleria Nazionale, GN 352.

45 Scannelli 1657, 278: 'Egli dopo haver dimostrato la gran difficoltà, che si ritrovava per esprimere una piangente al proposito proruppe finalmente nel dire, che una tal Maddalena del Correggio era un miracolo senza pari dell'arte, e quella veramente piangea senza sconcerto disdicevole del viso'. The comment on Correggio's *Lamentation* was made by Guercino.

46 Malvasia–Pericolo 2019, 1:72–73: 'Ch'ancor tragico caso è caro oggetto / e che spesso l'orror va col diletto'.

47 Florence, Gallerie degli Uffizi, inv. Sculture 1914 n. 294.

48 Malvasia–Pericolo 2019, 1:70–71 and 1:281, note 184.

49 Vasari–Bettarini and Barocchi 1966–97 (1976), 4:551.

50 Malvasia–Pericolo 2019, 1:54–55.

51 Ibid., 1:54–57: 'Poiché in quelli volledare a vedere a' malevoli che divulgavano in una o due figure al più non aver l'uguale, saperne anche porre assieme molte ed istoriare'.

52 Ibid.: 'Eseguito il tutto con una forza mista di tanta tenerezza, con uno sprezzo moderato così dalla giustezza, con movenze regolate in tal guisa dal decoro che nissuno mai gionse a quel segno'.

53 Ibid., 1:114–15: 'Quella grande invenzione, quella ferace composizione, que' giudiziosi ripieghi di sbattimenti favorevoli e di trapassi di lume, quella proprietà nelle figure ed espressioni di affetti'. On the *Pallione del Voto*, ibid., 1:295, note 217.

54 Ibid., 1:62–65. On the *Glory of Saint Dominic*, ibid., 1:271, note 152.

55 Ibid., 1:62–63: 'L'ampiezza di que' panni in que' personaggi celesti fare appunto quell'istesso effetto che gran strasico di manto attorno a no-

bile matrona, o gran coda alle cappe magne de' cardinali, a' quali esternamente ancor esse aggiongono tanto di decoro e di maestà'.

56 Ibid., 1:274, note 162, and 2:78–80.

57 Scannelli 1657, 113–14: 'Essere l'opera per se stessa bella, ma favolosa, per appunto in guisa dell'opere de gli hodierni Scrittori, i quali per l'ordinario co' Romanzi loro apportano alla consideratione un simile d'historia, ò favola, che vogliamo dire, così puntuale, e bene adornata, che il modo della particolare espressione allettando in estremo, fa, che goda parimente l'osservatore, benché per lo più davvero lontano'.

58 Malvasia–Pericolo 2019, 1:182–83 and 1:408–9, note 580: 'Affaticavasi anche, non mai saziandosi, ... nell'ultime sue pitture, mostrandocele sempre più erudite, con nuovi ricerchi e mille galanterie, con certi lividetti ed azzurrini mescolati fra le mezze tente e fra le carnaggioni..., quali si osservano nelle carni delicate, che rendono un certo diafano, ma più poi ed evidentemente qualora il lume cade sopra di esse, passando in particolare per finestre chiuse, massime di vetro, ... non essendo queste sue invenzioni chimeriche, ideali e senza appoggio, come ebbe a dire don Fabio della Cornia'.

59 Ibid., 1:184–85: 'Massime in quest'ultimo, usar l'ombre terribili e forzate, come cadenti d'alto e da finestra socchiusa, cagionate da lume di sole o di torchio acceso, artifiziose troppo ad ogni modo, violenti ed affettate, che non vediamo naturalmente e per l'ordinario salvo che in caso di rappresentare una notte, un incendio e simili'.

60 On the 'white manner', see Malvasia–Pericolo 2019, 2:36–45 and Pericolo 2019b.

61 Malvasia–Pericolo 2019, 1:182–83: 'Proposizioni aristoteliche infin negate ed all'evidenza dello sperimento ridotte'.

62 Ibid., 1:100–1 and 2:44–45.

63 Ibid., 1:494. 'Faceva solo mezze figure da godersi in camera e da presso'.

64 To my knowledge, the Providence *Lucretia* does not appear in any publication on Guido. For the Potsdam *Cleopatra*, see Pepper 1988, 260–61, no. 97.

65 On the *Samson Victorious*, see Malvasia–Pericolo 2019, 1:318–19, note 279. On the *Risen Christ*, ibid., 1:428–29, note 636, and 2:75.

66 See above, note 26.

67 New York, The Metropolitan Museum of Art, Gift of Herman and Lila Shickman, and Purchase, Lila Acheson Wallace Gift, 1997, 1997.167. See Malvasia–Pericolo 2019, 1:268, note 139.

68 On Guido's *non-finito*, see Pericolo 2019b.

69 Malvasia–Pericolo 2019, 1:166–67: 'Rispondeva ch'era obbligato a farvi anche di più che sapea e potea, se fosse stato possibile, venendone pagato più che mai altro pittore per lo passato'.

'LIKE A BEE AMONGST THE FLOWERS': YOUNG GUIDO RENI BETWEEN BOLOGNA AND ROME

Rachel McGarry

Like a bee amongst the flowers, so Guido went, savouring the exquisite and most perfect from all.[1]

Around the age of nine, Guido Reni (1575–1642) began his apprenticeship in the thriving workshop of Denys Calvaert (c. 1540–1619), a successful Flemish artist living in Bologna.[2] Calvaert had persuaded his father to allow the boy to train as a painter after seeing his gifts and passion for drawing and clay modelling. Guido came from a family of musicians: his father, maternal grandfather, and two uncles performed in the Signoria's celebrated wind ensemble, the Concerto Palatina, and were among its highest earners.[3] Guido likely had begun learning to play the cornet, trombone, and harpsichord while still in grammar school. As a testament to this youthful immersion in music, the artist often painted musical concerts, usually for holy figures ascending into heaven, as in the Frankfurt *Assumption of the Virgin*, the Madrid *Assumption and Coronation of the Virgin*, and the London *Coronation of the Virgin* [cat. 7–9], with angels playing superbly crafted instruments. Entering Calvaert's school meant that Guido would forego a musical career and forfeit the security of an inherited position and salary in the civic orchestra. But he had found his path. By thirteen, he had made such strides that Calvaert selected him to teach drawing to his fellow pupils.

Reni probably trained with Calvaert for nearly a decade, and his earliest works are deeply influenced by his master's manner, designs, and figural canon. The school was by all accounts a stimulating place to learn, and Guido received a rigorous foundation in *disegno* (drawing and design). Calvaert taught perspective, anatomy, optics, the orders of architecture, principles of design, and life drawing.[4] His pupils also benefitted from studying the master's rich collection of sculptures and casts, and Renaissance prints and drawings, including works by Raphael (1483–1520), Marcantonio Raimondi (c. 1470/82–1527/34), and Albrecht Dürer (1471–1528) – artists who had a profound influence on Reni, and whose works on paper he would one day collect.[5]

Guido also got plenty of hands-on experience in painting. Calvaert was preoccupied with a stream of major altarpiece commissions,[6] such that he relied heavily on his assistants to meet the high demand for his *rametti*, small paintings on copper. This was a favoured support of many Northern artists working in Italy in the period; Calvaert's coppers were recorded in prestigious collections in Bologna and Rome, exported abroad, and popular with 'novice nuns and new brides'.[7] Reni reportedly excelled at this work, even inventing some designs that the master retouched.[8] The skill proved formative in his early career. After moving to Rome and before he established a large studio as a salaried painter of Cardinal Scipione Borghese in early 1608, Guido painted *rametti*. The Prado's pair of Saint Apollonia paintings of about 1600–3 [cat. 13 and 14] exemplify the dazzling colour and polished finish he was able to achieve on this precious, portable medium. His most frequent subjects were celestial scenes filled with handsome miniature angels engaged in tender exchanges with the Virgin. Reni's *rametti* found their way into important Roman collections, notably those of the Aldobrandini and Borghese families. Perhaps the artist gave them as gifts: they would have been ideal advertisements of his distinctive artistic vision and the divine grace for which he would become famous. These paintings may well have helped secure his first major commissions from these papal families.

Before he struck out on his own as an independent painter around 1598, Reni joined the Carracci shop, probably in 1594–95. Carlo Cesare Malvasia and Giovan Pietro Bellori blame Calvaert's difficult personality and violent temper for Guido's decision to go[9] – Domenichino (1581–1641), too, left after Calvaert assaulted him for dropping a *rametto*. Reni's early Bolognese works never really aligned with the revolutionary naturalism of the Carracci in Bologna, but, Calvaert's personality aside, the ambitious Guido needed to spread his wings, and the reputation of the Carracci had surpassed Calvaert's. Annibale (1560–1609) and Agostino's (1557–1602) trip to Rome for a few months in the autumn of 1594, followed by Annibale's definitive move there by November 1595, could account for Reni's timing. With Annibale's departure imminent, Ludovico (1555–1619) must have been looking for help, and many young artists entered his studio at this time. As an experienced artist around nineteen years old, Reni is more accurately described as a journeyman. He did not stay long enough to participate in any significant Carracci workshop commissions, such as the oratory frescoes at San Colombano or the Aeneas frieze at the Palazzo Fava, where Ludovico's *bottega* of 'unproven disciples' collaborated loosely in Ludovico's manner.[10]

Nonetheless Guido's three years with the Carracci transformed his style. The studio's novel emphasis on life drawing and his immersion in the exceptional work of all three Carracci – paintings, drawings, and prints – were seminal. Reni assisted with studio tasks, studied and copied Carracci works, particularly Annibale's, and learned to etch, focusing on Parmigianino's (1503–1540) designs. As a journeyman, he was also free to take on independent work. His first major altarpiece, the *Coronation of the Virgin with four Saints* [fig. 16], painted for the Olivetan monks' church of San Bernardo, may date from these years. The *Judgement of Solomon* of around 1595–98, in a private collection, and the recently rediscovered *Assumption of the Virgin with Saints Francis, Dominic, Peter Martyr and Agnes* of around 1598–99, in the Klesch collection in London, may as well.[11] Blending quotations of works by Calvaert, the Carracci, Parmigianino, and other Emilian artists into single paintings, Reni created a novel style that was elegant and otherworldly. His languid figures seem to glow mysteriously. The high-keyed pastel palette – pale pink, dazzling yellow, pearly violet – combined with cool atmosferic effects, dark charcoal skies, and distant mountain landscapes reflect the enduring imprint of Calvaert, as do the compact figures with their sturdy, square heads (men) and teardrop faces with prominent noses (women). Reni typically restricted interaction and eye contact among his figures in these early works, so the forms appear as discrete units. The sculptural weight of the subjects (both celestial and earthly) in the Klesch *Assumption* contrast with the diaphanous forms and lustrous surfaces of Reni's other works, pointing to the next phase.

On 27 November 1598, Pope Clement VIII visited Bologna following the papal annexation of Ferrara. The city was transformed for the occasion: elaborate *apparati* were erected, palaces and arcades were adorned, and the squares were filled with Bologna's 60,000 residents. Reni, then age twenty-three, won the most prominent commission of the day, the decoration of the monument on the façade of the Palazzo Pubblico, where the papal procession would culminate. His mural, now lost but preserved in an etching by his hand, shows allegories, angels, narratives, and armorials majestically set into illusionistic architecture.[12] The two extant virtues, *Justice* and possibly *Fortitude* or *Hope*, which Guido frescoed inside the Palazzo Pubblico around 1598–99, might give a hint of this work.[13] These decorations by Bologna's native son held the spotlight, showcasing his talents to his hometown and members of the papal court. Two of Reni's most important early Roman patrons, Cardinal Paolo Emilio Sfondrato and Cardinal Pietro Aldobrandini, appear not to have been in attendance. Sfondrato was one of only a handful of cardinals to oppose the papal annexation – the Duke of Ferrara was Sfondrato's cousin on his mother's side[14] – and he is not listed as accompanying Clement.[15] Cardinal Aldobrandini, the pope's nephew, had been in Ferrara but accompanied the new Queen of Spain, Margaret of Austria, following her proxy wedding to Philip III there, travelling toward Milan.[16]

Reni's career in Bologna gained momentum in 1599. He was unanimously elected to the city's thirty-member council of the newly independent painters' guild.[17] His *Vision of Saint Hyacinth*, an altarpiece for the Dominican nuns' church of San Mattia, probably dates to about 1599 as well. Today the painting is known only from an etching by Claude Vignon (1593–1670) and, more spectacularly, from Guido's own *modello* [fig. 17]. The drawing is signed on the verso by the artist and four nuns, including Diodata Malvasia, prioress, Cinthia Locatelli, cited as 'current syndic', Faustina Bolognetti, and Livia Garisendi, probably the altarpiece's patron, as the painting was recorded on the Garisendi altar.[18] Based on the tenures of the prioress and

Fig. 16 Guido Reni, *Coronation of the Virgin with four Saints*, c. 1598–99. Oil on canvas, 261 × 206 cm. Bologna, Pinacoteca Nazionale di Bologna, inv. 440

syndic, the drawing must date between 1597 and 1599, and the painting would have been executed shortly thereafter.[19] The painterly technique is characteristic of Reni's early draughtsmanship – the soft chalk strokes that dissolve forms, the rippling, supple draperies. Also typical for Reni at this stage are the hidden feet and abbreviated treatment of hands. The figures are more cohesively integrated than in his earlier compositions, and the animated, lifelike Christ Child and angels make for a compelling devotional image.

Guido's masterpiece of the early period may be his luminous *Vision of Saint Eustace* [fig. 18], painted for the Olivetan monks' crypt at San Michele in Bosco. Eustace's pose recalls Hyacinth's but with heightened complexity and a new expressive force. Reni's meticulous description of Eustace's costume and weapons,[20] and his careful rendering of the animals and their attenuated proportions, seems to distance the painting from the Carracci orbit, leading some scholars to date it to around 1596.[21] These unique qualities, however, reflect the influence of Dürer's

Fig. 17 Guido Reni, *The Vision of Saint Hyacinth*, c. 1597–99.
Black chalk, lavender wash, and white heightening on blue paper,
371 × 220 mm. Stockholm, Nationalmuseum, inv. 1052/1863

1598 (when Clement VIII stayed at the monastery).[26] Reni's painting seems more likely to date to this later campaign. The misty midnight blue sky and shimmering mountain scenery, painted with layers of translucent glazes, demonstrate the artist's burgeoning interest in landscape painting, and hint at his future achievements in the genre – now better appreciated with the reappearance of two of his landscapes [fig. 23 and cat. 63].

The brisk pace of commissions shows Reni to be one of the most sought-after artists of his generation in Bologna. On 23 May 1599, he is recorded in Pieve di Cento, 34 kilometres away, as a witness in a contract with artisans to construct the parish church's high altar. His *Assumption of the Virgin* of about 1601–3 may have been commissioned at this time, but was probably completed a few years later. The high altar was under scaffolding until August 1600, when the Gallinari brothers were paid for frescoes there, and, while most of the altar was constructed by May 1600, artisans did not install the balustrade until December 1600.[27] Reni's undated payment of 432 lire, written in the notebook of the patron's executor, cannot be located in the city's archive.[28] Some scholars have observed the influence of Raphael's *Stanze* and other Roman works on the altarpiece,[29] suggesting a date after 1601, when Guido is first documented in Rome (or after 1600, when he probably took a brief undocumented trip).

Meanwhile, Reni had begun working for the Zani in Bologna, a noble family that had just completed their grand palace on Via Santo Stefano with the architect Floriano Ambrosini (1557–1621). Between 1600 and 1604, Guido is documented receiving eight payments in the family's account books.[30] He executed two ceiling frescoes, the *Fall of Phaethon* and *Separation of Night from Day* [fig. 19],[31] and reportedly designed nine oil paintings of illustrious men (now lost).[32] The payment from 1600 confirms Malvasia's report that Ambrosini introduced Reni to the Zani, as Ambrosini received 150 lire on 9 June to reimburse him for 100 lire to 'ms. Guido pitt.re', and 50 lire to 'Jeronimo Mattioli', another painter.[33]

While the various payments do not describe Reni's work in detail, it seems certain that the 100 lire payment in 1600 was for the *Phaethon* fresco, and most of the 300 lire he received in 1602 was for the larger *Separation of Night from Day*,[34] which is nearly twice the size and decorated the vault of the palace's largest reception hall, called the 'nobile Sala' (Malvasia) and 'Sala' or 'Sala Grande' (in the documents).[35] Five of Guido's six payments in 1602 – from May through October – refer to work in the 'Sala'.[36] The *Phaethon* fresco, instead, adorns the adjoining large antechamber, probably the 'Camerotto' in the accounts.[37] Reni

famous *Saint Eustace* engraving, which Reni updated by enlarging the soldier relative to the setting, turning him toward the spectator, and giving him a more fervent gesture. Such adjustments seem to call for a slightly later date. We know that the painting was part of a major restoration of the Olivetan monastery's 'paradiso' between 1596 and 1601. Other altarpieces commissioned for the crypt are dated: Gabriele Ferrantini's *Saint Lawrence* and Giovanni Battista Cremonini's *Saint John the Baptist* (both lost), completed in late 1596;[22] Calvaert's *Saint Clement*[23] and Ferrantini's *Mysteries of the Rosary* (lost), completed in spring of 1599;[24] and Lavinia Fontana's (1552–1614) *Five Female Martyr Saints*, signed and dated 1601.[25] The 1596 commissions went to artists already active in monastery projects, so it seems an unlikely moment for Guido to be hired given his inexperience. More work was underway in the crypt in 1599 and 1600 following a large donation from Father Clemente Cattanei, who had initiated the project in 1596 and served as abbot in is documented employing assistants for the first time in 1602, when he is reimbursed for payments to Vincenzo Gotti (c. 1580–1636) and Tommaso Campana (act. 1602–1619),[38] artists who also assisted him in Rome.[39]

The *Separation of Night from Day* is a self-consciously Roman work, whereas the *Fall of Phaethon* is deeply rooted in Bolognese art,[40] recalling elements of the Phaethon ceiling fresco by Pellegrino Tibaldi (1527–1596) formerly in the Palazzo Poggi and Ludovico Carracci's Phaethon fresco formerly in the Palazzo Montecalvi.[41] As is evident in Reni's *modello* of *Phaethon* [cat. 47], he achieved exciting drama in the lively movements of the figures. The forms are rendered in convincing relief with flourishes of pen work, precise cross-hatching, and painterly wash. Mentioned as a possible source is the Dioscuri on the Quirinal, which Reni could have seen on an unrecorded trip to Rome in 1600 or absorbed through prints.[42] Any Roman influence, however, is superficial compared to his *Separation of Night from Day*, executed in a grand manner deeply indebted to the famous fresco cycles and antiquities in Rome. The work draws directly from an engraving after Hendrick Goltzius (1558–1617) by Jan Muller (1571–1628), *Spirit separating Light from Darkness*, from 1589. Reni transformed the figures into heroic Roman types, with hulking physiognomies, idealised faces, and active poses that quote Roman works. Night recalls Raphael's *Galatea* in the Villa Farnesina and a recently excavated *Niobe* sculpture.[43] Day is reminiscent of Annibale's frescoes in the gallery of the Palazzo Farnese; Day's gesture, which prefigures Reni's Hippomenes figure [see cat. 61–62], draws from Michelangelo's (1475–1564) Sistine *Expulsion of Adam and Eve* and lost *Noli me tangere* cartoon.[44] The bold composition and colossal nude figures leave no doubt that Guido painted the fresco after spending time in Rome.

Between these two Zani frescoes, in 1600–1 Reni must have executed the *Vision of Saint Dominic and the fifteen Mysteries of the Rosary*, another painting for the nuns of San Mattia for their sanctuary of the Madonna di San Luca, Monte della Guardia (in situ) [fig. 20]. Vicaria Claudia Orsi commissioned it during her term of office (1599–1601) for the new chapel and Compagnia she founded to venerate the Rosary.[45] Reni created an innovative composition for this monumental painting, his largest to date, filling the lower third with an exquisite rosebush decorated with fifteen gold oval frames, each containing a miniature scene from the life of Christ and the Virgin. In the *sacre conversazione* above, Guido unexpectedly showed himself to be a new disciple of Annibale. The Virgin's solemn, weighty appearance and darkened profile are so reminiscent of Annibale's

Fig. 18 Guido Reni, *The Vision of Saint Eustace*, c. 1599–1600. Oil on canvas, 195 × 121 cm. Private collection

Three Marys at the Tomb of 1600,[46] that it seems Reni must have seen Annibale's painting in Rome.

Guido is first documented in Rome on 11 October 1601, in the account books of the church of Santa Cecilia in Trastevere, receiving 120 scudi 'for a painting of Saint Cecilia and other works'.[47] Cardinal Sfondrato, the church's titular cardinal, had undertaken a massive refurbishment and decoration of the basilica in the 1590s, which culminated in the discovery of Saint Cecilia's relics under the high altar in 1599. Between 1601 and 1606, Reni

Fig. 19 Guido Reni, *The Separation of Night from Day*, 1602. Fresco laid down on canvas, 450 × 420 cm. Dorset, Kingston Lacy (National Trust), Bankes Collection

received four payments from the cardinal, totalling 220 scudi. Four extant Reni paintings of Saint Cecilia are associated with the payments.[48] From the time Antonia Nava Cellini published the documents, the 1601 payment was thought to herald Reni's move to Rome. Instead they record only a brief foray, as the artist was back home working for the Zani in May, June, July, and October 1602. In November 1602 he was in Rome again, receiving 50 scudi for 'works he had made' at Santa Cecilia in Trastevere. Thus, in the early years Reni worked for Sfondrato, he was travelling frequently between Bologna and Rome.

Reni's copy of Raphael's *Ecstasy of Saint Cecilia*[49] of about 1600–1 and his *Coronation of Saint Cecilia and Saint Valerian* of about 1600, were probably painted for Sfondrato first.[50] According to Malvasia, Cardinal Facchinetti commissioned the Raphael copy in Bologna from Guido and sent it to Rome,[51] presumably to Sfondrato, 'il cardinale santa Cecilia' and the artist's eventual patron. Reni had painted a successful copy of Annibale's *Burial of Christ*[52] for Facchinetti's uncle, Astorre di Vincenzo Sampieri. Sampieri sent Reni's now lost copy to 'a great personage' in Rome, perhaps Cardinal Odoardo Farnese,

Rachel McGarry

as the work is later recorded in the Farnese collection in Parma.[53] Cardinal Federico Borromeo, who collected copies of important works in his *Musaeum* in Milan, also showed an interest in Guido. He was in contact with the artist in February and March of 1602, and Reni wrote twice from Bologna making excuses for delaying his trip to serve the illustrious cardinal.[54] Perhaps Borromeo wanted to enlist him to make copies, which could explain why Guido seems never to have gone.

Bellori and the Sienese historian Ugurgieri Azzolini suggest that Francesco Vanni (1563–1610) introduced Reni to Sfondrato. They report that the two artists met in Rome through a mutual friend, Antonio Scalvati (1557/59–1619/22), a Bolognese portrait painter working in that city with whom Guido had stayed (or even studied).[55] There is some basis for this theory, since Vanni not only executed eight paintings for Sfondrato, but he also designed Reni's *Coronation of Saint Cecilia and Saint Valerian* tondo for Santa Cecilia in Trastevere, Rome. Seven preparatory drawings by Vanni related to Reni's painting survive.[56] Vanni was in Rome for the 1600 Jubilee but back in Siena from 1600 to 1602, busy with various projects.[57] In 1603 he returned to Rome to paint an altarpiece for St Peter's and to be knighted by Sfondrato. If Vanni could not complete all of Sfondrato's commissions in 1600, he may have nominated Guido to paint the *Coronation* after his designs.[58] Reni's tondo was recorded in a 1600 chronicle on the ancient basilica of Santa Cecilia by the historian Antonio Bosio. He described it in the church's Cappella del Bagno, where it remains today, as 'a beautiful picture with the images of Cecilia and Valerian crowned by an angel with winter roses and lilies in the sky'.[59] If Reni received the commission in Rome in 1600, he might have returned home to paint it and make his copy of the Raphael. Maybe he sent the *Coronation* in time for Cecilia's feast day in 1600 and returned to Rome in 1601 to deliver the Raphael copy and collect payment.

Reni's stylistically more mature *Martyrdom of Santa Cecilia* [fig. 21], painted from his own design, probably relates to the 1602 payment of 50 scudi from Sfondrato.[60] The artist's autograph painting is preserved in the convent of Santa Cecilia in Trastevere, in a gallery near the cloister. The version on the altar of the Cappella del Bagno, which is often confused for Guido's painting, is a much later copy, and was mutilated in World War II.[61] (The saint's face and upper body were lost and replaced by yet another replica.) Reni's version is intact and differs in subtle ways from the copy: vapours of steam rise from the rectangular stones in the foreground, the executioner's right heel is nearly complete, and there is more space between Cecilia's hand and the right edge of the canvas.

Guido's activities in 1603 are virtually undocumented. He was still in Rome on 14 December 1602, recorded in a document appointing a cousin to oversee transactions pertaining to his father's estate in Bologna. On 17 July 1603, the cousin was registered as Reni's representative in Bologna in a land sale from the estate, presumably because the artist was out of town. Guido's presence at the funeral of Agostino Carracci in Bologna on 18 January 1603 cannot be established. He did not contribute to the elaborate funeral decorations by members of the Carracci studio, but Malvasia attributed to Reni the commemorative etchings published by Vittorio Benacci.[62] The etching style is distant from Reni's other prints, however, and the copper plates bore no attribution in the 1658 inventory of publisher Cesare Locatelli, even though other plates were listed as Reni's, in some cases ambitiously.[63] Guido may have been in Bologna in early 1603, busy with the *Orpheus and Eurydice* chimneypiece for the Lambertini,[64] the Pieve di Cento altarpiece, the Sampieri *Assumption of the Virgin* [cat. 7],[65] and any number of lost works. Or he may have been in Rome, working on the paintings recorded in the Farnese and Aldobrandini inventories[66] and the various *rametti* in the present exhibition [cat. 7–9, 13, and 14], as well as the recently rediscovered *Christ bearing the Cross* [fig. 22]. Here, Saint Veronica wears the same embroidered yellow dress shown in two of Reni's Cecilia paintings. Moreover, the executioner in the right foreground closely resembles a figure Guido drew in a study for the *Crucifixion of Saint Peter* discussed below, which can be dated to 1604–5.

In 1604 Guido was back in Bologna, recorded in January in a document related to his father's estate, and in April receiving a deposit of 16 lire from the Zani for an altarpiece he never painted. That summer he contributed a fresco to Ludovico's cloister project at San Michele in Bosco, *Saint Benedict receiving Gifts from the Peasants*. Only after this important Bolognese project was finished did the artist finally move to Rome. He was there on 18 September 1604, receiving 25 scudi from Sfondrato for some paintings. From then through 1612, Reni can be steadily recorded in Rome, except for a few short trips – to Loreto in October 1604, for instance, and to Bologna in April 1605 to collect his cloister payment.[67] (Between 1612 and 1614, he travelled between Bologna, Naples, and Rome until his public departure from Rome.)

Reni's surprising trip to Loreto helps to clarify some confusing details in this period. The artist ventured there on behalf of Cardinal Antonio Maria Gallo, protector of the city and active in the sanctuary decoration of the Santa Casa di Loreto. Reni was

Fig. 20 Guido Reni, *The Vision of Saint Dominic and the fifteen Mysteries of the Rosary*, 1600–1. Oil on canvas, 390 × 220 cm. Monte della Guardia (Bologna), Santuario della Madonna di San Luca

Rachel McGarry

recorded in Loreto on 24 October 1604, authorising a final payment of 40 scudi on Gallo's behalf to the painter Leonello Spada (1576–1622) 'for coming from Bologna' to paint the sacristy and 'for returning to Bologna'.[68] Guido had been sent by Gallo, who was seriously ill in Rome,[69] apparently to judge Spada's work, which had been underway for seven weeks. Reni appears to have dismissed Spada, and in 1605 Cristoforo Roncalli (c. 1553–1626) would be hired for the sacristy project, completing the frescoes in 1610. Roncalli also won the commission to fresco the cupola of the Loreto basilica (c. 1609/10–15, destroyed, fragments survive).

The 1604 document helps debunk the story that Caravaggio (1571–1610) and Guido competed for the Loreto project. In Malvasia's telling, Reni and Caravaggio competed for the Loreto dome fresco. Caravaggio reportedly threatened to break his skull when Guido offered to bow out or work with Caravaggio, and the commission went to Roncalli because he was favoured by another cardinal.[70] According to Giovanni Baglione, Caravaggio took revenge on Roncalli for being awarded the commission by hiring a Sicilian to slash his face.[71] Roncalli was indeed the victim of a knife attack, as newly discovered court documents reveal, but it happened in 1607. On 2 March, while walking through Rome's Campo Vaccino, Roncalli was wounded in the face, an assault arranged by Cavalier d'Arpino (1568–1640) over a longstanding dispute about their work in St Peter's.[72] The Loreto documents show that Reni was involved only tangentially in the Loreto sacristy commission. Caravaggio, who was inexperienced in fresco and dead before the dome project began, was probably never a serious candidate. Perhaps the early sources, eager for a better story, substituted the more famous, tempestuous artist for Spada, who was known as 'la scimmia di Caravaggio', or Caravaggio's ape.[73]

Reni had another connection to Gallo, who was also the titular cardinal of Santa Prassede in Rome. Bellori and Giovanni Battista Passeri reported that Guido stayed in rooms at the Santa Prassede monastery with his friend Francesco Albani (1578–1660) when they first moved to Rome.[74] Passeri included the presence of Domenichino, who was kept up at night by Reni and Albani's card playing and talking.[75] The Loreto document connecting Guido to Gallo in October 1604

suggests that the artists may have been living at Santa Prassede then.

Gallo was also bishop of Osimo, his hometown, just 15 kilometres from Loreto. Two altarpieces in Osimo have recently been attributed to Reni in connection with Gallo.[76] The *Trinity with the Madonna di Loreto and Cardinal Gallo* at Santissima Trinita was formerly attributed to the Bolognese painter Enea Campi and linked to payments from 1590–91,[77]

Fig. 21 Guido Reni, *The Martyrdom of Saint Cecilia*, 1602. Oil on canvas, 221 × 107 cm. Rome, Cloister of the Convent of Santa Cecilia in Trastevere

before Daniele Benati attributed it to Reni. It has been connected to Reni's 1604 Loreto trip.[78] Yet many aspects of the painting are difficult to reconcile with Guido's style, such as the pastiche-like composition, absence of landscape detail, figure types, and varied figural scale. If Reni was involved in the painting, he relied heavily on assistants (perhaps Campana and Gotti). The earlier *Christ crowned by Thorns among Saints*, made around 1598–1603 for San Leopardo, is a more convincing attribution to Reni,[79] although Albani is another strong candidate.[80] Gallo may have commissioned the picture after giving the Duomo the relic of the holy thorn around 1601.[81] Perhaps the painting helped Reni, or Albani, secure the Roman lodgings at Santa Prassede.

After Guido's definitive move to Rome in late 1604, he won his most prestigious commission to date, the *Crucifixion of Saint Peter* [fig. 10], for Cardinal Pietro Aldobrandini's newly reconstructed church of San Paolo alle Tre Fontane, just outside Rome's city walls. On 27 November 1604, Reni and another Bolognese painter, Passerotto de' Passerotti, each received a deposit of 50 scudi to execute an altarpiece there, and final payments of another 50 scudi each were recorded on 30 August 1605.[82] Passerotti's *Beheading of Saint Paul* (in situ) is lackluster, but Guido used the opportunity to produce a stunning picture that firmly established his reputation in Rome. Strikingly Reni imitates Caravaggio's manner, deploying forceful modelling and dramatic lighting, an effect enhanced over time by the darkening of the landscape background. Reni's naturalistic description of the figures – their bare feet, long toenails, wrinkled flesh – share the canvas with rough-and-tumble executioners and a young feathered-cap youth from Caravaggio's world. The tightly focused composition might recall Caravaggio's *Crucifixion of Saint Peter* of 1601–2, although that painting was probably not installed in the Cappella Cerasi at Santa Maria del Popolo until May 1605, a few months before Reni completed his.[83] Guido departed from Caravaggio in significant ways, however. His rigorously balanced, classicising composition contrasts with Caravaggio's snapshot of the toil and physical awkwardness that a crucifixion would entail. Reni's figures assume the graceful poses of dancers enacting a scene, whereas Caravaggio's subjects grunt and labour in their exertion, as evidenced by their indecorous poses. The compositional study in Budapest[84] reveals Reni's conceptual distance from Caravaggio at the preparatory stage, with little to suggest an intent to imitate Caravaggio's palette, figures, or manner.

It is possible that Guido's brief flirtation with Caravaggio's style attracted the attention of the Roman banker Ottavio Costa, an enthusiastic early collector of Caravaggio.[85] Costa hired Reni to paint the *Martyrdom of Saint Catherine of Alexandria* of about 1605–7 for the new church of Sant'Alessandro in the Costa fief of Conscente, Liguria, now in the Museo Diocesano at Albenga.[86] Previously the banker had commissioned Caravaggio's 1602 *Saint John the Baptist in the Wilderness* for this church,[87] but decided to keep it for himself and send a copy instead.[88] Perhaps Costa turned to Reni as a more economical, available artist, who could produce a work in the manner of his favourite artist. Because Costa was Sfondrato's banker, he was well acquainted with Guido and his early Roman work.[89] In fact, Reni's *Martyrdom of Saint Catherine* descends directly from his 1602 *Martyrdom of Saint Cecilia*, although with some considerable refinements. The beauty and grace of Catherine and the angels overwhelm the Caravaggesque executioner. Guido has tempered the chiaroscuro effect with a cool, grey atmosphere that bathes the coastal landscape.

Reni further perfected his famous conception of pious female martyred saints with upturned eyes in these years, as seen in his half-length paintings *Saint Catherine of Alexandria* [cat. 83] and *Saint Cecilia* [fig. 11], the latter which likely relates to Sfondrato's last payment to Guido in 1606 of 25 scudi for a 'quadro di Santa Cecilia'.[90] In these young women's faces, Reni created his inimitable expression of pathos as they gaze thoughtfully, serenely to God reassured by their faith. His brush relishes in their physical beauty and splendid attire, illuminating the glistening surfaces of their parted lips, gold pendants and crowns, silk dresses, and embroidered veils.

Reni's *David beheading Goliath* of about 1606–7 in the Arp Museum [cat. 17] may reflect a lingering interest in Caravaggio and a knowledge of his painting of about 1600 on the same subject in the Prado [cat. 15], although Guido painted a less horrific scene, before Goliath's decapitation. A more consequential influence is Raphael and his *David and Goliath* design of 1517–19 for the Vatican loggia, well known from Ugo da Carpi's (c. 1480–1532) chiaroscuro woodcut and Marcantonio Raimondi's engraving after Raphael's drawing. Like Raphael, Reni depicted David as a slender youth too small for the large-handled sword, and Goliath writhing on the ground just before the blow to his neck. Guido's open composition and panoramic view of a hilly landscape and cloudy sky further echo Raphael's model. He delighted, once again, in capturing details of dress with his exquisite handling, in this case the gleaming armour of Goliath.

Guido would experiment with Caravaggio briefly again in the following decade, probably stimulated by his acquisition of Caravaggio's *Denial of Saint Peter* of about 1610,[91] which he received in 1613 from Luca Ciamberlano as payment for a large debt.[92] In his two versions of *David and Goliath* in Paris, dated around 1609–11,[93] and Orléans [cat. 16] – which this author would date to about 1610–23 and suggest the participation of workshop assistants – and in *Lot and his Daughters leaving Sodom* of about 1615–16,[94] Reni revisits Caravaggio's manner selectively and analytically, often incorporating classical influences and infusing the compositions with grace and artifice. For his later and much copied treatment of David, for instance, Guido adopted the young hero's pose from an ancient sculpture, *Satyr in Repose* after Praxiteles, known from many Roman copies. Seeming to have sprung to life from marble, Reni's David, a beautiful youth, leans against a stone column, calm and aloof, as he clutches the hair of his hideous trophy.

Malvasia fervently promoted Guido as a prodigious success in Rome and a rival of Caravaggio and Annibale Carracci. Reni and Caravaggio were improbable enemies, however: at the time of Caravaggio's supposed jealousy, Reni's reputation was still modest and he was not yet established as a painter in Rome. Malvasia's reporting on this point must therefore be read critically. Guido's meteoric rise did not occur until these two towering figures vacated the competitive market – Caravaggio († 1610) in May 1606, after he committed murder, Annibale († 1609) after his catastrophic breakdown in 1605 made commissions difficult to fulfil.

Two sparkling landscapes by Reni have come to light, *Landscape with a Country Dance* of about 1603–6 [fig. 23] and *Landscape with Cupids playing* of about 1601–3 [cat. 63], enriching our understanding of this formative moment of his career.[95] Guido evokes a golden age in these masterful pictures, with brilliant blue mountains, emerald valleys, clear streams, and playful figures. Both canvases translate the light touch and shimmering aesthetic he mastered in his early *rametti*. Francesco Gatta traced *Cupids playing* to the Farnese collection, along with two other lost landscapes by the artist.[96] Reni's works decorated Cardinal Odoardo's Palazzetto Farnese on the Tiber, along with many other landscape paintings by Annibale and members of the Carracci school.[97] Reni's engagement in this project and interest in the new genre of landscape as it was being innovatively developed by Annibale and his

Fig. 22 Guido Reni, *Christ bearing the Cross*, c. 1599–1603.
Oil on copper, 45.1 × 31.7 cm.
Private collection

followers suggest that Guido and Annibale were more closely connected than Malvasia portrayed. The Bolognese biographer characterised Annibale as distrustful and envious of Reni, but it is clear from one of Guido's letters to Borromeo in 1602 that Annibale was helping Reni secure work.[98] That said, Reni's landscapes are entirely different in style from his Bolognese colleagues. Guido favoured the cooler palette and distant landscape vistas prominent in the background of his other paintings. Like a bee savouring the best nectar from every flower, Reni voraciously explored new influences and ideas, but always melded them to his unique vision. This would position him for success in the coming decade.

Fig. 23 Guido Reni, *Landscape with a Country Dance*,
c. 1603–6. Oil on canvas, 81 × 99 cm. Rome,
Galleria Borghese, inv. 609

1 Malvasia–Zanotti 1841, 2:56: 'Come l'ape da fiori, cosi da tutti ando egli delibando lo squisito e piu perfetto'; for discussion of Malvasia's bee metaphor, see Malvasia–Pericolo 2019, 1:211, note 10.

2 Malvasia–Zanotti 1841, 2:6; Bellori–Borea 1976, 488.

3 Gambassi 1989, 46, 162–90, and 626–28.

4 Malvasia–Zanotti 1841, 1:276–77 and 2:6; Bellori–Borea 1976, 488–89.

5 Malvasia–Zanotti 1841, 1:199; Hess 1934b, 80; Bellori–Borea 1976, 276. On Reni's collection and estate inventory, see Spike and Di Zio 1988, 58 and 63; Morselli 2008, 81–83. Malvasia believed that Reni had a book of Raphael drawings that was fraudulently taken before the estate inventory; see Malvasia–Zanotti 1841, 2:43.

6 Twiehaus 2002, 197–207.

7 Malvasia–Zanotti 1841, 1:197, 200: 'Per le Monache novizze e per le novelle spose'.

8 Ibid., 2:6; Bellori–Borea 1976, 489.

9 Malvasia–Zanotti 1841, 2:7 and 2:220; Bellori–Borea 1976, 307. Reni and Calvaert nonetheless remained on good terms until Calvaert's death in 1619.

10 Malvasia–Emiliani 1969, 110; Daniele Benati (1998, 8–9) dates San Colombano to about 1598–1600, after Reni left.

11 D. Benati in Cappelletti 2022a, 20–21.

12 A description of the major apparati and nine etchings by Reni were published by Vittorio Benacci in Descrittione degli apparati fatti in Bologna per la venuta di N.S. Papa Clemente VIII..., see Benacci 1598; see also Bartsch 1803–21 (1818), 18:24–32; Malvasia–Zanotti 1841, 1:92–93.

13 Bologna, Pinacoteca Nazionale di Bologna, inv. 929 and inv. 928, respectively. See G. P. Cammarota in Bentini et al. 2008, 46–48, nos. 29a–29b; Malvasia–Pericolo 2019, 1:242, note 87, and 2:figs. 10–11. Cammarota suggested that the allegory with the scepter or caduceus and the lilies might represent Fortitude, whereas Pericolo suggested Hope.

14 Pastor 1891–1953 (1933), 24:385–87; Weber 1994, 913.

15 Baldini 1598, Greco 1598, and Mocante 1598.

16 Röttgen 2002, 92.

17 Malaguzzi Valeri 1897, 312.

18 Birke 1981, 43–45. Per Bjurström (Bjurström, Loisel and Pilliod 2002, no. 1614) argues Reni's drawing does not represent Hyacinth, but Vignon turned Hyacinth into Dominic in his print, transforming an angel's banderole into a rosary. The early sources record Reni's San Mattia altarpiece as depicting Hyacinth (Cavazzoni 1603, 17; Masini 1666, 74; Malvasia–Emiliani 1969, 130). The Polish saint's cult flourished in Bologna, where he was a novitiate. Stephen Pepper (1969a, 472 and 481) attributed another drawing of Hyacinth to Reni in the Castello Sforzesco (Milan) that is more likely by Ludovico; see also Johnston 1974, 1:no. 6.

19 The terms of prioress and syndic were two years. Malvasia and Locatelli signed another document in these positions in May 1599. By August 1599 Costanza Garisendi (called Guastavillani) was prioress (Degli Esposti 1993, 139), another possible patron of the work, but she did not sign the drawing. An illegible name with 'fra' suggests a male representative of the nuns signed it.

20 The painting was probably cut down at the lower edge, with some losses around Eustace's weapons, in the eighteenth century when it was framed for the Palazzo Durazzo Pallavicini's symmetrical arrangement; P. Boccardo and E. Gavazza in Cattaneo Adorno et al. 1995, 23 and 59. It was sold by the monks to Marcello I Durazzo in 1716 (Puncuh 1984, 185, no. 63).

21 Pepper 1969a, 476; Pepper 1984, no. 2; Loire 1994, 225–29, no. 5; A. Emiliani in Cattaneo Adorno et al. 1995, 107–10; for later dates, see McGarry 2007, 151–61; Malvasia–Pericolo 2019, 1:225, note 44.

22 Some account books are extant, and an anonymous eighteenth-century manuscript about the monastery includes details from lost accounts books, see Notizie antiche spettanti al monastero di S. Michele in Bosco, Ms Malvezzi 51, Biblioteca Comunale dell'Archiginnasio, Bologna; Malaguzzi Valeri 1895, 61; Zucchini 1943, 38–70; McGarry 2007, 151–61. The 'Gabriele pittore' recorded here must be Gabriele Ferrantini, a former student of Calvaert's and the painter who taught Reni how to use oil in his Palazzo Pubblico mural (Malvasia–Zanotti 1841, 1:207 and 2:11), and not the often-named sculptor Gabriele Fiorini.

23 Church of San Alessandro in Copreno, on deposit from the Pinacoteca di Brera, Milan.

24 Bologna, Archivio di Stato di Bologna, Archivio damianale, S. Michele in Bosco [177-2349] (hereafter ASB, Bosco), 72r. The documents with Calvaert's payment are lost but transcribed with precision in Ms Malvezzi 51, 37v (see note 22), as 300 lire paid 'A fino Marzo 1599 a Ms. Dionisio Fiamengo'.

25 Bologna, Pinacoteca Nazionale di Bologna, inv. 787.

26 ASB, Bosco, 74r and 84r. The accounting of Cattanei's donation does not show it funding Calvaert's altarpiece, surely executed in honour of Cattanei's name saint.

27 Pepper 1969a, 482–83; Ariuli 1999, 116–17; Fortini 1999, 44.

28 Stephen Pepper (1969, 482, note 59) suggested that Reni's altarpiece may have been installed by 15 August 1600, the feast of the Assumption, but the other work in the church at the time makes this unlikely. Rossella Ariuli (1999, 163, note 29) reports that Pepper's citation of the executor's (Giuseppe Mastellari) notebook (Sezione della compagni di S. Maria, atti in registro, I, no. 35, 88v–102) does not correspond to the collocation numbers of the Archivio comunale di Pieve di Cento.

29 F. Valli in Emiliani et al. 1988, no. 11; Faietti, Oberhuber and Rosenauer 1990, 63–65.

30 Bologna, Archivio Storico Comunale, Patrimonio Ex Gesuitico, eredità Zani (hereafter ASCB, Zani), series 476, Libro giornale 1594–1617, series 477, Libro mastro, 1594–1617, series 478, Stracciafoglio del libro mastro, 1594–1617. Sonia Reggio (2000) and this author independently came upon these documents around the same time, with Reggio coming to different conclusions about Reni's payments than described here; see McGarry 2007, 299–316.

31 The Fall of Phaethon is in situ; the Separation of Night from Day was detached from the ceiling and transferred to canvas in 1840. Shortly thereafter it was acquired by William John Bankes for his country house, Kingston Lacy (Dorset), now part of the National Trust.

32 Malvasia–Zanotti 1841, 2:11–12.

33 ASCB, Zani, series 476, 80; series 478, 128. Malvasia reported that Reni was so grateful for the introduction, he painted a greatly admired Portia (lost) in Ambrosini's house (Malvasia–Zanotti 1841, 2:63).

34 ASCB, Zani, series 476, 80, 100, 105–9, and 124; McGarry 2007, 304–9. Giovan Pietro Bellori (Bellori–Borea 1976, 494) dated the Separation fresco with uncharacteristic exactness to 1602.

35 Reni's Phaethon measures 256 × 222 cm; Night and Day 450 × 420 cm.

36 For the second fresco Reni probably collected around 200 lire of the 300 he was paid in 1602, as 64 lire was designated as reimbursement for assistants (discussed below), and a 40 lire payment in January 1602, for 'varie pitt.re fatti et da farsi a bon conto', did not specify work in the 'Sala' like the others. Deliveries to the 'Sala' in 1602 for mortar before Reni worked and furnishings after further support this dating; McGarry 2007, 301–5.

37 ASCB, Zani, series 476, Libro Giornale, 109 and 111; McGarry 2007, 303, note 51.

38 ASCB, Zani, series 476, 105; series 478, 172. Reni was paid 64 lire in May 1602 to pay Gotti and Campana for 'work in the Sala'. Campana received direct payments from the Zani as well that year; one, a deposit for eight paintings, could relate to the execution of the illustrious portraits; see McGarry 2007, 305–9.

39 Malvasia–Zanotti 1841, 2:47 and 2:52.

40 Reni's *Phaethon* has traditionally been dated to 1599; see G. C. Cavalli in Gnudi and Cavalli 1955, 54, no. 5; Baccheschi 1971, no. 9; Loire 1994, 226; Takahashi 2001.

41 The fresco, detached in 1861, is now in Bologna, Biblioteca Comunale dell'Archiginnasio, inv. 64bis.

42 Hess 1934a; Bellori–Borea 1976, 494–95. An engraving published by Antonio Salamanca, and later by Antonio Lafreri in his *Speculum Romanae Magnificentiae*, offers a compelling comparison. While most scholars have dated Reni's *Phaethon* fresco to before the artist's move to Rome, some have argued that it must follow a Roman trip (Hess 1934a, 28; Johnston 1974, 1:59–62; Spear 1997, 279–80 and 384).

43 Florence, Gallerie degli Uffizi, inv. 294–Sculture (1914). See Johnston 1993, 14–15.

44 Hess 1967, 1:291 and 2:figs. 5–6; Spear 1997, 63–65.

45 Paolo Mattioli's nineteenth-century history of the Monte della Guardia and Madonna di San Luca records some of the details of the commission based on lost account books; *BV di S. Luca*, Ms Archivio Generale Arcivescovile, Bologna, Raccolta Breventani, card. F (1) XI, cap. 47, notes 15–21; see also Degli Esposti 1993. Mattioli notes that a lost *Vacchettino*, presumably written by Orsi, records 200 lire being taken out of the 1400 lire sum used to pay for the altar, and he speculates that it might refer to Guido's payment; Mattioli, cap. 47, note 20.

46 St Petersburg, Hermitage Museum, ГЭ-92.

47 See Nava Cellini 1969, 33–37 and 40–41, for all Santa Cecilia in Trastevere payments.

48 There is no documentary evidence supporting Stephen Pepper's theory (1984, 215; 1990, 39–40) that Reni's *Rest on the Flight into Egypt* formerly in the Borghese collection (c. 1602–3, private collection; Cappelletti 2022a, no. 14) and *Christ at the Column* [cat. 25] attributed to Reni were painted for Sfondrato. Lorenzo Pericolo (Malvasia–Pericolo 2019, 1:374, note 436) makes a more convincing suggestion that Camillo Borghese commissioned the *Flight into Egypt*.

49 Bologna, Pinacoteca Nazionale di Bologna, inv. 577.

50 Dublin, National Gallery of Ireland, NGI.70 and Rome, Santa Cecilia in Trastevere, respectively. Francesca Profili (2011) recently identified Reni's Raphael copy for Sfondrato in Dublin, tracing it to the Serbellini family, Milan, heirs of Sfondrato. This demotes the weak copy erroneously attributed to Reni in the Cappella Polet, San Luigi dei Francesi, Rome.

51 Malvasia–Zanotti 1841, 2:12. It is also possible Sfondrato knew Reni through monks at San Michele in Bosco; he stayed there in 1591 as papal legate and was a protector of the Olivetan monks.

52 New York, The Metropolitan Museum, of Art, Purchase, Edwin L. Weisl Jr. Gift, 1998, inv. 1998.188.

53 Malvasia–Zanotti 1841, 1:359 and 2:8; Bertini 1987, 101, no. 47, and 244, no. 159 (listed in the Farnese 1680 inventory with attribution to Annibale); Christiansen 1999, 416. There is also a copy of a century-old fresco in San Giacomo Maggiore, the *Madonna della Cintura*, attributed to Reni; Degli Esposti 1998, 90–91 and 105–7; Wimböck 2002, 103–10 and 276.

54 Jones 1993, 152 and 167; Spear 1997, 326; McGarry 2008.

55 Ugurgieri Azzolini 1649, 2:371; Bellori–Borea 1976, 496. Malvasia dismissed Reni's association with Scalvati, see his 1673 letter; Perini Folesani 1984, 223–24; Malvasia–Pericolo 2019, 1:421, note 614.

56 Riedl 1976, 40–42 and 48–49; Riedl 1978, 313–16. Vanni's 1601 drawing for a souvenir print for the church (Vienna, Albertina) also includes a version of his *Coronation* design. Reni's drawing in the Louvre distills Vanni's ideas; Loisel 2013, 102, no. 66.

57 Terzaghi 2007, 165–68. Maria Cristina Terzaghi notes that Sfondrato and Vanni became acquainted in Siena in 1599.

58 Further re-enforcing their relationship is Giulio Mancini's report that Vanni's son, Raffaello, worked in Reni's Rome studio in 1611 after Francesco Vanni died; Maccherini 1995; Sani 1998, 435.

59 Bosio 1600, 176. Antonio Bosio's book was probably published before Cecilia's feast day, 22 November 1600.

60 A payment in July 1600 of 24 scudi to Massimo Crugli for 'una copia … della Decollazione di S.ta Cecilia' cannot establish a *terminus ante quem* for Reni's *Martyrdom* (Nava Cellini 1969, 35–41; Pepper 1984, no. 12), since there are many works of this subject in the church; see McGarry 2007, 273.

61 The first record of two versions of Reni's *Martyrdom* being in the church is Picarelli 1904, 6–7. They were moved around the church frequently, but between 1934 and 1984 scholars identify the copy in the sacristy and Reni's in the Cappella del Bagno (McGarry 2007, 268–75). Reni's painting may have been relocated to the convent after the 1984–85 Rome exhibition, making it mostly inaccessible (see Fagiolo and Madonna 1984). The later copy was included in the Galleria Borghese exhibition (see Cappelletti 2022a, no. 1) and is represented by Lorenzo Pericolo as autograph (Malvasia–Pericolo 2019, 2:fig. 28). He illustrates Reni's autograph painting too, fig. 29, with the caption: 'before removal of saint's face'.

62 Morello 1603.

63 Morselli 1998, 290, nos. 380, 364–67, and 375. The plates for the 1598 festival for Clement VIII also appear without an attribution.

64 New Haven, Yale University Art Gallery, inv. 2019.29.1.

65 The Frankfurt *Assumption of the Virgin* [cat. 7], while dated by Bastian Eclercy to around 1598–99, is more mature than Reni's *Coronation of the Virgin with four Saints* altarpiece in the Pinacoteca Nazionale di Bologna [fig. 16] and *Assumption of the Virgin with Saints Francis, Dominic, Peter Martyr and Agnes* in the Klesch collection, London. With its weightier, more classicising figures, the Frankfurt painting seems more likely to date to about 1601–3. It typifies Reni's style after his first trips to Rome in 1600 or 1601 and is closer in date to the Prado *Assumption and Coronation of the Virgin* [cat. 8], the Pieve di Cento altarpiece, and the *Martyrdom of Saint Cecilia* in the cloister of the convent of Santa Cecilia in Trastevere [fig. 21].

66 D'Onofrio 1964, 210, nos. 319–21; Sparti 1998a, 47–48; Gatta 2017.

67 Reni's final payment (of 260 lire) from San Michele in Bosco, made in Bologna on 9 April, indicates that his first payment for the project (50 scudi) was sent to him in Rome, with no date recorded. Howard Hibbard's attempt to pinpoint the Roman payment – February–April 1603, based on a page number cited in a lost account book – cannot be substantiated based on other dated payments; see Hibbard 1965, 503; McGarry 2007, 424–25 and 378–82.

68 Posner 1963, 254–56.

69 Francucci 2013, 42.

70 Malvasia–Zanotti 1841, 2:13.

71 Baglione 1642, 291.

72 Sickel 2001.

73 Chiappini Di Sorio 1983, 12.

74 Hess 1934b, 80 and 264; Bellori–Borea 1976, 496. Bellori thought Sfondrato made the arrangements for Santa Prassede. Passeri, in his 'Life of Reni', said it was arranged by the titular cardinal of Santa Prassede, who knew Annibale. He does not name the cardinal, but erroneously identifies him as Sfondrato in his 'Life of Albani'. On the close relationship between Gallo and Sfondrato, see Francucci 2013.

75 Hess 1934b, 22–23.

76 Daniele Benati (2004–5, 231–47) attributed four paintings in Osimo to Reni; the two altarpieces discussed have gained more support; see also Terzaghi 2007, 169–70; Benati 2013b; Francucci 2020; Francucci 2021; D. Benati in Cappelletti 2022a, 22–24; L. Scanu in Cappelletti 2022a, 108–10.

77 Caldari Giovanelli 1992. For documents, see Grimaldi and Sordi 1988, 293–94. Campi was paid in 1590 and 1591 for various works, including 'dua quadri grandi fatti uno del ss.mo Rosario per la Chiesa di Loreto et l'altro per la ss.ma Trinita d'Osimo'. Daniele Benati suggested Campi's works are lost. They may have marked Gallo's appointment as bishop of Osimo in 1590. The *Trinity* also had a traditional attribution to Guercino (1591–1666).

78 Documents record the restoration of the high altar (1602–5) and the new altar complex near completion and ready for gilding in August 1604; see Francucci 2013.

79 Benati 2004–5, 240. An eighteenth-century source attributed it to Reni; see Martorelli 1705, 430–31.

80 It recalls Albani's *Holy Family with Saint Catherine* on slate (c. 1600–3, Rome, Galleria Doria Pamphilj).

81 M. Francucci in Sgarbi and Papetti 2013, 204.

82 Hibbard 1965, 503.

83 Bernardini 2001, 56–67.

84 Budapest, Szépművészeti Múzeum, D 2366.

85 Terzaghi 2007, 144–47 and 295–312. Costa's 1632 testament forbade his heirs from selling the Caravaggio paintings, especially his *Judith* (Rome, Palazzo Barberini, inv. 2533).

86 Matthiesen and Pepper 1970.

87 Kansas City (Missouri), Nelson Atkins Museum, inv. 52-25.

88 For the copy of Caravaggio's *Saint John the Baptist* (Albenga, Museo Diocesano), see Vannugli 2000; Terzaghi 2007, 296.

89 Terzaghi 2007, 169–81.

90 Nava Cellini 1969, 41.

91 New York, The Metropolitan Museum of Art, Gift of Herman and Lila Shickman, and Purchase, Lila Acheson Wallace Gift, 1997, inv. 1997.167.

92 Barbieri 2012. Reni may have owned it a decade; it is next recorded with Cardinal Savelli in 1624.

93 Paris, Musée du Louvre, inv. 519.

94 London, National Gallery, NG193.

95 Gatta 2017; Matthiesen 2017; Cappelletti 2022a, nos. 15 and 16; F. Gatta in Cappelletti 2022a, 72–83.

96 Gatta 2017.

97 Witte 2008.

98 Spear 1997, 20; McGarry 2008, 431–32 and 442. In 1612 Reni was hired by Farnese to retouch a Carracci school altarpiece at Grottaferrata, suggesting he may have worked for Farnese earlier as a member of Annibale's studio; Denunzio 2000, 372–73.

THE 'MOST DISTINGUISHED COMPATRIOT GUIDO RENI', GLORY OF BOLOGNA

Raffaella Morselli

Following his stay in Naples, after a brief stint in Rome – where in May 1621 he painted a portrait of the new Bolognese pope Gregory XV,[1] who had recently ascended to the papal throne[2] – Guido Reni (1575–1642) returned to Bologna intent on establishing himself permanently in his home town and shifting the centre of gravity of Bolognese painting. After nearly four decades in which Rome had played a key role in shaping at least two generations of painters, who had emigrated, as it were, from the second city of the Papal States to the capital, the advent of the Bolognese popes, the jubilees, and new professional opportunities signalled that the time had come for the most important painter of Bologna to present himself as an example for all his colleagues. Already by the late 1610s the city had started to become the new Athens mentioned by Giovanni Baglione in his *Vite de pittori, scultori et architetti* (1642), confirming the Vasarian adage – reformulated by Gaspare Celio in the *vita* of Bagnacavallo – that the Bolognese people, 'as usual', judged themselves to be 'the best in Italy' [fig. 24].[3] This time, however, Guido legitimised the statement on behalf of everyone.

Reni's return to his native city was not final, however, as he went back to Rome at least three times. Nevertheless, it was a well-thought-out decision that influenced the three parameters on which the painter had left a deep mark: 'the entire world', accomplished 'artists', and 'art lovers', according to Carlo Cesare Malvasia in his *Felsina pittrice* (1678).[4] In this transitional period in his career Guido championed a new *maniera moderna* or modern manner that was based not only on aesthetic considerations such as *bianchezza* (whiteness) – that is, the ability to lighten his palette – but also on skill at arriving at universal

consensus and earning unprecedentedly high profits.[5] The 'Cumpatriott' (compatriot or fellow citizen)[6] – as he was called by a friend of his, the Olivetan intellectual, scholar, musician, and composer Adriano Banchieri, an organist at the monastery of San Michele in Bosco – became the pride and glory of Bologna, and the city basked in his fame, which gave rise to considerable business of good quality. From 1620 onwards Reni came to be identified with Bologna, which was keen to protect its *genius loci*.

MAP OF RENI'S WORKS IN HIS NATIVE CITY

Beginning in 1614, Guido's Bolognese career, which was progressing in leaps and bounds towards the *seconda maniera* – that which was to the liking of 'the most learned', whereas his first manner appealed to 'the most curious'[7] – was notable for being perfectly interwoven with the local fabric. It was fuelled by his relationship with his clients – locals and foreigners – and pupils as well as with the whole network of people, intermediaries and dealers, admirers and intellectuals, that populated the painter's disorderly and unconventional life.

His full awareness of the value of his art, ability to impose on the market a set of completely new rules that corresponded to the appreciation of his work, and capacity to solve problems in accordance with his own vision of the world, even in the face of strong political pressure, come to light when we examine the circumstances surrounding his commissions in the city. Indeed, Guido must have enjoyed an extraordinarily high profile before

Fig. 24 Lorenzo Sabatini, *Map of the City of Bologna*, 1575.
Fresco. Vatican City, Palazzo Apostolico, Sala Bologna

the Napoleonic suppression of the religious orders that brought about the sale of their property and the market vicissitudes that led to the dispersal of various collections.[8] He was furthermore the bearer of an international message that honoured both the city and its public works.

Bologna's most important churches had chapels adorned with pictures by Reni and, as is only logical, his work was coveted by private collectors, dealers, and go-betweens alike; in addition, his mural paintings embellished public and private spaces. In the early 1620s Bologna boasted the exhibition of the *Pietà dei Mendicanti* [fig. 25], which was unique among Bolognese altarpieces as it was a collective public commission from the city's Reggimento (Senate) in 1613, when the painter had not yet put his Roman experience completely behind him. Placed on the high altar of the church of Santa Maria della Pietà near Porta San Vitale on 13 November 1616, the huge canvas showing the Virgin surrounded by the city's patron saints dominates the building erected to house the liturgical functions and private devotions of the local Compagnie delle Arti (guilds), the most powerful of which purchased a chapel that they decorated with images of their protective saints and their attributes.[9]

In addition to this huge public commission, there were other masterpieces by Guido dotted around the city: from the fresco of *Saint Benedict* in San Michele in Bosco, painted during a short trip to Bologna for Agostino Carracci's funeral in 1603,[10] to the tumultuous *Massacre of the Innocents* of 1611 [cat. 20], which was executed in Rome and sent to Bologna for the Berò family, patrons of a chapel in the church of San Domenico, and earned international fame in the 1620s thanks to the lines that Giovan Battista Marino devoted to it in his *Galeria* (1619).[11] After a short time the painting was brought into dialogue with the magnificent 1615 frescoes of the *Glory* of the saint on the dome of the chapel of the Rosary in that church.[12] In his annotations for the 1635 edition of Giovanni Zanti's guide (1583), Adriano Banchieri adds further paintings to the map of Reni's Bologna: the altarpiece of the congregation of San Salvatore, defining it as 'a treasure by Signor Guido Reni for posterity';[13] 'Signor Guido Reni's altarpiece' for the no longer extant church of San Tommaso di Strada Maggiore;[14] and, naturally, the most famous and 'most devout picture by the great Guido Reni' for the Capuchin fathers.[15] Malvasia, in addition to the abovementioned works, recalled as praiseworthy the altar painting executed during the artist's youth that hung in the church of San Bernardo:[16]

> ... on the wall to the right. In the upper part, where he depicted the Blessed Virgin crowned by God the Father and the Son within a glory of angels, he showed a persistent adherence to Calvaert's style, whereas in the figures of the lower portion he expressed a grandness and richness of brushstroke similar to those of Annibale [Carracci].[17]

HIS 'INTIMATE' FRIENDS

When he died, Reni was buried precisely in the basilica of the Dominicans thanks to one of the longest-standing relationships the painter had enjoyed in his native city: his friendship with the Guidotti family, who owned the chapel of the Rosary.[18] It is known that Guido had already come into contact with a few members of the family between 1601 and 1602, though his bond with them was based chiefly on his friendship with Saulo (1601–1665). Although as a painter Saulo enjoyed only 'middling success' – as Malvasia put it[19] – Guido had a soft spot for the young man, despite their age difference (a whole generation). They were very close from at least 1630 if we are to believe what Malvasia says about the choice of Saulo as a model for the Saint Francis in the processional plague banner known as the *Pala della Peste* or *Pallione del Voto* [fig. 30],[20] and, it seems, for all his future depictions of the saint, from the *Saint Francis in Ecstasy* for the Girolamini in Naples to the *Saint Francis in Prayer with two Angels* in the Galleria Colonna in Rome [cat. 42] and the *Saint Francis in Ecstasy* in the Louvre,[21] all datable to around 1631.

Guido and Saulo must have first met sometime before 1630–31. Saulo became essential to Guido, who entrusted him not only with the keys to his home but even with his most important contracts.[22] In fact, Guidotti also acted as the painter's spokesman in the almost fifteen-year lawsuit that pitted him against the Arte della Seta (silk guild) over the execution of the altarpiece dedicated to the patriarch Job for the church of Santa Maria dei Mendicanti, which Guido did not deliver until 1636 [cat. 44].[23]

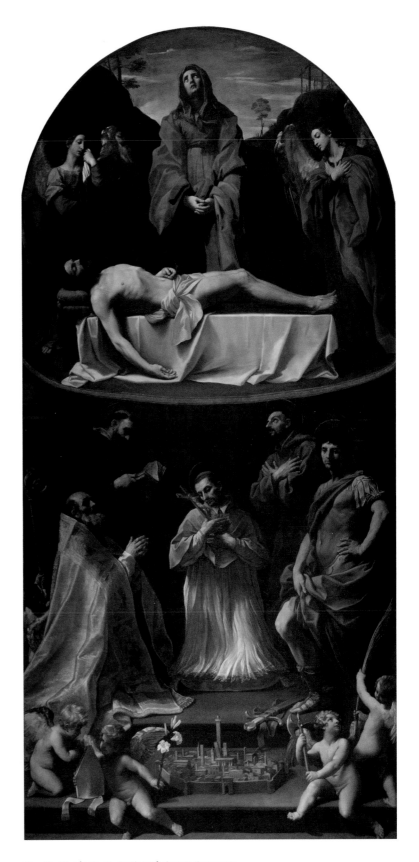

Fig. 25 Guido Reni, *Pietà with Saints Petronius, Francis, Dominic, Proculus and Charles Borromeo (Pietà dei Mendicati)*, 1613–16. Oil on canvas, 704 × 341 cm. Bologna, Pinacoteca Nazionale di Bologna, inv. 445

Fig. 26 Guido Reni, *The Baptism of Christ*, 1623. Oil on canvas, 263.5 × 186.5 cm. Vienna, Kunsthistorisches Museum Wien, Gemäldegalerie, inv. 222

His friend's face is captured in the *Portrait of Saulo Guidotti* (private collection), a painting that was located a few years ago and is dated to the early 1630s; its gestation was lengthy, dragging on until the final months of Guido's life. It shows Saulo standing in a stark room. His gaze is stern and profound, he is dressed in black, and his bony hands clasp a letter addressed to him: 'Al molto Ill.re Sig. Il Sig.r Saulo Guidotti. Bologna'.[24] The epithet, forcefully repeated twice, and the deliberate, necessary decision to omit any reference to rank (senator, doctor, or otherwise) define the intrinsic nature of the sitter and painter. Cutting a slim, almost gaunt figure, Saulo stands out from the overwhelming darkness of his mandatory black attire, enacting a *gravitas* that is human liturgy.

Guidotti was not the only friend to have the keys to Guido's house, a symbol of great trust. So did Jan Jacobs (1575–1650), a Flemish precious metalsmith and merchant who had settled in Bologna in 1607, where he soon became involved in the city's commercial life. These activities secured him sufficient funds to purchase a large house equipped with silk-throwing machines – two *filatoi* and one *torcitoio* – and accordingly to carve out a niche in Bologna's thriving silk trade, the most important local industry of the seventeenth century. In 1623 Jacobs moved into a house owned by senator Angelelli on the Via Calzolerie, the goldsmiths' and silversmiths' street, only a short distance from Guido's home and workshop.[25] That year Jacobs commissioned from Reni a *Baptism of Christ* [fig. 26] which he intended to send to Flanders to promote the painter's career internationally; for this purpose Jacobs enlisted the support of his brother-in-law, the printmaker Jan Meyssens (1612–1670), who was then drawing up a catalogue of the foremost European artists.[26] During those years Jacobs earned a growing reputation as a goldsmith in the Bolognese market: in 1625 he was commissioned to craft a golden frame and cover to protect the icon of the Virgin in the sanctuary of the Madonna di San Luca, and in 1626 he completed the rich reliquary for the Virgin's Sacred Belt, which contains the famous Bolognese relic preserved in the basilica of Santo Stefano, for which he was paid 1,200 lire.[27]

The goldsmith, who was 'dear to Guido for his good-heartedness and frankness', often put Reni up in his home, where he made 'many heads … at fifty scudi each', for which Jacobs was probably paid a percentage in commission.[28] Guido is well represented in Jacobs's picture collection, which was inventoried in the will he dictated before he passed away in September 1650. The finest piece is a 'head of a saint who is reading, by the hand of Signor Guido Reni',[29] which hung in the goldsmith's bedroom among the family portraits and was gifted to the Marquis Achille Albergati Vezza, his fiduciary heir. Guido's original was accompanied by a few copies by his school, inspired by autograph compositions in which Jacobs may have acted as an intermediary, such as the allegory *Drawing and Colour* [cat. 2], a picture purchased by Louis XIV in Flanders in 1685, of which the goldsmith wished to own a copy.[30]

After a decade, Guido succeeded in becoming one of the best paid painters of the artistic elite, though he managed his finances in a very particular manner: he never accumulated wealth and decided to rent rather than own property in order to be able to move quickly and easily into different apartments in the centre of Bologna. He kept some for several decades, such as his workshop – where he also lived – beside the apse

Raffaella Morselli

of Santa Maria della Vita in the parish of Sant'Andrea delle Scuole. It was owned by the priests of the church and Reni fitted it out simply with a few pieces of furniture. He had other rented premises 'in the Market' and another studio beside the Ospedale della Morte (now the Museo Civico Archeologico); in addition to these, there were places he used occasionally, such as a 'room … in the Accademia delle Porte', where he kept the *Abduction of Helen* [fig. 35], and three rented rooms in the Palazzo Fantuzzi,[31] which later became the workshop of his pupil Giovanni Francesco Gessi (1588–1649).

As part of this system of multiple premises in different locations for diverse purposes, Guido – in a sort of emulation of a courtly lifestyle – assigned some of his collaborators the role of pages or messengers, and others that of intermediaries. Among the former was Pietro Gallinari († 1664), also known as Pierino, the head servant or butler who passed on Guido's orders for the arrangement of copies of details of his pictures to be made by his pupils.[32] The men whom Malvasia defined as Reni's 'intimate' collaborators were the poet Cesare Rinaldi and the *cavalier* Andrea Barbazza, as well as the abovementioned Adriano Banchieri.[33] Rinaldi in particular had a constant relationship with the master, which specifically became one of service and assistance. Malvasia mentions the orders Guido gave him – as if he were his clerk – when he translated the literary efforts of the painter, who 'wrote incorrectly', albeit in an attractive cursive hand, in exchange for beautiful drawings.[34]

Count Barbazza accommodated the poet Giovan Battista Marino, 'making available to him the usual bedroom' when he arrived in Bologna and above all providing him with access to the court of Mantua in his capacity as first gentleman, close friend, and Bolognese agent of Duke Ferdinando Gonzaga.[35] It was through the count that Guido first came into contact with the duke in 1614 and, after extensive negotiations, painted for him the series of the *Labours of Hercules*.[36] The correspondence with the agent Barbazza tells us that he worked on the commission from July 1617 to July 1620, though the paintings were probably designed at the same time, as proven by the payment the artist received on 20 December 1617.[37] Experts currently agree that *Hercules on the Pyre* [fig. 27] was the first canvas to be sent to Mantua, followed by the rest between July 1619 and July 1620, though there has always been much uncertainty regarding the order in which they were executed. However, a recent detailed examination of the documents concerning Rinaldi has brought to light new elements that deserve to be analysed: in a letter of 1620, the poet comments that Guido 'at the present time' is painting *Hercules slaying the Hydra of Lerna*,[38]

Fig. 27 Guido Reni, *Hercules on the Pyre*, 1617–21. Oil on canvas, 260 × 192 cm. Paris, Musée du Louvre, inv. 538

leading us to think that it is the third or the fourth and last picture in the ensemble. Considering that *Hercules and Achelous*[39] is comparable to the last two paintings and that the only one that is not similar – it is much livelier and more poetic – is *Dejanira abducted by the Centaur Nessus*,[40] it has been suggested that this oil painting was the last to be sent, in July 1620, whereas the one Rinaldi saw is the third. It is interesting to note that these canvases were in Barbazza's Bolognese residence, and that there is a variant of the fourth now in Prague Castle Picture Gallery.[41]

On 3 November 1621 Ferdinando Gonzaga made a new request to the painter through Barbazza: a 'Trial of Paris' and 'a Venus served by the three Graces'.[42] The latter was almost finished and, indeed, it was the only one of the two – possibly designed as a pair – that arrived in Mantua in June 1623. The other one remained in Guido's workshop and was later listed in the 1642 inventory of his estate. Recent technical analyses of the *Toilet of Venus* [cat. 74] have revealed that the *putto* at the window was added after the painting was completed, confirming an observation made by Barbazza in a letter of January 1623 to the duke about the modification of an entire figure. The picture, which is very famous for its inventiveness, size, and composition, has experienced highly complex historical vicissitudes and critical fortunes: from the time it was devised for an impecunious duke who was a visionary to when, after passing through the hands of the most reputable and aristocratic seventeenth-century collectors, it returned to England, the country for which it was initially destined.[43]

BOLOGNA–ROME: HIGH-RANKING PATRONS AND COLLABORATORS/SERVANTS

In 1620 a by then famous Reni was called to Naples to paint a series of frescoes and three altarpieces for the Cappella del Tesoro in the cathedral.[44] Although the commission was prestigious and a contract had been entered into, the artist did not complete the undertaking and departed from Naples in April 1621. Through the mediation of his 'tailor friend' Domenico Lercaro, who left his estate to the convent of the Girolamini when he died in 1623,[45] a canvas by Reni, *Encounter of Christ with Saint John the Baptist in the Desert*, dated to between 1621 and 1631, arrived in Naples much later, between 1627 and 1633.

Meanwhile, Reni remained in contact with Rome. His most significant go-betweens were the high-ranking prelates who enjoyed privileged relations with Bologna and with Guido in particular due to their birth, career, or personal decisions. Notable among them was Ludovico Ludovisi (1595–1632), a cardinal and nephew of Gregory XV who, during his uncle's papacy – and possibly before that, during his formative years in Bologna (1615–19) – became Guido's patron for both public and personal works. Many pieces by the artist are found in the inventory of the paintings in Ludovisi's villa at Porta Pinciana in Rome and on the 1623 list of the movable assets in his *casino*.[46] In Bologna Reni also painted for the cardinal the large *Trinity* of 1625 that still hangs in the Roman church of Santa Maria dei Pellegrini [fig. 28]. The canvas, designed to decorate the high altar of the church, was commissioned to mark that year's Jubilee, but its execution was somewhat delayed; according to Malvasia, in August 1625 the artist undertook to complete it in twenty-seven days.[47] The composition, with a simple, monumental design and a towering frontality reminiscent of Masaccio, fully in keeping with Counter-

Reformation requirements of decorum, is embellished by the sumptuous elegance of the Trinitarians' robes. The canvas must have aroused great admiration when it arrived in Rome as Luigi Scaramuccia, commenting on the foremost works in the city in *Finezze de' pennelli italiani* (1674) much later, ranked Guido's *Trinity* second only to the *Transfiguration* by Raphael (1483–1520).[48] The work was transported from Bologna to Rome by Bartolomeo Omacci, known as Belcollare, who joined Guido's studio as a servant – according to Malvasia after the painter fired Giacomo Spostra, called Giacomazzo, who had posed for him as a model for the centaur in *Dejanira abducted by the Centaur Nessus* painted for Ferdinando Gonzaga in 1619–20.[49] Malvasia defines Omacci paradoxically as 'padrone di Guido' in order to explain his psychological influence and managerial sway over the artist. Belcollare's interests must have been divided, as he also worked as a servant in the household of the Zambeccari, for whom he acted as an intermediary in the purchase of a few paintings by Reni, securing them for a good price.[50] People such as Belcollare, who enlivened Guido's studio during the artist's peak period, played a role that was a mixture of servant, intermediary, and, in a few cases, even collector: it appears that Guido 'made a sleeping Cupid for Modona', and 'Belcollare had another painted which he bequeathed to his brother, who served Signor Cirro Marescotti, and which the latter then left to the aforementioned Cirro'.[51] As a result, Belcollare came to own another version of the *Sleeping Cupid*[52] that Cesare d'Este later purchased through his agent Rinaldo Ariosti. In fact, in January 1627 the Duke of Modena had asked for some finished court paintings according to a report of 8 February in which Ariosti suggested also purchasing the version of Belcollare, 'a friend of Reni', an idea that was dismissed as it was 'the least beautiful of them all'; in the end the negotiations proved unfruitful.[53] Nevertheless, the *Sleeping Cupid* entered the d'Este collections, and is identifiable as the one located by Daniele Benati.[54]

Guido lived in the midst of these contradictions: the members of his 'household' and his list of clients ranged from commoners and servants to nobles and high-ranking prelates. For example, during his term as papal legate in Bologna, Cardinal Roberto Ubaldini (1581–1635) also had Guido paint his well-known, highly elegant portrait,[55] probably in connection with the 1625 Jubilee.[56] A nephew of Alessandro de' Medici – who was Pope Leo XI for only twenty-seven days following his enthronement in April 1605 – Ubaldini also found favour with other popes, such as Paul V (Borghese) and Urban VIII (Barberini), who rewarded him with a long and fruitful term as apostolic nuncio in France, where he performed important diplomatic demarches. In France he was in contact with the queen consort, Marie de' Medici, who promoted his election as a cardinal.[57] His familiarity with the Florentine family, particularly Ferdinando Gonzaga's wife Catherine de' Medici, led him to act as an intermediary with Guido over an *istoria* that Catherine's brother, Cardinal Carlo, wished to buy in 1633, probably a painting depicting *Bradamante and Fiordispina* that Reni was undecided whether to finish.[58]

Cardinal Ubaldini acted as a go-between for one of the most important commissions of Guido's career. On 12 October 1626 the Congregazione della Fabbrica (works committee) of St Peter's, presided by Cardinal Domenico Ginnasi, wrote to Ubaldini in Bologna, requesting him to convince Reni to take part in Pope Urban VIII's ambitious project. The artist was asked to decorate one of the chapels of the Vatican Basilica, and of all the painters involved in the project he was the only one not to reside in Rome. Guido arrived in 1627 and, according to a recent reconstructive hypothesis, turned down the initial proposal that he paint a Trinity on the grounds of the fame of the Ludovisi canvas; instead, he asked to execute an altarpiece depicting Leo the Great and Atilla, snatching the commission from the Cavalier d'Arpino (1568–1640).[59] During his brief stay in Rome, Guido was given favourable treatment, as he had demanded: besides receiving a large down payment (400 scudi), the artist was not paid a sum established by contract but in accordance with each month's work. The committee's initial rejection of this offer was resolved with the intermediation of Francesco Barberini, who particularly wanted Guido to work on St Peter's.[60] Guido may have chosen the subject matter in order to measure himself against the divine Raphael of the Room of Heliodorus, but a few weeks later he decided not to complete the work and the only fragment he came to paint, a 'glory of angels', according to Malvasia, was scraped off on his orders before he returned to Bologna.[61]

ITALIANS, SPANIARDS, AND FRENCHMEN: ALL TOGETHER AT THE COURT OF GUIDO

Guido's fruitless Roman sojourn of 1627 nevertheless brought him further important commissions, particularly from the kingdom of Spain. Ambassador Íñigo Vélez de Guevara y Tassis, 5th Count of Oñate, enlisted him to paint for the Infanta Maria Anna of Spain an *Immaculate Conception* [cat. 55] that he completed in a very short time: the work became a centrepiece of the then very fierce debate on the tenet of Mary's Immaculate Conception. In the early 1600s the Spanish monarchs pressed for the

Fig. 28 Guido Reni, *The Trinity adored by Angels*, 1625. Oil on canvas, 564 × 301 cm. Rome, Santissima Trinità dei Pellegrini

proclamation of the dogma of the Virgin's conception without original sin, and in his *Sanctissimus* of 1622 Pope Gregory XV made it forbidden to claim, even privately, that the Virgin had been conceived in sin; his successor Pope Urban VIII, however, was unwilling to grant the request.[62] Reni's picture commissioned by Spain was therefore of particularly high value, above all because it gave shape to an iconography that was destined to enjoy huge success. The Virgin, standing on clouds and a half-moon, is an ethereal image set outside time and space, depicted without decorative detail, and is the sole element that emanates a light of its own in the painting. Guido, who was no doubt aware of the Renaissance versions of the theme – the best known of which is possibly that of Giorgio Vasari (1511–1574) for the church of the Santi Apostoli in Florence – pares down the composition following in the footsteps of Ludovico Carracci (1555–1619) in Bologna with the *Virgin and Child between Saint Jerome and Saint Francis* for Santa Maria degli Scalzi.[63] The painter returned to this iconography, with a few variants, in the canvas for the church of San Girolamo degli Zoccolanti in Forlì (now San Biagio, 1628–29)[64] and in other paintings that attest to the evolution of the theme of the Assumption, such as the well-known contemporaneous canvas for the high altar of Santa Maria Assunta in Castelfranco Emilia, and continued to explore it until the end of his days. Proof of the foregoing is the painting on silk, now in Munich,[65] commissioned by Marquis Rangoni on behalf of the confraternity of Santa Maria degli Angeli in Spilamberto, Modena, in 1631, which Guido did not deliver until March 1642, a few months before his death.[66]

One of Reni's fondest and most intelligent patrons was Cardinal Bernardino Spada (1594–1661), who hailed from a family from Brisighella, Ravenna. The Bolognese branch of the family, headed by Orazio Spada, had requested the services of Alessandro Algardi (1595–1654) during those years for the church of San Paolo Maggiore. Guido depicts the prelate in the *Portrait of Cardinal Bernardino Spada* [fig. 29], showing him seated on an armchair writing a letter to Pope Urban VIII, who had appointed him as a cardinal and was promoting his career. The painting was executed at the end of Spada's term as papal legate in Bologna (1627–31), as is confirmed by the payment of May 1631.[67] Reni and the cardinal often met during his legation, and their encounters were essential to establishing the painter's reputation during his mature period. One of these occasions was probably related to a new canvas, the *Abduction of Helen* now in the Louvre [fig. 35].

Philip IV of Spain had commissioned this *Abduction of Helen* from Reni in 1627 through both his ambassador the

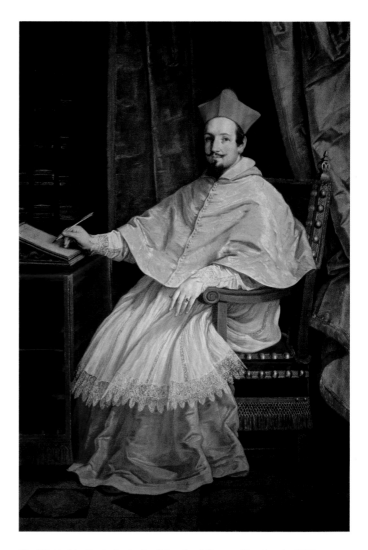

Fig. 29 Guido Reni, *Portrait of Cardinal Bernardino Spada*, 1631. Oil on canvas, 222 × 147 cm. Rome, Galleria Spada

Count of Oñate and Cardinal Francesco Barberini, and it soon became one of the most highly acclaimed paintings by the artist and, indeed, of the whole seventeenth century. The work's eventful collecting history is described by sources and recent critics, who provide the names of many of its previous owners and an account of how the iconography of the subject has been interpreted. Despite the title by which it is known, the canvas appears to be inspired not by Homer's version, in which Helen is indeed abducted, but rather by the version in Dictys of Crete's *Journal of the Trojan War*, in which Helen leaves her husband Menelaus of her own accord after falling in love with Paris, hypnotically following the object of her affection.[68]

Some scholars consider it to be a picture with a distinctly political slant, commissioned by the Barberini in an attempt to persuade the Spanish to call a truce in the Thirty Years' War and tone down their aggressive foreign policy.[69] Completed in 1628–29, the painting nevertheless remained in Guido's workshop; the artist was outraged by the behaviour of Oñate's successor – Manuel de Fonseca y Zúñiga, 6th Count of Monterrey – who had refused to purchase it despite the promise made, possibly because of the excessively high price the artist was asking for or, more likely, because it had been commissioned by his predecessor in the post, from whom the new ambassador wished to distance himself. Spada then arranged for the painting to find its way into the hands of Marie de' Medici, then queen mother of France, who later fell into disgrace and sought exile. All trace of the work was lost for nearly a decade, and in France it gained an almost legendary status and an iconographic meaning very different from the original one: indeed, the painting came to be identified with the misfortune of Marie de' Medici, who was doomed to an exile that ended with her death in Cologne in 1642, the same year Reni passed away.[70] Once again thanks to Spada, the queen had commissioned Guercino (1591–1666) to paint the *Death of Dido* (1629): unlike Reni's canvas, which arrived in France and came to be owned by a French secretary of state, Marquis Louis Phélypeaux de La Vrillière, Guercino's never left Bologna and remained in Spada's possession.[71] The cardinal gave instructions for a pupil, Giacinto Campana (c. 1600–c. 1650), to make a copy of the *Abduction of Helen*. Retouched by Guido, it arrived in Rome in 1632, and was proclaimed to be a second, almost autograph version of the original, though others of fine quality and a similar size progressively appeared over the years, such as the Rome work (Aeroclub).[72]

Cardinal Spada was a good friend and an important intermediary in the many opportunities that arose for Guido during those years. In 1627 Marie de' Medici again enlisted Spada to negotiate with Reni to get him to paint the gallery in the Luxembourg palace.[73] Instead, the queen obtained the delightful *Annunciation* of 1629 on which the artist had been working since 1627. She later gifted it to the Carmelite convent on the Rue Saint-Jacques, where it continued to be displayed until it was transferred to the Louvre.[74]

THE 'PAINTER OF PARADISE': SERIAL ICONOGRAPHIES AND THE LAST ALTARPIECES

After 1630 Guido's fame grew to the extent that everyone – nobles and members of the upper and lower bourgeoisie – yearned to have a work by the artist hanging in their home. That year the city's authorities swore a vow to the Virgin of the Rosary imploring her to intercede to put a stop to the plague. They enacted their vow on 27 December, staging a collective ceremony in which the grand celebratory *pallione* or banner depicting the *Virgin of the Rosary with the Child and the Patron Saints of Bologna* [fig. 30] that Guido had painted on silk was shown for the first time. Designed as a votive offering, from then onwards the banner was carried in a procession every year from the Palazzo Comunale, where it was kept, to the basilica of San Domenico. The choice of silk as a support enabled the artist to experiment with new, exquisite hues of colour while making a symbolic statement about the most flourishing market and the best sold product outside the walls of the city, which is portrayed at the patron saints' feet still shrouded in gloom due to the epidemic.[75]

More than as a history painter, Guido had earned fame as a 'painter of paradise', as his ability to capture the grace and mystic and ethereal aura of male and female saints was unrivalled. His recognisable signature feature is the position of these subjects' upturned face and heavenward gaze, which Malvasia describes as follows: 'he excelled in representing heads turned upward, and hence knew how to tilt them, inflecting all the parts toward the same curving line'.[76] His biographer tells us that the painter used to study close up the demeanour of women belonging to religious congregations to perfect his rendering of female heads,[77] though he never dared approach a beautiful and respectable young Bolognese woman ('one most beautiful girl, and a good citizen'). He therefore decided to rent a room behind Santa Maria Maggiore, in a building opposite where she lived, to be able to see her through the window and be able to 'draw her in different attitudes'.[78] Over the course of his compositional, painterly, and spiritual journey Guido gradually produced a huge series of half-figures of male and female saints and, at the same time, their profane version: the highly successful series of Lucretias and Cleopatras of which collectors were so fond. These compositions, like other famous ones dating from the 1620s, such as the Genoa *Saint Sebastian*,[79] were the most sought-after pictures on the market, so much so that they triggered a craze for canvases by Guido's hand ('di vera mano di Guido'). The copies produced by his studio, anonymous or signed by celebrated pupils of his such as Giovanni Andrea Sirani (1610–1670), Simone Cantarini (1612–1648), and Flaminio Torri (1620–1661) – some of which were retouched by the master and became valuable collectors' items in their own right – managed to keep pace with the high demand for Guido's oeuvre that the artist was unable to meet himself, or served as substitutes for buyers who could not afford original works.[80] Agents, friends, and intermediaries of his, such as the writer Giovanni Battista Manzini and the merchant Ludovico Mastri, undoubtedly played an important part in this process towards the late 1630s.[81]

Mastri had a key role in the complex history of one painting, the *Triumph of Job* for the silk merchants' chapel in the church of Santa Maria dei Mendicanti [cat. 44]. This canvas was one of the last truly important sacred paintings of Reni's late period, and the circumstances and chronology of the commission are known from the report drawn up by the Arte della Seta, which was published by Michelangelo Gualandi in 1840 and recently completed using archival documents.[82] The saint, whose life and miracles are recounted in the eponymous Old Testament book, dominates the scene in the upper part, seated on the right accepting gifts and honours from the people who flock there in veneration after he emerged triumphantly from the harsh trials to which he was subjected by Satan, with God's permission, to test his faith. His sores are miraculously transformed into silkworms, making him the patron saint of the guild. The canvas was commissioned in 1622 with a contract signed by the artist and Mastri, who then directed the guild, though Reni failed to honour his commitments and did not deliver the work until nearly fifteen years later.[83] On 28 February 1633 Jan Jacobs returned to the silk guild the down payment of 1,500 lire (300 scudi) – given to Guido by the guild's treasurer, Astorre Rizzardi – following a fruitless and fearful visit by the guild's council to the quarters of the painter, who was then lodging at the house of the silk merchant Simone Tassi. On 15 April 1633, the council of the silk guild was contemplating dispensing with Guido and turning instead to Domenichino (1581–1641) or to Guercino as third choice. At this point Pietro Martire Carli stepped in. Carli, who was a 'middleman and a mutual friend' of Astorre Rizzardi, the new rector of the silk guild, and also of Guido (and Domenichino), was a native of Como and had lived in Bologna for more than thirty years. Reni asked to be paid 10,000 Bolognese lire (2,000 scudi), but still did not deliver the work: only when there was talk of possibly replacing the commission with a canvas by Guercino did Guido decide to finish the picture. In the end he was paid 1,500 scudi for it – a sizeable sum for the guild, which did not see it completed until 1636: on 7 May that year the huge canvas was transferred to the Conservatorio di Zitelle, an institution for orphaned and abandoned girls near the church of Santa Caterina in Strada Maggiore, where it was mounted on a frame, retouched where necessary and varnished the following days. Guido made further improvements to the painting, for which he requested a further sum of

money that was denied him, leading Malvasia to state that Guido painted it 'more for the sake of spite than glory'.[84]

The 1630s were Reni's most difficult decade. Commissions were constant – as were his gambling losses, which sparked Malvasia's negative comment about the artist's output during this period. Critics have widely demonstrated that his last *maniera*, the style known as *non finito* or unfinished, was undoubtedly a deliberate strategy that enabled the painter to collect a down payment; he would then bring the painting to a degree of completion that made it impossible for it to be returned should the client demand his money back due to non-fulfilment of the contract.[85] The story of the delivery of the Spilamberto *Assumption* is as long drawn-out as that of the Job painting. This altarpiece was commissioned by Marquis Rangoni on 14 December 1632,[86] followed by payments on 12 December 1635 and 4 September 1639. The next annotation appears on 21 December 1640: 'the prior said he deemed it necessary to try to obtain the image Signor Guido Reni made such a long time ago'.[87] Fresh attempts were made on 14 July and 15 December 1641 before the picture was finally delivered. On 6 April 1642 Reni wrote to the prior telling him that if he did not like the picture he had a month to return it. On 9 April Guido is recorded as receiving 2,500 lire (500 scudi). Ten years had elapsed between the first advance and the final payment, but the painter, conscious of his non-compliance, expressed his readiness to keep the work, confident he would immediately find a buyer willing to pay more for it promptly.

1636 was a year of considerable public commitment for Reni: he grudgingly handed over the *Job* altarpiece, and another important canvas, the *Circumcision* for the Gori chapel in the church of San Martino in Siena, was shipped out of the city around the same time [cat. 21].[88] To these two works should be added the almost mirror-like altarpiece of the *Presentation of Jesus in the Temple*,[89] which replaced a picture by Dosso Dossi (c. 1486–c. 1542) in Modena cathedral, and a *Crucifixion* [cat. 32], for which the agent Girolami Resti paid 200 ducatons on 20 June 1636: the painting was displayed in Reggio Emilia, on the altar of the oratory of the Santissimo Sacramento, before 18 November 1636.[90]

Reni, who was resentful and had accounts to settle with Naples, waited until the time was right to avenge himself for what had occurred in 1621. When, at the end of his career, he was asked by the monks of the Naples charterhouse about a large 'painting of the *Nativity* for the Certosa of Naples' and 'how much it would cost them, if one thousand pieces of eight, believing it to be big money', Guido replied 'three thousand scudi

Fig. 30 Guido Reni, *The Virgin of the Rosary with the Child and the Patron Saints of Bologna: Petronius, Francis, Ignatius of Loyola, Francis Xavier, Proculus, Florian and Dominic* (*Pala della Peste* or *Pallione del Voto*), 1630. Oil on silk, 382 × 242 cm. Bologna, Pinacoteca Nazionale di Bologna, inv. 448

plus a gift from the prince', adding disdainfully, 'it is obvious ... that you Fathers are experts only in poverty'.[91] When the monks who had gone to speak to him at the Via delle Pescherie had left, Guido turned to his pupils and stated: 'I have spoken too proudly and said too much, but an inappropriate question requires an impertinent answer'.[92] The large canvas, which remains *in situ* in Naples [fig. 31], had not yet been delivered when the painter died, and was among the pictures found in his home-cum-studio when an inventory of his estate was drawn up.

THE 'RECALCITRANT HAND' OF THE FINAL YEARS

During this period of renewed vigour, Guido set to work on an important but troublesome commission for Henrietta Maria of France, the wife of Charles I of England: a large canvas in landscape format depicting the *Wedding of Bacchus and Ariadne* to adorn the ceiling of Henrietta Maria's bedroom in the Queen's House at Greenwich. The assignment came from Urban VIII and Cardinal Francesco Barberini through the papal legate Giulio Sacchetti: the intention was undoubtedly political, as the pope was then hoping to resume diplomatic relations with the English. The iconographic scheme of the painting, designed by Francesco Barberini, was intended to glorify the pair of sovereigns through the wedding of Bacchus and Ariadne, possibly suggesting a desirable link between England and Rome.[93] The picture, executed under Cardinal Sacchetti's watchful – and for Guido irksome – eye in the Palazzo Pubblico in Bologna, was finished in the summer of 1640 and sent to Rome, accompanied by a panegyric by Giuseppe Maria Grimaldi entitled *L'Arianna del Sig. Guido Reni*, where it proved a resounding success. The event led the people who had monitored the whole execution process to request several copies of the painting, both full-size and on a smaller scale. The largest copy – and possibly the one closest to the original, probably authorised by Reni himself – was painted for Sacchetti. After remaining in his heirs' home it passed to the Pinacoteca Capitolina and is now in the Accademia di San Luca; it was painted by Antonio Giarola (c. 1597–1674), known as Antonio Veronese, a copyist at Guido's workshop, and was retouched by the master himself, who received a chain as a gift.[94]

The collecting history of Guido's *Bacchus and Ariadne* is wrought with misfortune. It never reached England owing to the delicate political situation and the civil war, which forced the queen to seek refuge in France in 1644. The canvas ended up in the hands of the French king's finance minister, Michel Particelli d'Hémery, whose widow, according to the sources,

Fig. 31 Guido Reni, *The Adoration of the Shepherds*, 1640–42. Oil on canvas, 485 × 350 cm. Naples, Certosa di San Martino

reportedly cut it up into several pieces to sell them separately for more money. The fragment with the figure of Ariadne,[95] cut out with great precision, appeared in 2002;[96] another piece with the image of two dancing fauns that matches Reni's original canvas, as may be inferred from the print by Giovanni Battista Bolognini (1611–1688), was recently located.[97]

Guido had already addressed this theme twenty years earlier in two very small autograph versions – almost two cameos converted into paintings – of *Bacchus and Ariadne*.[98] The subject was inspired by Monteverdi's eponymous *favola in musica* with a libretto by Ottavio Rinuccini.[99] To have captured the very famous composition in an image so grammatically perfect made the painting an object of desire throughout courts from Bologna to Rome, giving rise to countless copies. In 1640 the freshness of this brilliant idea was dulled by the use of a canvas too large for the physical and psychological strength of the ageing master, who was losing his lustre and was burdened by the guilt of being a Catholic and a gambler, as well as harassed by the many creditors who came knocking on his door day and night. The protection of Guidotti, Jacobs, and the merchant Giovan Battista Ferri was not enough: the painter was nearing the end of his journey. Shortly after, it was Ferri who lodged Guido in his home during the brief illness that led to his death during the sweltering August of 1642.

There is little information about the end of that fatal year: Reni's cousin, Guido Signorini, travelled from Rome to Bologna to arrange the sale of the painter's unfinished works on the advice of Saulo Guidotti and returned the advances the artist had been paid; for the funeral Guido was dressed in his Capuchin habit and his coffin was paraded through the city's streets to San Domenico, where he was interred in the Guidotti chapel, the crowd attempting to touch his body, as if his mortal remains had miraculous powers; and Reni's assistants hurriedly made off with his drawings and personal objects, claiming that the painter had promised they could have them.

Despair gripped the mournful city, and the topographical detail Reni had painted in the lower part of the *Pala della Peste* seems to echo his departure from his beloved capital. We know how his many pupils felt from the first-hand testimony of one of them, Domenico Maria Canuti (1625–1684), which was reported by Malvasia. In his notes, undoubtedly dictated by Canuti, the historian tells how after Reni's death 'for a year [the painter] was beside himself, bursting into tears when he thought about Guido.'[100] And although the same was not true of them all, it took a long time to replace the Divine Guido, who had spawned devotees of his religion and of the myth of Felsina, the beautiful city of Bologna.

1 Wiltshire, Corsham Court, Methuen collection.

2 Malvasia–Pericolo 2019, 1:374, note 436.

3 Edited version of Gaspare Celio's *Le vite degli artisti* in Gandolfi 2021, 98–99.

4 Malvasia–Pericolo 2019, 1:17.

5 Puglisi 2021.

6 Zanti–Banchieri 1712, 60: 'Opera di Putt Mindicant, i qual tienin in la sua Chiesa una tavola all'Altar Mazor, fatta far dall'Illustrisim Reggimét d'Bulogna, dal sò insign Cumpatriott Guido Reni' ('Work of the Mendicanti, who have in their church a picture on the high altar commissioned by the most illustrious Senate of Bologna from its most distinguished compatriot Guido Reni').

7 Malvasia–Pericolo 2019, 1:183.

8 For an analysis of the presence of works by Guido and his school in private noble and bourgeois collections, see the inventories published in Morselli 1998.

9 A. Emiliani in Bentini et al. 2008, 57–61, no. 32.

10 On that occasion Guido himself made the prints of the other artists' paintings, in small format, and of some of the inscriptions on the temporary constructions erected for the funeral; see Sandri 2005.

11 For the painting, see the bibliography updated by F. Valli in Bentini et al. 2008, 50–57, no. 31; on the composition, see Cropper 1992.

12 Pepper 1988, 235, no. 43; Alce 1997.

13 *Christ the Saviour*, Bologna, Santissimo Salvatore.

14 For the altarpiece in San Tommaso di Strada Maggiore, see Zavatta and Bigi Iotti 2004.

15 It is the *Christ on the Cross with the Virgin, Saint Mary Magdalene and Saint John the Evangelist*, better known as the *Christ of the Capuchins*, now in Bologna, Pinacoteca Nazionale di Bologna, inv. 441.

16 It is the *Coronation of the Virgin with Saint Catherine, Saint John the Evangelist, Saint John the Baptist and Saint Benedict*, now in Bologna, Pinacoteca Nazionale di Bologna, inv. 440.

17 Malvasia–Pericolo 2019, 1:20–21, 1:225, note 43, and 1:463: 'Nel muro laterale a mano destra, ove nella parte superiore, che rappresenta la Beata Vergine coronata dal Padre Eterno e dal Figlio, con gloria d'angioli, mostrò aver anche ritenuto del far di Dionigi, là dove nelle figure sotto de' quattro santi diede in un grande e pastoso di Annibale'.

18 Guido's familiarity with the Guidottis can be traced back to the beginning of the century: he had painted one of the fifteen Mysteries of the Rosary, the *Resurrection*, around 1600–1 for the eponymous confraternity, which had been granted the 'temporary and revocable use' of the Guidotti chapel, where the large altarpiece was placed. It was later covered with a *sarasina*, a movable painting depicting the Virgin and Child with Saint Dominic and Saint John the Evangelist. For the artist's relationship with the Guidottis, see Morselli 2013.

19 Malvasia–Pericolo 2019, 1:163.

20 Morselli 2013, p. 60; Malvasia–Pericolo 2019, 1:181.

21 Paris, Musée du Louvre, inv. 533.

22 Malvasia–Pericolo 2019, 1:112–13: 'Fatto fabbricare molte chiave simili per la porta principale (che per assicurarsi da qualche insolenza fe' sempre star serrata) le distribuì al signor Saulo Guidotti' ('Although his door was always kept locked lest some abuse be perpetrated, Guido had the key to his house's main entrance duplicated and distributed to Signor Saulo Guidotti').

23 For this issue, studied in Morselli 2016, see the entry for cat. 44 in this catalogue.

24 The portrait, which nineteenth-century sources recall being in the home of the Guidotti heirs, reappeared in 2012 and was restored that year: see Morselli 2012a. Giordani remembers seeing it in the home of Francesco Guidotti Magnani in the notes to the *Felsina pittrice*; Malvasia–Zanotti 1841, 2:57; also Gardini 1876, 11, and Morselli 2013, 69–71.

25 Bologna, Archivio Generale Arcivescovile di Bologna, Parrocchie soppresse, S. Matteo delle Pescherie, Stati d'anime 30/8, fasc.1, 1623-57, fol. 6r; published in Bertoli Barsotti 2014, 17, note 48.

26 Pepper 1988, 251, no. 76; in Antwerp the painter Jan (or Jean) Meyssens published *Image de divers hommes d'esprit sublime qui par leur art et science devraient vivre eternellement et desquels la louange et renommée faict estonner le monde* (1649), in which he mentions Guido Reni, the only Italian artist represented in the gallery apart from Stefano della Bella (1610–1664) and Francesco Padovanino (1561–1617). The engraved image, taken from a lost self-portrait, shows the artist at an advanced age sporting a Flemish-style organza collar and gold chain; see Morselli, 2018b, especially 110–13.

27 The goldsmith's Bolognese commissions have been studied by Anna Maria Bertoli Barsotti (2014) based on the *Libro dei conti di bottega*

located in the archive of the Collegio dei Fiamminghi, founded by Jacobs, together with other unpublished documents held in different archives in the city.

28 Malvasia–Pericolo 2019, 1:97 and 1:107.

29 Bologna, Archivio del Collegio Jacobs de B16, letter 9, 1650, Codicilo, fol. 2v, in Bertoli Barsotti 2014, 53: 'Testa di un santo che legge di mano del S.r Guido Reni'.

30 The list of works inspired by Reni in Jacobs's collection, which subsequently passed to the Collegio dei Fiamminghi and are now preserved in different collections, is included in Bertoli Barsotti 2014, 59–62.

31 Iseppi (in press).

32 Malvasia–Arfelli 1961, 68.

33 Malvasia 1678, 2:61; Malvasia–Pericolo 2019, 1:139.

34 Malvasia–Pericolo 2019, 1:172–73: 'Scriveva anche scorretto ed in così poco buona forma che non mi è dato l'animo di tante che fra le altre possiedo, alcuna qui portare delle sue lettere, cavandone più tosto il succo … Credette, dico, che un alfabeto bello e ben condotto denotasse un animo ben composto; … Il perché, quando gli occorse rispondere a soggetti grandi, si valse del Rinaldi, che volentieri il serviva, riportandone in dono disegni' ('He [Guido] also wrote incorrectly and in such poor form that I cannot bring myself to reproduce here any of the many letters by him that, among others, I possess, preferring instead to extract their essence … he was convinced that a beautiful and well-traced lettering revealed a harmonious soul; … For this reason, when he needed to answer letters from great personages, he turned to Rinaldi, who willingly served him, receiving from him drawings as gifts'). On Reni's writing, see Morselli 2008.

35 Marino–Borzelli and Nicolini 1911–12, 1:127–29, letter LXXVII.

36 Now in Paris, Musée du Louvre, inv. 535–38, following its acquisition in 1662 for the collections of Louis XIV.

37 Pepper and Morselli 1993, 137, doc. III; Furlotti 2003, 173, doc. 287.

38 Paris, Musée du Louvre, inv. 535. Rinaldi 1620, 2:87–88. The issue is studied in Morselli and Iseppi 2021, 251–52.

39 Paris, Musée du Louvre, inv. 536.

40 Paris, Musée du Louvre, inv. 537.

41 Pepper and Morselli 1993, 129–45.

42 Mantua, Archivio di Stato di Mantova, Archivio Gonzaga, b. 1172, f. IV, fols. 673–74.

43 Pepper 1988, 248–49. For the vicissitudes of the work and the critical debate, see S. Lapenta in Morselli 2002, 191–92, no. 32. For the addition of the Cupid, Malvasia–Pericolo 2019, 1:287, note 196.

44 Malvasia–Zanotti 1841, 2:25; Malvasia–Pericolo 2019, 1:302–3, note 233.

45 Scaramuccia 1674, 69; Borrelli 1968, 50–51: 'Alcune bellissime Pitture in Quadri ad oglio della nobile mano di Guido Reni, quali dipinse, e donò, ad un suo caro amico Sartore, in quei tempi ch'egli per appunto colà per suoi interessi pervenne' ('Some very beautiful oil paintings by the noble hand of Guido Reni, which he painted and gave to a dear tailor friend of his, at a time when he had gone there out of interest'). The relationship between Reni and Lercaro and the string of commissions have been analysed using unpublished documents in Forgione 2020, 41–45; for the will, see 67–72, doc. 4.

46 Wood 1992 and Morselli 2022a, 35–36.

47 Vasco Rocca 1979, 97–99; Pepper 1988, 256, no. 89; Rice 1997, 212, note 8.

48 Scaramuccia 1674, 78: 'De' più bei Quadri, che siano in Roma In primo luogo dunque ti dico, che tu metta l'Opera famosissima del nostro Raffaello in S. Pietro in Montorio, nel secondo, quella di Guido alla Trinità di Ponte Sisto, nel terzo l'altra d'Annibale Caracci in S. Catterina de Fanari' ('Of the most beautiful pictures there are in Rome … Therefore, I say you should rank in first place the most famous work by our Raphael in S. Pietro in Montorio, and in second place that of Guido in the Trinità di Ponte Sisto, and in third place the other by Annibale Caracci in S. Caterina dei Funari').

49 Malvasia–Pericolo 2019, 1:318–19, notes 276 and 279.

50 Malvasia–Pericolo 2019, 1:491: 'v'andò Bartolomeo detto Belcolare, nel qual tempo fece i quadri del Giambeccaro, facendogli costui il mezano'; see also ibid., 1:318–19, note 279. One of the lost paintings was a *Beato Luigi Gonzaga*, see Pepper 1988, 354, Appendix IV, A18.

51 Malvasia–Pericolo 2019, 1:492: 'Fece un Amore che dorme per Modona; Belcollare se ne fece fare un altro rimasto a suo fratello che serviva il signor Cirro Marescotti che lo lasciò poi al sudetto signor Cirro'.

52 Modena, Banca Popolare dell'Emilia Romagna (BPER).

53 Venturi 1882, 194: 'Ho trattato con li padroni dei quadri di pittura, de' quali scrissi a Vostra A. Ser.ma et da tre ne ho inteso l'ultimo prezo che ne vogliono: il p[adr]one del San Gio. Battista è il S.re Pietro Zanetti, et vuole trecento ducatoni d'Argento, il p[adr]one del puttino che dorme è l'Abbate Sampietri, et ne vuole cento doppie, il padrone dell'Amorino è un tale Bartolomeo amico del Reni, et n'adimanda cento doppie, ma questo è il men bello di tutti, il p[adr]one della Santa Caterina è un Merchante nominato Tomaso Capelli, quale per nissun prezo lo vuole vedere' ('I have dealt with the owners of the paintings, about which I wrote to Your Most Serene Highness, and I know the last price they want for three of them: the owner of the Saint John the Baptist is Signor Pietro Zanetti, and he wants three hundred silver ducatons; the owner of the sleeping *puttino* is the Abate Sampietri, and he is asking for a hundred *doppie* for it; the owner of the Cupid is a certain Bartolomeo, a friend of Reni's, and he is demanding a hundred *doppie*, but this is the least beautiful of them all; the owner of the Saint Catherine is a merchant called Tomaso Capelli, who is unwilling to sell it at any price'). The agreements whereby Cesare d'Este purchased the Reni pictures are analysed in Sirocchi 2018.

54 Morselli 2022b, 71–72. On the *Sleeping Cupid*, see D. Benati in Benati and Peruzzi 2006, 106–8, and also L. Peruzzi in Casciu and Toffanello 2014, 212.

55 Los Angeles County Museum of Art, Gift of the Ahmanson Foundation, M.83.109.

56 Pepper 1988, 257, no. 90.

57 See Poncet 2020.

58 Fumagalli 1994, 244, notes 7 and 8.

59 This issue was recently analysed in Pierguidi 2019a.

60 Rice 1997, 163–64; Pierguidi 2019a, 152–53.

61 Malvasia–Pericolo 2019, 1:87.

62 Pierguidi 2019b.

63 Bologna, Pinacoteca Nazionale di Bologna, inv. 581.

64 Pepper 1988, 268, no. 113.

65 Munich, Bayerische Staatsgemäldesammlungen, Alte Pinakothek, inv. 446.

66 On the Castelfranco altarpiece, see *Assunta* 2016; on the Munich canvas, Pepper 1988, 295–96, no. 175. On Guido's use of silk, see Brady 2019 and Puglisi 2020.

67 Pepper 1988, 272, no. 121. On his Bolognese period, see Evangelisti 1983.

68 Colantuono 1997, 57–58.

69 The first was Pepper 1988, 127; the idea is taken up and expanded on in Colantuono 1997.

70 Pepper 1999a.

71 Rome, Galleria Spada.

72 The question was recently analysed in Pierguidi 2012b.

73 Letter from Marie de' Medici to Cardinal Magalotti, 28 May 1629, in Crinò 1963.

74 Paris, Musée du Louvre, inv. 521. Pepper 1988, 275, no. 129. See Loire 1996, 273–77, and, for the drawings, Bohn 2008, 65–66, nos. 50 and 51.

75 Puglisi 2020.

76 Malvasia–Pericolo 2019, 1:176–78: 'Più d'ogn'altro … intese le teste guardanti all'insù, onde ottimamente seppe girarle, facendo camminare tutte le parti per l'istesa linea rotonda'.

77 Ibid., 1:178–79: 'A certe solennità principali, nell'ore prime o intempestive osservò nelle chiese ogni fisonomia di donne ritirate, di giovanette più guardinghe, anche di parti alquanto eccedenti, e però non ingrate, per quella novità che sempre piace; sapendo poi egli ridurre all'ubbidienza di quella eccedente ogn'altra, ed in conseguenza all'armonia di che mancassero elleno, e diffettasse quella dall'altre abbandonata' ('At certain of the principal religious services, at early or unaccustomed times, Guido observed in the churches the features of women, whether discreet matrons or demure girls, taking note of their limbs even though they were slightly long, provided that they looked graceful in consideration of a certain novelty, which is always pleasant, for he was able to adjust all the other limbs to the long ones, thereby reducing all of them to the harmony they lacked in relation to one another').

78 Ibid., 1:178: 'Ricavarla più volte in varie positure'.

79 Genoa, Musei di Strada Nuova–Palazzo Rosso, PR 77.

80 Morselli 2012a, 140–42.

81 Morselli 2022b.

82 Morselli 2016.

83 Stephen Pepper (1988, 282, no. 148) writes that the first payment was dated 26 January 1601 and that the date of the painting is 1635. In his analysis of the 1988 Bologna exhibition, Richard Spear corrects this date based on documentary evidence: cf. Spear 1989 and Spear 1997, 346, note 87. Cf. Morselli 2016, 7–11.

84 Malvasia–Pericolo 2019, 1:114: 'Più per dispetto che per gloria'.

85 Emiliani 1988 and Spear 1997, chap. 15, 'Ultima maniera', 275–320.

86 Galvani 1864, 12.

87 Ibid.

88 Pepper 1988, 283, no. 150.

89 Paris, Musée du Louvre, inv. 522. Malvasia–Pericolo 2019, 1:324, note 290.

90 Stephen Pepper (1988, 297, no. 178) gave a date of 1639 based on the inscription that appears on the Resti altar, but the documentation recently found allows the payment and delivery of the altarpiece to be dated to 1636. Cf. Cadoppi 2011a; Malvasia–Pericolo 2019, 1:326, note 294.

91 Malvasia–Pericolo 2019, 1:152: 'la tavola del Presepe per la certosa di Napoli, l'interrogarono quanto gli la pagassero, se mille pezze da otto, credendosi di dire gran cosa ... che tre mila scudi ed un regalo da principe ..., si vede bene ... padri che non v'intendete che di povertà'.

92 Ibid.: 'ho pure parlato alto ... e detto troppo, ma ad una dimanda spropositata vi si richiede una risposta impertinente'.

93 Sources from Malvasia onwards recall that the opinion of another learned painter was required to specify the details of its content. For this purpose they enlisted 'Giovan Francesco da ritratti', identified as Giovanni Francesco Romanelli (1610–1662), and more recently as Giovan Francesco Negri (1593–1659), a Bolognese portraitist. Cf. Oy-Marra 2000; Montanari 2004; Biffis 2018.

94 This and other copies are analysed and discussed in Guarino and Seccaroni 2018, 39–48.

95 Bologna, Pinacoteca Nazionale di Bologna, inv. 10000.

96 See the reconstruction of the events in Guarino 2002a; also S. Guarino in Bentini et al. 2008, 74–76, no. 36.

97 In the Galleria Fondatico (2013) Daniele Benati presented the fragment as autograph; see Benati 2013a, 42–48; Benati 2018, 59–60.

98 Rome, Villa Albani, and Los Angeles County Museum of Art, Gift of the Ahmanson Foundation, M.79.63.

99 Morselli 2018a, 239–41.

100 Malvasia–Arfelli 1961, 31: 'Stette un anno che pareva fuori da sé stesso, mettendosi talvolta a pensare a Guido e direttamente a piangere'.

VICEROYS, AMBASSADORS, AGENTS, THEOLOGIANS: THIRTY YEARS OF (STORMY) RELATIONS BETWEEN GUIDO RENI AND SPAIN

Stefano Pierguidi

In a letter sent from Rome on 19 August 1627 to Antonio Galeazzo Fibbia, a Bolognese friend, Guido Reni (1575–1642) wrote: 'I have also agreed to make a large painting for the Spanish ambassador, and a small altarpiece for the Constable of Havard [sic], a Spaniard too'.[1] These were the first orders that the painter, then at the height of his fame, had received from a foreign monarch. In fact, the commission for these two canvases, which were to be sent to Spain, the greatest European power at the time, marked the apex of his career. The negotiations, by no means easy, were the culminating episode in Guido's long and intense but also trying relationship with Spanish viceroys and ambassadors.

AN UNREALISED PROJECT: THE CAPPELLA DEL TESORO DI SAN GENNARO IN NAPLES

Reni's relationship with Spain – or, to be more precise, with Naples, the capital of the Spanish viceroyalty – can be traced back to April 1612. That month the artist travelled there for the first time, probably to meet the delegates in charge of the Cappella del Tesoro, and was back in Rome by early May.[2] Also in Naples, at some point in 1612 or thereabouts, Guido painted a portrait of Pedro Téllez-Girón de Velasco, 3rd Duke of Osuna, who was appointed viceroy of Sicily that year. The portrait, now lost, was subsequently praised by Francisco de Quevedo in a sonnet.[3] In December of that year a notice from Rome announced that: 'This Catholic ambassador is sending two painters to Naples to make a few paintings for mosaics and more things in the church dedicated to Saint Gennaro which is being built there'.[4] We now know that in spite of Guido's initial contacts, the two painters recommended by the then ambassador of Spain in Rome, Francisco Ruiz de Castro Portugal, 8th Count of Lemos since 1622, were Orazio Borgianni (1574–1616) and Francesco Nappi (c. 1565–1630).[5] The decorative work, however, was not begun. In consequence, in 1616 the chapel delegates turned to the Cavalier d'Arpino (1568–1640), who never got round to climbing the scaffolding, leading to Reni receiving a fresh invitation in 1619.[6] After arriving in the city, however, Guido was forced to flee to Rome following the threat received early in 1621 from Belisario Corenzio (c. 1558–c. 1646),[7] a highly successful Naples-based painter who evidently aspired to secure such a prestigious commission. After years of negotiations and various trips to Naples, in the end Guido did not paint anything for the Cappella del Tesoro: the frescoes were later executed by Domenichino (1581–1641) and Giovanni Lanfranco (1582–1647).

DIPLOMACY AND ICONOGRAPHY: THE FRESCO OF THE INVESTITURE OF SAINT ILDEFONSUS

Giovan Pietro Bellori's biography of Reni, which was penned after he read Carlo Cesare Malvasia's in *Felsina pittrice* (1678) but remained in manuscript form, mentions a 1612 fresco by Guido depicting the episode of Saint Ildefonsus receiving the chasuble. The painting decorated one side of a lunette in the Cappella Paolina in Santa Maria Maggiore in Rome [fig. 32]:

Fig. 32 Guido Reni (and Giovanni Lanfranco), *Saint John Damascene
healed by an Angel* and *The Investiture of Saint Ildefonsus*, 1610–19.
Fresco. Rome, Santa Maria Maggiore, Cappella Paolina

In the chapel of Santa Maria Maggiore, in place of the
Madonna Guido had painted an angel holding out the chasuble to Saint Ildefonsus for him to celebrate mass; the pope
ordered that it be changed, and so, because of the departure
of Guido, who had gone away of his own accord, Lanfranco
was summoned to execute the pope's intentions in keeping
with the truth of the miracle; thus the same Lanfranco, having removed the angel, replaced it with the Virgin, as can be
seen today, to the displeasure of Guido, who rightly complained of the other's excessive temerity.[8]

This episode had not been reported by any previous sources
but Bellori had evidently been informed of these events by reliable witnesses, since there are documents confirming that it
was indeed Lanfranco who modified the fresco. The changes he
made, however, were not ordered immediately after the work

was completed in 1612, as the payment was not recorded until
August 1619.[9] Fernando Marías, who has analysed this episode
in detail, managed to locate a print published in 1621 showing
Guido's fresco with the appearance it had before Lanfranco's
intervention [fig. 33].[10]

The iconographic scheme of the Cappella Paolina had been
devised by two Oratorians, brothers Tommaso and Francesco
Bozio, who would presumably never have made such a mis-
take.[11] Guido had taken significant liberties and to maintain
the symmetry with the scene on the left side, where he was to
represent the scene of the miraculous restitution of Saint John
Damascene's hand, he depicted an angel handing something
to the saint in each painting. It is possible that the two
Oratorians were not present while the work was in progress
and that certain particular iconographic details, for which they
had established as a reference Laurentius Surius's *Vitae

Fig. 33 'The Cappella Paolina in Santa Maria Maggiore' (detail), in Paolo de Angelis, *Basilicae S. Mariae Maioris de urbe a Liberio papa I usque ad Paulum V Pont. Max. descriptio et delineatio*, Rome, Zanetti, 1621. Madrid, Biblioteca Nacional de España, 7/14351

dogma of the Immaculate Conception from Paul V.[13] The sovereign's special emissary was Juan Antonio de Trejo, the general of the Franciscan Order, who was received by the pope on 9 December 1618, and again in January and February 1619.[14] Although the endeavour proved unsuccessful (the dogma was not proclaimed until 1854), during those months the Spanish delegation even went to the lengths of striking a medal with the Eucharist on the obverse and the Immaculate Conception on the reverse. Thousands of these medals were confiscated in November 1619, while the pope strove to avoid breaking off relations with Philip III, who had not been informed of the initiative. It is no coincidence that it was precisely then that the pope issued orders for Guido's fresco to be retouched: given his fondness for the Virgin, Saint Ildefonsus was considered one of the earliest defenders of the dogma of the Immaculate Conception, and the whole programme of the Cappella Paolina culminated in the fresco on the dome, painted by Cigoli (1559–1613), which depicts this controversial subject.[15]

TWO WORKS FOR PHILIP III: THE *AGONY IN THE GARDEN* AND THE *ASSUMPTION AND CORONATION OF THE VIRGIN*

Between 1615 and 1619, when pressure was being heaped on to have the Roman fresco retouched, Guido may have already been known in Spain not only by name but also through his works:[16] in fact, one of his early pieces on copper seems to have arrived in Madrid very soon, before 1615. That year the body of Empress Maria of Austria was transferred from the lower cloister (where it had lain since her death in 1603) to the choir of the church of the convent of the Descalzas Reales in Madrid, and it is known from a contemporary account that 'above it was an altar with an image of the prayer in the orchard'.[17] The picture has been identified as a *Agony in the Garden* dated to around 1607 that is still in the Descalzas and is attributed to Reni [cat. 12].[18] The work has plausibly been linked to the *Assumption and Coronation of the Virgin* also by Guido, though the latter is painted on panel, larger in size, and only mentioned in the royal inventories from Philip IV onwards [cat. 8]. It is nevertheless significant that in 1632 Vicente Carducho (c. 1576–1638) should have recognised in the Madrid collection of *relator* Alonso Cortés, personal secretary to the king, two pictures on these themes as copies of Guido.[19] Perhaps it is possible to establish how those works found their way into Spain so quickly: Juan Alfonso Pimentel, 8th Count

sanctorum – which was repeatedly republished from the late sixteenth century onwards but until then always in Latin – were chosen by the painters. Whatever the case, one has the impression that when the frescoes were unveiled it was only the members of the Spanish colony in Rome who raised objections. The pope and the Curia do not appear to have been so sensitive – at least not in this case – to how faithful Reni was to the sources. In 1615 the ambassador Francisco Ruiz de Castro was urged to step in to ensure the painting was corrected, as descriptions of Guido's fresco had reached Toledo, Saint Ildefonsus' city of birth.[12] Even so, as stated earlier, Lanfranco did not retouch the fresco until 1619: evidently, the protests voiced to the Holy See in 1615 did not have an immediate effect. It is therefore likely that the turning point was marked by the work of the third mission of the royal committee sent to Rome by Philip III in 1618–19 to procure a definition of the and 5th Duke of Benavente and viceroy of Naples from 1603 to 1610 – known for having commissioned the *Crucifixion of Saint Andrew* by Caravaggio (1571–1610)[20] – was on very close terms with Paul V and his nephew Cardinal Scipione Borghese, so much so that the inventory drawn up of the count's possessions in 1611, when he returned to Spain, lists a number of artworks specifically described as gifts from the pope to the viceroy. These presents may possibly be traced back to a visit by Juan Alfonso's three children to the papal court in 1608.[21] Scipione Borghese, who in 1621 gave Cardinal Ludovisi two pictures on copper painted during Guido's youth,[22] may have likewise chosen those early pieces by the up-and-coming Bolognese painter as diplomatic gifts of extreme importance many years earlier. On returning to his country Benavente may have presented these paintings to Philip III (or perhaps they were intended for the king from the outset), who finally had the *Agony in the Garden* placed above his aunt Maria's tomb in 1615. In his *Felsina pittrice* (1678) Malvasia suggests that during his period of friction with the papal court over the works executed in the Cappella Paolina around 1612, Guido thought of 'fleeing to Spain or to France, where already those monarchs had honored him with invitations to their courts'.[23] Although it is likely that the author's statement is a backward projection of the European fame achieved by the artist in the late 1620s, when he was invited to work in France, the artist's name appears to have been known in Madrid during those years, by which time Philip III was on the throne.

That Reni's paintings were fit for the King of Spain was clearly spelled out in a letter of 1629 to Francesco Angeloni, Bellori's adoptive father, in which Giasone Vaccari writes that 'a head by Signor Guido drives [the agent Giovanni Battista Muti] wild, it being said to be consonant with his genius and so excellent that it could be placed at the bedhead of the King of Spain'.[24] In addition, around this time all the agents must have been well aware that Guido had received two important Spanish commissions a few years earlier.

THE *IMMACULATE CONCEPTION* FOR THE INFANTA MARIA ANNA OF SPAIN

David García Cueto must be credited with having identified the 'Constable of Havard, a Spaniard too' mentioned by Guido in his letter of August 1627 as Fernando Álvarez de Toledo y Beaumont. Fernando, the son of Antonio Álvarez, 5th Duke of Alba and at the time viceroy of Naples (1622–29), was the 7th constable of Navarre – a place name distorted to 'Havard'. The 'small altarpiece' (*tavolina*) commissioned from Guido might have been a piece intended for private devotion: the *Immaculate Conception* now in New York [cat. 55].[25] Malvasia, who had firsthand information about these events thanks to his close relationship with Cardinal Bernardino Spada, the papal legate in Bologna (who, as we shall see, had intently monitored the vicissitudes surrounding the *Abduction of Helen*),[26] reports that the work was intended for the Spanish infanta. He is referring to Philip IV's sister Maria Anna of Spain (1606–1646), who purportedly placed it in her chapel in the Alcázar.[27] It must therefore have been a gift from the viceroy, and as neither he nor his son lived in Rome the arrangements for the delivery and payment of the canvas were entrusted to the Spanish ambassador, Íñigo Vélez de Guevara y Tassis, 5th Count of Oñate. Relations between Oñate and Reni were fraught with tension from the outset. According to the *Felsina pittrice*, a reliable account that has been confirmed in all aspects – the agreed price of 400 scudi, and that the painting was sent to Bologna by Guido, annoyed at the delay in payment, but intercepted in Rimini by the Barberini envoys in December 1627 and returned to Rome[28] – it is likely that the negotiations between Guido and the client were conducted through the Barberini. The artist's patrons in Rome, they had invited him to paint one of the altarpieces for the new St Peter's, though he produced very little and the altarpiece ended up being crafted in marble by Alessandro Algardi (1595–1654).[29] Guido's behaviour – he seems to have deliberately sought a showdown with Oñate, even withdrawing the picture from sale – has been explained by the artist's huge pride or the state of diplomatic relations between Spain and the Holy See.[30] Nevertheless, this episode should possibly be understood first and foremost as a consequence of earlier brushes between the Bolognese artist and certain powerful Spaniards: the failure of the negotiations for the Cappella del Tesoro in 1612 due to the meddling of Ruiz de Castro, and later the censorship of his fresco in the Cappella Paolina which, if Bellori is to be believed, understandably upset Guido at having one of his works tampered with.[31] The client who commissioned the *Immaculate Conception* was furthermore the viceroy who had taken Corenzio under his wing in Naples[32] and who in 1621 had ultimately prevented Reni from painting the fresco in the Cappella del Tesoro. Reni must have built up a great deal of resentment over the years. The timely intervention of the Barberini nevertheless solved the incident and the canvas was shipped to Spain.[33]

There could have been no better choice than Reni for this altarpiece intended for the Spanish infanta's private chapel in the Alcázar, though it is reasonable to wonder what prompted the decision. The client had not previously made any prestigious commissions in Rome and cannot have been very familiar with the city's art scene: it is therefore likely that father and son put their trust in Oñate, who, as we shall see, was guided by precise instructions from the outstanding agent who arranged the concurrent commission of the *Abduction of Helen*.

The subject of the New York picture had always been complex and controversial, and became a particularly thorny issue in 1627. After the royal committee's third mission failed, Philip IV desisted from adopting significant initiatives to urge Urban VIII to acknowledge Mary's immaculate nature.[34] Nevertheless, in 1626 the pope blessed the first stone of Santa Maria della Concezione, the church of the Capuchin monks near the Palazzo Barberini alle Quattro Fontane, whose high altarpiece – lost but known through preparatory drawings and a surviving copy in the church – appears to have been painted between 1628 and 1630 by Lanfranco.[35]

Guido had never previously tackled the subject of the Immaculate Conception, but he must have been familiar with a few important models, notably the altarpiece of around 1590 by Ludovico Carracci (1555–1619) formerly in the church of Santa Maria degli Scalzi in Bologna.[36] Carracci's rendering of the theme was greatly simplified, leaving no space for the symbols generally associated with the Virgin Immaculate, which are often scattered around a landscape that is merely hinted at beneath her, on earth (from the *Hortus conclusus* to the *Porta Coeli*). Guido further pared down his version, dispensing with spatial allusions, and emphasised the transcendental and supernatural nature of the Immaculate Conception by representing both the Virgin and the two angels with their eyes directed at the heavens (in contrast to the usual depictions showing the Virgin in a devout pose, gazing downwards).

Guido's painting was not far removed from the iconography devised by Francisco Pacheco (1564–1644) in his work of 1619 in Seville cathedral and subsequently formalised in his treatise published in 1649.[37] But for the Spanish painter, who produced further versions of this subject, it was important for the crescent moon to be pointing downwards, as it was in Lanfranco's lost altarpiece in the Capuchin monastery in Rome – in fact it was a partially transparent sphere through which the landscape was visible; and he did not include

Fig. 34 Jusepe de Ribera, *The Immaculate Conception*, 1635. Oil on canvas, 502 × 329 cm. Salamanca, Agustinas de Monterrey, Iglesia de la Purísima Concepción

angels.[38] Reni's altarpiece did not conform to these guidelines, though it appears that painters always enjoyed a certain degree of freedom even when handling such delicate dogmatic issues: in 1635 Jusepe de Ribera (1591–1652), commissioned by Manuel de Fonseca y Zúñiga, 6th Count of Monterrey, painted a large *Immaculate Conception* featuring God the Father and the dove of the Holy Spirit, now in the church of the Purísima Concepción in Salamanca [fig. 34].[39]

THE ABDUCTION OF HELEN FOR THE NEW HALL OF THE ALCÁZAR

Guido received very precise instructions regarding the other picture to be sent to Spain, which, as he told Fibbia in his letter, he had agreed to paint in 1627. The 'large painting' (*quadro grande*) mentioned in the letter must have been the *Abduction of Helen* intended to be hung in the Salón Nuevo (New Hall) of the Alcázar[40] as part of a very cleverly and carefully designed cycle.[41] However, the painting never arrived in Spain; instead, it ended up in France and is still there, in the Louvre [fig. 35].[42] The ensemble in the New Hall, hung in the mid-1610s, albeit without the *Abduction of Helen*, was a matchless anthology of European painting of the period in which all or nearly all the Italian schools were represented, flanked by the Spanish and Flemish schools.[43] This ambitious plan to bring together many painters of different origins in a coherent cycle linked by the themes portrayed is not the only example of such important initiatives in Spain,[44] one of which is almost totally contemporaneous with the project for the New Hall.[45]

On 1 February 1629, barely two days before leaving for Naples to take up the post of viceroy, Fernando Afán Enríquez de Ribera, 3rd Duke of Alcalá, arranged to leave for the chapter room of the Seville charterhouse '13 paintings of the Apostles and our Saviour … each one by a different painter from among the most distinguished there were in Italy that year, whom I had paint them for this purpose'.[46] This cycle of paintings had been commissioned by the duke during his stint from 1625 to 1626 as ambassador in Urban VIII's Rome. In fact, the year 1626 emerged three times during the recent, albeit partial, reconstructions of this series: on the verso of the *Christ blessing the Children* by Artemisia Gentileschi (1593–c. 1652), now in Santi Ambrogio e Carlo al Corso in Rome, which was the central canvas in the cycle; on the *Saint Andrew* by the Neapolitan Giovanni Battista Caracciolo (1578–1635) belonging to a private collection; and on the *Saint James the Lesser* by Giovanni Baglione (c. 1566–1643) in a private collection in London, signed and dated 1626. Ribera's *Saint Peter* – known through many versions, of which the original is possibly a canvas that was put up for auction in Seville in 2016 – must have been commissioned by the duke when he was in Naples that year.[47] The Bolognese Guido worked on this cycle together with painters who were Roman by birth (Artemisia and Baglione) or by choice (Lanfranco),[48] or Neapolitan (native like Caracciolo or adoptive like Ribera). The fact that he was entrusted with depicting what was undoubtedly the most dearly loved apostle in Spain, *Saint James the Greater*

[cat. 39], attests to the prestige the artist enjoyed during those years. Furthermore, in 1625, during his Italian sojourn, the duke had precisely received a painting by Reni as a diplomatic gift from the Ludovisi.[49]

Returning to the *Abduction of Helen*, the Spanish Crown's decision to commission Guido to paint not one of the large paintings due to hang in the highest part of the New Hall but one of the smaller ones designed for the lower level might seem surprising.[50] Around this time Domenichino, for example, was asked to produce one of the large paintings, the lost *Solomon and the Queen of Sheba*, which was to engage in dialogue with the *Jacob and Esau*[51] by Peter Paul Rubens (1577–1640), canvases measuring approximately 320 × 280 centimetres. Domenichino's fame was by no means comparable to Reni's, but the *Abduction of Helen* was designed to be a painting with a poetic accent, a celebration of beauty and love, that would contrast with Rubens's lost *Mucius Scaevola*, known through sketches and copies [fig. 36], an example of heroic and manly steadfastness.[52] Entrusting Guido with this canvas and assigning to Domenichino the solemn tale of *Solomon and the Queen of Sheba* was the result of deliberate and extraordinarily fortunate decisions. Although this cycle of paintings, which can be reconstructed through the 1636 inventory of the Alcázar,[53] has been analysed in several studies, until now no attempt has been made to locate the mastermind of this programme,[54] whom we propose identifying as Giovanni Battista Crescenzi (1577–1635). The full importance of this formidable aristocrat and enthusiast of painting and architecture, on whom much has already been written, has yet to be recognised.[55] Crescenzi was the promotor of an academy that taught painting from nature (especially still-life scenes) and later became 'superintendent' of the paintings of Pope Paul V, particularly those of the Cappella Paolina where, as mentioned, Reni worked.[56] In 1617 he departed for Madrid as part of the retinue of Cardinal Antonio Zapata y Cisneros, taking with him one of his protégés, Bartolomeo Cavarozzi (c. 1587–1625), a follower of Caravaggio.[57] The nobleman returned to Italy in 1619 with letters of recommendation, among other things, from the sovereign and the viceroy (then the Duke of Osuna) to hire workers for the construction of the Pantheon of the Kings at El Escorial,[58] of which he was supervisor in his capacity as an architect. Together with the painter Juan Bautista Maíno (1581–1649), who had lived in Italy from 1600 to 1608 (and, it seems, had met Reni),[59] in 1626 Crescenzi commissioned Diego Velázquez (1599–1660), who had beaten his rivals Vicente Carducho (the Florentine Vincenzo Carducci) and another Tuscan, Angelo Nardi (1584–1665), to paint the lost *Expulsion*

Fig. 35 Guido Reni, *The Abduction of Helen*, 1631. Oil on canvas,
253 × 265 cm. Paris, Musée du Louvre, inv. 539

of the Moriscos, one of the large history paintings intended for the upper level of the New Hall.[60] Although the episode marked the emancipation of the Spanish school, driven by the accomplishments of the great master, it is evident that comparison with the Italian models still carried weight: indeed, the two members of the committee were Italians, or Italianised, and the two other aspirants were Italians too. The iconographic scheme

of the new pictures that were ordered for the New Hall was based on the logic of contrasting pendants: Guido's *Abduction of Helen*, whose protagonist, Paris, had given rise to the long siege of Troy by recklessly abducting the Greek queen, was set against Rubens's lost painting illustrating the heroism of Mucius Scaevola, who had impressed the Etruscan King Porsenna by thrusting his hand into fire, convincing him to lift the siege of

Fig. 36 Peter Paul Rubens and Anthony van Dyck, *Mucius Scaevola before Lars Porsenna*, c. 1618–20. Oil on canvas, 187 × 156 cm. Budapest, Szépművészeti Múzeum, inv. 749

Rome.[61] The other pair of paintings on the lower level showed the heroic Achilles who, although dressed in women's clothing, revealed his identity as a hero warrior on unsheathing his sword among the daughters of Lycomedes – the canvas was by Rubens and Anthony van Dyck (1599–1641)[62] – and, on the other side, Hercules, the hero par excellence, compelled to perform a woman's task, spinning, opposite Queen Omphale (the painting, now lost, was commissioned from Artemisia Gentileschi).[63] The famous 1597–1601 cycle of frescoes by Annibale Carracci (1560–1609) on the ceiling of the Galleria Farnese was based on the same mechanism of contrasting pairs.[64] The two pictures executed by Guercino (1591–1666) in 1617, which belonged to the Ludovisi collection and were bequeathed to Philip IV in 1664,[65] illustrate a similar approach: in *Susannah and the Elders*,[66] two old men attempt unsuccessfully to seduce a young woman and, conversely, in *Lot and his Daughters*,[67] two young women manage to fool an elderly man; and there are many more examples.

Velázquez's most Italianate paintings, the *Forge of Vulcan*[68] and *Joseph's Bloody Coat brought to Jacob* [fig. 63], produced during his stay in Rome in 1630,[69] are based on the same logic: the former reveals a deceit (Venus's betrayal of Vulcan with Mars); while in the other a different kind of trickery is perpetrated (Joseph is sold by his brothers behind their father's back). It must have been an Italian who devised the programme for the New Hall and it is likely that that Italian lived at the court of Madrid, as the commissions for these canvases, whose themes were carefully chosen, appear to have been sent simultaneously to Rome (Domenichino, Reni, and Artemisia), Milan (Camillo Procaccini), Naples (Ribera), and Antwerp (Rubens).

As has partly been pointed out, the painters were assigned the themes to which they seemed best suited. Artemisia, a *femme forte* par excellence, was entrusted with *Hercules and Omphale*, where a woman subdues a man.[70] It is known that shortly after 1611 – the year she was raped by Agostino Tassi (1580–1644), followed by a trial that must undoubtedly have caused a stir – Gentileschi painted her first version of the subject of Judith beheading Holofernes,[71] which was interpreted almost as a programmatic declaration (the woman who defeats and decapitates the man). More sophisticated still was the choice of Domenichino as a history painter and of Guido as a painter of grace and beauty. This contrast between the two great Bolognese masters, who were contemporaries and former pupils of the Carracci academy, first emerged in 1608–9, when Reni and Domenichino painted in fresco and on canvas, respectively, the *Saint Andrew led to Martyrdom* and the *Flagellation of Saint Andrew* in the oratory of Sant'Andrea beside San Gregorio al Celio in Rome. It appears to have been Annibale himself who characterised the styles of the up-and-coming stars of Italian painting immediately afterwards.[72] It is significant that for the above works, an initiative of Scipione Borghese, it was Crescenzi who supervised the estimates for the tasks performed by the architects and stonemasons[73] and therefore witnessed the contrast between Guido's and Domenichino's styles from the outset. Indeed, there is every indication that Crescenzi played a key role in devising the iconographic programme for the New Hall and in selecting the painters active in Rome who were to be involved. That is why he may even have played some part in the fortunate choice of Guido to paint the *Immaculate Conception*. It should also be borne in mind that, as stated, Giovanni Battista had returned to Italy for a short stint in 1619 and had had the chance to refresh his knowledge of the Roman art scene.

As pointed out earlier, however, the *Abduction of Helen* never arrived at its destination and its place in the New Hall was occupied, a few years later, by the *Finding of Moses*[74] by Orazio Gentileschi (1563–1639). We know from Malvasia that when the picture was finished it was publicly shown in Bologna before being sent to Rome, where Monterrey, who had taken over from Oñate as ambassador to the papacy, was in charge of the negotiations. In his *Felsina pittrice*, Malvasia states that a dispute arose over the price of the picture, even though, according to the letter to Fibbia, it had been agreed on from the outset. Once again, the painter seems to have sought confrontation with the Spanish Crown, and this time the Barberini did nothing to repair the rift; indeed, they allowed the canvas to be returned to Bologna. It was probably around that time (the spring of 1629), during the Thirty Years' War – when the pendulum swung decisively towards the French following the failure of the Spaniards' attempt to besiege Casale – that Urban VIII, the Cardinal Nephew Francesco, and Bernardino Spada used the *Abduction of Helen* for political ends, once again revealing their sympathies with France.[75] In fact, on 28 May 1629 Marie de' Medici wrote to Spada, the former nuncio in Paris, telling him that she wished Guido to go to France to paint a cycle of canvases for the Luxembourg palace, her residence; on 2 July the cardinal took the opportunity to propose that she purchase the *Abduction of Helen*. An astute diplomat like Spada would never have dared make such a bold move (offer France a work commissioned by Spain … in the throes of the Thirty Years' War!) had it not been for the backing of Cardinal Francesco, to whom he continued to report on the queen's negotiations with Guido.[76] The painting was thus purchased by Marie' de Medici, who never got to see Reni's masterpiece as she was defenestrated by Richelieu and forced into exile. After remaining in Lyons for about ten years, around 1642, immediately after the queen's death, the picture passed to the French secretary of state Louis Phélypeaux de La Vrillière, who hung it in the picture gallery of his Paris mansion alongside a marvellous selection of masterpieces of Italian painting of the period (Guercino, Alessandro Turchi, Pietro da Cortona, Carlo Maratta, and adoptive Roman Nicolas Poussin).[77] The transfer of the painting from Spain to France towards the end of the Thirty Years' War, when power relations between the two major European nations were changing, became steeped in political significance, confirming the huge prestige of the painting and its maker. However, it is likely that Reni's sympathies did not lie with either country. Malvasia reports a telling reply the painter gave when asked: "'if you had to choose one or the other [France or Spain], which one would it be?" "The one," he answered, "that would be the more useful or at least less harmful to our Italy."'[78]

PHILIP IV'S LAST AND FAILED COMMISSION

Malvasia reports that when Guido died a silk cloth was found in his studio with 'the fable of Latona for the King of Spain, who, knowing full well what had happened with the *Abduction of Helen*, after complaining about it with his ambassadors, had ordered this new painting'.[79] Although there is no mention of a painting on this subject in the inventory of Reni's estate, this information appears to be confirmed somewhat by the mention in the 1653 inventory of Monterrey's collection of a 'fable with a woman, two children and a man transformed into a frog', which was held in great esteem.[80] However, this picture was recently identified as the large canvas by the Genoese artist Orazio De Ferrari (1606–1657) that appeared in a private collection in Spain, purchased or commissioned by Monterrey in Genoa shortly before returning to his home country in July 1638.[81] It is difficult to explain how Malvasia could have known about De Ferrari's *Latona* and it is telling that an important canvas on a subject that was certainly not very popular should have been commissioned in Italy around the same time, and precisely by Monterrey. In short, this picture appears to have been somehow linked to a possible *Latona* commissioned from Guido, which would confirm what is reported in the *Felsina pittrice*. It is likely that Monterrey really did attempt to get hold of another painting by Reni for the king and that at the same time or immediately after this attempt failed he had commissioned a canvas on the same subject (possibly chosen independently) for himself from a less prestigious painter.[82] It should be pointed out that negotiations had begun with Reni in the spring of 1637 for the execution of a huge canvas for the French Queen of England, Henrietta Maria. Once again, the Rome-based Cardinal Barberini and the cardinal legate in Bologna, Giulio Sacchetti,[83] acted as intermediaries with the painter. The news may have opportunely reached the courts of Madrid and Naples, and would explain why contact was then resumed with Guido so that Philip IV too could finally own a 'royal' canvas by the master.

This is not surprising: for the large altarpiece for the Purísima Concepción in Salamanca – the church that, thanks to Monterrey, assembled one of the most outstanding public collections of seventeenth-century Italian painting in Spain – the count had previously turned to Guido for a *Saint John the Baptist in the Wilderness* [cat. 22]. This picture, together with canvases by Alessandro Turchi (1578–1649) and other masters yet to be identified, was to flank the abovementioned *Immaculate Conception* by Ribera (the cycle, like that of the New Hall, was based around the theme of comparison between schools of painting).[84] In addition, during his term as viceroy of Naples, Monterrey, with the collaboration of his wife,[85] commissioned a series of imported canvases for the Buen Retiro, chiefly from painters who were active, or had trained, in Rome. One of these pictures was the *Women Gladiators*[86] now attributed to a pupil of Reni, Giovanni Giacomo Sementi (1583–1636), a canvas that was indeed listed in the 1701 inventory of the Spanish royal collections as 'of the school of Guido'.[87] All in all, the count's interest in, and appreciation of, Guido Reni[88] is confirmed by many aspects and, according to Malvasia, it may be deduced that Philip IV put pressure on the person who had let the *Abduction of Helen* slip away, that is, Monterrey.

In a letter of 20 August 1639 Philip IV's secretary, Antonio Carnero, informed the historian Virgilio Malvezzi, then in Madrid, of the king's wish to 'provide a measurement of the size of a painting that Signor Guido is to make in Bologna, which shall be on the subject of which Your Lordship is to notify him. This measurement shall be sent by courier from here to the Duke of Medina de las Torres'.[89] Shortly after Monterrey's departure, by which time the plans to obtain the abovementioned *Latona* had come to nothing, no efforts were spared to maintain the artist-client relationship with Guido, enlisting the aid of the new viceroy Ramiro Núñez Felípez de Guzmán, Duke of Medina de las Torres. Furthermore, just after the Count of Monterrey returned to his native country, in September 1638, Spada had tried in vain to sell his own copy of the *Abduction of Helen* (now still in the Galleria Spada in Rome) precisely to Medina de las Torres, almost as if it were the original, which was then held up in Lyons.[90] This confirms that it was common knowledge that the Spanish Crown was still interested in acquiring a painting by Guido. It seems odd that the measurements of the canvas to be commissioned had already been established by August 1639, as if the picture were intended to be hung in a specific place, possibly alongside another work or several others (as with the *Abduction of Helen*), yet the choice of subject matter was left to Malvezzi's discretion. It appears that the theme of *Latona* had also been a favourite of Monterrey's: what Madrid was basically aiming for during those years was to obtain a picture by Reni to put on show; the subject was not a particular concern. Whatever the case, Bellori refers precisely to this stage in the failed negotiations when he writes that Philip IV 'ordered Guido to paint him another, larger picture with the fable of Samson; however, because it was delayed too long it remained unfinished at his death'.[91] The author was familiar with the *Felsina pittrice*, yet ignored Malvasia's reference to a *Latona*, claiming instead that

Philip IV had commissioned Reni to paint a *Samson*. If he reported a different version it must have been because he possessed certain information. Actually, although he could not have known this, Philip IV and his court were particularly fond of this subject.[92] For one thing, the cycle of paintings for the New Hall included three canvases, paired with three others on different subjects, depicting Samson (one had been commissioned from Camillo Procaccini).[93] And it seems to be no coincidence that another, more important Italian work on the same subject had been gifted to the king years earlier: Giulio Cesare Procaccini's *Samson and the Philistines*,[94] a canvas slightly larger (263 × 263 centimetres) than those of the series for the New Hall, to which the *Abduction of Helen* belonged (about 250 × 250 centimetres). Once again, it arrived in Spain through the mediation of Monterrey, to whom it appears to have been delivered in June 1622 while he was passing through Italy as head of the delegation sent to pay tribute to the newly elected Gregory XVI.[95] As the picture is not listed in the inventory of Monterrey's possessions, and Philip IV had just succeeded his father on the Spanish throne in March 1621, it may be assumed that it was immediately interpreted as a diplomatic gift for the new king.[96] In addition, a 1666 inventory of the Alcázar in Madrid lists a lost 'Samson when they gouged out his eyes' (some 180 centimetres wide), attributed to an unspecified Procaccini – it is not known whether Giulio Cesare (1574–1625) or Camillo (1551–1629).[97] The latter canvas may have been devised in connection with Guilio Cesare's masterpiece that is now in the Prado. And lastly, more significant still is the mention of another lost 'Samson when he killed the Philistines' by Paolo Finoglio (c. 1590–1645), the same size as the 'Samson when they gouged out his eyes' listed in the Spanish collections.[98] This painting was also commissioned through viceroy Monterrey and should be dated approximately to between 1633 and 1638.[99] The *Samson* theme must have been conceived as an extension of the Procaccini paintings that had been in the royal collections for some time, and possibly also of the *Samson* that, according to Bellori, Guido never finished for Philip IV. Among other things, Malvezzi must have been familiar with the *Samson Victorious* of about 1617–19 by Guido in Zambeccari's Bolognese collection [fig. 15], which was one of the artist's masterpieces – and, incidentally, a heroic male figure similar to the Salamanca *Saint John the Baptist*. Reni is at his best in such simple and majestic creations.

In July 1636 Malvezzi, who had been firm friends with Guido since the early 1630s,[100] departed for Madrid. This trip enabled the historian to at last put to good use his deep-rooted sympathies with Spain, which had caused him considerable problems during Barberini's papacy.[101] When Malvezzi set about securing the long-desired Reni painting for Philip IV's collection, Guido had probably just started on the abovementioned canvas for the Queen of England, a *Bacchus and Ariadne* that was nevertheless sent to Rome in August 1640.[102] As for the negotiations on that other picture that was supposed to be sent to Madrid, however, there is no further news after the letter of 1639. Nor does the carefully drawn up inventory of Reni's estate specify any canvases commissioned by the Spanish Crown. Once again, things had not gone as Madrid expected.

1 Prohaska 1988, 646: 'Ho anco accettato a far un quadro grande per l'Ambasciatore di Spagna, e una tavolina per il Contestabile di Havard pure spagnolo'. The letter, printed in the eighteenth century by Giovanni Gaetano Bottari, has repeatedly been republished with comments, see Emiliani et al. 1988, 202; Cf. the translation in Malvasia–Pericolo 2019, 1:295, note 218.

2 A document dated 12 April 1612 attests to the presence in Naples of Guido, who entrusted Luca Ciamberlano with handling his affairs in Rome; see Bologna 1960. The hypothesis that the Neapolitan trip of April 1612 was related to the work on the Cappella del Tesoro was suggested in Prohaska 1988, 646.

3 García Cueto 2006, 208 and 240, note 448; G. Finaldi in Spinosa 2011, 180.

4 Orbaan 1920, 1:206: 'Quest'ambasciatore Cattolico manda a Napoli due pittori per fare alcune pitture di musaico et altro nella chiesa, che si fabrica colà sotto l'invocatione di San Genaro'.

5 Pupillo 1998, 303–4. On Borgianni's relationship with Spain, see in particular Gallo 1997.

6 Strazzullo 1978, 49–50 and 104.

7 Ibid., 108.

8 Bellori–Borea 1976, 512–13: 'Aveva Guido nella cappella di Santa Maria Maggiore in vece della Madonna dipinto un angelo che porge la pianeta a San Ildefonso per celebrare la messa; il papa ordinò che si mutasse, onde per la partenza di Guido che di sua volontà s'era allontanato, fu chiamato il Lanfranco ad eseguire l'intentione del papa conforme la verità del miracolo; siché il medesimo Lanfranco tolto l'angelo vi rifece la Vergine, come si vede con dispiacere di Guido, che del troppo ardire dell'altro si dolse giustamente'. For the English translation, see Bellori–Wohl 2005, 359.

9 The payment specified the following information: 'per havere accomodato alcune pitture nella cappella di Sua Santità in Santa Maria Maggiore' ('for fixing some paintings in the chapels of His Holiness in Santa Maria Maggiore'); cf. Orbaan 1920, 1:331; Ostrow 1996a, 224; Marías 2014, 64.

10 Marías 2014, 64, fig. 5.

11 The iconographic programme reads: 'En el otro [arco de descarga] S. Ildephonso Arzobispo de Toledo. *S. Ildephonsum qui haereticos pro gloria Virg. Confutarat, sacra veste ornat*. Surio en las vidas de los santos antes mencionados'; see Ostrow 1996a, 282.

12 Nicolau Castro 2007; Marías 2014, 64–68.

13 Stratton 1994, 84–86.

14 Ibid., 84.

15 Ostrow 1996b. On Reni and the popularity of the theme of the Immaculate Conception during the papacy of Paul V, see also Mann 1993.

16 Prominent among Reni's first Spanish collectors was Juan de Lezcano, who may have purchased directly from the painter in Rome, in 1610, two

17 of the three paintings by Guido that were in his possession in 1631; see Vannugli 2009, 352–55.

17 García Sanz 1992, 59.

18 Ibid., 59; Colomer 2006, 214–16.

19 Burke and Cherry 1997, 1:287, nos. 13 and 14: the paintings were valued at quite a significant sum compared to the rest in the collection.

20 The Cleveland Museum of Art, Leonard C. Hanna, Jr. Fund 1976.2.

21 Denunzio 2004, 76–79.

22 They were a *Virgin sewing in the Temple* (lost) and a *Virgin and Child with the Infant Saint John* (Paris, Musée du Louvre, inv. 524). Wood 1992, 519, note 109; Malvasia–Pericolo 2019, 1:40 and 251, note 105.

23 Malvasia–Pericolo 2019, 1:58–59 and 271–72, note 153: 'Pensiero di fuggirsene in Ispagna o in Francia, già che nell'una e nell'altra corte era onorevolmente stato invitato da quelle Maestà'.

24 Sparti 1998a, 78: 'Una testa del S.ʳ Guido lo fa pazziare, essendo disse conforme al suo genio, e che per essere cosa eccellente può stare a capo letto del Re di Spagna'.

25 This identification of the *tavolina* as the *Immaculate Conception* has been questioned by other scholars; see, for example, Malvasia–Pericolo 2019, 1:87.

26 On the relationship between Malvasia and Bernardino Spada, see Colantuono 1997, 25–38.

27 Pierguidi 2019b, 82–83, note 9. The destination of the *Immaculate Conception* has been disputed by other scholars; see, for example, Rafael Japón's entry for this painting in this catalogue [cat. 55].

28 Malvasia–Pericolo 2019, 1:86–88.

29 Pierguidi 2019a.

30 Colantuono 1997, 52–110; Pierguidi 2012b, 18–19.

31 See note 8.

32 Palos 2016, 101–7.

33 Colantuono 1997, 19–20; Pierguidi 2012b, 63–64.

34 Stratton 1994, 88–92.

35 Schleier 1983, 137–39, no. XXVI.

36 Bologna, Pinacoteca Nazionale di Bologna, inv. 581. Morello, Francia and Fusco 2005, 220, no. 60.

37 Polvillo 2009–10, 60–64.

38 Pacheco–Bassegoda 1990, 575–77; Moretti 2005, 85–86.

39 See *infra*.

40 This connection between the letter of 1627 and the *Abduction of Helen* has been questioned on various occasions; see Malvasia–Pericolo 2019, 1:295, note 218.

41 Pierguidi 2012b, 44–56; Malvasia–Pericolo 2019, 1:296, note 218.

42 The bibliography on the *Abduction of Helen* is almost endless; in addition to the references quoted in the following notes, see in particular Colomer 1990 and Loire 1996, 324–28.

43 Pierguidi 2016a, 22–23; Pierguidi 2020, 121–23.

44 Pierguidi 2016a.

45 Concerning this aspect of the Alcalá series of *Apostles*, see Pierguidi 2020, 114–15.

46 Forgione and Saracino 2019, 5; Japón 2019, 360–61: '13 cuadros de los Apóstoles y el nuestro Salvador … que cada uno es de diferente pintor de los más insignes que se hallaron en Italia aquel año, a quien con este intento los hize pintar'.

47 For a reconstruction of the whole cycle, see the articles quoted in note 45 above.

48 Papi 2021.

49 Brown and Kagan 1987, 239 and 248, no. 18. There was also a *Cleopatra* by Reni, now lost, in the Duke of Alcalá's collection.

50 For a reconstruction of the layout of the paintings in the Salón Nuevo according to the inventory of 1636, see Orso 1986, 74–87; Pierguidi 2012b, 44–46; Barbeito 2015, 32–34; Martínez Leiva and Rodríguez Rebollo 2015, 68–70.

51 Bayerische Staatsgemäldesammlunge, Staatsgalerie im Neuen Schloss Schleißheim, inv. 1302.

52 Pierguidi 2012b, 49–53.

53 Martínez Leiva and Rodríguez Rebollo 2007.

54 On the iconographic programmes devised by the Spanish Crown during the same period, see Lapuerta Montoya 2002, 281–82, 320–21, and 621–27.

55 On Crescenzi see above all Brown and Elliott 1980, 44–45; Harris 1980; Spezzaferro 1985; Bernstorff 2013; Bernstorff 2017.

56 Baglione 1642, 365.

57 Bernstorff 2017, 7–8.

58 Ibid., 22

59 Finaldi 2009, 51.

60 Martín González 1958, 61; Orso 1986, 113. In 2009 it was proposed attributing to Reni a drawing whose subject has been identified as 'Don John and the battle of Lepanto', and the hypothesis was put forward of its possible connection with a picture that may have been intended for the New Hall; see Sutherland Harris 2009. The attribution of the drawing has not been subsequently discussed by critics and does not seem to be unquestionable (Daniele Benati expressed a negative opinion). Nor is the subject securely identified. Indeed, the New Hall already featured a canvas by Titian (*Philip II offering the Infante Fernando to Victory*, now in the Prado, P-431) that commemorated the historic naval battle won against the Turks: it therefore seems odd that a second one should have been envisaged, among other reasons because only figures of sovereigns appear in those pictures, Philip IV and his main predecessors. The format, subject and layout of the design (with the protagonist in the foreground and a battle scene in the background) are in fact much closer to the history paintings intended for the Hall of Realms in the Buen Retiro palace, a grand cycle executed exclusively by Spanish painters between 1634 and 1635 (quoted in Sutherland Harris 2009, 159); for example, there is a striking similarity to the *Defence of Cádiz against the English* (Madrid, Museo Nacional del Prado, P-656) painted by Francisco de Zurbarán (1598–1664). Only Spanish painters worked on that cycle, beginning with Velázquez, and we therefore cannot rule out the possibility of attributing the design to a Tuscan-trained artist like Carducho.

61 Pierguidi 2012b, 53.

62 Madrid, Museo Nacional del Prado, P-1661.

63 In relation to the picture by Rubens and Van Dyck, see also Mann 2017, 170–76.

64 Pierguidi 2012b, 111; Pierguidi 2016b, 9–11.

65 Bassegoda i Hugas 2002, 228–29, no. PQ-67-9, and 233–34, no. PQ-81-10; Redín Michaus 2013, 681.

66 Madrid, Museo Nacional del Prado, P-201.

67 Patrimonio Nacional. Colecciones Reales. Real Monasterio de San Lorenzo de El Escorial, inv. 10014629.

68 Madrid, Museo Nacional del Prado, P-1171.

69 In the past it has been hypothesised that Velázquez may have negatively judged Guido's *Abduction of Helen* (he may have viewed it in Bologna, see Salort Pons 2012, 619), and that echoes of his criticisms reached Monterrey (Mancini 2004, 214; Rivas Albaladejo 2014b, 319–20 and 336, doc. 6), but in fact the count was probably forced to find an excuse to account for the failure of the negotiations with Guido; see Pierguidi 2019b, 84, note 15. On the close relationship between these masterpieces by Velázquez and the contemporaneous works of Guercino and Reni, see, at least, Salort Pons 2002 and Prasad 2003.

70 Pierguidi 2012b, 24 and 52–53.

71 Naples, Museo e Real Bosco di Capodimonte, Q 378.

72 McTighe 2008; Malvasia–Pericolo 2019, 1:253–54, notes 109 and 110, and 256, notes 114 and 115; Pierguidi 2022a.

73 Fumagalli 1990, 69.

74 Madrid, Museo Nacional del Prado, P-147.

75 Pierguidi 2012b, 67–69.

76 Dirani 1982, 85–87.

77 Colantuono 1997, 36–38; Pierguidi 2012b, 119–20 and 121–41 (for the Galleria La Vrillière collection); Malvasia–Pericolo 2019, 1:296, note 218.

78 Malvasia–Pericolo 2019, 1:170–71 and 398, note 534; Ciammitti 2000, 198: 'Se dovesse ella aderire ad una di queste, qual saria ella? Quella, replicò, che fosse per esser la più utile o almeno la men nociva alla nostra Italia'.

79 Malvasia–Pericolo 2019, 1:130–31: 'La favola di Latona pe'l Re di Spagna che, risaputo il successo del Ratto di Elena, dolutosene co' gli ambasciadori, avea fatto ordinargli questo'.

80 Colantuono 2008, 215–16, note 33: 'fabula Con una muger dos Niños y un hombre Conbertido En rrana'. The scholar proposed identifying Guido's painting with a canvas in a private collection, but his proposal has not been supported; see Malvasia–Pericolo 2019, 1:356–57, note 387.

81 The *terminus ante quem* for dating De Ferrari's painting comes from the description in the *Ragguagli d'Amore del Regno di Cipro* by Luca Assarino (Bologna, 1642); see Boccardo 2016, 35–37. In 1639 Assarino (*Sensi d'humiltà e di stupore*) had published an account of a visit to Reni's studio in Bologna, where, among the many unfinished canvases, he described a few (such as *Bacchus and Ariadne*, cf. note 83 and Malvasia–Pericolo 2019, 1:342, note 344), but without mentioning a *Latona* or a *Samson* (see *infra*).

82 Boccardo 2016, 35–37.

83 On the complex vicissitudes of the *Bacchus and Ariadne*, which ended up being destroyed (there is a surviving fragment of Ariadne on long-term loan to the Pinacoteca Nazionale di Bologna), but it is well known through many copies, drawings, and prints; see Malvasia–Pericolo 2019, 1:341–42, note 343.

84 Madruga Real 1983, 155–57 and 226; Finaldi 2007, 756; Pierguidi 2016a, 23–27.

85 On the types of commissions for the Buen Retiro, in which the wives of Monterrey and Olivares played a leading role, see Simal López 2011, 253–54.

86 Madrid, Museo Nacional del Prado, P-472.

87 Pierguidi 2010, 88–89.

88 On Monterrey's collecting, see also the more recent Rotatori 2020.

89 Colomer 1996, 203 and 212, note 6; García Cueto 2006, 262, 267, and 365, doc. 110: 'entregar una medida del tamaño que ha da tener una pintura que ha de hazer el Sr. Guido en Bolonia, la qual ha de ser del sugeto que V.S. le debe avisar. Esta medida se remite con el correo desta al Duque de Medina de las Torres'.

90 Dirani 1982, 91–92; Pierguidi 2012b, 89–90.

91 Belori–Borea 2009, 527; Pierguidi 2012b, 43–44: 'Ordinò che Guido li dipingesse un altro quadro più grande con la favola di Sansone, la quale per essersi troppo tardata, restò nella sua morte imperfetta'. For the English translation, see Bellori–Wohl 2005, 366.

92 Two sculptures are also highly relevant to the fortunes of this theme in Spain, *Samson slaying a Philistine* (London, Victoria and Albert Museum, A.7-1954) and *Samson and the Lion* (Art Institute of Chicago, 1997.335), by Giambologna and Cristoforo Stati, respectively, both of which formerly adorned the fountains at the residences of the 1st Duke of Lerma (1533–1625); see Loffredo 2012.

93 Around 1627, the governor of Milan, Gonzalo Fernández de Córdoba, had received instructions from Madrid to commission two canvases, a *Cain and Abel* and a *Samson and the Philistines*, from the best painter in Milan: Giulio Cesare Procaccini was dead by then and Camillo was considered the main local artist. The second of the two canvases (147 × 141 cm), part of the cycle for the New Hall, in whose inventory of 1636 they are mentioned, was recently identified; see D'Albo 2017, 72–74.

Stefano Pierguidi

Hanging in the same hall were Ribera's *Samson and Delilah* and Rubens's *Samson slaying the Lion*; see Orso 1986, 109; Vergara 1999, 45–46; and Pierguidi 2012b, 44.

94 Madrid, Museo Nacional del Prado, P-3794.

95 This was one of the most important works by the leader of the Milanese school, originally executed for Cosimo II de' Medici, subsequently sold to Lorenzo de' Medici, and finally given by him to Monterrey, cf. D'Albo 2018, 80. That same year, 1622, Monterrey was elected as president of the Council of Italy, cf. Rivas Albaladejo 2014a, 87. On 22 June 1622, while staying in Florence, the count attended the performance of Jacopo Cicognini's *Il martirio*.

96 Surprisingly, the picture is not documented in the Spanish royal collections until 1794, when it was located in the Buen Retiro; see Brigstocke and D'Albo 2020, 373, no. 137.

97 'Sansón cuando le sacaron los ojos'. Martínez Leiva and Rodríguez Rebollo 2015, 436, no. 545; D'Albo 2017, 75, note 39; Brigstocke and D'Albo 2020, 447.

98 'Sansón cuando mató a los filisteos'. The work first appears in the inventory of 1701, together with other canvases by the Neapolitan artist that belonged to two very specific cycles commissioned for the Buen Retiro, that of the *Costumes of the Ancient Romans* and that of the *Histories of Saint John the Baptist*; see Úbeda de los Cobos 2005, 204, no. 40.

99 Among the paintings then commissioned from Finoglio was also a *Masinissa mourning over the Death of Sophonisba* (Museo del Prado, P-2280), whose subject (isolated from all the other canvases intended for the Buen Retiro) can be read in relation to that of Guercino's masterpiece, the *Death of Dido* (Rome, Galleria Spada), whose story is connected with that of Reni's *Abduction of Helen*; see Colantuono 1997, 30–31; Pierguidi 2010, 80–81.

100 Colomer 1996, 201–3.

101 On Malvezzi, see in particular García Cueto 2006, 253–82 (especially 259).

102 See note 83.

'A MAN WHO PERPETUALLY CONSULTS NATURE': GUIDO RENI AND DRAWING

Viviana Farina

It is illusory to think that the true conceptual and technical scope of Guido Reni (1575–1642) can be understood without in-depth reflection. Like all truly great artists, Reni stands out in particular for his embodiment of the virtue that Giorgio Vasari summed up with the term *sprezzatura*. The modern word that best expresses that sixteenth-century concept is 'nonchalance', the ability to conceal the huge effort underlying the perfection of a result that is simple only in appearance. This opinion was expressed early on by the seventeenth-century critic Francesco Scannelli, who describes Guido as a master of great 'ease' and 'grace', qualities capable of camouflaging his 'studied effort' – tireless work – and very keen application.[1] Scannelli implied that the artist achieved these results through the persevering practice of drawing. Indeed, drawing was the basic principle of the artistic training provided by the Bolognese school of the Carracci, where a twenty-year-old Guido arrived around 1595 after spending his early years as a painter in the Bolognese workshop of Denys Calvert (c. 1540–1619), a master originally from Antwerp.

On entering the most impressive room of the recent Reni exhibition at the Galleria Borghese in Rome,[2] visitors were astonished by the silent dialogue between Guido's 1611 canvas, the *Massacre of the Innocents* [cat. 20], and the marble group of *Apollo and Daphne* (1622–25) sculpted by Gian Lorenzo Bernini (1598–1680).[3] Stepping inside the gallery and coming face-to-face with this block of marble, they were immediately drawn into the 3D optical effect created by the interaction of the arms raised in movement and the sequence shot of the sculpted nymph and the mother at the left edge of the painting with their mouths open wide in amazement. This effect, the product of an exhibition layout that was both congruous and intelligent, was more than mere suggestion. It stemmed from the fact that the two works, created only a few years apart and completely independently from each other, with thoroughly different stylistic results, were equally capable of illustrating to Early Modern beholders a representation that engaged the emotions, a key principle of seventeenth-century aesthetics. Reni mitigates the feeling of death by carefully gauging the forms of the canon of Praxiteles, while Bernini heightens the turmoil with his voluptuous handling of the marble. There is a huge distance between the methods used by the artists to achieve their objectives – but not between the objectives themselves. Indeed, emotion is the aspect of the painting that was praised in 1619 by the prince of the Baroque poets, Giambattista Marino, in his adaptation of a madrigal initially penned for another work: 'horror often goes with pleasure'[4] – fear can also be a source of enjoyment, and this also applies ideally to Daphne's unyielding despair. The true extent of Guido's modernity, however, becomes apparent when the picture is viewed from a few centimetres away and we note his enormously skilled handling of the paintbrush, with its flowing movement capable of reinterpreting the classical universe, restoring the truth of the flesh and blood imitated on the canvas. This is Reni's intense and subtle way of following 'the natural course' of painting during the years of Caravaggio (1571–1610) and Peter Paul Rubens (1577–1640), and not only a tribute – in the mother standing on the right – to the screaming boy in Merisi's *Martyrdom of Saint Matthew* in the Contarelli chapel at San Luigi dei Francesi in Rome.

Reni's works on paper speak of this personal interpretation, sometimes attesting to a pursuit of 'realism' that leaves behind the angelical forms that earned him extraordinary fame during his lifetime. This aspect may not have escaped the attention of the first true admirer of Guido's graphic work, Pierre-Jean Mariette, who refers to Guido in the *Description* of the Crozat collection (1741) as a 'man who perpetually consults Nature'.[5]

The *Massacre of the Innocents* is a perfect, flawless work. The artist painted it for the Bolognese Counts Berò, possibly in Rome given his paraphrase of the teachings of antiquity and of Raphael (1483–1520) – Roberto Longhi spoke of bodies of 'marble reminiscences'[6] – and the precise reference, in the heavenward-gazing mother kneeling in the foreground, to the *Head of Niobe* that was discovered in the Eternal City, where it remains on view. Where, then, are the dozens of preparatory studies that would necessarily have been involved in creating such a divine work? Especially because the only drawing that Otto Kurz first considered to be related to the painting – the *Kneeling Woman* identified as no. 1429 E in the Uffizi – seems to belong more to an adoration scene.[7]

This digression on the *Massacre of the Innocents* is, in fact, a necessary introduction to Reni's career as a draughtsman, evidence of which is fairly incomplete considering that he is known to have constantly practised graphic art. In the *Felsina pittrice* (1678), his biographer Carlo Cesare Malvasia puts his professional mastery down to 'strenuous labour' and 'unceasing study', and notes that he specifically made studies of heads of ancient statues 'continuously for eight years' and 'from every angle'.[8] At the end of his career, 'dreading the debilities of old age', Guido worked tirelessly every evening, gathering his students in his 'rooms' to sketch nudes from life or bas-reliefs, and spending as many as four hours on end drawing 'heads from various viewpoints, of every gender and age, as well as hands, feet, ideas for narrative compositions'.[9]

Only a small portion of the thousands of sheets Reni must have produced throughout his career have survived. While the Florentine Filippo Baldinucci remarked on the sizeable presence of drawings in the possession of the painter's heirs,[10] the inventory of Guido's studio, drawn up on 11 October 1642, not long after his death, lists less than 2,000,[11] perhaps too small a number to document his long and prolific activity. Today his known corpus of drawings amounts to some 300 examples.

In view of the foregoing, it seems too bold to hypothesise that Guido progressively relied less on drawing from the early 1620s onwards. Nor, perhaps, is it useful to state that he departed from the Carracci academy's practice of creating pictures only after careful preparation based on a live model.[12] There are too many unknown factors to be able to draw such drastic conclusions.

Besides, Reni soon distinguished himself for his less systematic approach to painting. The real problem continues to be that his activity as a draughtsman at the height of his mature period is sparsely documented. The shift – towards greater modernity – in his painting technique over the years would in itself explain a lesser need for preparatory studies. However, this does not mean to say that he stopped drawing, merely that he changed his approach. The Guido described by Malvasia, the man who was 'initiated on the path' (*incamminato*), could never have deprived paper of its role as a field for experimentation. It is evident that those initial ideas did not always deserve to be developed and passed on for posterity or became dispersed in other ways.

There is an abundance of literature on this subject. After Otto Kurz's pioneering studies and catalogue of the Windsor Castle drawings,[13] and Catherine Johnston's various contributions later merged in her unpublished doctoral thesis defended at the Courtauld Institute,[14] the reference work that most resembles a monograph continues to be the catalogue compiled by Veronika Birke in 1981,[15] partly updated by her own effort to the major exhibition of 1988.[16] The studies conducted by Babette Bohn on the Uffizi collection[17] and by Catherine Loisel at the Louvre complete the picture of where research currently stands.[18]

The terminology in Italian employed here and in the catalogue entries for drawing media other than pen and ink and/or wash deserves a preliminary note. Bohn chose to describe the sketches in the Uffizi as being executed in red or black *pietra naturale* (natural stone), or a combination of both colours. This definition matches more closely the French *pierre* and the English 'chalk'. Here we prefer to use the terms found in seventeenth-century sources. Filippo Baldinucci speaks of *matita* (pencil) in his *Vocabolario toscano dell'arte del disegno* (1681). He defines the red variety, *matita rossa*, as 'a sort of soft stone' found in 'pieces' that need to be cut and shaped into points, the best kind being German, as Vasari stated. This author likewise describes the black variety, *matita nera*, as a natural stone available in chips that need to be sharpened, excellent if it is French – once again according to Vasari – and better still if it is Spanish.[19]

Earlier on, referring precisely to Reni, Scannelli had explained that he 'drew first with a *pietra amatite* and then with a pen'.[20] The alphabetical entry for *amatita* in Baldinucci's glossary describes it as a 'soft stone like gypsum, which is used for drawing; and there is black and red',[21] subsequently referring to the definition of *lapis amatita* and *matita*, also known as *cinabro minerale* (mineral cinnabar), 'a very hard natural stone' that is red in colour and, if ground, produces a red ink similar to lake that is also very useful for 'colouring fresco'.[22] It may be deduced from this that Baldinucci regarded both definitions as synonymous. And that in Florence, the cradle par excellence of drawing in Italy, *lapis* was an equivalent term to *matita* may also be inferred from the descriptions of Reni's designs put forward between 1671 and 1675 as possible purchases for Cardinal Leopoldo de' Medici's collection.[23] Comparing the biography written by Malvasia, we furthermore find that Reni used red lapis (*lapis rosso*), red and black chalk (*carbone nero e rosso*), white chalk (*gesso*), pen and wash, and pastel (*pastello*). All these media are documented in this exhibition, except for the last one.

It is hard to define Reni's manner not only of painting but also of drawing during the period he collaborated with Calvaert, and it is equally difficult to trace the steps of the *incamminato* artist during the last years before he moved to Rome. Now that the date of the *Coronation of the Virgin with four Saints* for the church of San Bernardo in Bologna [fig. 16] has been moved from 1595 to approximately 1598,[24] we need to establish which drawings could precede its respective preparatory study in the British Museum.[25] Using black chalk, grey-brown wash and white heightening on blue-grey paper, Guido presented a composition that was consonant with the Carracci's practices in terms of support but departed from them in the flowing lines and the majestic Raphaelesque grace, which surpasses that of the related painting. Indeed, Reni's marked fondness for Raphael's Bolognese *Ecstasy of Saint Cecilia*,[26] even before he executed the copy now in Dublin,[27] is accepted by critics as a fact. It is worth noting that further traces of Raphaelesque inventiveness, subsequent and unpublished, are found in the red chalk *Study of a Foot* in the Uffizi.[28]

The drawing in the British Museum is linked to a second *Coronation of the Virgin* on the recto side of a double-faced sheet in Edinburgh [cat. 10]. The open contours and light wash point to a close affinity with Ludovico Carracci (1555–1619) and show the changeability of Guido's language within a short space of time. The same can be said of other drawings executed on blue paper like the London one, which presumably share the same date of 1598–99. One example is the delicate *Holy Family with Saint Francis* in the Louvre [fig. 37], which, significantly, was formerly attributed to Parmigianino (1503–1540).[29] Another is the *Vision of Saint Hyacinth* in the Nationalmuseum of Stockholm [fig. 17],[30] whose verso displays the important contract Reni entered into with the Dominican nuns of San Mattia to paint a picture, now lost but documented through a print by Claude Vignon (1593–1670).[31] Both, in different ways, are subsequent tributes to the world of Ludovico.

The only sound basis that provides a useful guide for establishing the timeline of Reni's stunning graphic overture is what

Fig. 37 Guido Reni, *The Holy Family with Saint Francis*, 1598–99. Black chalk, brown wash, and lead white on blue paper, 278 × 228 mm. Paris, Musée du Louvre, Département des Arts graphiques, inv. 12101

remains of the ephemeral *apparati* devised by him to celebrate the passage through Bologna of Pope Clement VIII Aldobrandini on 27 November 1598. The print showing the façade of the Palazzo del Senato,[32] adorned with figurines with an unmistakeably Mannerist appearance, displays the same extreme refinement as the *Coat of Arms of Cardinal Sforza*,[33] a study for an etching that furthermore shows traces of indentation for transfer.[34] Around this time Guido was particularly fascinated by Parmigianino's extenuated elegance. This is attested not only by some of his prints,[35] or the paraphrasing embodied by the *Vision of Saint Eustace*, a canvas that hung in San Michele in Bosco [fig. 18],[36] but also by other even more Mannerist drawings such as the *Annunciation* in the English royal collection, all on blue paper.[37]

Reni likewise executed one of the cornerstones of his entire graphic corpus on a sheet of cerulean blue paper: the *Assumption of the Virgin* in the Medici collections, faded on the recto side – as it is part of the historical core of drawings that

Fig. 38 Guido Reni, *The Crucifixion of Saint Peter*, 1604. Pen, brown ink, brown wash, and traces of red chalk on paper, 230 × 137 mm. Budapest, Szépmüvészeti Múzeum, inv. 2366

during the resurgence of the cult of the Christian protomartyrs that was so important in Cardinal Cesare Baronio's Rome.[41]

Before arriving in the papal city, Guido, as is only logical, had also studied the graphic work of the other Carracci who stayed on at the Bologna academy following the departure of Annibale (1560–1609) in 1595: Agostino (1557–1602). Reni successfully assimilated his hatching to the extent that it is difficult to distinguish drawings sometimes mistakenly attributed to Agostino – such as the beautiful *Saint Sebastian in a Landscape with Angels* in the Uffizi[42] – from others that should be ascribed to Guido's youth, though not all of them can be associated with known compositions.[43] At the height of his fame in Rome, where he had arrived in 1601, the artist proved he still had very much in mind Agostino's teachings of a flowing calligraphy, producing finished drawings – even though they were always rough sketches – for key pictorial compositions. This is apparent in the study for the decoration of the apse of the oratory of Santa Silvia in San Gregorio al Celio depicting *God the Father and Playing Angels*[44] – a prestigious commission from Cardinal Scipione Borghese around 1609. It can likewise be seen in the two drawings, on a single sheet, of the *God the Father borne by Angels* executed between 1609 and 1611 for the dome of the chapel of the Annunciata in the Palazzo del Quirinale, Pope Paul V Borghese's private residence, whose mastermind was Reni.[45]

At the same time, the artist insightfully reinterpreted Ludovico Carracci's drawing stratagems. It is almost surprising to discover that in his most evident rivalry with Caravaggio – for the *Crucifixion of Saint Peter* in the Pinacoteca Vaticana [fig. 10], commissioned in 1604 by the Cardinal Nephew Pietro Aldobrandini for San Paolo alle Tre Fontane – Guido designed the work in a drawing style characteristic of Ludovico. Indeed, his take on Caravaggio's *Crucifixion* in Santa Maria del Popolo is a far cry from its model in terms of painting technique on account of the pale ground layer that achieves a very luminous result. However, it is the Budapest drawing [fig. 38][46] that documents the real ontological gap separating Reni from Merisi, as it shows a very carefully calculated preliminary study of the work that would never have been characteristic of the Lombard. It was recently defined as one of the closest drawings to Ludovico executed after 1600 on account of the dense hatching, the geometrical definition of the bodies, and the wash chiaroscuros that greatly recall Ludovico's studies for the cycle of San Michele in Bosco in Bologna, in which Guido was also involved in 1604, leaving Rome for a brief period.[47]

The vigorous chiaroscuro in the manner of Ludovico, achieved by diluting brown ink, is characteristic of other drawings by Guido. A few examples are the Haarlem *Birth of the*

were 'exhibited'[38] – but not on the verso, which displays an *Annunciation* of a type different from the British work.[39] The swirling effect of the line – in two different shades of black, achieved by going over and emphasising the gesture – merely sketches the position of the apostles; the figures executed subsequently in the related painting of 1599–1600 in Santa Maria Maggiore in Pieve di Cento have a very severe appearance.[40] The greatest differences are found in the upper part of the paper, where the figure of Mary stands out, svelte and sinuous like a *Nike*, stylistically comparable to the angel in the contemporary tondo of the *Coronation of Saints Cecilia and Valerian* in Santa Cecilia in Trastevere painted for Cardinal Paolo Emilio Sfondrato

Viviana Farina

Virgin,[48] the Windsor Castle *Battle of Samson and the Philistines*[49] – the initial idea for the fresco in the Sala delle Nozze Aldobrandini in the Vatican, another commission for Paul V from 1608–9 – the studies for the Cappella Paolina in Santa Maria Maggiore, and those of 1613 for the famous *Pietà dei Mendicanti* [fig. 25].[50]

Meanwhile, the drawings for the paintings to decorate the pope's funerary chapel, paid for between 1610 and 1612, spur us to reflect on the gap that exists between Reni's initial ideas and the final solutions he adopted. This not only involved reducing from five to three the number of figures on the wall panels to adapt to the limited space available;[51] in addition, the drawn and painted forms are underpinned by different aesthetic ideals. The elongated bodies of the *Five Crowned Saints* [fig. 39] and the *Five Greek Bishop Saints*[52] do not in fact match the types found in the frescoes, which are extensively modelled and based more closely on Raphaelesque parameters than what is seen in the studies on paper. They attest to a pursuit of longitudinality – devoid of any twisted spiralling that might denote a reference to his beloved Parmigianino – that is particularly evident in *Narses Victorious over Totila*,[53] the study for the lunette on the left-hand wall of the Cappella Paolina. We should thus ask what inspired Reni when he designed his work for a basilica that was also an object of interest in the context of the resurgence of early Christian worship. If we focus on the Uffizi *Five Crowned Saints* from this different perspective, we might even admit that the brown wash sculpts the draperies, paraphrasing the angular folds of the *Coronation of the Virgin*, the mosaic by Jacopo Torriti (act. c. 1270–1300) of around 1295 that is a prominent feature of the ceiling of the apse of Santa Maria Maggiore. The iconic elegance of the female saints furthermore seems to be adapted to the late classicism of the oldest mosaics of the magnificent fifth-century triumphal arch that may have caught Guido's attention when he sought pure inspiration for his repertoire. Take, for example, the three svelte Magi in oriental garb who appear before Herod in the second tier of the decoration on the right of the arch. Reni's curiosity must have been merely experimental and speculative, but it nevertheless gives the impression of still being partly alive in the drawing related to the *Pieta dei Mendicanti* in Genoa's Palazzo Rosso.[54]

Conversely, we find the flowing pen strokes learned from Agostino Carracci in the two drawings where Reni – in varying degrees of completeness – sketched the design for the fresco of *Aurora* for the ceiling of the central hall of the building that later became known as the Casino dell'Aurora but was then in the garden owned by Cardinal Scipione Borghese, on the Quirinal hill. Completed in 1614 and marking the ascent of a further rung

on his successful career ladder in the capital, the design is a genuine expression of the classical legacy of Raphael in Annibale Carracci's gallery in the Palazzo Farnese. There had never been a particularly good rapport between the two artists, and with this very impressive accomplishment Reni had now snatched from Annibale the title of 'new Raphael'. The same impression is conveyed by the charming procession of small figures, particularly in the Louvre drawing [fig. 40],[55] which shows the paratactic frieze from a better focus and a close viewpoint, but without the essential right-hand portion containing the rosy goddess of the morning that is, however, included in the Albertina drawing.[56] In the first drawing the supple bodies do not allow us to imagine the full turn of the chariot, only the rhythm and movement of the fresco. Guido drew them in red chalk, which he then went over in ink applied with a fine pen that can be seen to flow over

Fig. 39 Guido Reni, *Five Crowned Saints* (for a panel in the Cappella Paolina), 1610–11. Pen, brown ink, brown wash, and traces of red chalk on paper, 173 × 105 mm. Florence, Gallerie degli Uffizi, Gabinetto dei Disegni e delle Stampe, inv. 12461 F

Fig. 40 Guido Reni, *Study for the Chariot of Apollo guided by Aurora*, 1612–14. Pen and brown ink over red chalk on paper, 185 × 265 mm. Paris, Musée du Louvre, Département des Arts graphiques, inv. RF 5344

the sheet in a continuous gesture executed with amazing ease, recalling the grace of the ancients and, precisely, following in the wake of Raphael's graphic legacy.

A further testament to the artist's long, complex relations with the Borghese family is a drawing of Pope Paul V, to which scholars have barely paid attention, acquired with an attribution to Reni by the National Museum in Stockholm [fig. 41].[57] This portrait of the pope's head – a surviving *tessera* from the painter's documented activity as a portraitist, which is little known especially in the field of drawing[58] – was executed in rapid strokes of black chalk but owing, among other things, to the skilful touches of white heightening, it treats us to a moment of good-natured confidence granted by His Holiness. Once again, the artist chose blue paper – this time also in consonance with the Roman portrait tradition of the early 1600s[59] – and achieved a likeness that rivals in introspection with the face of Cardinal Antonio Maria Gallo painted at some point around 1604 at the foot of the altarpiece of the church of the Santissima Trinità in Osimo.[60]

Portraiture is the genre that offered the best proof of the mimetic competition established with nature. But Reni, as is well known, earned extraordinary fame above all for his drawings of heads of all kinds and ages. We find more idealised faces celebrated for their heavenward-gazing eyes[61] and others with a striking expressive effect, all executed in red or black chalk or a combination of both colours. In some the artist employs white chalk heightening or, more often, he simply makes use of the background of the white paper. The exhibition features a few drawings of heads related to known paintings and some without secure links, all of them attributable to the height of the master's mature period. Of the examples dating from the first decade of the century, it is worth recalling at least the memorable study in red chalk for the head of the servant woman holding a jug in the fresco painting of the *Birth of the Virgin* in the chapel of the Palazzo del Quirinale;[62] a preparatory drawing of the face of one of the three bishops[63] for the abovementioned mural painting in the Cappella Paolina;[64] the two different studies for the head of the saint depicted in the *Martyrdom of Saint Andrew* fresco in San Gregorio al Celio (1608);[65] and the two studies for the same gaunt face of an old woman proposed as possible initial ideas for what was subsequently a seated young woman with her face partially concealed by a hood in the bottom right area of the Roman fresco.[66]

The abovementioned five drawings, all in the Louvre – and mostly executed on blue paper – are an excellent example of Guido's experimental approach with respect to both technique and subject matter. In sheet no. 8923, where Saint Andrew is framed from the right, foreshortened to the torso, the artist not only used dry black chalk and white chalk, but also added a second, darker black pigment with a visual effect similar to pastel – possibly an oily charcoal,[67] which is more common in Reni's drawings than has been previously noted. The bearded head is one of the most interesting responses to the Venetian-style repertoire of Ludovico Carracci,[68] but can also be perfectly interpreted in parallel with Jusepe de Ribera's (1591–1652) repertoire of senile subjects.

The mention of this Spanish-born Neapolitan artist is no coincidence, as drawing no. 18460 in the Louvre, one of Reni's two studies for an old woman, bears a handwritten attribution to 'Lespagnoleta'. Indeed, during the first half of the seventeenth century in Italy Reni and Ribera were the two leading painters of old age, practising a naturalism that went beyond the parameters established by Caravaggio. The Spaniard took the baton from the Bolognese. Their paths had crossed in Rome between about 1606 and 1614, and they had to keep a watchful eye on each other for a long time as rivals in this topic and ideal field of which Reni's finest example is possibly the sculpture *Head of Old Man*, known as *Head of Seneca* [cat. 36].[69] The *Bishop* no. 8913 in the Louvre is a portentous example of a plump face that shows the ravages of time in the cheeks and neck. But no. 811 E in the Uffizi – the *Head of Saint Peter* for the *Assumption* in the church of Gesù e dei Santi Ambrogio e Andrea in Genoa, dated 1617[70] – is one of the works on paper that best fit Malvasia's technical description.[71] Reni has an astonishing ability to sculpt facial features using two chalks, media in which it is intrinsically more difficult to lend body and volume to figures than in paint. More impressive still are the skill of the hatching and the unique marks that bring to life the creases and ripples of the flesh,[72] the beard, and the hair, thanks also to the application of a deeper black in places. Such a reading is likewise possible for another of Reni's masterpieces, this one from a much later date: the *Head of Saint Andrea Corsini* related to the picture in Florence's Palazzo Corsini of 1629–30,[73] also in the Louvre.[74] With its prestigious pedigree as a work transferred from Pierre Crozat's collection to that of Mariette – as documented by the original passepartout that is still in place – the drawing is astounding for its exploration of such minute detail, which coincides in the 'photographic shot' of the left eye. There is no way of reproducing here these details of the complete images of both designs. But we do not hesitate to confirm that they are two miracles of a naturalist culture, so in keeping with Ribera's universe, which remind us all that it is always in drawing that we find the greatest examples of artists' freedom of expression. This even holds true for a staunch classicist like Guido.

The inscription 'Spagnioletto' is also found on another work that is worth bearing in mind: the Uffizi *Study for Dying Hercules*

Fig. 41 Guido Reni, *Portrait of Pope Paul V*, 1605–10. Black chalk heightened with white on blue-grey paper, 179 × 129 mm. Stockholm, Nationalmuseum, NMH 524/2016

[fig. 42],[75] the most complete surviving sketch related to a picture that was part of the cycle of four scenes of the hero painted between 1617 and 1621 for Ferdinando II Gonzaga, Duke of Mantua [fig. 27].[76] Once again turning to an oily medium to achieve a visual effect similar to pastel, Reni went over the contour line, succeeding in capturing the sinuousness of the human body, the rotundity of the muscles, and the creases of the skin. His careful study of the lights, alternating white chalk with blank spaces left in the paper, accentuates the naturalistic appearance. Acknowledging the drawing to be the work of Reni, Catherine Johnston accounted for its misattribution to Ribera by the pose characteristic of a martyrdom scene, typical of the Spaniard's repertoire.[77] The leaning posture of the figure is a reworking of an unidentified ancient model of a faun that Reni may have seen through early Bolognese drawings made before his day.[78] Any comparison – formally so convenient, even with respect to the robustness of the bust – with the famous *Barberini Faun*[79] is unfortunately only theoretic, as the statue had not yet been discovered in 1617.

It has been suggested that sheet no. 8920 in the Louvre [fig. 43], which belonged to Malvasia's collection and later to that of Crozat-Mariette, can also be linked to the Gonzaga cycle, specifically with the painting of *Dejanira abducted by the Centaur Nessus*[80] or, alternatively, the second version of the subject in Prague castle or the *Apollo and Marsyas* in Munich's Alte Pinakothek,[81] all of which date from 1620–22.[82] None is a complete match, however, as the drawing is a study of expression,

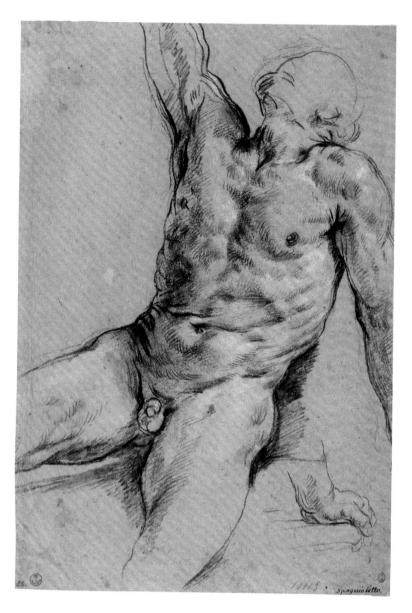

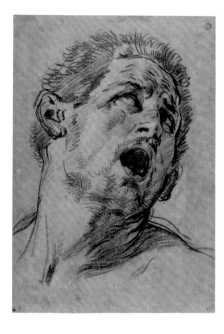

Fig. 42 Guido Reni, *Study for the Dying Hercules*, 1617. Black chalk, white chalk, oily black chalk, and traces of red chalk on faded blue paper (?), 390 × 267 mm. Florence, Gallerie degli Uffizi, Gabinetto dei Disegni e delle Stampe, inv. 10113 S

Fig. 43 Guido Reni, *Head of a Screaming Man*, 1620–22. Black chalk, red chalk, oily black chalk, and white chalk on faded blue paper, 375 × 263 mm. Paris, Musée du Louvre, Département des Arts graphiques, inv. 8920

made in a combination of three colours – red, grey/black, and white – over which, once again, the deep, velvety black of an oily chalk is predominant.[83] It is a supreme example of skill, which borrows motifs from antiquity – the flung-back head of the *Laocöon*[84] – and also captures the emotional moment in accordance with the lessons that Caravaggio more than any other artist had taught his century. While the previously mentioned drawings fill us with amazement, this one leaves us completely awestruck. Photography is incapable of capturing the emotional impact or properly reproducing the effect of the quivering flesh. Once again, the parallel belongs to the realm of the ideal. However, Reni's screaming man and the weeping Proserpina with a contrite expression struggling to escape Pluto's violent clutches in another marble group crafted by Bernini for Scipione Borghese in 1621–22[85] are the offspring of the same era.

1 Scannelli 1657, 85 and 349–50.

2 Cappelletti 2022a.

3 Rome, Galleria Borghese, inv. CV.

4 Farina 2002, 38, note 227; Malvasia–Pericolo 2019, 1:56: 'Spessol'orrorva col diletto'. For the English translation, ibid. 1:57.

5 Mariette 1741, 55: 'Un homme qui consulte perpétuellement la Nature'.

6 Longhi 1935, 132: 'Ricordo marmorato'.

7 Bohn 2008, 38–40, no. 27. However, according to Carel van Tuyll, it is the work of Sisto Badalocchio (1585–c. 1647): Sutherland Harris 1999, 28, note 11. This opinion is not considered by Bastian Eclercy in Eclercy 2022a, 198–200, no. 70.

8 Malvasia–Pericolo 2019, 1:68 and 1:70: 'Con incessante studio e con ostinata fatica … per otto anni continui … in ogni veduta'. For the English translation, ibid., 1:69 and 1:71.

9 Ibid., 1:180: 'teste in varie vedute, e d'ogni sesso, d'ogni età, mani, piedi, pensieri di storie'. For the English translation, ibid., 1:81.

10 Baldinucci–Ranalli and Barocchi 1974–75 (1974), 4:25.

11 John T. Spike and Tiziana Di Zio (1988, 56) pointed out more than 900. But the loose sheets numbered no less than 1855, as well as the six sketchbooks (Morselli 2007, 79 and 81).

Viviana Farina

12 See Bohn 2008, XV–XVI.

13 Kurz 1935–36; Kurz 1937; Kurz 1955.

14 Johnston 1974.

15 Birke 1981.

16 Birke 1988a.

17 Bohn 2008.

18 Loisel 2013, 97–130, nos. 58–136.

19 Baldinucci 1681b, in the alphabetical entries.

20 Scannelli 1657, 349: 'Disegnò prima colla pietra amatite e poi colla penna'.

21 Baldinucci 1681b, 9: 'Pietra tenera come gesso, con la quale si disegna; e ne è della nera e della rossa'.

22 Ibid., 79: 'colorire a fresco'.

23 M. Faietti in Bohn 2008, VII.

24 Benati 2022, 19.

25 London, The British Museum, inv. 1946,0713.237; Birke 1981, 24–25, no. 1.

26 Bologna, Pinacoteca Nazionale di Bologna, inv. 577.

27 Dublin, National Gallery of Ireland, NGI.70. See Benati 2022, 16; A. Brady in Eclercy 2022a, 132–34, no. 27.

28 Florence, Gallerie degli Uffizi, Gabinetto dei Disegni e delle Stampe, inv. 1573 F; Bohn 2008, 143, no. 9.

29 Loisel 2013, 98, no. 58. Despite the different dating, there are considerable similarities between the figure of the saint of Assisi and the small painting on copper depicting *Saint Francis comforted by a Musical Angel* of 1606–7 (Bologna, Pinacoteca Nazionale di Bologna, inv. 32531).

30 B. Eclercy in Eclercy 2022a, 122–23, no. 24.

31 Birke 1981, 43–45, in no. 17 (*The Vision of Saint Dominic*). Lorenzo Pericolo (Malvasia–Pericolo 2019, 1:227, note 49; 2:164, fig. 8), argues that the work is a *Vision of Saint Hyacinth*, refuting Stephen Pepper's opinion (1988, 214–15, no. A6). Daniele Benati (2022, 27, note 23) stresses that the print shows the angel holding the rosary, further emphasising the presence of Dominic de Guzmán; this opinion is shared by Loisel 2022, at the height of note 42.

32 Birke 1987, no. 7.

33 London, The British Museum, inv. 1862,0712.523.

34 Birke 1981, 38–39, nos. 11–12.

35 Cf. Faietti 2015.

36 Malvasia–Pericolo 2019, 1:225, note 44.

37 Royal Collection Trust, RCIN 902189; Birke 1981, 37, no. 10.

38 Florence, Gallerie degli Uffizi, Gabinetto dei Disegni e delle Stampe, inv. 1654 E.

39 Bohn 2008, 12–15, no. 8; B. Eclercy in Eclercy 2022a, 126–28, no. 25.

40 Pepper 1988, 216, no. 10.

41 Ibid., 218–19, no. 13.

42 Florence, Gallerie degli Uffizi, Gabinetto dei Disegni e delle Stampe, inv. 1427 E; Bohn 2008, 19, no. 12.

43 Sutherland Harris 1999.

44 Milan, Castello Sforzesco, inv. 5683.

45 Florence, Gallerie degli Uffizi, Gabinetto dei Disegni e delle Stampe, inv. 14941 F; Bohn 2008, 19–23, nos. 13–14.

46 Birke 1981, 51, no. 22; A. Rentzsch in Eclercy 2022a, 148–49, no. 37.

47 See Loisel 2022, at the height of note 72. The stylistic link with Ludovico is also stressed in Bohn 2008, 24–26, no. 16.

48 Haarlem, Teylers Museum, inv. B8; Birke 1981, 33–34, no. 8.

49 Royal Collection Trust, RCIN 903410; Birke 1981, 48–49, no. 20; S. Albl in Eclercy 2022a, 162–63, no. 45.

50 Bohn 2008, 34–37, nos. 23–25, the design of the Palazzo Rosso (Genoa), in particular. On the painting, see Pepper 1988, 236–37, no. 46.

51 For an *excursus* on the vicissitudes of the chapel decoration, see Malvasia–Pericolo 2019, 1:264–65, note 133.

52 Windsor Castle, Royal Collection Trust, RCIN 903409: see more recently A. Rentzsch in Eclercy 2022a, 168–71, no. 50.

53 Vienna, Albertina, inv. 2793: A. Rentzsch in Eclercy 2022a, 168–69, no. 49.

54 See note 50 above.

55 Birke 1981, 74, no. 43; Loisel 2013, 108–9, no. 78.

56 Vienna, Albertina, inv. 24550; Birke 1981, 73–74, no. 42. On the two drawings, see S. Albl in Eclercy 2022a, 172–73, nos. 52–53.

57 Martin Olin (2016, 107) proposes dating it to 1605–10; Catherine Loisel (2022, note 80) also accepts the attribution.

58 Summed up in Bohn 2008, 61–62, no. 46; Malvasia–Pericolo 2019, 1:374, note 436. For another portrait drawing of the pope in red and black chalk (private collection), see N. Turner in Costamagna, Härb and Prosperi Valenti Rodinò 2005, no. 90.

59 Martin Olin (2016, 109–10) compares it with Ottavio Leoni's portrait of the pope when he was still Cardinal Camillo Borghese (New York, The Morgan Library, inv. I, 24; Primarosa 2017, 285, no. 39).

60 The authorship was restored to the master by Daniele Benati. See L. Scanu in Cappelletti 2022a, 108–11, no. 4.

61 Malvasia–Pericolo 2019, 1: 178–79.

62 Chatsworth House (Derbyshire), inv. 485; Birke 1988a, no. B8; L. Wolk-Simon in Eclercy 2022a, 212–13, no. 81.

63 Paris, Musée du Louvre, Départment des Arts graphiques, inv. 8913.

64 Loisel 2013, 107, no. 74; Rosenberg et al. 2019, I, 1027, no. 1698.

65 Paris, Musée du Louvre, Départment des Arts graphiques, inv. 8911 and 8923; Loisel 2013, 104–5, nos. 70–71; Rosenberg et al. 2019, 1:1026–27, no. 1697.

66 Paris, Musée du Louvre, Départment des Arts graphiques, inv. 8919 and 18460 ; Loisel 2013, 106, nos. 72–73 ; Rosenberg et al. 2019, 1:1033, no. 1707; B. Eclercy in Eclercy 2022a, 220–21 and 223, no. 89 (inv. 8919: 'ca. 1630–40 [?]').

67 Loisel 2013, 104–5, no. 71: 'pierre noir grasse'.

68 The parallel applies to the head of Saint Jerome in the canvas formerly in the Bentivoglio chapel in Santa Maria degli Scalzi (*Virgin and Child with Saints Jerome and Francis*, Bologna, Pinacoteca Nazionale di Bologna, inv. 581).

69 On the relationship between Reni and Ribera, see Farina 2014, 72–97, where numerous references to the *Seneca* are also discussed. For a summary of Guido's sculpture, see Malvasia–Pericolo 2019, 1:279, note 177.

70 Bohn 2008, 45–46, no. 33.

71 Malvasia–Pericolo 2019, 1:178: 'Quelle anche de' vecchi non lasciò lisce ed unite, come l'altre, ma con botte maestre, piene di mille gentilezze osservate in quelle pellicciuole cadenti quali s'imparano dal rilievo Famoso detto comunemente il suo Seneca'.

72 Ibid., 1:279, note 177.

73 Now in Florence, Gallerie degli Uffizi, inv. 1890 n. 10072.

74 Paris, Musée du Louvre, Départment des Arts graphiques, inv. 8922; Loisel 2013, 115, no. 86; Rosenberg et al. 2019, 1:1032–33, no. 1706.

75 Bohn 2008, 47–49, no. 36; M. Aresin in Eclercy 2022a, 228–30, no. 93. Executed on faded cerulean blue paper, as confirmed by the Uffizi's restoration laboratory.

76 Paris, Musée du Louvre, inv. 535–38; Pepper 1988, 246–47, no. 67; for an overall description of the drawings related to the cycle, see also Benati 1991, 2:134–45; Loire 2017.

77 Johnston 1966.

78 Johnston 1974, 136–39, in no. 103; Keazor 2001, 147–55. For a more recent analysis of Guido's relationship with antiquity, see Morselli 2022e.

79 Munich, Glyptothek, inv. 218.

80 Paris, Musée du Louvre, inv. 537.

81 Munich, Bayerische Staatsgemäldesammlungen, Alte Pinakothek, inv. 513.

82 Birke 1988a, no. B42; Loire 2017, 27.

83 Loisel 2013, 112–13, no. 82; Rosenberg et al. 2019, 1:1032, no. 1705.

84 Vatican City, Musei Vaticani, inv. 1059.

85 Rome, Galleria Borghese, inv. CCLXVIII.

PAINTING FOR POSTERITY: GUIDO RENI'S MATERIALS AND TECHNIQUE

Aoife Brady

In a conversation some years ago with Elizabeth Cropper and the late Charles Dempsey about research on the workshop of Guido Reni (1575–1642), Dempsey asserted frankly that 'Guido is difficult'.[1] This, of course, was a reference to the complexity of the artist's practices rather than a criticism of his personality, though if the remarks of early biographers are anything to go by, the statement could be applied equally in both cases. Reni's 'difficulty' is undeniable, and yet makes his working methods all the more worthy of investigation. Guido and his studio created some of the most technically astounding works of seventeenth-century Italy. The artist was recognised by seventeenth-century sources as having possessed extraordinary manual skill, which surpassed even that of his masters. Count Carlo Cesare Malvasia, Reni's primary biographer, described an occasion on which a frustrated Annibale Carracci (1560–1609) struggled to complete a passage of drapery to his satisfaction, and ordered Reni, then under his tutelage, to complete it for him. On Annibale's return, he 'saw the resolution with which Guido had managed to execute his orders so rapidly and without difficulty', and noted the 'intelligence and mastery' with which the young artist painted, leading the master to 'praise him to the highest in unequivocal terms'.[2]

The study of Reni's workshop proves complex on several counts. There is a lack of substantial contemporary reports describing the artist's studio practices, and when such descriptions appear in seventeenth-century texts, it is difficult to establish whether they are 'true' accounts or literary devices. Then, there are the obstacles presented by the large and ever-changing number of artists working in his Bolognese workshop, the proliferation of copies of Reni's compositions that the studio produced, and the problems of attribution associated with such works. In an attempt to meet these challenges, a twofold approach is required – detailed examination of seventeenth-century texts, and methodical analysis of Guido's paintings. The interpretation of the former has been greatly aided by Lorenzo Pericolo and Elizabeth Cropper's recent work on the Malvasia Project: the publication of their annotated translation of the *Life of Guido Reni* included in the biographer's *Felsina pittrice* (1678) has enriched our understanding of this nuanced seventeenth-century *vita*.[3] The practice of close looking, on the other hand, is today supported by the work of scientists and conservators and by the development of new analytical techniques, allowing us to understand more about the processes involved in creating works of art.

This text offers an overview of Reni's painting technique, combining information from seventeenth-century authors, modern scholarship on the artist, and scientific analysis and reports kindly shared by the conservation departments of various public institutions. It focuses on the production of oil paintings, rather than his work in fresco or on paper (the latter subject is addressed in Viviana Farina's essay in this catalogue). Though not all-encompassing, the present writer hopes that what follows conveys the varying nature of the artist's approach to creating paintings, and the experimental spirit with which he and his studio made use of materials.

Guido Reni, *Saint John the Baptist in the Wilderness*
(detail of cat. 23), c. 1633–34

PREPARATIONS

> No talent, however great and highly favoured by genius, has ever of itself inspired wonder for excellence without the skill of art, which is acquired through application and hard work.[4]

According to his biographers, Guido engaged in intensive study while preparing his paintings. Both Malvasia and Giovan Pietro Bellori described the artist's frustration at being praised for his perceptibly natural talents, to which he responded: 'These gifts are acquired by dint of labors … I have studied more than anyone ever did'.[5] Reni's studies certainly included the practice of drawing: an inventory taken of the artist's possessions on his death listed almost nine hundred drawings stored in his home, hundreds more than those identified to date, illustrating the artist's dedication to careful preparatory work in ink and chalk.[6] These preparations also involved the careful consideration of his painting supports and priming materials, which often carry specific functions and offer distinct visual effects.

SUPPORTS

Guido's usual choice of support was fabric, namely linen canvas, though he also used hemp, copper, silk, and wood as surfaces on which to paint.[7] Canvas was, of course, a conventional painting material in the seventeenth century. Many artists favoured fabrics of specific thread densities or weaves; Reni's preference varied between coarse and fine and twill and plain weave canvases with little consistency. Generally speaking, the surface effects achieved by different kinds of canvas varied according to the dimensions of the finished work: large canvases tended to be executed with thinner paint layers than their smaller counterparts, and the thickness of the paint layer (as well as the coarseness of the fabric) dictated the level of visibility of the canvas threads. For example, while the canvas weave has been obscured on the surface of Reni's *Bacchus and Ariadne* of about 1619–20 in Los Angeles,[8] this has been facilitated by the painting's relatively small size (96.5 × 86.4 centimetres). The threads of the artist's monumental *Pietà dei Mendicanti* [fig. 25], which was painted around the same time, on the other hand, are clearly visible through a thin paint layer, a necessity to prevent the surface from cracking due to the imperceptible movement inherent in a support of this size (704 × 341 centimetres).

Reni is well known for his paintings on copper, usually realised on a small scale. His first master Denys Calvaert (c. 1540–1619) was a particularly important advocate of the use of copper supports in Bologna, and taught his student the technique. Guido began to use the metal support in the early 1590s and was considered especially successful in it. Copper supports proved very popular on the Iberian Peninsula, where Spanish collectors were familiar with the material through the proliferation of Flemish imports. It has been noted that copper panels seem to have been used extensively, although not exclusively, for paintings to be gifted to patrons. When Reni was introduced to Paul V, for example, he gave the pope two small paintings on copper: a *Virgin and Child with Saint John* and a *Virgin sewing with three Angels,* known today only through engravings.[9] The artist exploited this material for the meticulous effects obtainable on its hard, smooth, non-absorbent surface, which made it particularly suitable for small, detailed compositions, and therefore for portable gifts.[10] These visual effects are not particularly distinct from those achievable on a well-prepared wooden panel, and indeed, both supports were utilised by Guido in the creation of small Marian paintings, including the *Assumption of the Virgin* today in the Städel Museum [cat. 7] and the *Coronation of the Virgin* in the National Gallery, London [cat. 9], both on copper, and the Prado *Assumption and Coronation of the Virgin* [cat. 8], on wood panel. However, copper supports offered a less absorbent surface than wood panels, and was also reflective, resulting in a more luminous paint layer. This contrast is perceptible between the three early devotional works in Frankfurt, London, and Madrid, the latter of which appears more matte and chalky than its copper counterparts.

A common misconception exists that paintings on copper are inherently fragile, though there is evidence to support the notion that well-prepared and soundly executed compositions on copper are actually more durable than comparable works on wood panel or canvas.[11] Indeed, today many of Reni's works on copper remain startlingly bright and fresh in appearance, with minimal cracking or flaking of the paint surface. Guido's frequent use of the support is therefore in keeping with his apparent desire for longevity in his work, evident in his selection and exploitation of specific materials. His use of silk as a support for several paintings appears to relate similarly to a desire to extend the life of his works.[12] Convention exists for western painting on silk since the early Renaissance, examples of which were generally associated with processional standards, flags, and liturgical decorations, though many of these objects were ephemeral and are now known only through contemporary descriptions.[13] Cennino Cennini gave instructions on how to 'work on silk' in *Il libro dell'arte* (1437), highlighting its suitability for 'banners and ensigns', presumably because it was lightweight, and the members of the *Gonfalone*, founded in the 1260s and considered to be the oldest confraternity in Rome, were known to have marched behind large silk banners in public processions.[14] Reni famously used silk as an alternative fabric support for three major commissions: the so-called *Pala della Peste* or *Pallione del Voto* of 1630 now in the Pinacoteca Nazionale di Bologna [fig. 30], the *Archangel Michael* of 1635–36 in Santa Maria della Concezione dei Cappuccini in Rome, and the *Assumption of the Virgin Mary*, commissioned and completed before 1642, now in the Alte Pinakothek in Munich.[15]

Silk was an incredibly expensive material in comparison with other fabric or panel supports, and, while its smooth fibres might arguably facilitate detailed application of paint, it does not produce a surface effect so distinct from finely woven linen or hemp canvas so as to justify its relative price. Both Malvasia and Bellori tell their readers that Reni's use of silk supports was linked to his desire for durability in his works, part of an effort to ensure their longevity. They relate an incident that Guido witnessed involving the exhumation of a tomb, in which the body had been reduced to dust, but the silk robe remained perfectly preserved.[16] Malvasia notes that, as a result of what he saw, Reni came to believe 'that silk was much more invulnerable to damage from decay than linen', and this is what inspired the artist to use silk as a painting support.[17] There is both anecdotal and scientific evidence to support this belief. His famous *Pala della Peste*, for example, functioned as a votive banner, and was paraded through the streets of Bologna for over one hundred and fifty years after its creation in an annual civic procession celebrating the abatement of the 1630 plague. Despite a long history of movement and disturbance, its paint layer survives in astoundingly good condition. Modern scientific studies on the properties of silk suggest that the fabric ages relatively well, maintaining a higher level of elasticity over time than other fabrics, and showing resistance to the process of biodeterioration.[18] The artist's beliefs, therefore, appear to have been well placed. We will revisit the topic of durability later in an examination of Reni's palette.

PRIMING AND GROUND LAYERS

The next step in Guido's preparation – the priming of supports – likely fell to studio assistants. Different supports required different kinds of preparation. Canvases would first have been

covered in an animal glue, rendering their fibres non-absorbent. Ground layers were then applied. Like many of his contemporaries in the seventeenth century, Reni favoured coloured grounds, ranging from orange to brown to dark red, which could be left exposed in certain passages to act as a mid-tone. While some artists applied a single ground layer to their support, Reni's paintings often present a double layer, usually composed of some mixture of chalk, earth pigments, charcoal or bone black, and lead white.[19] These double layers were generally of similar composition and both orange or reddish-brown in colour, as is the case of the Louvre *David holding the Head of Goliath* of about 1604–6,[20] as well as the later versions of *Saint Sebastian* in the Prado [fig. 44] and Dulwich Picture Gallery,[21] but occasionally these ground layers were different in colour and makeup.[22] Analysis of the *Christ at the Column* at the Städel Museum [cat. 25], for example, demonstrates the use of a lighter-coloured lower ground layer, while the upper one is tinted orange. This bright underlayer was perhaps first applied in an attempt to impart some luminosity to the finished painting, since it also includes reflective minerals, such as quartz.[23] In certain later works, including the Louvre *Christ giving the Keys to Saint Peter* of about 1620–25[24] and the *Abduction of Helen* of 1631 [fig. 35], Reni employs a single ground layer, perhaps having been influenced by Roman trends during his time there in earlier decades, or for reasons of economy during a busy period in his Bolognese studio.[25]

Malvasia describes Guido's technique in using these coloured ground layers as a space 'to play upon' where he could leave areas uncovered to create shadow or delineate forms.[26] While exposed ground layers are evident in small passages of Reni's earlier works, it is not until his late period that the artist begins

Fig. 44 Cross-section of paint sample from saint's white drapery revealing two orange-brown ground layers in Guido Reni, *Saint Sebastian*, c. 1619 [cat. 19]

to exploit the tinted grounds to their greatest effect. In the Dulwich Picture Gallery *Saint John the Baptist in the Wilderness* of around 1633–34 [cat. 23], for example, Reni makes great use of the ground in optical effects in the sky, employing widely streaked grey scumbling through which the ground can be seen [see detail on p. 102]. The group of background figures to the left of the Baptist 'consist almost entirely of the ground roughly outlined with coloured strokes'.[27]

The preparation and composition of ground layers differed in the case of panel supports, particularly copper. The copper support of the National Gallery, London *Coronation of the Virgin* [cat. 9], for instance, was coated with pewter, a metal alloy, as part of its preparation.[28] The practice of applying metal-alloy coatings to copper plates (often described as 'silvering' or 'tinning') was unusual, though certain artists did favour coated plates, including Guido and his contemporaries, Guercino (1591–1666) and Domenichino (1581–1641), as well as Adam Elsheimer (1578–1610) and Claude Lorrain (1600–1682).[29] Reni's reasoning behind using such coatings may be related again to his desire for durability in his materials – such tinning apparently provides resistance to corrosion with minimal increase in thickness or weight.[30] Another effect of the use of these silver-coloured alloy layers is the luminosity in the paint surface that they produce. An unusual tonal quality is created by the metallic brightness beneath the ground and paint, which intensifies the clarity and brilliance of these masterpieces.[31]

Most paintings on copper appear to have a thin, pale-toned preparatory layer between the paint film and tinned or bare copper support. This coating is far thinner than the ground layers applied to the artist's canvases. The lack of absorbency of copper meant that the preparation necessary for cloth supports to prevent fibres from absorbing paint unevenly and to provide saturation of colour was unnecessary: copper allowed paint to be applied in a manner that appears smooth and highly saturated without the need for thick ground layers.

CREATING COMPOSITIONS

The next steps in Reni's process involved laying out the basic format of his compositions. The nature of this process varied considerably, depending on the dimensions of the work (large altarpieces, for example, required more careful laying out, while smaller single-figure compositions might have been painted freehand) and the period of the artist's career from which it originated. We know that Guido 'dead coloured' most of his works, that is, blocked in various aspects of his composition with flat colours to suggest shapes and explore spatial relationships before adding colour, tone, and detail later.[32] These basic elements in some instances were adapted from preparatory drawings, like the detailed sketch created for the *Coronation of the Virgin with four Saints* in the British Museum,[33] while in later years, simple, single-figure compositions such as the *Cleopatra* at the National Gallery of Ireland [cat. 91] appear to have been created *alla prima*, worked up directly on the canvas without the aid of this kind of step-by-step process.

Underdrawings have been detected using infrared reflectography in a small number of Reni's works. An infrared reflectogram of the Prado *Apostle Saint James the Greater* [fig. 45], for example, reveals underdrawing in the form of freehand brushstrokes in black paint or ink, as does the *Toilet of Venus* in the National Gallery, London [cat. 74].[34] Faint traces of underdrawing may be identifiable around the left-hand-side of Christ's chest in the Städel *Christ at the Column*, though infrared analysis is not conclusive in this regard.[35] Imaging also reveals *pentimenti* nearby on the left shoulder of Christ, suggesting that this part of his anatomy proved a challenging passage for Reni to complete, and perhaps required the guidance of underdrawing to assist the artist in arriving to a resolution.

Infrared imagery of later works from Reni's studio, including the Auckland, Prado, and Dulwich *Saint Sebastian* canvases,[36] do not make visible any significant evidence of underdrawings, suggesting that some paintings from Reni's post-Roman years were worked up without the guidance of a sketch.[37] The absence of identifiable freehand underdrawings in these depictions of Saint Sebastian may alternatively be due to the fact that at least two of these works are copies (for which the prime version remains the subject of debate), and would therefore have been executed based on a pre-existing composition. The mechanical means by which Reni and his studio reproduced outlines for such copies – which are often replicated with a high degree of accuracy – is unknown. There are no surviving cartoons or gridded drawings related to the artist's frequently repeated compositions, or extant documentary evidence from the seventeenth century that might illuminate the procedures involved in the replication of their outlines, while analysis of the paintings themselves does not reveal evidence of traced drawings, pouncing, or incision lines on the canvases. We may infer, therefore, that Guido and his workshop transferred the outlines of compositions using non-destructive, ephemeral, and undetectable means, perhaps replicating them using a transparent piece of cloth, known as a *velo,* which could be used to trace

Fig. 45 Detail of infrared reflectogram revealing evidence of painterly underdrawing in Guido Reni, *The Apostle Saint James the Greater*, c. 1626 [cat. 38]

designs from paintings in chalk, before transposing the faint outlines onto a new support by rubbing.[38]

During the height of the artist's success in the 1620s and early 1630s, Reni's studio developed formulae for the creation of new works, recycling figures and other elements from earlier compositions, which were adapted according to new subject matters. This facilitated increased workshop participation in the creation of compositions during busier periods, while also maintaining a cohesive and recognisable visual language – a brand, if you will. The *Toilet of Venus* offers a good example of a work in which the basic structure of the composition

appears to have been developed by studio assistants based on fragmentary tracings of earlier paintings, and was later adjusted and retouched by Reni himself.[39]

APPLICATION OF PAINT

> … no painter has ever made heads with a more beautiful air, nor fleshier and more tender little *putti*, nor hands and feet better drawn, nor more appropriate and magnificent draperies, nor nudes more profoundly understood and researched.[40]

PALETTE AND PIGMENTS

Guido employed a palette of pigments that was very much conventional in the seventeenth century, and remained consistent throughout his career. These included natural mineral blue pigments, ultramarine and azurite; yellow, red, and brown earth pigments; manufactured pigments, such as vermilion (also seen to occur naturally), lead white, red lead, lead-tin yellow, smalt, and verdigris; artificially prepared blue and green copper pigments; red and yellow lake pigments; insoluble blue plant dyestuff, indigo; and a number of different blacks.[41] His earth pigments would appear to be Italian in origin – very good quality earth pigments were produced in Italy – while his cochineal pigments and ultramarines would have been imported.[42] These were usually bound in linseed oil, though walnut oil has also been identified in one work: *The Adoration of the Shepherds* of about 1640 in the collection of the National Gallery, London.[43]

While the contents of Reni's palette are largely standard, the manner in which he exploited this range of colours changes from painting to painting, and evolves as the artist's career progresses. In the first decades of the seventeenth century, Reni's tonalities were bright and intense. The Bologna *Massacre of the Innocents* of 1611 [cat. 20] utilises opaque, highly pigmented primary colours – the blue of the sky contrasting with the deep red and bright yellow of the foreground figures' drapery. Similar colouring is seen into the 1620s, in Reni's Potsdam *Lucretia* of 1626,[44] again with bright, bold primary colours dominating, especially in the drapery. The artist's palette begins to lighten considerably in the 1630s, when compared to these earlier works, and he makes use of a palette consisting of lighter, cool, pastel colours, as seen in the *Rape of Europa* of 1637–39 at the National Gallery, London.[45] In Reni's latest works, such as the aforementioned *Adoration of the Shepherds* painted around 1640, also at the National Gallery, there has been no identifiable change in the pigments and binders from those that he used in previous decades. The artist does, however, begin to use these materials in different ways, employing increased amounts of lead white and painting in a heightened key. Reni's late palette continues to evolve in his final years, becoming cooler, more restricted and, at times, more sombre, when compared to that in his early works, as illustrated by the Pinacoteca Capitolina *Portrait of a Girl with a Crown* [fig. 48], rendered almost exclusively in shades of white, blue, yellow, and brown.

LEAD WHITE

Reni's increased employment of lead white during the final decades of his career proves a distinctive characteristic of his palette. The artist's exploitation of this pigment was indeed so conspicuous that it is addressed at some length by the seventeenth-century sources. Though apparently being advised against the overuse of this material by one of his masters, Ludovico Carracci (1555–1619), and 'contrary to the good masters of the past', Guido 'did not hesitate to use white lead to excess'.[46] Malvasia claims that this was a method employed by Reni to discourage his works from ageing poorly, claiming that 'while the paintings of others would lose a great deal over the years, [Guido's] pictures would gain as the white lead would yellow, and they would take on a certain patina reducing all the pigments to a true and good natural colour, whereas those other works would blacken to excess'.[47] Francesco Scannelli, however, apparently disapproved of the employment of such preventative measures, and wrote that painters should concern themselves with depicting the present reality, instead of preparing for 'the uncertainties of future effects'.[48] Malvasia also links Reni's increased use of lead white in later decades to the artist's newly emerging style, where he 'refused to use those tremendous or contrived shadows' which were 'excessively artificial' but 'instead he used sweet and pleasant shadows, as though cast by a bright and open light, such as we see every day in the streets'.[49]

While some of Reni's pigments have inevitably suffered darkening over time, for the most part his paintings have retained their colour, and they are generally cited as being in excellent condition by conservators who examine them. Indeed, lead white as a material is said to maintain a fresh appearance and resists moisture damage, therefore creating a durable paint surface.[50] Reni's *Immaculate Conception* of 1627 [cat. 55] provides an unusual example of the durability of lead white. The work is recorded as having been part of the Duke of Bridgewater's collection in 1823, which was fire bombed in World War II, leaving the painting badly damaged.[51] According to the late Sir Denis Mahon, who saw the painting being sold at auction, the work was 'entirely black with paint falling off everywhere', and appeared 'totally unsalvageable'.[52] Having been acquired by the Metropolitan Museum in 1959, it was lined, cleaned, and restored, and while the work is, as the conservation report phrases it, 'peppered with losses', it remains in remarkable condition given its history. Dorothy Mahon, the author of the report, notes that the 'durability' of the painting is 'a testament to a well-crafted product, very directly executed with paints containing a large admixture of lead white'.[53] That the conservator attributes this painting's survival directly to Reni's technique and his use of lead white demonstrates the soundness of the artist's practice, and supports his belief that the use of *biacca* would extend the life of his paintings.

FLESH TONES

The composition of Reni's flesh tones varies considerably from painting to painting, and often contains unexpected pigments. In his Birmingham *Lady with a Lapis Lazuli Bowl* of 1638–39,[54] conservators note that 'green paint [has been] applied over warmer tones within the sitter's face and neck area (surprisingly)'.[55] This inclination toward cooler flesh tones can be observed in both early and late works. Pigment analysis of two versions of Guido's frequently repeated *Saint Sebastian* compositions at the Prado [cat. 19] and Dulwich Picture Gallery illustrate this. Though the paintings are ascribed disparate dates – the Madrid work is dated to around 1619, but may have been painted even earlier, while the London canvas is generally dated to around 1630–35 – the composition of the flesh paint in both is strikingly similar, dominated by lead white and green earth.[56] In Reni's *Susannah and the Elders* of around 1623–24 in London [cat. 89], Susannah's flesh is painted using lead white, green earth, and black pigments, again producing the cool, green tones that were previously noted. In contrast, the flesh of the men is painted using earth pigments and lead white, giving their faces a much warmer, ruddy tone, contrasting with the purity of Susannah's skin.[57] Reni's flesh tones caught the attention of Malvasia, who wrote about this unusual practice of adding cooler pigments to his figures' skin colours (though he calls attention to the use of violet-greys and pale blues as opposed to green), as has been noted in his comments that Reni used these cool colours 'mixed in amidst the half-tints and flesh colors', producing delicate skin tones which reflect 'a diaphanous glow'.[58]

Malvasia's explanation of this practice of adding cool colours to his flesh tones so as to impart a 'diaphanous' quality is a plausible one. In *Susannah and the Elders*, for example, it is not immediately evident in viewing the work that Reni has used green or black pigments in Susannah's flesh. Her skin colour, however, has a radiant quality to it that could indeed be described as 'diaphanous'; a luminous paleness that is associated with skin which is semi-transparent, through which the veins of a person's hands and wrists might be visible. The radiance and clearness of Susannah's skin gives her a purity which contrasts with the ruddy faces of the men who surround her. This may be a rhetorical device used by Guido, the bright paleness of Susannah alluding to the character's purity and innocence, contrasting with the lustful, lecherous men surrounding her, emphasising the erotic nature of the scene.

BRUSHWORK

Reni's brushwork is an aspect of his technique that developed in stages over the course of his career. This evolution, however, was not an entirely linear one, and he adjusted his handling of paint from one work to another, according to the medium and support employed, the format and subject matter, and, of course, the intended recipient. At times, his brushwork was adapted in response to the demands of his growing business. Malvasia relates that, upon Guido's return to Bologna from Rome around 1614, he made a number of paintings quickly and cheaply, adjusting his handling accordingly, adopting a more painterly technique using 'bold strokes and hatching'.[59] Richard Spear recognises a direct correlation between Reni's style and his economic objectives early on in his career, saying that this is understood to have occurred well before the 1630s, when such a link became more apparent.[60] Furthermore, busier periods naturally necessitated increased studio involvement in the production of paintings today attributed to Reni. For all of these reasons, we should be wary in attempting to determine exact dates for works on the basis of levels of 'tightness' or 'looseness' in the painter's brushstrokes. That being said, what follows will cautiously track Reni's progression to a more painterly style as his career progressed, a shift discussed at some length in seventeenth-century literature.

Generally speaking, Guido's application of paint in the early years of his career was more measured, with finer brushwork that appears tight and controlled when compared to that of the subsequent decades. Among the artist's earliest works is his first public commission, the *Coronation of the Virgin with four Saints* of around 1598, now in the Pinacoteca Nazionale di Bologna

[fig. 16], which is rendered in exceptional detail, particularly visible in the ornate crozier held by Saint Bernard and the scroll on the Baptist's reed cross. There is a certain soft, atmospheric quality and a texture to the artist's brushwork in areas of this painting reminiscent of the work of Annibale Carracci. Reni had moved to the Carracci academy around 1594, having 'not yet turned twenty'.[61] This work illustrates a moment of departure from the Mannerist tendencies of his earlier master, Calvaert, toward the naturalistic manner of the Carracci, which had a profound impact on the young painter. Malvasia writes that this work shows the manner of Calvaert in its upper half (in passages depicting the 'Blessed Virgin crowned by God the Father and the Son within a glory of angels'), while the figures in the lower half – the four saints – yield to the *pastoso*, or softness, of Annibale.[62]

Three years after his departure from the Carracci academy around 1598, the artist spent periods working in Rome before returning to Bologna around 1614. Rome had a profound impact on his handling of paint. In response to the popularity of Caravaggism in the city, Guido made a departure from the 'softness' of Annibale toward a more polished manner, applying paint in even, smooth strokes with little visible impasto. The influence of the Caravaggesque is readily apparent in works like the Pasadena *Saint Cecilia* of 1606 [fig. 11] and the Frankfurt *Christ at the Column* of about 1604 [cat. 25], both set against a dark background and modelled with the exacting brushwork that lends itself to Caravaggio's (1571–1610) style of extreme naturalism, bringing to his paintings 'a certain rigorous imitation of reality'.[63]

Reni's brushwork over the second decade of the seventeenth century characteristically varied between tight and detailed to loose and painterly. Some works from the years following the artist's return from Rome in 1614 continue to reflect the influence of the Caravaggesque in their tight handling and naturalistic modelling of figures, for example, the *Lot and his Daughters leaving Sodom* of about 1614–15 now in the National Gallery, London.[64] His treatment of the *Samson Victorious* of about 1617–19 at the Pinacoteca Nazionale di Bologna [fig. 14], on the other hand, illustrates the initial moves toward a looser handling of paint – the brushwork used to paint Samson and the other characters in the foreground is relatively fine, though it becomes visibly less so in the background figures. This variation allows the artist to draw attention to aspects of the composition most essential to the narrative, while also effectively creating the impression of distance and depth in the painting.

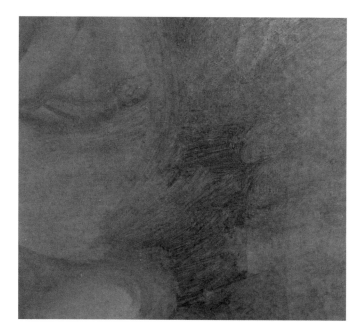

Fig. 46 Detail of the figure of the Baptist blended with the foliage in Guido Reni, *Infant Jesus and Saint John*, 1640–42. Oil on canvas, 86.5 × 69 cm. Rome, Musei Capitolini, PC 188

From around 1620 onwards, Guido began to move towards his *seconda maniera*, a painterly style which would continue to develop until his death in 1642. This late manner becomes more apparent from 1630 onwards, when his brushwork becomes very free, loose, and rich in impasto. At this time, Reni began modelling the surface of some figures with extensive parallel and zigzag hatching that recalls his handling of chalk.[65] These distinctive passages of brushwork are particularly evident in works such as the *Fall of the Giants* of around 1637–40 in Pesaro [cat. 45] and the *Saint Sebastian* of around 1640 in Bologna,[66] the latter of which features areas of especially painterly, visible brushwork and impasto, particularly in the saint's robes. The culmination of this late style can be found in works like the *Flagellation* in Bologna [cat. 94], where areas of the painting are merely suggested with summary brushwork, as opposed to fully formed brushstrokes.

NON FINITO

Works produced late in Guido's career are often described as 'unfinished' because of their sketchy, loose brushwork, muted palette, and lack of detail. It has been argued, however, that many of these works were, in fact, completed by the artist, and that the contrast in technique from Reni's earlier paintings is the result of a distinct shift in the artist's psychology. Malvasia asserts that the change in Guido's later works was brought about by

'extreme necessity' caused by 'excessive [gambling] losses, which exceeded his financial means'. He goes on to describe Reni's late painting methods, writing that the artist 'took to painting half-figures and heads *alla prima*, without priming; he thoughtlessly dashed off history paintings and more considerable works'.[67] The *Infant Jesus and Saint John* of 1640–42 in the Musei Capitolini features several passages which appear unfinished. The robe of the kneeling Baptist at the extreme right of the composition, for example, fades into murky green foliage in the background, and has not been delineated in the dark brown brushstrokes with which Reni has treated the rest of the figure [fig. 46]. Close examination of the paint surface in this area suggests that this was, in fact, deliberate. The green background paint has been actively blended with the drapery using a large, stiff bristled brush, while both colours were still wet. No other area of either figure sees this kind of blending with the background paint. Were it the case that the artist simply left this part of the painting unfinished, this passage would presumably see the figure's flesh blocked out, but not deliberately mixed with neighbouring passages of paint.

That the background paint has been blended with the figure's drapery while still wet suggests that this work was executed rapidly. There is a disorganised, frenzied appearance to this area of the composition, evident in the irregular, zigzagging brushstrokes with which Reni has blended the passages, perhaps suggesting a frustration on the artist's part. It appears as if Guido has 'scribbled out' this part of the composition, rather than abandoned it unfinished. It is possible that he deliberately blurred the boundary between the saint's robe and background to make it appear softer and less stark. It is equally possible that this passage forms an example of the irresoluteness of Reni in the latter years of his life, in which Scannelli says he struggled to complete compositions to his satisfaction.[68]

FINISHING TOUCHES

> If [patrons] knew how much it takes and how one has to rack one's brains to apply a brushstroke well to the canvas, they would not talk this way.[69]

The final stages of Reni's painting process involved adjustment to the contours of his compositions, such as those visible in the arms of the figures in an infrared reflectogram of the Los Angeles *Joseph and Potiphar's Wife* of about 1630,[70] or, occasionally, a complete repositioning of some elements, which appear in technical imaging as dramatic *pentimenti*. Such significant revisions were often made at a late stage in the painting process to make a composition appear more balanced, as may have been the case for those visible in infrared imagery of his Bologna *Massacre of the Innocents* [fig. 47]. There are many minor *pentimenti* evident in this painting, which is to be expected from such a large and complex composition: Reni took some time to work out certain aspects, like the hands of the woman kneeling in the foreground to the right-hand side. A more significant *pentimento* appears in the figure on the extreme right – the woman's face has been repainted at a relatively late stage in the painting process, changing its position on the canvas significantly. This brings it more in line with the corresponding female figure whose hair is being pulled on the left-hand-side of the work, creating a more symmetrical composition.

Once the final structure of the composition was revised to Reni's satisfaction, the finishing touches were then applied as highlights and other incidental details on the uppermost layer of paint. In many works, the artist applied highlights to flesh tones using rows of tightly zigzagging or parallel brushstrokes, visible, for example, on the arm of Christ in the Vienna *Baptism of Christ* of 1622–23,[71] and the thigh off the Dulwich *Saint Sebastian* of about 1630–35. This method of highlighting becomes increasingly visible on the surface in his works from the 1630s onward, for example on the chest of the Rome *Girl holding a Wreath* [fig. 48]. This served to give skin a textural quality by diffusing light hitting the surface of the raised impasto created by the dynamic strokes.

The finishing touches often give the impression of having been applied with spontaneity. French art critic Roger de Piles described Reni's handling as, for the most part, highly controlled, but states that he 'was so convinced that freedom of the hand was necessary for a pleasing result that, after having sometimes toiled on a work, he would splatter a few bold and free strokes over it to remove all hint of the time and great effort it had cost him.'[72]

Indeed, Guido finishes some of his works with a flair. The exquisite *Christ crowned with Thorns* of the early 1630s in Detroit,[73] for example, is painted on copper with careful, meditative brushstrokes, supplemented at the very final stages with some carefree opaque highlights dragged down the length of the wooden cane and arcing through Christ's beard, along with some daring splashes of blood which interrupt the porcelain glow of the figure's skin, forcing the viewer to redirect their gaze.

Fig. 47 Infrared reflectogram revealing dramatic *pentimenti* in Guido Reni, *The Massacre of the Innocents*, 1611 [cat. 20]

PAINTING FOR POSTERITY

What emerges in examination of Reni's painting materials and techniques is an overarching preoccupation with the longevity of his materials, and a desire to create works that would stand the test of time. It appears as a recurring topic that runs through many of the seventeenth-century writings on Reni when referring to his use of silk supports and large quantities of lead white pigment, but might be equally relevant to other practices employed by the artist, such as the pewter coatings

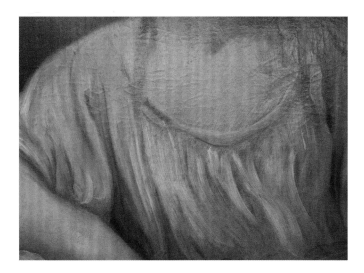

Fig. 48 Detail of brushwork on chest in Guido Reni,
Girl holding a Wreath, 1640–42. Oil on canvas,
91 × 73 cm. Rome, Musei Capitolini,
Pinacoteca, PC 181

applied to some of his copper panels. A letter from Guido to Ferrante Trotto dated 11 July 1639 confirms the artist's preoccupation with longevity – in an assessment of Carlo Bononi's (1569–1632) *Ascension* in San Salvatore, Bologna, Reni made the following astute observations: 'the painting here in San Salvatore has greatly suffered on account of the priming, excessively corrosive because it was perhaps made with earth pigment'.[74] Reading almost like a modern conservation report, the letter illustrates Guido's keen understanding of painting materials and the manner in which they can impact the ageing of a work of art.

The artist's aim to create works that would remain in good condition for posterity seems, at least for the most part, to have been successful – his oeuvre today is in generally good condition, and even works that have suffered known damage over the course of their respective histories, such as the aforementioned *Immaculate Conception* and the *Pala della Peste*, survive in a surprisingly good state. And despite Malvasia's report that Reni abandoned his careful working methods in the final moments of his career, paintings from the last five years of the artist's life do not present any major adverse effects noted by conservators to coincide with the artist's change in style and technique. Reni was a master of his preferred medium, oil, and has created works that have survived remarkably well for hundreds of years, to tell of his technical excellence in painting as 'the Bolognese Apelles, to whose brush the world pays reverence'.[75]

1 Meeting with the late Prof. Emeritus Charles Dempsey and Prof. Dr Elizabeth Cropper, Museo del Prado, Madrid, 3 March 2016. The contents of this essay are based on a chapter of the present author's doctoral dissertation, which provides a more detailed account of Reni's workshop practices: see Brady 2017. For additional information on the artist's workshop, see Iseppi 2020.

2 Malvasia–Pericolo 2019, 1:22: 'Veduto la risoluzione con che avea saputo eseguir ben tosto e senza difficoltà veruna il comando, ma più la intelligenza e la maestria con che sì bene avea adattato … non poté come non apertamente lodarlo in estremo'. For the English translation, ibid., 1:23.

3 Malvasia–Pericolo 2019.

4 Bellori–Wohl 2005, 367.

5 Ibid. See also Malvasia–Pericolo 2019, 1:68–69.

6 Spike and Di Zio 1988, 46. The topic of Reni's drawing practice is addressed elsewhere in this volume: see Viviana Farina's essay, '"A man who perpetually observes Nature": Guido Reni and Drawing', in this catalogue.

7 While no works on stone can today be attributed to the artist, his Roman account books record the purchase of a type of polished hard stone described as *parangoni*, potentially acquired to exploit as a painting support. See Pepper 1971a, 316, nos. 57 and 58, and 317, no. 71. I am grateful to Sir Nicholas Penny for kindly drawing my attention to these references.

8 Los Angeles County Museum of Art, M.79.63.

9 Schaefer 1988, 7.

10 Bowron 1999, 16.

11 Komanecky 1999b, 4.

12 For more on Reni's use of silk as a support, see Brady 2019 and Puglisi 2020.

13 Spear 1972, 389, note 87.

14 Cennini–Thompson 1960, 106–7; Wisch and Newbigin 2013, 1–2.

15 Munich, Bayerische Staatsgemäldesammlungen, Alte Pinakothek, inv. 446.

16 Bellori–Wohl 2005, 368; Malvasia–Pericolo 2019, 1:128–29.

17 Malvasia–Pericolo 2019, 1:128: 'Chiaritosene occularmente Guido, formò questo concetto presso di lui invincibile, come che appoggiato alla dimostrazione, che la seta fosse più privilegiata assai contro i danni della corruttibilità della tela'. For the English translation, ibid., 1:129.

18 Ljaljević Grbić et al. 2014, 132.

19 Glanville 1995.

20 Paris, Musée du Louvre, inv. 519.

21 London, Dulwich Picture Gallery, DGP268.

22 Sophia Plender, Conservation Record for Guido Reni, *St Sebastian*, Dulwich Picture Gallery, analysis carried out by Ashok Roy of the Scientific Department at the National Gallery, London, 1998; Hillary and Kisler 2009, 210; Maite Jover de Celis and María Dolores Gayo, Pigment Analysis Report (optical microscopy, SEM-EDX, XRF) for Guido Reni, *Saint Sebastian*, Museo del Prado, Madrid, 2022.

23 Lilly Becker, Scientific Report for Guido Reni, *Christ at the Column*, Städel Museum, Frankfurt, 2022.

24 Paris, Musée du Louvre, inv. 526.

25 Martin 2008.

26 Malvasia–Pericolo 2019, 1:178: 'si servì di quel primo colore, quasi di letto, per scherzarvi sopra'. For the English translation, ibid., 1:179.

27 Helen Glanville, Notes on Condition and Recommendation for Treatment for Guido Reni, *St John the Baptist in the Wilderness*, London, Dulwich Picture Gallery, 1988.

28 Personal correspondence with Helen Howard of the Scientific Department of the National Gallery, London, April 2014.

29 Horovitz 1999, 68.

30 Ibid., 67.

31 Spear 1982, 1:297; Horovitz 1999, 68.

32 Brady 2017, 1:111; Mandy et al. 2019, 24.

33 London, The British Museum, inv. 1946,0713.237.

34 Personal correspondence with Ana González Mozo, Museo del Prado, Madrid, September 2014; Mandy et al. 2019, 24.

35 Lilly Becker, Scientific Report for Guido Reni, *Christ at the Column*, Städel Museum, Frankfurt, 2022.

36 Auckland Art Gallery Toi o Tāmaki, M1882/2/3; Madrid, Museo Nacional del Prado [cat. 19]; and London, Dulwich Picture Gallery, DPG268.

37 It is worth noting that underdrawings, even if indeed present, are not always identifiable using infrared analysis.

38 Brady 2020, 12.

39 See Brady 2020.

40 Malvasia–Pericolo 2019, 1:176: 'Nissuno perciò fece mai più belle arie di teste, nissuno puttini più carnosi e teneri, mani e piedi meglio disegnati, panni più propri e magnifici, nudi più profondi e ricerchi'. For the English translation, ibid., 1:177.

41 Kirby 1999, 30.

42 Personal correspondence with Helen Howard of the Scientific Department of the National Gallery, London, April 2014.

43 London, National Gallery, NG6270. Mandy et al. 2019, 28. Limited analysis has been carried out on Reni's binding materials, making it difficult to ascertain how frequent his use of walnut oil or other alternative binders might have been.

44 Potsdam (Germany), Neues Palais, GK I 5388.

45 London, National Gallery, NG6642.

46 Malvasia–Pericolo 2019, 1:184: 'al contrario de' buoni maestri passati, s'è arrischiato oprar smoderatamente la biacca'. For the English translation, ibid., 1:185.

47 Ibid.: 'che dove le pitture de gli altri perdono tanto col tempo, le sue acquistariano, ingiallendosi quella biacca e pigliando una certa patena che riduce il colore ad un vero e buon naturale, ove l'altre annerendosi troppo'. For an exploration of the potential reasons underpinning Reni's increased use of lead white in his *seconda maniera,* see Puglisi 2021.

48 Scannelli 1657, 114: 'Mà lasciamo una tal ragione per insufficiente, perché deve chi opera dopo la debita preparazione sodisfare con ogni potere in ordine alla presente prima veduta, e poi tra lasciare alla prima causa del tutto gl'incerti effetti del futuro'.

49 Malvasia–Pericolo 2019, 1:184: 'non volle … usar l'ombre terribili e forzate; ma dolci e piacevoli, come partorite da un lume chiaro ed aperto, quali cotidianamente si veggono nelle strade'. For the English translation, ibid., 1:185.

50 Taylor 2015, 178.

51 Dorothy Mahon, Examination and Treatment Record for Guido Reni, *The Immaculate Conception*, The Metropolitan Museum of Art, New York, 1987.

52 Quote from Sir Denis Mahon, cited ibid.

53 Ibid.

54 Birmingham Museums Trust, inv. 1961P30.

55 Haydn Roberts, Examination Report for Guido Reni, *Portrait of a Woman, perhaps Artemisia* or *Lady with a Lapis Lazuli Bowl,* Birmingham Museums Trust, Birmingham, 1988.

56 Sophia Plender, Conservation Record for Guido Reni, *St Sebastian*, Dulwich Picture Gallery, analysis carried out by Ashok Roy of the Scientific Department at the National Gallery, London, 1998; Maite Jover de Celis and María Dolores Gayo, Pigment Analysis Report (optical microscopy, SEM-EDX, XRF) for Guido Reni, *Saint Sebastian*, Museo del Prado, Madrid, 2022.

57 Personal correspondence with Helen Howard of the Scientific Department of the National Gallery, London, April 2014.

58 Malvasia–Pericolo 2019, 1:182: 'con certi lividetti ed azzurrini mescolati fra le mezze tente e fra le carnaggioni … quali si osservano nelle carni delicate, che rendono un certo diáfano'. For the English translation, ibid., 1:183.

59 Ibid., 1:54: 'lavorandole di botte e di tratti, con certa sprezzatura da gran maestro'. For the English translation, ibid., 1:55.

60 Spear 1972, 211.

61 Malvasia–Pericolo 2019, 1:20: 'Se ne passò dunque a' Carracci che non compiva il vigesimo anno'. For the English translation, ibid., 1:21.

62 Ibid.: 'ove nella parte superiore … mostrò aver anche ritenuto del far di Dionigi, là dove nelle figure sotto de' quattro santi diede in un più grande e pastoso di Annibale'.

63 Passeri 1772, 59.

64 London, The National Gallery, NG193.

65 Spear 1972, 311.

66 Bologna, Pinacoteca Nazionale di Bologna, inv. 446.

67 Malvasia–Pericolo 2019, 1:104: 'Il maggior danno però l'ebbe sempre dal giuoco …; poichè, ridottosi in estreme necessità per le perdite eccessive ed eccedenti la sua possibilità, per pagare i debiti ponevasi a lavorare mezze figure e testi alla prima, e senza il letto sotto; a finire inconsideratamente le storie e le tavole più riguardevoli'. For the English translation, ibid., 1:105.

68 Scannelli 1657, 359: 'non potendo allo spesso sodisfare, massime giunto nell'ultima età, annullava più volte il principiato, e con gran fatica riduceva l'opere al desiato compimento'.

69 Guido responding to criticism of his high fees. See Bellori–Wohl 2005, 356.

70 Los Angeles, Getty Museum, 93.PA.57.

71 Vienna, Kunsthistorisches Museum, Gemäldegalerie, inv. 222.

72 Piles 1715, 322, cited by Spear 1972, 300.

73 Detroit Institute of Arts, Gift of James E. Scripps, inv. 89.23.

74 Gaye 1839–40, 3:545, cited by Malvasia–Pericolo 2019, 1:356, note 386.

75 Malvasia–Pericolo 2019, 1:190: 'Il bolognese Apelle, al cui pennel fa riverenza il mondo'. For the English translation, ibid., 1:191.

GUIDO RENI: A MASTER WITHOUT A SCHOOL?

Daniele Benati

Although commonly used, the term *scuola* (school) is not entirely appropriate to define the complex productive apparatus that Guido Reni (1575–1642) set in motion in Bologna after returning from Rome for good.[1] Or at least this label cannot be used in the same sense in which it is employed in connection with the Carracci, particularly Ludovico (1555–1619) and Annibale (1560–1609). Indeed, so great was Ludovico's fame as a teacher that it overshadowed his excellent painterly skills. For his part, Annibale – consciously or otherwise – was comparable to Raphael (1483–1520) in his large number of pupils, one of the aspects on which the latter's greatness was based. However, it seems that for Guido, who was very soon praised as 'divine' – an epithet previously given to Raphael – establishing a school was not such a strong imperative. In fact, all his biographers agree that others were excluded from both taking part in and disseminating the 'laboratory of the ideal' to which he devoted himself throughout his career. Granted, Reni had numerous assistants on whom he increasingly relied, and many later artists in Bologna and the whole of Europe drew inspiration from his unmatchable masterpieces. But his art was inextricably bound up with his ideas and was not something that could be taught.

If we are to believe what Carlo Cesare Malvasia claims in a manuscript note to have learned from Marco Bandinelli, the servant Guido called 'Marchino', who stayed with the master until his death, the artist was aware that even those who professed to be his disciples had merely admired and imitated him rather than truly understood him. It is not that Guido did not like teaching: helping the younger painters and correcting their work, sometimes sparing no fierce criticism, was possibly the occupation to which he devoted himself with greatest relish during his breaks from painting. It displeased him that youngsters did not wish to properly learn his *maniera*, only steal and imitate it. In his day – he had confided to Marco – disciples studied their master's way of working in depth, endeavouring to apply it to their own compositions; and this, in his opinion, constituted true learning, on which the passing on of skills from master to pupil should be based. When he died, instead, his teachings would disappear, as his pupils had merely emulated the pictures in front of them.[2] This might sound like a paradoxical statement made by an elderly artist disillusioned with life, but it is difficult to refute: instead of assimilating the mental processes that had guided his art, most of Guido's disciples had simply settled for plagiarising some of his visible formulas, such as his unrealistic palette and the ever-upturned gaze of his female saints.

Actually, it must have been quite difficult for young artists to assimilate Reni's conviction that 'beautiful ideas need be in the head',[3] and that accordingly one model was as good as another. This is what Guido himself proved to Count Filippo Aldrovandi, who, possibly egged on by Guercino (1591–1666), asked him whom the woman who posed for his pictures of the Virgin or the Magdalen was. Ordering his colour grinder, 'who had the ugly mug of a criminal',[4] to sit in front of him and look up, Reni painted such a beautiful head of a female saint that it appeared miraculous to the count. Studying from life, then, was for Guido the starting point for the pursuit of an otherworldly beauty that is unknowable to the senses. It is therefore possible that the troubled face of his friend Saulo Guidotti (1601–1665) suggested to Reni the physiognomy of Saint Francis in the processional votive banner known as the *Pallione del Voto* [fig. 30] and that certain beautiful Bolognese ladies, such as the countesses De' Bianchi and Barbazza, had fired his imagination, though the facial features of his *Cleopatras* and *Lucretias* are so idealised that it is impossible to consider them portraits. It is also hard to believe Malvasia when he writes in his *Felsina pittrice* (1678) that to be able to comfortably paint a young woman whose parents did not wish her to sit for him the artist went to the lengths of renting a room opposite her windows. To study the male musculature, which was particularly difficult, Guido may have sought his models among porters or labourers, some of whom are mentioned by Malvasia (a certain Sansone in Rome and a Giacomazzo dall'Olle in Bologna); though it is significant that the artist should finally have made do with a certain Battistone, 'who was poorly built and with flat muscles' – that is, anything but athletic – but served 'to refresh his memory';[5] he then corrected his physical flaws with his brush. He occasionally used his pupils as models too; for the Bacchus in the picture that belonged to the Davia family,[6] he had Emilio Savonanzi (1580–1666) stripped, as his 'nude body was so well muscled' that he found it comparable to ancient torsos.[7]

Nor does it appear from these episodes that Guido enjoyed the same jocular rapport with his pupils as the Carracci did with theirs. Reni, who was shy by nature, had been the target of joking as a boy, when Ludovico found it amusing to make him blush with his compliments, remarking that he would make a perfect model for one of his angels.[8] In addition, pupils' practices at the Carracci's workshop, such as secretly making portraits of each other while they went about their tasks or sitting for each other as models, must have been one of the aspects of the jovial and fun atmosphere 'between equals' that characterised the teaching given to those who considered themselves to be on the path – *incamminati* – to the natural. Reni, however, had not cultivated such amiable relationships with his young pupils, 'perhaps more out of fear of himself than hatred of others', noted Bandinelli.[9] On feast days he did not like to be seen in their company and preferred to go for strolls on his own, avoiding the busiest streets; he even criticised his colleagues, who would strut around with their retinues of disciples.[10] Even today experience shows that pupils like to be acknowledged as such; it must therefore have been highly frustrating for the young men who frequented his workshop not to be seen out and about in the city with their master, on whom they lavished attentions of all kinds in private, to the extent of fighting over who would hand him his brush or palette.

Indeed, Reni's almost painful awareness of his own excellence, which had guided his decisions since the start of his career, manifested itself in an inability to show his true feelings, making him appear aloof and disdainful. This was also the likely cause of his loneliness, which he was unable to remedy except by allowing himself to be possessed by the demon of gambling, a 'vice' that is stressed by all his biographers, though it never sullied his huge prestige. When he died those who had remained at his side for varying lengths of time went down different avenues, and it was clear to them all that his passing marked the end of an era. Despite competing openly with him throughout his career, Francesco Albani (1578–1660), an artist who was an apprentice at the same time as Reni, first at the workshop of Denys Calvaert (c. 1540–1619) and later with the Carracci, stated in this connection that never again would 'a new Guido come into this world'.[11] Reni's pictures lived on and continued to supply the flourishing market for copies which the artist, under pressure from his debts and an overabundance of commissions, had never been able or willing to hinder.

It is therefore striking, in the light of the above statements, that Reni should have ended up adopting a teaching model he himself had harshly criticised on leaving the – overly coercive – workshop of Calvaert, who would order his pupils to make replicas of his paintings without any variations.[12] But times had changed and the fashion for pictures known as *quadri da stanza* – which had only just appeared in Bologna in Calvaert's day, generally in relation to small cabinet paintings – had fully caught on. In addition to major public commissions, for which it was essential to be able to rely on assistants, private tastes in decoration were shifting from frescoes and fabric or embossed leather wall coverings to increased orders for easel paintings to embellish mansions. This spurred the emergence of new types of pictures:[13] a demand that proved highly promising for painters, of whom Guido was precisely one of the most dedicated and sought-after.

As for the first of these qualities, the 'account book' Reni kept from 1609 to 1612 records the amounts paid to the assistants who had cooperated with him on the major public commissions dating from those years.[14] They were painters who already enjoyed a reputation, such as Antonio Carracci (c. 1583–1618), Francesco Albani, and Giovanni Lanfranco (1582–1647), to whom he entrusted the parts he calculated he would not be able to finish himself. As a consequence, the resulting works were not fully coherent: for instance, the frescoes executed by other artists in the Cappella dell'Annunziata in the Palazzo del Quirinale clearly illustrate his various assistants' stylistic leanings.

Daniele Benati

Fig. 49 Giovanni Francesco Gessi and Giovanni Giacomo Sementi after cartoons by Guido Reni, *Christ in Glory and Angels*, 1614–16. Fresco. Ravena, Duomo, Cappella del Santissimo Sacramento

A good example is the lunette with 'seven *puttini*' that Albani felt at liberty to paint in the gentle, naturalistic style he had learned from his long stint with Annibale Carracci.[15] Pope Paul V, who had commissioned the paintings, complained, though Guido managed to extricate himself from the predicament with a brilliantly witty remark, to which we will return in due course.

Back in Bologna, Reni found it necessary to take on young painters who, although already trained by other masters, were more flexible in complying with his requests and could even stand in for him. That is how his workshop came to be joined by the Bolognese Francesco Gessi (1588–1649) and Giovanni Giacomo Sementi (1583–1636), painters who had initially trained with Calvaert and started out on their own under the influence of Ludovico in particular. Together with the less known Bartolomeo Marescotti (c. 1590–1630), from 1614 to

1616 they all helped Guido decorate the chapel of the Santissimo Sacramento in Ravena cathedral, a commission from Cardinal Pietro Aldobrandini, and executed a large proportion of the frescoes after Reni's preparatory cartoons to the client's full satisfaction [fig. 49].[16] Reni also enlisted their help later on: in 1617, replying to the request to decorate some ceilings in Mantua at the behest of Duke Ferdinando Gonzaga, Guido gave the names of his two collaborators, whom he declared to be 'masters' and accordingly capable of working autonomously – that is, without needing to use his cartoons.[17] He likewise took them with him to Naples in 1621 to assist him with the decoration of the Cappella del Tesoro in the cathedral; however, following his hasty departure from the city due to threats from local artists, it appears that Gessi attempted to take his place there, sparking the first quarrel with the master.[18] As for Sementi, in 1624 he entered the service of Cardinal Maurice of

Fig. 50 Giovanni Giacomo Sementi, *The Holy Family with the Infant Saint John and three Angels*, c. 1630. Oil on canvas, 97 × 134 cm. London, private collection

Savoy and pursued an important career in Rome, remaining there until his death [fig. 50].[19] Gessi and Sementi are among the first of many artists for whom frequenting Guido's *stanza* for a period of varying length served as a springboard for a career pursued along personal paths that were not always consonant with the results sought by their master.

Besides altarpieces and large fresco decorations, in Rome Reni had already begun to take an interest in painting heads or half-length figures that emphasised the expressions of biblical or mythological characters, conveying an action solely through gestures and gazes. Of course, this was by no means new, as similarly conceived paintings had been produced throughout the sixteenth century, especially in northern Italy. They also enjoyed great success in Rome in response to the new demand for medium-sized pieces to hang in the rooms of homes where the *quadreria* (picture collection) was displayed. Guido contributed unquestionably original features to this type of painting, thanks in particular to his early reflections on Raphael's *Ecstasy of Saint Cecilia* (then in the church of San Giovanni in Monte and now in the Pinacoteca Nazionale in Bologna).[20] What the young Guido most admired about this extraordinary painting was the expressiveness of the saint's heavenward gaze, in silent communion with the divinity. Reni's *Saint Cecilia playing the Violin* painted for Cardinal Odoardo Farnese during his early years in Rome, of which several examples with a problematic autograph status are known,[21] is a good illustration of the potential that Guido attempted to harness from the sublime Raphaelesque

model with a view to producing a type of picture in which a single, isolated, half-bust-length figure could convey an entirely inner and spiritual 'action'. Reni's intense explorations in the field of *quadri da stanza* were along this path. The intensity of his *arie delle teste* (literally 'airs of the heads', outward expressions of inner emotion), capable of representing the ineffable solely through the force of the gaze, earned him outstanding fame. As a result, the young assistants who helped him with more demanding commissions also had to produce replicas of inventions of this kind, which aroused such enthusiasm among collectors.[22]

The fullest information about the running of his workshop – or *stanza*, as he preferred to call it – comes from Carlo Cesare Malvasia, who had the chance to get to know personally both Reni and many painters who frequented it. The truth is that not even the term *stanza* is appropriate, as Guido worked in different places throughout his lifetime, none of which he owned but rented, and there were periods when he even painted in more than one at the same time.[23] The house where he died belonged to his friend Giovan Battista Ferri and was located behind the basilica of San Petronio;[24] Guido had previously worked in several premises located in what was called the Mercato di Mezzo, adjoining the Piazza Maggiore, and for a time rented several rooms in the Palazzo Fantuzzi on the Via San Vitale, which were later occupied by Gessi.[25] According to the inventory of Guido's estate,[26] the last house that also doubled as a studio was on the Via delle Pescherie in the Mercato di Mezzo and consisted of many rooms: on the ground floor were the studios used by his pupils and the one where 'Signor Guido painted'; and on the upper floor, in addition to the kitchen and storerooms, were his bedroom and those of Bandinelli and a servant. Guido's houses-cum-workshops were not decorated with fine furniture; instead, they were crammed with disorderly piles of unfinished or roughed out paintings, primed canvases, stretchers, and tools of his trade: he replied to those who reproached him for this untidiness that the great personages who visited him did not come looking for luxurious furnishings.[27] What is more, not having any children or close relatives, he did not deem it necessary to accumulate possessions to bequeath.[28]

What is impressive is the number of young people Guido surrounded himself with, allowing them to work in his own home-cum-studio. As Malvasia put it, 'It is impossible to draw up a register … of all the students in Guido's school', since if they were all counted they would number two hundred.[29] Although evidently an exaggeration, this statement is based on a sound truth. So generous was Reni's hospitality that he never expelled any pupils unless they had given him good reason to do so, and Bandinelli, Loli, Lauri, and Sirani worked in Reni's home until he died.[30] However, it was inevitable that the commotion caused by bringing so many young men from different places together under the same roof, sometimes so careless that they ruined his paintings, ended up annoying the master. He finally decided that only the most trustworthy could work in his studio, allowing the rest to occupy other parts of the house.[31] Among the first group were the Bolognese Lorenzo Loli (c. 1612–1691) and Giovanni Andrea Sirani (1610–1670), whom, as he had done formerly with Gessi and Sementi, he used to jokingly call 'his masters of the chamber'.[32]

It is therefore difficult to ascertain what Reni's *bottega* was like and what type of teaching was imparted there. Few painters appear to have trained fully with him, going from mere apprentices to assistants and then to masters in their own right, as was common practice at traditional workshops. This was true, for example, of Sirani and the abovementioned Bandinelli; nearly all the rest were painters who hailed from different backgrounds and were therefore already trained. In exchange for their assistance, Guido offered them the chance to use his home and studio, allowing them to grow professionally by following his example and advice. To use a present-day academic term, we might say that Guido's workshop, more than a place where basic teaching of any kind was imparted, was a sort of specialist 'school for further training' open to young men wishing to gain access to a prestigious career. In fact, it often so happened that, unable to accept all the commissions he received, Reni would recommend a pupil to his client, who managed to save a considerable amount of money and achieved results that were guaranteed in some way by the master's supervision.

The case of Gessi and Sementi being sent to work for the Duke of Mantua was repeated, for example, in 1637, when Guido was engaged to paint three altarpieces for Pope Urban VIII for the church adjoining the Forte Urbano in Castelfranco (now Castelfranco Emilia, between Bologna and Modena). Already busy with the huge painting of *Bacchus and Ariadne* commissioned by Cardinal Francesco Barberini as a gift for Henrietta Maria, the wife of Charles I of England,[33] Reni put forward the names of Michele Desubleo and Pietro Lauri, and recommended the Pesarese Simone Cantarini (1612–1648) for the most challenging painting on the subject of the *Transfiguration*.[34] Cantarini, who had joined Guido's workshop around 1633–34, executed the picture in his master's studio and when Reni saw it he did not hesitate to point out its flaws, particularly the excessively large proportions of the figure of Saint Peter in the

Fig. 51 Simone Cantarini, *The Transfiguration*, 1645. Oil on canvas, 310 × 200 cm. Vatican City, Palazzo Apostolico, Cappella Paolina

foreground [fig. 51]. In front of Simone and the other disciples, Guido marked in chalk the part which, in his opinion, should have been smaller, much to the annoyance of the young man, who, irked by the criticism, turned the painting towards the wall so that nobody else could comment on it; he later left Reni's workshop and looked for somewhere else to live and work.

The case of Cantarini is paradigmatic. Trained in Pesaro with Giovanni Giacomo Pandolfi (1567–after 1636) and the Veronese artist Claudio Ridolfi (1570–1644), he was gifted with a talent that had enabled him to establish a reputation as a painter in his homeland, and his presence alongside Reni certainly does not indicate he was a pupil of his. Indeed, like Gessi, Sementi,

Fig. 52 Michele Desubleo, *Allegory of Truth*, c. 1630.
Oil on canvas, 100 × 94 cm. Private collection

Desubleo, and others, he was an artist with a style of his own that was largely indebted to the experience gained before joining Guido's workshop. His admiration for Reni had undoubtedly grown thanks to the pictures the latter had sent to the Marche region, such as *Christ giving the Keys to Saint Peter*, painted for Fano in 1626,[35] and the *Pala Olivieri*, formerly in Pesaro cathedral;[36] however, it is difficult to believe what Malvasia says about Cantarini passing himself off as a novice in order to be taken on by Reni and benefit from his teachings. It seems more likely that the painter from Pesaro, whose boastful nature Malvasia himself stresses, would have attempted to artfully win the painter's appreciation only to then fall out with him through constant provocation and effusiveness. Even in terms of pictorial results, Cantarini's achievements during his period of closest contact with the master are distinguished by an inclination towards naturalism that shows him to be alien to Reni's ideal thrust.

After Gessi and Sementi, Reni was joined by other painters who had trained elsewhere and already proved their worth. The Fleming from Maubeuge Michel Desoubleay, whose name was soon Italianised as Michele Desubleo (1602–1676), had probably been a pupil of Abraham Janssens (c. 1575–1632) in Antwerp and had travelled to Rome in 1624 with his stepbrother Nicolas Régnier (1591–1667); this explains why there was a work of his in Vincenzo Giustiniani's collection by 1638.[37] Although his heroines always have heavenward gazes, the glazed, almost porcelain-like appearance of the brushwork in his paintings is very different from the master's agitated, vibrant execution [fig. 52]. As for the Troyes native Jean Boulanger (1608–1660), whom Malvasia reports as having been with Reni 'for ten years', it is known that he learned the rudiments of the profession from his father, Olivier, who had a reputation above all as a painter of *destrempe*. This technique, similar to gouache, undoubtedly accounts for the extraordinary freedom of execution that characterises Boulanger's paintings, especially his frescoes.[38] In the case of the Frenchman Pierre Laurier, who was known as Pietro Lauri (act. in Bologna 1639–69), it is reasonable to think that he was not trained in Guido's teachings, though he enjoyed his support for a long time.[39] Another artist with a very personal style was the Milanese Pier Francesco Cittadini (1616–1681), who above all geared his activity to genres that neither Reni nor any other fellow disciples wished to practise, such as still life and everyday scenes [fig. 53].[40]

As in the case of Cantarini and the other artists mentioned so far, a more or less long spell with Reni did not result in a lasting conversion to his style. In this connection we find the surprising example of the Veronese artist Antonio Giarola, known as 'Il cavalier Coppa' (c. 1597–1674), who is documented in Rome between 1617 and 1619 in the workshop of Carlo Saraceni (c. 1570–1620) and was subsequently active in his homeland, where he practised a heightened naturalism.[41] Veronese sources also report a subsequent stay in Bologna, first with Albani and later with Reni, who had him copy his paintings. Giarola's most impressive result in this field is the replica he made between 1636 and 1638 of the *Allegory of Fortune* executed by the master for Abbot Giovanni Carlo Gavotti [fig. 54].[42] As Giarola had not complied with the conditions established by Reni – he not only showed the picture in public before it was finished but also instructed Girolamo Scarselli to secretly make a print of it – out of spite Guido transformed the copy painted by the Veronese artist into a new version, an autograph replica of his own picture, simply by replacing the bag of coins held by Fortune with a crown.[43] Recently identified as the canvas that arrived at the Accademia di San Luca in Rome,[44] Giarola's copy is surprisingly similar in style to the master's, whose brushwork

Daniele Benati

he imitates perfectly, achieving a result that is slightly softer and less crystalline in appearance, also evidently influenced by his knowledge of Albani's style. However, Giarola's mastery of Reni's manner did not prevent him painting in his usual style, as attested by the beautiful altarpiece of *Verona imploring the End of the Plague* sent to his home city (Verona, San Fermo) in 1636 and the *Presentation in the Temple* still on view in the church of the Voto in Modena.[45] The inspiration drawn from Guido's famous model[46] is expressed in an original manner, with touches of an almost rustic naturalism. Giarola therefore proves himself to be a painter capable of using different manners of execution: completely mimetic when copying Reni's pictures and absolutely personal when working independently.

The abovementioned example brings us to the tricky issue of copies, a task to which the collaborators who frequented Reni's workshop were assigned. In order to defend his favourite painter's reputation, Malvasia states that these copies were mostly made secretly, possibly at the behest of a disloyal servant or dishonourable dealer who aimed to sell them later as the master's originals.[47] Actually this was not the case, as it was Guido himself who encouraged the production of copies to disseminate his famous paintings outside Bologna. The success his

models enjoyed was gauged by the number of copies ordered of them: in the case of the *Christ on the Cross with the Virgin, Saint Mary Magdalene and Saint John the Evangelist*, painted for the Bolognese church of the Cappuccini,[48] Boulanger was chosen to produce a copy for Flanders, while Gessi painted two for Modena and Giovanni Battista Bolognini (1611–1688) another for Parma.[49] Small copies (*in piccolo*) were also made, such as the one executed by Reni himself for Cardinal Gessi, who placed it on the altar of his chapel in the church of Santa Maria della Vittoria in Rome, though it differs in part from the original because the 'great talent' could not bring himself to make an exact replica of his own work.[50] Besides copies of the entire compositions, many were produced of the heads of individual figures, each of which was intended to express a particular emotion and convey it to the viewer.

With respect to the *Allegory of Fortune*, existing sources allow us to solve the problem of distinguishing an autograph painting by Reni from a copy. In other cases we must rely solely on the connoisseur's expert eye, with all the difficulties entailed by judging paintings that survive in varying condition and are almost never available for comparison. In general, a copy differs from the original in that the copyist merely imitates the end result – that

Fig. 53 Pier Francesco Cittadini, *Vulcan and Bacchus*, c. 1640. Oil on canvas, 115 × 150 cm. Private collection

Fig. 54 Guido Reni, *Allegory of Fortune*, 1635–36. Oil on canvas, 158 × 130 cm. Private collection

is, without repeating the elaborate execution process involved in creating the model. It is not simply a case of *pentimenti* or corrections, which can also occur when copying another painting, but manners of execution characteristic of a particular artist. Following a detailed comparison of the more than fifteen surviving examples of the composition Guido adopted for the *Lucretia* he painted between 1622 and 1623 for the Patrizi family in Rome,[51] it seems to me that only one [fig. 55][52] displays the highly intelligent application of paint characteristic of the autograph pictures from this stage in Guido's career. According to this process, to construct the figure the artist began with a quick sketch *alla brava* using a brush dipped in grey paint that was designed to be visible beneath successive layers of colour. It can be seen, for example, in the knuckles of Lucretia's right hand and in the folds of her chemise, which has a dazzling white appearance owing to the abundant lead white finish.[53]

These stages of execution follow the dictates first of the mind and then of the hand; copies merely transcribe the effect, failing

to grasp the intrinsic necessity. In comparison, other examples of the same composition, although also of fine quality, are inevitably no more than copies produced by skilled imitators who worked in the master's studio.[54] It is nevertheless surprising to discover a perfect interpretation of Reni's manner of painting in a picture by Carlo Maratta (1625–1713) in which the theme of Lucretia's suicide is handled very similarly [fig. 56].[55] It is evident that this great artist from the Marche region, a leading figure on the Roman cultural scene from the late 1600s to the early 1700s, had the opportunity to reflect on Reni's *Lucretia*, then in the Patrizi collection; and also that Malvasia was right to include Maratta among the artists who, despite belonging to other schools, had assimilated Guido's example in both form and execution technique, particularly in the manner of applying the whites, endlessly using 'white lead to excess'.[56] There are other interesting cases where artists of an unusually high standard compete, as it were, with Guido, and even aim for personal effects when imitating his compositions. Rather than dwell on the examples provided by Cantarini, which are well known,[57] I would like to comment on how the Fleming Jan van Dalen (act. 1632–1670), who possibly spent a stint in Reni's workshop, measures himself against the Bolognese master in *Salome receives the Head of Saint John the Baptist from a Page*, a painting that is unfortunately only known through copies.[58] Van Dalen imbues his version [fig. 57] with a dynamic painterly quality, employing rapid, highly visible brushstrokes that sometimes create an 'unfinished' effect.[59]

In Reni's output the dialectic between autograph paintings and copies is further complicated by his increasingly systematic use of the procedure of *ritocco*, or retouching. This term, which Malvasia consistently uses, must have been very common: it refers to copies executed by pupils which the master then retouched in order to turn them into 'autograph' works in a sense. This was a well-known practice in Renaissance workshops but inevitably gained fraudulent connotations at a time when the art market was growing progressively more demanding. Guido had to come up with a witty remark to justify its use in a somewhat embarrassing situation that occurred during his youth. It so happened that Pope Paul V unexpectedly came across Lanfranco working in Reni's place atop the scaffolding in the Cappella dell'Annunziata in the Palazzo del Quirinale. The pope reproached Guido for being more interested in money than work, reminding him that the frescoes had been commissioned from him and therefore had to be made 'with his own hands'. With considerable audacity, Reni replied to the pope that transferring the drawing from cartoons to wall, roughing out the

Daniele Benati

figures, and painting the backgrounds did not make the 'work', just as a papal chirograph could not be called as such until the pope had put his signature to it.[60]

The episode refers to frescoes, but Guido's reply is also applicable to easel paintings. His 'signature' – that is, the distinctive mark that made the work autograph – could therefore consist of adding the finishing touches to a picture painted by another artist. Reni began to put this principle into regular practice in order to deal with his numerous commissions and gambling debts, as it spared him having to repeat himself and saved time. If we had to name all his *ritocchi*, the list would be endless, as Malvasia reminds us,[61] adding that in some cases it was his own disciples who sold as 'retouchings' – that is, as substantially autograph works – practice copies made by them and simply corrected by Guido. When the master found out he expelled them from the workshop.[62] As can be seen, it was quite a slippery issue.

Indeed, whereas the use of Giarola's copy to make the second version of the *Allegory of Fortune* is a very interesting case in that some judged the new picture to be even better than the one painted entirely by Reni, the same was not true of the second version of the *Abduction of Helen*, which Cardinal Bernardino Spada ordered from Reni in 1631. For this purpose the artist used a copy previously made by Giacinto Campana (c. 1600–c. 1650), guaranteeing that he would retouch it to bring it up to the standard of the original: compared to the latter, now in the Louvre [fig. 35], the copy housed in the Galleria Spada in Rome has a lifeless appearance, and Reni's promised involvement may therefore be suspected to have been very scarce.[63]

A different matter is the case of the *abbozzi* or sketches, a large number of which appear on the list of the possessions found in the artist's home following his death. Once again according to Malvasia, they were pictures that Reni had begun to

Fig. 55 Guido Reni, *Lucretia*, c. 1622–23. Oil on canvas, 84.5 × 73.5 cm. London, private collection

Fig. 56 Carlo Maratta, *Lucretia*, c. 1685. Oil on canvas, 82.5 × 77.5 cm (with later additions, 112.5 × 86.5 cm). Patrimonio Nacional. Colecciones Reales. Palacio Real de La Granja de San Ildefonso, inv. 10027850

Fig. 57 Jan van Dalen after Guido Reni, *Salome receives the Head of Saint John the Baptist from a Page*, c. 1645. Oil on canvas, 167 × 130 cm. Whereabouts unknown

rough out, taking them to a degree of finish equivalent to the value of the down payment received so that they could be delivered if his clients, tired of waiting so long, asked for a refund. For each of the canvases found in this state, the executors of his will took it upon themselves to approach the respective clients and ask them if they wished to be refunded the money they had advanced or keep the sketched-out works and nearly all of them, Malvasia reports, chose the *bozzi* rather than the money.[64] Others were acquired by collectors and dealers and Cardinal Giulio Cesare Sacchetti (1587–1663) also purchased many of them, as a result of which paintings such as the *Blessed Soul* [cat. 96] and the *Girl holding a Wreath* [fig. 48], together with part of his collection, later passed to the Musei Capitolini in Rome. The Hercolani princes acquired the *Flagellation* [cat. 94] and the

Madonna della Ghiara adored by Saint Francis – canvases now housed in the Pinacoteca Nazionale di Bologna – the latter having been commissioned by the presidents of the Monte di Pietà de Reggio Emilia for their altar in the sanctuary of the Madonna della Ghiara. Many other *bozzi* are now in museums and private collections. Apart from the contingent reason why they were left in an unfinished state – an issue to be discussed at length in subsequent literature – there is no doubt that these paintings are one of Guido's most fascinating achievements as they reveal what Roberto Longhi matchlessly defined in 1934 as the 'almost Buddhist motive' of his art, which is characterised by 'a yearning for ecstasy, where the body is but a murmured recollection, a trace'.[65]

1 The term *scuola* is used in the title of the book edited by Emilio Negro and Massimo Pirondini (Negro and Perondini 1992), which contains reports – not always correct – about the activity of many painters who came into contact with Guido Reni in very different ways.

2 This bitter reflection is found in a passage of notes that were made by Malvasia for his *Felsina pittrice* (1678) but never used (*Scritti originali del conte Carlo Cesare Malvasia spettanti alla sua Felsina pittrice*, Bologna, Biblioteca Comunale dell'Archiginnasio, Ms B16; Malvasia–Pericolo 2019, 1:503).

3 Malvasia 1678, 2:80: 'Le belle idee bisogna averle qui in testa'. For the English translation, see Malvasia–Pericolo 2019, 1:181.

4 Malvasia 1678, 2:80: 'Ch'avea ceffo di rinnegato'. For the English translation, see Malvasia–Pericolo 2019, 1:181.

5 Malvasia 1678, 2:80: 'Ch'era di corporatura infelice, e di muscoli bassi, ma che a bastanza a lui serviva, valendosene in quest'ultimo per rinfrescamento di memoria'. For the English translation, see Malvasia–Pericolo 2019, 1:181.

6 On the difficulties of identifying this picture, see Malvasia–Pericolo 2019, 1:333, note 311.

7 Malvasia 1678, 2:79: 'Nudo sì ben risentito'. For the English translation, see Malvasia–Pericolo 2019, 1:181. For all the information provided here on Reni's use of models, see Malvasia 1678, 2:79–80; Malvasia–Pericolo 2019, 1:178–81.

8 Malvasia 1678, 2:7.

9 Malvasia–Pericolo 2019, 1:495: 'Forse più per più timore di se stesso che [per] odio al prossimo'.

10 Malvasia 1678, 2:61.

11 Ibid., 2:84: 'un altro Guido'.

12 Ibid., 2:5–6.

13 Danesi Squarzina 1998.

14 Pepper 1971a and 1971b; Morselli 2022c. This booklet, which entered the holdings of the Pierpont Morgan Library in New York (MA 2694) in 1968, was known to Malvasia, as it had been a gift from Giovanni Andrea Sirani, and there are considerable references to it in his *Felsina pittrice*; Malvasia 1678, 2:17.

15 Puglisi 1999, 124, no. 37. The heterogeneousness of the styles that characterises the Cappella dell'Annunziata is also commented on in Malvasia 1678, 2:20.

16 Hibbard 1965, 508–10. Reni's authorship of the lunette with *Elijah and the Angel* is rightly argued by Faietti 1988.

17 Generally assigned to the lost decoration of the Villa Favorita in Mantua (Askew 1978, 283–84; Malvasia–Cropper and Pericolo 2013, 212, note 329), the involvement of Gessi and Sementi has correctly been identified

in the ceiling of the Gallery of Mirrors in the Palazzo Ducale (Berzaghi 1995; L'Occaso 2003, 55–57).

18 On Gessi, see Malvasia–Cropper and Pericolo 2013.

19 On Sementi, see Pellicciari 1984; Francucci 2014, 73–80 and 83–88; Francucci 2015; Serafinelli 2015.

20 Bologna, Pinacoteca Nazionale di Bologna, inv. 577.

21 Gatta 2022, 77.

22 Essential readings on the pricing policy Reni pursued throughout his career are Spear 1997 and Morselli 2008.

23 Malvasia 1678, 2:60.

24 Morselli 2022d, 96–97. His commemorative tombstone is located in a building at the corner of what is now Via Farini (formerly Via del Libri) and Via del Cane.

25 Morselli 2008, 78.

26 Spike and Di Zio 1988.

27 Malvasia 1678, 2:60.

28 Ibid., 2:47.

29 Ibid., 2:58: 'De gli Allievi della sua Scuola è impossibile il metterne assieme un registro'. For the English translation, see Malvasia–Pericolo 2019, 1:133.

30 Malvasia 1678, 2:69.

31 Ibid., 2:32, who this time quotes the names of Pietro Lauri (Pierre Laurier), Jean Boulanger, Lorenzo Loli, Giuliano Dinarelli, and Giovanni Andrea Sirani.

32 Ibid., 2:64: 'I suoi maestri di camera'. For the English translation, see Malvasia–Pericolo 2019, 1:147. More than as a painter, Lorenzo Loli is known as an etcher, an activity in which he finally replaced Cantarini, on whom Guido relied, but as he himself stated 'preferiva tagliare le cose proprie, non le altrui' ('he preferred to make etchings of his own things, not those of others') (ibid., 2:440). On Loli and, in general, Reni's prints, see Candi 2016.

33 For the eventful history of the huge canvas, of which only a few fragments survive, see Madocks 1984.

34 A. Emiliani in Emiliani 1997, 96–102, no. I.14.

35 Paris, Musée du Louvre, inv. 526.

36 Vatican City, Musei Vaticani, MV.40389.

37 Salerno 1960, 97. Suggested in Peruzzi 1986, Desubleo's Roman stay has been demonstrated by research on the stati d'anime, records of the people who, house by house, had received Communion during Easter (Lemoine 2007, 372). On the artist, see Cottino 2001; Girometti 2022.

38 Sirocchi 2018.

39 On Pietro Lauri, see M. Cellini in Negro and Pirondini 1992, 295–99.

40 On Cittadini's activity in the field of still life, see Benati 2000. His skill as a painter of figures too is illustrated by the Vulcan and Bacchus reproduced here [fig. 53], also decorated with large sections of fruits.

41 For his Veronese production, see Brognara Salazzari 1974; Marinelli 1982.

42 Recognised in Pepper and Mahon 1999, Reni's original reappeared on the international market in 2013 (Dorotheum, Vienna, 15 October 2013, no. 595).

43 Carlo Cesare Malvasia mentions the episode (Malvasia 1678, 2:32 and 2:41), and Filippo Baldinucci (Baldinucci–Ranalli 1845–47 [1846], 4:29–30) speaks of it in greater detail in 1686: according to the latter, the picture painted by Giarola was 'd'assai maggior pregio di quello del Gavotti' ('much more valuable that Gavotti's'), a work entirely by Reni. Completed in 1639 (Assarino 1639, 27–28), the second painting was acquired by Monsignor Jacopo Altoviti of Florence while passing through Bologna to visit his cousin, Cardinal Sacchetti, the papal legate in Bologna from 1637 to 1640.

44 Francucci 2017. In addition, on the painter, see G. C. Cavalli in Cavalli 1954, 101–2, no. 38; Baldi, Cibrario and Jatta 2015.

45 Benati 1987; also Mazza 1996.

46 Paris, Musée du Louvre, inv. 522.

47 Malvasia 1678, 2:44.

48 Bologna, Pinacoteca Nazionale di Bologna, inv. 441.

49 Malvasia 1678, 2:30.

50 Ibid.: 'Sì grand'ingegno'. For the English translation, see Malvasia–Pericolo 2019, 1:73.

51 Pedrocchi 2000, 267, no. 137.

52 Oil on canvas, 84.5 × 73.5 cm. Previously in the Politzer collection, Vienna; Politzer sale, Glueckselig & Wanderfer, Vienna, 7–9 December 1920, no. 78; Relarte, Milan, autumn 1964, 74, fig. 75. See Pepper 1984, in no. 89.

53 The particularities of Reni's style of execution are described at length in Malvasia 1678, 2:80–82.

54 For example, the picture in a private collection in New York, wrongly identified by Stephen Pepper (1984, no. 89, fig. 113) as the original version.

55 M. Mena in Redín Michaus 2016a, 241–43, no. 44.

56 Malvasia 1678, 2:84: 'Caricando anch'essi sterminatamente di biacca'. For the English translation, see Malvasia–Pericolo 2019, 1:189.

57 More recently, Morselli 2012a.

58 For the one in the Ringling Museum in Sarasota, see Tomory 1976, no. 132.

59 Oil on canvas, 167 × 130 cm. Formerly at Christie's, Monaco, 2 December 1989, no. 25 (as 'Giovanni Andrea Sirani, attr.'); and Sotheby's, New York, 31 January–1 February 2013, no. 169 (as an eighteenth-century copy of Guido Reni). The group of paintings I reclassified under the provisional name 'Master of the Death of Dido' (Benati 2001, 1:165) was rightly reassigned to Jan van Dalen by Crispo 2018.

60 Malvasia 1678, 2:19: 'di sua mano'. For the English translation, see Malvasia–Pericolo 2019, 1:147.

61 Malvasia 1678, 2:70.

62 Ibid., 2:32.

63 Ibid., 2:39. The issue of the two paintings is studied in Pierguidi 2012b.

64 Malvasia 1678, 2:57.

65 Longhi 1973, 203.

GUIDO RENI AND SEVENTEENTH-CENTURY SPANISH PAINTING

Javier Portús

Guido Reni (1575–1642) was one of the most famous and influential painters of his day. Several of his major works belonged to Spanish private collections and religious institutions; Spanish painters who travelled to or worked in Italy had firsthand knowledge of his art; and his compositions were widely disseminated through copies and prints. Yet until only a few decades ago his name was seldom mentioned in the literature of Spanish painting or monographs on Spanish artists.[1]

The reasons for this are varied and stem from the idiosyncrasy of the historiography of Spanish painting, a 'school' that did not gain visibility in Europe until the late 1700s and whose history was told in endogenous terms that facilitated its consideration and postulation as a unique phenomenon. The characteristics stressed in this connection, chiefly naturalism and love of colour, served to grant it a status of its own. Titian (c. 1488–1576), Caravaggio (1571–1610), Peter Paul Rubens (1577–1640), and Anthony van Dyck (1599–1641) were readily quoted during this process, whereas the names of artists held to be the aesthetic opposites of the Spaniards, such as Raphael (1483–1520), the Carracci, and Reni, were rarely mentioned. In addition, during the height of affirmation of the Spanish 'naturalists', beginning in the mid-1800s, the general prestige of the classicists dipped to its lowest point. The exceptions to this absence of references were those made by historians who, due to their origin and training, were aware of the role Reni had played in the European art of his day, such as the Britons William Stirling-Maxwell and Walter Armstrong, the Spaniard Aureliano de Beruete, and the German Carl Justi, all of whom point out or discuss general influences, albeit predominantly in a context of national 'authenticity'.

In 1916, Roberto Longhi, in a commentary on Juan Bautista Maíno (1581–1649),[2] and subsequently August L. Mayer in 1938, ushered in an awareness of Guido's influence on Spanish painting. The German scholar showed the specific ways in which Bartolomé Esteban Murillo (1617–1682) was indebted to Reni's compositions,[3] and a few years later affirmed the influence of the Bolognese school on Spanish painting, commenting that this was a chapter 'yet to be completed'.[4]

The above task was gradually carried out during the following decades. These efforts progressively grew in intensity, spurred by the adoption of a more open-minded approach to the history of Spanish art and the incorporation of increasingly varied phenomena into the field of study. Scholars accordingly shifted away from the 'endogenous' mindset and examined the history of the painting related to Spain as a phenomenon inextricable from the developments that were taking place in Europe. In addition, the more detailed knowledge gleaned of Baroque artistic practices highlighted how the supposed opposites that underpinned the theoretical discussion of art (naturalism–classicism, drawing–colour, old–modern) were often superseded by everyday artistic practice, which was often more eclectic and drew from very diverse sources.

Beginning in the mid-twentieth century, with impetus from researchers such as Martin Soria, Charles de Tolnay, and Diego Angulo, a prospective approach caught on and more and more cases were reported of Spanish artists who found inspiration for their compositions in prints. The large number of examples provided until now attests to the chronological and topographical variety of intaglio compositions involved and their generally

Guido Reni, *The Immaculate Conception*
(detail of cat. 55), 1627

indiscriminate use by Spanish artists, who did not usually stop to consider the aesthetic 'affinities' of their creators and employed them at their own discretion. Prints after Reni are documented as having been used by Luis Tristán (1580/85–1624), Murillo, Alonso del Arco (c. 1635–1704), and Juan de Valdés Leal (1622–1690), among others.

Along with this interest in graphic sources, the period witnessed an increase in studies on early picture collections aimed at gleaning greater knowledge of the provenance of their artworks and incorporating collecting into the realm of art history as a phenomenon in its own right. The number of inventories of large, medium-sized, and even small collections that were unearthed and analysed grew exponentially within a matter of decades, allowing art historians to gain an accurate picture of the paintings in circulation in Golden Age Spain. The abundance of masterpieces by foreign artists in the Spanish royal collections was common knowledge, as many still remain in the country, but studies on collecting confirmed a similar tendency (albeit on a different scale) among noble collectors. All this made it possible to stress the international context to which much of Spain's pictorial ecosystem belonged and paved the way for a task that would mark an about-turn and breakthrough in the historiographical literature produced in the country: save for exceptions – such as Gregorio Cruzada Villaamil's studies on Rubens or those of Pedro Beroqui on Titian – Spanish art historians had focused on local painters, but the mid-century saw the emergence of an interest (largely spurred by Diego Angulo) in studying the presence of foreign painters and works in the country. This provided the means to document the abundance of such works and sparked a concern with seeking traces of their impact on Spanish artists. Indeed, nowadays references to received 'influences' are de rigueur in monographs on Spanish painters.[5]

In Guido's case, the endeavour to identify works of his on the Iberian Peninsula culminated in Alfredo E. Pérez Sánchez's book on seventeenth-century Italian painting in Spain, *Pintura italiana del s. XVII en España* (1965). Of the more than two hundred pictures it brings together, the author classifies thirty-five as originals, more than forty as copies, and a hundred or so as unidentified works.[6] The list has been subsequently enlarged and fine-tuned in a process to which various historians have contributed and which has so far materialised in this exhibition. During these years scholars have not only succeeded in linking further works by Reni with Spain but have also gained a better idea of the degree of authorship, provenance, and importance of works that were already known.[7] An increasing number of

Spanish paintings have likewise been found to be related in some way to the Italian painter, and thanks to the interest that has lately arisen in the phenomenon of 'copies' of pictures, a large corpus has already been compiled of copies of Reni's compositions in Spain.[8]

In his essay on Reni and Spain published in 1988, the above-mentioned Pérez Sánchez provided an overview of the importance the painter enjoyed in the country during the 1600s and 1700s and of how he left his mark on local artists.[9]

All this, together with the study of the documentary sources of the period, give us an approximate idea of Guido's place in the Spanish imaginary and painting practice in the seventeenth century, a long and uneven period. The writings of Francisco Pacheco in the 1630s, Father Francisco de los Santos in the mid-1600s, Jusepe Martínez around 1675, and Antonio Palomino in his early eighteenth-century treatise attest to the reputation the painter had gained as one of the most prestigious artists of his day, which earned him adjectives such as 'famous', 'celebrated', 'great', and 'illustrious' from Spanish writers.

The circulation of prints and copies and firsthand knowledge of the Italian's works multiplied Spanish artists' possibilities of seeking sources of inspiration in his oeuvre. This process was not progressive; that is, the increase in originals, copies, and prints did not make the artists active in the central and final decades of the century more receptive to the influence of Guido. On the contrary, it was the Spanish artists born in the late 1500s and around 1600 on whose art Reni had more of an influence (active or passive), for several reasons. The first is chronological: Guido was born in 1575 and died in 1642. The second is biographical: many of those artists (Maíno, Velázquez, Jusepe Martínez…) travelled to Italy or pursued their entire careers there (Ribera), and they all had the chance to see very important works for themselves and appreciate the prominent status Reni had attained in the Italian artistic community. A further reason is related to artistic languages: as the century progressed, Spanish painting shifted towards increasingly colourful formulas that had more in common with the formal and compositional aspects of Rubens or Van Dyck than with Roman–Bolognese classicism.

Greater knowledge of Spanish Golden Age art and broader approaches to studying it have led to new information about Reni's impact and works. However, these increasingly abundant findings in turn need to be put into perspective and subjected to a comparative analysis in order, for example, to gauge the presence and influence of his oeuvre and models in relation to that of other artists (contemporary and earlier) who also had an effect on their Spanish counterparts.

In addition, when objective data is gathered, it needs to be interpreted and assessed in connection with a broad variety of variables that can give rise to differences of opinion. For example, Guido is an important figure for understanding Jusepe de Ribera (1591–1652), and various circumstances link the two artists and their works, which contain similar elements. However, contrary to the recent critical trend of searching for and stressing the connections between them, a few specialists in the Spanish-born artist use the same information to defend his uniqueness, underline their differences, and claim that they had different narrative temperaments. The same is true of Diego Velázquez (1599–1660), with respect to whom specialists tend to either emphasise or downplay Reni's influence, depending on their own interests or perspectives. Therefore, although it is accepted that the Bolognese artist's works were generally known and used, it remains to be gauged to what extent he was a driving force behind the development of individual artists or Spanish painting in general.

During the early 1600s, when several Spanish artists were in Italy, Guido enjoyed a prominent role among the local painters and his reputation grew as the century progressed, especially following the deaths of Annibale Carracci and Caravaggio respectively in 1609 and 1610. Not only had he breathed new life into classicism and updated it compositionally and emotionally, but with his attitude to life and relationships with powerful members of society he was also seen to stand for a sort of artistic ideal. He was the Italian and classicist counterpart to Rubens, who was almost an exact contemporary. This made him an unavoidable figure for any painter living in Italy during that period and a point of reference to be emulated or reacted against.

A few contemporary sources speak of specific relationships between Reni and several Spanish painters. The most explicit link is with Jusepe Martínez (1600–1682), who often drew on his own professional experience in his treatise on painting, *Discursos practicables del nobilísimo arte de la pintura* (c. 1675). From 1623 to 1627 Martínez lived in Italy, where he came into contact with Guido and witnessed the huge prestige he had earned. He calls him 'famous', 'great', 'most famous', and 'celebrated', lavishing these adjectives on him more than on any other artist. He praises Reni's ability to judge compositions, actions, and expressions (implicitly citing him as belonging to the lineage of Raphael) and tells an anecdote that links him to the pope. Besides stating of himself that he 'had much communication' with Guido and Domenichino (1581–1641), Martínez refers to the contact Maíno also had with the former: 'a few years ago a most splendid talent emerged called Fray Juan Bautista Maíno,

who was a pupil and friend of Annibale Carracci and a great companion to our great Guido Reni, who always followed his manner of painting'.[10]

This comment led Maíno's oeuvre to be scrutinised by critics from a very early date with a view to identifying his Italian sources. Numerous names have been put forward, some at the opposite end of the aesthetic spectrum to the two great artists Martínez cites: Giovanni Girolamo Savoldo (c. 1480–after 1548), Domenichino, Francesco Albani (1578–1660), Agostino Tassi (1580–1644), and Annibale Carracci (1560–1609). However, the main names around which the discussion on Maíno and Italy revolves are Reni, Caravaggio, and Orazio Gentileschi (1563–1639). Borrowings from, or similarities with, all of them have been detected in his work, and together they remind us that the categories that have sometimes been established by artistic treatises and art historical literature are difficult to apply to certain painters, who chose what interested them irrespective of stylistic affinities.

Martínez's comment set Maíno in the context of Roman–Bolognese classicism and for some time now critics have been detecting specific influences of Reni in some of his works, such as the *Virgin of Bethlehem* formerly in Fuentes de Andalucía (Seville) – currently unlocated – whose angels are reminiscent of Guido's. So are those depicted in the area beneath the choir loft in the church of San Pedro Mártir in Toledo, whose decoration indicates a familiarity with Reni's Roman wall paintings, such as those executed in 1608–9 for the church of San Gregorio al Celio. A few compositional devices sometimes employed by Maíno likewise link him to the Bolognese master, for instance the use of a high horizon and the conception of landscape as a series of horizontal colour fields, as in *Saint John the Evangelist in Patmos* [fig. 58] and the *Penitent Magdalen in the Grotto of Saint-Baume*.[11]

But despite these and other connections with Reni and Martínez's comments, Maíno is known in the history of Spanish painting for having seen Caravaggio's works firsthand and being an early practitioner of his style. Factors which have contributed to this consideration are his sparing descriptive detail, certain lighting effects (especially in works such as *Saint John the Baptist*),[12] and a few resemblances found between the emotional mood of early compositions by the Italian (such as the *Rest on the Flight into Egypt* in Rome[13]) and scenes by Maíno. However, one of the aspects that most strongly back this connection is the similarity between Maíno's art and the oeuvre of the Caravaggist Orazio Gentileschi, which can be clearly seen if we compare these painters' palettes and contrasts as well as their highly characteristic modelling of volumes and figures.[14]

One of Maíno's distinguishing features is that although he can be classed as a member of the large family of Caravaggists, most of his compositions lack one of the traits that best define the mature Caravaggio and a good many of his followers: a penchant for drama, expressed by accentuating the contrasts of light and using a range of emotions steeped in tension, sorrow, and foreboding. Very few paintings by the Dominican convey such a mood: the aforementioned *Saint John*, the *Tears of Saint Peter* in the Louvre,[15] and above all, the lower part of the Prado *Adoration of the Shepherds*.[16] Out of Maíno's entire oeuvre, the two shepherds in the latter work, lost in thought and oblivious to what is going on around them, as if taken from a scene of Mercury and Argos, strike the most unsettling note and come closest to Caravaggesque emotion. Otherwise Maíno's paintings generally abound in smiles, gentle emotions, delicate facial and bodily expressions, and a climate of intimate devotion. Indeed, they form a corpus that comes close to Reni's emotional classicism in its tendency towards stereotyping and codification, and the emotional mood created.[17] This suggests that when Martínez stated that Maíno 'always followed his manner of painting' he was probably referring to their similarities when it came to putting together narratives (*istorias*).

Maíno marked the establishment in Spanish painting of a string of artists with a fondness for gentle and delicate emotions and intimate scenes. Some of the practitioners of this type of painting are Francisco de Zurbarán (1598–1664), Alonso Cano (1601–1667), and Murillo, who are comparable to Guido in this respect.

One of the Spanish artists active in Italy when Maíno worked there was Jusepe de Ribera, whose name is associated to Reni's in two important pieces of contemporary writing. One is Francisco Pacheco's treatise on painting, *Arte de la pintura* (published posthumously in 1649), which includes a famous paragraph where the author defends painting from life, citing as examples of this tendency Caravaggio, Ribera, and his own son-in-law Velázquez. He states that 'among all the great paintings owned by the Duke of Alcalá, [Ribera's] figures and heads alone seem to be living, and the rest painted, even if compared to paintings by the Bolognese Guido'.[18] By doing so he implicitly acknowledges Reni to be the benchmark, at the same time comparing him to those who imitate nature. In 1715 Palomino again likened the two artists in a paragraph where he compares Spanish painters with their foreign 'peers' and places both almost at the top of a pyramid, just below Titian, Velázquez, and Juan Carreño de Miranda (1614–1685).[19]

The two names are connected in another treatise on painting, *Considerazioni sulla pittura* (c. 1620), where Giulio Mancini drew a distinction between the Roman–Bolognese artists, who were characterised by 'the intelligence of their art, with charm and expression in feelings, and propriety and composition in the narrative', and the followers of Caravaggio, who always worked from life, although, he states, they were flawed in their composition of the *istoria* and in the expression of feelings.[20] While he classifies Ribera among the latter, he notes that 'Signor Guido' regarded him very highly and 'thought a great deal of his determination and handling of paint [*colorito*], which for the most part follows the path of Caravaggio, but is more experimental and bolder'.[21]

Although Reni's opinion of Ribera is documented, we do not know what Jusepe thought of Guido, though we can venture a guess. The seventeen-year age gap between them meant that during the Spaniard's formative period and early years as an artist in Rome, the Bolognese became an unavoidable point of reference owing to his prestige in breathing new life into classicism, which had secured him a social and economic status and special treatment by the powerful members of society. The Italian art scene was highly competitive and a keen creative awareness had spread among painters, who wore their aesthetic creeds on their sleeves. The oeuvre of a foremost representative of the group who was securing particular prestige was necessarily a model for Ribera to learn about, study, and emulate or challenge. Having established himself in Naples, Ribera coincided with Reni during the Italian's sojourn there in 1621.

Although, as we saw with Mancini, Ribera was clearly classed among the Caravaggists, at least two characteristics distinguish him from other naturalists and bring him closer to the classicists. One is his overriding interest in drawing, which he sometimes used as a starting point for paintings and which equipped him with impressive compositional skills. The other is that his interest in expressing emotions led him to seek a means of codifying them, and he produced a series of prints showing gestures or anatomical details which eventually gave rise to handbooks of drawings.[22]

The consequences of his practice of drawing and pursuit of expressive codification were a marked compositional balance and an ability to represent the *istoria*, which explains historians' interest in seeking links between Ribera and Reni since the mid-twentieth century. A starting point was established by Elizabeth du Gué Trapier in 1952, when she drew attention to the similarities between Ribera's *Crucifixion* in the collegiate church of Osuna (Seville) and an *Ecce Homo* by Reni,[23] and

Fig. 58 Juan Bautista Maíno, *Saint John the Evangelist in Patmos*, 1612–14. Oil on canvas, 74 × 163 cm. Madrid, Museo Nacional del Prado, P-3128

related the Spaniard's *Adoration of the Shepherds*[24] to the one the Bolognese produced for the charterhouse of San Martino in Naples [fig. 31].[25] Over time these connections have progressively been studied in greater depth. Closer similarities have been found between Ribera's Osuna *Crucifixion* and Reni's homonymous work for the Capuchin monks of Bologna,[26] and both paintings have in turn been related to a famous drawing by Michelangelo (1475–1564),[27] though given the closeness of their dates of execution some historians prefer to speak of them both being inspired by this same Michelangelesque model.[28] Following Trapier's study echoes of Reni have been detected in several more of Ribera's paintings, such as the Osuna *Saint Sebastian* [cat. 18], the *Christ on the Cross* and *Saint Peter* and *Saint Paul* in the Museo Diocesano de Arte Sacro in Vitoria,[29] the Strasbourg *Saint Peter and Saint Paul*,[30] the depictions of Saint John the Baptist as an adolescent, the Nancy *Baptism of Christ*,[31] the Prado *Martyrdom of Saint Philip*,[32] the *Immaculate Conception* of the Augustinian nuns of Salamanca [figs. 34 and 75], and the Brussels *Apollo and Marsyas*,[33] which is greatly indebted to Guido's painting on the same subject in Toulouse [cat. 57].[34] These and other connections have been discussed, with fairly contradictory opinions,[35] and almost always need to be studied in depth in order to specifically ascertain whether Ribera had access to Reni's proposed models and thereby

distinguish between influences and affinities. But regardless of the category to which they belong, the existence of such associations allows us to define Ribera as an artist who shares important compositional and expressive aspects with the classicists and to single him out among the painters belonging to the extended family of 'imitators of nature'.

To determine what unites and what divides Ribera and Reni, it is useful to compare the gestural codes of the latter's 1611 *Massacre of the Innocents* [cat. 20 and fig. 60] with the former's 1646 *Miraculous Escape of Saint Januarius from the Fiery Furnace* [fig. 59], to whose parallels several Ribera specialists have drawn attention.[36] They are both tumultuous scenes dominated by a huddle of people prostrate on the ground, from which some emerge on foot. In addition, both compositions display an abundance of violent bodily gestures and expressions of horror, violence, and surprise in the form of gaping mouths, wide-open eyes, and tensed arms. Ribera's painting is the culmination of his explorations of extreme expressions in paintings and drawings, to which he wished to lend a normative status through prints that could be used as models by other artists. Apart from these notable similarities with respect to expressive devices, there are a few significant differences between the two pictures, such as Guido's use of colder, more synthetic colours, whereas Ribera employs a highly nuanced palette and is much

Fig. 59 Jusepe Ribera, *The Miraculous Escape of Saint Januarius from the Fiery Furnace*, 1646. Oil on copper, 320 × 300 cm. Naples, Duomo, Reale Cappella del Tesoro di San Gennaro

pieces of pictorial composition of his time. Ribera's narrative aim is different, however, as the story has a main character, Saint Januarius, to whose calm, engrossed, and devout gesture the group of astonished or horrified bystanders provides a counterpoint.

Another of the Spanish artists who had the chance to study Reni's works in Italy was Diego Velázquez, who first stayed in the country from 1629 to 1631 and visited cities that had played a part in Guido's career, such as Rome and Naples. When he set off on his journey Velázquez had just turned thirty and only a few months earlier had bid farewell to Rubens, who was himself departing for Antwerp and probably encouraged him to visit Italy. The Fleming was a key contact for Velázquez – not only from a strictly artistic viewpoint but also because he provided him with a living model of what the Sevillian artist aspired to become in terms of honours and prestige. In these respects the equivalent to Rubens in Italy was Reni, and Velázquez no doubt paid keen attention to Guido's works and was on the lookout for news and comments about him.

We can gain an idea of how Velázquez most likely regarded Reni from Pacheco's abovementioned comments. Although his treatise was published posthumously in 1649, part of it was written in 1632, as he hints at one point.[37] Indeed, although his son-in-law went on to play a very important role in Philip IV's service during the following years, Pacheco does not point this out or mention anything later than the Italian trip, which, in contrast, he does describe in detail. Those comments, shared and most likely encouraged by Velázquez, suggest that the latter considered himself a member of an artistic lineage to which Caravaggio and Ribera also belonged, characterised by an interest in painting from life and distinct from that of Guido, whose paradigmatic status was nevertheless acknowledged.

The process described at the beginning of this chapter, whereby the history of Spanish painting was progressively shaped as an almost autonomous phenomenon with a tendency to underline the traits that set it apart, is particularly evident in the case of Velázquez, who was long treated as the 'solitary bird' to which Ramón Gaya referred. Reni's role in this process was considered to be merely residual. His name seldom appeared in the main monographs published on the painter beginning in the late 1800s. As could not be otherwise, Justi quotes him as an important presence in his extensive mosaic of the Italian and Roman art scene but avoids linking him with Velázquez and even considers them to be opposites. Indeed, his book includes an apocryphal letter where Velázquez writes that Guido 'is the painter of his school who has most distanced himself from

more painstaking in his rendering of bodies and clothing. Similarly, Reni's human figures are based on a longstanding code of idealised types whereas Ribera's belong to the extensive naturalist family; this is related not only to the fact that Guido's are mostly female but also to the aesthetic identity of both artists. In Reni's case, the simplification to which he subjects both colour and form, combined with an emphasis on the gesture and idealisation of types, is perfectly adapted to portraying an action with collective protagonists and gives rise to one of the master-the healthy truth, certainly in colour, but in everything else too'.[38] A few years later Armstrong noted a relation with *Joseph's Bloody Coat brought to Jacob* [fig. 61], and in 1904 Beruete, while not completely denying these connections, considered that their temperaments were radically at odds.[39] As for more recent scholars, José López-Rey does not take him into account when surveying the painter's artistic career; Enriqueta Harris (well-versed in Italian art) merely draws attention to the traces of Reni in *Christ contemplated by the Christian Soul*,[40] and in Jonathan Brown's monograph his name appears in connection with the authorship of works related to the Spanish royal collection and among the Roman–Bolognese painters who cultivated the subject of the 'Sibyls'.[41]

In recent decades the pendulum has swung in the other direction and scholars have focused on seeking links between the two, to the extent that it has been claimed that in Rome Guido was 'the aesthetic reference for his brushes', and that it was from him that Velázquez purportedly acquired his 'majestic, serene, and balanced spirit'.[42] Julián Gállego paved the way for this search when he considered the cold light of the *Forge of Vulcan*[43] to be a starting point for a Reni invigorated by Velázquez.[44] This line of thought was taken up by scholars who have found the overall influence of Guido in works such as *Joseph's Bloody Coat* and *Christ on the Cross*,[45] or have pointed out specific borrowings in the *Coronation of the Virgin*,[46] the *Temptation of Saint Thomas Aquinas*,[47] and *Las Meninas*.[48] Of the varied sources suggested to account for the gesture of Ambrosio Spínola and Mauricio de Nassau in the *Surrender of Breda*,[49] Marc Fumaroli even alluded to Reni's *Encounter of Christ with Saint John the Baptist in the Desert* of 1621–31.[50]

The quotation from Pacheco, which suggests an aesthetic polarisation between naturalists and classicists, should warn us against the tendency to consider that in Italy Velázquez converted to Roman–Bolognese classicism, as the abovementioned enthusiastic comment suggests. Throughout his career the painter proved to be highly receptive to influences and very skilled at assimilating them. Around 1630 Italy saw the development of an interest in large history paintings that provided painters with an opportunity to express 'feelings'.[51] The painter paid attention to these concerns and responded by producing the abovementioned *Joseph's Bloody Coat* and the *Forge of Vulcan*, which,

Fig. 60 Guido Reni, *The Massacre of the Innocents* (detail from cat. 20), 1611. Oil on canvas, 268 × 170 cm. Bologna, Pinacoteca Nazionale di Bologna, inv. 439

together with the works of Reni, Guercino (1591–1666), Pietro da Cortona (1596–1669), and Nicolas Poussin (1594–1665), bear witness to a particularly intense period of reformulation of pictorial narration. However, Velázquez was not only attentive to what contemporary artists were doing but also drew on the city's Renaissance and classical past.

As for Reni, it is useful to compare his large history painting dating from 1631, the *Abduction of Helen* [fig. 35], with Velázquez's *Joseph's Bloody Coat* to see to what extent the painters' artistic temperaments differed. Both compositions are arranged in frieze fashion, with the figures positioned on a plane very close to the spectator and a marked emphasis on gesture; there is even a little dog in the foreground of both, with a significance that is more than anecdotal. If we look beyond this intention to create expressive, clearly legible, and monumental compositions with a sharp diction, we find many differences in a variety of aspects: Velázquez shows a greater wish to clearly separate the spatial planes and individualise the repertoire of expressions and a more naturalistic handling of anatomies and faces, which are more stereotyped in Reni's work, as befits a classicist. In addition, the palette employed in *Joseph's Bloody Coat* is a faithful reflection of the Neo-Venetianism that was spreading across Italy, and the scene in general is expressed in terms of everyday experience. With respect to colouring, as scholars since Juan Allende-Salazar and Denis Mahon have pointed out, Velázquez's picture is closer to Guercino than to Reni. Guercino is the artist who is most often cited when explaining the genesis of the painting, though names such as Jacopo Tintoretto (1518–1594), Gerard von Honthorst (1590–1656), Cortona, Masaccio (1401–1428), and Andrea Sacchi (1599–1661) have also been bandied about.

As mentioned above, two of the most striking aspects of the work are the painter's ability to distinguish between spatial planes in a composition with a frieze-like arrangement and the emphasis on expression. A contributory factor to the former is the prominent role given to the two figures on the left, whose semi-naked bodies create a more credible space than if they were dressed. The expressivity of the picture stems from the gestures of those two figures and the patriarch Jacob. Velázquez may have found models for both devices at the Villa Medici in Rome, whose façade overlooking the gardens displayed an outstanding group of Roman reliefs that also had frieze-like compositions and used the interplay of clothed and naked figures to create space. In its gardens was the ancient sculpture of the *Niobids*,[52] full of clearly legible 'gestures of sorrow' similar to that of Ruben at the far end of Velázquez's canvas.[53]

The main consequence of Velázquez's first trip to Italy was his intense contact with classical tradition through both the primary sources and their different reformulations since the Renaissance. Studying them enabled him to overcome his lingering problems of spatial construction and aroused his interest in history painting and the theory of gestures. But at the same time he retained 'imitation of nature' as a distinguishing feature and what is particular about the works deriving from that trip is their blend of classicism and naturalism. We may infer from Pacheco's comment that Velázquez was highly attentive to and appreciative of Reni's work, and it is possible to identify specific formal borrowings. Nevertheless, what prevails in him is a wish to distance himself from the codes of idealisation characteristic of the Roman–Bolognese artists and propose an alternative based on everyday experience, which is what he does in both *Joseph's Bloody Coat* and the *Forge*, compositions that are a continuation of the *Feast of Bacchus* in their mixture of 'history' and 'experience'.[54]

Returning to Pacheco's comment on imitators of nature – when he writes that the Ribera paintings 'owned by the Duke of Alcalá … seem to be living, and the rest painted, even if compared to paintings by Guido Reni' – there is every indication that this is not an abstract comparison, as other works by these artists in the duke's possession include an apostle series that he gifted to the charterhouse of Seville. The latter included pieces by Ribera, Giovanni Battista Caracciolo (1578–1635), Artemisia Gentileschi (1593–c. 1652), and Reni, copies of which served as a basis for similar sets housed in Granada and Zamora cathedrals.[55] Such a mixture of artists and styles in the same ensemble illustrates the flexibility of Spanish artists and collectors.

An example of the foregoing is the work by which Guido was represented in the apostles series: a *Saint James the Greater* [cat. 39] similar to the one in the Museo del Prado [cat. 38]. Zurbarán was probably familiar with it, as suggested by his *Saviour blessing* in the Prado,[56] which was signed in 1638 and despite its naturalistic rendering bears several similarities with respect to the scale and frontality and the execution of the backgrounds.

During the period in which Zurbarán continued to be called 'the Spanish Caravaggio', a few historians also drew attention to certain affinities with Reni. In 1848 Stirling-Maxwell quoted Reni, Titian, and Correggio (c. 1489–1534) to explain the San Diego *Virgin and Child with Saint John*.[57] Over time this idea has been further backed by claims of specific borrowings, such as the presence of singing boys clearly reminiscent of Reni in the Grenoble *Adoration of the Shepherds*[58] and in the Prado *Virgin Immaculate as a Child* of 1656 [fig. 62].[59]

Fig. 61 Diego Velázquez, *Joseph's Bloody Coat brought to Jacob*,
c. 1630. Oil on canvas, 213.5 × 284 cm. Patrimonio Nacional.
Colecciones Reales. Real Monasterio de San Lorenzo
de El Escorial, inv. 10014694

Apart from these and other formal similarities, what has served to associate Reni's name with Zurbarán and other painters is the Italian's conversion into a representative par excellence of an artistic trend with well-defined formal and above all expressive traits. This trend is characterised by a fondness for agreeable and delicate feelings, a certain codification and idealisation of gestures and faces, and harmonies of colour; and a dislike for jarring movements and marked contrasts. A substantial portion of Zurbarán's oeuvre shares these same features (though the language is different), and the same is true of several of his contemporaries.

Among them, the one traditionally considered closest to the Bolognese master is Alonso Cano. Francisco Preciado de la Vega stated in 1765 that Cano 'had a "harmonious" and beautiful manner, after Guido's taste' and the following decade Antonio Ponz remarked that 'he can be called the Guido Reni of Spain'.[60] These similarities had been reflected in collecting: Marian images by both hung side by side in the sacristy of the royal chapel at the Alcázar in Madrid.[61] However, despite Cano's 'undisguised' use of other artists' models and the fact that his fondness for prints and his sojourns in Granada, Seville, Madrid, and Valencia must have brought him into contact with originals by Reni and copies of his work, his connection with this master is not based on specific borrowings.[62]

Of the artists of the generation born around 1600, Zurbarán and Cano have traditionally been held to represent two of the trends that pervaded Spanish painting in the central decades of the century as summed up by the two nicknames by which they were known: one was dubbed the 'Spanish Caravaggio' and the other the 'Guido Reni of Spain'.[63] Naturally it was not quite as simple as that: these artists' late output had significant aspects in common and both explored similar affects. Some of the characteristics they shared and others in which they differed are found in Murillo, who, like Cano, regarded drawing as the essential basis for painting, was a sound composer and, like Zurbarán, considered nature to be the source of inspiration for his art. His, like theirs, was a world of tempered passions and

Fig. 62 Francisco de Zurbarán, *The Virgin Immaculate as a Child*, 1656. Oil on canvas, 194.3 × 157 cm. Madrid, Museo Nacional del Prado, P-8220

intimate feelings. Murillo differed from both in his technical daring and bold colours that were partly rooted in Venetian and Flemish painting and in his extraordinary narrative skills, which made him one of the artists of his time who most obviously achieved 'unity of action'.

This had been one of the aspirations of western painting since the days of Leon Battista Alberti (1404–1472) and had particularly interested the classical artists, who sought to build a well-codified vocabulary of recognisable expressions. Guido excelled in this field, using powerfully idealised faces and bodies as vehicles for these expressions. With his ability to clearly convey emotions and moods, and to interrelate all the participants in a story, merging them in a unity of action, Murillo belonged to the same lineage as Reni. He also shared with him a penchant for a range of calm and agreeable emotions, though this did not prevent him from depicting violence and horror in a lifelike manner when the subject so required. But like Velázquez, Murillo differed from Guido in two important aspects. The first is his naturalistic leanings reflected in both the facial features and the gestural codes of his human figures, which resulted in a much more spontaneous appearance and meant that his work appealed to a more varied audience. The distance between Murillo's naturalism and Reni's classicism is illustrated by the fact that, although they were artists with many things in common, the period in which the Sevillian reached the height of his posthumous fame (the mid-1800s) coincided with the moment when the Bolognese's prestige was beginning to wane. It is nevertheless telling that they were both viewed negatively by John Ruskin, who found them guilty of false sentimentalism. A further difference between Reni and Murillo lies in their concept of colour, which is directly linked to the above aspect insofar as colour and naturalism were concepts that were traditionally associated. In general, in Guido's oeuvre colour distinguishes and prescribes, whereas in Murillo's works, especially those of his mature period, it integrates and unifies, facilitating the merger of emotions and actions he achieved so well. This, coupled with the different expressive codes the artists used, causes Reni's *istorie* to be perceived as more intellectual whereas Murillo's are more immediately comprehensible and associable with everyday experience.

Murillo is one of the points of reference for the history of Reni's influence in Spain; indeed, he was the subject of the first article to be devoted to the theme.[64] In this monograph and in subsequent studies Mayer drew attention to the traces of the Bolognese master found in several of the Sevillian's Immaculate Conceptions, the link between the latter's *Saint Felix of Cantalice*

Fig. 63 Bartolomé Esteban Murillo, *The Infant Christ and Saint John the Baptist with a Shell*, c. 1670. Oil on canvas, 104 × 124 cm. Madrid, Museo Nacional del Prado, P-964

with the Child[65] and the former's *Saint Joseph and the Child* [fig. 5], the importance of Reni's angels with respect to those that appear in Murillo's *Angels' Kitchen*,[66] and the fact that the Spaniard's *Infant Christ and Saint John the Baptist with a Shell* [fig. 63] is inspired by a widely circulated etching by the Italian. The list of works by Murillo with links to Reni has been enlarged over time by a drawing of *Studies for Saint John the Baptist*,[67] the various versions of the *Christ Child asleep on the Cross*,[68] and an *Archangel Saint Michael*.[69] A further addition is the group of Immaculate Conceptions, which recall Guido's version now in New York [cat. 55] – Murillo was familiar with the original as well as copies – in their narrative simplicity, divested of allegorical elements.[70] As in other cases mentioned earlier, several of these connections are tentative and whereas some scholars underline the existence of a relationship of dependence, others, like Angulo, speak more of a 'reflection of the style of the same period'[71] and deny a specific interest in Reni.

But aside from seeking specific links, historians have drawn attention to the existence of a number of themes of which both artists were fond and which served to disseminate their prestige. These are devotional scenes with a focus on intimacy, and include examples where agreeable sentiments are predominant and others that combine resignation and sorrow: depictions of the Virgin with the sleeping Child, Mater Dolorosas and Ecce Homos, Immaculate Conceptions, and the abovementioned Baby Jesus asleep on the cross, among others.[72] In Murillo's case this repertoire (which in the nineteenth century was taken as evidence of a link with Raphael)[73] is also a sort of updated, revamped version of that in which his colleague Zurbarán had specialised and which had had such a good reception on the Sevillian art scene.

The list of Spanish seventeenth-century artists whose work shows signs of familiarity with Reni does not end here. Constantly evolving, it could be extended to include Pedro de Orrente (1580–1645) [fig. 64], Pedro Núñez del Valle (c. 1597/98–1649), Luis Tristán, Antonio de Lanchares (c. 1586–1630), Angelo Nardi (1584–1665), Antonio del Castillo (1616–1668), Sebastián Martínez (c. 1615–1667), Juan de Valdés Leal,

Fig. 64 Pedro Orrente, *Saint Sebastian*, c. 1616. Oil on canvas, 306 × 219 cm. Valencia, Iglesia Catedral Basílica Metropolitana de Nuestra Señora Santa María, Capilla de San Sebastián Mártir

Juan Carreño, Claudio Coello (1642–1693), Alonso del Arco, Francisco Ignacio Ruiz de la Iglesia (1649–1704), Pedro Núñez de Villavicencio (1640–1695), Antonio Palomino (1655–1726), and others. As a whole, it encompasses a considerable portion of the history of Spanish painting, particularly the artists active in the middle of the century. And given the paradigmatic and exemplary nature of the Bolognese's painting, it serves as a touchstone for gauging and assessing the genesis and nature of the contributions of many Spanish artists, especially in the field of devotional images.

1 I would like to thank David García Cueto and Juliette Guez for their kind help in locating information for this text.
2 Longhi 1916, 245.
3 Mayer 1938.
4 Mayer 1947, 280.
5 A general reflection can be found in the papers delivered by Peter Cherry and Enrique Valdivieso in 2005 at a conference on 'Foreign Art in Spain: Presence and Influence' (Arte foráneo en España: presencia e influencia). The subject of Italian influences has not only been studied with respect to specific artists but also in connection with large production centres, such as Rafael Japón's highly exhaustive study on Andalusia (Japón 2022b). On Bolognese painting in Golden Age Spain, see as a reference work García Cueto 2006.
6 Pérez Sánchez 1965a, 176–90.
7 An overview updated in the chapter 'El lugar de la pintura boloñesa en las colecciones españolas del siglo XVII' by García Cueto 2006, 192–212. For the works related to the Spanish royal collection, see Colomer 2006; Redín Michaus 2013. For other pieces and other collectors, see Burke and Cherry 1997; Vannugli 2009; García Cueto 2016a.
8 References to copies, for example, in García Cueto 2014; Aterido Fernández 2015, 57 and 109; García Cueto 2019 and 2021a; Japón 2022b; etc.
9 Quoted from Pérez Sánchez 1993, 95–119. For the case of Seville, see Japón 2020b.
10 Martínez–Manrique Ara 2006, 242–43: 'comuniqué mucho', 'pocos años atrás floreció un lucidísimo ingenio llamado fray Juan Bautista Maíno, discípulo y amigo que fue de Annibale Carracci y gran compañero que fue de nuestro gran Guido Reni, que siguió siempre su manera de pintar'.
11 Madrid, Museo Nacional del Prado, P-3225.
12 Basel, Kunstmuseum Basel, inv. 164.
13 Rome, Galleria Doria Pamphilj, inv. 428.
14 Maíno's relationship with Italian painting has been dealt with since the beginning of modern literature on the painter. An up-to-date review can be found in Finaldi 2009 and Ruiz Gómez 2009a.
15 Paris, Musée du Louvre, RF 2011 58.
16 Madrid, Museo Nacional del Prado, P-3227.
17 Finaldi 2009, 51.
18 Pacheco–Bassegoda 1990, 443: 'sus figuras y cabezas en todas las grandes pinturas que tiene el duque de Alcalá parecen vivas y lo demás pintado, aunque sea junto a Guido Boloñés'. For a survey of Reni's presence in Spanish writings on art, see Pérez Sánchez 1993, 95–119.
19 Palomino [1715–24] 1947, 74: 'A Correggio en la solidez, y buen color, los dos racioneros andaluces, Pablo de Céspedes y Alonso Cano; a Guido Reno [sic] nuestro insigne Españoleto José de Ribera'.
20 Mancini–Marucchi 1956–57 (1956), 1:108–9.
21 Ibid., 1:249: 'facendo gran conto della sua risolution e colorito, qual per il più è per la strada del Caravaggio, ma più tento e più fiero'. For the English translation see Felton 1991, 72. See Milicua [1952] 2016, 153–61.
22 J. M. Matilla in Cuenca García, Hernández Pugh and Matilla 2019, 261–65.
23 Bologna, Pinacoteca Nazionale di Bologna, inv. 10004.
24 Paris, Musée du Louvre, inv. 939.
25 Trapier 1952, 20–23 and 11, respectively.
26 Bologna, Pinacoteca Nazionale di Bologna, inv. 441.

27 Pérez Sánchez 1993, 106. The links between the two works have been examined in greater depth, among others, by Japón 2020b, 179.

28 For example, Lange 2004, 132–34.

29 Vitoria, Museo Diocesano de Arte Sacro, inv. 393, 295, and 327, respectively.

30 Strasbourg, Musée des Beaux-Arts. G. Finaldi in Milicua and Portús Pérez 2011, 156.

31 Nancy, Musée des Beaux-Arts, inv. 574.

32 Madrid, Museo Nacional del Prado, P-1101.

33 Brussels, Musées royaux des Beaux-Arts de Belgique, inv. 3445.

34 See, among others, Pérez Sánchez 1993, 105ff.; Benito Doménech 1991, 38–40, 102, 109, 114–15, 131, 156, and 172.

35 In contrast to the tradition embodied by Elizabeth du Gué Trapier, Alfonso E. Pérez Sánchez, and Fernando Benito, which has tended to seek similarities, some specialists underline the differences between them with respect to pictorial conception and narrative temperament. Notable among the latter is Nicola Spinosa (2008, 101, 114, 116, 118, 172, 181, 206, 260, and 291), who only finds circumstantial links.

36 See Spinosa 2008, 247.

37 Pacheco–Bassegoda 1990, 191, alludes to the date and to the fact that Velázquez was a recent informant when he writes: 'Añado a esto (por relación de mi yerno, deste año de 1632) que estando el caballero Josefino...' ('I add to this [as reported by my son-in-law, this year 1632] that while the gentleman Josefino...').

38 Justi 1953, 275.

39 Armstrong 1897; Beruete 1906, 36–37.

40 London, The National Gallery, NG1148.

41 Brown 1986, 161.

42 Salort Pons 2002, 50.

43 Madrid, Museo Nacional del Prado, P-1171.

44 Gállego 2011, 266.

45 Madrid, Museo Nacional del Prado, P-1167.

46 Madrid, Museo Nacional del Prado, P-1168.

47 Orihuela, Museo Diocesano de Arte Sacro, inv. 1.

48 Madrid, Museo Nacional del Prado, P-1174. Mena Marqués 1996; Salort Pons 2002, 60–77.

49 Madrid, Museo Nacional del Prado, P-1172.

50 Naples, San Filippo Neri dei Girolamini. Fumaroli 1997, 53; Boesten-Stengel 2015, 162.

51 Colomer 1999.

52 Florence, Gallerie degli Uffizi, inv. Sculture 1914 nn. 289–94, 297–300, 302, 304–6.

53 On the inspiration drawn from the Villa Medici sculpture, see Portús Pérez 2017, 58–60.

54 Madrid, Museo Nacional del Prado, P-1170.

55 Japón 2019; Forgione and Saracino 2019; Japón 2022b, 94–97.

56 Madrid, Museo Nacional del Prado, P-6074.

57 The San Diego Museum of Art, Gift of Anne R., Amy and Irene Putnam, 1935.22. Stirling-Maxwell 1848, 2:775–76; quoted from Glendinning 2010, 202.

58 Grenoble, Musée de Grenoble, MG 1324.

59 Pérez Sánchez 1965b; Pérez Sánchez 1993, 108–9 (also 121–27).

60 Aterido Fernández 2002, 533 and 539 respectively: 'tuvo una manera "vaga" y bella, según el gusto de Guido', 'puede llamarse el Guido Reni de España'.

61 They were there in 1686. Ibid., 490.

62 Quoted from Pérez Sánchez 1993, 110. There are possible exceptions, such as his *Virgin of Bethlehem* in Seville cathedral, as pointed out in Japón 2018c, 35.

63 The expression comes from Ponz 1988–89 (1988), 3:181. See Mayer 1947, 389–90.

64 Mayer 1938.

65 Seville, Museo de Bellas Artes, CE0119P.

66 Paris, Musée du Louvre, MI 203.

67 London, The British Museum, 1873,0614.212; Brown 2012, 68.

68 Serrera 1982, 132.

69 Vienna, Kunsthistorisches Museum Wien, Gemäldegalerie, inv. 9821; Hereza 2019, 296.

70 José Luis Colomer (2006, 217) considers him to be the Spanish painter most similar to Reni in temperament and draws attention to the parallels in their respective critical fortunes. For the Immaculate Conceptions, see also Ayala Mallory 1983, 43; Japón 2018c, 35–36.

71 Angulo Íñiguez 1981, 1:175.

72 Quoted from Pérez Sánchez 1993, 112.

73 García Felguera 1989, 201–6.

CATALOGUE

'I, GUIDO RENI, BOLOGNA'

By the late sixteenth century, the wealthy, cultured city of Bologna – part of the Papal States since 1506 – had become one of Europe's leading centres of art, celebrated in particular for the activity of its school of painting. Steeped in the Counter-Reformation spirit, local artists sought to blend long-standing traditions with a number of radical innovations pioneered by the Carracci family. These painters rejected the then-fashionable Mannerist aesthetic in favour of a more natural style, enhanced by a rereading of works by great masters such as Raphael, Correggio, Titian, and Veronese. In doing so, they created a beautiful, innovative language that could also convey the most profound religious sentiments.

It was against this backdrop that Guido Reni (1575–1642), the son of a local musician, was eventually to raise painting in Bologna to a level of perfection hitherto unattained. A shy, well-behaved child, he began to train as a painter in his early teens. Guided by the principles of the Carracci academy, Reni came to be known as 'the divine' on account of his talent for capturing spiritual qualities on canvas. He himself never regarded this skill as an innate gift, but rather as the result of enormous effort in the pursuit of beauty, a quest in which he achieved a harmonious symbiosis of line and colour.

1   Guido Reni

Self-Portrait

1595–97
Oil on canvas, 64.5 × 52 cm
London, private collection

Provenance: Sent by Guido Signorini to Ginevra Pucci (or Pozzi), Guido Reni's mother, from Rome to Bologna in 1621.

Selected bibliography: Brown 2001, 145, no. 145 (as Domenichino); Petrucci 2008, 3:721; Whitfield 2008, 40–45; Clark and Whitfield 2010, 86–88; Morselli 2012b, 289–90; Malvasia–Pericolo 2019, 1:358, note 389, and 1:364, note 408.

The history of this exceptional portrait is in part revealed by a letter (illegible in some sections) that was pasted onto the back of the canvas and re-emerged only recently, when a lining, applied at an indeterminate time, was removed and the painting cleaned. Although the entire contents of the written communication are unclear, a relevant passage can be read with relative clarity: 'With the present letter I send the portrait of Signor Guido to be given to Signora aunt Ginevra, and tell her that it is from life and he did it when he showed a little bit of beard, and tell the Signora aunt that he sends it because the secretary of the Borghese wanted Signor Guido to give it to him.'[1] A misreading of the Italian text had led to the assumption that the letter did not offer clues about the identity of its author, and that the

'Signor Guido' mentioned in it was to be identified with the painter's cousin, Guido Signorini († 1644). If correctly read, the text however indicates that the letter was penned by Signorini himself and sent to the printmaker Bartolomeo Coriolano (c. 1599–c. 1676) on 2 April 1621 – the date and addressee are noted at the beginning of the missive.

The son of Augusto Signorini and Ippolita Pucci (or Pozzi) – the sister of Guido's mother, Ginevra Pucci (1555–1630) – Guido Signorini was naturally entitled to call Ginevra 'signora zia'.[2] That Signorini was the author of the letter is also suggested by the historical context. Described in archival documents as a native of Bologna, Signorini appears as Guido's agent in transactions carried out in Rome in 1615 and 1620.[3] Guido remained very close to his cousin throughout his life. On 5 July 1641, he donated to Signorini the part of the house he had inherited from their common grandmother, Orinzia Trevisi.[4] Guido also made Signorini his universal heir, and upon the master's death, Signorini went to Bologna to take care of his inheritance.[5] When the letter was written in April 1621, Guido was in Naples, where he had been called upon to decorate the cathedral's Cappella del Tesoro. Having left Bologna in December 1620, Guido spent only a few months in Naples, and by June 1621 he was back in his native city.[6]

Well documented, Guido's relationship with Coriolano is first mentioned in this letter. Coriolano was certainly working with and for Guido in 1627, when he produced one of his memorable chiaroscuro prints for the master, *Peace and Abundance*.[7] The 1621 letter also mentions Giovan Giacomo da Mano, a disciple of

Fig. 65 Attributed to Annibale Carracci,
Self-Portrait. Oil on canvas, 45 × 35 cm.
Milan, Porro & C., sale 64, 31 May 2011, lot 110

Guido who apparently never practiced painting as a profession. Devoted to Guido, Da Mano occasionally served as an agent between the artist and his patrons outside Bologna, as he did in 1627 when he delivered a *Lucretia* by Guido in Rome that was destined for Cardinal Francesco Barberini (1597–1679).[8] From the letter on the back of the self-portrait, it is evident that Guido himself wanted the painting to be sent to Bologna during his absence from the city lest Ferrante Carlo (1578–1641), the 'secretario delli Burghesi', put his hands on it. The missive also implies that Carlo's request to obtain the painting had occurred rather recently, which may suggest that Guido stopped in Rome before heading to Naples in late 1620 or soon afterward. In all likelihood, he returned to Rome in late May–early June 1621, on his way back from Naples, in time to paint the *Portrait of Gregory XV*.[9] In his *Felsina pittrice* (1678), Carlo Cesare Malvasia records a *Portrait of Ferrante Carlo* made by Guido (most probably in 1603–5).[10] Carlo's greed for works of art is also notorious, and it is not surprising that he would press Guido to donate his self-portrait to him.

It is noteworthy that, in his letter, Signorini briefly recounts the history of the work, saying that it was executed by Guido ('l'a fatto') from life ('naturale'), and that it was painted even as Guido was growing a beard – Signorini's comment on the 'pocho di barba' would not make sense otherwise, since Guido does not seem to have ever dispensed with his usual moustache and goatee in the Spanish style. This therefore implies that the portrait was executed at the end of Guido's puberty, and because he was born in 1575, this would lead to a dating around 1593–97. Revealed through X-ray analysis, the composition that lies beneath the pictorial surface of Guido's self-portrait may be useful in further fixing the chronology. It has been remarked that Guido painted his likeness over what seems to be his own copy of Federico Barocci's (c. 1535–1612) *Saint Francis receiving the Stigmata*, a work produced in 1594–95 for a Capuchin church outside Urbino.[11] Guido might have been familiar with this altarpiece through an engraving after it executed by Francesco Villamena (1564–1624) in 1597.[12] There is another possibility. In 1595, Guido was collaborating with the Carracci, and Malvasia stresses his proximity with Agostino (1557–1602). That very year, Agostino reproduced Barocci's *Aeneas and his Family fleeing Troy* in an ambitious engraving.[13] While the history of Barocci's painting is complex, it is almost certain that the artist supplied Agostino with a drawing of the composition. Malvasia relates that Agostino sent two copies of the print to Barocci, who, dissatisfied with it, expressed his discontent in an incensed letter.[14] In light of this, it is not impossible that Agostino might have received other drawings by Barocci for reproduction in print, perhaps also the one with the then most recent *Saint Francis receiving the Stigmata*, enabling Guido not only to become acquainted with the composition, but also to develop it into a painted replica.

Be that as it may, the self-portrait betrays the uncertainties of a very young artist struggling with the technical aspects of this pictorial genre. Although little is known about his training in portraiture prior to his arrival in the Carracci workshop in late 1593–early 1594, it is fair to assume that Guido did not have much experience in painting likenesses since this did not count among Denys Calvaert's (c. 1540–1619) specialisations.[15] In a letter of about 1608 to his cousin Ludovico (1555–1619), Annibale (1560–1609) noted:

> He [Guido] is what he is thanks to us, for when he came out of [his training] under the Flemish [Calvaert], we know well what he was doing, and in the end he is not who he considers himself to be nor who everyone claims he is, since he lacks several parts [necessary] to be a true master.[16]

There might be exaggeration in Annibale's bitter remarks, but also a parcel of truth. Blinded by the myth of Guido's precocity, we tend to forget that entering the Carracci workshop must have been a great shock for Guido. It must have taken him years to catch up with the variety of technical skills taught and mastered by the Carracci, from drawing to painting and printmaking. This self-portrait may attest to the difficulties of these years. X-ray analysis shows that the palette – along with the hand that holds it – was added subsequently. Rather archaic in format, Guido's self-portrait reminds us (deliberately?) of those painted by Annibale in the early 1580s, such as the so-called *Self-Portrait* in a private collection [fig. 65].[17] But even by these works' standards, Guido's likeness relies more heavily on draughtsmanship, with the outlines sharply defining the main features as opposed to a more evocative modelling through brushstroke, and this increases the impression of hieratic fixity determined by the rather conventional three-quarter view. While the expression and pose are far from spontaneous, the self-portrait is already imbued with the graceful pride and sense of majesty that would become Guido's trademark. The young man that appears before us is not only a handsome youth, but a prefiguration of the master-to-be, his black jacket, black *ferraiolo* (mantle) – he would wrap it around his arm while painting before visitors in subsequent years – and organza white collar (a subtle chromatic counterpoint) bespeaking the social status he aspired to reach through success.[18]

Lorenzo Pericolo

1 The text reads as follows: 'Invio con la presente il Ritrato del sig[n]or Guido a darlo alla sign[o]ra zia Genevra e dirle che è naturale e l'a fatto nel mentre [?] lo mostrava un pocho di barba, e dirle alla sig[n]ora zia che lo manda perché il secretario delli Burghesi voleva che il sig[n]or Guido lo donase a lui'. Mine is a diplomatic-interpretative transcription.

2 On Ginevra Pucci (or Pozzi), see Malvasia–Pericolo 2019, 1:217, note 22, and 1:373–74, note 434.

3 Nicolaci and Gandolfi 2011, 56–57 and 149–50, docs. 9–10.

4 Morselli 2007, 77 and 127, note 19.

5 For Malvasia on Signorini, see Malvasia–Pericolo 2019, 1:331, note 305; 1:350, note 370; 1:358, note 389; 1:360, note 394; 1:378, note 457; 1:432, note 643; and 1:523, note 109.

6 For the details of Guido's stay in Naples, see Malvasia–Pericolo 2019, 1:302–3, note 233.

7 On Guido and Bartolomeo Coriolano, see Malvasia–Pericolo 2019, 1:357–58, note 388.

8 Malvasia 1678, 2:36; Malvasia–Pericolo 2019, 1:251, note 105; 1:307–8, notes 247–48; 1:334, note 315; 1:338, note 498; and 1:514, note 27.

9 Wiltshire, Corsham Court, Methuen collection. On this portrait, see Pepper 1988, 248, no. 71; Malvasia–Pericolo 2019, 1:374, note 436.

10 Malvasia–Pericolo 2019, 1:375, note 442.

11 Urbino, Galleria Nazionale delle Marche, inv. 1990 D 81. For the painting, see Lingo 2008, 185–86.

12 Kühn-Hattenhauer 1979, 172–73.

13 Malvasia–Cropper and Pericolo 2017, 1:307, note 304.

14 Malvasia 1678, 1:401.

15 For the date of Guido's arrival in the Carracci workshop, see Malvasia–Pericolo 2019, 1:224, note 41.

16 Malvasia–Pericolo 2019, 1:475, note h.

17 Posner 1971, 2:3, no. 1.

18 On Guido's habit of wrapping the mantel around his arm while painting, see Malvasia 1678, 2:63–64.

2 Guido Reni
Drawing and Colour

c. 1624–25
Oil on canvas, 120.5 cm (diam.)
Paris, Musée du Louvre, Département des peintures, inv. 534

Provenance: Nicolaes Sohier, Amsterdam, 1626; purchased in the Low Countries by Gabriel Blanchard and sold to the King of France, Louis XIV, in 1685; mentioned in the French royal collection, Versailles, 1695, 1709–10, 1737, 1760, 1784, and 1794; transported to the Louvre, 1797; on display at the Musée Central des Arts, Paris, 1798; on deposit at the Château of Maisons-Lafitte (France), 1912–44 and 1948–89.

Selected bibliography: Baccheschi 1971, 100, no. 102; Pepper 1988, 348, no. B3 (as not by Guido Reni); Pepper 1991, 89 (as by Guido Reni); Loire 1996, 303–7 (with extensive bibliography); B. Eclercy in Eclercy 2022a, 190–91, no. 65.

In his *Osservationi* (1632), the poet and novelist Francesco Belli (1577–1644) relates the most relevant events of his journey in Germany, the Low Countries, and France, undertaken at the instigation and in company of the Venetian ambassador at the French court Giorgio Zorzi (b. 1582). During his stay in Amsterdam in 1626, Belli visited the houses of two local merchants with strong ties to Italy, Guglielmo Bartolotti (Willem van der Heuvel, 1602–1658) and Nicolaes Sohier (1588–1642), noting: 'I saw there, among other things, a work by Reni that represents Painting and Drawing, which is held in the greatest esteem'.[1] While Belli does not specify whether Guido's painting was in the Bartolotti house (on Herengracht canal) or in Sohier's Huis met de Hoofden (House with the Heads, on Keizersgracht canal), documentary evidence confirms that the work belonged to Sohier: in the inventory of his estate drawn up on 9 August 1642, there is mention of 'two half-figures by Guido from Bologna'.[2] Sohier might have ordered or obtained the painting through his brother, Wilhelm (1587–1657), who lived in Padua, where he married a certain Isabella Zorzi in 1626.[3] In his testament, Sohier bequeathed his entire collection to his son, Constantijn (1624–1671), on the condition that it remain inalienable. Upon Constantijn's death in 1671, Guido's painting was most probably inherited by Constantijn's son, Nicolaes II (1645–1690), who, although bounded by his grandfather's will, might have managed to sell the work to the French painter Gabriel Blanchard (1630–1704) during the latter's trip to the Low Countries in 1685.[4] Guido's *Drawing and Colour* is first listed in the account books of the French royal household on 18 September 1686: 'To the painter Blanchard, for having fixed

[*raccommodé*] a painting by Guido that represents Drawing and Colour, 115 livres'.[5] The French verb *raccommoder* may indicate that Blanchard restored the painting, but also that he modified its format. The latter seems plausible since it is known that the painting had preserved its almost square format (81 × 87 centimetres) during its time in Amsterdam (its current circular format is made up of additions on all four sides). A drawing by the Flemish painter Jan de Bisschop (1628–1671) and a mezzotint print by the French-Dutch painter Wallerant Vaillant (1623–1677) confirm this.[6] In reproducing the composition, Vaillant also enlarged it laterally, perhaps because the outermost parts of the figures' sleeves and mantles were cropped in the original.

Guido does not seem to have been particularly interested in expressing his ideas on painting through allegory but *Drawing and Colour* is not exactly an exception among his allegorical compositions. In his testament of 1662, the archbishop of Santiago de Compostela, Pedro Carrillo de Acuña y Bureba (1595–1664) bequeathed to Burgos cathedral 'two large paintings for the capitular hall, one The Triumph of David and the other Sculpture and Painting, both by Guido with golden frames'.[7] While the attribution to Guido cannot be confirmed – both paintings remain unidentified – it is noteworthy that one of them was an allegory, 'Sculpture and Painting', a subject that was equally treated by Guercino (1591–1666) in a painting of 1637 now in the Palazzo Barberini.[8] More interestingly, another allegory by Guido, *Cupid crowning Painting*, was in Amsterdam in 1653–58 in the collection of the Dutch merchant Gerrit Reynst (1599–1658), as documented by an engraving executed by Theodor Matham (1605/6–1676) [fig. 66].[9] In all likelihood, Guido's painting was purchased by Gerrit's brother, Jan Reynst (1601–1646), who lived in Venice from about 1625 until his death. It is unknown when the painting reached Amsterdam, but for many years it might have been on display not far from *Drawing and Colour* – the Reynst house was also on Keizersgracht. A good quality copy of about 1630 of this composition, reduced in size and usually ascribed to Guido's disciple, Giovanni Francesco Gessi (1588–1649), is to be found in the Fondazione Carisbo.[10]

In the Reynst picture, the personification of Painting, a young woman, gazes upon a Cupid perched on a sort of pedestal, his quiver laden with arrows lying nearby as if momentarily dismissed. Unaware of the solemn act performed by Cupid, she remains indifferent to the laurel crown bestowed upon her, her eyes revealing her true passion, love for painting, as suggested by her hand pointing toward her palette and brushes. If in the Reynst allegory Guido made the amorous

Fig. 66 Theodor Matham after Guido Reni, *Cupid crowning Painting*, c. 1650. Engraving, 403 × 285 mm. Amsterdam, Rijksmuseum, RP-P-OB-23.311

Fig. 67 Caravaggio, *The Fortune Teller*, 1575–1600. Oil on canvas, 99 × 131 cm. Paris, Musée du Louvre, inv. 55

theme explicit through the insertion of Cupid, in *Drawing and Colour* love is summoned through the exchange of gazes that occur between the two half-figures in the painting. A handsome young man, Drawing fixes his eyes on Colour, a beautiful girl, as if filling his sight with her likeness, ready to draw her face on a sheet of paper on the table on which his hand rests while holding a stylus. Absorbed in her beloved, Colour cannot stop looking at him, her devotion to him symbolised by the gesture of her left hand planted on her breast. It is no coincidence that, in staging the amorous dialogue between Drawing and Colour, Guido adopted a half-figure format and arrangement inspired by Caravaggio's (1571–1610) *Fortune Teller* in the Musée du Louvre [fig. 67].[11] As in Guido's work, the young man and the gypsy are enthralled in one another's eyes, the former as an effect of seduction, the latter however ensuring the gullible boy is distracted so as to slip out the ring from his finger. By switching the position of the man and woman, Guido in a sense suggested that his work was a reversal of Caravaggio's: an evocation of imperishable, chaste attraction as opposed to a low-life comedy of equivocations. In depicting Drawing about to execute the likeness of the beloved woman, Guido introduces the theme of the portrait of love, of neo-Platonic ascent, which, rooted in Italian lyrical poetry, was also specific to the artistic tradition as exemplified by Michelangelo's divine heads.[12] In a remarkable manner, Guido dissolves the dichotomy between drawing and colour (Rome and Venice) that divided artists and art theorists in seventeenth-century Italy, by proposing a union between them, one where neither predominates but both coexist in mutual interdependence.

This might be Guido's own take on the Carracci's 'synthesis of styles'.[13] The vigorous handling of the brushstrokes, the bright palette marked by the predominance of yellow-orange in opposition to violet-blue, and the effects of broken colour place *Drawing and Colour* in close proximity to Guido's *Trinity adored by Angels* in the Santissima Trinità dei Pellegrini in Rome, executed in 1625 [fig. 28].[14] The work was thus executed in 1624–25 and might have been still 'fresh' when it was admired by Belli in Sohier's house in Amsterdam.

Lorenzo Pericolo

1 Belli 1632, 120: 'Vi osservai tra l'altre un pezzo del Reni che rappresenta la Pittura e 'l Disegno, tenuto in singolarissimo pregio'. See further Meijer 1992, 287.
2 Ploegaert 2018, 53: 'Twee beelden halve lijven van Guido Bollones'.
3 Zen Benetti 1972, 51, note 4.
4 Brejon de Lavergnée 1987, 458–59, no. 481.
5 Ibid., 458: 'À Blanchard peintre, pour avoir raccommodé un tableau du Guide representant le dessin et le coloris 115 livres'.
6 Loire 1996, 304–5.
7 Fernández Gasalla 1992, 431–32: 'Dos quadros grandes para la sala capitular: el uno El Triunfo de David y el otro La escultura y pintura, ambos de Guido, con cornixas doradas'.
8 Rome, Galleria Nazionale d'Arte Antica di Palazzo Barberini, inv. 813. See Turner 2017, 526, no. 236.
9 Logan 1979, 143–44, no. 26.
10 Bologna, Fondazione Carisbo, M3086. See Negro and Pirondini 1992, 246 and 255.
11 For an interpretation of Caravaggio's painting, see Pericolo 2011, 135–55.
12 On Michelangelo's 'divine heads', see Pericolo 2017.
13 On the Carracci synthesis of styles, see Malvasia–Pericolo 2019, especially 2:45–50.
14 On this painting, see Malvasia–Pericolo 2019, 1:281–82, note 185.

II

THE ROAD TO PERFECTION

Guido Reni was first apprenticed to Denys Calvaert, a Flemish painter based in
Bologna, who favoured an elegant version of late Mannerism with northern
European overtones. A harsh master, Calvaert was quick to exploit his student's
talents. Under his tutelage, Reni became an accomplished draughtsman, and
developed a striking, sensual approach to colour; he also acquired the business
acumen of his master, who had built up a flourishing trade in small oil paintings
on copper. In 1594, dissatisfied with his situation, Guido decided to further his
studies under Ludovico, Annibale, and Agostino Carracci, who around 1582 had
founded a studio – the Accademia degli Incamminati – offering practical and
theoretical training for young artists. There, Reni attended classes in life drawing
and learned printmaking and terracotta modelling techniques; he also started to
produce his own paintings, not just as part of Ludovico's team but sometimes
working independently for private clients and the clergy, or on official
commissions for the local authorities in Bologna.

3   Guido Reni

**Rest on the Flight into Egypt with
the Infant Saint John** (recto)
**Studies for Holy Martyrs, an Angel,
a Landscape and the Virgin and Child** (verso)

c. 1598–1600
Pen and brown ink on two sheets of paper glued together,
352 × 538 mm (recto horizontal; verso vertical)
Madrid, Museo Nacional del Prado, D-2131

Provenance: Isidoro Brun?; Pedro Fernández Durán; in the Museo del Prado
since 1931.

Bibliography: Mena Marqués 1983, 237, fig. 249; V. Farina in *Italian
Masterpieces* 2014, 116–17; Gatta (in press).

This drawing, remarkable for its imposing format and very rare
for its landscape theme in Guido Reni's entire production, is relatively well known [see cat.10]. The design of the early mount
– deep blue, edged with narrow gold tape embossed with a
pattern, followed by a double-ruled border in ink – and the up-
per-case handwritten attribution – 'BARBIERI (DIT LE GUERCHIN)'
– document its probable provenance, hitherto unrecorded, from
the collection of the painter Isidoro Brun (1819–1898), before
moving to the collection of Pedro Fernández Durán (1846–1930)
and from there, as a legacy, to the Museo del Prado. More specifically, the reference in French to Guercino shows that it could
be part of a group of works on paper purchased by Brun at the
Hôtel Drouot – the celebrated Parisian auction house – in
the 1860s and 70s. The passepartout bears no trace of any written annotation about the merit of the drawing, possibly given to
Brun by the painter Valentín Carderera y Solano (1796–1880),
as is frequent on the drawings sharing this provenance.[1]

Its attribution to an artist from the Emilia region – albeit the
wrong one – may have been prompted by the predominance of
the landscape over the sacred scene, a model popular in
Bolognese circles. It was correctly given to Reni by Catherine
Johnston, as Manuela Mena states after reading her handwritten
note on a mount – I suppose modern – which has been impossible to find. Accepting this attribution, Mena suggested that the
drawing was made before Guido moved to Rome because of
the strong echoes of the landscapes and the graphic style
of Annibale Carracci (1560–1609), as well as its resemblance, in
terms of execution, to three drawings of the same topic already
ascribed to the young Reni: the well-known Louvre landscapes[2]
and the *Coronation of the Virgin* in the National Galleries of

Scotland, Edinburgh [cat. 10]. This last comparison was
considered useful to date the Prado drawing to around 1595,[3]
in view of its similarity to the *Coronation of the Virgin with four
Saints* in the Pinacoteca Nazionale di Bologna, originally from
the church of San Bernardo [fig. 16], for which a later date from
around 1595 to around 1598 has only recently been proposed.[4]

Commenting on the reverse of the Prado drawing – which
can be read both vertically and horizontally, even turning it several times – Mena recognised a Saint Cecilia. In my view, the
upper part of the sheet contains three different sketches for
Saint Catherine of Alexandria (the poses in the first and third
one match that of the Saint Catherine on the left of the Bologna
Coronation, while the second more closely resembles Saint
John in the same picture), and the lower part four sketches for
Saint Lucy. In all, there are ten female figures: in the upper part
of the sheet, beside an angel emerging from a cloud with a martyr's palm and a dense view of buildings surrounded by trees,
there is also a female saint in prayer, repeated three times with
variations, of which the central version, in addition, recalls Saint
Bernard in the Bologna painting. The arrangement of her drapery in antique-looking concentric arcs in the area of the mid-
riff – visible also in the four sketches of Saint Lucy – is the same
in the Saint Catherine in the Bologna *Coronation*. The distinctive line of the praying, as well as of the various versions of
Saint Lucy, the peculiar distended modelling of the faces, and
the large eyes strongly recall the graphic style of Agostino
Carracci (1557–1602), as I already pointed out elsewhere – as
an alternative to Annibale – to explain the recto of the Prado
sheet. Comparisons can readily be made with a number of
Windsor Castle drawings which Ann Sutherland Harris moved
some time ago from Agostino's catalogue to Reni's. I refer particularly to the *Holy Family*, published with a chronology before 1600.[5]

Returning to the sketches for Saint Catherine on the verso of
the Prado sheet, I recognise another very appropriate parallel

Cat. 3 recto

with the *Draped Female Figure Standing in a Niche* also at Windsor Castle.[6] This drawing, hypothetically a personification of Peace,[7] provides a secure connection to the decorative project for the façade of the Palazzo Pubblico in Bologna, executed by Reni on the occasion of Pope Clement VIII's visit to the city in 1598, a work now known only through an etching by Guido himself.[8] A third useful comparison, albeit in a different medium, can be made with the red-chalk *Saint Catherine* in the Uffizi, which must be regarded as contemporaneous with the few works by Reni that can be dated to 1598.[9]

By contrast, the handling both of the angel and of the Virgin and Child also featured on the verso of the Prado sheet seems to point to a later date: specifically, to the fresco of *God the Father and Playing Angels*[10] over the apse of the oratory of Santa Silvia in San Gregorio al Celio in Rome, completed by Guido in 1609.[11] Reni's pen drawings, however, are known to display significant variations, so it is by no means easy to establish a consistent chronology. Moreover, there will always be differences between a rapid sketch and a complete, finished composition. Finally, it should be borne in mind that, from the Virgin to

Cat. 3 verso

the several sketches of Saint Lucy, the Prado work displays a language and a style reminiscent of certain images intended for private devotion, possibly produced in the mid-1590s, such as the *Virgin and Child with Saint Catherine and Saint Hyacinth* painted around 1595 for the Fioravanti family (now in a private collection) – which marked the high point of Guido's collaboration with Ludovico Carracci (1555–1619)[12] – and the *Virgin crowned by Angels, adored by Saint Paul and Saint Catherine of Alexandria* (also in a private collection).[13] We can thus safely conclude that the verso of the Prado drawing originated in Bologna.

So, were the recto and verso drawings produced at the same time? It is entirely possible that Guido pasted together two sheets of existing sketches when he needed to produce a large horizontal composition, such as the recto of the Prado drawing. I should stress that, in my view, this was an independent project, although conceptually related paintings exist.[14]

The wildness of nature, the twisted trunk, the boulders, and the dense shading are elements reminiscent of Agostino Carracci's vocabulary; yet the flowing line of the drapery and the full forms of the central figures – especially the treatment of the Virgin – point to Ludovico. In terms of these latter features, the recto of the sheet too can be compared to the Bologna *Coronation*, and particularly to the depiction of Mary surrounded by the Trinity: in the characteristic fall of the drapery over the legs, stressing the rounded forms; in the elderly heads of God the Father and of Saint Joseph; in the fleshy body of the angel seen in rear view, perched on a cloud to the left, and of the Christ Child. Despite the different technique, careful examination reveals harmonious echoes of the preparatory study for the Bologna *Coronation*, a superb drawing on blue paper in the British Museum,[15] which Otto Kurz was the first to recognise as the work of Reni.[16]

Commenting on the recto of the Prado sheet, Francesco Gatta has rightly noted that it departs from the 'classical, ideal' landscape model established in Rome by Annibale Carracci, suggesting a chronology during Guido's early years in Rome or shortly before, prior to the magnificent small copper paintings of *Saint Jerome with two Angels in a Landscape* (1601–2) now in the Breslau Trust[17] and the *Return from the Flight into Egypt* (1602–3) proceeding from the Sfondrato collection and later in the Borghese one.[18]

Reni addressed also the theme of the *Holy Family in a Landscape (Rest on the Flight into Egypt?)* in another drawing at Windsor Castle,[19] originally attributed to Agostino Carracci. On stylistic grounds, this drawing has been dated to around 1607,[20] making the Prado design the earlier of the two. Finally, it is interesting that the typology of the figure of John the Baptist and the setting in untamed nature, which still carry the Carracci imprint, are also to be found in an etching by Guido of the *Christ Child and the Infant Saint John*.[21]

Viviana Farina

1 On this provenance, see Turner 2004, 27–28.
2 Paris, Musée du Louvre, nos. 8926 and 8927.
3 V. Farina in *Italian Masterpieces* 2014, 116–17.
4 Benati 2022, 19. Alessandro Brogi (2018, 82) still opts for 1595–96.
5 Windsor Castle, Royal Collection Trust, RCIN 902284. Sutherland Harris 1999, 8, note 28.
6 Windsor Castle, Royal Collection Trust, RCIN 903457.
7 Kurz and McBurney 1988, 115–16, no. 335.
8 Bartsch 4005.007. Birke 1987, 298, no. 7.
9 Florence, Gallerie degli Uffizi, Gabinetto dei Disegni e delle Stampe, inv. 4206 S. See Bohn 2008, 10–11, no. 6 (Reni); Johnston 2009 ('copy'); Loisel 2022, fig. 4 (Reni).
10 Milan, Castello Sforzesco, inv. 5683-B.1990 P.
11 Bohn 2008, 19 and 21, no. 13; S. Albl in Eclercy 2022a, 164–65, no. 46.
12 S. Pepper in Emiliani et al. 1988, 18–19, no. 5.
13 Benati 2004–5, 232–33 and pl. 6; Benati 2022, 17, 26, note 10.
14 I am grateful to Francesco Gatta for drawing my attention to the small copper (*Holy Family with the Infant John the Baptist*) at Kedleston Hall, reattributed to Reni by Brogi (2018, 82 and 87, figs. 17 and 88) for being 'such an affectionate and above all daily' compositional idea dating from 1600–1, and as an expression of the influence of Ludovico Carracci on Guido. This latter issue, crucial to our understanding of Reni, is also explored in Benati 2004–5; Toscano 2009; Brogi 2017.
15 London, The British Museum, inv. 1946,0713.237.
16 Birke 1981, 24–25, no. 1; Kurz and McBurney 1988, 116.
17 A. Iommelli in Cappelletti 2022a, 148–51, no. 13.
18 F. Gatta in Cappelletti 2022a, 152–55, no. 14. On these observations, see Gatta (in press).
19 Windsor Castle, Royal Collection Trust, RCIN 902282.
20 Sutherland Harris 1999, 10, figs. 9 and 12. The attribution to Reni had already been proposed by Turner and Pepper. See https://www.rct.uk/collection/902282/the-holy-family.
21 Bartsch 4005.027 S2. Birke 1982, 163, no. 13 (287).

Denys Calvaert
(Antwerp c. 1540–1619 Bologna)

Abraham and the three Angels

c. 1578–85
Oil on canvas, 147 × 161 cm
Madrid, Museo Nacional del Prado, P-3329

Provenance: Possibly not from the Spanish royal collection since the only inventory number it bears is the one assigned to it when it entered the Museo del Prado in the nineteenth century. In 2021 Isadora Rose-de Viejo related it to a canvas recorded in the collection of Manuel Godoy (no. 875; CA 441), where it was listed as a product of the 'Italian school', with no further details.

Selected bibliography: Madrazo 1843, 80, no. 397; Madrazo 1858, 98, no. 397; Madrazo 1872, 321, no. 568; Rose-de Viejo 1983, 2:617, no. 875; *Museo del Prado* 1990, I, 122, no. 397; Diéguez Rodríguez 2010; Rose-de Viejo 2021, CA. 441.

The composition is structured around the oak of Mamre, whose leafy boughs form a canopy beneath which the scene from Genesis (18:1–15) unfolds. Abraham, the central figure, serves as a metaphor for the presence of God in this prefiguration of the Eucharist. He welcomes three approaching pilgrims, offering them a place to rest beneath the oak, where he has set up a table bearing bread and wine. After eating, the pilgrims – angels sent by Yahweh – depart, but not before announcing that one of them will return, by which time Abraham's wife Sarah will have borne a child. This news astounds both Abraham and Sarah – who, hidden inside the tent, has heard the angel's revelation – since they are both very old.

The monumental figures, which occupy virtually the entire foreground, and the predominance of saturated shades of indigo, yellow, pink, and mauve are typical of the Italian school. It is hardly surprising, then, that the painting should always have been listed as a Florentine work in the inventories of the Museo del Prado. But other features – such as the technical precision and attention to detail, the depiction of nature, the careful rendering of hair and beard, an interest in capturing the subtle effects of light as it passes through the wine bottle and reflects onto the tablecloth, and the luminosity of the sunrise in the background, bathing the fields and hills in a hazy mist – are more characteristic of the Flemish school in which Denys Calvaert trained. He first studied under the landscape painter Christian van den Queborn (1515–1578) in Antwerp, entering his workshop as an apprentice in 1556 and staying there until 1558 at least.[1] Little is known of his subsequent training, though he probably continued to study in Italy. After spending some years in Rome, in 1568 he is recorded as working with Lorenzo Sabatini (c. 1530–1576) in Bologna, where he appears to have settled permanently by 1575.[2]

The Florentine influence discernible in Calvaert's work can be attributed to the years he spent working under Sabatini, and before that under Prospero Fontana (1512–1597).[3] It was the seamless blend of the Italian language with an essentially

Fig. 68 Possibly Denys Calvaert, *Abraham and the three Angels*, 1578–85. Pencil and brown wash with white highlighting on paper, 167 × 173 mm. Paris, Musée du Louvre, Département des Arts graphiques, inv. 9437

Flemish heritage which led to Calvaert eventually being appropriated by the Bolognese school of painting.

Abraham and the three Angels is closely related to the paintings Calvaert produced once he had established his own workshop in Bologna, in around 1575. There are, for example, strong resemblances – in terms of facial features, gestures and compositional schemes – to the drawing of *Jacob and Rachel at the Well* in the Musée du Louvre, dated 1578,[4] and to two versions of *Noli me tangere,* one in the Pinacoteca Nazionale di Bologna[5] and the other, dated 1585,[6] in the church of Santa Maria Maddalena di Cazzano in Budrio.

The scene depicted in the Prado canvas is repeated in an inverted drawing in the Louvre, which differs slightly from the final painting [fig. 68]. The most significant variations are found in the figure of Sarah – who in the drawing is pictured emerging from the tent holding a tray – as well as in the foreground vegetation and some items on the oblong stone over which the cloth has been laid. Michele Danieli was the first to relate this drawing to Calvaert's oeuvre, in private correspondence with the Louvre in 2020,[7] though without linking it specifically to the Prado painting.

As Wouter Kloek noted in 1993,[8] Calvaert used mirror images of figures and entire compositions both for teaching purposes at his studio-academy in Bologna and for experimentation; inverted images are common in his large-format compositions, since many of his drawings were used for engravings.[9] A drawing with the same orientation as the Prado canvas may well survive, though it has yet to be located.

Ana Diéguez-Rodríguez

1 Rombouts and Lerius 1961, 199.

2 Malvasia–Brascaglia 1971, 165.

3 Twiehaus 2002, 22.

4 Paris, Musée du Louvre, Département des Arts graphiques, inv. 19838. Available at https://collections.louvre.fr/en/ark:/53355/cl020109982 [accessed: 14 June 2022].

5 Bologna, Pinacoteca Nazionale di Bologna, inv. 494.

6 Twiehaus 2002, 67, 209, and 215.

7 On this drawing, see https://collections.louvre.fr/en/ark:/53355/cl020006512 [accessed: 14 June 2022].

8 Kloek 1993, 67 and 70.

9 Andrews 1985; Kloek 1993, 63; Twiehaus 2002, 147; Danieli 2010, 471–72.

5   Ludovico Carracci
(Bologna 1555–1619)

The Vision of Saint Francis

c. 1601–3
Oil on canvas, 200 × 147 cm
Madrid, Museo Nacional del Prado, P-70

Provenance: First mentioned in an inventory of Luigi Zambeccari's estate, in Bologna, in 1630; in the Zambeccari collection until 1787 at the latest, when it is listed as part of the Spanish royal collection in the Casita del Príncipe, El Escorial (no. 205); queen's dressing room in the Palacio Real de Aranjuez by 1818 (no. 205), whence it subsequently entered the collections of the Museo del Prado.

Selected bibliography: Pérez Sánchez 1965a, 111–12; Brogi 2001, 1:188–89, no. 75; J. Riello in Beaven 2014, 96.

Ludovico Carracci's *Vision of Saint Francis* is first described on the altar of the chapel in the Zambeccari family palace 'behind Santa Maria Maggiore', Bologna, in 1630: 'An altarpiece of Saint Francis with the Blessed Virgin and Our Lord'.[1] It is almost certain that the painting was commissioned by Luigi Zambeccari (1570–1630), perhaps soon after his marriage to Pantasilea Bentivoglio in 1600. The erudite Marcello Oretti (1714–1787) saw this *Vision* in another Zambeccari palace (formerly Casa Danzi), mentioning it twice in his notes.[2] This painting is undeniably the same as the one described in the inventory of the estate of Francesco Maria Zambeccari, drawn up in 1752.[3] It is unknown when and how the future King of Spain, Charles IV, acquired the picture, but this might have occurred even before his departure from Italy (where he was born) in 1765. Ludovico's *Vision of Saint Francis* is listed in the Casita del Príncipe, at El Escorial, around 1787. It was then transported to the palace of Aranjuez, where it is mentioned in 1818.

The painting seems inspired by an episode related in the *Little Flowers of Saint Francis* (a text written by Brother Ugolino Brunforte in 1327–37), where a young novice witnesses a miraculous event in the forest:

> And reaching the place where Saint Francis was praying, he began hearing many voices speaking, and moving closer so that he might see and understand what he was hearing, he happened to see a marvellous light, which surrounded Saint Francis, and within it he saw Christ and the Virgin Mary, and Saint John the Baptist, and the Evangelist, and a great multitude of angels, who were conversing with Saint Francis.[4]

Although Ludovico took his cue from this account, he most probably bore in mind another episode also recorded in the *Little Flowers*, the vision of Brother Pietro.

'One day', Ugolino writes, 'Brother Pietro, while praying and thinking most devoutly about Christ's Passion, and how the most blessed Mother of Christ and John the Evangelist, his most beloved disciple, and Saint Francis were painted at the foot of the cross, crucified with Christ as a result of their suffering [with him] through their minds, he was overtaken by a desire to know who of the three of them had endured the greatest pain from Christ's Passion, whether his mother, who had birthed him, or his disciple, who had rested over his chest, or Saint Francis, who had been crucified with Christ, and while dwelling on this devout reflection, the Virgin Mary appeared to him with Saint John the Evangelist and Saint Francis'.[5]

Brother Pietro learned then that first the Virgin, then Saint John, experienced the greater pain on that occasion, but almost equal to theirs was Saint Francis' agony, and his adherence to evangelical poverty even greater than Saint John's.

By omitting the figure of Saint John the Baptist, and by stressing the theme of Christ's Passion through the depiction of Jesus' foot and hand wounds aligned with Francis' stigmatised hand deployed in a gesture of devotion, Ludovico steers away from literally representing any of these two episodes from the *Little Flowers*, conflating them instead as a visual reflection on Francis' *imitatio Christi* – his modelling himself entirely upon Christ – and exalting the uniqueness of his sainthood. In the painting, Ludovico stages a sort of *disputatio*, with the Virgin pointing to herself as a reminder of her motherly suffering, and Christ indicating Francis as if adding him to the group of those who, along with the Virgin and Saint John the Evangelist, 'suffered with him' during the Passion. Prominently displayed, Christ's palm, pierced through the nail wound, is directed to Francis below, enraptured in his vision, reminding the viewer of the famous episode of Francis' stigmatisation at La Verna. In this manner, Ludovico highlights Francis' role as *alter Christus*, while his appearing on the lower tier of the representation reinstates his different status within the theological hierarchy.

Ludovico's *Vision of Saint Francis* might have been executed in 1601–3.[6] Although Guido Reni was in Rome at the time, he had been competing with Ludovico, his former master, for different jobs since 1597–98, when he quit the Carracci workshop. In 1600, for instance, Guido had sought to snatch from Ludovico the commission of a *Birth of Saint John the Baptist* for the church and convent of San Giovanni Battista in Bologna to no avail.[7] It is interesting that the patron of Ludovico's *Vision of Saint Francis*, Luigi Zambeccari, became a great supporter of Guido's, commissioning from him important paintings, such as a *Samson Victorious* [fig. 14] and a *Bacchus and Ariadne* [cat. 58].[8]

Lorenzo Pericolo

1 Cammarota 2001, 107: 'Un'ancona di S[an] Francesco con la Beata Vergine et Nostro Signore'.

2 Marcello Oretti, *Le pitture che si ammirano nelli palazzi e case de' nobili nella città di Bologna e di altri edifici in detta città*, manuscript, Bologna, Biblioteca Comunale dell'Archiginnasio, Ms B 104, 1:87 and 143: 'Una tavola da altare con Chr[ist]o, la Madonna, S[an] Giovanni Vang[elist]a, sotto S[an] Francesco d'Assisi, è de' Carracci'; 'una tavola d'altare con S[an] Francesco inginocchioni avanti alla Madonna S[antissi]ma, S[an] Giovanni Evangelista con angioli, è opera di Ludovico Carracci, figure come il vero'.

3 Cammarota 2001, 175: 'Un quadro che rappresenta Gesù Cristo, la Beata Vergine, S[an] Giovanni in gloria, e S[an] Francesco. Cornice dorata. Del Carazzi'.

4 Brunforte–Cesari 1860, 40–41 (chapter XVII): 'E giugnendo presso al luogo ove san Francesco orava, cominciò a udire un gran favellare; e appressandosi più per vedere e per intendere quello ch'egli udiva, gli venne veduto una luce mirabile, la quale attorniava san Francesco, e in essa vide Cristo, e la Vergine Maria, e san Giovanni Batista, e l'Evangelista, e grandissima moltitudine d'angeli, li quali parlavano con san Francesco'.

5 Ibid., 98 (chapter XLIV): 'uno dì istando frate Pietro in orazione, e pensando divotissimamente la Passione di Cristo, e come la Madre di Cristo beatissima, e Giovanni Evangelista dilettissimo discepolo, e san Francesco erano dipinti appiè della Croce, per dolore mentale crocifissi con Cristo, gli venne desiderio di sapere, quale di quelli tre avea avuto maggiore dolore della Passione di Cristo, o la Madre, la quale l'avea generato; o il Discepolo, il quale gli avea dormito sopra il petto suo; o san Francesco, il quale era con Cristo crocifisso: e stando in questo divoto pensiero, gli apparve la Vergine Maria con san Giovanni Evangelista, e con san Francesco'.

6 See Brogi 2001, 1:188–89, no. 75.

7 Malvasia–Pericolo 2019, 1:238–39, notes 77–78.

8 On Guido's Zambeccari *Samson Victorious*, see Malvasia–Pericolo 2019, 1:318–19, note 279.

6 Annibale Carracci
(Bologna 1560–1609 Rome)

The Assumption of the Virgin

1588–90
Oil on canvas, 130 × 97 cm
Madrid, Museo Nacional del Prado, P-75

Provenance: Spanish royal collection, first mentioned in the Real Monasterio de San Lorenzo de El Escorial in 1656; it stayed there until 1813, when it was sent to the Real Academia de Bellas Artes de San Fernando; it subsequently entered the Museo del Prado in 1839.

Selected bibliography: Pérez Sánchez 1965a, 99; Posner 1971, 2:19, no. 39; D. Posner in Perini Folesani 1986, 275–78, no. 90; A. Brogi in Benati and Riccomini 2006, 210, no. IV.13; Robertson 2008, 12–14; J. Riello in Beaven 2014, 98.

Annibale Carracci's *Assumption of the Virgin* now in the Museo del Prado is first mentioned in the so-called 'Memoria de Velázquez', a list of the paintings in the possession of King Philip IV that were sent at his behest to the monastery of San Lorenzo de El Escorial in 1656. Here, Annibale's picture, which is said to be in the sacristy, is described as a gift to the king brought from Italy by Manuel de Fonseca y Zúñiga, 6th Count of Monterrey (1588–1653).[1] In 1657, the historian monk Francisco de los Santos describes it in the same place: 'It is a painting of great renown, by Annibale Carracci, very similar to those by Tintoretto in the blotches and colours; as well as in the composition of the story'.[2] In 1668, the writer and diplomat Lorenzo Magalotti reports that Cosimo III de' Medici, Grand Duke of Tuscany, saw the painting in the sacristy of El Escorial.[3] The painting remained there until it was put on deposit at the Academy of Fine Arts of San Fernando, Madrid, in 1813; it was given to the Prado in 1839.[4]

Nothing is known about who might have commissioned the painting, or when. Given its relatively small size, it was likely to be destined for a private chapel. More certain is its unrelatedness to another *Assumption of the Virgin* by Annibale in Dresden's Gemäldegalerie which is dated 1587, and for which it was erroneously believed to be preparatory.[5] Made for the Confraternity of San Rocco in Reggio Emilia, the Dresden work is profoundly infused with reminiscences of Correggio (c. 1489–1534). Quite differently, the Prado *Assumption* reflects Annibale's fascination with Venetian painting, in particular Titian (c. 1488–1576) and Jacopo Tintoretto (1519–1594) – the latter's 1554–55 *Assumption of the Virgin* in Santa Maria Assunta in Venice [fig. 69] must have impressed

Fig. 69 Jacopo Tintoretto, *The Assumption of the Virgin*, 1554–55. Oil on canvas, 440 × 260 cm. Venice, Santa Maria Assunta (I Gesuiti) (from Santa Maria Assunta dei Crociferi)

Annibale – although Paolo Veronese (1528–1588) could also qualify as a source of inspiration.[6] Another *Assumption of the Virgin* by Annibale, executed in 1592 for the Bonasoni chapel in San Francesco, Bologna,[7] is also indebted to Venice, whose influence nevertheless appears entirely metabolised here, as opposed to the Prado painting, where Annibale seems to be experimenting with the 'blotches' and 'colours' – as acutely suggested by Santos – characteristic of the Venetian pictorial tradition.[8] On a preliminary basis, it can generally be assumed that the Prado *Assumption* was executed between 1587 and 1592. To be more specific, the painting was almost certainly made in 1588–90: that is, between Annibale's *Madonna of Saint Matthew*,[9] dated 1588 – where Correggio's imprint is still discernible – and the *Virgin and Child in Glory with Saints Louis, Alexius, John the Baptist, Catherine, Francis and Clare*, known as the *Madonna of San Ludovico*,[10] which is usually dated after Annibale's sojourn in Venice in 1588, and was probably executed in 1589–90.[11]

As a disciple and collaborator of Annibale, Guido Reni considered both Correggio and Venetian painters such as Titian, Tintoretto, and Veronese canonical models to learn from and improve upon. In Guido's eyes, however, Annibale's engagement with these two pictorial traditions (the 'Venetian' and the 'Lombard', to which Correggio belonged) was at times too exclusive. In praising the 'broader' vision of painting of Ludovico Carracci (1555–1619), Guido pointed out that he,

> unlike his cousins [Annibale and Agostino], had not been so attached to the Lombard and the Venetian schools that it could not be seen that he had studied the Roman school as well, and that the other two had been taken up with a manner that was similar to Titian and Correggio, whereas Ludovico, despite having also studied the manners of Andrea del Sarto, Tibaldi, Primaticcio, and having a liking for all the other masters, had then formed a new manner that was distinctive and truly his own.[12]

Whether or not Guido might have thought this was the case, the notion that Annibale and Agostino did not manage to create a fuller synthesis of styles by going beyond Titian and Correggio is as unfair as it is inaccurate. It is nonetheless true that Ludovico was more open to various styles, and in some cases bolder in fusing them together.

Lorenzo Pericolo

1 Cruzada Villaamil 1885, 210: 'De las pinturas que el Conde de Monterey trajo de Italia y dió a S[u] M[ajestad] … Una de Aníbal Carracci, de la Subida de Nuestra Señora a los cielos'. It is noteworthy that the anonymous author of this list describes Annibale's work with words used by Francisco de los Santos in his *Descripción breve* of 1657.

2 Santos 1657, 46r: 'Es pintura de gran nombre, de mano de Anibal Carache, muy semejante en las manchas y tintas y en la disposición de la historia a las de Tintoreto'.

3 Magalotti 2018, 175–76, note 214: 'En la sacristía, que es muy grande y rica, hay … pinturas de inestimable valor … también hay … la Asunción de Anibal Carracci'.

4 Bassegoda I Hugas 2002, 124, no. S12.

5 Dresden, Gemäldegalerie Alte Meister, Gal.-Nr. 303. See for instance Posner 1971, 2:19, no. 39: 'In my opinion, it is close in style to the Dresden picture, and its more dynamic composition should be considered as a kind of experiment made in connection with the Dresden altarpiece'. On the Dresden *Assumption of the Virgin*, see Posner 1971, 2:19, no. 40.

6 On Tintoretto's *Assumption of the Virgin*, see Pallucchini and Rossi 1982, 1:168, no. 170.

7 Bologna, Pinacoteca Nazionale di Bologna, inv. 455.

8 On Annibale's *Assumption of the Virgin* for San Francesco, Bologna, see Posner 1971, 2:29–30, no. 69; Robertson 2008, 86.

9 Dresden, Gemäldegalerie Alte Meister, Gal.-Nr. 304.

10 Bologna, Pinacoteca Nazionale di Bologna, inv. 471.

11 On Annibale's *Madonna of Saint Matthew*, see Posner 1971, 2:20–21, no. 45; Robertson 2008, 85–86. On Annibale's *Virgin and Child in Glory with Saints Louis, Alexius, John the Baptist, Catherine, Francis and Clare* (*Madonna of San Ludovico*), see Posner 1971, 2:19–20, no. 41; A. Brogi in Benati and Riccomini 2006, 190–91, no. IV.3; Robertson 2008, 89.

12 Malvasia 1678, 1:491: 'Perché non era stato come cugini tanto attaccato alla scuola lombarda e alla veneziana che anche la romana aver osservato non dimostrasse, ché que' duo s'eran dilettati d'una maniera a Tiziano ed al Correggio simile, ma Lodovico, nonostante l'aver quelle osservato di Andrea del Sarto ancora, del Tibaldi, del Primaticcio, e d'ogn'altro compiaciutosi, avevasi poi composto una maniera nuova e propria che poteasi dir la sua, e da ogn'altra diversa'; Summerscale 2000, 233–34.

7   Guido Reni

The Assumption of the Virgin

c. 1598–99
Oil on copperplate, 58 × 44.4 cm
Frankfurt, Städel Museum, inv. 2434

Provenance: Sampieri collection, Bologna (Malvasia 1678, 1743 inventory); acquired by Eugène de Beauharnais, Duke of Leuchtenberg,[1] after 1795 (catalogue 1851); thence by descent; purchased by the dealer Nordiska, Stockholm, 1917; Rudolph Poeschel collection, 1925; sold by Leo Spik auction house, Berlin, to Martin Schoenemann, Lugano, 1961; then in another private Swiss collection; sold by Koller Auctions, Zurich, to Jean-Luc Baroni, London, 2013; acquired by the Städelscher Museums-Verein, Frankfurt, 2014.

Selected bibliography: Andrews 1961, 462 and fig. 35; Pepper 1969a, 475–79, note 23; Pepper 1984, 209, no. 3; Pepper 1988, 214, no. 3; Baroni 2014, 16–21, no. 4; Eclercy 2015; Malvasia–Pericolo 2019, 1:20ff. and 226, note 46; Eclercy 2022a, 100–1, no. 8; Eclercy 2022b (with exhaustive discussion and full bibliography).

No subject matter is better suited to demonstrate the 'celestial ideas', the divine, angelic, and paradisal qualities of Guido Reni's art, than the Assumption of the Virgin – a life theme that preoccupied Guido again and again from his early years in Bologna to his last phase. His very first version of the topic, a painting on copper introduced by Keith Andrews and Stephen Pepper to modern Reni scholarship, was acquired for the Städel Museum in 2014.[2] Its provenance can be traced back to the Sampieri collection in Bologna, where it is mentioned by Carlo Cesare Malvasia in his *Felsina pittrice* (1678): 'un'Assonta in rame, oggi nel copiosissimo museo de' signori Sampieri'.[3] The exquisite copper was presumably commissioned by the jurist Astorre di Vincenzo Sampieri (1547–1610), the abbot of Santa Lucia di Roffeno (Castel d'Aiano) and canon of the cathedral of San Pietro in Bologna, who was active as a patron and collector in the 1590s. While still in the Carracci academy, Guido had painted a copy after Annibale Carracci's (1560–1609) *Burial of Christ* of 1595[4] for Sampieri – probably the initial encounter that led to further commissions.[5]

The Virgin is seated at the centre of the composition on an immaterial throne of fluffy clouds. She has her arms spread wide in the *orans* posture, her gaze transfigured and pointed upwards in the manner so typical of our painter. And it was presumably in this work that Reni first used the motif of the heavenward gaze for the main figure so decisively. Little angels lift Mary toward the light entering the scene from the top centre through clouds pushed to the left and right like a curtain. A rich gold produced entirely with paint points to the celestial character of this light, which virtually becomes a substitute for God himself, who receives Mary in heaven (*assumptio*) but is present in the scene only in the form of the splendour he emanates. Here the medieval gold background has returned, virtually transformed into pigment.[6] A vividly poetic allegory of the celestial spheres, this sea of clouds and light is populated with countless angels who appear in part to merge with their surroundings. Almost all are engaged in music making of various kinds, joining in the *musica coelestis* that, in the theological conception, pervades heaven.[7] We might also detect a subtle competition here between the arts of painting and music. Guido himself came from a family of musicians, a circumstance which may explain his special affinity to the theme as well as the organological knowledge evident in his depictions of instruments.

No two angels in the painting are alike. Yet behind the variegated manyness of these small beings, a cleverly devised order prevails, lending the composition structure and an astounding monumentality. The two lute players at the bottom, depicted on the same figural scale as the Virgin, serve to stabilise the pictorial construction while at the same time subtly guiding the eye of the viewer with the directions of their own gazes. Three angels have been tasked with assisting Mary directly. Their obvious exertion is not just an amusing detail, but illustrates quite manifestly the *bodily* assumption of the Mother of God into heaven – a matter hotly disputed by theologians and only elevated to the status of papal dogma centuries later, in 1950.[8] A gently curving bank of clouds forms a backdrop to Mary, and the music-making angels fairly dissolve in its golden light; clouds and bodies merge.

For this sensitively thought-out composition, Reni clearly took above all the two large altarpieces of the *Assumption of the Virgin* by Annibale and Agostino Carracci now in the Pinacoteca Nazionale di Bologna as his point of departure.[9] However, Guido's conception of the theme is also fundamentally different from that of his teachers, and indeed revolutionarily new. Whereas the Carracci adhered to the pathos of Mary's dramatic ascension modelled on the High Renaissance, Reni translated it into an entirely different mood – a gentle upward floating accompanied by spherical strains and full of poetic harmony. He also made major changes to the traditional iconography of the Assunta with its horizontal division into a celestial zone accommodating Mary and the angels, and a terrestrial one with the apostles gathered around the empty grave. Reni boldly left out the apostle group and limited himself solely to the vision of the Mother of God surrounded by choruses of angels and ascending into heaven. In place of the complex relationships between the Carracci's restlessly interacting figures, we now encounter a simple, clear order based on geometric forms. This little painting (that I date to c. 1598–99 for stylistic reasons)[10] thus provides fascinating insights into a historical turning point in Reni's oeuvre: his emancipation from pupil to master.

Remarkably, the early Frankfurt *Assumption* already forms the nucleus of Guido's later pictorial ideas. Time and again throughout his career, he returned to his first version, transforming it in the process. The most closely related works are the two likewise small-scale renditions of the same subject in the Prado and the National Gallery in London [cat. 8, 9], both dating from Reni's Roman phase. For these compositions, the painter clearly drew on the Städel picture, but without repeating so much as a single detail verbatim. He rethought every figure. These paintings are therefore not replicas but free variations on the Frankfurt version. Even in his much later Assumptions or Immaculate Conceptions from the 1620s and 1630s [cat. 55], Reni returned to his own early model. Detached from the more complex context of the Frankfurt composition and its successors, the central figural group finds its way into the monumental format of altarpieces in modified form. The Städel copperplate thus proves to be a kind of sum of Guido's pictorial inventions, marking not the end but the outset of his career. It teaches us to conceive of Reni's art from the perspective of its beginnings.

Bastian Eclercy

1 Eugène de Beauharnais, Viceroy of Italy and Duke of Leuchtenberg (1781–1824).
2 Andrews 1961; Pepper 1969a.
3 Malvasia–Pericolo 2019, 1:20.
4 New York, The Metropolitan Museum of Art, Purchase, Edwin L. Weisl Jr. Gift, 1998, inv. 1998.188.
5 Malvasia–Pericolo 2019, 1:24ff.; Christiansen 1999.
6 See Wimböck 2002, 251–56.
7 See Krüger 2017.
8 See Stoichita 1997, 41–46.
9 Annibale Carracci, *Assumption of the Virgin*, 1592, Bologna, Pinacoteca Nazionale di Bologna, inv. 455; Agostino Carracci, *Assumption of the Virgin*, 1592–93, Bologna, Pinacoteca Nazionale di Bologna, inv. 469. E. Fiori in Bentini et al. 2006, 293–95, no. 195; D. Benati, ibid., 306–8, no. 202.
10 Eclercy 2022b.

8   Guido Reni
The Assumption and Coronation of the Virgin

1602–3
Oil on panel, 77 × 51 cm
Madrid, Museo Nacional del Prado, P-213

Provenance: First mentioned in an inventory of the Real Alcázar, Madrid, in 1666; listed in the court painters' workshop in the Real Alcázar, Madrid, in 1686, 1694, 1700 (no. 570), and in the queen's new chambers in 1703 and 1734; Palacio del Buen Retiro, Madrid, brought from the Casas Arzobispales, in 1747 (no. 1010); gallery hall and back rooms at the Palacio Real, Madrid, in 1772 (no. 1010); first room in the new building, Palacio Real, Madrid, in 1794 (no. 1010).

Selected bibliography: Mayer 1934, 294; Pérez Sánchez 1965a, 173–74; Pérez Sánchez 1965b, 274; Pérez Sánchez 1970, 452; Baccheschi 1977, 91; Pepper 1984, 214; *Museo del Prado* 1985, 539–40; *Museo del Prado* 1990, 1:259, no. 928; Pérez Sánchez 1993, 103; Salvy 2001, 145; Ruiz Gómez 2009b, 19; Finaldi 2013, 57; Finaldi 2014, 51; Martínez Leiva and Rodríguez Rebollo 2015, 485, no. 689; Japón 2020a, 1:594; Eclercy 2022a, 100–1, no. 9; Eclercy 2022b, 25–29.

This was one of the first paintings by Guido Reni to enter the Spanish royal collections during the reign of Philip III. It is widely thought to have been sent to Madrid from Rome in the early seventeenth century – together with an Agony in the Garden by the same artist [cat. 12][1] – as a gift from Cardinal Camillo Borghese, the future Pope Paul V, to Empress Maria of Austria. More recently, however, Stefano Pierguidi has suggested that both paintings were entrusted to his nephew Cardinal Scipione Borghese, who gave them to Juan Alonso Pimentel de Herrera, 5th Duke of Benavente and Viceroy of Naples from 1603 to 1610,[2] to deliver to the king. In 1615, Philip III arranged for the remains of the empress – who had died in 1603 – to be transferred to the choir in the convent church of the Descalzas Reales in Madrid; since then, the *Agony in the Garden*, painted on copper, has hung above her tomb. While the two paintings may have been intended as a pair – being similar in terms of size, composition, and style – they were to have different destinies. There is no record of the *Assumption* until a 1666 inventory of the Alcázar in Madrid, where it is listed as hanging in an upstairs room of the Tower.[3] It remained there until the end of the seventeenth century, when it was inventoried in the court painters' workshop, alongside Reni's *Saint Sebastian* [cat. 19], in 1700. It was then listed in the Cuarto Nuevo de la Reina (Queen's New Apartments) in 1703 and 1734. Saved from the fire that destroyed the Alcázar in 1734, the panel was taken to the Casas Arzobispales (Archbishop's Residence) and from there to the Buen Retiro

Fig. 70 X-ray image of *The Assumption and Coronation of the Virgin* [cat. 8]

compositions by one of his masters, Ludovico Carracci (1555–1619), are readily discernible, together with the first fruits of techniques with which he experimented in Rome, stirred by the artistic trends then in vogue. The complex, carefully designed composition is divided into three sections, whose figurative elements lead the viewer's eye towards the central area. The gazes of the four angels in the corners – two playing instruments in the lower section, and two parting the clouds above – converge on the seated figure of Mary, her arms crossed over her breast and her eyes raised towards heaven. It is at this point where the X-ray study conducted by the Museo del Prado reveals a major change in the proportions of the figure of the Virgin [fig. 70]. While Reni certainly achieved a powerful devotional image, it is somewhat marred by its excessive frontality and lacks the lightness of touch characteristic of later versions. Nowhere is this more apparent than in the upper section of the *Assumption* at the church of Gesù e dei Santi Ambrogio e Andrea in Genoa. Reni's style gradually evolved towards simpler, less cluttered compositions, thus making it easier to appreciate the idea of ascension associated with this iconography; here, the sense of upward motion is impeded by the inclusion of the two *putti* bearing the crown. In technical terms, too, Guido is still clearly dependent on the approach favoured by his masters, a trait shared by other painters – among them Giovanni Lanfranco (1582–1647)[6] – who followed a similar path after leaving the Accademia degli Incamminati.

At least two other autograph versions are known, both painted on copper: one, which probably also came from Spain, in the National Gallery, London [cat. 9], and the other, which originally belonged to the Sampieri collection in Bologna, in the Städel Museum, Frankfurt, since 2019 [cat. 7].

Rafael Japón

palace; it was later transferred to the newly-completed Royal Palace, where it remained – hanging in the 'first room' of the new building and elsewhere – until it entered the Museo del Prado in 1854.

Alfonso E. Pérez Sánchez identified this *Assumption* as the *Madonna* which, according to Carlo Cesare Malvasia in his *Felsina pittrice* (1678), was given to the King of Spain and was expressly requested by Queen Margaret of Austria for her bedchamber.[4] Other scholars later claimed that Malvasia's *Madonna* was in fact the *Virgin of the Chair* [cat. 52], which was among the works sent to decorate the monastery of El Escorial in the seventeenth century. José Luis Colomer rejected both hypotheses, suggesting that Malvasia was referring to the Raleigh *Virgin and Child* [fig. 4], which was recorded in El Escorial prior to being looted during the French invasion.[5]

Critics agree that the panel was painted during Guido's first sojourn in Rome, between 1602 and 1603, since it displays a number of formal features found only in his early works. Echoes of

1 García Sanz 1992, 59.

2 See Stefano Pierguidi's essay, 'Viceroys, Ambassadors, Agents, Theologians: Thirty Years of (Stormy) Relations between Guido Reni and Spain', in this catalogue.

3 There are grounds for this hypothesis: in 1631, the Madrid collection of *relator* Alonso Cortés, personal secretary to Philip IV, boasted two copies – very possibly painted on copper – identical in size to Reni's *Assumption* and *Agony in the Garden*. It is worth noting that the painter entrusted with identifying and appraising these works was Vicente Carducho (c. 1576–1638), who was probably familiar with the originals; see Burke and Cherry 1997, 1:286–90.

4 Malvasia 1678, 2:30: 'Come fece la Regina di Spagna, che d' una Madonna donata al Rè, ed a lui chiesta instantemente, ed ottenuta, arrichì il suo Regio quarto'; Pérez Sánchez 1965a, 173–74.

5 Colomer 2006, 224. More recently, Lorenzo Pericolo lent his support to the view that Malvasia was referring to the *Virgin of the Chair*; see Malvasia–Pericolo 2019, 1:288, note 197.

6 Pérez Sánchez 1970, 452.

9   Guido Reni

The Coronation of the Virgin

c. 1607
Oil on copperplate, 66.6 × 48.8 cm
London, The National Gallery, Bequeathed by William Wells,
1847, NG214

Provenance: Spanish royal collection (?), Madrid; Sir Thomas Lawrence, London; William Wells, before 1831 until 1847, when he bequeathed it to the National Gallery.

Selected bibliography: Waagen 1854, 1:337; Gnudi and Cavalli 1955, no. 14; Matthiesen and Pepper 1970, 458; Baccheschi 1971, 91, no. 41a; Pepper 1984, 222, no. 26; Malvasia–Pericolo 2019, 1:226, note 46; Eclercy 2022a, 100–1, no. 10; Eclercy 2022b, 25–29.

Combining two iconographies in a single composition, Guido Reni achieved an iconic devotional image whose success is evident from the numerous known copies of this *Coronation of the Virgin*. Mary appears at the centre of the copperplate, surrounded on all sides by an angelic choir engaged in various activities: in the lower foreground, angels play musical instruments; in the centre, they assist her in her ascension; in the upper section they part the heavens so that two *putti* may descend through the opening, bearing her crown. Although the other two autograph versions in the Städel Museum [cat. 7] and the Museo del Prado [cat. 8] are very similar in composition, significant variations in the treatment of these figures mean that they cannot be classified as replicas. Critics agree that they date from different years, though all three were produced early in Reni's career. The Städel version, identified as the picture referred to by Carlo Cesare Malvasia in the Sampieri collection in Bologna, was painted around 1598–99 and is thought to be the first in the series; a key difference with regard to the later versions is the absence of the Coronation scene. The Prado picture was painted around 1602–3, during Guido's first sojourn in Rome, while the London version was probably produced some five years later, around 1607. This hypothetical dating is borne out by certain technical and stylistic differences between the latter two: the third painting, compositionally bolder and more accurate – the result of much more careful study – also employs a more

vibrant palette. During this period, Reni made further use of the choir of angels in the apse of the oratory of Santa Silvia al Celio in Rome, which also includes the trio of *putti* holding a sheet of music and singing. This latter detail is copied in an eighteenth-century canvas in the holdings of the Real Academia de Bellas Artes de San Fernando in Madrid; however, subtle yet discernible differences between the two paintings confirm that the London version was the model.[1]

The presence of this and other copies in Spain indicates that the original may have belonged to a Spanish collection.

Fig. 71 Workshop of Guido Reni, *The Assumption and Coronation of the Virgin*, 17th century. Oil on panel, 82 × 55 cm. Peñaranda de Bracamonte (Salamanca), Convento de las Madres Carmelitas

Although the idea that it hung in Seville cathedral in the seventeenth century is clearly erroneous,[2] it may have been in that city at the time, judging from the number of surviving reproductions to be found there. They all display certain compositional features found only in this version, particularly the lute-playing angel in the foreground, looking out at the viewer. Of all the copies located, that of the collegiate church of the Divino Salvador in Seville stands out for its large size and identical use of colours.[3] The Spanish provenance is supported by a note accompanying the title of this work in the catalogue for an exhibition staged in 1831 by the British Institution for Promoting the Fine Arts in the United Kingdom. The note states that the picture, which belonged at the time to the shipbuilder and art collector William Wells (1768–1847), was 'from the Royal Collection at Madrid'.[4] However, inventories of the royal residences mention only the Prado panel from 1666 until it entered the Museo del Prado in the nineteenth century, and the possible coexistence of two versions over the centuries cannot therefore be confirmed. Nevertheless, in 1631 *relator* Alonso Cortés, personal secretary to Philip IV, owned an *Assumption* on copper measuring two *tercias* (roughly 60 centimetres) in height, which Vicente Carducho (c. 1576–1638) regarded as a copy of the Reni painting; as court painter since 1609,[5] he would have been familiar with the other version. Carducho also identified in the Cortés collection an *Agony in the Garden* which was a pendant of that *Assumption*, just as the copperplate on the same theme in the Musées de Sens [cat. 11] could at some point have been paired with this London *Assumption*.[6] Further research into the widespread diffusion of this model in Spain unearthed, in the twentieth century, another copy in the T'Serclaes collection in Madrid,[7] as well as one in the convent of the Discalced Carmelites of Peñaranda de Bracamonte in Salamanca [fig. 71].[8] The latter is an interesting reproduction on panel which includes a number of variations, mostly affecting the figure of the Virgin and the lower section of the composition, to which a landscape has been added. In view of its quality, the picture can be attributed to Reni's workshop.

Rafael Japón

1 Madrid, Real Academia de Bellas Artes de San Fernando, inv. 0552; Pérez Sánchez 1965a, 188.
2 Pedro José Respaldiza Lama (2002, 213, no. 13) mistakenly identified the National Gallery painting as the *Assumption with two Angels* belonging to G. W. Taylor, sold in London in 1823 by Christie's, whose auction catalogue stated that it had come from Seville cathedral. But this assertion was based on an iconographical misinterpretation; in fact, the auction catalogue referred to the *Immaculate Conception* now at the Metropolitan Museum of Art in New York [cat. 55].
3 Japón 2018c, 35–36; García Cueto and Japón 2019, 540–43.
4 *Catalogue of Pictures* 1831, 13, no. 29: '*The Coronation of the Virgin*, from the Royal Collection at Madrid'; Pepper 1984, 222, no. 26.
5 Burke and Cherry 1997, 1:286–90.
6 Pepper 1984, 222, no. 27. Among the existing copies of this work, Stephen Pepper lists a picture signed and dated in 1626 by Domenico Zampieri, Domenichino (1581–1641), in the Musée Bonnat-Helleu, Bayonne (CM 99), and another oil on copper in the Szépművészeti Múzeum, Budapest (inv. 958).
7 Pérez Sánchez 1965a, 190.
8 J. Ramos Domingo in Mesonero 2002, 54.

10   Guido Reni

The Coronation of the Virgin (recto)
A Landscape (verso)

c. 1598–1600
Pen, grey-brown ink and wash on paper, 325 × 263 mm
(recto vertical; verso horizontal)
Signed on verso
Edinburgh, National Galleries of Scotland, David Laing Bequest
to the Royal Scottish Academy transferred 1910, D 702

Provenance: Pierre Crozat, until 1740; Pierre-Jean Mariette (L. 1852), 1741; François Joullain (1697–1778) or François Charles Joullain (c. 1735–1790); Charles Gilbert Paignon Dijonval (1708–1792); Thomas Lawrence (1769–1830) (L. 2445); David Laing (1793–1878); Royal Scottish Academy, Edinburgh, 1879 (L. 2188); National Galleries, Edinburgh, 1910.

Selected bibliography: Andrews 1961, 461 and figs. 29 (recto) and 31 (verso); Andrews 1968, 1:104 and 2:124, figs. 708 (recto) and 709 (verso); Johnston 1969, 377–79, note 2, fig. 64 (verso); Johnston 1974, 1:49–50, no. 24; Birke 1981, 26–27, no. 3; A. Weston-Lewis in Bolognese Drawings 1993, no. 41; Bohn 2008, 31 and note 79, in no. 20; Loisel 2013, 101, in no. 64, and 116, in no. 88; Rosenberg et al. 2019, 3:1029, no. I1701; Loisel 2022, at the height of note 13; Rosenberg and Choueiry 2022, II, no. I1701; Gatta (in press).

The work number assigned to this sheet by Pierre Crozat (1665–1740) is visible in the lower right corner of the recto: '82'. The drawing, then attributed to Guido Reni, was purchased by Pierre-Jean Mariette (1694–1774) at the famous 1741 auction of Crozat's collection, as part of lot 524. In the subsequent sale of Mariette's estate held in 1775, the sheet – which today lacks the original mount – was included in lot 642. In the catalogue compiled by Pierre-François Basan, it is described as 'A beautiful landscape on the recto … on the verso is the Coronation of the Virgin',[1] suggesting that Mariette attached greater importance to the landscape on the back than to the religious scene on the front. We shall therefore look first at the verso.

Keith Andrews, the first historian to draw attention to the drawing, recognised the importance of the subject matter within the artist's oeuvre, noting that it is 'the only pure landscape drawing by Reni known to exist'.[2] After removal of the passepartout, two squiggles in the lower right corner – which might have been taken for grass – were revealed as the top arches of the letters G and R, part of Guido Reni's full signature, in the same ink as the drawing.[3] Andrews recognised in the vigorous style echoes of the landscapes by Annibale Carracci (1560–1609) datable to around 1590–95. Also, the three figures almost hidden on the right recalled drawings by both Annibale and Agostino Carracci (1557–1602). He regarded it, in short, as exactly what one would expect Guido to have produced in the Carracci workshop towards the end of the sixteenth century.

The Coronation of the Virgin on the recto presented more complex problems, since Reni had tackled this subject, sometimes transformed into an Assumption of the Virgin, throughout his early career. The graphic style could be traced back to Ludovico Carracci (1555–1619), whose name – understandably and significantly – cropped up when the drawing was purchased by the National Galleries of Scotland. At that stage it was viewed as an echo, but certainly not a prefiguration, of the Coronation of the Virgin with four Saints in the British Museum,[4] the preparatory study for the canvas now in the Pinacoteca Nazionale di Bologna [fig. 16]. Compositional similarities could also be discerned in the mystery on the same theme depicted in the Vision of Saint Dominic and the fifteen Mysteries of the Rosary of 1600–1 in the sanctuary of the Madonna di San Luca [fig. 20]. The connection with the Coronation of the Virgin by Annibale Carracci,[5] painted in Rome in 1595–97, appeared equally evident, so the Edinburgh drawing could be dated no earlier than Guido's arrival in the capital. After examining parallels with several of Reni's treatments of the Assumption of the Virgin, Andrews goes on to suggest a particularly significant link with the version in the National Gallery, London [cat. 9]. He concludes that the drawing may have been made in 1604–5 or, alternatively, at an earlier stage, between 1595 and 1598, when Guido was still at the Carracci workshop.

Shortly afterwards, by contrast, Catherine Johnston stressed that the recto of the Scottish sheet could not be linked to any known painted composition. On that occasion, she explored the verso in conjunction with three other landscapes also purchased by Mariette – the two now in the Louvre and one in the Szépművészeti Múzeum[6] – concluding that these were unrelated drawings, different from the landscape backgrounds painted by Guido in the early 1610s, and particularly from the view in the Aurora ceiling fresco executed in 1612–14 for the central hall of the Casino Pallavicini-Rospigliosi in Rome.

Cat. 10 recto

Cat. 10 verso

Given that the style is perfectly in keeping with the Carracci tradition, she suggested that these designs were produced when Reni was still at the Accademia degli Incamminati, or certainly no later than the early 1600s. This dating seemed to be borne out by the quality of the pen strokes – Johnston was referring strictly to the Louvre drawings nos. 8926 and 8927 – which hinted at the hand of an engraver, a speciality in which Guido is known to have trained in Bologna. In an entry compiled for her doctoral thesis later,[7] Johnston argued that the verso of the Edinburgh drawing should undoubtedly be viewed as a worthy response to advice offered by the Carracci, who were fond of Venetian *vedute*. According to her, the heavily graphic nature of the style, especially in the background, bespoke the particular influence of Agostino, the master from whom Reni had learned the art of engraving.

In a 2017 opinion, Aidan Weston Lewis agreed that the drawing could be dated to before 1601, acknowledging the evidence of a cultural link to landscapes by Agostino Carracci.[8] It is an opinion also shared by Catherine Loisel and Francesco Gatta.

In the light of what is currently known of Reni's early career, the Bologna influence in the drawing certainly seems evident: on the recto, in the forms rendered in broad strokes and delicate washes according to Ludovico's style; and on the verso, in the contrast – recalling Agostino – between the shade of the trees and the open landscape. The early dating of the work would appear wholly justifiable. The upper part of the sacred scene on the recto unquestionably bears a certain resemblance not only to the *Coronation of the Virgin* of around 1598 in the Pinacoteca Nazionale di Bologna, but also to the small mystery in the *Vision of Saint Dominic* at the sanctuary of the Madonna di San Luca of about 1600;[9] while in the lower part there are echoes of the *Assumption* on copper produced around 1598–99 that belonged to the Sampieri family, which was recently purchased by the Städel Museum [cat. 7],[10] a painting which itself recalls the *Assumption of the Virgin* dated to 1599–1600 in Santa Maria Maggiore in Pieve di Cento.

We may readily conclude, on stylistic grounds, that the famous *Landscape with Erminia* and *Landscape with a Windmill and a Castle* in the Louvre (inv. 8926 and 8927) – both of which still retain the original Mariette mount, and belonged to Count Carlo Cesare Malvasia[11] – must have been drawn later than the verso of the Edinburgh sheet.[12] The same fine, precise lines are a distinctive feature of the Uffizi *Mountain Landscape with a Village*,[13] which itself displays a harmonious overall affinity to

the often-overlooked *Landscape with two Castles* in the Louvre, from the collection of Alfonso IV d'Este.[14] Years ago, Johnson dated the Florence drawing to around 1612, thus coinciding with the naturalistic sweep of the *Aurora* in the Casino Pallavicini-Rospigliosi; this date, subsequently accepted by Babette Bohn, would seem decidedly late in terms of the current reconstruction of Reni's production of *vedute* in the early 1600s. By this time, Guido – like other Bolognese artists living in Rome – had shown himself able to observe and respond in his own way to the serene, light-filled view of nature conveyed in such a masterly fashion by Annibale Carracci in Rome.[15]

It is more difficult to establish whether or not the verso of the Edinburgh sheet predates the *Rest on the Flight into Egypt with the Infant Saint John* in the Museo del Prado [cat. 3], these being the only known examples of Reni's foray into the landscape genre in the manner of the Incamminati. In the current absence of suitable parallels in Guido's paintings, we can at least note that the 'wild' setting bears some resemblance to the rough, rocky landscape of the *Vision of Saint Eustace*, formerly in the crypt at San Michele in Bosco and now in a private collection in Genoa [fig. 18]; this altarpiece, Reni's superb tribute to Parmigianino (1503–1540), has tentatively been dated to 1599–1600.[16]

Viviana Farina

1 Rosenberg et. al. 2019, 1029: 'Un beau Paysage en Travers … au verso se trouve le Couronnement de la Vierge'.
2 Andrews 1961, 461.
3 The presence of the signature, also noted in Birke 1981, was confirmed by Pierre Rosenberg and Marie-Louise Choueiry (2022), to whom it was pointed out by Aidan Weston-Lewis.
4 London, The British Museum, inv. 1946,0713.237.
5 New York, The Metropolitan Museum of Art, Purchase, Bequest of Miss Adelaide Milton de Groot (1876–1967), by exchange, and Dr and Mrs Manuel Porter and sons Gift, in honor of Mrs Sarah Porter, 1971, 1971.155.
6 Rosenberg et al. 2019, 3:1030–31, nos. I1702, I1703, and I1704.
7 Johnston 1974, 1:49–50, no. 24.
8 See Rosenberg et al. 2019, 3:1029, no. I1701.
9 Malvasia–Pericolo 2019, 1:226–27, note 48.
10 Pepper 1988, 213–14, no. 3; Malvasia–Pericolo 2019, 1:226, note 46.
11 Loisel 2013, 99–101, nos. 62 and 64.
12 See most recently F. Gatta in Eclercy 2022a, 155–57, nos. 42 and 43, 'around 1601–5'.
13 Florence, Gallerie degli Uffizi, Gabinetto dei Disegni e delle Stampe, inv. 588 P; Bohn 2008, 30–31, no. 20.
14 Paris, Musée du Louvre, Départment des Arts graphiques, inv. 8143; Loisel 2013, 102, no. 65.
15 On this issue, see Gatta 2017 and Gatta (in press).
16 Benati 2004–5, 232–33; Malvasia–Pericolo 2019, 1:225, note 44.

11 Guido Reni

The Agony in the Garden

c. 1607
Oil on copperplate, 57 × 43.5 cm
Sens, Musées de Sens, inv. 527 (on long-term loan from the Musée du Louvre)

Provenance: Gaspard Marsy collection; collection of Louis XIV of France, 1668; Musée du Louvre, Paris, 1793; Musées de Sens, Sens (on long-term loan from the Musée du Louvre), 1895.

Selected bibliography: Dézallier d'Argenville 1762, 2:109; Matthiesen and Pepper 1970, 459–60 and 492, note 45; Baccheschi 1971, 90–91, no. 40; Pepper 1984, 222, no. 27; S. Pepper in Pirovano 1985, 176–78, no. 52; Muti 2006.

The Louvre *Agony in the Garden* is a superb example of the sheer elegance and consummate technical virtuosity which Guido Reni attained in this type of small-format devotional paintings in his early years in Rome from 1602 onwards. This masterly result can be ascribed to his application of highly precise brushstrokes to render certain details – folds of drapery, strands of hair, shining eyes – and to the use of copper as a support. Although Reni's technique is widely attributed to his early training in Bologna under the Flemish master Denys Calvaert (c. 1540–1619), this approach was already well established in Rome in the second half of the sixteenth century, and was particularly favoured by the circle of Marcello Venusti (c. 1512–1579) and other followers of Michelangelo (1475–1564); it was even adopted by El Greco (1541–1614) during his stay in Rome from 1570 onwards.

In the late sixteenth century, at the start of his career in Bologna, Guido had tackled the same theme in the manner of Titian in one of the fifteen Mysteries accompanying the *Madonna of the Rosary* painted for the sanctuary of the Madonna di San Luca [fig. 20]. Subsequently, once he had settled in Rome, this highly innovative composition painted on copper met with considerable success: discussing the artist in his *Felsina pittrice* (1678),[1] Carlo Cesare Malvasia included the *Agony in the Garden* – making no mention of its owner – among the Reni paintings most widely reproduced by print-makers. The best proof of its commercial success, however, are Guido's two currently-known autograph versions – this one and the painting in the convent of the Descalzas Reales in Madrid [cat. 12], which must have been produced at almost the same time – together with several workshop copies,[2] as well as the various engravings which, as Malvasia noted,[3] appeared in the course of the seventeenth century.

Stephen Pepper rightly dates the painting to around 1607:[4] Reni had by then grown familiar with the ground-breaking style of Caravaggio (1571–1610), and his attention was shifting – as he sought his own ideal classicist idiom – toward artists with a very different approach, such as the Cavalier d'Arpino (1568–1640). Reni must have studied some of the small devotional pieces produced by the Cavalier or by Ludovico Carracci (1555–1619), which provided good examples of how to simplify scenes in small-scale compositions without undermining the emotional impact of the subject.

Christ is shown here with his hands clasped on his lap, in an attitude that conveys serene expectation and acceptance of torment; while his pose strongly resembles that of the Virgin in Reni's *Pentecost* fresco of 1607–8 in the Vatican's Sala delle Dame (Hall of the Ladies), the intense yet contained emotion conveyed in his heavenward gaze was to serve as a starting point for future models of Christ in his suffering. The placing of the kneeling Christ and the young angel holding out the bitter cup enabled Guido to highlight the carefully layered folds arranged on the crest of the hill, recalling his training under Calvaert. Echoes of Caravaggio are apparent in the marked contrast between the divine golden glow outlining the figure of Christ and the darkness of the night in the right of the picture, where the three sleeping apostles and the group coming to arrest Christ are barely visible. Interestingly, this part of the landscape is handled very differently in surviving prints, where all the figures involved are clearly discernible.[5] The delightful company of angels, bearing the symbols of the Passion, features in the three frescoes painted by Reni in 1609–10 for the chapel of the Annunciation at the Palazzo del Quirinale in Rome, and also in his 1607 drawing for an engraving after Luca Cambiaso's (1527–1585) *Glory of Angels*. A very similar garlanding of angels around the central figure is to be found in Guido's *Coronation of the Virgin* in the National Gallery in London [cat. 9],[6] a picture so close in support, size, and style that some critics regard it as a pendant to this *Agony in the Garden*.

The earliest written reference to the Louvre *Agony* dates from 1668, when the sculptor Gaspard Marsy (1624–1681) sold it to Louis XIV for 3000 livres;[7] it remained in the French royal collections until the Louvre was established as a museum in 1793. Some scholars[8] mistakenly identified it as the painting recorded in the collection of Cardinal Jules Mazarin (1602–1661) in 1661; on the cardinal's death later that year, the collection passed to his nephew, the Duc de Mazarin, thence to the Duchess of Chevreuse, who – according to some historians – subsequently sold it, though this seems unlikely. In any case, Mazarin's version was painted on canvas,[9] while the one purchased by Louis XIV was on copper, like this one. The muddle was solved with the discovery, reported by Laura Muti,[10] of a hitherto-unknown high-quality replica in a private collection,[11] possibly painted by Reni himself; this painting is a much closer match, in terms of support and measurements, to the picture mentioned in Mazarin's will.

Carmen García-Frías Checa

1 Malvasia–Zanotti 1841, 1:97. The first known engraving of the *Agony in the Garden* was made in 1637 by Pierre Scalberge (c. 1592–1640).
2 In addition to the Descalzas Reales version, which he regards as a workshop copy, Stephen Pepper (1984) mentions a further copy in the Pierre Rosenberg collection in Paris, another whose whereabouts is unknown (though also in France), and a fourth copy on the New York art market; one of these might be the painting hailed by Laura Muti (2006) as the original.
3 Francesca Candi (2016, 184–86, nos. 21–23) lists the three engravings so far identified: Pierre Scalberge (1637), Jeremias Falck (1639–55), and François de Poilly (1669–93).
4 Pepper 1984, 222, no. 27; Stephen Pepper in Pirovano 1985, 176–78, no. 52.
5 See note 3.
6 Patrick Matthiesen and Stephen Pepper (1970, 459–60), and again Stephen Pepper (1984, 222, no. 26) suggest that the London painting came from the Spanish royal collection; however, the version now in the Prado [cat. 8], painted around 1602–3, is in fact the painting recorded at the Madrid Alcázar in 1666, as noted in Pérez Sánchez 1965a, 173. For further information, see Rafael Japón's entry for the latter in this catalogue.
7 Bailly-Engerand 1899, 156, no. 17.
8 Matthiesen and Pepper 1970, 459–60; S. Pepper in Pirovano 1985, 176–78, no. 52.
9 Cosnac 1884, 319, no. 1106.
10 Muti 2006.
11 Oil on canvas, 57.9 × 44.1 cm.

12   Guido Reni
The Agony in the Garden

c. 1607
Oil on copperplate, 50.5 × 43.5 cm
Patrimonio Nacional. Colecciones Reales. Monasterio de las Descalzas Reales de Madrid, inv. 00610862

Provenance: Monasterio de las Descalzas Reales, Madrid, 1615.

Selected bibliography: Pepper 1984, 222, no. 27; S. Pepper in Pirovano 1985, 176–78, no. 52; García Sanz 1992; Colomer 2006, 214–16 and 236; C. García-Frías Checa in Moya Valgañón 2011, 184–85; Redín Michaus 2016b, 21–22 and 43, note 33.

This painting in the convent of the Descalzas Reales is an exact replica of the Louvre version, now on long-term loan to the Musées de Sens [cat. 11]; the two pictures, painted on copper, are almost identical in both size and colour scheme. Because of its awkward location above the choir stalls in the convent church of the Descalzas Reales in Madrid, which was closed to the public until 1960, and given that until 2021 it hung at a considerable height, physical examination of the painting has proved something of a challenge to specialist historians. As a result, it is still sometimes catalogued as a copy of the Louvre original by Guido Reni.[1] Ana García Sanz was the first scholar to highlight the painting's artistic quality following its restoration in 1992, while José Luis Colomer has insisted on hailing it not only as an autograph work but also as the first version to reach Spain, since its presence in the convent church, beside the tomb of Empress Maria of Austria (1528–1603), can be traced back to 1615.

The meticulous technical execution of this painting points unmistakeably to Reni as the sole executor of the work during his early years in Rome. His hand is evident in the highly precise rendering of the cherubs and of Christ's face, the gleam in his beautifully upturned eyes, and the painstakingly depicted drops of blood, unique to this version. Differences in shades and glazes with respect to the Louvre picture, noticeable in the golden background, in the ultramarine of Christ's billowing cloak, or in the whites turning into unstable greys, are due to changes undergone by the painting in the course of its history.[2] These alterations are particularly evident in the dark night scene on the right of the painting, where the sleeping apostles and the soldiers about to arrest Christ can barely be discerned.

Following her death on 26 February 1603, Maria of Austria was buried in the convent church of the Descalzas Reales 'with only a plain, flat stone on top', as stipulated in her will.[3] The

Cat. 11

Catalogue

Cat. 12

The Road to Perfection

tomb was placed beneath an altar bearing a painting of the *Agony in the Garden* of 1586 by Diego de Urbina (1516–c. 1595), in the northeast corner of the lower cloister.[4] But Philip III, feeling that this was not a suitable resting-place for his aunt, decided that her remains should be moved to the southern end of the choir, where a niche was opened behind the choir stalls[5] to a design by Juan Gómez de Mora (1586–1648).[6] During the transfer ceremony held on 11 March 1615, the corpse was placed 'in a not very large chest, on which an imperial crown was laid'.[7] Father Juan Carrillo, confessor to the Empress's daughter Sister Margaret of the Cross (1567–1633) and to the Descalzas community, wrote that in 1615 'an altar was placed over the tomb, with a picture of the Agony in the Garden, surmounted by a very rich black canopy and many lights'.[8] While this complied with his aunt's wish to be buried beneath an *Agony in the Garden*,[9] the empress's preference for this new location was prompted by the fact that the altar with Urbina's painting, located on the eastern side of the lower cloister, was set aside for tombs. The new home behind the choir stall proved to be temporary; the definitive niche was not completed until June 1622, while the jasper urn – produced to a design by Giovanni Battista Crescenzi (1577–1635) resembling those in the Royal Pantheon at El Escorial – was not finished until the autumn of 1631.[10] The Empress's remains were kept in the Niño Jesús chapel in the upper cloister until the following year, when they were transferred, possibly with Reni's painting on copper, to their final place of rest.[11]

As for its provenance, the painting is commonly thought to have been commissioned by Pope Paul V;[12] there are good grounds for this view, since the pope – like his nephew Scipione Borghese – was among Guido's major clients during the artist's time in Rome. Given the period in which it was painted, the picture was probably intended as a gift from the pope to Philip III, entrusted to one of his ambassadors in Rome: either Gastón de Moncada, 2nd Marquis of Aytona (1554–1626), who held the post from 1606 to 1609, or Francisco Ruiz de Castro, 8th Count of Lemos (1579–1637), who was ambassador from 1609 to 1615.

But following the death of her mother in 1603, Sister Margaret of the Cross also received diplomatic gifts – particularly holy relics – from Paul V, delivered by representatives of the Holy See.[13] While the idea that the painting entered the Spanish royal collection alongside Reni's *Assumption and Coronation of the Virgin*[14] now in the Prado [cat. 8][15] is certainly appealing, there is no record of its presence in the royal collections before the 1666 inventory of the Madrid Alcázar, whereas the *Agony in the Garden* is documented in the collection as early as 1615.

Carmen García-Frías Checa

1 Stephen Pepper (1984, 222, no. 27, and Pepper in Pirovano 1985, 176–78, no. 52) admits that he has not seen it himself, but relies on information provided by Alfonso E. Pérez Sánchez. See Redín Michaus 2016a. There is a seventeenth-century copy, attributable to the Italian school, in a private collection in Nájera (La Rioja); see Fernández Pardo 1996, 75–76, fig. 59.

2 There is some paint loss along the lower and right sides of the copper support, caused by extreme heat. Rather than the fire that ravaged part of the church in 1862, which mainly affected the chancel, the heat probably came from occasional candles; alternatively, losses might have been caused by the drying agent used in the dark areas of the painting, where the most extensive flaking is to be found.

3 Carrillo 1616, 218r.

4 A papal brief issued by Clement VIII granted permission for her to be buried in the cloister of the Descalzas Reales, as noted in Carrillo 1616, 218r–221r.

5 Ibid., 221v–223r.

6 Tovar Martín 1979, 85–96; Blanco Mozo 2015, 17; Toajas Roger 2016, 366.

7 As reported by Cassiano dal Pozzo, who accompanied Cardinal Francesco Barberini on a visit to the choir of the Descalzas Reales on 30 May 1626; see Anselmi 2004, 116–19.

8 Carrillo 1616, 223r: 'un altar, con una imagen de la Oracion del huerto, sobre el qual avia un muy rico dosel negro, y muchas luzes'.

9 García Sanz 1992.

10 Blanco Mozo 2015, 16–21.

11 Father Juan de Palma (1636, 254v–255r) refers to the transfer, but gives no date.

12 Ana García Sanz (1992, 59) suggests that the painting may have been a gift from Cardinal Camillo Borghese, the future Pope Paul V, when he was papal legate in Spain (1593–96), although this would mean that it was produced much earlier than previously thought.

13 García-Frías Checa (in press).

14 See the entry for the Louvre *Agony in the Garden* [cat. 11].

15 Pérez Sánchez 1965a, 173; Pepper 1984, 219, no. 14.

III

IN ROME: BETWEEN RAPHAEL AND CARAVAGGIO

After the Jubilee year of 1600, perhaps driven by arguments with his master Ludovico Carracci, Guido Reni made his first trip to Rome, then the undisputed art capital of Europe. The city was to have a crucial impact on his subsequent career, for it was there that he discovered the outstanding legacy of classical antiquity; there, too, he was able to examine at first hand the work of Raphael, an artist he greatly admired. But the most remarkable feature of his sojourn in Rome was his insistence on emulating the art of Caravaggio, the most radical, ground-breaking artist then active in the city. On seeing Caravaggio's work, Guido promptly modified his own approach, with the avowed intention of outdoing Caravaggio by imitating his very particular style, an attitude which turned him for a time into a kind of 'anti-Caravaggio'. Reni's interest was shared by a contemporary Spanish painter who would also go on to become a leading figure on the seventeenth-century art scene: Jusepe de Ribera. But this experimental phase proved transitory, just one more step in the shaping of his own identity. Nowhere is this more apparent than in his superb altarpiece depicting the *Massacre of the Innocents* [cat. 20].

13 Guido Reni
The Martyrdom of Saint Apollonia

c. 1600–3
Oil on copperplate, 28 × 20 cm
Madrid, Museo Nacional del Prado, P-214

Provenance: Carlo Maratta, Rome, 1712; collection of Philip V, Palacio Real de La Granja de San Ildefonso, Segovia, 1723 (no. 162) and 1727; oratory at the Palacio Real de La Granja de San Ildefonso, Segovia, 1746 (no. 248); small oratory at the Palacio Real, Aranjuez, 1794 (no. 248), and king's small oratory, 1818 (no. 248); Museo del Prado, Madrid, since 1819.

Selected bibliography: Pérez Sánchez 1965a, 177; Pepper 1984, 217–18; *Museo del Prado* 1990, 1:240; Pierleoni 1991, 152 and 206; Aterido Fernández, Martínez Cuesta and Pérez Preciado 2004, 2:20; Colomer 2006, 227–28; R. Japón in Cappelletti 2022a, 104–7, no. 3.

Saint Apollonia lived in Alexandria in the first half of the third century AD. As the daughter of a civil servant, she received a broad intellectual education. She is thought to have converted to Christianity as a child, on learning that her mother, anxious to conceive, had besought the assistance of the Virgin Mary. According to Dionysius, Bishop of Alexandria, Apollonia devoted herself from an early age to preaching the Christian faith, and was even appointed *parthénos presbytis*, a post probably equivalent to that of deaconess. During festivities held in the reign of Emperor Philip the Arab to commemorate the millennium of the founding of Rome, a series of popular revolts took place against the Christians, which the authorities made no attempt to subdue. In the course of one such uprising, Apollonia was seized by the mob and beaten on the face until all her teeth were broken; she was then taken to a place beyond the city gates and ordered to blaspheme and renounce her faith in Jesus Christ. Though aware that failure to do so would lead to her being burnt alive, Apollonia refused to recant, preferring to throw herself into the flames and thus end her life.

The heirs of Carlo Maratta (1625–1713) sold part of his collection of paintings to the Spanish crown in 1722, offering Philip V three original works by Guido Reni: a *Saint Catherine* [cat. 84], this *Martyrdom of Saint Apollonia*, and a *Saint Apollonia at Prayer* [cat. 14]. The latter two formed a pair, for in addition to addressing the same theme, they were both painted on copper and were exactly the same size. Here, the saint is shown with her hands tied to a tall stake which rises up behind her, flanked by two tormentors. One uses his left hand to pull her head back by her hair, brandishing in his right hand a pair of pincers holding a tooth, while the other uses both hands to lift his pliers towards Apollonia's mouth with the intention of pulling out more teeth.

Jacobus de Voragine wrote in some detail about the torture of Apollonia, testifying to the widespread popularity of her story in the Middle Ages, when prayers addressed to her were thought to cure toothache. The best-known accounts of her martyrdom, including the biography in Voragine's *Golden*

Fig. 72 Guido Reni, *The Martyrdom of Saint Apollonia*, c. 1632–33. Oil on copperplate, 44.5 × 34.5 cm. Dresden, Staatliche Kunstsammlungen, Gemäldegalerie Alte Meister, Gal.-Nr. 377

Legend compiled around 1260, report that her teeth were knocked out rather than extracted in an attempt to silence her, both literally and symbolically, and thus stop her from actively spreading Christianity in her community. Here, however, the two executioners wield pliers, indicating that Reni drew on the iconographic tradition rather than on literary sources. The pincers had long been the attribute by which Saint Apollonia was identified, appearing in numerous paintings even before the fourteenth century. Guido's picture is similar, in terms of composition, to a miniature painted by Simon Marmion (c. 1425–1489) in the mid-fifteenth century,[1] which features the same elements, including the stake.

This is by no means the only difference between the painting and the written sources. Reni, again following the visual cultural tradition, portrays Apollonia as a young virgin with a pale, smooth complexion, wearing a flowing, figure-hugging dress; in fact, at the time of her death she was an old woman. Guido's treatment of the saint's body may well have been based on the central figure in the *Ecstasy of Saint Cecilia* by Raphael (1483–1520),[2] with which he would have been familiar since his youth in Bologna. Apart from the position of the hands, the posture of the two saints is identical; they have the same facial expression, and their garments are very similar in design. According to Carlo Cesare Malvasia in his *Felsina Pittrice* (1678), Guido even copied Raphael's painting, which hung at the time in the church of San Giovanni in Monte in Bologna; some historians believe that Reni's copy is the *Ecstasy* in the church of San Luigi dei Francesi in Rome, while others identify it as the version in the National Gallery of Ireland.[3] The two paintings display a similar compositional balance: Raphael's Saint Cecilia is flanked by two pairs of saints, those nearest to her being depicted in profile, like the two tormentors in Reni's picture.

Guido addressed this episode in at least one other painting, which was in the Barberini collection in Rome until the eighteenth century, when it was purchased by the Duke of Orléans. Though its whereabouts is now unknown, a surviving copy that had also hung in the Palazzo Barberini – and is regarded as an autograph version too – can now be seen at the Dresden Gemäldegalerie [fig. 72]. The original, probably painted in around 1606–7, differs considerably from this Prado *Martyrdom* with regard to both the placing of the saint and the background – which in the later painting features a highly-elaborate landscape with ruins – while the style has also become noticeably brighter. By contrast, the Prado *Martyrdom* displays a certain technical naiveté and a greater reliance on the impact of the Caravaggio-like use of chiaroscuro, suggesting that it must have been painted some years earlier, probably around 1600.

Rafael Japón

1 Amsterdam, Rijksmuseum, RP-T-1961-100.
2 Bologna, Pinacoteca Nazionale di Bologna, inv. 577.
3 Dublin, National Gallery of Ireland, NGI.70; Malvasia–Pericolo 2019, 1:37.

14   Guido Reni
Saint Apollonia in Prayer

c. 1600–3
Oil on copperplate, 28 × 20 cm
Madrid, Museo Nacional del Prado, P-215

Provenance: Carlo Maratta, Rome, 1712; collection of Philip V, Palacio Real de La Granja de San Ildefonso, Segovia, 1723 (no. 47) and 1727; oratory at the Palacio Real de La Granja de San Ildefonso, Segovia, 1746 (no. 249); small oratory at the Palacio Real, Aranjuez, 1794 (no. 249) and king's small oratory, 1818; Madrid, Museo Nacional del Prado, since 1819.

Selected bibliography: Pérez Sánchez 1965a, 177; Pepper 1984, 217–18; *Museo del Prado* 1990, 1:240; Pierleoni 1991, 152, 206; Aterido Fernández, Martínez Cuesta and Pérez Preciado 2004, 2:20; Colomer 2006, 227–28; R. Japón in Cappelletti 2022a, 100–3, no. 2.

This painting, a pendant to the *Martyrdom of Saint Apollonia* also in the Museo del Prado [cat. 13], depicts an episode immediately following the beating during which the saint's teeth were knocked out. The young woman kneels in prayer, her hands folded on her breast and her mouth half open to display the consequences of her torture; her upward gaze rests on an angel, emerging from the clouds to present her with the martyr's palm and the saint's crown. Prominently placed in the foreground are the pincers with which she was tortured and the fire that alludes to the manner of her death, whose rising smoke merges into the burst of glory.

By including these objects, Guido Reni recreates the moment, just before the saint's death, when she accepts God's will, thus resigning herself to her tragic destiny. The scene exudes a serenity somewhat at odds with the violence described in the literary sources, for at that very moment the torturers were threatening to cast her into the flames if she refused to blaspheme against Jesus Christ. Unintimidated by their threats, Apollonia chose instead to throw herself onto the fire, thus meeting her death without losing her faith. Here, by contrast, Guido depicts a young woman fearful at the thought of dying, being comforted by the angel. The sombre atmosphere, enhanced by the dark background, conveys a sense of contemplation, the idea that the saint is captured in a moment of introspection, in direct dialogue with God. This device is found in other works from this period attributed to Reni, such as the *Martyrdom of Saint Cecilia* in the Museo della Certosa,[1] and was widely used by other seventeenth-century artists as an ideal resource for visually translating miracles and mystical visions. Nowhere is this more apparent than in the work of Francisco de

Zurbarán (1598–1664), a good example of which is the Prado *Vision of Saint Peter Nolasco*.[2]

Interestingly, the saint's attire differs in each picture: in the *Martyrdom* she is dressed in a green and yellow robe, whereas here she wears a red gown with orange-tinted sleeves and a delicate white scarf around her neck. With this change, Guido may have sought to draw a parallel between her gown and the colour

of the flames which were to bring to an end her earthly existence. In depicting scenes from the lives of saints, artists often used clothing to identify the central figure in different situations; these two paintings may therefore have formed part of a larger series on the life of Apollonia, which was subsequently dispersed.

Although both pictures were confidently attributed to Reni by Alfonso E. Pérez Sánchez[3] – albeit classed as minor works produced in his youth – Stephen Pepper later dismissed them as copies of lost originals.[4] At present, however, critics agree that they are autograph paintings executed around 1600, when the young Guido, who had just arrived in Rome, was discovering the naturalism practiced by Caravaggio and his followers. While not displaying the flawless technique evident in Reni's work from 1605 onwards, these pictures are regarded as providing rare evidence of the experimental phase – and the stylistic transition – through which the artist was going at that time. Indeed, some critics even see similarities between this *Saint Apollonia* and the nymph in *Landscape with Cupids playing* painted during the same period [cat. 63].[5] Another work displaying an undeniable resemblance, in terms of composition and technique, is the *Assumption and Coronation of the Virgin* in the Museo del Prado [cat. 8], where the positioning of the main figures and of the angels hovering above is very similar. The *Assumption* dates from around 1602–3, suggesting that the two Saint Apollonia paintings may have been produced slightly earlier.

These two pictures confirm that, at an early stage in his career, Guido had already begun to shape his own highly personal image of saintliness, one which was to prove highly successful because it perfectly reflected post-Tridentine thought. Once in Rome, he was involved in several commissions for images of martyrs, whose veneration had spread due to the discovery, among other things, of the incorrupt remains of Saint Cecilia.[6] In works of this kind, Reni liked to portray saints with their eyes raised towards heaven, an expression that would come to be associated with the triumph of Christian heroes, and of which he would make use throughout his career.

The Spanish monarchs thought very highly of these paintings from the moment they were acquired in 1722, as attested by their placing in the oratory at the royal palace at La Granja de San Ildefonso in Segovia together with a *Saint Catherine* by the same artist [cat. 84]. There they would remain until 1794, when they were recorded in a chapel at the royal palace of Aranjuez.

Rafael Japón

1 Pavia, Museo della Certosa, inv. 407.
2 Madrid, Museo Nacional del Prado, P-1237.
3 Pérez Sánchez 1965a, 177.
4 Pepper 1984, 218.
5 Pulini 2019, 39–43.
6 Terzaghi 2022, 31.

15 Michelangelo Merisi da Caravaggio
(Milan 1571–1610 Porto Ercole, Italy)

David with the Head of Goliath

c. 1600
Oil on canvas, 110.4 × 91.3 cm
Madrid, Museo Nacional del Prado, P-65

Provenance: Estate of Charles III, Palacio del Buen Retiro, Madrid (attr. Caravaggio), 1794; storage rooms at the Palacio Real, Madrid (attr. school of Caravaggio), 1814–18; Museo del Prado, Madrid, 1849.

Selected bibliography: Madrazo 1872, no. 77; Venturi 1927, 369; Longhi 1943, 39; Ainaud de Lasarte 1947, 385; *Mostra del Caravaggio* 1951, 21; Pérez Sánchez 1970, 122, no. 32; *Museo del Prado* 1972, 115–16; Pérez Sánchez 1973, no. 2; Marini 1974, 149 and 380–381; Cinotti 1983, 454 (with earlier bibliography); Gregori 1985, 268–70; Gregori 1989, 122–23; Gregori 1991, 22 and 28–29; Marini 1996; Milicua 2005, 56–59; Cappelletti 2009, 47; Van der Sman 2016, 76–77; Vodret Adamo 2021, 158.

Compared with the many other treatments of this well-known biblical episode, the scene depicted in the Prado picture is somewhat unusual. It captures the moment when the young David, having felled the giant Goliath by striking him on the forehead with a stone hurled from his sling, 'ran and stood upon the Philistine, and took his sword, and drew it out of the sheath thereof, and slew him, and cut off his head therewith. … And David took the head of the Philistine, and brought it to Jerusalem' (1 Samuel 17:51 and 54). The young man, emerging from a shadowy background, straddles the giant's body, reaching down to seize Goliath's severed head – lying in the immediate foreground – by the hair, and tie it with a rope.

The Prado *David with the Head of Goliath*, one of the least popular paintings in the much-explored Caravaggio canon, has enjoyed mixed critical fortune, and considerable doubt persists as to its provenance. The documentary history of the painting only really begins in 1794, when it was listed in the inventory of the Buen Retiro palace under the reference number '1118', clearly visible in the lower right corner of the canvas: 'David triumphing over the Philistine, two and a quarter *varas* high and one *vara* wide, Michelangelo Carabacho'.[1] Yet these measurements do not match those of the canvas in question; taking the Castilian *vara* as equivalent to 83.49 centimetres, the painting should be well over 167 centimetres high, rather than the present 110 centimetres.[2] The difference could be due to an error either in measurement or in transcription. But it could also undoubtedly be attributed, wholly or in part, to the removal of a strip of canvas from the lower section, perhaps effected before 1794, when the number '1118' was inscribed in the lower

right corner. Early copies provide some idea of the appearance of the original canvas, which was considerably larger. In 1951, Roberto Longhi noted that there were 'several good seventeenth-century copies in various collections in Madrid … including one in the Medina-Daza collection'.[3] Later, Alfred Moir drew attention to a copy in the Haen collection,[4] while Maurizio Marini added a canvas seen in a Rome collection and another, judged to be of higher quality, in the United States.[5] In both, the hilt of Goliath's sword is shown in its entirety, together with the pebbles which, according to the biblical account, David kept in his pouch, and which are barely visible in the lower section of the original. In the Prado, this canvas was first listed as item '2081', attributed to Caravaggio, in the inventory drawn up in 1849; the reference number is still legible in the lower left corner of the painting. The attribution was repeated in 1872, and again in 1901 (inv. 77) and 1910 (inv. 65).[6] In any case, the presence of old copies in Madrid suggests that the Prado canvas must have been in Spain at an early stage. Yet it fails to match the descriptions provided in any seventeenth-century inventories. It certainly bears little resemblance to the 'half-length figure of David' by Caravaggio reported by Giovan Pietro Bellori in the collection of Juan de Tassis, Count of Villamediana;[7] judging by the description, and the fact that it is thought to date from Caravaggio's sojourn in Naples, this is much more likely to be the picture on the same theme in the Kunsthistorisches Museum, Vienna.[8] As for the original provenance of the painting, a mention in the will of Galeotto Uffreducci (or Eufreducci, 1566–1643) may shed some light on the issue. In his testament, drawn up on 26 January 1643,[9] Uffreducci – a canon at the church of Santa Maria Maggiore in Rome – bequeathed to his friend Monsignor Giulio Rospigliosi, the future Pope Clement IX, 'a David by Caravaggio'.[10] The picture is not listed in any known inventories of the assets of Rospigliosi, who was a leading figure in artistic, literary, and musical circles. It should be borne in mind, however, that in 1632 he was appointed to the chapter of Santa Maria Maggiore, where he must have met Uffreducci, and that in the spring of 1644 he travelled to Madrid as papal nuncio to the Spanish court, taking with him – according to letters to his family – many items from Rome to furnish a dwelling worthy of his rank.[11] During his nine years in Spain, Rospigliosi had the opportunity to engage closely with Philip IV and see his collection, and some of the *objets d'art* he brought from Italy may well have found their way into Spanish art-collecting circuits. At present, however, the only certainty is that the *David* listed in the Alcázar inventories from 1666 onwards as 'school of Caravaggio' is not this painting but rather – judging by the description and measurements – a canvas by Tanzio da Varallo (c. 1580–1632/33), which was on loan to the Spanish embassy in Buenos Aires.[12]

Attribution of the Prado canvas to Caravaggio has not always been unanimous: general, if sometimes reluctant, acceptance of the painting's authorship was achieved only after it had been restored in 1946–47, and once Roberto Longhi had rehabilitated the painting in 1951.[13] Major confirmation came with the publication, by Mina Gregori, of an X-ray of Goliath's head: in Caravaggio's initial composition, the giant was depicted immediately after his death, wild-eyed, his mouth open in a scream, in that respect closely resembling Holofernes in the *Judith and Holofernes* at the Palazzo Barberini, or the Uffizi *Medusa*.[14] The final version, however, is more restrained, whether at the request of the client or by choice of the artist, if Caravaggio was still unsure how to proceed. And in fact the whole poetic substance of the picture lies precisely in that sensitive balance 'between delicate idyll and atrocious drama'.[15] The still-firm brushstrokes and controlled facture, the ochre-based palette, the depiction of David using the lost profile technique – reminiscent, for example, of the angel accompanying Saint Matthew in the Contarelli chapel at the church of San Luigi dei Francesi in Rome, or of Isaac in the Uffizi painting[16] – all suggest that it cannot have been painted much later than the turn of the century.

Maria Cristina Terzaghi

1 Pérez Sánchez 1970, 122, no. 32; Pérez Sánchez 1973, no. 2: 'David triunfante del filisteo, dos varas y cuarta de alto y una vara de ancho, Michelangelo Carabacho'.
2 By contrast, the difference in width (9 cm) is wholly compatible.
3 R. Longhi in *Mostra del Caravaggio* 1951, 21.
4 Moir 1976, 107, no. 54, and 138–39, note 235. Moir, however, doubts that the Prado painting is an original.
5 Marini 1996, 135–42, figs. 221–25; Marini 2001, 577.
6 Pérez Sánchez 1970, 122, no. 32; Pérez Sánchez 1973, no. 2; Cinotti 1983, 454.
7 Bellori–Borea 1976, 214: 'La mezza figura di Davide'.
8 Vienna, Kunsthistorisches Museum Wien, Gemäldegalerie, inv. 125. On Caravaggio's commission from the Count of Villamediana, see Terzaghi 2021, with earlier bibliography. The suggestion that the canvas was brought to Spain by Giovan Battista Crescenzi (1577–1635) when he took up residence in Madrid in 1617 would appear equally arbitrary; it is a view no longer held by Marini, who canvassed it in the most recent edition of his monograph (Marini 2005, 429–30).
9 A similar view is expressed by Rosella Vodret Adamo (2021, 158).
10 Marini 2005, 430: 'un David del Caravaggio'.
11 On his collection, see Negro 2007.
12 For the 1666 inventory entry, see Marini 2001, 431, who also lists entries in later inventories, already discarded as possible references to this painting in Pérez Sánchez 1970, 122, no. 32
13 Doubts were still being expressed by Ainaud de Lasarte 1947, 385, no. 14; and also in *Museo del Prado* 1945, 111, no. 65.
14 Rome, Gallerie Nazionali, Palazzo Barberini, inv. 2533; Florence, Gallerie degli Uffizi, inv. 1890 n. 1351, respectively. Gregori 1989, 122–23; Gregori 1991, 22, 28, and 29.
15 R. Longhi in *Mostra del Caravaggio* 1951, 21.
16 Florence, Gallerie degli Uffizi, inv. 1890 n. 4659.

16 Guido Reni and workshop (?)
David with the Head of Goliath

c. 1630–31
Oil on canvas, 228 × 163 cm
Orléans, Musée des Beaux-Arts, inv. 1177

Provenance: Collection of Louis Phélypeaux de La Vrillière, until 1681; by inheritance, his son Balthazar, until 1700; by inheritance, his son Louis II, until 1705; by purchase, Louis Raulin Rouillé, until 1713; by purchase, Louis Alexandre de Bourbon, Count of Toulouse, until 1737; by inheritance, Louis Jean Marie de Bourbon, Duke of Penthièvre at Châteauneuf-sur-Loire, until 23 October 1793, when it was moved by revolutionaries to the Louvre in Paris; on permanent loan in Orléans, Musée des Beaux-Arts, from 1872; owned by the city of Orléans since 2007.

Selected bibliography: Cotté 1985, 92, nos. 14 and 21; Haffner 1988, 33–34; Pepper 1988, 222, no. 8; Loire 1990, 29; Pepper 1992, 139 and 144, note 47; Loire 1996, 412; Klinka-Ballesteros 2009, 44–45; Szanto 2011, 229–31; Malvasia–Pericolo 2019, 1:320–21, note 282; C. Dury in Eclercy 2022a, 144–45, no. 33.

This canvas, one of Guido Reni's most famous compositions, shows the young hero David – the future King of Israel – leaning against a broken column, holding the severed head of the giant Goliath, which rests on a rectangular stone block. By means of a cunning stratagem, David had succeeded in defeating the giant, thus saving his people. On the corner, the sword lays at the young man's feet, like the brute strength of the giant which has given way to the hero's meditation on the fate of the defeated.

The painting's provenance can be reliably traced up to 1872, when it entered the Musée des Beaux-Arts in Orléans, following the change of ownership of the Hôtel de La Vrillière in Paris. The 1681 post mortem inventory of the estate of Louis Phélypeaux, first Seigneur de La Vrillière and owner of the house, contains the following entry: 'Item a large painting in height painted on canvas with its carved and gilded frame representing a "David holding the head of Goliath", said to be from the Guide, valued at four hundred livres'.[1] For La Vrillière, secretary of state to two successive kings – Louis XIII and Louis XIV – Italian art was a lifelong passion. Among contemporary artists, he was particularly fond of Guido, and indeed managed to acquire one of the artist's masterpieces, the *Abduction of Helen* [fig. 35] intended for Marie de' Medici, the French queen regent. The history of the *Abduction* is inextricably linked to the queen's mixed but well-charted fortunes.[2] Due to a plague outbreak in 1630, followed by Marie's exile to the Château de Compiègne after a series of political intrigues

aimed at ousting Cardinal Richelieu, the painting took some time to reach Paris. In July 1631, having escaped from Compiègne, the queen took refuge at the court in Brussels, and from there attempted to regain possession of the painting, which was still in Bologna. A record of the negotiations can be found in the correspondence between Cardinal Bernardino Spada and the queen's agent, the abbot of San Luca in Bologna. On 27 July 1631, Spada wrote to the abbot, bemoaning the queen's fate and lamenting the fact that in Bologna:

> I had found a David recently executed by Guido Reni and sold for 200 ducatons, modelled on the first one, but reported to be far more beautiful; and at the same time I learned that, while the painting belonging to Theodosio Porta had been retouched by Guido, it was in any case not the true original, which he claims is in Genoa.[3]

The rush of events forced Marie de' Medici to abandon her claims on Reni's masterpiece, even though she had paid for it generously: the *Abduction of Helen* eventually reached Paris, but was purchased by Louis Phélypeaux de La Vrillière, who – as we have seen – also owned this *David*. Copies of both paintings are recorded in the collection of Michel Particelli d'Hemery, La Vrillière's father-in-law, as early as 1650.[4] They also shared a common destiny, being moved to the Louvre in the late eighteenth century; but unlike the great canvas intended for Marie de' Medici, the Museum had no qualms about parting with the *David*, which was placed on loan to Orléans, since the French royal collection had long boasted an older version of the same theme. The correspondence mentioned earlier clearly shows there were various versions of Guido's *David*, whose autograph status was unclear even to his contemporaries; charting their provenance thus poses something of a challenge.[5] Of the twelve known versions to date, the earliest is generally agreed to be the canvas now in the Louvre,[6] on which this *David* is only partially based: here, Goliath's head is turned towards, rather than away from, his enemy, in a position that more closely resembles that of the Uffizi version,[7] recorded in the collection of Carlo de' Medici at least since 1666.[8] In the late 1630s, then, two versions of Reni's masterpiece were to be found in Paris. Spada's advice regarding the purchase of a *David* for the queen was therefore unlikely to be a chance suggestion. The cardinal may have been aware that Marie de' Medici wished to own something similar to the painting she had seen in the collection of Marshal Charles de Créquy, which would later enter the collection of Marie's own son, Gaston, Duke of Orléans.[9] But while Créquy may have acquired his painting in the course of his Italian wanderings, it is less easy to chart the route by which the Orléans *David* came to France. Given the co-incidences noted so far, it would be tempting to imagine that the *Abduction of Helen* and the Orléans *David* travelled together from one collection to another; however, a letter written in January 1633 by Cornelio Malvasia, to the Duke of Modena, Francesco I d'Este, seems to prove that the picture referred to by Spada was still on the market in Bologna:

> There is also another painting for sale, showing David with the head of the slain Giant, which is much larger than the other [the *Saint Sebastian*], but to my mind the beauty of this one is unrivalled, and now the Cardinal legate is having a copy made of it. This painting deserves to enter the gallery of your Highness, although the Owner is very fond of it, and I imagine will not part with it for less than three hundred silver ducatons.[10]

The painting was duly sold to Francesco I d'Este and, after numerous changes of ownership, has been reliably identified as the version formerly on loan to the National Gallery, London, and now in a private collection.[11] However, Malvasia's letter mentions that, before selling the picture to the Duke of Modena, the cardinal legate Antonio Santacroce had a copy made of it, just as Spada had commissioned a copy of the *Abduction of Helen* from Giacinto Campana (c. 1600–c. 1650).[12] As with the latter painting, which mysteriously disappeared for a long period of time, it is hard not to suspect that what was sent to France was actually a workshop copy of *David* – perhaps touched up by the master – rather than the original. Even so, and quite apart from the question of provenance, there is a further doubt regarding the claim of the London version to be the canvas that was first in Bologna and later in Modena: its attribution to Simone Cantarini (1612–1648), whose movingly vibrant painterly style remarkably resembles that of the English *David*; so much so, indeed, that the young hero's superbly characterised head has been seen as a self-portrait of Cantarini.[13] On the other hand, recent restoration of the Orléans picture has highlighted its considerable quality, to the extent that some critics, instead of classifying it as a workshop copy, now regard it as an autograph work.[14] Whatever the case, Reni certainly worked on the picture at very different times; the

initial composition can be dated to the 1610s, and was certainly completed before 1619, when the famous poet Giovan Battista Marino included a sonnet devoted to the painting in his *Galeria*, which was published that year in Venice.[15] He returned to it at the end of the 1620s or around 1630, producing a number of autograph replicas as well as retouched versions, whose quality was always checked by the great master.

Maria Cristina Terzaghi

1 Cotté 1985, 92, no. 21: 'Item un grand tableau en hauteur peint sur toille avec sa bordure taillé et dorée representant un "David tenant la teste de Goliath", soy-disant du Guide, prisé quatre cens livres'.

2 In addition to Malvasia 1678, 2:30, see Dirani 1982; Pepper 1988; Colantuono 1997, with earlier bibliography; Pierguidi 2012b. See also Stefano Pierguidi's essay, 'Viceroys, Ambassadors, Agents, Theologians: Thirty Years of (Stormy) Relations between Guido Reni and Spain', in this catalogue.

3 Dirani 1982, 89; Pepper 1992, 129: 'Havevo trovato un David, fatto nuovamente da Guido Reni e venduto 200 ducatoni sull'andar del primo, ma secondo ch'ei dice assai più bello, e con quest'occasione avevo imparato che, se bene il quadro del Theodosio Porta era stato ritoccato da Guido, ad ogni modo non era il vero originale, il quale professa che si trovi in Genova'.

4 Szanto 2011, 229–31. There is, in any case, no evidence that the painting passed from the collection of Michel Particelli d'Hemery and his daughter Marie, to that of her husband Louis Phélypeaux de La Vrillière, a possibility suggested in Gilet and Moinet 1996, 370, no. 422, and by C. Dury in Eclercy 2022a, 144–45, no. 33.

5 Stephen Pepper (1992) lists the most important copies.

6 Paris, Musée du Louvre, inv. 519.

7 Florence, Gallerie degli Uffizi, inv. 1890 n. 3830.

8 This is noted in Loire 1996, 412. For the Uffizi canvas, see A. Jommelli's recent essay in Cappelletti 2022a, 142–45.

9 Boyer and Volf 1988, 34–35. In the eighteenth century, Pierre-Jean Mariette saw the picture in the Palais du Luxembourg, claiming that it had been taken to Versailles in 1743, and that the Bologna version was then in the collection of Eugene of Savoy in Vienna (Mariette 1851–60 [1858], 4:361).

10 Venturi 1882, 185–86: 'È anco in vendita un altro quadro nel quale vi è un Davide con la testa del Gigante ucciso d'assai maggior grandezza del altro, ma questo pare a me che non habbi paragone in bellezza et hora il S.r Card.le legato ne fa cavar copia. Questo quadro merita di venire nella galleria di V.A. se bene è ancor lui caro assai, che stimo non lo lascij il Padrone per meno di trecento ducatoni d'argento'.

11 Pepper 1992; London, Sotheby's, 2012, lot 32; Malvasia–Pericolo 2019, 1:320–21, note 282. Raffaella Morselli (2012a, 147) displays some caution regarding the picture that was in London.

12 Venturi 1882, 185–86.

13 Pulini 2002; Morselli 2012a, 146–47.

14 Malvasia–Pericolo 2019, 1:320–21, note 282.

15 Marino–Pieri 1979, 1:51: 'Ecco l'Alcide Hebreo / se già trà rozi armenti ancor Garzone / fù sbranator di fere, / ora tra squadre guerrere hà lodi e vate / d'uccisor di Giganti. / Quel teschio, che sostien tremando e reo / del crudo Filisteo / ben fora a gli occhi miei novo Gorgone, / ma s'io ben miro il vincitore, e'l vinto. Più bello è il vivo, ch'orrido l'estinto' ('Behold the Jewish Alcides / who once among rough flocks when still a Boy / was a slayer of wild beasts, / now among warring hosts wins praise and fame / as a slayer of Giants. / That skull he holds, huge and evil, / of the brutish Philistine / could well be a new Gorgon to my eyes, / yet looking hard at the victor and the vanquished / more beautiful is the one alive, than hideous is the one dead').

17 Guido Reni
David beheading Goliath

c. 1606–7
Oil on canvas, 174.4 × 133 cm
Remagen (Germany), Arp Museum Bahnhof Rolandseck /
Sammlung Rau für UNICEF, inv. GR 1.261

Provenance: Collection of Agostino Giusti (?), Verona, 1620; by inheritance, collection of Gian Giacomo Giusti (?), until 1641; by inheritance, his sons Francesco and Marcantonio Giusti (?); Silvano Lodi Gallery; Gustav Rau collection, 1984.

Selected bibliography: Pepper 1984, 221; Schleier 1986, 109; F. Valli in Emiliani et al. 1988, 48; Restellini 2001, 32; Dossi 2008, 119; Malvasia–Pericolo 2019, 1:282–83, note 186; A. Röstel in Eclercy 2022a, 146–47, no. 35.

This canvas, which is in a good state of repair, depicts the beheading of the giant Goliath, cunningly defeated by the young David in order to save his people. Guido Reni opted for a pyramidal composition, the apex of which is formed by the hero's raised arms, wielding the heavy drawn sword with which he is about to behead the fallen giant. Goliath's prostrate body forms the horizontal base of the pyramid; his helmet lies close to his body, and David rests one knee on his back. A beautiful silent landscape stretches into the distance. Reni's palette focuses entirely on the colour contrast between the red of the cloak around David's slender body, the blue of the background, and the dark hues of Goliath's head and armour. By placing the life-size figures in the immediate foreground, and highlighting the violent contrast between David's lithe form and the giant's graceless bulk, Guido undoubtedly produced one of the most fascinating treatments of the Old Testament episode, clearly in tune with the naturalist poetics brought to Rome by Caravaggio (1571–1610) in the early seventeenth century.

The painting's documented history is recent: it passed in 1984 from the collection of Silvano Lodi to that of the great philanthropist Gustav Rau, who upon his death in 2002 bequeathed his collection to UNICEF, in whose headquarters the picture now hangs. Its critical history is equally recent. In fact, the canvas was first hailed as an autograph work by Reni in 1984, by Stephen Pepper,[1] who credited Mina Gregori with the initial attribution (it was presumably suggested to him in person, since there is no written record of it). Given her familiarity with the Lodi collection, Gregori may well have seen the picture before it entered the German collection, where Pepper encountered it.

It would be futile to comb the sources in search of this painting, for it was wholly overlooked by Guido's biographers. However, a David slaying Goliath is recorded in the collection of Agostino Giusti in Verona; as Francesco Pona remarks: 'I do not ask you the author of this beautiful David, who has struck down and slain the dreaded giant, for I know that I myself saw it being painted in Bologna, by our own Guido Rheni'.[2] The inventory of Giusti's paintings indeed lists 'A life-size figure of David by Reni',[3] and the matching dimensions add significant weight to the idea that the inventoried canvas is in fact the painting in the Rau collection. A manuscript by Marcello Oretti also refers to this source: 'Verona, in the house of Count Giusti dal Giardino, David slaying the giant, a picture that Francesco Pona, the Verona doctor, saw being painted, and mentioned in his book Sileno'.[4] Hence Pepper's unquestioning belief that the Rau David was the canvas in the Verona collection;[5] yet such a hypothesis must be treated with the utmost caution. Pona certainly reports seeing a David being painted in Bologna, where he is known to have stayed in 1615,[6] which would indicate a fairly late date for the picture. In the absence of documentary evidence, however, critics tend to date it to the early 1600s: while some art historians suggest it was produced after 1607, recent research points to a date of around 1605,[7] which would mean that it was painted in Rome. As for the genesis of the painting itself, in which Mannerist influences are evident – with echoes not only of the Sistine chapel ceiling by Michelangelo (1475–1564), but also of Daniele da Volterra (c. 1509–1566) and even Pordenone (1483/84–1539)[8] – a number of surviving drawings are regarded as preparatory sketches for the picture. Some are in the Biblioteca Vallicelliana, together with an album of studies for engravings by Luca Ciamberlano (c. 1570/80–c. 1641) of Episodes from the Life of Saint Philip Neri, whose attribution to Reni is by no means universally accepted; these engravings have also been linked to another set of drawings now in the Uffizi.[9] Two of the drawings focus on the story of David and Goliath. The attribution to Guido of the Uffizi drawing – which shows David dragging the giant's head by the hair – has rightly been rejected.[10] By contrast, the drawing in the Biblioteca Vallicelliana may well be a preliminary draft of Reni's David.[11]

In addition to the sixteenth-century influences mentioned earlier, Reni also appears to have been familiar with the David with the Head of Goliath by Caravaggio now in the Prado [cat. 15], but perhaps the most closely-related contemporary paintings are the beautiful David and Goliath by Orazio Gentileschi (1563–1639) in the National Gallery of Ireland[12] and – despite

significant variations – the *David and Goliath* by Orazio Borgianni (1574–1616) in the Real Academia de Bellas Artes de San Fernando in Madrid,[13] both of which can be dated to around 1605. Reni's canvas shares – especially with Gentileschi – the poetic, light-filled interpretation of Caravaggio's painterly idiom, as well as the naturalistic setting which assumes a dominant role in Guido's picture. Indeed, research into Reni's work as a landscape artist during his early years in Rome enables us to date the canvas to this hectic stage in his career. It shares certain characteristics with other large-format paintings produced at around this time, particularly the *Martyrdom of Saint Catherine of Alexandria* in the Museo Diocesano of Albenga (Italy), formerly owned by the wealthy banker Ottavio Costa, which displays a similar use of colour and a comparable taste for landscape; even the torturer's pose, with sword drawn, resembles that of David. The Albenga masterpiece was undoubtedly painted around 1605, and I believe that this *David* – remarkable for its greater compositional synthesis – was produced afterwards. Guido travelled frequently between Rome and Bologna during this period, so it is not easy to determine where he began the painting; however, it may be – particularly if we accept that it later entered the Giusti collection – that Reni worked on the canvas in both cities, or that it was taken from Rome to Bologna, where Pona may also have seen it at some later date. Whatever the case, comparison with the versions of *David* mentioned above highlights the uniquely innovative language of Guido's painting: engaging both with Mannerism and with Caravaggism, it is ultimately his focus on nature that allows him to distance himself from both.

Maria Cristina Terzaghi

1 Pepper 1984, 221.

2 Pona 1620, 21: 'Ma di questo bellissimo Davidde c'ha lo spaventoso gigante atterrato, e morto, non vi chiedo il maestro, poiché so haverlo io stesso veduto a dipingere in Bologna al nostro Guido Rheni'. His description of the collection takes the form of a dialogue between a native of Verona – Francesco Pona himself – and a stranger from Bologna. For the collection, see particularly Dossi 2008, 119; Dossi and Marcorin 2020.

3 Guzzo 2004, 403. On the death of Count Agostino Giusti in 1615, his son Gian Giacomo should have drawn up a list of all his father's *objets d'art* in the Verona house; however, he failed to do so. It was not until 1697 that an inventory was published of the *Quadri acquistati dal Sig. Conte Giovan Giacomo Giusti padre comune che deve esser divisi col sig. Marco Antonio mio fratello*, which provided a summary of the art collection in 1641, on the death of Gian Giacomo, when his estate was divided between his sons Francesco and Marcantonio; see Guzzo 2004, 401–4.

4 Marcello Oretti, *Le pitture che si ammirano nelli palazzi e case de' nobili nella città di Bologna e di altri edifici in detta città*, manuscript, Bologna, Biblioteca Comunale dell'Archiginnasio, Ms B 104: 'Verona, presso li conti Giusti dal Giardino, Davide che fa morto il gigante pittura che vidde dipingere Francesco Pona medico veronese citato nel suo libro il Sileno'. Oretti's quotation, transcribed here for the first time, was mentioned in Pepper 1984, 221.

5 Pepper 1984, 221.

6 Bondi 2015.

7 Stephen Pepper (1984, 221) opted for 1607–8, while Lorenzo Pericolo (Malvasia–Pericolo 2019, 1:283, note 186) has suggested an earlier date.

8 An influence first noted by Carlo Cesare Malvasia; see Pepper 1984, 221.

9 For the drawings in the Biblioteca Vallicelliana, see particularly Parma Armani 1978–79; Papi and Zicarelli 1988; Melasecchi and Pepper 1998; Pampalone and Barchiesi 2017.

10 Florence, Gallerie degli Uffizi, Gabinetto dei Disegni e delle Stampe, inv. 1579F. Babette Bohn (2008, 167) tentatively attributes this drawing – earlier thought to be by Guido (Petrioli Tofani 1991–2005 [2005], 2:267) – to the school of Giovanni Francesco Gessi (1588–1649).

11 Rome, Biblioteca Vallicelliana, Cod. O 23, fol. 448v (other sketches on this theme can be found in fols. 482, 485, 486, and 491). The plate has only been published by Elena Parma Armani (1978–79, 143 and 375, fig. 86), who is not familiar with Reni's picture, and thus traces no link between the drawing and the painting.

12 Dublin, National Gallery of Ireland, NGI.980.

13 Madrid, Real Academia de Bellas Artes de San Fernando, inv. 93.

18 Jusepe de Ribera
(Játiva, Valencia 1591–1652 Naples)

Saint Sebastian

1617
Oil on canvas, 179 × 139 cm
Osuna, Antigua Colegiata de Osuna

Provenance: Commissioned in 1617 by Pedro Téllez-Girón y Velasco Guzmán, 3rd Duke of Osuna, and his wife, Doña Catalina Enríquez de Ribera; donated by Doña Catalina to the Colegiata de Nuestra Señora de la Asunción of Osuna in 1627; kept in the presbytery until 1770, when the painting was incorporated into a new high altar.

Selected bibliography: Pérez Sánchez and Spinosa 1992, 71–72, no. 13; Spinosa 2003, 260, no. A36; G. Finaldi in Milicua and Portús Pérez 2011, 162–66; Farina 2014, 128–29; Farina 2018, esp. 62 and 66.

Jusepe de Ribera's *Saint Sebastian* was part of a group of ten paintings donated by Doña Catalina Enríquez de Ribera (1582–1635) to the collegiate church of Osuna in 1627.[1] Among these pictures, there were five works by Ribera: a *Saint Jerome and the Angel of the Last Judgement*, a *Martyrdom of Saint Bartholomew*, a *Saint Peter in Tears*, a *Crucifixion*, and this *Saint Sebastian*. They were all executed between 1617 and 1618 for Doña Catalina and her husband, the Viceroy of Naples, Pedro Téllez-Girón y Velasco Guzmán, 3rd Duke of Osuna (1574–1624).[2]

Ribera's *Saint Sebastian* is first mentioned in an entry in the account book of Juan Miguel Igún de la Lana, the Duke of Osuna's treasurer, on 12 July 1617.[3] In a letter of 13 January 1618 to Andrea Cioli (1573–1641), the secretary of Cosimo II de' Medici, Grand Duke of Tuscany, Cosimo del Sera, the Grand Duke's agent in Naples, expressed his doubts about the skills of the Neapolitan painter Fabrizio Santafede (c. 1560–after 1628), praising Ribera instead, especially in light of the 'three paintings of saints for the viceroy' he had recently executed, and which were 'held in great esteem'.[4] Further evidence indicates that these paintings, destined for the duke's oratory in Osuna, were Ribera's *Saint Jerome, Saint Sebastian*, and *Saint Peter*.[5]

Describing the Osuna *Saint Sebastian* in 1992, Alfonso E. Pérez Sánchez remarked on its affinity with the Bolognese and Caravaggesque styles, and underscored the treatment of the nude body, which he said recalled the manner of Guido Reni.[6] No doubt, Ribera and Reni were well acquainted. In his *Considerazioni sulla pittura* (c. 1617–21), the physician and art theorist Giulio Mancini observes: 'He [Ribera] is held in high

esteem by Signor Guido, who greatly appreciates his resolution and colour, which is mostly in the vein of Caravaggio, but darker and fiercer'.[7] In his manuscript notes, the Florentine art biographer Filippo Baldinucci records that Ribera 'went to Rome, where he set out to draw after the works of good masters and particularly copy things by Guido, from which he learned the way of fine colouring'.[8] In his life of Ribera, Bernardo de Dominici relates that upon the arrival in Naples of Guido's unfinished *Adoration of the Shepherds* for the Certosa di San Martino (still in situ) [fig. 31], Ribera secretly and unwillingly 'commended [Guido's] excellence in art and his unattainable nobility'.[9] Of course, De Dominici's account is inaccurate, if nothing else because Ribera's painting, executed in 1637, precedes the arrival in Naples of Guido's *Adoration* (which was left unfinished in his workshop upon his death in 1642).

It can be assumed that Guido met Ribera in Rome, perhaps as early as 1606, upon the latter's arrival in the city. A document of 6 April 1614 reports that Guido, Ribera, and other members of the Accademia di San Luca had pledged one hundred scudi each for the construction of the church consecrated to the academy's patron saint.[10] Guido was most likely in Rome from January to October 1614, and it was probably during those months that he expressed his appreciation for Ribera to Mancini.[11] In 1621, Reni spent a few months in Naples, in all likelihood meeting Ribera there again.[12] Despite De Dominici's recollection of Ribera's jealousy toward Guido, there is no reason to believe that their relationship was not amiable. Ribera's works undoubtedly manifest his fascination for Guido, although it is sometimes difficult to pin down the scope of the Bolognese artist's imprint on him.

This *Saint Sebastian* has been compared to a homonymous composition by Guido replicated in many versions, one of them now at the Museo del Prado [cat. 19]. The focus on the almost nude body of the saint, depicted up-close and three-quarter length; the contrast between the brightly illuminated body in the foreground and the fading glow of dusk in the distant horizon; and the stark opposition between the flesh tones and the ambient semidarkness, besides the martyr's heavenward gaze, point to a strong connection between the two masters. Yet, all the versions of Guido's *Saint Sebastian* cannot be dated prior to 1619, and by then Ribera had already produced his painting for Osuna.[13] It could be conjectured that Ribera's *Saint Sebastian* inspired Guido, but this too is a problematic assumption on many counts since, among other things, the former artist was living in Naples, the latter in Bologna, and it is highly unlikely that Guido could have seen Ribera's painting before 1621. The question of who inspired who thus remains open, but it ought to be further explored, since Guido's and Ribera's affinities are key to understanding the evolution of their respective art.

Rafael Japón and Lorenzo Pericolo

1 Rodríguez-Buzón Calle 1982, 73 (13 April 1627).

2 G. Finaldi in Milicua and Portús Pérez 2011, 162–66. The dating of Ribera's *Crucifixion* has been the object of debate. See Finaldi 1991 and G. Finaldi in Milicua and Portús Pérez 2011, 167–68, no. 26.

3 Bouza Álvarez 2012, 218: 'A Giuseppe Ribera, pintor de Su Excelencia, ducados 35 para el recaudo de un Sant Sebastian que ha de hazer'.

4 Parronchi 1980, 40.

5 See more recently Farina 2014, 128–31. Ribera's *Martyrdom of Saint Bartholomew* was presumably finished after Del Sera wrote his letter, certainly by 15 November 1618, when the painter was reimbursed for three frames.

6 A. E. Pérez Sánchez in Pérez Sánchez and Spinosa 1992, 71–72.

7 Mancini–Marucchi 1956–57 (1956), 1:249.

8 Santi 1980, 1:392.

9 De Dominici 1742, 3:13.

10 The History of the Accademia di San Luca, c. 1590–1635: Documents from the Archivio di Stato di Roma, 6 April 1614. Accessible at www.nga.gov/accademia.

11 Malvasia–Pericolo 2019, 1:271, note 152.

12 Ibid., 1:302–3, note 233.

13 On Guido's different versions of *Saint Sebastian*, see Malvasia–Pericolo 2019, 1:323, note 288.

19   Guido Reni
Saint Sebastian

c. 1619
Oil on canvas, 172 × 134.5 cm
Madrid, Museo Nacional del Prado, P-211

Provenance: Recorded in the collection of Isabella Farnese, Queen of Spain, in the Palacio Real de La Granja de San Ildefonso, Segovia, in 1746 and 1766 (no. 620); oratory of the Palacio Real, Aranjuez, 1794 (no. 620); Palacio Real, Madrid, 1814–18 (no. 620); listed among the paintings in the Museo del Prado in 1834.

Selected bibliography: Pérez Sánchez 1965a, 176; Baccheschi 1971, 94, no. 63b; G. degli Esposti in Emiliani et al. 1988, 68, no. 24; Pepper 1988, 240, no. 54; G. Finaldi in Boccardo and Salomon 2007, 108–11, no. 5; Malvasia–Pericolo 2019, 1:323, note 288.

The Museo del Prado *Saint Sebastian* is one of five paintings of identical or similar composition that are traditionally ascribed to Guido Reni, and whose attributions and dating have sometimes been the object of heated debate – the four other works are in the Musée du Louvre, the Dulwich Picture Gallery, the Museo de Arte de Ponce, and the Auckland Art Gallery Toi o Tāmaki.[1] Stylistically, the Madrid, Paris, and (possibly) Ponce versions can be dated to about 1619, while the impressive London 'replica' was most certainly executed in the late 1630s – the highly intriguing Auckland painting presents many singularities, which makes its attribution to Guido a matter of great complexity.

Assuming that the first known versions of this composition were produced around 1619, it is possible to identify one of them with a *Saint Sebastian* commissioned from Guido by Pellegrino Lintrù, the descendant of a Flemish family that had settled in Bologna by the end of the sixteenth century.[2] In a letter of 23 February 1619, the Bolognese poet and friend of Guido, Cesare Rinaldi, wrote to the master:

'Our Signor Pellegrino Lintrù is waiting with extreme desire for the image of the arrow-pierced Martyr [Saint Sebastian], made by Your Lordship; the ornament [frame] is already finished, though it is not commensurate with such a precious work for it would require a frame of solid gold, and not just decorated with the thinnest gilding on the surface'.[3]

It is impossible to establish whether this *Saint Sebastian* might be the same as the one mentioned by Cornelio Malvasia, Carlo Cesare's cousin, in a letter of 20 January 1633 to Francesco I d'Este, Duke of Modena, on whose behalf he was looking for paintings.

'I have also seen', he writes, 'the painting of Saint Sebastian, a work by Guido, which was however made many years ago, approximately three *braccia* high, or a little more, and of a proportionate width, with around it a gilded frame of mediocre quality. This is considered most beautiful by people of the art, but his owner also recognises it as such, and keeps its price high, saying to me that he will not give it up for less than two hundred scudi of our currency, which will be exactly a hundred sequins'.[4]

The Bolognese *braccio* is approximately 64 centimetres; the *Saint Sebastian* described by Cornelio Malvasia was over 192 centimetres high, which may correspond to the average size (170 centimetres) of Guido's versions of this composition if the frame was included in the measurements. It may be a coincidence, but the 'mediocre' quality of the frame remarked upon by Cornelio Malvasia resonates with Rinaldi's description of the Lintrù painting's frame as 'decorated with the thinnest gilding on the surface'.

It is usually believed that the Prado *Saint Sebastian* originally belonged to Juan Alfonso Enríquez de Cabrera, 9th Admiral of Castile (1599–1647). In the inventory of his estate, drawn up on 25 June 1647, there is mention of 'a canvas of Saint Sebastian, half-figure, by Guido Reni', decorated with a rich frame.[5] Because the measurements are omitted, this mention may or may not refer to the Prado work, which instead is certainly listed in 1746 as part of the collection of Isabella Farnese, Queen of Spain (1692–1766), in her palace at La Granja de San Ildefonso.[6] A recent cleaning carried out by the conservators of the Prado has opportunely removed later repaints such as an elaborate addition to the loincloth – made to better cover the saint's lower abdomen – thereby revealing the previously overpainted contour of the upper left arm that extends down almost to the level of the diaphragm, as well as the silhouette – blocked out directly from the red brownish priming – of the left hand behind the right hip along with the loop of a rope. It is now possible to appreciate the compacted modelling of Sebastian's nude torso – which, more vulnerable to shadows than Hippomenes' in the almost contemporaneous Prado *Hippomenes and Atalanta* [cat. 61], is not yet eroded by darkness like the

Fig. 73 Guido Reni, *Study for Saint Sebastian's Head*. Black chalk. Liverpool, Walker Art Gallery, WAG 1995.64

rippling brushstrokes, a few touches of lead white – on the chin, the bridge of the nose, and below the left eye – contrasting with the vermilion infused in the flesh, or fully displayed on the lips.

While the Prado painting is not as extensively worked over as its counterpart at the Louvre, and although, at that point in Guido's career, the multiple reiterations of a composition no doubt required the workshop's contribution, there are no grounds to consider it a studio copy.[11] It is nevertheless true that, in particular, Sebastian's loincloth in the Prado version, even after the removal of its repaints, may fail to reach the standards of the master's craftsmanship due to an excess of chromatic saturation and definition slightly at odds with the nude body's more nuanced chiaroscuro and modelling. In any case, it is urgent to renounce the notion that there is an original *Saint Sebastian* from which the others would have stemmed. The point is that paintings such as the Prado and the Louvre *Saint Sebastian* might have been sketched on the canvas and begun contemporaneously, the artist finishing them at different moments and to differing degrees, most likely in accordance with the requests of the customers who visited his workshop.

Lorenzo Pericolo

Saviour's in the Malta *Risen Christ embracing the Cross* of about 1620 [fig. 15].[7] Despite some abrasions determined by excessive cleaning in the past, the torso shows Guido's sophisticated handling of 'thinly applied paint with quite highly impastoed, broadly hatched highlights', which accentuate the grandiose torsion of the upper body in exposing itself to the intense lighting of the foreground.[8]

A black chalk drawing at the Walker Art Gallery in Liverpool [fig. 73] has been rightly regarded as a preliminary study from life for Sebastian's foreshortened head – Guido seems to have portrayed here the same model as the one he used for the Luigi Zambeccari *Bacchus and Ariadne* [cat. 58].[9] It is noteworthy that, in modifying the foreshortening of Sebastian's head as initially captured in the drawing, Guido bore in mind the famous marble bust of the so-called *Dying Alexander* from the Medici collection now in Florence.[10] This Roman copy of a Hellenistic prototype must have caught Guido's imagination, for in the painting he clearly evokes the thrust of Alexander's elongated neck, the strenuous upward tilt of his head in the throes of agony, his low triangular forehead crowned with curly hair. But whereas the antique exalts Alexander's masculine vigour by stressing, for instance, the jaw's massive relief, Guido smooths out his hero's features into ephebic softness. In the Prado painting, Sebastian's head, beautifully distorted in foreshortening, is delicately caressed by subtly

1 Paris, Musée du Louvre, inv. 532; London, Dulwich Picture Gallery, DPG268; Ponce (Puerto Rico), Museo de Arte de Ponce, Luis A. Ferré Foundation; and Auckland, Art Gallery Toi o Tāmaki, M1882/2/3. For the Louvre version, see Loire 1996, 296–99, and S. Loire in Boccardo and Salomon 2007, 114–16, no. 6. For the Dulwich version, see X. F. Salomon in ibid., 100–4, no. 4. For the Auckland version, see M. Kisler in ibid., 94–96, no. 3. For the Ponce version, see R. Aste in ibid., 118–20, no. 7. I have not had the opportunity to examine the Ponce painting in the flesh, and must suspend my judgment on it.

2 See Morselli and Iseppi 2021, 244–45.

3 Rinaldi 1620, 1:141–42: 'Con un desiderio estremo attende il nostro Sig. Pellegrino Lintrù l'imagine del saettato Martire, opera di V. Sign. già l'ornamento è finito, benché non proporzionato a così pretioso lavoro, che ci vorrebbono le cornici massiccie d'oro, e non con oro di sottilissima foglia superficialmente segnate'. See further Malvasia–Pericolo 2019, 1:323, note 288.

4 Venturi 1882, 185 (with a few corrections after my own transcription from the original): 'Ho anche veduto il quadro del S[an] Sebastiano, pittura di Guido, ma fatta molti anni sono, d'altezza di tre braccia in circa o poco più, e di larghezza proporzionata, con cornice atorno dorata di mediocre qualità. Questo viene da persone del arte stimato bellissimo, ma chi lo possiede lo riconosce per tale e tienlo alto di prezzo, dicendomi non volerlo lasciare per meno di ducento scudi di nostra moneta, che serano cento cechini giusto'.

5 Burke and Cherry 1997, 1:432, no. 587.

6 Aterido Fernández, Martínez Cuesta and Pérez Preciado 2004, 2:64, no. 620.

7 Valletta, National Art Museum MUŻA. For Guido's *Risen Christ*, see Malvasia–Pericolo 2019, 1:428–29, note 636.

8 G. Finaldi in Boccardo and Salomon 2007, 112.

9 For the drawing and its relation to the *Saint Sebastian*, see M. Kisler in Boccardo and Salomon 2007, 96.

10 Florence, Gallerie degli Uffizi, inv. Sculture 1914 n. 338.

11 See in this regard Gabriele Finaldi's defense of the painting in Boccardo and Salomon 2007, 110–11.

20 Guido Reni

The Massacre of the Innocents

1611
Oil on canvas, 268 × 170 cm
Bologna, Pinacoteca Nazionale di Bologna, inv. 439

Provenance: Painted for the Cappella Berò in the church of San Domenico, Bologna, whose patronage passed to the Ghisilieri family in 1734; transferred during the Napoleonic looting of works of art to the Musée du Louvre, Paris, in 1796; recovered by Antonio Canova in 1815; entered the Pinacoteca Nazionale di Bologna in 1817.

Selected bibliography: Marino 1620, 58; Malvasia–Zanotti 1841, 2:14–15, 17–18, 37, and 232; G. C. Cavalli in Cavalli 1954, 69–71, no. 10; Gnudi and Cavalli 1955, 21–22 and 63, no. 26; Pepper 1984, 27, 40–41, and 225–26, no. 34; Emiliani 1988, pp. XXVI, XXXIV, LVIII–LX, and LXV–LXVI; F. Valli in Emiliani et al. 1988, 50, no. 17; Valli 1988; Emiliani 1990, 103–6; A. Emiliani in Borea and Gasparri 2000, 2:346–47, no. 6; F. Valli in Bentini et al. 2008, 50–57, no. 31; Malvasia–Pericolo 2019, 2:ad indicem; M. Cavalli in Cappelletti 2022a, 130–33, no. 9.

A masterpiece unique among his body of work, Guido Reni's *Massacre of the Innocents* was painted for the family chapel of Agostino and Ercole Berò in the church of San Domenico in Bologna. It can reliably be dated to 1611 on the basis of an entry in Guido's account book for the period 1609–12, when he was working in Rome as a salaried artist for Cardinal Scipione Borghese.[1] On 26 April 1610, alongside numerous payments for his frescoes at the palace of Monte Cavallo and at the Paolina chapel in Santa Maria Maggiore, Reni records an advance of twenty scudi on account for the picture for 'Signori Berò';[2] the payment was made almost one year to the day after Counts Agostino and Ercole Berò assumed patronage of the chapel on 25 April 1609.[3] Although his somewhat onerous commitment to Cardinal Borghese led Guido to refuse commissions and return deposits, he agreed to paint this altarpiece for the Berò family – which he quickly completed – for a final sum of one hundred scudi,[4] as Carlo Cesare Malvasia reports in his *Felsina pittrice* (1678), 'on account of the affection he had for these signori'.[5]

Malvasia also notes that Domenichino (1581–1641) – in a letter dated 6 May 1612 to Francesco Poli, master of ceremonies to Cardinal Pietro Aldobrandini – reports having seen, when passing through Bologna, 'the works of the great Guido in S. Domenico, and in S. Michele in Bosco';[6] this provides us with a conclusive *terminus ante quem* for the painting. Domenichino's fulsome praise for these canvases by a fellow-artist, which seemed to have been 'painted by the hand of an angel', foreshadows the glittering renown later achieved by the *Massacre of the Innocents*, to which the Baroque poet Giambattista Marino dedicated a poem in his volume *Galeria* (1620), ending with an immensely effective oxymoron: 'horror goes often with delight'.[7]

Although there is no record of where the *Massacre* was produced, art scholars agree that it was painted in Rome rather than – as Malvasia claimed – in Bologna.

This Roman link is a crucial consideration for any thorough analysis of this remarkable moment in the history of painting; it

Fig. 74 Infrared reflectogram of
The Massacre of the Innocents [cat. 20]

marks the birth of the classical Reni, establishing – for the first time in the seventeenth century – the canons of an ideal beauty 'inspired by Raphael and antique art',[8] paradigms he explored and reinterpreted in the quest for a new, personal idea of perfection.

The works from antiquity conceptually underpinning the *Massacre* include the *Laocoön* group,[9] the Hellenistic marble *putti*, and above all the *Niobids*, the famous sculptures discovered in 1583 in Rome, between the Esquiline Hill and San Giovanni in Laterano, and taken to the Villa Medici.[10] A special relationship can be discerned between the mother looking up in the right foreground and *Niobe,* in the shared figurative representation of consternation and despair, of serene and timeless grief. But Guido's references to ancient art are intended to do more than simply illustrate a canon of beauty; in stark contrast with the 'clamour' and 'turmoil' surrounding the slaying of the protomartyrs,[11] these classical allusions provide a means of transcending the visible in search of a higher order, eternal and ideal, in which to set his reflections on earthly sentiments and dramas.

Giovan Battista Passeri reports that Reni owned plaster casts of various Roman antiquities, including the *Niobe* and the *Venus de Medici*,[12] evidently taken from Rome to Bologna, which he presented to his students as the epitome of his personal poetics.[13] Critics down the ages – from Giovan Pietro Bellori and Malvasia to contemporary scholars – have recognised and examined the central importance of classical sculpture to Guido's view of art.[14]

In its design, the Berò altarpiece echoes certain famous engravings; from the *Bacchanal with a Wine Vat* by Andrea Mantegna (c. 1431–1506),[15] Reni borrowed the overlapping bodies of the two infants in the lower foreground; from a print of the *Massacre of the Innocents* by Marcantonio Raimondi (c. 1470/82–1527/34) after a drawing by Raphael (1483–1520), he reworked postures, expressions, and the balanced arrangement of spaces, always ensuring not to quote directly from his sources. Nowhere is Guido's approach to reworking more clearly displayed than in the relationship between the woman in the lower left of the painting and the matching figure in the left foreground of the engraving. A number of parallels can also be drawn, despite the intellectual distance, with Raphael's tapestry on the same theme, part of the so-called 'Scuola Nuova' set at the Galleria degli Arazzi (Tapestry Hall) in the Musei Vaticani:[16] yet Raphael's asymmetrical composition, its space crammed with compressed, writhing figures, contrasts strongly both with the perfectly-articulated, geometric conception and with the air of

suspended tragedy conveyed in the Bologna *Massacre*, where the whole drama is condensed in the raised dagger in the empty space at the centre of the composition, poised to commit the deed. Reni constructs the flawless equilibrium of this superb scene around the 'balance of that dagger about to fall'.[17] The action is frozen, the violence narrated rather than represented, by analogy with classical tragedy; the scene expresses the idealised truth that shuns all excess, blending Raphael and antique art as obligatory references from which Reni extracts the rules required to sublimate – in the 'perfection of the inimitable'[18] – the Christian drama.

It was in Rome that Reni fully assimilated Raphael's legacy; the latter's *Ecstasy of Saint Cecilia*[19] was essential to the Berò altarpiece in defining the circularity of the closed, inward-looking space, bounded by the wailing mothers, who, 'like stone pillars block ... all centrifugal movement'.[20]

Infrared analyses carried out in 1988 at the time of the last restoration[21] revealed a different earlier treatment of the mother standing on the right, wrapped in a cloak and protecting the child through the twist of her body, placed some 35 centimetres lower than in the final version [fig. 74]. By offering a glimpse of a key phase in the supremely balanced structuring of the *Massacre*, this major variant helps to make up for the scarcity of preliminary drawings; in any case, the authorship of some known drawings remains a matter of critical debate.[22]

Six years after Reni painted the *Crucifixion of Saint Peter* for the church of San Paolo alle Tre Fontane [fig. 10] now in the Musei Vaticani, regarded by critics – though with reservations – as the painting in which his approach most closely resembles that of Caravaggio (1571–1610), echoes of the Lombard artist unexpectedly resurfaced in the idealised atmosphere of the *Massacre*. The specific reference here is to the *Martyrdom of Saint Matthew* in the Contarelli chapel at San Luigi dei Francesi in Rome, from which Reni takes Caravaggio's frightened child as a model for the woman in the background on the right in the *Massacre* and also, in part, for the woman with the grey-pink cloak in front of her. Although endowing them with a nobility all his own, Reni gives both women 'a more human expression of grief'.[23] While this marks a minor departure from his usual philosophy, it bears eloquent testimony to Reni's all-encompassing spirit of enquiry during his time in Rome. Over the six years since the *Crucifixion of Saint Peter*, Guido had become fully aware of his own artistic personality, far removed from Caravaggio's naturalistic approach and his well-known fondness for chiaroscuro. By quoting the anti-classical Caravaggio in a painting otherwise notable for its classical air, Reni seems to be

openly declaring that he has left behind, for good, a style explored on several occasions during the first decade of the seventeenth century. Yet Caravaggio clearly continued to exercise a certain appeal, not least in financial terms; in 1613, Reni agreed to accept his *Denial of Saint Peter*[24] from Luca Ciamberlano (c. 1570/80–c. 1641) in part payment of a debt.[25]

Mirella Cavalli

1 Morselli 2022c.
2 Pepper 1971a, 315. Information on the payments made for the *Massacre of the Innocents* was first published by Malvasia, who claims to have received Guido Reni's account book from Giovanni Andrea Sirani; see Malvasia–Zanotti 1841, 2:14; Malvasia–Pericolo 2019, 1:44 and 1:257–58, note 121.
3 Landolfi 1992.
4 Malvasia–Zanotti 1841, 2:14–15; Malvasia–Pericolo 2019, 1:55 and 1:258, note 121.
5 Malvasia–Zanotti 1841, 2:14–15; Malvasia–Pericolo 2019, 1:44 and 1:257–58, note 121.
6 Malvasia–Zanotti 1841, 2:232.
7 Marino 1620, 58: 'Spesso l'orror va col diletto'. Marino's poem is transcribed in Malvasia–Zanotti 1841, 2:18; Malvasia–Pericolo 2019, 1:56 and 270, note 150.
8 C. Gnudi in Gnudi and Cavalli 1955, 22.
9 Vatican City, Musei Vaticani, inv. 1059.
10 Florence, Gallerie degli Uffizi, inv. 289–94, 297–300, 302, and 304–6–Sculture (1914).
11 Malvasia–Zanotti 1841, 2:14; Malvasia–Pericolo 2019, 1:55 and 1:270, note 147.
12 Florence, Gallerie degli Uffizi, inv. 224–Sculture (1914).
13 Passeri 1772, 765.
14 Malvasia–Zanotti 1841, 2:22; Bellori–Borea 1976, 526. Examples include Emiliani 1988; Pagliani 1990.
15 Emiliani 1990, 103.
16 Vatican City, Musei Vaticani, inv. 43864.
17 G. C. Cavalli in Gnudi and Cavalli 1955, 63.
18 Emiliani 1990, 106.
19 Bologna, Pinacoteca Nazionale di Bologna, inv. 577.
20 Valli 1988, 101.
21 Emiliani 1990, 105.
22 F. Valli in Bentini et al. 2008, 50–51.
23 Emiliani 1990, 105.
24 New York, Metropolitan Museum of Art, inv. 1997.167.
25 Nicolaci and Gandolfi 2011; Cappelletti 2022b, 49.

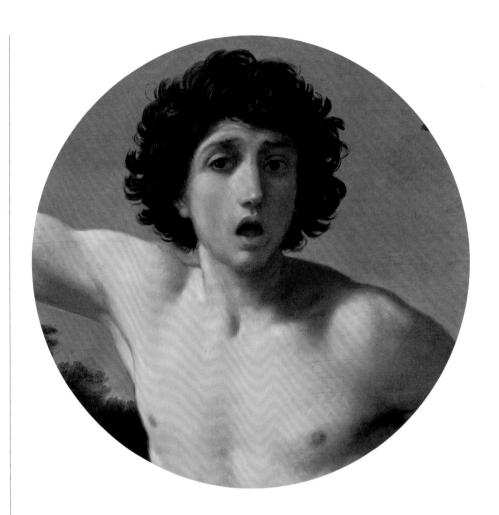

IV

THE BEAUTY OF THE DIVINE BODY

Guido Reni's talent for bringing the viewer closer to divinity was unanimously acknowledged even in his lifetime. His biographer, Carlo Cesare Malvasia, likened him to a 'generous eagle' taking 'sublime flight to the spheres', and afterwards bringing 'celestial ideas' back to earth. For the writer Francesco Scannelli, Guido's painting 'transcended the human' to approach the divine. Malvasia described his holy figures as 'divinity humanised', noting the power of certain paintings to involve the viewer in transcendent scenes. This is what made Reni such a remarkable interpreter of the life and Passion of Christ, by presenting him as a man of great physical beauty capable of harbouring a divine soul. At the same time, certain gospel themes, such as those featuring the young John the Baptist, allowed him to explore a crucial stage in human development, the physical transition from adolescence to adulthood.

21 Guido Reni

The Circumcision

1636
Oil on canvas, 371 × 216 cm
Siena, Arcidiocesi di Siena-Colle di Val d'Elsa-Montalcino.
Chiesa di San Martino

Provenance: Commissioned by the Gori family, Siena, in 1626; first mentioned in the church of San Martino in Siena in 1636.

Selected bibliography: Malvasia 1678, 2:31 and 2:36; G. C. Cavalli in Cavalli 1954, 109–10, no. 47; Gnudi and Cavalli 1955, no. 90; Baccheschi 1971, no. 172; F. Torchio in Ciatti, Martini and Torchio 1983, 212–13; Pepper 1988, 283, no. 150; Malvasia–Pericolo 2019, 2:324–25, note 291.

The painting hangs over the second altar on the right at the church of San Martino in Siena. As early local guidebooks noted,[1] the altar was originally sponsored by the Goris, a wealthy burgher family with contacts in the Emilia region: Fabio Gori commissioned it in 1617,[2] and in 1621 Silvio Gori, then in Ferrara as auditor to Cardinal Francesco Cennini, formally established the family's patronage.[3] At that stage, the altarpiece featured an 'ancient panel' – a polyptych comprising five statues by Jacopo della Quercia (c. 1374–1438) – described by Fabio Chigi as 'broken' in 1626, which was later returned to the church proper.[4] As Chigi noted, at that time (*hora*) a painting was commissioned from Guido Reni for 800 scudi; delivery, however, took much longer than expected. Girolamo Gigli reports that Fabio Gori's son Giovan Battista Gori Pannilini (1604–1662), papal vice-legate in Bologna from 1634 to 1639, played an active role in arranging the commission, and may also have intervened to hasten the completion of the canvas and its delivery to Siena.[5] The *Circumcision* reached the city in the summer of 1636, as noted in a letter by Abbot Gherardo Saracini to an unknown recipient, dated 12 July, where he remarked that 'Signor Guido's panel, made for the Signori Gori, arrived a few days ago'.[6] A protégé of Catherine de' Medici – wife of Ferdinando Gonzaga, Duke of Mantua and rector of the University of Siena[7] – who had been appointed Governess of Siena in 1627, the monk and Marinist poet Saracini may also have acted as intermediary. The abbot, fully informed about the progress of the painting, was able to contact Reni through the poets that gravitated around the court at Mantua (especially Giambattista Marino and Andrea Barbazza), and received from the unknown addressee a drawing by Reni, to be given to Duke Leopoldo de' Medici. One month later, on 28 August – the feast-day of Saint Augustine, patron saint of the Augustinian friars who then governed the church – the canvas was placed over the Gori altar,

framed by a marble altarpiece, the work of Cortona stonemason Ascanio Covatti († 1632).[8] According to Giovacchino Faluschi's guidebook, the final payment may have amounted to 1000 scudi, 100 for each painted figure; Marco Ferri, transcribing the entry from a church account book, gave the even higher figure of 1500 scudi, which would match the real increase in price of Reni's paintings towards the end of his life.[9] Faluschi (in 1784, though not in 1815) also reports that Reni, as though to compensate for this exorbitant price, apparently gave the Goris two additional paintings, one depicting the *Eternal Father*, which was placed over the altar (their heirs later replaced it with a copy) and a *Saint Catherine of Siena* which ended up in the estate of the branch of the family living in Via Camollia, who still owned it in 1840.[10] However, this significant information is not confirmed either in later local guidebooks or by biographers, making it difficult to identify the two works.

Guido again offers a softened but richly detailed depiction of an episode of the life of Christ to which there is no more than a passing reference in the Gospel (Luke 2:21). The Child, undergoing circumcision at the centre of the composition, is surrounded by priests; to the right, Mary and Joseph look on, while at the lower left the infant Saint John the Baptist embraces a lamb which – taken in conjunction with the angel holding a dish to catch the first drops of blood shed by Jesus – enables the event to be read as a prefiguration of the Passion. The circumcision, a rite which according to Jewish law must be performed eight days after birth, probably took place in Bethlehem, even though the Corinthian columns hint at the Temple in Jerusalem, reflecting an iconographic tradition that since the fifteenth century had tended to link the setting of the Circumcision with that of the Presentation in the Temple, forty days later. In his *Felsina pittrice* (1678), Carlo Cesare Malvasia mistakenly located the 'Presentation in the Temple' in Siena and a 'Circumcision' in Perugia, an error – repeated by Filippo Baldinucci – perhaps prompted by confusion with the *Presentation of Jesus in the Temple* recorded at one stage in Modena.[11]

Mentioned by Malvasia among Reni's 'undoubtedly autograph' late works, the canvas – though admired by foreign travellers[12] and appreciated by nineteenth century biographers[13] –

came under heavy criticism at the start of the last century. Seeing it in an exhibition of Italian painting at the Palazzo Pitti, Margherita Nugent felt that it marked the start of a decline in Guido's style, while Heinrich Bodmer regarded it as typical of the artist's 'last infelicitous period'.[14] The canvas was cleaned for the first monographic exhibition of Reni's work in 1954, when Gian Carlo Cavalli helped to revive its faltering reputation; he defined the figures gathered around Jesus as 'a magic circle of poetry' where light and colour – tempered by Reni's new approach, in which Malvasia had detected a certain 'weariness' (*fiacchezza*)[15] – defined the complex personal outlook underpinning his style.[16] The almost dazzling radiance of the angels in the foreground, together with the three cherubs above, heighten the lyricism characteristic of Guido's late manner, which still retains that 'literary decorum',[17] that poetic erudition that has only recently been re-assigned to him. Here, as in other paintings, Reni also drew on the New Testament apocrypha – and especially on Pseudo-Matthew 15:1, from which he may have taken the detail of the doves ('And when the infant had received parhithomus [circumcision] … they offered for Him a pair of turtle-doves, or two young pigeons'; see also Luke 2:24). He devised a rather crowded scene including Simeon – possibly the figure standing behind Jesus – by then one hundred and twelve years old, in the cloak in which he would later wrap Jesus and kiss his feet, as well as the high priests Annas and Caiaphas. Malvasia, alert to this intellectual process, noted of this and other contemporary works that 'deeper knowledge and an unattainable perfection are revealed every day'.[18]

This canvas is part of a group of paintings that were all delivered in around 1636, but which had taken some time to finish. Beset by financial difficulties, Reni had been charging large advances without completing commissions. The *Circumcision* shares with the *Presentation of Jesus in the Temple*, the *Triumph of Job* commissioned in 1622 [cat. 44], and the Modena *Crucifixion* [cat. 32] – all delivered, late or reluctantly, in 1636 – a number of stylistic features: a velvety chromatic range, a complex scenic structure inherited from the Carracci, and a distinctive approach to drapery.

In 1980, an attempt was made to steal the painting: the figure of the infant Saint John the Baptist was cut off, resulting in some loss of colour, but the rest of the picture has been preserved in excellent condition. It was restored in 1983, when the cut-off portion was reintegrated, the canvas was lined, and the paint surface was cleaned.

Giulia Iseppi

1 Pecci 1752, 86; Pecci 1759, 100; Pecci 1761, 100; Faluschi 1784, 121; Faluschi 1815, 102–3; Romagnoli 1822, 91; Romagnoli before 1835, 5:84–85; Romagnoli 1836, 39; Romagnoli 1840, 32, no. 152.
2 Ferri 1832, 111.
3 Ugurgieri Azzolini 1649, 1:492. Fabio Torchio (in Ciatti, Martini and Torchio 1983, 212) gives the following signature for the records: Archivio Arcivescovile di Siena, Ms 3611, fols. 50–63, but following a recent rearrangement of the archive, this signature now refers to different records, and those cited by Torchio have not yet been traced.
4 Biblioteca Apostolica Vaticana, Ms Chigiano 1.1. 11, 217v., in Bacci 1939, 316; F. Torchio in Ciatti, Martini and Torchio 1983, 212.
5 Gigli 1723, 2:447.
6 Bottari 1754–73 (1766), 5:LXXV, 153: 'Da pochi giorni in quà è arrivata la tavola del sig. Guido, fatta per i signori Gori'. Romagnoli before 1835, 10:83; Malvasia–Pericolo 2019, 2:325.
7 Saracini 1629; Gigli 1723, 1:52.
8 F. Torchio in Ciatti, Martini and Torchio 1983, 212.
9 Faluschi 1815, 103; Ferri 1832, 111.
10 Faluschi 1784, 121, note to Romagnoli 1840, 50.
11 Now in Paris, Musée du Louvre, inv. 522. Malvasia 1678, 2:31 and 2:36; Baldinucci 1681a, 12:75; Pepper 1988, 283, no. 150; Malvasia–Pericolo 2019, 2:324–25, note 291.
12 Cochin 1769, 1:228; Lalande 1769, 2:599.
13 Bolognini Amorini 1839, 17; Giordani 1840, 49.
14 Tarchiani 1922, 152; Nugent 1925–30 (1925), 1:83; Bodmer 1929, 97.
15 Malvasia 1678, 2:32.
16 G. C. Cavalli in Cavalli 1954, 109–10.
17 Ibid., 123.
18 Malvasia 1678, 2:42: 'Si scuoprano poi ogni dì d'un più profondo sapere, di una inarrivabile finitezza'.

22 Guido Reni

Saint John the Baptist in the Wilderness

c. 1636
Oil on canvas, 230 × 140 cm
Salamanca, Madres Agustinas Recoletas, Convento de la Purísima

Provenance: Commissioned by Manuel de Fonseca y Zúñiga, 6th Count Monterrey, in 1633–35; Augustinian church of La Purísima Concepción, Salamaca.

Selected bibliography: Villar y Macías 1887, 2:364; García Boiza 1945, 26; Prota Giurleo 1957, 149; Pérez Sánchez 1965a, 756; Gómez Moreno 1967, 299; Madruga Real 1983, 157.

An astounding painting, the Salamanca *Saint John the Baptist in the Wilderness* has not always been acknowledged by scholars as an original by Guido Reni. In a letter of 30 November 1957 to Ulisse Prota Giurleo, Roberto Longhi, basing his opinion on a black and white reproduction of the main altarpiece in the church of the Augustinian nuns in Salamanca, remarked in relation to the 'Saint John the Baptist, standing, in a landscape': 'The composition certainly derives from Reni; the quality seems good and it is not impossible that it is an original by Reni himself in his later years, no doubt after 1630'.[1] In 1965, Alfonso E. Pérez Sánchez, refuting an attribution to Domenichino (1581–1641) by Manuel Gómez Moreno, noted that 'it was closer to Cantarini or Reni himself'.[2] More recently, in 2007, Gabriele Finaldi described it to be 'in the style of Reni (possibly by Simone Cantarini)'.[3] The latest opinion, given by Massimo Pulini when he published the picture online in 2020, is that it is an original by Guido.[4]

A better understanding of this painting may be had from the history of the altarpiece of which it forms a part. On 8 November 1633, the Viceroy of Naples, Manuel de Fonseca y Zúñiga, 6th Count Monterrey (1588–1653), commissioned Cosimo Fanzago (1591–1678) to execute 'the marble ornamentation for the main altar of the chapel that His Excellency is building in the city of Salamanca, in the convent of the nuns of Saint Ursula'. Fanzago pledged to deliver the work by May of the following year. A receipt on the margin of the contract, signed and dated by Fanzago in 1634, confirms that he received 1500 ducats, possibly the final instalment of the agreed amount of 5000 ducats.[5] Fanzago's monumental framework for the altarpiece was originally destined for the church of the Anunciación in the Ursuline convent

in Salamanca, where it was to decorate the chapel in which Monterrey and his wife wished to be buried. Shortly after engaging Fanzago, the count changed his mind and decided instead to build a brand-new church and convent across the main entrance of his palace in Salamanca for the Augustinian nuns that were under his family's protection. The foundation agreement of this religious complex was drawn up in Naples in December 1634 and validated by the Augustinian nuns in Salamanca in January 1635.[6] Construction on the church began soon after, but it was only in 1685, when a new cupola was erected after the previous one collapsed, that this architectural project came to completion.[7] It is unlikely that Fanzago modified the layout of the retable as a result of the new location. Rather, in all probability Curzio Zaccarella (c. 1588/89–1641) and Bartolomeo Picchiatti (1571–1643) must have taken into account the proportions of the marble framework which Fanzago had already executed, though the height of the new building was in no way proportionate to Fanzago's decorative scheme. In a new

Fig. 75 Main altarpiece of the Augustinian church of La Purísima Concepción, Salamaca

contract drawn up in Naples on 1 April 1636, Fanzago committed to execute five more altars of lesser dimensions and a pulpit for the church.[8] In the meantime, between 1635 and 1637 Giuliano Finelli (1601/2–1653) was tasked with the execution of the funerary marble sculptures of the viceroy and his wife, Leonor María de Guzmán (1590–1654), which still stand on either side of the main altarpiece.

There is evidence that Monterrey started ordering canvases for the altarpiece in 1634–35 [fig. 75]. From his favourite painter, Jusepe de Ribera (1591–1652), he commissioned a *Pietà* (1634) and a majestic *Immaculate Conception* (1635) over five metres high.[9] Placed at the centre of the retable, Ribera's huge composition not only represented the holy mystery to which the Augustinian church was consecrated, but also was the object of eternal contemplation for the sculpture of Monterrey and his wife.

On the sides, in the upper tier, two paintings introduce the theme of the Virgin's family: the *Embrace at the Golden Gate* (the moment when Mary was conceived through the miraculous embrace of Anne and Joachim) by an unidentified painter – traditionally held to be Giovanni Lanfranco (1582–1647) – and a *Saint Joseph with the Child* by Alessandro Turchi (1578–1649). In the lower tier, to the left, Guido's *Saint John the Baptist* also refers to the Virgin's family, for John was the son of Mary's cousin, Elizabeth. On the right, the *Saint Augustin* by a Flemish master relates to the cult of the Augustinian nuns. This *Saint Augustin* did not belong to the original series; the 1676 inventory of the altarpiece paintings makes specific mention of an untraced *Saint Francis* in its place.[10] Obviously, this work, which alluded to the previous destination of the retable – the church and convent of the Ursulines, who belonged to the Franciscan order – was replaced.

In view of his personal involvement in the selection of the decorative items for the church, it is extremely likely that Monterrey ordered the *Saint John* directly from Guido. That the count should have approached the master for a painting is nonetheless curious given their strained relations. A few years earlier, in 1630, Monterrey's arrogance and stubbornness had led Guido to sell his *Abduction of Helen* [fig. 35][11] to the French queen regent, Marie de' Medici (1575–1642), in spite of the fact that the painting had been commissioned by the King of Spain.[12] In a letter dated 22 May 1630, Philip IV wrote to Monterrey: 'From what you say in your letter of 10 February, I have seen that the painting of the Abduction of Helen … has turned out to be inappropriate, and the price asked for it by Guido of Bologna is excessive, and I want to advise you that, if it has as many flaws as you mention, then it should not be shipped'.[13] Only a few months later, in October 1630, the king tried to correct course, asking the count to purchase the painting as soon as possible, but the deal was definitely compromised by then.[14] In spite of Monterrey's initial aversion to the master, the possibility of having a painting by an artist of the stature of Guido for his own church must have induced Monterrey to change his attitude, and given the outcome, he could not have made a better decision.

The Salamanca *Saint John* is an inspired work. Verging on the brink of overexposure, the larger than life-size body of the Precursor illuminates the entire foreground with a radiance seldom attempted by Guido. Barely perceptible and limited to a few areas, semi-transparent shades caress the delicate ivory of the saint's nude

Fig. 76 Infrared reflectogram of *Saint John the Baptist in the Wilderness* [cat. 22]

The Beauty of the Divine Body

flesh, imbuing the whiteness of his elongated torso, arms, and legs with a pearl-like luminescence. Similar to a loincloth, the furry strip of the mantle, which, by drooping sideways, counteracts the hip's leftward tilt, barely covers the saint's nudity; indeed, the soft fur on hairless flesh conjures up for the imagination, almost haptically, the nudity it pretends to conceal. In a pose inspired by ancient statuary, the body leans against a rocky outcrop; balance is ensured through the contrapposto of the legs, the left crossed behind the right. A recent reflectogram executed by the Prado Laboratory reveals Guido's difficulty in anchoring the figure to the ground, as evidenced by the shifting outlines and differing profiles of John's thighs, legs, and feet [fig. 76]. The surface of the body is animated by myriad delicate brushstrokes, the pictorial equivalent of extensive chiselling in sculpture. In his carnal beauty, the figure of John is the religious counterpart to the ephebic body of antiquity. The suspended, thoughtful expression of John's face betokens his superhuman ardour in delivering the sacred prophesy: 'Ecce agnus Dei'. Stylistically, the *Saint John* bears affinity with works executed by Reni in 1636, such as the Notre-Dame *Triumph of Saint Job* [cat. 44] and the Louvre *Presentation in the Temple*,[15] as evidenced not only by the luminous palette, delicate brushstrokes, and compact forms, but also by the similarity of the crowd gathered in the background of the Salamanca painting with the figures depicted in these two works.[16] In this regard, the reflectogram suggests that Guido added the crowd on the left at a later stage. Monterrey ended his tenure as Viceroy of Naples in November 1637; the following year, he embarked on his way back to Madrid. These must be the dates by which the *Saint John* was shipped to Spain.

Lorenzo Pericolo and Ángel Rivas Albaladejo

1 Prota Giurleo 1957, 149.
2 Pérez Sánchez 1965a, 131–32. Prota Giurleo 1957, 149: 'San Giov. Battista in piedi in un paesaggio. É una composizione certamente di origine reniana; la qualità ne sembra buona e non è impossibile si tratti di un originale del Reni stesso nel suo periodo avanzato; certo dopo il '30'.
3 Finaldi 2007, 756.
4 Pulini 2020.
5 Madruga Real 1983, 175, doc. VII.
6 Ibid., 54–56.
7 Ibid., 91–99.
8 Ibid., 176, doc. VIII.
9 On Monterrey and Ribera, see Rivas Albaladejo 2015, 559–68. It is noteworthy that Ribera's *Saint Januarius* and *Saint Augustine* for the lateral altars in La Purísima were executed in 1636.
10 Madruga Real 1983, 226, doc. XL.
11 Paris, Musée du Louvre, inv. 539.
12 For an updated reconstruction of this commission, see Malvasia–Pericolo 2019, 1:295–97, note 218.
13 Rivas Albaladejo 2014b, 336, doc. 6.
14 For Philip IV's letter of 22 June 1630, see Rivas Albaladejo 2014b, 336, doc. 7.
15 Paris, Musée du Louvre, inv. 522.
16 On this painting, see Malvasia–Pericolo 2019, 1:324, note 290.

23 Guido Reni

Saint John the Baptist in the Wilderness

c. 1633–34
Oil on canvas, 225.4 × 162.2 cm
London, Dulwich Picture Gallery, DPG262

Provenance: First mentioned in the Balbi collection, Genoa, in 1678; purchased by Andrew Wilson in Genoa in 1804–5; sold to Noël Desenfans soon afterward; bequeathed to Dulwich College, London, by Francis Bourgeois in 1811.

Selected bibliography: Pepper 1969b; C. Casali Pedrielli in Emiliani et al. 1988, 316, no. 63; Pepper 1988, 302, no. 196 (dated 1640–42); Malvasia–Pericolo 2019, 1:452, note 679; B. Eclercy in Eclercy 2022a, 268–69, no. 116.

In his *Felsina pittrice* (1678), Carlo Cesare Malvasia records a *Saint John the Baptist* by Guido Reni in the house of 'Signor Giovan Francesco Maria Balbi' in Genoa.[1] Malvasia refers here to the Genoese nobleman Francesco Maria Balbi (1619–1704). In an inventory of the paintings in his possession compiled in 1688, there is mention of a 'Saint John the Baptist by Guido Reni'.[2] In his *Istruzione* (1766), the Genoese painter and biographer Carlo Giuseppe Ratti (1737–1795) singles out Guido's *Saint John* in the Balbi collection as a 'life-size figure' and 'a singular work'.[3] Guido's painting remained in the Balbi collection until the very beginning of the nineteenth century. In a letter from Genoa of 8 May 1804 to the art collector William Buchanan, the Scottish painter and art dealer James Irvine (1757–1831), who had learned about the Balbi's intention to part with their collection, remarked: 'The Saint John and Saint Jerome by Guido are the only pictures that are untouched, and worth about 700 guineas each'.[4] Reference is made here to Guido's *Angel appearing to Saint Jerome* now in the Detroit Institute of Arts [cat. 41]. While Irvine's attempt to buy the paintings fell through, his fellow painter Andrew Wilson (1780–1848), who was in Genoa in 1803–5, succeeded in this enterprise. Soon afterward, he must have sold Guido's *Saint John* to the French art dealer Noël Desenfans (1741–1807). At an indeterminate date, the painting was in fact in his collection:

Went next to see Mr. Desenfans' famous and numerous collection … Desenfans' best picture, I think, is a single full-length figure of Saint John in the Wilderness by Guido Reni. He bought it from Andrew Wilson for a thousand guineas. There is a fine landscape in the background, with some clever little figures at a great distance. The superhuman expression of John uttering his prophecies is most admirable, and his body most nobly painted. His mouth is painted with peculiar beauty and elegance, open.[5]

Although the author of this annotation is unknown, its description of the *Saint John* reveals the enthusiasm for Guido's art in early nineteenth-century England. Desenfans bequeathed his collection to his friend, the British landscape and history painter Francis Bourgeois (1753–1811), who in turn donated it to Dulwich College upon his death.

Guido scholars have traditionally dated the Dulwich *Saint John the Baptist in the Wilderness* to 1636–37, that is, after works such as the *Triumph of Saint Job* at Notre-Dame in Paris [cat. 44] and the *Circumcision* for San Martino in Siena [cat. 21].[6] This date seems to be rather advanced. The closest affinity to the Dulwich painting is to be found in the two versions of Guido's

Saint Francis in Prayer with two Angels, the first in the Galleria Colonna [cat. 42] and the second in the Galleria Estense, where it is erroneously attributed to Giovanni Francesco Gessi (1588–1649).[7] These paintings are characterised by a restrained chromatism, with a predominance of grey, brown, and dark green tints – deployed with staggering subtlety – in contrast to the bright hues of the pale blue sky and the flesh tones, the latter occasionally highlighted with soft filaments of white lead. Like the Dulwich painting, the Colonna *Saint Francis* – the only version that is cleaned – presents a certain degree of indefiniteness, especially in the modelling of the head and hands of the holy figure. No doubt, the Dulwich *Saint John* is a more inspired work, as is the Detroit *Angel appearing to Saint Jerome*, which, as already mentioned, also belonged to the Balbi, was displayed face-to-face with it as its pendant, and might have been executed around the same time. From this point of view, it can be said that the Colonna *Saint Francis* presents a stylistic tendency that would culminate in the Balbi paintings. In fact, the Colonna work is also stylistically linked with the *Penitent Magdalen* now in the Palazzo Barberini [cat. 86], which was certainly produced in 1633,[8] and is marked by a higher degree of polish and more brilliant chromatism. Keeping in mind Guido's unrelenting proclivity to experimentation – and the swiftness and versatility with which he modifies his style – it is possible to date the Dulwich painting to 1633–34, in any case before the 1635 *Saint Michael Archangel* for Santa Maria della Concezione in Rome.[9]

Lorenzo Pericolo

1 Malvasia 1678, 2:91.
2 Belloni 1973, 69: 'S[an] Gio[vanni] Batt[ist]a di Guido Reni'.
3 Ratti 1766, 189: 'figura naturale … opera singolare'.
4 Buchanan 1824, 2:151.
5 Sparkes 1876, 75, note *.
6 For the *Triumph of Saint Job*, see Malvasia–Pericolo 2019, 1:338–39, note 335. For the *Circumcision* in San Martino, Siena, ibid., 1:324–25, note 291.
7 Modena, Galleria Estense, S28. On the Colonna *Saint Francis with two Angels*, see Malvasia–Pericolo 2019, 1:445, note 671.
8 The date of the *Penitent Magdalen* has been disputed by other scholars; see, for example, Aoife Brady's entry for this painting in this catalogue [cat. 86].
9 On Guido's *Saint Michael Archangel*, see Malvasia–Pericolo 2019, 1:306–7, note 245.

24 Guido Reni
Saint John the Baptist in the Wilderness

c. 1634–35
Oil on canvas, 216 × 144 cm
Bologna, Palazzo Bentivoglio

Provenance: Louis-Joseph Reynoird, 1768; mentioned in the Irvine collection, Temple Newsam House, Leeds, 1808, 1816, 1822, 1854, 1865, 1879, 1897, 1898, 1902, 1950–51, 1954, and 1976; Palazzo Bentivoglio, Bologna.

Selected bibliography: Temple Newsam 1951, 93–94; Adamson and Musgrave 1954, 54; Pepper 1988, 286, no. 156 (as possibly by Simone Cantarini);[1] Beddington 2020 (unpublished catalogue entry).

The splendid *Saint John the Baptist in the Wilderness* now in the Palazzo Bentivoglio, Bologna, had been on display until the early 1980s in Temple Newsam House, Leeds, the historical mansion of the Ingram family (Viscounts Irvine) in the United Kingdom. It is first mentioned there as a work by Guido Reni in an inventory of the Irvine estate of 1808: 'Saint John preaching in the wilderness, size of nature; the figure is sitting, the left hand holding a slight cross; embraces the Agnus Dei; the right hand points to heaven'.[2] Most likely, the painting was purchased by Charles Ingram, 9th Viscount Irvine (1727–1778), from Louis-Joseph Reynoird (1727–1803). The 'abbé Reynoird' (whose family name was spelled variously as Renouard, Renoir, or Renoux) was a canon of Cambrai cathedral and a successful art dealer in mid-to-late eighteenth-century Paris.[3] His name appears in an engraving by Pedro Pascual Moles (1741–1797) that reproduces the Bentivoglio *Saint John* 'after an original painting by Guido in the cabinet of Monsieur Abbot Reynoird'.[4] Dated to 1770, Moles' engraving indicates that by that year the painting was still in Reynoird's possession. It is thus unlikely that Sir Joshua Reynolds (1723–1792) acquired Guido's Bentivoglio *Saint John* in 1768, while on a two-month trip to Paris. During his sojourn in that city, he certainly tried to buy the painting through the intermediary of his friend, the French painter Gabriel-François Doyen (1726–1806). From Reynolds's pocketbook, we in fact learn that he had seen Guido's work on 30 September 1768 at Reynoird's place. A note inserted in the journal, half in Italian half in English, reveals his intentions: 'Il Giovanni di Guido, 300; Parrocell, 50; Due Mole, 80; paiessi di Rembrandt, 20. A copy of a paper I gave to Mr Doyen to buy those pictures at the Abbé Renoux at St. Sulpice'.[5] Further documentation confirms that Reynoird possessed paintings by Pier Francesco Mola (1612–1666), Joseph (1646–1704) and Charles

The Beauty of the Divine Body

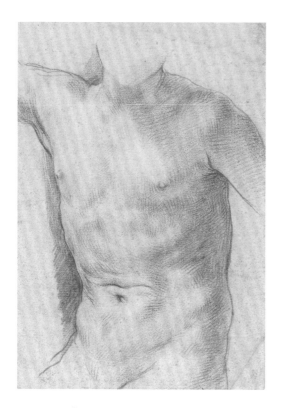

Fig. 77 Guido Reni, *Study of a Torso*. Red chalk on paper. New York, Sotheby's, sale 26 January 2011, lot 547 (with an attribution to Simone Cantarini)

(1688–1752) Parrocel, Rembrandt (1606–1669), and Guido Reni (a *Lucretia* and a *Saint Jerome* 'peint au premier coup et très librement').[6]

Even if Reynolds did not manage to purchase Guido's *Saint John the Baptist in the Wilderness* in 1768, he might have been responsible for its acquisition by Charles Ingram at a later date. Reynolds' acquaintance with the nobleman and his family is well known, and Ingram seems to have bought another painting by Guido from Reynolds: a *Saint Margaret* now in the LWL–Museum für Kunst und Kultur in Münster [fig. 98].[7] Even less certain is the identification of the Bentivoglio *Saint John* with a painting by Guido of the same subject in the collection of Vittorio Amedeo I, Duke of Savoy (1587–1637). In an inventory of the ducal gallery in Turin of 1635, there is mention of a 'Saint John the Baptist naked in the desert, his mouth open, whole length figure, by Guido Reni … high 3 ½ feet, wide 2 ½ feet'.[8] Sensibly smaller than the Bentivoglio painting, the Savoy *Saint John*, which apparently measured 180 × 128 centimetres (the *piede liprando* being approximately 51.3 centimetres), may or may not be, on account of the 1635 inventory's inaccuracies, the same work as the Bentivoglio painting. The question remains open, especially because the untraced paintings present in the 1635 inventory of the

Savoy collection might have been dispersed, stolen, or destroyed in the 1659 fire of the Turin ducal palace.

Until recently, the Bentivoglio painting has been deemed a variant of Guido's *Saint John the Baptist in the Wilderness* now in the Dulwich Picture Gallery [cat. 23], made by Simone Cantarini (1612–1648), a student of Guido's. This attribution, advanced by Stephen Pepper among other scholars, likely resulted from the existence of another version of the Bentivoglio painting that was once in the Zambeccari collection and is now in the Pinacoteca Nazionale di Bologna.[9] This *Saint John the Baptist in the Wilderness*, which the Zambeccari inventories ascribe alternatively to Cantarini or Flaminio Torri (1620–1661), another disciple of Guido's, is on one occasion recorded as an unfinished work by Guido completed by Torri.[10] Technical analysis would help clarify the attribution of this intriguing painting, which indeed presents some unfinished parts, and whose sketchy, quick strokes are not inconsistent with Torri's. A red chalk *Study of a Torso*, sold at Sotheby's, New York, with an attribution to Cantarini [fig. 77], has been recently ascribed to Guido by Charles Beddington. This drawing relates to both the Bentivoglio and the Dulwich *Saint John*, without corresponding exactly to either. Likely a work by Guido, it bears affinity in particular with some of his drawings from life of the 1610s such as the *Study for the Apollo in the Casino dell'Aurora* now in the Uffizi, Florence.[11] If this is the case, then it is important to reconsider Guido's work process in the early 1630s, for here he might have revisited an earlier drawing by using it as a linchpin for two different paintings: ones that are almost antithetical in terms of style. While the Dulwich *Saint John* is characterised by a certain degree of pictorial indefiniteness, with a subtle exhibition of *sprezzatura*, the Bentivoglio painting is diligently modelled and coloured with richness of impasto. While the Dulwich *Saint John* is highly evocative – the saint's averted eyes magnify the impression of elusiveness determined by the slightly out-of-focus rendition of the face, as if the prophecy and its utterance pertained to an intimate act of introspection – the Bentivoglio Precursor is fixed in a gesture of unmediated fervour, as if paradoxically paralysed, his eyes anxious to catch the viewer's attention, his divine revelation impressed upon us through the mask-like expression of his face pierced by the hypnotic circle of his shouting mouth: 'vox clamantis in deserto'.

It is perhaps no coincidence that, stylistically, the Bentivoglio *Saint John* bears affinity with Guido's *Angel appearing to Saint Jerome* now in the Kunsthistorisches Museum in Vienna.[12] Even if they are not pendants, they in a sense 'work together' as the counterparts to the Balbi paintings: the Dulwich *Saint John* and the Detroit *Angel appearing to Saint Jerome* [cat. 41]. Because the Vienna painting is documented as being for sale in 1635, when it was in the collection of a 'French tailor', it must have been executed in 1633–34, and this may also apply to the Bentivoglio *Saint John*.

Lorenzo Pericolo

1 In a letter dated 8 July 1993, Stephen Pepper expressed his conviction that the painting, counter to his previous assessment, was an original by Guido Reni. Ever since, other scholars have confirmed this attribution: Denis Mahon, Keith Christiansen, Erich Schleier, and, on the basis of colour transparencies, Andrea Emiliani and Daniele Benati.

2 Beddington 2020 (unpublished catalogue entry).

3 Michel 2007, 111.

4 The caption reads: 'D'après un tableau original par le Guide du cabinet de M. l'Abbé Reynoird'.

5 Leslie and Taylor 1865, 1:288, note 4.

6 The Getty Provenance Index® Databases, F-A191 (1767) and F-A589 (1780). Accessible at: https://www.getty.edu/research/tools/provenance/search.html.

7 Pepper 1988, 329, no. 11; Beddington 2020 (unpublished catalogue entry).

8 Baudi di Vesme 1897, 43, no. 210: 'S[an] Giovanni Battista nudo al deserto, con bocca aperta, figura intiera. Di Guido Reni … A[lto] p[iedi] 3 ½; L[argo] p[iedi] 2 ½'.

9 Bologna, Pinacoteca Nazionale di Bologna, inv. 428

10 R. Morselli in Emiliani 1997, 184, no. I.86; M. Cellini in Bentini et al. 2008, 427–29, no. 249.

11 Florence, Gallerie degli Uffizi, Gabinetto dei Disegni e delle Stampe, inv. 11720 F. For the Uffizi drawing of Apollo, see Bohn 2008, 33–34, no. 22. For a related drawing in the Royal Collection, Windsor Library, see V. Birke in Ebert-Schifferer, Emiliani and Schleier 1988, 291, B13.

12 Vienna, Kunsthistorisches Museum Wien, Gemäldegalerie, inv. 9124. On the history of this painting, see Malvasia–Pericolo 2019, 1:290–91, note 205.

25 Guido Reni
Christ at the Column

c. 1604
Oil on canvas, 192.7 × 114.4 cm
Frankfurt, Städel Museum, inv. 1103

Provenance: Trackert collection (?), Frankfurt; Johann Theodor Wiesen, Frankfurt, until 1875; acquired by the Städel Museum, Frankfurt, 1875.

Selected bibliography: Kugler 1850; Weizsäcker 1900, 275; Pepper 1971c, 326–27 and 339; Spear 1982, 129–30, no. 7; Pepper 1984, 215; Pepper 1988, 220; Terzaghi 2007, 315; Malvasia–Pericolo 2019, 1:246, note 96; Francucci 2020, 156–57; Becker 2022; Benati 2022, 22; B. Eclercy in Eclercy 2022a, 138–41, no. 32; Terzaghi 2022, 33.

Although there are few certainties regarding the origin of this superb canvas, it can reliably be dated to Guido Reni's early years in Rome. Attempts to trace its history can go no further back than the mid-nineteenth century. On 8 June 1875, it was purchased by the Städel Museum, Frankfurt, at an auction of the estate of Johann Theodor Wiesen (1794–1875). No records have yet been unearthed to confirm its earlier presence in the Trackert collection in Frankfurt, a claim advanced in 1850.[1]

The composition, remarkable for its powerful vertical thrust, is based entirely on the contrast between Christ's light-bathed, muscular body, tightly bound to a half-column of light marble, his poignant expression, and the dark background.

Its widely accepted attribution to Guido appears in the Museum's earliest catalogues.[2] Stephen Pepper brought this work to the attention of Reni scholars in the early 1970s, in an article that sheds crucial light on the artist's first sojourn in Rome, when he was beguiled by the *maniera* of Caravaggio (1571–1610).[3] Studies of this painting have invariably highlighted the influence of Caravaggio's style, noting that the composition, centred on a single life-size figure, the dark setting, and the naturalistic rendering of Christ's body all echo the pictorial grammar brought to Rome by Caravaggio in the early 1600s. More recently, research has focused on its possible origin in the context of the Vallombrosian monastery of Santa Prassede in Rome. The first art historians to study the painting stressed its connection with the relic of the column to which Christ was bound at the time of his flagellation; the relic has been kept in the basilica of Santa Prassede in Rome since the thirteenth century, and has always been the object of special veneration. According to the account provided by Carlo Cesare Malvasia in his *Felsina pittrice* (1678), and repeated in various forms by all the early biographers, Guido lodged at the monastery of Santa

Prassede on his arrival in Rome. Cardinal Paolo Emilio Sfondrato, one of the artist's earliest patrons in Rome, also arranged lodgings at the monastery for two other protégés, Domenichino (1581–1641) and Francesco Albani (1578–1660).[4] It is no coincidence that Domenichino tackled the same subject in a painting dated 1603, whose composition bears a strong resemblance to Reni's canvas.[5] The two pictures share the same format and compositional structure: Jesus is depicted standing, his hands bound to a column which certainly recalls the relic preserved in Santa Prassede. Domenichino, however, departs from Guido's choice of a dark background, opting instead to paint some buildings in the distance, including the basilica of San Giovanni in Laterano.[6] Both paintings appear to be a joint tribute by the two Bologna artists to the monastery which provided them with accommodation, and to the kindness of their protector; so much so, in fact, that one might imagine a hypothetical competition between two rival artists. Scholars have often drawn attention to the link between the two works. Pepper suggests that the Reni canvas – which in his view was painted at around the same time as Domenichino's – may be one of several unspecified works for which the artist received payment from Cardinal Sfondrato on 18 September 1604.[7] Doubt has recently been expressed concerning the Sfondrato commission on the grounds that, at the time when the artists lodged there, the Cardinal Protector of the monastery of Santa Prassede was not Sfondrato but another of Guido's patrons, Antonio Maria Gallo.[8] Given that the two cardinals were friends and shared similar views, they may both have been involved in encouraging the young artists to honour the monastery that afforded them lodging, and the relic venerated there.[9] Both Reni and Domenichino departed from the more traditional iconography of the Flagellation – in which Jesus, bound to the column, is scourged by his torturers – to be found, for example, in another beautiful painting of disputed authorship, also in Santa Prassede, with which both artists were evidently familiar.[10] Although Guido focuses particularly on the expression of the suffering Christ, his face veiled in sadness, he does so without over-dramatising or outstepping the bounds of muted melancholy. It is with this remarkable restraint that Reni set out on his career: naturalism became a means of expression, but never shaped the secret core of his painting, which – in a matter of months – became pure, unalloyed harmony.

Maria Cristina Terzaghi

1 Kugler 1850.
2 Weizsäcker 1900, 275. The attribution to Reni is rejected by Richard E. Spear (in Strinati and Mignosi Tantillo 1996, 378, note 4).
3 Pepper 1971c, 326–27 and 339.
4 A brief account is provided in Malvasia–Pericolo 2021, 1:247, note 98.
5 This painting recently appeared in the London art market (Christie's, London, auction 20552, 7 July 2022, lot 22. Available with complete bibliography at https://www.christies.com/lot/lot-6381787?ldp_breadcrumb=back&intObjectID=6381787&from=salessummary&lid=1).
6 For this painting, see, among others, the entry by R. E. Spear in Strinati and Mignosi Tantillo 1996, in which he questions the attribution of the Frankfurt painting to Reni; and the detailed catalogue entry for auction 20552 at Christie's, mentioned in note 5 above.
7 Archivio di Stato di Roma, Corporazioni Religiose, Santa Cecilia, b. 4092, Libro dei Mantati del 1604, no. 15 (Pepper 1971c, 339, note 5). The document was first published in Nava Cellini 1969, 41, note 39. The payment order has been sought in vain; Terzaghi 2007, 315.
8 Francucci 2020; Benati 2022, 24; Terzaghi 2022, 32–33. Gallo was Cardinal Protector of Santa Prassede from 30 August 1600 to 1 June 1605.
9 Terzaghi 2007, 173.
10 For the painting previously attributed to Giulio Romano (c. 1499–1546), to Simone Peterzano (c. 1535–1599), and even – albeit misguidedly – to Caravaggio, see M. Calvesi in Vodret Adamo 2011–12 [2011], 1:102–5.

26 Anonymous,
after a model by Alessandro Algardi

The Flagellation of Christ

1650–75
Gilded bronze; wooden base with lapis lazuli inlays,
47.5 × 42.5 × 16 cm (including the base)
Toledo, Madres Clarisas Capuchinas. Federación Inmaculada
Concepción. Convento de la Purísima

Provenance: Donated by Cardinal Pascual de Aragón to the convent of the Purísima Concepción de las Madres Capuchinas in Toledo (?).

Selected bibliography: Nicolau Castro 1990, 6; Carrió Invernizzi 2017, 186; Nicolau Castro 2014, 136–37.

This *Flagellation of Christ* is part of a series of groups in bronze or other materials based on two very similar prototypes, both produced in Rome in the 1630s.[1] Their attribution is a particularly thorny issue, which may be summarised as follows: the central figure of Christ bound to a column – very similar in both versions – is flanked by the two flagellators who are scourging him in poses that differ from one prototype to the other. On the basis of that difference, Jennifer Montagu draws a distinction between the two: in what she terms type A, exemplified by the model in the Musées royaux d'Art et d'Histoire in Brussels, the figure on the viewer's left holds his right arm aloft and his left arm by his side, while his partner on the right holds his left hand away from his waist; in type B, exemplified by the model in the Schatzkammer, Vienna,[2] the figure on the left wields the scourge with both hands, while his partner rests his left hand on his hip. Montagu suggests – albeit tentatively – that the model of Christ at the column is in both cases by Alessandro Algardi (1595–1654), that the type A flagellators are the work of François du Quesnoy (1597–1643), as claimed by Giovan Pietro Bellori, and that their type B counterparts are by Algardi himself.[3] Montagu's grounds for regarding Bellori's views as somewhat unreliable in this case are wholly admissible, although – as she herself acknowledges – the question remains open.

The *Flagellation* group in the convent of the Purísima Concepción de las Madres Capuchinas in Toledo belongs to type B, and is therefore after a model by Algardi. Indeed, it was attributed to him when it was first published by Juan Nicolau Castro in 1990, when it was still housed in a cloistered space.[4] The very appearance of this piece proclaims its worth, in both artistic and monetary terms. Quite apart from the bronze itself – a costly material invariably requested by patrons – the wooden base of the *Flagellation* is inlaid with lapis lazuli, a rare hard stone enjoying enormous prestige. Such a display of opulence tells us something about the donor, the convent's founder Pascual de Aragón (1626–1677), who was ordained cardinal in 1660.[5] From 1646, when he moved to Toledo, throughout his time in Italy and later at the court in Madrid, where he remained until his death, Aragón maintained close links with the Capuchin nuns, to whom he sent *objets d'art* and other gifts.[6] The most noteworthy of these was a group of artworks from Italy which presumably included this *Flagellation*, whose material value hints at an illustrious patron. The Farnese collection in Rome boasted another *Christ at the Column* attributed to Algardi, though in ivory, 'on a black base with lapis lazuli compartments' (in Stefano Lolli's inventory dated 1708),[7] a mounting similar to that of the Toledo *Flagellation*. Though of little value in terms of attribution, this information sheds some light on the life of these objects in a specific place – Rome – at a particular moment, the mid-seventeenth century. The prestigious provenance and opulent mounting of this piece do not, in themselves, imply that it must be a work by Algardi. As Montagu has shown, objects of this kind were rarely cast in person by the masters; more often, they were produced by highly-specialised workshops which replicated existing models, sometimes under the creator's supervision, other times even without his authorisation. The Toledo *Flagellation* is a fine work, but as one of a series it cannot be attributed with any certainty to Algardi; it is more likely to have been made by a Roman workshop which continued to reproduce this model, perhaps even after Algardi's death.

In terms of style and composition, the figure of Christ in this *Flagellation* group clearly engages with the aesthetics of Guido Reni. The positioning of the head, leaving the neck and collarbone exposed and vulnerable, echoes the supremely delicate *Ecce Homo* in the Fitzwilliam Museum, Cambridge [cat. 29], while the advanced right leg and posture recall the monumental *Christ at the Column* in the Städel Museum, Frankfurt [cat. 25].

Fernando Loffredo

1 Montagu 1967.

2 Vienna, Kunsthistorisches Museum Wien, Schatzkammer GS D 187.

3 Montagu 1985, 2:315–16.

4 Nicolau Castro 1990, 6.

5 See Villarreal y Águila 1686; Estenaga y Echevarría 1929–30; Nicolau Castro 2014.

6 Nicolau Castro 1991.

7 Coiro 2013, 168: 'Sopra piedistallo nero con comparti di lapislazuli coronato di rami dorati e piccole pietre rosse, con un pomo d'agata nel cassetto, vi è in avorio a tutto rilievo un Cristo che viene legato alla colonna da un ladrone; dell'Algardi'.

27 Guido Reni
Ecce Homo

c. 1639–40
Oil on canvas, 79 × 65 cm
Dresden, Staatliche Kunstsammlungen, Gemäldegalerie
Alte Meister, Gal.-Nr. 330

Provenance: Collection of the painter Charles-Antoine Coypel, 18th century; acquired by Maria Josepha of Saxony, Dauphine of France, 1753; collection of Augustus III, Prince-Elector of Saxony and King of Poland, 1754; missing since 1945, it is in the Gemäldegalerie Alte Meister, Dresden, since 1974.

Selected bibliography: Mariette 1753, 6–7, no. 11; Jähnig 1929, 156, no. 330; Baccheschi 1977, 113, no. 195b; Pepper 1984, 274, no. 161; G. J. M. Weber in Henning and Weber 1998, 45–46, no. 14; Spenlé 2008, 171; A. Henning in Maaz, Koch and Diederen 2014, 140, no. 56; B. Eclercy in Eclercy 2022a, 260–63, no. 111.

This picture is among the finest of Guido Reni's successful series of *Ecce Homo* paintings, a disparate set of works on canvas, copper, or panel, in a variety of formats – head, half-length, or three-quarter length bust – intended to meet the devotional requirements of private clients. Although none of them are dated, the irrefutable similarities between this canvas and the depictions of the dying Christ in the *Crucifixions* in the Galleria Estense, Modena, of 1636 [cat. 32] and in the church of San Lorenzo in Lucina, Rome, of about 1637–38 [fig. 79], suggest that it must have been produced at around the same time.

While there are no records prior to the eighteenth century that might help us to establish who commissioned the painting, this may well be the canvas referred to by Carlo Cesare Malvasia who in his *Felsina pittrice* (1678) mentions an *Ecce Homo* painted for a merchant by the name of 'Gnicchi' – perhaps Matteo Gnetti – and adds that the Pamphilj collection in Rome boasts a 'Christ crowned with thorns holding a reed sceptre' whose description fits this painting, though the measurements differ.[1] The inventories of certain noble art collections feature other works on the same theme by Reni, among them a painting owned by Ferrante III Gonzaga, Duke of Guastalla, and another sold in 1649 by the procurator Girolamo Resti to Aurelio Zanelletti.[2] Guido also produced an *Ecce Homo* for the Bologna senator Saulo Guidotti, but this work has been identified as the one now hanging in the Pontifical Irish College in Rome.[3]

The first reference to the Dresden painting places it in Paris, in the collection of the court painter Charles-Antoine Coypel (1694–1752). On his death, the canvas was acquired by Maria Josepha of Saxony, Dauphine of France (1731–1767); she in turn gave it to her father Augustus III, Prince Elector of Saxony and King of Poland (1696–1763), whose fabulous art collection provided the basis for the present-day Gemäldegalerie in Dresden. Following the bombing and looting of the gallery during World War II, the work was considered lost until 1974, when it was recovered for the collection.

Reni tackled this *Ecce Homo* – a favourite theme of Counter-Reformation piety – with remarkable economy of means, reducing the composition to a foregrounded half-length figure. In keeping with the Gospel account, Christ is depicted with his hands tied and holding the reed sceptre, wearing the crown of thorns and the purple cloak, rendered here with delicate pinkish tones. The absence of secondary figures and spatial references endows the image with a certain iconic power and a sense of timelessness. The dramatic use of light – harking back to Guido's time in Rome – stresses the beauty of the unflawed anatomy, barely tainted by signs of martyrdom, a hallmark of Reni's particular idealistic poetics. Both the placing of the figure against a dark background and the golden glow of his aureole recur in a second *Ecce Homo*, painted on copper, also in the Gemäldegalerie in Dresden.[4] In the latter version, however, Christ's eyes are downcast and his expression despairing, whereas here he is depicted with the distinctive heavenward gaze common to Reni's holy figures.

This painting was reproduced as a print, much later on, by the German engraver Christian Gottfried Schultze (1749–1819), but it must have been known in Spain years earlier, probably through painted copies, such as the two discovered by David García Cueto in the convent of the Descalzas Reales in Madrid.[5] In any case, this was apparently not the most widely published version of Reni's *Ecce Homo,* the shoulder-length figure achieving greater popularity. Prints of this type circulated as early as the seventeenth century[6] and a number of mosaic versions also survive, including one given to the future Charles III by Clement XII in 1738, now in the palace of Aranjuez.[7]

Although this portrayal of Christ with lips parted and eyes half-closed had a number of precedents in Spanish and European art, it was consolidated in Reni's work as an effective

The Beauty of the Divine Body

alternative to the traditional iconography of the contemplative Christ. The new model was later adopted, albeit loosely, by certain Spanish Golden Age painters; in his *Christ, Man of Sorrows* in the Museo del Prado,[8] Antonio de Pereda (1611–1678) seems to blend elements reminiscent of prints by Albrecht Dürer (1471–1528) with the haunting expressiveness of Guido's images. Echoes have also been noted in an *Ecce Homo* by Francisco Camilo (c. 1615–1673), part of a private collection recently placed on long-term loan at the Museo de Segovia, as well as in a small painting, now in a private collection, attributed to Bartolomé Esteban Murillo (1617–1682).[9] Thanks to new prints and lithographs, the model achieved even greater popularity in the nineteenth and twentieth centuries, and was copied by academic painters such as Elías García Martínez (1858–1934), author of the ill-fated mural in the sanctuary of La Misericordia in Borja, Zaragoza.[10]

Manuel García Luque

1 Malvasia–Pericolo 2019, 1:162–63 and 1:202–3, notes 504 and 664. Malvasia also recalls a third *Ecce Homo* in the collection of Count Segni in Bologna; this, however, was an oval painting showing only the head. Malvasia–Pericolo 2019, 1:198–201.

2 Ibid., 1:319 and 1:326, notes 280 and 294. The 'Ecce Homo, testa al naturale di Guido Reni' owned by Count Andrea Barbazza must have been one of the reduced versions. Ibid., 1:435, note 652.

3 Albl 2014.

4 Dresden, Staatliche Kunstsammlungen, Gemäldegalerie Alte Meister, Gal.-Nr. 329.

5 Patrimonio Nacional, inv. 00615985 and 00616036. Stephen Pepper (1984, 274) also mentions a copy on copper in the Kunsthistorisches Museum, Vienna.

6 Including engravings by Robert Nanteuil (1623–1678) and Adrian van Melar (1633–1667). Candi 2016, 190.

7 Colomer 2006, 230–31.

8 Madrid, Museo Nacional del Prado, P-1047.

9 García-Hidalgo Villena 2022.

10 The painting was defaced in August 2012 in a disastrous intervention by an amateur painter. Gracia Rivas 2010.

28 Titian

(Tiziano Vecellio, Pieve di Cadore c. 1488–1576 Venice)

Ecce Homo

c. 1546–47
Oil on slate, 69 × 56 cm
Madrid, Museo Nacional del Prado, P-437

Provenance: Given by Titian to Charles V in 1548, and kept thereafter in the monastery of Yuste until Charles' death in 1558; apartments of Philip II (king's library), Alcázar, Madrid, until 1734; king's antechamber, Palacio Real Nuevo, Madrid, 1772; entered the Museo del Prado in 1821.

29 Guido Reni

Ecce Homo

c. 1639
Oil on canvas, 113 × 95.2 cm
Cambridge, The Fitzwilliam Museum, inv. 2546

Provenance: Collection of Prince Lucien Bonaparte until 1815, when it was purchased at auction (New Gallery, 60 Pall Mall, London) by Sir Thomas Baring 1st; bought in 1848 by his second son Thomas Baring, who bequeathed it to his nephew Thomas George Baring, 1st Earl of Northbrook, 1873; inherited by his son Francis George Baring, 2nd Earl of Northbrook, 1904; Christie's, London, 12 December 1919, bought by Sigismund Goetze; donated by his widow Mrs Constance Goetze to the Fitzwilliam Museum in 1943.

Selected bibliography: Falomir 2003, 224–25, no. 36; Falomir 2007; González Mozo 2018, 36–38, 60–62, 65–66, 69–72, 75–78, 84–94, 100–6, and 115–23; B. Eclercy in Eclercy 2022a, 260–63, no. 112.

The words 'Ecce Homo' ('Behold the Man')[1] – spoken by Pontius Pilate when he presented Jesus to the crowd so that they might decide on his fate – became synonymous with the image of Christ's humiliated, scantily clad body,[2] either surrounded by other relevant figures or entirely alone, sacrificing himself to save mankind. As a guide for artists, based on the account in the Gospel of John, the mocking of Christ was narrated in graphic detail in the *Meditations on the Life of Christ* written in around 1300 and attributed to pseudo-Bonaventure;[3] it was also recounted in the *Vita Christi* by Ludolph of Saxony (c. 1295–1377), which additionally quoted a letter sent by the governor of Judea, Publius Lentulus – Pilate's alleged predecessor – to the Roman Senate, providing a precise description of Jesus' physical appearance.[4] It was among the iconographies favoured by the Church to appeal to the piety of the faithful,[5] and was used by the *devotio moderna* spiritual movement as a means of fostering individual meditation assisted by descriptions – written, painted, or sculpted – of holy figures in torment which, when portrayed in total solitude, heightened the empathy between those at prayer and the object of their veneration.[6] Depictions of the episode, which could be traced back to Byzantine icons of the ninth and tenth centuries, were elaborated over the following centuries from two different perspectives: the Northern European and Spanish schools focused on the battered and bleeding Christ, while Italian artists adopted a more serene, sensual, and intimate approach.

Although the sacred nude played a major role in the Christian educational programme, its ambiguous status – hovering between the erotic and the devotional, often depending on the treatment of the anatomy – ran counter to Church interests,[7] especially after the Council of Trent,[8] for it was pleasing to the eye and distracted the prayerful from their purpose. In their treatments of the *Ecce Homo*, both Titian and Guido Reni avoided depicting the extreme violence implicit in the scene, creating elegant busts that fulfilled the visual aspirations of even the most erudite viewers, without defying the restrictions imposed by the most orthodox Catholicism. Their Christs are barely wounded, with only a few drops of blood visible near the crown of thorns. The pathos is instead defined, in each case, by the grief of a man forsaken, helpless in his nakedness. It was a theme to which both artists returned throughout their careers, and their approach gradually evolved away from elaborate compositions with a large cast[9] to solitary pensive Christs in abstract spaces. Titian always used the same pattern with variations,[10] while Reni created different models.

The two artworks on show here were produced almost a hundred years apart, in distinct personal circumstances and for very different purposes. Both were painted by artists at the height of their powers, at the age of around sixty; but Guido was coming to the end of his career, while Titian was at his peak, having found during his sojourn in Rome between 1546 and 1547 sources of inspiration that were to consolidate his style and provide scope for innovation over the following decades. When he began the painting in 1546, in Rome, Titian sought only to please Charles V by giving him a picture that would appeal to his restrained piety. He chose a support – slate – with which he had never worked before; it was one of the materials over which the fierce *paragone* debate was then raging,[11] and it also required a highly complex painting technique.[12] In his only two paintings on stone – the other is the *Mater Dolorosa with her Hands Apart*[13] – Titian cleverly created the visual effect of statuary and antique painting, but tempered it by retaining an icon-like appearance appropriate to the traditional personification of holy figures.[14] In the *Ecce Homo,* he achieved his purpose by replacing the emaciated bodies of the Byzantine Christs with the

muscular power of the ancient marble torsos that were then being unearthed in the countryside around Rome; the face recalls the Vatican *Dionysus Sardanapalus*,[15] while the expression of resignation and weariness is identical to that of the statues of Dacian warriors in the Farnese collection and on the Arch of Constantine, both of which Titian was able to study during his time in Rome.[16]

It is not known whether Reni had a specific client for the Cambridge painting, or whether this was just one of the well-known sketched half-length figures that he stored ready for urgent completion, either for a commission that would provide him with money to pay his debts[17] or to demonstrate his skills to visitors to his studio with just a few hours' work.[18] Far removed from Titian's robust Christ on stone, Guido's version appears to draw on the *Ecce Homo* now in Dublin [fig. 78]. Moving and vibrant, it is the epitome of a simple yet effective composition, wholly in keeping with Counter-Reformationist doctrine, and displays the masterly brushwork and superb quality that a seasoned artist can achieve by combining speed and experience.

Both painters, while seeking to stir the viewer with expressions of suffering, also used the body of Christ to display their skill at

Fig. 78 Titian, *Ecce Homo*, 1558–60. Oil on canvas, 73.4 × 56 cm. Dublin, National Gallery of Ireland, Purchased, 1885, NGI.75

Cat. 28

Cat. 29

The Beauty of the Divine Body

modelling torsos with realistically rendered flesh, this being one of the aspirations of artistic theory and practice, especially among Venetian painters, whose views regarding the educational and demonstrative purposes of religious art were rather more heterodox, and who – ever since the late fifteenth century – increasingly judged the worth of a painting not just in terms of the subject depicted or its formal and emotional impact, but also for its material quality and the manner in which it was executed. By the sixteenth century, other approaches to painting – and other ways of seeing pictures – had become established in Venice, and attention was starting to focus on certain painterly qualities for which new terms were devised. Three such terms are important for understanding the ideas behind Titian's *Ecce Homo*, and could equally define Reni's version: the first was *proprietà*,[19] or verisimilitude achieved by simulating the colours and textures of bodies and objects using brushstrokes that enhanced certain optical effects of the paint itself; the second was *vaghezza*, or the blurring of forms, the softening of outlines in order to emulate the way nature was perceived, lacking precise contours;[20] and the third was *morbidezza*, or the softness of bodies, inviting us to sink our fingers into them. Implicit in these concepts was the ability to capture, understand, and convey in a painting the play of light on natural and artificial surfaces, in such a way that the viewer would recognise them as such; this was something at which both Titian and Reni excelled, not through imitation but through suggestion. In this context – in which new editions of texts by Aristotle and of Pliny's *Natural History* played a key role[21] – the realistic rendering of flesh, echoing the Greeks' speculations concerning colour, became a central issue in Venetian thought and praxis; in this respect, too, Guido was remarkably gifted. Pietro Aretino alludes in his letters to the lifelike appearance of Titian's figures[22] and especially of the *Ecce Homo* that Titian gave him for Christmas in 1548, which he describes as 'vivo e vero'; while Carlo Cesare Malvasia occasionally notes that Reni's figures were very true to life. Unsurprisingly, therefore, both artists were hailed as 'new Apelles',[23] in allusion to the celebrated Greek painter of the fourth century BC famous for his rendering of flesh tones, whose works were known only through classical texts. The difference is that, for Titian, this comparison with Apelles represented a personal challenge; in his letters, in his outlook on life, and in his art, he expressed an explicit desire to surpass him.[24] Nowhere, perhaps, is that competitive drive better displayed than in this *Ecce Homo*, in which – emulating the skills of his 'rival' – he uses just four colours, and above all handles the material in such a way that in reproducing Christ's flesh he manages to breathe life into the picture. In Reni's case, the comparison with Apelles was more of a standard formula used by certain contemporary writers when highlighting the beauty – *grazia* – of his forms.[25] Only

Pierfrancesco Minozzi was more specific in praising his brushwork and the poetry of his colours.[26] Undoubtedly, these two paintings invite reflection on such matters and, in particular, on the appearance of the flesh on different male bodies: that of Titian's hero in his physical prime, albeit defeated and bruised, and that of Guido's gaunt and ageing Christ.

Both were superb colourists, and their versions of the *Ecce Homo* are a clear example of how a very wide range of colours can be achieved with just a few pigments, by exploiting all the components of the paint, varying densities and allowing underlying colours – including, in Titian's case, the coarse support – to show through, thus integrating them into the visible image.

The two Christs share the contrast between the corporeal – conveyed through the heavy application of opaque paint in the more highlighted areas – and the ethereal, captured by light oil layers in the shaded areas; they also use a reduced palette, yet they are very different in appearance. During the two years it took Titian to finish his painting – he completed it in Venice in 1547 – he worked on the bust and the cloak, applying multiple layers of oil and resin. The dark, translucent ground layer tempers the coldness of the stone support, but does not completely cover the grain. It also varies in thickness: Titian allowed the bluish-grey of the slate to show through the primer in very specific places, beneath the ochre of the flesh, in order to create the deeper shadows that model Christ's facial features and the muscles of his chest and arms, whose nuances are the result of subtle tonal transitions. Finally, he enriched the texture by spreading the oil with his fingers on the shoulder and torso. The result was a rounded, solid Christ that seems to emerge from the stone; it resembles a bas-relief whose outlines blur as they gradually merge into the background.[27] Guido made no attempt to exploit the weave of the canvas; the movement of his *Ecce Homo*, at once fragile and more human, is achieved by varying the length and direction of the brushstrokes. This is particularly apparent in the purple cloak, the arms, and the face, where multiple tones have been generated by overlaying and interweaving irregular long and short brushstrokes, and by alternating thicker paints with more transparent oils that allow the layers beneath to show through. The softening of outlines, even on the body itself, is done much less subtly than in Titian's painting; to integrate the torso with the background, Reni scratched the lighter areas in all directions with a stiff-bristled brush, leaving a brownish base visible through the scratches. This underlying colour serves to enhance the greenish-grey and bluish appearance of the mid-tones. Although it is not clear what pigments were used here, the Bolognese is known to have added blues and greens when nuancing flesh tones,[28] a practice confirmed by chemical analysis of many of his works in the Museo del Prado.

Malvasia compared the vigorous brushstrokes and use of colour in Reni's early seventeenth century paintings with Titian's early murals for the Fondaco dei Tedeschi and his late *Transfiguration* in the church of San Salvatore[29] – both in Venice – as well as with works by Paolo Veronese (1528–1588) and even Jacopo Tintoretto (1519–1594),[30] whose paintings, significantly, were not to Guido's taste.[31] In my view, though Reni's 'Venetian style' may be associated to this kind of thick, rapid brushstroke, it is actually more Venetian in its attempt to ensure verisimilitude by controlling the play and absorption of light on and by the materials distributed irregularly over the picture plane,[32] an effect he achieved in this *Ecce Homo*.

Close examination of Reni's canvases, and of many of the infra-red reflectograms made of them, reveals a working practice similar in some respects to that of Titian and Tintoretto.[33] However, two considerations should be borne in mind: first, many artists arrive independently at the same solutions; and second, despite Reni's familiarity with the great Venetian masters and his well-documented friendship with Palma Giovane (c. 1548/50–1628), he was paradoxically reluctant to send works to Venice and refused a number of commissions from the city, claiming that he did not want to paint like Tintoretto and did not know how to paint like Veronese, much though he admired his work.[34] He certainly never endowed his figures with the physical force of theirs; his painting was brighter and more airy, although – like Tintoretto – he used loose, swift brushstrokes to enliven his scenes, and – like both Tintoretto and Titian – he overlaid layers of paint and built up the picture by visibly combining successive stages in the creative process.

Stripped of all artifice, these two versions of the *Ecce Homo* prove that with four colours, an intelligent technique, and a successful formal model, the artist can create an illusion of life and move the viewer. Titian and Guido, each in his own way, transcended the violent dimension of the sacred nude; rather than focusing on bodies disfigured by martyrdom, they offered the public an intimate vision of the Passion, with solitary grieving figures presented as examples of the nude anatomically appropriate to the physical build – athletic or frail – chosen by the artist. While still fulfilling the requirements to be met by a religious image, these works stand both as a proof of their authors' skill and as a statement of their painterly aspirations and achievements. Titian's personal ambitions – unconstrained in those days by post-Tridentine restrictions – led him to take advantage of the emperor's spiritual leanings to further develop his interpretation *dell'antico* and thus pursue his personal duel with Apelles. His *Ecce Homo* lies on the borderline between the canonically correct and the erotic *morbidezza* roundly condemned following the Council of Trent.[35] Reni's

work undoubtedly lacks the painterly conceptual reflection that preceded Titian's and also, to be fair, its virtuoso technique; yet it is no less effective. The two paintings were intended to meet different challenges, to fulfil different aims, and to please different recipients, but they share two key features of the art of their time: the ability to arouse the viewer's emotions, and the formal and technical innovations – *technè* – involved in doing so.

Ana González Mozo

1   John 19:5.
2   Gasnier 1992.
3   Puente [1605] 1935, part four, Introduction, points 1 and 2; Meditation 30, points 1 and 5; Meditation 35, points 2 and 3; Meditation 36, points 2 and 37. For an updated attribution, see Sajonia–Dadreo 1853, 632–36; Tóth and Falvay 2014.
4   Baxandall 1978, 78; Bizzarri and Sainz de la Maza 1994.
5   Baxandall 1978, 60–61.
6   Thomas à Kempis, *The Imitation of Christ*, c. 1418–27, Book IV, ch. XX.
7   Baxandall 1978, 60 and 78; Arasse 2005, 409–10.
8   Arasse 2005, 410–12; Belting 1994, 1–9.
9   Titian, *Ecce Homo* (1543, Vienna, Kunsthistorisches Museum Wien, Gemäldegalerie, inv. 73) and Guido Reni, *Christ crowned with Thorns* (c. 1600, Osimo, cathedral of San Leopardo).
10 Falomir 2003, 224; Falomir 2007; González Mozo 2018, 117, note 438.
11 Mendelsohn 1982; Hendler 2013.
12 González Mozo 2018, 69–92.
13 Madrid, Museo Nacional del Prado, P-444: oil on white marble.
14 González Mozo 2018, 117, note 440.
15 Vatican City, Musei Vaticani, MV.2363.
16 González Mozo 2018, 35–38 and 113–22.
17 Scannelli [1657] 1989, 1:112; Malvasia–Pericolo 2019, 1:432, note 644. This painting matches the description of the picture that Reni gave to Camillo Pamphilj to thank him for a loan, although the dimensions differ. Malvasia–Pericolo 2019, 1:440, note 664.
18 According to his biographer Malvasia, Reni was in the habit of giving away 'works entirely by his hand to those who pleased him [and] knew how to win his sympathies', including an *Ecce Homo* given to a merchant known as Gnicchi. Malvasia–Pericolo 2019, 1:162–63.
19 González Mozo 2018, 177.
20 Ibid., 106.
21 Ibid., 32–33.
22 Aretino and Vasari–Zuffi 2008, 24.
23 The epithet was first used by Petrarch, referring to the Sienese Simone Martini (c. 1284–1344).
24 González Mozo 2018, 30–31.
25 Spear 1997, 103ff.
26 Minozzi 1641, 211–13.
27 Ludovico Dolce and Marcantonio Michiel referred to this as 'soft-brush impasto', a technique for which they praised both Giorgione (1477/78–1510) and Titian. Michiel–Morelli 1800, 80, 86ff., and 98; Roskill 1968, 142–43, 155, and 181.
28 Malvasia–Pericolo 2019, 1:182–83 and 1:408, note 579.
29 Ibid., 1:54 and 1:70.
30 Ibid., 1:68.
31 Ibid., 1:28 and 1:281, note 184.
32 Ibid., 1:182–83.
33 Ibid., 1:276, note 167, and 1:280, note 178.
34 Ibid., 1:170–71 and 1:399, note 541.
35 Borghini 1584, 109–10.

30 Guido Reni

Head of Christ

1620

Red chalk on paper, 344 × 267 mm
The Royal Collection / HM King Charles III, Windsor Castle,
The Royal Library, RCIN 905283

Provenance: Silvestro Bonfiglioli, 1696; Zaccaria Sagredo, 1728; consul Joseph Smith, 1751–52; King George III of Great Britain, 1762.

Selected bibliography: Schilling and Blunt 1971, no. 384; Johnston 1974, 1:147, no. 110; Birke 1981, 104, no. 68; V. Birke in Ebert-Schifferer, Emiliani and Schleier 1988, 339–40, no. B36; Kurz and McBurney 1988, 90, no. 72, pl. 17; Pepper 1988, Appendix II, 347, no. A11; Whitaker and Clayton 2007, no. 119; Malvasia–Pericolo 2019, 1:303–4, note 237, and 2:307, fig. 171; H. Damm in Eclercy 2022a, 214–15, no. 84.

This iconic drawing – featured on the front cover of Veronika Birke's catalogue for the 1981 retrospective *Guido Reni: Zeichnungen* in Vienna – is a superb example of the profound sense of beauty and grace characteristic of Guido Reni's art.

The larger-than-life male head, seen from below, looking downwards and slightly to its right, was first recorded in an inventory of the British Royal Collection around 1800–20[1] as the work of the Bolognese artist Giacomo Cavedone (1577–1660), since it formed part of an album of fifty 'heads' all attributed to him.[2] The drawing was summarily catalogued and reproduced with that attribution by Otto Kurz in 1955. Catherine Johnston subsequently identified the sheet as a study by Reni for the *Salvator Mundi*, painted to Guido's designs by his assistant Giovanni Francesco Gessi (1588–1649) for the high altar of Santissimo Salvatore in Bologna (where it still hangs today), according to Carlo Cesare Malvasia's *Felsina pittrice* (1678).[3] Reni – who had received the commission and was paid between October and December 1620 – gave Gessi a set of patterns on paper. However, on learning that his pupil had been slandering him, Guido refused to pay him before their departure for Naples in 1621, as reported by Malvasia.[4] In his later *Pitture di Bologna* (1686), Malvasia explicitly mentioned the 'drawing, a pastel of the head' by Reni, retouched by Gessi, who executed the painting.[5] The allusion to 'pastel' – despite not being the medium used for this drawing – must be regarded as a specific reference to the Windsor Castle sheet by the biographer, who probably knew it at first hand. This was the view advanced by Stephen Pepper.[6] Malvasia's 1686 reference has therefore been reasonably linked to the description provided in the 1696 inventory of Silvestro Bonfiglioli's collection, which lists a 'Drawing of the Head of the Saviour by the hand of Guido, in a gilt frame with glass', besides taking into account that other artworks formerly in the Bonfiglioli collection ended up in the British Royal Collection.[7]

Compared with the original drawing, the head of Christ in Gessi's painting – though seen from below – displays a less marked foreshortening; the gaze, originally more imperial than imperious, has been trivialised in the expression; and the languid sensuality of Christ's sketched face, descendant yet again of true *venustas*, beauty in its noblest form, has been lost. Indeed, Reni's distinctive reinterpretation of the antique style has yet to be explored in connection with this drawing.

Critics have also overlooked that the British drawing appears to resume the composition of the head of Christ carrying the cross at the centre of the fresco decorating the cupola of the Aldobrandini chapel in the cathedral of the Resurrezione di Nostro Signore Gesù Cristo in Ravenna, paid by Cardinal Pietro Aldobrandini between 1614 and 1616 to Reni, who worked with his pupils Gessi, Giovanni Giacomo Sementi (1583–1636), and Bartolomeo Marescotti (c. 1590–1630) through to 1619–20.[8] Guido appears to have focused his efforts there between 1615 and 1616, and there is no doubt that he had to provide his own compositional drawings for the project. Two surviving autograph cartoons for the cupola show angels carrying the symbols of the Passion.[9] One of these, the *Angel with the Veil of Saint Veronica*,[10] suggests a link – at least in terms of typology – between the bearded image on the Turin Shroud and a drawing often mentioned in relation to Gessi's painting in the church of Santissimo Salvatore in Bologna: a *Male Bearded Head* in black and red chalk on grey (faded blue?) paper in the collections of the Victoria & Albert Museum.[11] Bearing very little resemblance to the Bologna altarpiece, it has been variously regarded as probably by Reni,[12] as the work of Gessi,[13] or as closer in style to Cavedone.[14] Catherine Loisel argues that it displays stylistic features characteristic of Gessi.[15] It would thus seem more likely that the Victoria & Albert sheet was made during the work at Ravenna cathedral.

Viviana Farina

1 Windsor Ms, Inventory A (c. 1800–20), 84, as among: 'Teste di Cavedone: Although slight yet Drawn with great Fire and Spirit, most as large as Life'.

2 London, Royal Library, RL 5244-5293.

3 Pepper 1988, Appendix II, 347, no. A11, fig. 54.

4 See Malvasia–Cropper and Pericolo 2013, 126–27 and 212–13, note 330; Malvasia–Pericolo 2019, 1:82 and 1:303–4, notes 237–39.

5 Malvasia 1686, 168–69: 'Disegno, pastello della testa'.

6 See note 3 above. By contrast, Lorenzo Pericolo (Malvasia–Pericolo 2019, 1:303, note 237) suggests that the drawing referred to by Malvasia is now lost.

7 1696 Bonfiglioli inventory: 'Dissegno con Testa del Salvatore mano di Guido in cornice dorata, e vetro'. Whitaker and Clayton 2007, no. 118.

8 See Pepper 1988, 236, no. 45.

9 Bohn 2008, 42–45, nos. 31–32.

10 Modena, Galleria Estense, R.C.G.E. 4281.

11 London, Victoria & Albert Museum, DYCE.316; Ward-Jackson 1979, 77, no. 790, as 'School of Reni'.

12 Pepper 1988, Appendix II, 347, no. A11.

13 See V. Birke in Ebert-Schifferer, Emiliani and Schleier 1988, 339, no. B36.

14 Whitaker and Clayton 2007, no. 118.

15 Personal communication with the author.

31   Guido Reni

Christ holding the Cross

c. 1619–20
Black and white chalk on grey paper, 341 × 241 mm
The Royal Collection / HM King Charles III, Windsor Castle,
The Royal Library, RCIN 903289

Provenance: King George III of Great Britain, 1762.

Selected bibliography: Kurz and McBurney 1988, 118, no. 346, pl. 59; Pepper 1988, 244, in no. 64; Malvasia–Pericolo 2019, 1:429, note 637; A. Raub in Eclercy 2022a, 232–33, no. 95.

This drawing appears to have entered the collection of George III (1738–1820) in 1762, and was first listed in the early-nineteenth-century royal inventory, alongside works by fourteen different followers of Guido Reni.[1]

Otto Kurz, in his 1955 catalogue of seventeenth- and eighteenth-century Bolognese drawings at Windsor Castle, was the first to recognise it as a study of the famous *Christ carrying the Cross* executed by Michelangelo (1475–1564) in 1519–21 for Santa Maria sopra Minerva in Rome. Consulting eighteenth- and nineteenth-century literary sources, Kurz was able to establish that one of Guido's pupils had used the drawing as a model for a painting made for the door of the tabernacle at the church of the Santissimo Salvatore in Bologna. Sir Joshua Reynolds (1723–1792) had seen it and praised its colours. According to Kurz, the pictorial work could be identified with the canvas in the Musée des Augustins in Toulouse, where it was taken after Napoleon's campaign in Italy.[2] This painting should be attributed to a certain Castellino, presumably Giacomo Castellini, who is mentioned in Carlo Cesare Malvasia's *Felsina pittrice* (1678) as one of Reni's assistants. Finally, Kurz also knew the attested fact that on 8 January 1621 Guido retouched the 'little Christ that goes in the tabernacle'.[3]

Stephen Pepper was the first to link the Windsor Castle drawing with the *Risen Christ embracing the Cross* in the National Museum of Art MUŻA in Malta [fig. 15], a picture unknown to Malvasia but independently recognised as a Reni original by Sir Denis Mahon and Pierre Rosenberg, and first published in 1970 by Erich Schleier, who proposed a chronology around 1620. Even then, a key reference to the painting had been found in a letter from Mattia Preti (1613–1699) – sent from Malta on 23 April 1669 – to the well-known collector Prince Antonio Ruffo of Messina. Therefore Pepper suggested that the canvas was directly commissioned by the Grand Master of the Order of the Knights of Malta, Alof de Wignacourt (1547–1622). In the meantime, in 1965 Alfonso E. Pérez

Sánchez drew attention to a second copy in the Real Academia de Bellas Artes de San Fernando in Madrid,[4] which had originally belonged to the royal collection in the Alcázar (1666),[5] suggesting that it may have come from Naples, according to a reconstruction by Erich Scheleier.[6]

Interestingly, Christ's pose in the Windsor Castle drawing varies with respect to the Michelangelo statue. Although Guido retained the spiral movement of the torso, he modified the turn of the head and brought the legs closer together. In the drawing, at the height where the figure is framed below the knees, the right leg is placed slightly in front of the left, yielding a pose which is less faithful than the subsequent paintings to the prototype. In Reni's day, Michelangelo's statue was placed in – or directly in front of – a niche; the artist therefore had to examine it from the left, with the result that in Guido's study Christ's knees appear to touch. This view, however, is incompatible with the position of the head in the sculpture, that Reni, without considering the point of view from below (obligatory for anyone studying the statue at first hand), changed and drew frontally and in a three-quarter profile.

For an artist trained at the Accademia degli Incamminati, the almost literal reworking of a landmark expression of the *maniera moderna* such as Buonarroti's sculpture cannot by any means be dismissed as mere coincidence. In reproducing the typology associated with the risen Christ carrying the cross, Reni was deliberately paying tribute to the Michelangelo prototype, praised also in Francesco Scannelli's *Microcosmo della pittura* (1657),[7] and readily recognised both by the public and by the artist's clients.[8] Reni was thus expressing a feeling almost of devotion, which might be read as the ideal pendant to the faithful copies he produced in his youth of a work by another father of modern art: Raphael (1483–1520) and his *Ecstasy of Saint Cecilia*.[9]

Viviana Farina

1 Windsor Ms, Inventory A (c. 1800–20), 79: 'Guido &c. Tom. 2', among '14 of different Scholars of Guido as Giovan.Andrea Sirani, Gessi&c ... a Christ'.
2 Toulouse, Musée des Augustins, 2004 1 21.
3 Malvasia–Pericolo 2019, 1:428, note 636.
4 Madrid, Real Academia de Bellas Artes de San Fernando, inv. 0291.

5 Martínez Leiva and Rodríguez Rebollo 2015, 257–58, no. 141.

6 Pérez Sánchez 1970, 450–51, no. 146. On the painting, the copies made of it, and Antonio Vannugli's later hypothesis that the Madrid copy came from the collection of Marquis Giovan Francesco Serra di Cassano (1609–1656) via that of the Spanish Viceroy of Naples, Gaspar de Bracamonte y Guzmán, Count of Peñaranda, see also Malvasia–Pericolo 2019, 1:428–29, note 637.

7 F. Scannelli (1657, 280–81) bases his view on an opinion already expressed by Giovanni Paolo Lomazzo in his *Trattato dell'arte della pittura* (1584). On all this, see Malvasia–Pericolo 2019, 2:73–74.

8 Lorenzo Pericolo (Malvasia–Pericolo 2019, 2:75) tends more towards the view that the adverse criticism of the *Christ* in Santa Maria sopra Minerva voiced by the scholar and collector Marquis Vincenzo Giustiniani in his *Discorso* (shortly after 1610) may to some extent have influenced Guido's decision to adapt Michelangelo's 'divine' model in search of a beauty even more perfect. Seen from that perspective, Reni's *Christ holding the Cross* could be regarded as a kind of artistic manifesto.

9 Bologna, Pinacoteca Nazionale di Bologna, inv. 577.

32 Guido Reni
The Crucifixion

1636
Oil on canvas, 260.3 × 174.6 cm
Modena, Ministero dei Beni e delle Attività Culturali
e del Turismo / Gallerie Estensi, RCGE 414

Provenance: Oratory of the Confraternita del Santissimo Sacramento e delle
Cinque Piaghe, Reggio Emilia, 1636; collection of the Dukes of Este, Palazzo
Ducale, Modena, 1783; Galleria Estense, Modena, 1854.

Selected bibliography: Scannelli 1657, 352; Malvasia 1678, 2:43; Malvasia–
Zanotti 1841, 2:31–32; Venturi 1882, 335 and 398; Pepper 1984, 286; A.
Colombi Ferretti in Benati and Frisoni 1986, 176–77; S. Ebert-Schifferer in
Ebert-Schifferer, Emiliani and Schleier 1988, 217–19; Pepper 1988, 297 (with
earlier bibliography); Spear 1997, 196–201; F. Trevisani in Benati and Mazza
2002, 206–9; Cadoppi 2011b; Ferriani 2011; Malvasia–Pericolo 2019, 2:326,
note 294, and 2:519, note 61; B. Eclercy in Eclercy 2022a, 264–67, no. 114.

Guido Reni's life-size *Crucifixion* is among the masterpieces at
the Galleria Estense. It entered the collection of the Dukes of Este
in 1783, during the suppression of convents and religious com-
munities decreed by Ercole III d'Este, Duke of Modena and
Reggio (1727–1803). The following year, in his *Descrizione de'*

quadri del ducale appartamento di Modena,[1] Count Giacomo
della Palude listed the painting among those hanging in the
Palazzo Ducale of Modena. In view of its outstanding devotional
value, the canvas was placed in the duke's bedroom. Before that,
it had adorned the high altar of the oratory of the Confraternita
del Santissimo Sacramento e delle Cinque Piaghe in Reggio
Emilia, beside the church of Santo Stefano, as part of an austere
marble altar which the Duke donated to Reggio Emilia cathedral
in 1788, to be placed in the Estense funerary chapel. The top
moulding bears the inscription 'REDEMPTUS / REDEMPTOREM /
ADORA / HIERONIMUS RESTA / EREXIT / ANNO / MDCXXXIX'.

It was probably this inscription that led Carlo Cesare Malvasia
to date the painting to 1639 in his *Felsina pittrice* (1678).
Nevertheless, Alberto Cadoppi's careful reconstruction of events
shows that the work was taken to Reggio Emilia towards the end
of 1636. The date on the inscription, 1639, refers to the year of
completion of the altar itself, which is made of Portoro, a valuable gold-veined black marble also known as Porto Venere after
the place where it is quarried. It was commissioned by Girolamo
Resti, who – like his father Teodato and his brother Simone –
was a member of the brotherhood. Some time after 1645, Simone
sponsored the construction of the church of San Girolamo in
Reggio Emilia, modelled on the Holy Sepulchre complex
in Jerusalem; the work was entrusted to the master builder
Girolamo Beltrami (c. 1615–c. 1690), working from plans drawn
up by Gaspare Vigarani (c. 1586/88–1663/64).

Girolamo Resti, who hailed from a wealthy aristocratic family in Reggio Emilia, wished to be buried in the main chapel of
the oratory. The contract for the marble altar was drawn up in
1635, with delivery scheduled for the following year. The work
was commissioned from the Carrara sculptor Attilio Palmieri,
remembered in the sources for having twice supervised the
transport to Madrid of bronze sculptures made by his brother-
in-law and colleague Pietro Tacca (1577–1640). The one-year

Fig. 79 Guido Reni, *The Crucifixion*, c. 1637–38.
Oil on canvas, 340 × 220 cm. Rome,
San Lorenzo in Lucina

The Beauty of the Divine Body

deadline was not met due to the difficulties involved in hauling the stone across the Apennine passes: the last marble elements reached Reggio at the beginning of 1639, and the installation of the altar was completed in early July of that year.

As for the painting, we know that on 20 June 1636 Reni was paid 200 silver ducatons, to which an ex gratia payment of 320 lire was added. On 1 October of that year, he received a further unexpected payment of 24 silver ducatons. In a letter dated 18 November 1636, Girolamo Resti informed Attilio Palmieri that the large painting for the altarpiece had arrived in Reggio. On that occasion Guido also delivered a 'head of Christ' which Resti later gave to his close friend Aurelio Zanetti, a collector of works by Guercino (1591–1666). Girolamo, who himself owned a large number of paintings, also commissioned ecclesiastical vestments and a black velvet baldachin for the Good Friday procession, which he bequeathed to the oratory in his 1662 will.

Reni painted numerous Crucifixions. He was particularly fond of this theme, which allowed him, as Malvasia remarked, 'to show off his great knowledge of the torso'.[2] Compared to the famous Crucifixion[3] he probably executed in 1619 for the Capuchin Order – in which Christ is attended by the canonical figures of the Virgin, Saint John, and Mary Magdalene, the reds, blues and ochres of their garments offering a rather sombre contrast in lighting – and also to the dazzling crucifixion depicted in Guido's monumental Trinity of 1625 for the church of the Santissima Trinità dei Pellegrini in Rome [fig. 28], the versions Guido produced towards the end of his career testify to a progressive formal catharsis.

Two further Crucifixions date from the 1630s: one now in the Pinacoteca Ambrosiana in Milan,[4] featuring a skull in the foreground and a city in the background, and another decorating the high altar at San Lorenzo in Lucina [fig. 79], which entered the church in 1669 as a bequest from Cristiana Duglioli Angelelli († 1669), a noblewoman who left Bologna in some haste to settle in Rome, but soon recovered the paintings that had formed her collection.[5]

The tendency toward formal abstraction characteristic of these paintings, a hallmark of Reni's so-called maniera argentina, culminated in this masterpiece in the Galleria Estense. The canvas is remarkable not only for its chromatism and light palette – the shimmering delicacy of its cold silky whites, its exquisite greys and the pearly sheen of its violets – but also for the extreme dematerialisation of the figure. Over time, Guido's highly-evocative treatment breathed new life into this iconic image which between the eighteenth and twentieth centuries was loved and venerated, though equally despised both for its

unwavering espousal of academic precepts and for its Pietist overtones. Be that as it may, it was to have an enormous influence on Catholic imagery. Both the purity of Christ's unsullied body – on which only a few drops of blood appear, despite being held to the cross by three nails – and the formal clarity of the delicately-modulated tones in which it is rendered erase all impression of pain and shun all sense of despair. Similarly, the vertical alignment of the figure – wholly at odds with the writhing forms typical of contemporary iconographies – makes no attempt to convey the final contortions of death. The body's timeless stillness is countered only by the swirling loincloth. The expression on Christ's face as it is raised towards heaven, that 'divine upturning of the eyes'[6] which other artists would later seek in vain to emulate, has been described as 'the most divine that can be depicted on human features'.[7] In that countenance, as Luigi Lanzi has remarked, 'death itself appears beautiful'.[8]

As some critics have suggested, that new sensibility may well owe much to the Crucifixion with the city of Urbino in the background painted by Federico Barocci (c. 1535–1612) for Duke Francesco Maria II della Rovere, who in his 1628 will bequeathed it to King Philip IV.[9] Certain aspects of Reni's crucifixion also call to mind the famous drawing that Michelangelo (1475–1564) gave to Vittoria Colonna, described by Ascanio Condivi as 'Christ on the cross, not in the semblance of death, as he is usually depicted, but in a divine attitude, his face raised up towards the Father'.[10] By removing the city in the background and the skull from the foot of the cross – both of which feature in the Angelelli canvas in San Lorenzo in Lucina, then the residence of the General Curia of the Clerics Regular Minor – Guido imbued the image with an ideal essence, leading the devout viewer to focus on the saving figure of the living Christ, captured in its last throes, as intangible as a vision of ecstasy.

Angelo Mazza

1 Palude 1784, 37–38.

2 Malvasia 1678, 2:78; Malvasia–Zanotti 1841, 2:56; Malvasia–Pericolo 2019, 1:177: 'Mostrare in que' torsi il suo grand'intendere'.

3 Bologna, Pinacoteca Nazionale di Bologna, inv. 441.

4 Milan, Pinacoteca Ambrosiana, inv. 1184.

5 The first reference to the painting, in 1643; see Cammarota 2001, 111; Curti 2007, 26, 29, 71, 72, 74, and 116.

6 De Dominici 1742–45 (1745), 3:149: 'Divin girar degli occhi'.

7 P. Malgouyres in Franck and Malgouyres 2015, 124: 'La plus divine que l'on puisse représenter sur des traits humains'.

8 Lanzi 1823, 5:130: 'Par bella la morte stessa'.

9 Madrid, Museo Nacional del Prado, P-7092. Montanari 2009, 221; Moretti 2014, 515–27.

10 Condivi [1553] 1823, 78: 'Gesù Cristo in croce non in sembianza di morto, come comunemente s'usa, ma in atto divino, col volto levato al Padre'.

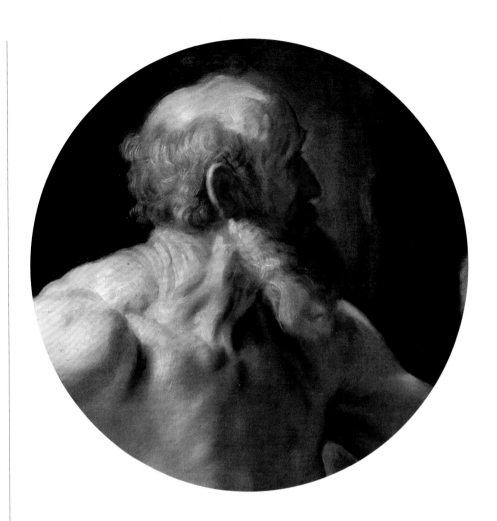

THE POWER OF SAINTS
AND THE BEAUTY OF OLD AGE

In Baroque society, saints were assigned a crucial role in protecting the Catholic faithful and interceding on their behalf. Echoing this religious sentiment, Guido Reni became remarkably adept at producing beautiful, moving depictions of saints, and of scenes from their lives, both as single figures and as part of more elaborate compositions. Nowhere is his skill in constructing hagiographical narratives better displayed than in his magnificent *Triumph of Job* [cat. 44], where the wealth of secondary elements serves to highlight the saint rather than undermining his importance. But it was in his representations of single holy figures – apostles, evangelists, ascetics – that Reni fully projected his own sensibility, tackling a concept at which he excelled: the lasting beauty of the body beyond youth. The exquisite care and painterly intensity lavished on these ageing faces, these sagging bodies, endows them with a singular charm. Guido's approach – shared by other leading contemporary artists – reflects the Christian idea that the beauty of the soul outlasts the flesh.

33 Guido Reni
Saint Peter

1633–34
Oil on silk, 76 × 61 cm
Madrid, Museo Nacional del Prado, P-219

Provenance: Collection of García de Haro Sotomayor y Guzmán, 2nd Count of Castrillo; Spanish royal collection, located in the prior's chapter room at the Real Monasterio de San Lorenzo de El Escorial, 1667.

Selected bibliography: Ponz 1772–94 (1773), 2:140–41; Pérez Sánchez 1965a, 175; Pérez Sánchez 1970, 460; Andrés 1971, 53; Baccheschi 1977, 104, no. 30; Pepper 1984, 270–71, no. 147; *Museo del Prado* 1985, 541; S. Ebert-Schifferer in Ebert-Schifferer, Emiliani and Schleier 1988, 161–94, no. A-25a; *Museo del Prado* 1990, 1:125, no. 411; Bartolomé 1994, 20; Salvy 2001, 125; H. Damm in Eclercy 2022a, 216–17, no. 85.

This painting and its pendant – the *Saint Paul* also in the Museo del Prado [cat. 34] – formed part of the Spanish royal collection as early as the seventeenth century, when Father Francisco de los Santos described them as hanging in the Chapter Rooms at the royal monastery of San Lorenzo de El Escorial in 1667. Both were placed in the Prior's Chapter Room, where this *Saint Peter* hung below a depiction of the *Adulterous Woman*[1] from the workshop of Paolo Veronese (1528–1588) and near another celebrated painting by Guido Reni, the *Virgin of the Chair* [cat. 52]. They had previously belonged to García de Haro Sotomayor y Guzmán, 2nd Count of Castrillo (1585–1670), who – among other appointments – held the post of Viceroy of Naples from 1653 to 1659. Both were listed in an inventory of his possessions, drawn up in Naples two years before his return to Spain, which records two octagonal paintings portraying the two apostles.[2]

Father Santos praised this *Saint Peter*, describing it as admirable and 'superior in Art',[3] and drawing attention to the distress conveyed by Peter's realistic gestures. In this bust-length depiction within an oval frame, Peter gazes heavenward, his head resting on his right hand and his mouth half open. The pathos is heightened by Reni's rendering of the signs of old age in the saint's face, the deep wrinkles serving as channels for the tears that fall from his weary eyes, as well as the grey hair and the unkempt beard. His left hand presses against his chest with such strength that it makes furrows in the skin, following the line of his fingers.

All these elements suggest that the theme was in fact the so-called 'tears of Saint Peter', the moment when the apostle implores Christ's forgiveness after denying him three times. The subject became popular within the Catholic Church during the Counter-Reformation since it conveyed several of the values espoused by the Council of Trent, such as repentance and the ensuing sacrament of penance. Guido was among the artists who best succeeded in adapting their painterly approach to the new Catholic ideology, developing a compositional formula ideally suited to the production of profoundly devotional images. Like this portrait, Reni's holy figures aroused the empathy of the faithful by reflecting a range of emotions drawn from their own reality. The painting thus became a means of teaching the principles debated by theologians; here, the penitent Saint Peter embodies human weakness and illustrates the mercy shown by the Church in forgiving it.

The skilled handling of compositional resources evident in this picture – a hallmark of Reni's treatment of holy figures – together with certain technical features, including the loose yet accurate brushstrokes, suggest that it was painted fairly late in his career. Notwithstanding, Alfonso E. Pérez Sánchez dated it to the mid-1610s, noting similarities with the physical models in the lower part of the *Assumption* at the church of Gesù e dei Santi Ambrogio e Andrea in Genoa, painted around 1616.[4] However, critics now agree that it was painted in 1633–34 in view of certain anatomical features; the masterly use of the pictorial mass to shape the neck, for example, hints at a certain abstraction far removed from the perfect outlines of his earlier work.[5] It has been suggested that Guido may have taken as his model a classical sculpture of the *Death of Seneca*, which he could have seen in the Villa Borghese, where it had stood since at least 1613.[6] According to Carlo Cesare Malvasia, Reni had a copy of this marble, which he could also have used as a model for the figure of Saint Peter in the Genoa *Assumption* mentioned above.[7] By placing the bust in an oval frame, against whose dark background only the figure and the halo stand out, Guido succeeded in creating a sense of depth, thus demonstrating his awareness of the particular effects that can be achieved with different formats.

Recent technical examination carried out at the Museo del Prado has revealed that the support is silk, cut to a circular shape and relined on a rectangular fabric, with the joins modified and the space at the corners painted green.[8] Although it is impossible to determine exactly when these changes were made, the inventory of the 2nd Count of Castrillo alludes specifically to the unusual octagonal format of the pictures, but neither Father Santos nor Antonio Ponz (1725–1792) – who saw them in the late eighteenth century – make any reference to it.[9] While this does not in itself confirm a later modification, the two copies made by Ponz himself – now in the minor cloisters at the monastery of El Escorial – are rectangular in format, and the figures have been extended into the lower section.[10] This suggests that the canvases may have undergone two changes in format, the first probably in the seventeenth century, after entering the Spanish royal collection, and the second in the nineteenth or twentieth century.

Rafael Japón

1 Madrid, Museo Nacional del Prado, P-495.

2 Bartolomé 1994, 20.

3 Santos 1667, 75v; Bassegoda i Hugas 2002, 167, CP14.

4 Pérez Sánchez 1970, 458.

5 S. Ebert-Schifferer in Ebert-Schifferer, Emiliani and Schleier 1988, 191, no. A-25a.

6 Paris, Musée du Louvre, Département des Antiquités grecques, étrusques et romaines, Ma 1354.

7 On this comparison and the sculpture in Reni's studio, see Malvasia–Pericolo 2019, 1:279, note 177.

8 For this information I am grateful to Laura Alba Carcelén, who carried out the X-ray examination of this canvas in May 2022.

9 Ponz 1772–94 (1773), 2:140–41.

10 Patrimonio Nacional, inv. 10014807 and 10014769.

34 Guido Reni
Saint Paul

1633–34
Oil on silk, 76 × 61 cm
Madrid, Museo Nacional del Prado, P-220

Provenance: Collection of García de Haro y Avellaneda, 2nd Count of Castrillo; Spanish royal collection, prior's Chapter Rooms at the Real Monasterio de San Lorenzo de El Escorial, 1667; friary of Nuestra Señora del Rosario, Madrid, after 1808; Real Academia de Bellas Artes de San Fernando, Madrid, 1813, from whence it entered the Museo del Prado.

Selected bibliography: Ponz 1772–94 (1773), 2:140–41; Pérez Sánchez 1965a, 175; Pérez Sánchez 1970, 460; Andrés 1971, 53; Baccheschi 1977, 104, no. 129; Pepper 1984, 270–71, no. 148; *Museo del Prado* 1985, 541; S. Ebert-Schifferer in Ebert-Schifferer, Emiliani and Schleier 1988, 161–94, no. A-25b; *Museo del Prado* 1990, 128, no. 420; Bartolomé 1994, 20; Salvy 2001, 125; H. Damm in Eclercy 2022a, 216–17, no. 86.

This *Saint Paul* shares with its pendant – the *Saint Peter* also in the Museo del Prado [cat. 33] – a number of technical characteristics which indicate that they were produced by Guido Reni at the same time, around 1633–34. Chief among these is his masterly construction of volume using swift brushstrokes that allow the picture layer beneath to show through, creating a vibrant effect. This is particularly apparent in the saint's left hand, which assumes great prominence on account of its position in the foreground grasping the sword, one of Paul's attributes. His fingers are rendered in patches of colour employing a very limited palette and using fragile glazes that make precise contours unnecessary. This testifies to the vast technical knowledge of an artist at the height of his career, whose paintings during this period are notable both for their speed of execution and for an economy of resources which – contrary to what one might imagine – never undermines the quality of his work.

This piece contains several compositional elements that contrast with those of *Saint Peter*, probably in order to convey different, though complementary, Counter-Reformation values. Here, the Apostle to the Gentiles is depicted in early middle age, his maturity hinted at only by a few grey hairs, executed with fine brushstrokes against his dark locks. Though the two saints are facing in opposite directions, both raise their eyes towards heaven, but Paul's gaze bespeaks a wholly different intention; his firm, haughty expression and his grip on the sword underline his commitment to the defence of Christianity. The colour of their garments is also in keeping with their attitudes: while Peter wears an ochre robe that stresses his grief, Paul's bright

Cat. 33

Cat. 34

The Power of Saints and the Beauty of Old Age

red cloak stands out against the green background, heightening the sense of movement conveyed by the turning of his head. In terms of composition and use of colour, the picture strongly resembles the *Saint Paul* designed by Fra Bartolomeo (1472–1517) and completed by Raphael (1483–1520) for the church of San Silvestro al Quirinale in Rome, now hanging – alongside a *Saint Peter* by the same artists – in the Musei Vaticani.[1] Reni employed an identical combination of clothing in other portrayals of the two apostles, making excellent use of all the technical resources at his disposal to create two very different but interrelated works that were part of a shared programme.

While Paul of Tarsus was not among the twelve apostles who had personally known Jesus, he was a key figure both as a missionary and as the author of the epistles, which were to achieve canonical status. The sword, usually intended as a reference to his martyrdom, reflects a phrase from one of his letters, 'the sword of the Spirit, which is the word of God',[2] alluding to the power of the divine message as a defensive spiritual weapon, but also as an offensive one to be used in spreading the gospel. For that reason, following the Council of Trent the image of Paul came to symbolise militant Catholicism, complementing the figure of Saint Peter as founder of the early Church. Reni also depicted the two apostles together in a single scene, engaged in theological discussion.[3] Although according to Carlo Cesare Malvasia that canvas was produced early in the artist's career for the Sampieri family in Bologna,[4] the saints physically resemble their counterparts in the Prado paintings, albeit in a register much more reminiscent of Caravaggio, typical of Guido's first sojourn in Rome. Malvasia notes that, while in Rome, the artist produced a complete *Apostles* series,[5] pointing to an early specialisation in this kind of devotional image.

This painting together with its pendant were placed in the prior's chapter room at El Escorial, perhaps as part of the redecoration programme undertaken by Diego Velázquez (1599–1660); they were hung beneath a *Virgin and Child with the Infant Saint John* by Paolo Veronese (1528–1588), now unidentified.[6] During the Peninsular War, both pieces were taken to the friary of Nuestra Señora del Rosario for safe keeping, remaining there until 1813, when they entered the Real Academia de Bellas Artes de San Fernando, from where they were transferred to the Museo del Prado.[7] Recent technical analysis has revealed an identical change of format in both works, and has established that they may have been painted on a silk fabric support, a procedure not uncommon in Reni's oeuvre.[8] In addition to the copies made by Antonio Ponz (1725–1792), now in El Escorial, Alfonso E. Pérez Sánchez identified further copies painted in the eighteenth century by Luis Planes (1772–1799) in storage at the Museo de Bellas Artes in Valencia.[9] The Prado register of copyists shows that in the late nineteenth century at least three applications were received to copy *Saint Paul*, while only one was made to copy its companion piece.[10] The interest of other painters in these pictures appears to date back to their creation; it has been suggested that Jusepe de Ribera (1591–1652) may have been inspired by them.

Rafael Japón

1 On these two paintings by Fra Bartolomeo and Raphael, see Borgo 1987.
2 Ephesians 6:17.
3 Milan, Pinacoteca di Brera, inv. 357.
4 On this painting, see D. Benati in Zeri 1991, 238–41; Malvasia–Pericolo 2019, 1:258, note 122.
5 Malvasia–Pericolo 2019, 1:474.
6 Santos 1667, 76; Bassegoda i Hugas 2002, 167–68, CP15.
7 Vignau 1903, 375.
8 For this information I am indebted to Laura Alba Carcelén, who performed the X-ray examination of this canvas in May 2022.
9 Pérez Sánchez 1965a, 190.
10 Japón 2022a, 66.

35 Guido Reni
Saint Luke

c. 1625
Oil on canvas, 76.5 × 63.5 cm
Madrid, Fundación Casa de Alba, Palacio de Liria, P.129

Provenance: Acquired by Carlos Miguel Fitz-James Stuart, 7th Duke of Berwick and 14th Duke of Alba, Naples, 1816.

Selected bibliography: Barcia 1911, 125; Pita Andrade 1960, 1:54–58; Pérez Sánchez 1965a, 181.

This painting is regarded as an autograph replica of the *Saint Luke* in the Bob Jones University Museum and Gallery in Greenville, South Carolina, produced as part of a set including the other three evangelists: *Saint John, Saint Mark*, and *Saint Matthew with the Angel*. This series, formerly in the collection of the Duke of Beaufort, is thought to have been commissioned, together with three sibyls, by the Bologna art dealer Girolamo Manzini, who sent them to France to be sold.[1] In his *Felsina pittrice* (1678), Carlo Cesare Malvasia refers to this commission in an account of an argument between Reni and his patron, who had contracted him to produce a set of half-length figures.[2] While Malvasia provides no specific date for these works, it can be inferred that pictures of this type by Guido Reni were by then highly prized, and that the four pictures were painted around 1620.

The *Saint Luke* in the Fundación Casa de Alba differs somewhat from the Greenville version, thought to be the first of the series. Though it is slightly smaller, the figure is similarly positioned and outlined. However, the space between the figure and the upper border has been enlarged and the background colour is subtly lighter in the area around his head, thus better defining the contours. The bull, a symbol of Saint Luke, is in both cases very faint and blurred. Reni may have fixed the composition by tracing the preliminary drawing, as he did on several occasions; for that reason, differences mainly affect the use of colour and final brushstrokes. Here, the shining eyes and the highlights on the nose and forehead are more emphasised, while the curling hair and beard convey a greater sense of movement. Moreover, the book is somewhat smaller and the gap formed by the folded spine as it lies open is more realistic in design. In view of these compositional variations, and of a discernible shift towards looser brushstrokes and greater precision when capturing the effects of light and shade, it can be assumed that this canvas was produced a few years later, perhaps around 1625.

Although the Greenville series is the only complete set to have survived, reproductions and variants of the individual paintings have been recorded in a number of collections; some of these may have been produced as a set, being dispersed at a later date. There is no documentary evidence as to whether this *Saint Luke* belonged to such a group or whether it was intended as a single devotional image; nonetheless, the existence in different locations of three paintings identical in size and similar in facture, each depicting one of the other three evangelists, suggests that this canvas formed part of a series.[3] Sets of evangelists were sometimes assembled using works by different painters: in 1668, for example, the Venice collection of Alvise Molin included a series comprising a *Saint Mark* by Jusepe de Ribera (1591–1652), a *Saint Matthew* by Guercino (1591–1666), a *Saint Luke* by Girolamo Forabosco (1605–1679), and a *Saint John* by Reni.[4] It would not be the first time that several renowned artists – among them Guido – had been commissioned to produce a single set.[5] In this case, however, the Ribera painting was larger than the rest, confirming that Molin did not commission the four pictures as a set. This would also account for the participation of a younger painter like Forabosco.[6] Although these paintings have not been identified, Reni's *Saint John* is likely to have been a version of its Greenville counterpart, whose composition is very similar to *Saint Luke*, although the saint faces the other way and is looking down at the book. To judge by the number of surviving copies, it was among the most widely reproduced representations of the evangelists; a copy has even been attributed to one of Guido's most gifted followers, Simone Cantarini (1612–1648).[7]

The present canvas was acquired in Naples by Carlos Miguel Fitz-James Stuart, 14th Duke of Alba (1794–1835), in 1816 for 3600 francs.[8] The records mention several complete sets in Naples, including one now in the Pio Monte della Misericordia – all four paintings of which are regarded as copies – and another in the Palazzo Filomarino della Rocca,[9] whose provenance cannot be reliably traced due to insufficient information.

Rafael Japón

1 Pepper 1984, 241; Malvasia–Pericolo 2019, 1:336–37, note 322.

2 Malvasia–Pericolo 2019, 1:504.

3 The other canvases which might belong to this set are the *Saint Matthew with the Angel* now in the Pinacoteca Vaticana (MV. 40395), the *Saint John* now in the Muscarelle Museum of Art, Williamsburg, Virginia (acquired with funds from the Board of Visitors Muscarelle Museum of Art Endowment, 2015.013), and a *Saint Mark* recently sold by Sotheby's London (*Old Master Paintings*, 23 September 2020, lot 28). I am grateful to Professor Lorenzo Pericolo for pointing out the possible link between these paintings.

4 Borean 1998, 501, doc. 157; Marin 2015, 346–47.

5 A good example was the *Apostles* series belonging to Fernando Afán Enríquez de Ribera, 3rd Duke of Alcalá de los Gazules; on this subject, see cat. 39 in this catalogue and Japón 2022b, 92–99.

6 Malvasia–Pericolo 2019, 1:396–97, note 532.

7 Pepper 1984, 242.

8 Redín Michaus 2017, 174.

9 Pepper 1984, 241.

36 Anonymous, after a model by Guido Reni
Head of Old Man, known as Head of Seneca

17th or 18th century
Bronze, height 40 cm
Madrid, Museo Arqueológico Nacional, inv. 2941

Provenance: Spanish royal collection; Gabinete de Antigüedades de la Biblioteca Nacional, Madrid; Museo Arquelógico Nacional, Madrid, 1867.

Selected bibliography: Castellanos de Losada 1847, 41, no. 115; Villaamil y Castro 1876; Rada y Delgado 1883, 222, no. 2941; Mélida 1895; Bernoulli 1901, 2:166; Álvarez Ossorio 1925, 120; Kurz 1942; *Velázquez y lo velazqueño* 1960, 153, no. 233; Bacchi 2004.

As Carlo Cesare Malvasia recalls in his *Felsina pittrice* (1678), among his many skills Guido Reni was something of a sculptor: '[He] modeled in relief and was good at it, as proven by the famous head of the so-called *Seneca*, which circulates in every workshop, and for which Guido used as a model a Slav [Dalmatian] in Rome he had met at the Ripa [district], modeling and exaggerating his features in that manner'.[1] The Italian term used by Malvasia, *modelleggiare*, literally meaning 'to make models', can be interpreted as modelling in the sense of working with ductile materials such as clay, or perhaps wax or plaster. While this suggests a painter conversant with the plastic arts – a versatility famously displayed by Leonardo da Vinci (1452–1519) – though not necessarily one skilled at working hard materials such as marble or bronze, it nevertheless testifies to Reni's multifaceted creativity, placing him squarely in the Carracci tradition. In fact, Malvasia notes that both Agostino (1557–1602) and Ludovico Carracci (1555–1619) had also produced clay models.[2] In tackling the various challenges posed by *Seneca* – the old, bald man's heavily wrinkled face and neck, the play of shadows on his skin – Guido skilfully combined an antique model with a study *del naturale*. Although the original head made by Reni seems to have disappeared, its immense success both in contemporary art academies – as reported by Malvasia – and in later periods is borne out by the large number of surviving drawings and replicas in a range of materials, among them this bronze head in the Museo Arqueológico Nacional in Madrid.

The lost original head can in all probability be dated to one of Reni's sojourns in Rome, in the 1610s. According to Richard Spear, echoes of the study for *Seneca* can be found in Reni's frescoes of saints on the arches of the Cappella Paolina at Santa Maria Maggiore, painted around 1611–13, and particularly in the head of Saint Ildefonsus receiving the chasuble [fig. 32] and that

of the companion of Saint Dominic. To these, we could perhaps add the bishop to the left of Saint Cyril, although he is not gazing upwards. The features of *Seneca* can also be discerned in Guido's *Saint Charles Borromeo* in the church of San Carlo ai Catinari in Rome, painted shortly after the frescoes at the Cappella Paolina.[3] It is impossible to determine with any certainty whether these frescoes offer a reliable *terminus ante quem* for the production of Reni's *Seneca*, for he may have worked from drawings, and only modelled the three-dimensional head at a later stage.[4] However, it seems likely that he produced the head before 1617, when – according to Malvasia – he repeated Seneca's wrinkled neck in his depiction of Saint Peter for the *Assumption* in the church of Gesù in Genoa.[5] Whatever the case, Guido continued to make use of the model throughout his career, and visual references to *Seneca* are often to be found in his oeuvre: in the *Fathers of the Church disputing the Dogma of the Immaculate Conception*, painted in 1624–25;[6] in his celebrated portraits of the Blessed Andrea Corsini, produced in the 1630s;[7] unmistakeably in the Siena *Circumcision* [cat. 21]; and even in the *Adoration of the Shepherds* at the Certosa di San Martino in Naples [fig. 31], one of the last works painted before his death in 1642.[8]

After a long period of oblivion, the first head to be recognised as a replica of Reni's *Seneca* was the plaster version at the Accademia Clementina in Bologna.[9] In 1942, Otto Kurz found the bronze head in the Museo Arqueológico Nacional in Madrid, thinking it might be the original cast by Guido. That possibility, however, must be ruled out, since Malvasia refers to a ductile material. Together with the Madrid piece, Kurz published two further versions: a plaster in the library of the Stadtpalais Liechtenstein in Vienna, and a stone version in the Palais de la Légion d'honneur in Paris: in both cases, it was regarded first and foremost as a portrait of the writer and philosopher Seneca, and its origins as an academic study by Reni had been completely forgotten.[10] This bronze head entered the Gabinete de Antigüedades as a portrait of Seneca, cast from a Roman original found at Herculaneum and brought to Madrid by Charles III.[11] It soon became apparent, however, that this was not an ancient work, and it was catalogued as a Renaissance sculpture until it was reattributed to Reni by Kurz.[12]

As well as through sculptural replicas, the most distinguished of which is the terracotta version in the Museo di Palazzo Venezia in Rome,[13] Reni's *Seneca* is also known through a large group of drawings (for example, the one in the Royal Collection at Windsor[14]) and paintings (such as the canvas in the Galleria Spada[15]). *The Painter's Studio* in the Galleria Nazionale d'Arte Antica di Palazzo Barberini, a picture attributed to Michael Sweerts (1618–1664), features a particularly charming backlit representation of the head.[16] In addition to its widespread diffusion in Italian academies and collections, Reni's *Seneca* must have had a certain impact in Spain. It occupies a prominent place in a drawing entitled *Allegory of Painting* by Juan Conchillos (1641–1711), made around 1694–1700, now in the Museo del Prado.[17] There, the head of Seneca is centrally positioned in the immediate foreground, as though it were the most obvious embodiment of the art of painting. This drawing may open up new avenues of research into the circulation and success of Guido's model in Spain.

Fernando Loffredo

1 Malvasia 1678, 2:82: 'Fece di rilievo, e se diportò bene, come dalla famosa testa detta del Seneca, che cammina per tutte le scuole, e che cavò da uno schiavo in Roma che trovò a Ripa, modelleggiandolo, e caricandolo in quella guisa'. For the English translation, see Malvasia–Pericolo 2019, 185.
2 Bacchi 2004.
3 Takahashi 2002.
4 Spear 1997, 282.
5 Pierguidi 2015, 373.
6 St Petersburg, State Hermitage Museum, ГЭ-59.
7 Florence, Gallerie degli Uffizi, inv. 1890 n. 10072; Bologna, Pinacoteca Nazionale di Bologna, inv. 443; Pierguidi 2018.
8 Bacchi 2004.
9 Malaguzzi Valeri 1926.
10 Kurz 1942, 222–23 and 225–26.
11 Castellanos de Losada 1847, 41, no. 115; Villaamil y Castro 1876; Rada y Delgado 1883, 222, no. 2941.
12 Mélida 1895; Bernoulli 1901, 2:166; Álvarez Ossorio 1925, 120.
13 Rome, Museo Nazionale del Palazzo di Venezia, PV 10588; Giometti 2011, 38–39, no. 11.
14 Windsor, Royal Collection, RCIN 905165.
15 Zeri 1954.
16 Rome, Galleria Nazionale d'Arte Antica di Palazzo Barberini, inv. 2212; Papi 1990, 174; Pestilli 1993, esp. 131.
17 Madrid, Museo Nacional del Prado, D-127; Pérez Sánchez 1972b, 87–88; Marco García 2021, 40.

37 Anonymous

One of the Seven Sages of Greece

2nd century AD (head); 17th century (bust)
Marble, 88.5 × 55.7 × 25.5 cm
Madrid, Museo Nacional del Prado, E-399

Provenance: Spanish royal collection.

Selected bibliography: Hübner [1862] 2008, 137, no. 237; Barrón 1908, 260–61, no. 399; Blanco and Lorente 1981, 122, no. 399; Schröder 1993–2004 (1993), 1:80–82.

A saltire carved into the right shoulder of the bust tells us that this marble figure belonged to King Philip V, and must therefore have been in the royal collection since at least the eighteenth century; however, since it has not yet been clearly identified in any of the early inventories, its exact provenance remains unknown.

The piece comprises two different parts: the head, its nose a later replacement, and the bust draped in a *paludamentum*, presumably of Baroque origin. The marble displays some greyish streaks, but the blackened debris visible on the surface was caused by fire, suggesting that the figure survived the blaze which destroyed the Alcázar in Madrid in 1734.

Stephan Schröder has dated the head to the second century AD, noting a number of specific features – such as the way the curls fall over the forehead – reminiscent of other figures produced at that time, which might provide some indication of its possible authorship. However, even the iconographic identification of the portrait is unclear. Given its resemblance to the head of a double herm at the Villa Albani in Rome, whose reverse bears a portrait of Periander of Corinth (7th century BC), one of the so-called 'Seven Sages of Greece', this may well be another illustrious member of that select group, though his exact identity has yet to be confirmed.

As we are often reminded, Pliny credited Asinius Pollio with the idea of placing portraits of well-known authors in Rome's public libraries, alongside their books. The aim was somehow to capture their soul through their likeness, so that readers might fruitfully engage not just with their written work but also with their physical presence.

Ever since, the major figures of classical antiquity – not just intellectuals but also politicians, military strategists, and artists – have graced our galleries and graphic repertoires, illustrating our need to identify excellence through a tireless quest for a plausible likeness that might ultimately enhance the credibility of the written word. It was that same need to 'engage' with those now in a higher order of being which prompted, from the Middle Ages onwards, the assembly of collections of busts-reliquaries, endowing the anthropomorphic representations with all the transcendence required in order for a mortal to communicate with the immortal.

Picture galleries, of course, served the same function, and the parallels are obvious. We can trace clear links between these 'illustrious men' of classical antiquity and the ensuing time-honoured, quintessential 'apostle series': mature, usually bearded figures in classical dress, adopting reflective poses, clothed with the dignity of age and exuding a wisdom discernible not just in their physical features but also in the portrait of their inner selves as role models and sources of spiritual guidance.

Guido Reni's use and interpretation of classical sculpture – what Malvasia termed the palpable 'benefit of the ancient statues'[1] – is evident throughout his oeuvre,[2] and the immense skill that he brought to this discipline strongly suggests that busts like this were a direct source of inspiration when seeking models for his representations of saints. Indeed, he displayed a highly personal approach to conveying physical attributes, blending the study from life with the lessons provided by classical sculpture collections, as the best and most effective of academies.

Manuel Arias Martínez

1 Malvasia 1678, 2:74–75; Malvasia–Pericolo 2019, 1:169.
2 Pagliani 1990.

38 Guido Reni

Saint James the Greater

c. 1626
Oil on canvas, 135 × 89 cm
Madrid, Museo Nacional del Prado, P-212

Provenance: Collection of Isabella Farnese, Palacio Real de La Granja de San Ildefonso, Segovia, 1746 (no. 318); king's apartments – quarters occupied by the infante at the Palacio Real de La Granja de San Ildefonso, Segovia, 1766 (no. 318); oratory and elsewhere at the Palacio Real, Aranjuez, 1794 (no. 318); Infante Francisco's quarters – first room at the Palacio Real, Madrid, 1814–18 (no. 318); Real Museo, Madrid, 1854 and 1858.

Selected bibliography: Gnudi and Cavalli 1955, 83; Pérez Sánchez 1965a, 177–78; Baccheschi 1977, 97, no. 82; *Museo del Prado* 1990, 1:234, no. 836; 'Prado disperso' 1994, 88; A. Pancorbo in *Italian Masterpieces* 2014, 108; Japón 2019, 354–57; Forgione and Saracino 2019, 11; Japón 2022b, 94–96.

James the Greater, a senior apostle and one of Jesus' closest disciples, had strong ties with Spain. He is said to have travelled to the peninsula after the events at Pentecost in order to preach the gospel. According to tradition, his remains were interred in Santiago de Compostela, where from the Middle Ages onwards his shrine became a popular place of pilgrimage, as a result of which he was named patron saint of Spain. He is also deemed to have played a central role in several miracles associated with battles against the Moors. Accordingly, he was held in special esteem by the Spanish monarchy, in whose territories the image of this saint, in its various iconographies, soon spread. In this half-length frontal representation, the brilliant rendering of colour against a neutral background combines with the chosen perspective to endow the figure with a sculptural presence. James is portrayed here as a pilgrim, with the staff as his only attribute, pinned diagonally against his body by his right arm, and his hands folded in prayer. His head is slightly tilted backwards, emphasising his upward gaze. Above him, the golden heavens open in a dramatic gesture underlining his role as God's intercessor.

For this version, Guido Reni turned to a model first used around 1617 in a canvas that was more demanding in terms of composition: the *Assumption of the Virgin* in the church of Gesù e dei Santi Ambrogio e Andrea in Genoa, in which the position of one of the apostles in the lower left, gazing up at Mary, is identical to that of Saint James in this painting. Guido had earlier made successful use of this pose – and this setting – for similar figures, for example in the frescoes of *Saint Francis in Ecstasy* of about 1611 for the Cappella Paolina in Santa Maria Maggiore, Rome, and in the *Glory of Saint Dominic* for the apse

of the Cappella dell'Arca, in the church of San Domenico, Bologna, of around 1613.

The first mention of this canvas in an inventory of the Spanish royal collection appears in 1746, when it is listed among Queen Isabella Farnese's paintings at the palace of La Granja de San Ildefonso. It was later transferred to Aranjuez, together with several other works by Reni, including a *Saint Catherine* [cat. 84] and a *Saint Sebastian* [cat. 19], beside which it was placed in the

Fig. 80 X-ray image of *Saint James the Greater* [cat. 38]

oratory. The painting was subsequently moved to the Royal Palace in Madrid, where it hung in the 'first room', and more specifically in the Infante Francisco's quarters, and kept the same inventory number. It was taken to the Museo del Prado in 1834. In the twentieth century, Bernard Berenson and Hermann Voss agreed that this was an original work by Reni, a view officially adopted in 1955 in a book by Cesare Gnudi and Giancarlo Cavalli.[1]

This composition achieved considerable success in the seventeenth century. The presence of copies in several major Spanish religious buildings, including the cathedrals of Granada and Zamora,[2] led some to believe they were based on the Prado canvas, which must therefore have been in Spain before it entered the royal collection. However, it is now known that the model for these copies was another autograph version that formed part of an *Apostles* series commissioned in Rome around 1625 by Fernando Afán Enríquez de Ribera, 3rd Duke of Alcalá de los Gazules (1583–1637), for the family pantheon at the monastery of La Cartuja in Seville.[3] This canvas, now in the Museum of Fine Arts, Houston [cat. 39], displays several subtle traits that also appear in the reproductions to be found in Spain but not in the Prado version, confirming that the Houston work was the painting in the duke's collection. X-radiography of the Madrid painting, carried out at the Museo del Prado, has revealed neither *pentimenti* nor substantial changes in composition [fig. 80], both of which have been detected in the Houston canvas, suggesting that the Prado version was produced later, with greater ease and technical assurance.

The Prado register of copyists shows that between the nineteenth and twentieth centuries fifteen applications were received to copy this canvas, making it the third most copied Reni work in the Prado. Prominent copyists included Natalio Hualde (1873–1951) – a Navarre painter who made a copy in December 1890, at the age of only seventeen – and the Granada sculptor Pablo de Loyzaga (1872–1951), who produced a copy in 1943.[4]

Rafael Japón

1 Gnudi and Cavalli 1955, 83; A. Pancorbo in *Italian Masterpieces* 2014, 108.
2 Navarrete Prieto 2005, 324; Rivera de las Heras 2013, 92; Japón 2020a, 1:378, figs. 160 and 161.
3 Japón 2019, 354–57; Forgione and Saracino 2019, 11; Japón 2022b, 94–96.
4 Japón 2022a, 65.

39 Guido Reni
Saint James the Greater

c. 1626
Oil on canvas, 132.3 × 98.8 cm
Houston, The Museum of Fine Arts, Museum purchase funded by the Agnes Cullen Arnold Endowment Fund, inv. 2002-10

Provenance: Commissioned by Fernando Afán Enríquez de Ribera, 3rd Duke of Alcalá, in Rome in 1625; chapter room in the Monasterio de Santa María de las Cuevas, Seville, 1629; Louis Philippe d'Orléans, Paris; Christie's sale, London, 21 May 1853, purchased by Nieuwenhuys; Charles Scarisbrick, Scarisbrick Hall and Wrightington Hall, Lancashire; Christie's sale, London, 13 May 1861, purchased by Graves; private collection, Ireland; Christie's sale, London, 9 December 1988, purchased by Richard L. Feigen of New York; acquired by the Museum of Fine Arts, Houston, 2002.

Selected bibliography: Japón 2019, 354–57; Forgione and Saracino 2019, 11; Japón 2022b, 94–96.

This portrayal of James the Greater beseeching God's intercession formed part of an *Apostles* series commissioned in Rome around 1625 by Fernando Afán Enríquez de Ribera, 3rd Duke of Alcalá de los Gazules (1583–1637), then Philip IV's ambassador to the Holy See. The set – placed in the family pantheon at the Carthusian monastery of Santa María de las Cuevas in Seville about 1629 – comprised a further twelve canvases by some of the leading contemporary artists in Italy, including Artemisia Gentileschi (1593–c. 1652), Jusepe de Ribera (1591–1652), Giovanni Battista Caracciolo (1578–1635), and Giovanni Baglione (c. 1566–1643).[1] After its dispersal, probably at the time of the French invasion, all record of the series was lost. Since then, some of the paintings in the set have been located, and copies found in Spain provide a good idea of what the untraced ones looked like.[2] Close comparison with these copies strongly suggests that the version of *Saint James the Greater* produced by Guido Reni for the Duke of Alcalá is the painting now in Houston, which is identical in size to the other surviving canvases, whereas the Prado picture is somewhat smaller [cat. 38]. There are a number of subtle compositional differences between the two, particularly affecting the right shoulder, which are also found in the copies. In the Houston work, for example, the pilgrim's staff is placed further to the apostle's right than in the Prado version, creating a space between the stick and the apostle's neck which Reni used to add curls to the hair, achieving a more dynamic effect. In the Houston painting too, the clothing is executed with a highly-nuanced range of colour, more closely resembling other works produced by Guido around 1625, whereas in the Madrid canvas

Cat. 38

Cat. 39

the colours are flatter, to the point that significant folds in the cloak – for instance, over the shoulder against which the staff rests – have been omitted. The walking stick itself is more delicately worked, capturing the impact of light from above, and what appears to be a *pentimento* is visible at a glance, suggesting that at one stage the staff was even further away from the head, while the decorative knot has been raised to eye-level. These particular features are discernible in the copies forming part of the *Apostles* series in the cathedrals of Granada and Zamora.[3] The Zamora set is in fact a complete reproduction of the original series, so its *Saint James the Greater* must undoubtedly have been modelled on the painting now in Houston. Its Spanish provenance would appear to be confirmed by its temporary presence in the collection of Louis Philippe d'Orléans, who resided in Andalusia after his marriage to Maria Amalia of Naples – a niece of Charles IV – and created the Spanish Gallery at the Louvre between 1838 and 1848, with almost five hundred paintings acquired in Spain by Baron Taylor and the painter Adrien Dauzats following the disentailment of church-owned properties under Mendizábal.[4]

The canvas was largely overlooked by art historians until 1988, when Stephen Pepper and Denis Mahon attributed it to Reni, though suggesting that it was painted around 1635.[5] However, since it was part of the Duke of Alcalá's commission, it must unquestionably have been produced between 1625 and 1626. Guido based the composition on a model he himself had created for one of the apostles in his *Assumption of the Virgin* in the church of Gesù e dei Santi Ambrogio e Andrea in Genoa, painted around 1617.

This version is likely to have been known at the Spanish court before the other painting – the one belonging to Queen Isabella Farnese [cat. 38] – entered the Spanish royal collection, given that the Museo del Prado has a high-quality copy of the Houston canvas [fig. 81]. Although it is in a rather poor state of repair, it appears to have been painted in the seventeenth century and that – since it spent some time in the Museo de la Trinidad[6] – it must earlier have hung in a church in or near Madrid.

Reni succeeded in creating a devotional image very much to the Spanish taste; indeed, it was the most widely-copied painting of the set commissioned by the Duke of Alcalá, partly because it represents the country's patron saint. Guido had been painting *Apostles* series since his youth,[7] but on this unusual occasion he had to adapt – as did all the participating artists – to a pre-established programme; this has led scholars to think that each artist might have been required to paint two pictures, with the exception of Artemisia Gentileschi, who produced the most representative work of them all, *Christ blessing the Children*.[8]

Rafael Japón

Fig. 81 Copy after Guido Reni, *Saint James the Greater*, 17th century. Oil on canvas, 114 × 80 cm. Madrid, Museo Nacional del Prado, P-5176 (on permanent loan to the Museo de Huesca)

1 Japón 2019, 354–66; Japón 2022b, 92–99.
2 The most recently identified painting from the series is a *Saint Bartholomew* by Giovanni Lanfranco (1582–1647), published in Papi 2021. However, in a study of the copies surviving in Spain, Rafael Japón had already attributed the lost original to Lanfranco; see Japón 2020a, 1:392.
3 Japón 2020a, 1:378, figs. 160 and 161.
4 Marinas 1981, 13–18.
5 Christie's, London, *Important Old Master Pictures*, 9 December 1988, lot 13.
6 *Museo del Prado* 1990, 2:245, no. 797.
7 According to Carlo Cesare Malvasia, Reni painted a series of twelve apostles during his first sojourn in Rome, in a style heavily influenced by Caravaggio; see Malvasia–Pericolo 2019, 1:474.
8 Japón 2020a, 1:362–99; Japón 2022b, 91–99.

40 Guido Reni
The Conversion of Saul

c. 1621
Oil on canvas, 222 × 160 cm
Patrimonio Nacional. Colecciones Reales. Real Monasterio
de San Lorenzo de El Escorial, inv. 10033839

Provenance: Villa Ludovisi, Rome, before 1633 until 12 May 1665; Real Monasterio de San Lorenzo de El Escorial, 1681.

Selected bibliography: Redín Michaus 2013; Redín Michaus 2016b, 22–23; D. Benati in Redín Michaus 2016a, 145–50, no. 13; B. Eclercy in Eclercy 2022a, 186–89, no. 62.

The *Conversion of Saul* was first attributed to Guido Reni in 2013 by Gonzalo Redín; since then, its authorship has never been questioned. It can be dated to the early 1620s on the grounds of its stylistic similarity to well-known works such as the *Hercules* series which Reni painted for Ferdinando Gonzaga's (1587–1626) Villa Favorita in Mantua (1615–26).[1] The figure of Saul shares Hercules' heroic appearance, though its impact is perhaps somewhat diluted by his contrived, Mannerist pose – arms raised above his head, legs spread wide – and by the innovative use of colour for his *all'antica* clothing.

The theme had proved highly popular among Mannerist painters, including some well known to Reni, such as his master Denys Calvaert (c. 1540–1619);[2] this enables us to better appreciate certain novel features of Guido's interpretation. Saul's pose recalls that of Heliodorus in Raphael's (1483–1520) *Expulsion of Heliodorus from the Temple* fresco of 1512–14 in the Vatican Stanze, while the composition echoes a *Conversion of Saul* painted in 1527 by Parmigianino (1503–1540) in Bologna,[3] repeated with some modifications by Ludovico Carracci (1555–1619) in 1587–88 for the Zambeccari chapel in the church of San Francesco in Bologna.[4] The horse with its elongated neck and mottled leather saddle is also reminiscent of Parmigianino, though Saul's expressive strength, the positioning of his legs, and the placing of his hand on the ground[5] more closely resemble those of Carracci's version.

Although we cannot be sure when the painting was commissioned, or by whom, it was listed in a 1633 inventory of the contents of the Villa Ludovisi al Pincio in Rome, where it was correctly attributed: 'A conversion of Saul, full-length and life-size alone with a horse, gilt frame about ten p. high and seven and a half wide, by the hand of Guido Reni'.[6] Returning to Rome after an ill-starred visit to Naples, Guido worked for Pope Gregory XV's nephew, Cardinal Ludovico Ludovisi (1595–1632), who

in 1624 commissioned him to paint a high altarpiece of the *Trinity* for the church of La Santissima Trinità dei Pellegrini in Rome [fig. 28]. But prior to that, in 1621, he had received 100 scudi for two paintings on unknown subjects; one of these may have been the *Conversion of Saul*, even though it was not recorded in the Villa Ludovisi until 1633. Reni was by then an established artist, and though less influenced by Caravaggio (1571–1610) since his death ten years earlier, the Bolognese artist must have borne in mind his pioneering treatment of the *Conversion* for the Cerasi chapel in Santa Maria del Popolo, Rome (1600). This led Guido to focus on the figure of Saul, struck to the ground by a divine light, and on his horse, wholly omitting the military escort mentioned in the Acts of the Apostles (9:1–9). Eschewing Caravaggio's dramatic contrast of light and shadow, Guido instead draws attention to the sky, traversed by thick vertical clouds that bathe the whole composition in a bluish penumbra. Greater importance is also attached to the startled horse, foaming at the mouth, its head raised towards the sky.

As a token of his gratitude to the King of Spain, Ludovico's nephew and heir Niccolò Ludovisi (1610–1664), Prince of Venosa and Piombino and formerly Spanish Viceroy of Aragon and Sardinia, bequeathed to Philip IV six paintings from his collection, and two further works by Titian (c. 1488–1576).[7] Visiting the villa on 9 May 1665, the Spanish ambassador Pedro Antonio Ramón Folch de Cardona and Cardinal Niccolò Albergati-Ludovisi selected at least three paintings to be sent to Spain: *Susannah and the Elders*[8] and *Lot and his Daughters*,[9] both by Guercino (1591–1666), and this *Conversion of Saul* by Reni, which hung in 'the second room'. The three paintings were first recorded together in the Spanish royal collection in 1681, when they were described as hanging in the Quadra de Mediodía at El Escorial,[10] and attributed to Guercino.[11] This is somewhat surprising, since Philip IV's palace boasted a number of canvases by Reni; perhaps it simply arrived at an inopportune moment, the king having died only recently.[12] The three pictures must have been sent to El Escorial in 1676, as part of a batch of paintings chosen by the court painter Juan Carreño de Miranda (1614–1685) to 'decorate the Royal Apartments at the Palace' on the occasion of Charles II's first visit.[13]

Surprisingly few copies have been recorded or preserved. Seventeenth-century copies include one by Francesco Graziani, recorded in the collection of Carlo Maratta (1712),[14] an anonymous canvas from the Pepoli's Palazzo Vecchio in Bologna, now hanging in the Museo Regionale Agostino Pepoli in Trapani,[15] and a similar version painted by Pier Francesco Cittadini (1616–1681) for the choir at the church of San Paolo in Bologna. Three versions are known to have been produced in the eighteenth century: an exact copy by Francisco Martínez Bustamante (1680–1745) for the altarpiece of the San Pablo chapel in Oviedo cathedral (1717–45); a further copy auctioned by Isbilya Subastas in 2021;[16] and a free interpretation produced in 1767 by Nicolas-Bernard Lepicié (1735–1784), now in the John Mitchell & Son Gallery, London.

Carmen García-Frías Checa

1 Paris, Musée du Louvre, inv. 535–538.

2 A version known from a drawing by the artist in 1579, now in Paris, Musée du Louvre, Département des arts graphiques, inv. 19837.

3 Vienna, Kunsthistorisches Museum Wien, Gemäldegalerie, inv. 2035.

4 Bologna, Pinacoteca Nazionale di Bologna, inv. 467.

5 The artificial arrangement of arms and legs can be found in a preparatory drawing for the figure of Sisera (1602–3) by the Cavalier d'Arpino (1568–1640): Lyon, Museé des Beaux-Arts, inv. 1962-666.

6 Garas 1967a, 289; Pepper 1984, 307: 'Una conversione di San Paolo figura intiera, e grande del naturale sola col cavallo, cornice dorata alta p. dieci in circa larga sette e mezzo, mano di Guido Reni'.

7 Partially published in García Cueto 2006, 203, note 238.

8 Madrid, Museo Nacional del Prado, P-201.

9 Patrimonio Nacional, inv. 10014629. Real Monasterio de San Lorenzo de El Escorial.

10 Antonio Ponz (1988–89 [1988], 2:121) later saw it in the upper cloister, whence it was removed during renovation work at the palace under the Bourbons. Following the French invasion of Spain, the painting was taken to the Depósito del Rosario (1813) (Madrid, Archivo General de Palacio, Fernando VII, caja 357/2, no. 729); on its return to El Escorial, according to Damián Bermejo (1820, 193), it was placed in the 'Sala Prioral'.

11 Santos 1681, 82v; Santos 1698, 97v. Guercino's *Susannah and the Elders* was mentioned even earlier, in Santos 1667, 100v–101r.

12 The vexed question of authorship was further complicated by Charles II's will, drawn up in 1700 (Fernández Bayton 1975–85 [1985], 3:95, no. 26), in which the painting was attributed to Luca Giordano (1634–1705), having mistakenly identified 'Luca de Olanda'. Following Andrés Ximénez (1764, 175), it was widely held to be a work by Giordano in the style of Guercino, and is listed as such in Charles II's 1794 testament (Fernández-Miranda 1988–91 [1988], 1:394, no. 91), in Ceán Bermúdez 1800, 2:342, and in Poleró 1857, 102, no. 405. Only Antonio Ponz (1988–89 [1988], 2:121 [1777]) and Antonio Conca (1793, 2:81) continued to attribute it to Guercino.

13 Santos 1680, 257 and 261–63; García-Frías Checa 2001, 22–23.

14 Galli 1928, 17.

15 Redín Michaus 2013, 682, note 43.

16 Seville, Isbilya Subastas, 29–30 June 2021, lot 43, undoubtedly painted in the 18th century.

41 Guido Reni

Angel appearing to Saint Jerome

c. 1633–34
Oil on canvas, 199.7 × 147.9 cm
Detroit, Detroit Institute of Arts, Founders Society Purchase, Ralph Harman Booth Bequest Fund, Henry Ford II Fund, Benson and Edith Ford Fund and New Endowment Fund, inv. 69.6

Provenance: First recorded in the Balbi collection in 1688, 1766, and 1804; purchased in 1804–6 by Andrew Wilson and sold soon afterward to Walsh Porter; sold at the Porter auction in 1810; acquired by Edmund Higginson and sold in 1846 to John Rushout, 2nd Baron Northwick (Thirlestaine House); sold at the Spencer-Churchill auction, Christie's, London, 28 May 1965; purchased by the Detroit Institute of Arts in 1969.

Selected bibliography: Pepper 1969b; C. Casali Pedrielli in Emiliani et al. 1988, 316, no. 63; Pepper 1988, 302, no. 196; Malvasia–Pericolo 2019, 1:452, note 679; Pericolo 2019, 631–32; C. Puglisi in Eclercy 2022a, 258–59, no. 110.

Guido Reni's *Angel appearing to Saint Jerome* is listed in the 1688 inventory of paintings in the possession of the Genoese nobleman Francesco Maria Balbi (1619–1704). There, the Saint Jerome is paired with another painting by Guido, a *Saint John the Baptist in the Wilderness* now in the Dulwich Picture Gallery in London [cat. 23].[1] Describing the works on display in the 'terzo salotto' of the Balbi Palace, Genoa, the art biographer

and painter Carlo Giuseppe Ratti (1737–1795) singles out Caravaggio's *Conversion of Saul* on the main wall,[2] with two paintings by Guido placed on the adjacent walls face to face. 'On the other wall', Ratti writes in his *Istruzione* (1766), 'there is a Saint John the Baptist, a life-size figure by Guido Reni, a singular work'; 'on the other wall, the pendant to the Saint John the Baptist, where there is Saint Jerome with an angel who speaks with him, an equally beautiful work by Guido Reni'.[3] By the same token, the French astronomer and writer Joseph-Jérôme Lefrançois de Lalande (1732–1807), mentioning the most prominent paintings in the Balbi Palace, pairs the two works together: 'Saint John and Saint Jerome by Guido: these are two large paintings that are drawn in a beautiful manner, but whose colour is faint'.[4] The Balbi *Angel appearing to Saint Jerome* is sometimes confused with a painting by Guido quoted by Carlo Cesare Malvasia in his *Felsina pittrice* (1678): 'In the house of Signor Giovan Francesco Maria Balbi, a Saint Jerome Reading a Book and a Saint John the Baptist'.[5] This work is also recorded in the Balbi inventory of 1688.[6] In his *Istruzione*, Ratti also mentions this painting in the 'quarto salotto' of the Balbi Palace: 'On the other wall there is a painting of Saint Jerome reading by Guido Reni'.[7] This *Saint Jerome reading* remains untraced. In 1804, the Scottish painter and art dealer James Irvine (1757–1831) noted that the Balbi were trying to sell Guido's *Angel appearing to Saint Jerome* and *Saint John the Baptist in the Wilderness* [cat. 23].[8] Around the same time, the Scottish landscape painter Andrew Wilson (1780–1848) managed to obtain Guido's *Angel appearing to Saint Jerome*. In his *Memoirs* (1854), William Buchanan published a list of paintings imported by Wilson from Italy, where Guido's work is praised: 'This most admirable performance was selected from the Balbi Palace as one of the first objects of solicitude. Afterwards purchased by Walsh Porter, Esq[uire]'.[9] Upon Porter's death in 1809, the painting was sold at auction and entered a few British collections, until it was purchased by the Detroit Institute of Arts in 1969.[10]

In terms of size, the Dulwich *Saint John the Baptist* and the Detroit *Angel appearing to Saint Jerome* cannot be deemed pendants, the former being perceptibly larger than the latter. However, besides working well in tandem through their opposition of a youth to an elderly man and the complementarity

Fig. 82 Guido Reni, *Saint Jerome*, c. 1600–40.
Etching on paper, 216 × 140 mm. New York,
The Metropolitan Museum of Art, The Elisha Whittelsey
Collection, The Elisha Whittelsey Fund, 1959, inv. 59.570.603

The Power of Saints and the Beauty of Old Age

of the saints' dispositions, they may well have been executed at the same time, most likely in 1633–34. In both works, Guido plays with forms on the brink of the *non-finito*. A lack of sharp definition and certain elusiveness in contouring and modelling the bodies characterise both paintings, which showcase Guido's prodigious *sprezzatura* in avoiding polish while calibrating the degree of finish through a variety of solutions: from the neatly rendered featheriness of the angel's right wing in the *Saint Jerome* to the slightly out-of-focus face of the prophesying Precursor in the *Saint John* and the coarsely outlined lost profile of the elderly author of the Vulgate in the Detroit painting.

Some details are just breathtaking on account of their technical handling. Jerome's robust neck takes on the appearance of a gorge encircled by waves of thick flesh delicately highlighted in white lead, while a gouge of dark separates the neck from the chest or engulfs itself beneath the beard. In particular, the chromatic blending of flesh and hair visually signals the dissolution of the human figure as a result of ascetic deprivation; aesthetically, it merges Correggio (c. 1489–1534) and Titian (c. 1488–1576) (the masters of soft hair and living flesh) to the extremes of paradox, with hair treated like flesh and flesh occasionally combed like hair.[11] In his *Felsina pittrice*, Malvasia stresses Guido's ability to beautify the aging skin and flesh of his elderly figures. Describing Guido's destroyed *Saints Anthony Abbot and Paul the Hermit with the Madonna and Child* of 1613–17, Malvasia singles out the 'tiny wrinkles and overlapping creases' of these saints' bodies as an example of Guido's 'sprezzatura in bold strokes' in the style of Titian and Jacopo Tintoretto (1519–1594).[12] Similarly, in listing Guido's etching of a *Saint Jerome* [fig. 82], Malvasia lingers on 'the skin and wrinkles of an old man' that, it can be added, are so magisterially achieved through cross-hatching.[13] In Malvasia's eyes, Guido was perhaps following in the footsteps of his master, Ludovico Carracci (1555–1619). In admiration of Ludovico's dexterity in allying vigorous relief and delicacy, Malvasia praised the 'accentuated muscles' and 'delicate and gracious contours' he used to display so 'appropriately', 'sometimes bringing them together mysteriously or rather setting them off against one another'.[14] In Ludovico's *Saint Anthony Abbot preaching to the Hermits* of 1614–15 in the Pinacoteca di Brera,[15] Malvasia goes as far as to praise the depiction of the elderly hermits' hands, 'all callous and gnarled, which would appear tortuous and unsightly if others had painted them, whereas here they appear marvellous, learned, and singular in their beautiful monstrosity [*bella mostruosità*]'.[16] Guido's *Angel appearing to Saint Jerome* is a most eloquent example of the *bella mostruosità*: the 'tortuous' and 'unsightly' essence of the aged body are here transfigured into an aesthetic spectacle, a pyrotechnics of what the brush can pull off when given free rein.

If a member of the Balbi family purchased both the *Saint John* and the *Saint Jerome* – this may have been Giacomo Balbi, the father of Francesco Maria – then he must have been willing to disburse a small fortune. In 1636, Prince Karl Eusebius of Liechtenstein (1611–1684) paid 600 silver ducatons for a different version of Guido's *Angel appearing to Saint Jerome* now at the Kunsthistorisches Museum in Vienna.[17] Equally a pictorial feat, the painting had been fought over by, among others, Francesco I d'Este, Duke of Modena, and Charles I, King of England.[18]

Lorenzo Pericolo

1 Belloni 1973, 69: 'un San Girolamo del detto [Guido Reni]'. The painting is mentioned just after the Balbi *Saint John the Baptist in the Wilderness*.
2 Rome, Odescalchi Balbi collection.
3 Ratti 1766, 189: 'In altra facciata è S[an] Giovanni Battista, figura al naturale di Guido Reni, opera singolare … Nell'altra facciata il Quadro compagno al S[an] Giovambattista entrovi S[an] Girolamo con un angiolo parlantegli. È opera egualmente bella di Guido Reni'.
4 Lalande 1769, 8:484: 'S[aint] Jean et S[aint] Jérôme du Guide: ce sont deux grands tableaux dessinés d'une belle manière, mais dont la couleur est fade'.
5 Malvasia 1678, 2:91: 'Presso il Sig. Gio. Francesco Maria Balbi S. Girolamo che stà leggendo un libro: Un S. Gio. Battista'.
6 Belloni 1973, 69: 'Un San Girolamo di Guido Reni'.
7 Ratti 1766, 191: 'Nell'altra facciata è un quadro di S[an] Girolamo che legge di Guido Reni'.
8 Buchanan 1824, 2:151.
9 Ibid., 2:201.
10 See Pepper 1969b.
11 These passages are taken from Pericolo 2019, 631–32.
12 Malvasia 1678, 2:29: 'Toccati con gran sprezzo tutti di colpi … con quelle pellicciuole, e cresparelle raddoppiate'. See further Malvasia–Pericolo 2019, 1:282–83, note 186.
13 Malvasia 1678, 1:115: 'Con quelle pellicciuole, e crespe, che mostra un vecchio'. See further Malvasia–Cropper and Pericolo 2013, 238–39, no. 14.
14 Malvasia 1678, 1:435: 'Risaltati muscoli, quanto i gentili, e graziosi contorni aplicando gli uni, e gli altri a tempo e luogo, talora misteriosamente unendoli, o per meglio dire, contraponendoli'; Summerscale 2000, 210–11.
15 Milan, Pinacoteca di Brera, inv. 122.
16 Malvasia 1678, 1:435: 'Mani incallite, e nodose, che tormentate, e difettose per mano d'altri diverriano, là dove qui riescono nella loro bella mostruosità così ammirabili, dotte, e singolari'; Summerscale 2000, 211. On Ludovico's *Preaching of Saint Anthony*, see Brogi 2001, 1:226–27, no. 114.
17 Vienna, Kunsthistorisches Museum Wien, Gemäldegalerie, inv. 9124.
18 On the history of this painting, see Malvasia–Pericolo 2019, 1:290–91, note 205.

42 Guido Reni

Saint Francis in Prayer with two Angels

c. 1632
Oil on canvas, 196 × 117 cm
Rome, Galleria Colonna, inv. 117

Provenance: Cardinal Girolamo I Colonna, prior to 1645.

Selected bibliography: Malvasia 1678, 2:90; Baccheschi 1971, 116–17, no. XXIV; Safarik 1981, 109–10, no. 151; Pepper 1988, 272–73, no. 125, pl. 116; Safarik 1999, 233, fig. 412; Di Meola 2003, 118 and 122, fig. 6; A. Emiliani in Baldassari 2007, 126–27, no. 14; Paoluzzi 2014, 147–48, figs. 20 and 71; M. C. Paoluzzi in Piergiovanni 2018, 227–29, no. 204.

One of the undisputed masterpieces in the Galleria Colonna collection, *Saint Francis in Prayer with two Angels* has enjoyed pride of place in the gallery since it was first founded in the early eighteenth century. Commissioned from the artist himself by Cardinal Girolamo I Colonna (1604–1666) during his term as archbishop of Bologna between 1632 and 1645, it is recorded in a 1648 inventory of Colonna's estate: 'A picture of St. Fran.c[is] with his hands joined, in a gilt frame, by the hand of Guido Reni'.[1] In 1678, Carlo Cesare Malvasia reported the presence in Rome of a 'Saint Francis from the Pallione del Voto, a half-figure', which might be the same canvas, even though the format appears to differ.[2]

The 1648 inventory of the Cardinal's estate includes six further paintings on sacred themes regarded as autograph works by Reni, among them his superb *Salome receiving the Head of Saint John the Baptist* of about 1638–42 [cat. 82], which remained in the Colonna collection until the late eighteenth century, when it was sold for the huge sum of 6000 scudi; it is now owned by the Art Institute of Chicago [cat. 82].

As Girolamo was well aware, his illustrious forebears had always professed a heartfelt and deep-rooted devotion to Saint Francis, one which could be traced right back to the first cardinal in the family, Giovanni I Colonna (elected in 1195), a contemporary of Francis himself. Giovanni helped to secure papal approval for the Franciscan Rule, and in 1215 granted Francis one of his properties near the village of Piglio (in the province of Frosinone), where the first friars settled and where Francis himself founded a monastery – still active today – devoted to Saint Lawrence. But Girolamo's most charismatic ancestor was undoubtedly Margherita Colonna (1255–1280), one of the earliest members of the Order of Saint Clare (beatified by Pope Pius IX in 1848), who – according to her brother Cardinal Giovanni II (elected in 1206) – bore the stigmata on her side

only a few decades after they were received by Saint Francis at La Verna.

This canvas faithfully reproduces Guido's depiction of Saint Francis at the centre of the *Pallione del Voto*, a votive processional banner painted on silk, commissioned by the Bologna Senate to be carried in procession every year from the Palazzo Pubblico to the church of San Domenico, in thanks for the ending of an outbreak of the plague in 1630 [fig. 30].

Reni, too, is known to have been highly devoted to the saint of Assisi, so much so that he wished to be buried in the Capuchin habit. Significantly – as Malvasia noted, and as Raffaella Morselli has also stressed – Guido was anxious to endow the saint with the physical features of his friend and spiritual *alter ego*, the Bologna nobleman and senator Saulo Guidotti (1601–1665), who was twenty-nine when this painting was produced. As though seeking to immortalise him, Reni repeated the likeness of Guidotti – with whom he enjoyed a close friendship that went beyond the purely professional – in a number of autograph replicas produced in around 1631: the gaunt features, pale complexion, thinning hair at the temples and large, deep-set eyes are to be found not only in the Colonna canvas, but also in the earlier *Pallione del Voto* and in versions now in the Girolamini church in Naples and in the Louvre.[3] Andrea Emiliani also noted a physical resemblance to the central figure in Reni's *Saint Andrew Corsini at Prayer* now in the Gallerie degli Uffizi.[4]

The composition is one that Reni had already used with some success in paintings produced for other sophisticated ecclesiastical clients in Bologna. It echoes, for example, the staging of the *Penitent Magdalen*, painted at around the same time for the recently appointed Cardinal Antonio Santacroce, during his residence in Bologna as papal legate between 1631 and 1634; on his death in 1641, the canvas entered the collection of Cardinal Antonio Barberini [cat. 86]. In both cases, the anchorite saints are depicted inside a narrow rocky cave, surrounded by the same elements alluding to prayer: a humble altar carved into the bare stone bearing a skull and rosary in front of a cross of intertwined branches; a few root vegetables in the foreground symbolise fasting and abstinence. Two hovering angels witness their mystical ecstasy, observing their heavenward gaze. Both paintings belong to what Malvasia defined as the artist's *seconda maniera*, characterised by a lighter palette that would give way to the silvery tones of his later career. In the brightly coloured background – contrasting with the brown hills of the middle ground, where we can discern the small figure of Brother Leo in meditation – soft, milky clouds sail across a characteristically intense blue sky.

Reni made extensive use of this archetypal depiction of Saint Francis in the cave, kneeling in prayer before receiving the stigmata on Mount La Verna, the three knots visible on the rope belt of his habit clearly alluding to the vows of poverty, chastity, and obedience. The presence of autograph replicas and numerous copies – tracked down in 1988 by Stephen Pepper[5] – suggests that it achieved widespread renown at an early stage. Several versions crossed the Alps for devotional purposes, among them a canvas given by Prince Camillo Pamphilj to Louis XIV in 1665, now in the Louvre,[6] and the three versions known in Spain: one inventoried in 1794 as autograph and valued at 3000 escudos[7] and two copies in Seville's Alcázar[8] and in the Museo Colegial at Daroca.[9]

The Colonna composition provided the basis for an etching signed in the lower right corner by 'Canutus F',[10] which was made by Domenico Maria Canuti (1625–1684) in around 1640, when he was still employed at Reni's workshop. Interestingly, although the print is in all other respects a faithful copy, the apprentice – presumably on the orders of the master himself – has given the saint an older face. This would support the portrait hypothesis: some ten years had elapsed since the original version, and the sitter – probably still Saulo Guidotti, to whom Guido was deeply attached – would by then have a more mature appearance. The hypothesis is further borne out by comparison with a likeness of Guidotti recently rediscovered by Morselli, who has dated it to the early 1640s (now in a private collection).[11] The Canuti print in turn served as the source for an eighteenth-century black pencil drawing, with touches of red chalk, made by one of the Gandolfis, which was donated to the Museo del Prado[12] in 1931 by Pedro Fernández Durán y Bernaldo de Quirós.

Patrizia Piergiovanni

1 Inventory of 1648, 44, no. 64; Safarik 1996, 70, no. 64: 'Un' quadro di sa. fran.c[esc]o che tiene le mani giunte con cornice indorata mano di Guido Reni'.
2 Malvasia 1678, 2:90; Malvasia–Pericolo 2019, 1:204–5: 'San Francesco del Palione, mezza figura'.
3 Morselli 2013, 60–61. See note 6 below.
4 Florence, Gallerie degli Uffizi, inv. 1890 n. 10072; A. Emiliani in Baldassari 2007, 126.
5 Pepper 1988, 272–73, no. 125, pl. 116.
6 Paris, Musée du Louvre, inv. 533.
7 Formerly in Barcelona, Palacio de Pedralbes, 231.
8 Patrimonio Nacional, inv. 10020824.
9 See Pérez Sánchez 1965a, 187.
10 Bartsch 1803–21 (1819), 19:223–24, no. 2.
11 Morselli 2013, 70, fig. 8.
12 Madrid, Museo Nacional del Prado, D-1180.

43 Guido Reni

Study for the Figure of Saint Ignatius of Loyola (for the Pallione del Voto)

1630
Black chalk with traces of white on grey (faded blue) paper,
385 × 252 mm
Madrid, Biblioteca Nacional de España, DIB/13/11/102

Provenance: Valentín Carderera Solano (L. 432); purchased in 1867 by the Biblioteca Nacional de España.

Selected bibliography: Johnston 1974, 1:185–86, no. 157; Birke 1981, 166–67, no. 120; Mena Marqués 1988, 65, no. 40.

The famous plague epidemic of 1630 also ravaged Bologna. For this reason, in the summer of that year, the local authorities decided to make a vow to the Virgin of the Rosary, praying that she might intercede in her grace to save the city from this scourge. The dissolution of the vote took place on 27 December with a public ceremony attended, among a large number of religious figures, by Cardinal Bernardino Spada, then papal legate in Bologna, whom Guido Reni immortalised in the superb portrait of 1631 now in the Galleria Spada in Rome [fig. 29].[1] Reni was the most famous painter in Bologna at that moment, so he was asked to produce a *pallione*, the votive standard to be carried in the procession, which he painted in oil on silk, following the usual procedure for this genre. The *pallione*, depicting the *Virgin of the Rosary with the Child and the Patron Saints of Bologna: Petronius, Francis, Ignatius of Loyola, Francis Xavier, Proculus, Florian and Dominic*, assumed the value of an ex-voto, displayed at the church of San Domenico on that occasion and carried in procession amongst a crowd of people from there to the chambers of the *gonfalonier* at the Palazzo Pubblico. As long as it remained in the local government headquarters, Guido's standard continued to be carried in the annual procession, until it was replaced by a copy commissioned from Pier Francesco Cavazza (1677–1733). The original was transferred from the Palazzo Pubblico to the Pinacoteca Nazionale di Bologna, where it still hangs today [fig. 30].[2]

The so-called *Pala* or *Pallione della Peste*, characterised by its imposing dimensions – it measures 382 × 242 centimetres – is a composition divided into three registers. In the central one, the city's protector saints – Petronius, Francis of Assisi, Proculus, Florian, and Dominic – are arranged in a semicircle, either standing or kneeling, together with two further saints who had been recently canonised, the founders of the Society of Jesus, Ignatius of Loyola and Francis Xavier, whom the civic authorities had included in December 1630 in their appeal to the Virgin. In the upper register, the Virgin is seated on clouds with the Child on her lap, surrounded by a glory of angels bearing roses and garlands in allusion to the specific cult of the rosary. Mary's feet rest on a rainbow, whose light brings peace into the deathly atmosphere of the city, conveyed symbolically by Reni in the leaden colour of the sky. Finally, the lower register provides a view of Bologna, surrounded by the city walls from which wagons carrying plague victims come out.

The votive function of the painting is heighted by Reni's use of light, ranging from the oppressive grey gloom of the plague-ridden city to the splendid golden glow radiating from the Virgin. In Francesco Scannelli's *Microcosmo della pittura* (1657), the *Pala della Peste* was already mentioned as the epitome of Guido's *seconda maniera* – the 'light' style that characterised his late mature period – for its 'really incomparable grace, ease of manner and harmonious beauty'.[3]

The drawing exhibited here, remarkable for its measurements, is a preparatory study for Saint Ignatius of Loyola, who appears on the far left of the painting, standing behind the kneeling figure of Saint Petronius. Catherine Johnston was the first to suggest a link to the *Pallione del Voto,* accepting the traditional attribution to Reni but dismissing Ángel María de Barcia's identification of the figure as Saint Andrew Corsini.[4] An inscription in black chalk on the recto reads 'Guido Reni'; on the verso, also in black chalk, are the words 'Guido // P.[ar]ᵃ el cuadro de S. / Andrés Corsini en S. Juan de Let[rán]'. The inscription in Spanish could have been added either by Barcia, curator at the Biblioteca Nacional in the early twentieth century,[5] or perhaps more likely by the painter and scholar Valentín Carderera y Solano (1796–1880), an intellectual and a keen collector of drawings, many of which – including this one – later entered the Biblioteca Nacional de España and the Museo Nacional del Prado. It is hardly surprising that Carderera, who had trained in Rome from 1822 to 1831, should have associated the painting of the *Ecstacy of Saint Andrew Corsini* in the Palazzo Corsini, Florence,[6] to the mosaic copy on the altar of the chapel dedicated to the saint in the church of San Giovanni in Laterano, Rome.

As in other late drawings, Guido focused primarily on the refined folds of the saint's mantle, merely sketching the head. The essential features defining the figure in the final painting are clearly represented here. The paper was originally cerulean blue, a support favoured by the Carracci and commonly used by Reni for his drawings.

Finally, another sheet linked to the *Pala della Peste* is the better known *Study for the Head of Saint Proculus* at Christ Church, Oxford,[7] equally impressive for its dimensions (338 × 262 millimetres) and a superb example of Guido's unwavering attention and observation when drawing from life.[8]

Viviana Farina

1 Pepper 1988, 272, no. 121.
2 Ibid., 273–74, no. 127; E. Fiore in Bentini et al. 2008, 69–74, no. 35; Malvasia–Pericolo 2019, 1:295, note 217.
3 Scannelli 1657, 349: 'grazia, facilità e vaghezza veramente impareggiabile'.
4 Johnston 1974, 1:185–86, no. 157.
5 Barcia 1906, 606, no. 8017: 'San Andrés Corsino (?)'.
6 Now in the Gallerie degli Uffizi, inv. 1890 n. 10072. Pepper 1988, 270–71, no. 117.
7 Oxford, Christ Church, Picture Gallery, inv. 0528.
8 V. Birke in Ebert-Schifferer, Emiliani and Schleier 1988, 392–93, no. B60.

44   Guido Reni
The Triumph of Job

1636
Oil on canvas, 415 × 265 cm
Paris, Cathédrale Notre-Dame, Direction régionale
des affaires culturelles d'Île-de-France, NDP 774

Provenance: Cappella dell'Arte della Seta, Santa Maria dei Mendicanti, Bologna.

Selected bibliography: Pancaldi 1637; Gualandi 1840–45 (1840), 1:118–40; Malvasia–Zanotti 1841, 2:37; Gnudi and Cavalli 1955, 88, no. 83; C. Casali Pedrielli in Emiliani et al. 1988, 150–51; Pepper 1988, 282, no. 148; Morselli 2016.

The history of this *Triumph of Job*, one of the most complex of Guido Reni's later works, can be traced through various records which suggest that its completion and subsequent delivery to the clients – representatives of Bologna's Silk Guild – was a lengthy and somewhat eventful process. Entries in an account book kept by the wardens of the chapel for which the altarpiece was destined, in the church of Santa Maria dei Mendicanti, were first published by Michelangelo Gualandi; they were subsequently cited by later critics,[1] partially analysed,[2] and more recently examined in their correct order and supplemented with further documentary notes.[3] The painting was intended to manifest the public image and wealth of the guild in the building which had become a place of worship and exhibition for the city's corporations. The first contract between Guido and the rector Ludovico Mastri was signed on 21 April 1622, but the canvas was not delivered until fourteen years later. Carlo Cesare Malvasia summed up the attendant vicissitudes, remarking that the painting was 'worked on more out of spite than for glory';[4] after a payment made in 1625 to Reni's servant Bartolomeo Belcollare, the composition appeared to have been partially completed, but in 1633 the silversmith Jan Jacobs – a close friend and agent of Guido's – returned to the guild an advance of 1500 lire received by Reni, acknowledging non-performance of the contract. In 1634, when the commission was about to go either to Domenichino (1581–1641) or to Guercino (1591–1666), Guido decided to finish the painting; however, he demanded a total of 2000 scudi (200 per figure) for the work, a very high sum which was eventually – after several meetings with secretaries and refusals by the artist – knocked down to 1500, on which an advance was paid through the good offices of senator Filippo Sampieri. On 23 December 1635, the wardens visited Reni's studio on Via delle Pescherie, only to find that the canvas had not been finished. They had to wait a further six months to see the

painting, which was exhibited in Santa Maria dei Mendicanti on 10 May 1636, the feast-day of Saint Job. After two weeks, it was placed over the altar, but only a month later Guido made changes to the saint's head and added the ram on the ground – perhaps a symbol of the guild – which had been left out of earlier negotiations. Stolen by the French in 1796, the painting has been in Notre-Dame since 1811, but had been considered lost until it was recognised by Denis Mahon.[5]

The theme is drawn from the epilogue to the book of Job, widely circulated in an Italian translation by Giovanni Diodato (Geneva, 1607). Job, a wise and wealthy man inexplicably subjected to afflictions of various kinds until God acknowledged his total innocence, is shown seated on a throne, receiving gifts including gold, precious vessels, and even a calf. The image of a righteous man rewarded by God – a sapiential parable – highlights the wisdom and mastery displayed in the late works by Reni, who reflected on the narrative passages of the Scriptures not just with feeling but with a scholarly awareness in a year of feverish activity – 1636 – in which he also finished other paintings including the *Circumcision* [cat. 21] and the *Presentation of Jesus in the Temple*.[6] To mark its completion, a slim volume was published by Giovanni Pellegrino Pancaldi (Bologna, 1637), containing a sonnet on the picture – which the author had presumably seen in person – together with an analytical description focussing on Guido's breadth of learning and offering a pious reading of the painting.

Always somewhat unconvinced by Reni's *seconda maniera*, Malvasia gave the canvas a rather lukewarm reception, bemoaning the absence of 'that great invention, that fertile composition, the well-judged deployment of appropriate shadow and play of light' characteristic of his *prima maniera*;[7] even so, he could not help praising 'the beautiful drapery and the felicitous brushwork'.[8] Although Malvasia complained about the nude figures made from life on the left, 'straining as though they were carrying an elephant',[9] they were admired by Giovan Pietro Bellori.[10] The painting was hailed as extraordinary by Luigi Scaramuccia and regarded as one of the most 'scientific, agreeable, and refined' of canvases by Giampietro Cavazzoni Zanotti;[11] in the twentieth century, its rhythm was viewed as over-fragmented,[12]

The Power of Saints and the Beauty of Old Age

and the altarpiece was shown only once, at the 1988 monographic exhibition of Reni's work, for which it was restored. In fact, Guido organised the space in masterly fashion, creating a complex interweaving of filled and empty spaces, in which figures placed on different planes are rendered in their correct proportions, resulting in a lively choral scene. The foreground is dominated – as in the *Circumcision* – by a youthful figure; here, a page in white silk stockings rests his right foot on a bale of yarn on which cocoons – the symbol of the Silk Guild[13] – can be discerned.

The spatial arrangement partly echoes that of the *Saint Benedict* painted by Reni at an early stage for the cloister at San Michele in Bosco (1604), known through prints [fig. 9]: a pyramidal structure in which the figures are crammed in the lower register in no apparent order, their gestures and poses converging on the central figure, placed in a higher register[14] and displaced to one side, leaving a free area beyond a balustrade that separates the narrative space from an outdoor architecture reminiscent of Veronese. Malvasia attributed the latter to Reni's pupil Giovanni Maria Tamburini (c. 1575–c. 1660), describing Guido as 'not greatly gifted for architecture',[15] although the master had earlier made use of a similar resource in his *Judgement of Solomon* (1596, private collection).[16]

Despite its uneven critical fortune, the altarpiece was praised by foreign travellers[17] and widely known through reproductions: a smaller contemporary copy, in darker tones, has been attributed to Giovanni Battista Bolognini (1611–1688),[18] and a copy of the same size was made by Pietro Rotari (1707–1762) in 1740;[19] two further copies have been identified by Federico Zeri.[20] Engravings by Giuseppe Maria Mitelli (1634–1718), from 1679, Domenico Maria Fratta (1696–1763), and Giuliano Traballesi (1727–1812) testify to the painting's educational value for both Italian and foreign artists. Drawings were also made of the whole picture and of its details; at least two, by Reni's school or circle, may well have been contemporary;[21] a third was made later by Ludovico Mattioli (1662–1747);[22] and still others were produced by Gaetano Gandolfi (1734–1802), Charles-Joseph Natoire (1700–1777) and Jean-Honoré Fragonard (1732–1806).[23]

Giulia Iseppi

1 Gualandi 1840–45 (1840), 1:118–40, in incorrect order; Malaguzzi Valeri 1929, 51; Gnudi and Cavalli 1955, 88, no. 83.
2 Spear 1989; Stanzani 1992, 142–46; Stephen Pepper (1988, 282, no. 148) mistakenly indicates that it was commissioned in 1601.
3 Morselli 2016. See also Malvasia–Pericolo 2019, 1:338–39, note 335.
4 Malvasia–Zanotti 1841, 2:36: 'Lavorate più per dispetto che per gloria'.
5 Malaguzzi Valeri 1929, 51. As reported in Zucchini 1953, 55; Gnudi and Cavalli 1955, 88.
6 Paris, Musée du Louvre, inv. 522.
7 Malvasia–Zanotti 1841, 2:37: 'Quella grande invenzione, quella ferace composizione, que' giudiziosi ripieghi di sbattimenti favorevoli e di trapassi di lume'; C. Casali Pedrielli in Emiliani et al. 1988, 150, no. 62.
8 Malvasia 1686, 77: 'Bei panneggiamenti, e nel felice maneggio del pennello'.
9 Malvasia–Zanotti 1841, 2:37: 'Come se fossero attorno ad un Elefante'.
10 Bellori–Borea 2009, 2:513–14.
11 Scaramuccia 1674, 55; Cavazzoni Zanotti 1710, 14–16.
12 Gnudi and Cavalli 1955, 88, no. 83.
13 Morselli 2016, 18.
14 C. Casali Pedrielli in Emiliani et al. 1988, 150, no. 62.
15 Malvasia–Marzocchi 1983, 219; Malvasia–Pericolo 2019, 1:501.
16 Morselli 2016, 19, no. 53.
17 Cochin 1759, 2:122; Dézallier d'Argenville 1762, 2:106–7.
18 St Petersburg, State Hermitage Museum, ГЭ-2714; Vsevoložskaja 2010, 241.
19 Bologna, Pinacoteca Nazionale di Bologna, inv. 6330; S. Marinelli in Bentini et al. 2011, 428–29.
20 Morselli 2016, 15 and 26, with bibliography.
21 Windsor Castle, Royal Library, RCIN 903476; Paris, Musée du Louvre, Département des Arts graphiques, inv. 8951.
22 Florence, Gallerie degli Uffizi, Gabinetto dei Disegni e delle Stampe, inv. 20325 F.
23 Auzas 1958, 305–9; for all these, see Morselli 2016, 16–17, with bibliography.

VI

THE SUPERHUMAN ANATOMIES
OF GODS AND HEROES

In Rome, Guido Reni saw and studied a number of landmark artworks that
offered a grandiose, monumental view of the human anatomy, among them the
famous *Belvedere Torso* and, particularly, Michelangelo's frescoes in the Sistine
Chapel. In his own masterly handling of certain mythological themes, Reni opted
for a similar interpretation of the male body, painting anatomies which – though
plausible – bordered on the superhuman. This approach to the human body was
well suited to depicting certain episodes from classical mythology, such as the
fall of the giants or the labours of Hercules. His pictures on themes of this kind
were mostly commissioned or collected by aristocrats keen to highlight the
splendour of their own ancestry. The Spanish monarchy, too, ordered paintings
of mythological scenes for self-representational purposes from artists such as
Francisco de Zurbarán and the Bolognese sculptor Alessandro Algardi, who
was to be remembered as a 'new Guido in marble'.

45 Guido Reni

The Fall of the Giants

1637–40
Oil on canvas, 208.5 × 189 cm
Pesaro, Palazzo Mosca, Musei Civici, inv. 3916

Provenance: Mentioned in the Palazzo Isolani, Bologna, around 1760; listed in the collection of Marchese Piriteo Malvezzi in 1806 and inherited by his daughter, Maria Malvezzi, wife of Astorre Ercolani; in the Ercolani-Malvezzi collection in 1812, 1824, 1867; obtained in 1868 by Gioachino Rossini, among other works of the Malvezzi-Ercolani collection, as settlement for credits; purchased by the city of Pesaro in 1879 as part of the Rossini collection.

Selected bibliography: Cavalli 1955, 97–98, no. 106; Baccheschi 1971, 112, no. 190; Ebert-Schifferer, Emiliani and Schleier 1988, 212–14, no. A32; Pepper 1988, 284, no. 154; Malvasia–Pericolo 2019, 1:358, note 388.

In listing the paintings housed in the Palazzo Isolani in Bologna, the art historian Marcello Oretti (1714–1787) singles out 'The Fall of the Giants, life-size figures, believed to be a work by Guido Reni'.[1] In the same place, Oretti mentions two other works by or attributed to Guido: 'the most beautiful portrait of an old man, perhaps a cavaliere of the said house [Isolani], clad in black with collar in the Spanish fashion, half-figure, life-size … said to be by Guido Reni' and 'a Virgin with the child Jesus that looks like a sculpture, painted in monochrome by Guido Reni, but seems to be a work by the Carracci'.[2] Both paintings remain untraced. In his *Felsina pittrice* (1678), Carlo Cesare Malvasia records 'the

famous Assumption of the Virgin, which Guido likewise made as a gift to Signor Count and Senator Alamanno Isolani, in place of the extremely bad Virgin executed by Pietro Faccini in that large painting, where she hovers above the most beautiful apostles'.[3] By the time Malvasia penned his *Felsina*, Guido's *Assonta* had become an *Assontina* (still untraced): a 'beautiful little head' (*bella testina*) that had been cut out from Pietro Faccini's (c. 1562–1602) original *Assumption*.[4] Nothing is known either about Guido's relationship with Alamanno Isolani (1572–1657) or the latter's art collection. It is thus impossible to establish whether and to what purpose he might have ordered Guido's *Fall of the Giants*. Nor is it possible to verify whether the other works by Guido mentioned by Oretti had belonged to Alamanno Isolani himself.

As successors to the Lupari family, the Isolani came into possession of what is still called the Palazzo Isolani on Via Santo Stefano only in 1671.[5] It is thus possible that Guido's work belonged not to Giacomo Isolani, Alamanno's son, but to his wife, Francesca Maria Lupari, who in fact had inherited the collection of paintings of her father and uncle, Marcantonio († 1667) and Bartolomeo († 1668) Lupari.[6] Guido's *Fall of the Giants* might initially have been conceived of as a ceiling painting, although, in its current state, it looks like an unfinished fragment of a larger composition, cut out and rearranged through the insertion of an out-of-scale smallish Jupiter. Its measurements (208.5 × 189 centimetres) are, for instance, slightly inferior to those of Guido's 1600 *Fall of Phaethon* (256 × 222 centimetres) in the Palazzo Zani, Bologna.[7] If the *Fall of the Giants* was commissioned by a member of the Lupari family, then it cannot be ruled out that it was made for a ceiling of the Palazzo Lupari (later Isolani). There is no reason to assume that the painting was destined for one of the ceilings of the

Fig. 83 Guido Reni, *The Fall of the Giants*.
Red chalk on paper, 290 × 393 mm.
Florence, Gallerie degli Uffizi, Gabinetto
dei Disegni e delle Stampe, inv. 12448 F

Isolani castle and villa in Minerbio, near Bologna. While many rooms of the 'new palace' in Minerbio were decorated with frescoes, most notably by Amico Aspertini (1474–1552), in the late 1530s, there is no indication that the Isolani commissioned any decoration there in Guido's time.[8]

The *Fall of the Giants* is listed again in the 1806 inventory of the estate of Marchese Piriteo Malvezzi (1734–1806).[9] Upon Piriteo's death, the painting was inherited by his daughter, Maria Malvezzi (1780–1865), and entered the Ercolani collection as a result of her marriage with Count Astorre Ercolani (1779–1828). Guido's *Fall of the Giants* ended up in the possession of the opera composer Gioachino Rossini (1792–1868), who obtained it from Maria Malvezzi as part of a settlement for previous credits. In 1879, the city of Pesaro bought Rossini's entire collection of paintings, including Guido's *Fall of the Giants*.

Malvasia, who seemingly did not know about this work, relates in his *Felsina pittrice* (1678) that upon Guido's death in 1642 many autograph drawings were found at his house, among them one that represented the *Giants struck down by Lightning* 'in oil on canvas in chiaroscuro so that it would reach France safely for one of those skilful engravers who had requested it, and whose prints satisfied Guido more than the woodcuts executed so laboriously in three states by Coriolano'.[10] Malvasia refers here to the *Fall of the Giants*, a large chiaroscuro print over four sheets of paper executed first in 1638, then in 1641 (with variations) by Bartolomeo Coriolano (c. 1599–c. 1676) after a drawing by Guido.[11] 'In this print', Malvasia notes;

> Guido wished to indulge his fancy, to make known that he equalled all other great masters in his understanding of the muscles and of the nude, just as the other [Michelangelo] had demonstrated in his Judgement, but with a uniform proportion and delicacy of form.[12]

In his life of Guido, Malvasia also quotes an 'extremely large drawing of the Giants, which is kept covered with great care and veneration' by the Sacchetti in Rome.[13] While this drawing (which according to a 1705 inventory of the Sacchetti collection measured approximately 234 × 172.7 centimetres) should not be confused with the 'oil on canvas in chiaroscuro' previously mentioned, it is possible that it was identical in composition (neither work has been traced).[14] This may or may not have differed from the version of the *Fall of the Giants* reproduced by Coriolano in his chiaroscuro print. In any case, the Pesaro painting represents (in reverse) the four bottommost Giants in Coriolano's composition.

A red chalk drawing in the Gallerie degli Uffizi, convincingly ascribed to Guido, depicts three of the Giants featured in the Pesaro painting [fig. 83].[15] As pointed out by Malvasia, Guido undertook to play with the idea of the Herculean body as a pictorial challenge late in his life. With his usual mordancy, Francesco Albani (1578–1660), once a friend then an archenemy of Guido, defined the elaborate bodies of the Giants as 'little sausages' (*salsicciotti*), alluding to the master's inability to modulate the muscles' reliefs through appropriate chiaroscuro.[16] In reality, Guido's enterprise aimed to demonstrate that, through his trademark softness, he could paradoxically succeed in rendering the exceptional vigour of an over-muscular body. Like Albani, but with greater nuance, Malvasia also considered Guido's undertaking a failure. The *Fall of the Giants* must have been executed around the time when Coriolano produced his chiaroscuro prints, that is, in 1637–40. The painting bears affinity with Guido's *Hercules and the Hydra* now in the Palazzo Pitti, Florence [cat. 48], and *Polyphemus throwing a Rock* now in the Pinacoteca Capitolina, Rome.[17]

Lorenzo Pericolo

1 Marcello Oretti, *Le pitture che si ammirano nelli palazzi e case de' nobili nella città di Bologna e di altri edifici in detta città*, manuscript, Bologna, Biblioteca Comunale dell'Archiginnasio, Ms B 104, 1:73.

2 Ibid., 1:72–73.

3 Malvasia 1678, 2:88: 'La famosa Assonta, che fece similmente in dono al Sig. Conte, e Senatore Alamanno Isolani, in luogo di quella così cattiva, che sovra gli Apostoli così belli avea dipinto in una gran tavola Pietro Faccini'.

4 Malvasia–Arfelli 1961, 77.

5 Cuppini and Roversi 1974, 302.

6 The Getty Provenance Index® Databases (accessible at: https://www.getty.edu/research/tools/provenance/search.html), GPI, I–1193 and I–1196.

7 On the *Fall of Phaethon*, see Malvasia–Pericolo 2019, 1:242–43, note 88.

8 Cuppini and Matteucci 1969, 346–47.

9 Ghelfi 2002, 19, no. 15: 'Li Giganti fulminati abbozzo di Guido Reni lire 300'. See further ibid., 21 and 23.

10 Malvasia 1678, 2:56: 'In tela di chiaroscuro a olio, perche salvi fossero gionti in Francia ad uno di que' bravi intagliatori che gli ne avea richiesto, e ne' quali erasi più soddisfatto che ne gl'intagliati in legno, con tre stampe e tanta fatica dal Coriolano'.

11 On the print, see Malvasia–Pericolo 2019, 1:357–58, note 388.

12 Malvasia 1678, 1:116: 'Volendose in essi sbizzarrire Guido, e far conoscere se al pari d'ogn'altro gran maestro intendesse i muscoli e'l nudo, come lo dimostrò l'altro nel suo Giudicio, ma dando anch'egli in una troppo uniforme proporzione, e dilicatezza'.

13 Ibid., 2:90: 'Il disegno grandissimo de' Giganti che tiene coperto con gran riguardo e venerazione'.

14 On these works, see Malvasia–Pericolo 2019, 1:357–58, note 388.

15 Bohn 2008, 68–69, no. 53.

16 Malvasia 1678, 2:56.

17 Rome, Pinacoteca Capitolina, PC 241. See Malvasia–Pericolo 2019, 1:447, note 673.

46 Alessandro Algardi
(Bologna 1595–1654 Rome)

Jupiter Victorious over the Titans

1650–54
Patinated and gilded bronze, 112 × 60 × 53 cm
Private collection

Provenance: Unknown.

Selected bibliography: Unpublished.

This bronze group, featuring Jupiter felling the Titans with his thunderbolt, is linked to Alessandro Algardi's last and most prestigious commission: four pairs of firedogs, ordered by Diego Velázquez (1599–1660) during his second sojourn in Rome (1649–51), destined for the collection of Philip IV of Spain.[1] Each pair was to represent one of the Olympian deities associated with the four elements: Jupiter (fire), Juno (air), Cybele (earth), and Neptune (water).[2]

Algardi completed the bronzes of Jupiter and Juno before his death in June 1654. A year later, the Spanish sovereign decided that the Cybele and Neptune models should be finished, on terms that were remarkably demanding.[3] The work was entrusted to Algardi's most gifted assistants, Ercole Ferrata (1610–1686) and Domenico Guidi (1625–1701), who were required not only to meet a very tight deadline (three months) but also to present their work on three separate occasions for the approval of Rome's most celebrated sculptor, Gian Lorenzo Bernini (1598–1680).[4] Once in Madrid, the firedogs did not fulfil their intended function; instead, seven of them were used to decorate a fountain in Aranjuez.[5] The eighth, a Jupiter, was placed first in the Alcázar of Madrid (1686)[6] and then in the Buen Retiro palace[7] before it subsequently disappeared, probably during the Peninsular War (1808–14). Two of the Aranjuez bronzes (a Juno and a Neptune) were also looted during that war, while a further two (a Jupiter and the other Juno) were stolen in 1943. The remaining pieces – a Neptune and two Cybeles – are now in the care of Patrimonio Nacional.[8]

Unsurprisingly, given Algardi's fame and the fact that the theme illustrated the concept of absolute monarchy embodied by Louis XIV, the models of Jupiter and Juno were promptly copied in France. The bronze sculpture on show here, however, differs from the French copies. All the figures – Jupiter as well as the Titans – have smooth eyeballs without pupils, as in all Algardi's representations of mythological figures. The sphere into which the eagle sinks its claws is not the globe but rather a celestial vault marked by constellations, an iconography more consistent with Jupiter's status as ruler of the heavens. Moreover, if we ignore three nineteenth-century interventions – the replacement of the right arm and the left leg, and the addition of a piece of rock under the globe – the fluid, organic, uniform modelling of this bronze is characteristic of Algardi's autograph works.

Any tentative attribution of this Jupiter to Algardi raises the question of whether it was one of the versions commissioned by Velázquez. It is unlikely to have belonged to the Aranjuez group, especially since it shows no signs of prolonged exposure to water, as would be the case if it had decorated a fountain. The possibility that this is the version recorded at the Buen Retiro palace deserves further consideration: replacement of the protruding parts may have been prompted by damage sustained during looting, while the rock under the globe may have been added in order to reinforce the stability of the group. Alternatively, it may be another version made in Rome, although this would mean that the firedogs were not commissioned exclusively for Philip IV. The contract, if found, might perhaps cast some light on this matter.

The superb modelling directly recalls that of Guido Reni, hailed as Algardi's *alter ego*[9] in a stylistic pairing similar to that traced two centuries later between Lorenzo Bartolini (1777– 1850) and Jean-Auguste-Dominique Ingres (1780– 1867).[10] Algardi's bronze sculpture echoes Reni's *Fall of the Giants* of 1637–40 [cat. 45] in terms of the placing of the Titans and the treatment of their anatomies.[11] Algardi could not have seen this canvas, since he was living in Rome at the time it was painted in Bologna; however, he may have set eyes on drawings of it, and the two chiaroscuro engravings by Bartolomeo Coriolano (c. 1599–c. 1676), although richer in figures and more ambitious in composition, may have provided him with an initial idea.[12] The subject was historically associated with the Spanish monarchy, and had earlier been addressed in two Italian frescoes in honour of Charles V: one by Perino del Vaga (1501–1547) at the Villa del Principe in Genoa, and the other by Giulio Romano (c. 1499–1546) at the Palazzo Te in Mantua, where Algardi spent some years before moving to Rome.

Grégoire Extermann

1 Montagu 1985, 1:133–34, 2:404–5, and 2:409–15; García Cueto 2011; C. Giometti and D. García Cueto in Redín Michaus 2016a, 212–13, nos. 34 and 35; Warren 2016, 2:610–13.
2 Bellori–Borea 1976, 415–16.
3 García Cueto 2011.
4 Ibid., 50–52.
5 Portús Pérez 2004, 56–57.
6 Bottineau 1958, 308.
7 Ponz 1787–93 (1793), 6:133.
8 C. Giometti and D. García Cueto in Redín Michaus 2016a, 212–13, nos. 34 and 35.
9 Malvasia–Emiliani 1969, 131; Montagu 1985, 1:64.
10 Extermann 2011, 78.
11 Montagu 1985, 1:133.
12 Malvasia–Takahatake and Pericolo 2017, 261, fig. 622; Malvasia–Pericolo 2019, 1:357–58, note 388.

The Superhuman Anatomies of Gods and Heroes

47   Guido Reni

The Fall of Phaethon

Before 1600
Pen and brown ink, grey wash, heightened with lead white over
black chalk on faded brown-grey paper, 372 × 324 mm
Edinburgh, National Galleries of Scotland, Purchased 1974, D 5011

Provenance: Sir Archibald Campbell, 2nd Baronet of Succoth (1769–1848);
Sir Ilay Campbell; purchased by the National Galleries of Scotland in 1974.
Selected bibliography: Kurz 1935–36, 14, pl. 19; Kurz 1955, 116, no. 336;
Pepper 1968, 368–69; Johnston 1974, 1:59–62, no. 30; Birke 1981, 46, no. 18;
V. Birke in Ebert-Schifferer, Emiliani and Schleier 1988, 271–72, no. B3; Pepper
1988, 214, no. 5; Macandrew 1990, 54–55, no. 17; A. Weston-Lewis in *Bolognese
Drawings* 1993, no. 43; Malvasia–Pericolo 2019, 1:242–43, note 88.

The biographer Carlo Cesare Malvasia reports on Guido Reni's
work at the Palazzo Zani on via Santo Stefano in Bologna, where
he frescoed three life-size figures representing the *Separation of
Night from Day* [fig. 19] for the vault of the main hall, and in the
adjoining antechamber, the *Fall of Phaethon*, complete with horses
'in an excellent *di sotto in sù*'.[1] It is clear from this account that the
first of the two frescoes – the *Separation of Night from Day*, detached from the ceiling and transferred to canvas in 1840 and subsequently sold to William John Bankes, who reinstalled it at
Kingston Lacy, in Dorset, where it can still be seen[2] – was completed in 1599, and that Malvasia believed the *Phaethon* was painted
at the same time. According to Giovan Pietro Bellori, however, the
commissions from the Earls Zani were carried out shortly before
the artist left for Rome, in 1602.[3] While this date is erroneous –
Guido was paid in Rome already in January 1601[4] – both sources
agree about the Bolognese chronology for the two paintings.

Nevertheless, Stephen Pepper preferred to backdate the
Phaethon fresco to 1596–97 on stylistic grounds; Catherine
Johnston and Veronika Birke opted for 1603 – after Reni's return
from Rome to Bologna for the funeral of Agostino Carracci
(1557– 1602) – also noting the possible citation of the horses of
the group of the two *Dioscuri*, then in the Piazza del Quirinale.
Following the discovery of the Zani family's account books, we
now know that Guido received the first payments between
26 May and 9 June 1600. It would therefore be reasonable to
assume that both frescoes were completed at around that time,
as indicated by Malvasia.[5]

The Edinburgh drawing bears an old handwritten attribution
to Lelio Orsi da Novellara (1508/11–1587), as does the preparatory drawing for the *Separation of Night from Day*, pointing to
a possible shared provenance.

The Windsor Castle collection has a second work on paper
– from the so-called Domenichino volumes[6] – of the young
Phaethon, shown half-length, plunging to earth with his four
horses after having been struck by a thunderbolt from Jupiter. The
status of the drawing remains controversial: it has been regarded
as an unfinished sheet intended for subsequent tracing;[7] as a
copy;[8] as a drawing started by Guido and never completed;[9] as
'not a copy … but maybe a later stage in the preparation of a fresco';[10] or as no more than a tracing of drawing no. D 5011 in the
Scottish National Gallery of Modern Art in Edinburgh.[11]

Finally, it should be noted that Pepper was the first critic to fully explore, in 1968, the possible connection between the Zani frescoes and a sheet in the Uffizi containing several *Studies for Figures*
on the recto, whose fame rests chiefly on the presence of some
signatures by Guido Reni.[12] The drawing, proof of a style wholly
reflecting Guido's training under Agostino Carracci, thanks to the
male nude in the centre of the paper, could be a first thought for
the *Fall of Phaethon*; while several other elements on the same
sheet could be connected with the *Resurrection of Christ*, one of
the small canvases making up the *Fifteen Mysteries* surrounding the
sculpture of the Virgin in the chapel of the Rosary at the church of
San Domenico in Bologna. In Pepper's view, both painting commissions had to be dated to around 1596–97.[13] Although unaware
of the documentary records discovered in 1960 relating to the joint
production of the paintings in San Domenico, completed by August
1601,[14] he was certainly the first to connect the Uffizi work on paper with the small *Resurrection* in San Domenico.[15]

Viviana Farina

1 Malvasia–Pericolo 2019, 1:34–35: 'Cavalli egregiamente di sotto in su'.
2 Pepper 1988, 216, no. 9. The preparatory drawing for the entire composition
   (Paris, Musée du Louvre, Départment des Arts graphiques, inv. 6681) bears
   a handwritten attribution to Lelio Orsi, but was recognised as an original
   Reni by Dominique Cordellier. Catherine Johnston (1993) traced it to the
   collection of Count Ranuzzi in Bologna: see Loisel 2013, 98, no. 59.
3 Bellori–Borea 1976, 493–94.
4 Terzaghi 2007, 170 and 419–20.
5 Malvasia–Pericolo 2019, 1:242–43, note 88. The *Fall of Phaethon* is still
   in situ, with a frescoed *quadratura* frame added in the eighteenth century. The records of the year 1600 complicate still further any attempt to
   trace Reni's stylistic development in parallel to his works. The Louvre
   drawing – see note 2 above – certainly seems to express an *imagerie*
   wholly compatible with that of a painting regarded as later: *Orpheus and
   Eurydice*, which Malvasia saw at the Lambertini home, and which – significantly – was attributed to Ludovico Carracci (1555–1619) until it was
   correctly identified by Catherine Johnston in 1993 (Yale University Art
   Gallery, 2019.29.1); see Benati 2015, 40–44, no. 8: '1596/1597'; Benati
   2022, 16–17, fig. 1: '1595'.
6 Windsor Castle, Royal Collection Trust, RCIN 901535: pen and brown ink
   on paper, 413 × 252 mm.
7 Kurz and McBurney 1988, 116, no. 336.

8 Johnston 1974, 1:62 (possibly by Donato Creti); Birke 1981, 47, no. 19.

9 V. Birke in Ebert-Schifferer, Emiliani and Schleier 1988, 271–72, no. B3.

10 Pepper 1988, 214, no. 5.

11 See https://www.rct.uk/collection/search#/4/collection/901535/the-fall-of-phaethon: 'After Guido Reni. c. 1600–1700'. In a verbal communication, A. Clark (1994) suggested that it might be a copy by Raymond La Fage (1656–1684).

12 Florence, Gallerie degli Uffizi, Gabinetto dei Disegni e delle Stampe, inv. 1587 F.

13 Pepper 1968, 367–68, pl. 10.

14 Pepper 1988, 214, no. 4. On this issue, see Malvasia–Pericolo 2019, 1:351, note 375 and 2:176, fig. 20.

15 When classifying the Uffizi drawing, Babette Bohn (2008, 15–16, no. 9) appears to misread Pepper's view: 'Although Pepper has indicated that these sketches may be studies for a Resurrection, no historian to date has suggested any connection between the drawing … and this painting [in San Domenico]'. On this drawing, see most recently M. Aresin in Eclercy 2022a, 92–93, no. 3.

48 Guido Reni

Hercules and the Hydra

c. 1620–25
Oil on canvas, 224 × 175 cm
Florence, Gallerie degli Uffizi, 1890 n. 7810

Provenance: Cardinal Giovan Carlo de' Medici, Casino Mediceo in Via della Scala, Florence, 1647; Palazzo Pitti, Florence, 1688–1836; Villa del Poggio Imperiale, Florence, 1836–c. 1890; Palazzo Pitti, Florence, c. 1890–1932; Pistoia, 1932–74; Cenacolo di San Salvi, Florence, 1974–2001; Palazzo Pitti, Galleria Palatina, Florence, 2001.

Selected bibliography: Borea 1975, 146, no. 103; Chiarini 2001, 137–39; R. Maffeis in Gregori and Maffeis 2007, 39 and 62, notes 142–43; Mosco 2007, 154–55; Padovani 2009; G. Badino in Lo Bianco 2016, 204–5, no. 49; Malvasia–Pericolo 2019, 1:506, note 107.

This painting depicts the second labour of Hercules: the hero is captured in a thoughtful pose, resting his weight on the blood-ied club with which he has slain the poison-breathing monster; the vanquished Hydra lies headless at his feet.

Hercules and the Hydra has been identified as the 'Hercules' by Guido Reni mentioned in the 1647 inventory of the Casino in Via della Scala, Florence, in the collection of Cardinal Giovan Carlo de' Medici (1611–1663): 'Large painting containing a life-size Hercules, his club resting on a rock, and the dead Hydra at his feet, with carved and gilded ornamentation, by the hand of Guido Reni'.[1] This is undoubtedly the canvas purchased by Giovan Carlo de' Medici for his collection; he and his brother Leopoldo may have bought half-shares, as they often did. In his recent critical commentary on Malvasia's life of Guido Reni, Lorenzo Pericolo put forward the interesting suggestion that the work may originally have been painted for Count Girolamo Ranuzzi of Bologna – who turned it down – as a pendant to a *Sisyphus* by Guercino (1591–1666), whose whereabouts is now unknown.

In the Casino it hung beside the *Three Graces* by Francesco Furini (c. 1604–1646),[2] the deliberate juxtaposition of the two artists – as Rodolfo Maffeis has stressed – echoing a 'collector's rule' that had emerged in Venice some years earlier. Both pictures are recorded, as a pair of similar dimensions, in the 1663 inventory drawn up on the death of Cardinal Giovan Carlo.[3]

In keeping with the refined Medici penchant for commissioning frames with decorations relating to the subject of the painting, Guido's canvas – later to join the collection at the Palazzo Pitti – was placed in a superbly carved 'thematic' frame (not in the exhibition). Attributed to Carlo Galestruzzi, a carver in the employ of Cardinal Leopoldo,[4] it featured various elements of the Hercules iconography, such as the Hydra's scaly coils and the lion's skin.

In the Palazzo Pitti, where it is recorded from 1688, the painting was moved on several occasions. At the time of the 1716–23 inventory it hung on the second floor, in the apartments of Prince Mattias;[5] when the Galleria Palatina was established in 1828, it was placed in the Sala delle Belle Arti (Hall of Fine Arts), part of the so-called Quartiere de Volterrano; later, in 1836, it was among the pieces placed in storage, and was in fact transferred to the Villa del Poggio Imperiale. However, an engraving of it was made by Augusto Bedetti (act. 1835–1864) for Luigi Bardi's comprehensive print collection, the *Imperiale e Reale Galleria Pitti*;[6] for twentieth-century critics,[7] Bedetti's print provided key evidence about the painting, which was by then regarded as lost. In fact, the canvas – which returned to the Palazzo Pitti in the late nineteenth century, stripped of its frame, and was later placed in external storage (Cenacolo di San Salvi) – is recorded in contemporary inventories, though they list only the subject, with no mention of the artist. In 2001, despite the poor condition of the paint surface, Marco Chiarini recognised it as the work of Reni, reconstructed its provenance, and suggested a provisional date of around 1636–37. After the painting was cleaned in 2006, the picture proved easier to read and was dated to the early 1620s on the basis of stylistic affinities with the *Labours of Hercules* series (particularly the first three canvases: *Hercules on the Pyre* [fig. 27], *Hercules slaying the Hydra of Lerna*, and *Hercules and Achelous*, all three now at the Musée du Louvre),[8] painted by Reni between 1617 and 1621 for Ferdinando Gonzaga, Duke of Mantua, and intended for the Villa La Favorita. Common to all of them, despite differences in background and lighting, is the towering nude figure of Hercules, inspired by ancient statuary and the paintings of Peter Paul Rubens (1577–1640), in which Reni displayed renewed interest at around that time.

In its powerful muscle structure, this Hercules recalls several drawings by Guido of the mutilated *Belvedere Torso*,[9] the celebrated Hellenistic marble statue usually identified as Ajax contemplating his suicide. Although he interprets it loosely, Reni must have taken this as a model when seeking to depict Hercules as a weary, melancholy hero, captured in a meditative pose following the death of the Hydra. The violently dramatic treatment of the figure, perhaps also reminiscent of nudes by Annibale Carracci (1560–1609) at the Galleria Farnese in Rome, conveys Reni's freedom of approach as a mature artist for whom the grandiose style was best suited to the subject matter.

Cristina Gnoni Mavarelli

1 Florence, Archivio di Stato, Possessioni 4279, Inventario delle masserizie del giardino di Via della Scala del Serenissimo Prencipe Cardinale Giovan Carlo, Camera Terza con la finestra sulla strada e riesce sulla sala grande, 41: 'Quadro grande entrovi un Ercole al'naturale con il bastone che posa sopra un masso, e l'Idria morta a piedi con adornamento intagliato e dorato di mano di Guido Reni'.
2 St Petersburg, State Hermitage Museum, ГЭ-5556.
3 Florence, Archivio di Stato, MdP 2697, Stima di quadri che si ritrovano nel Casino di Via della Scala del Serenissimo Signore Principe Cardinale Giovan Carlo di gloriosa memoria.
4 See Mosco 2007, 154–55.
5 Florence, Archivio Biblioteca Uffizi, Ms 79.
6 Bardi 1837–42, IV (1842).
7 Borea 1975, 146, no. 103.
8 Paris, Musée du Louvre, inv. 538, 535, and 536, respectively.
9 Vatican City, Musei Vaticani, inv. 1192.

49   Francisco de Zurbarán

(Fuente de Cantos, Badajoz 1598–1664 Madrid)

Hercules and Cerberus

1634
Oil on canvas, 132 × 151 cm
Madrid, Museo Nacional del Prado, P-1247

Provenance: Palacio del Buen Retiro, Madrid, 1701 (no. 260); Palacio del Buen Retiro, Madrid, 1794 (no. 531).

Selected bibliography: J. M. Serrera in Serrera 1988, 244, no. 43; Caturla 1994, 114; L. Ruiz Gómez in Úbeda de los Cobos 2005, 164, no. 33; Brown and Elliott 2016, 222; Japón 2020b, 182.

This was one of a series of ten paintings – all now in the Museo del Prado – commissioned from Francisco de Zurbarán in 1634 to decorate the area over the windows of the Salón de Reinos (Hall of Realms) in the Buen Retiro palace, whose iconographical programme also included a set of royal portraits and battle scenes by various artists. In the case of Zurbarán's paintings, the composition, framing, and modelling of the figures reflect the fact that all these canvases were to be hung at a height of over three metres and against the light.

The cycle was connected to an iconographical tradition instituted by the Habsburg dynasty in Spain during the reign of Charles V, intended to highlight their claimed descent from Hercules. But it is also related to two other monumental series focussing on the Theban hero, both exceptional for their time. The first is a set of ten canvases, albeit in different formats, painted by Frans Floris (c. 1519–1570) in Antwerp around 1553.[1] Floris' cycle – for which there was no precedent in the Northern pictorial tradition – was commissioned by the merchant Nicolaas Jonghelinck (1517–1570) for one of the rooms in his suburban villa. Jonghelinck belonged to a family in the service of the Habsburgs; his brother Jacob Jonghelinck (1530–1606) held the post of sculptor and medallist to Philip II of Spain. In a letter written in 1571 to the royal secretary Gabriel de Zayas, the humanist Benito Arias Montano noted that the king himself had been impressed by the cycle during his sojourn in the Netherlands; he added that the pictures were then in Brussels – at the house of Jacob Jonghelinck, who had inherited them from his brother – and recommended that the king purchase them.[2] Zurbarán would have been familiar with them through ten prints by Cornelis Cort (1533–1578), which went through several editions, starting in 1563;[3] he may well have taken them as the basis for his own compositions, and particularly for his depiction of Cerberus.[4]

The second monumental series to which Zurbarán's cycle is related is a set of four paintings depicting scenes from the Labours of Hercules, painted by Guido Reni between 1617 and 1621 for Ferdinando Gonzaga, Duke of Mantua, and intended for the Villa La Favorita. Reni's *Hercules slaying the Hydra of Lerna* of about 1620–21[5] displays certain marked stylistic affinities, particularly as regards colour, with Zurbarán's *Hercules and Cerberus*.[6] These similarities, however, may be due simply to chance, and to a common environment or *Zeitgeist*, rather than indicating any direct link. Both series focus on the virtues of the hero as a reflection of those of the prince, while the use of chiaroscuro enhances a Christian moral reading in which the central figure vanquishes vice and defeats the enemies of the faith. Zurbarán is unlikely to have had access to Reni's composition, through either copies or prints. The Mantua paintings were sold in 1627, along with the rest of the Duke's collection, to Charles I of England, and remained in his possession until his death in 1649. The first known engraving of the Reni painting was made by Gilles Rousselet (1610–1686) in around 1677, when the picture was in the collection of Louis XIV of France.[7] However, Zurbarán may possibly have seen some sketch or drawing, brought to Madrid during negotiations for the sale of the Duke's collection, since there was still a chance that it might be purchased – at least in part – by Philip IV.[8] In any event, Zurbarán is known to have been influenced by Reni's style through originals and copies of his work in Spain.[9] Significantly, the 1794 inventory of the Buen Retiro palace attributes the Hercules cycle to the school of Giovanni Lanfranco (1582–1647), who worked with Reni on several occasions, and it has also been linked to Jusepe de Ribera (1591–1652)[10] – whose style was also influenced by Reni – and more specifically to his *Tityus* and *Ixion*, which in 1634 were also acquired for the new palace.[11]

Eduardo Lamas

1 Wouk 2018, 335–39.
2 Ibid., 709, note 54.
3 Ibid., no. H.67-76.
4 Soria 1955, 14.
5 Paris, Musée du Louvre, inv. 535.
6 Japón 2020b, 182.
7 Birke 1988b, 417.
8 Elliott 2002, 556.
9 Pérez Sánchez 1993, 108; Japón 2020b, 181.
10 Soria 1955, 14; Angulo Íñiguez 1964, 80.
11 Madrid, Museo Nacional del Prado, P-1113 and P-1114.

VII

MARY, OR DIVINITY MADE HUMAN

In the late 1620s, Guido Reni received two important commissions for the
Spanish court. The first was an *Abduction of Helen* [fig. 35], intended for
the main hall at the Alcázar in Madrid, then known as the 'Salón Nuevo' or
New Hall. Owing to a series of disagreements, the painting – which achieved
considerable renown at the time – never reached Spain. The second was an
Immaculate Conception [cat. 55] commissioned for the Infanta Maria Anna
of Spain, the sister of Philip IV, which was subsequently donated to Seville
cathedral, where it remained until the Napoleonic invasion, providing a source
of inspiration for Murillo. In producing this painting, Guido was obliged to
tackle the controversial issue of the Immaculate Conception of Mary, a doctrine
fiercely defended by the Spanish monarchy but rejected by the Dominican order.
The artist interprets this theme with the sensitivity that marks all his depictions
of Mary, reflecting his own lifelong, fervent devotion to the Virgin. Reni's
brushwork brings Mary closer to the viewer, as the most beautiful human
idealisation of a divine being.

50   Giovanni Battista Manzini (compiler)
(Bologna 1599–1664)

Il trionfo del pennello. Raccolta d'alcune Compositioni nate a gloria d'un ratto d'Helena di Guido
[The triumph of the brush. Collection of some compositions written in praise of an Abduction of Helen by Guido]

Bologna, by Nicolò Tebaldini and Paolo Veli, 1633
54 pages, fol. in 4to.
Inscription: 'Ex legato D. Equitiis Antonij Francisci de Marmij'
Florence, Biblioteca Nazionale Centrale, A-D⁴ E⁴ (-E4) F-G⁴

Selected bibliography: Malvasia 1678, 2:39–40; Colomer 1990; Colantuono 1997, 112–40; Borghi 2018; Malvasia–Pericolo 2019, 1:92–96 and 1:314–17, notes 266–73.

This slim volume contains a collection of epistles in praise of Guido Reni's highly-celebrated *Abduction of Helen* [fig. 35], a painting commissioned towards the end of 1627 by the Spanish ambassador to the Holy See, Íñigo Vélez de Guevara y Tasis, 5th Count of Oñate (c. 1573–1644), for the Salón Nuevo [New Hall] at Philip IV's Alcázar in Madrid. In spite of attempts at mediation entrusted to Cardinal Bernardino Spada, papal legate in Bologna from 1627 to 1631, and Cardinal Francesco Barberini, negotiations between Reni and the Count were broken off and the canvas – which reached Rome in 1628–29 – was offered to the new Spanish ambassador, Manuel de Fonseca y Zúñiga, 6th Count of Monterrey (1588–1653), who probably refused to reconsider the price.[1] As a result, on 2 July 1629 Spada offered the painting to Marie de' Medici, the French queen regent (1575–1642), who bought it in 1631 but never actually took delivery, being forced to flee following the failure of her coup d'état against Cardinal Richelieu.[2] Held up in Lyon, the work did not reach Paris until after the queen's death in 1642, and was eventually purchased by Louis Phélypeaux de La Vrillière (1598– 1681).[3]

All the dated epistles were composed in the autumn or winter of 1632–33, by which time neither the painting nor the copy made for Spada by Giacinto Campana (c. 1600–c. 1650) – despatched to Rome in April 1632[4] – were to be seen in Bologna. The book on show here, which belonged to Anton Francesco Marmi (1665–1736), keeper of the Biblioteca Magliabechiana, is a first edition, published in 1633 in Bologna (Tebaldini), Venice (Tomasini), and Parma (Magri). It includes letters by Luigi Manzini, Jacopo Gaufrido, Lanfranco Furietti, Claudio Achillini (two) and Virgilio Malvezzi, as well as two by Giovanni Battista Manzini himself. The enterprise earned a comment from Reni's biographer Carlo Cesare Malvasia, who in his *Felsina pittrice* (1678) described the authors as 'the most celebrated prosaic pens of our city, and of the whole century';[5] Malvasia must have been using the second edition of the *Trionfo* (1634), since among the authors he lists Annibale Marescotti, whose *Panegyric* to Cardinal Santacroce – which had been published independently in 1633 – was only included in the reprint.[6]

Regardless of Malvasia's specific reference, scholars have only recently recognised the importance of this volume in view of the light it sheds on the relationship between the artist and the authors involved. In 1953 Guido Giongo mentioned it in passing, alluding to Achillini[7] though not to the other writers; in recent years it has been reappraised within the framework of a political reading of the painting's iconography, in the context of the Salón Nuevo.[8] Examination of the book in its historical context, and of the financial or patronage-related links existing at the time between the authors and Reni, has revealed that the publishing operation was based on a network of relationships involving the Manzini brothers, Gaufrido, Fieschi, Furietti, and Achillini.[9] The exception was Malvezzi, a prominent man of letters, client of Reni's and close acquaintance of Manzini,[10] who spent many years in his service, whose 'highly learned' letter lent prestige to the edition.[11] The authors – all of whom were members of the Accademia della Notte, founded in 1622 under the aegis of Maffeo Barberini, the future Pope Urban VIII – gave the *Trionfo* an unashamedly pro-French orientation. According to Malvasia, the artificer of the project was Giovanni Battista Manzini, a versatile man of letters and art expert, who set the enterprise in motion with a view to obtaining a painting by

Reni;[12] if so, then the promotion of such an illustrious venture at an early stage in his career may be seen as part of an ambitious quest for social advancement. Publishing it as an appendix to the second volume of his *Furori della gioventù* (Bologna, 1634), Manzini sent the *Trionfo* to Cassiano dal Pozzo in 1634, thus embarking on a correspondence which would gain him entry into Barberini's entourage.[13] Manzini was well aware that Cassiano thought highly of the epistle *De raptu Helenae* that Gaufrido had published independently in 1632, which was later included in the anthology.[14] Gaufrido was a modest French littérateur, but a skilled diplomat at the Farnese court in Parma: both his introductory ekphrastic epistle and the second letter by Manzini were dedicated to the abbot Claudio Fieschi, who played a crucial role in the publication of the anthology, not only as the addressee of the letters but also as their promoter. Fieschi, the French-born son of a lady-in-waiting to Marie de' Medici, was acquainted with Achillini and Gaufrido through their relationship with the Farnese family, and wished to be kept 'informed in detail about this painting',[15] in which the queen regent had shown interest; it was he who prompted the composition of the epistles. In January 1633, Gaufrido sent Achillini another epistle on the *Abduction of Helen,* offering a highly precise description of the actions portrayed in order to satisfy his curiosity. Achillini's second epistle (4 January 1633) must be the reply to this first letter. Finally, Marescotti's epistle – also published independently in 1633 – opened with a dedication by Bartolomeo Cavalieri to Fieschi, thus confirming that he was among the book's sponsors.[16]

Giulia Iseppi

1 Pierguidi 2012b, 21–25; Malvasia–Pericolo 2019, 1:295–97, note 218.
2 Dirani 1982, 85–91; Pierguidi 2012b, 93–96.
3 Pierguidi 2012b, 119–21.
4 Dirani 1982, 90–91; Colantuono 1997, 112–40; Pierguidi 2012b, 79–82.
5 Malvasia 1678, 2:40: 'Le penne prosaiche più celebri della nostra Città, ed insiem di quel secolo'.
6 Colantuono 1997, 112–13; Borghi 2018, 482.
7 Giongo 1953, 354.
8 Colomer 1990; Pepper 1999; O. Bonfait in Bonfait 1994, 128–35.
9 Colantuono 1997, 112–40.
10 Colomer 1996, 201–6; García Cueto 2006, 256–63.
11 Borghi 2018, 496–501; Malvasia–Pericolo 2019, 1:92.
12 Malvasia–Zanotti 1841, 2:29–30; Malvasia–Pericolo 2019, 1:91–94 and 1:317, note 273.
13 Colantuono 1997, 206–36; Unglaub 1999, 39; Borghi 2018, 488–89.
14 Unglaub 1999, 40.
15 Manzini 1633, 16: 'Raguagliato minutamente di questo quadro'.
16 Colantuono 1997, 120.

51 Guido Reni

The Annunciation

1629
Oil on canvas, 237 × 154 cm
Ascoli Piceno (Italy), Comune di Ascoli Piceno. Musei Civici, inv. 399

Provenance: Santa Maria della Carità, Ascoli Piceno, the Marches.

Selected bibliography: Lazzari 1724, 67; Orsini 1790, 167–70; Rossi 1850–51; *Guida della Galleria* 1919, 27; Cavalli 1954, 107, no. 44; Gnudi and Cavalli 1955, no. 80; Baccheschi 1971, no. 151; S. Pepper in Perini Folesani 1986, 514, no. 183; Pepper 1988, 268, no. 114; Papetti 2007; R. Morselli in Papetti 2012, 162–65, no. 47; Papetti 2013; M. Francucci in Sgarbi 2015, 216–17, no. 67.

The Virgin kneels at a prie-dieu, her right hand placed delicately at her breast while her left falls naturally on the book lying on the armrest, as though to keep it open. She is wrapped in a blue mantle, with a diaphanous veil draped over her shoulders. The archangel Gabriel stands before her, floating on a cloud that prevents his feet from touching the floor. His white wings, elegantly outspread, complete this celestial apparition in the privacy of a small, humble dwelling. In the upper left of the composition, two *putti* riding on a cloud look diagonally down on Mary; above them, the clouds have parted to reveal a soaring heavenly dove.

The painting was commissioned by Marquise Eleonora Alvitreti for the family chapel she had erected in 1624 in the church of Santa Maria della Carità, also known as the 'Chiesa della Scopa', attached to the Confraternità dei Disciplinati, a brotherhood devoted to the care of the sick and of those condemned to death. The stucco decoration of the chapel (the first in the left-hand nave), the work of Sebastiano Ghezzi (c. 1580–1647), was inspired by the late Mannerist designs introduced by Federico Zuccari (1539–1609) for the chapel of the Dukes of Urbino in Loreto.[1] In Ghezzi's ornamental structure, the canvas is framed by two columns displaying a vine-shoot motif, thus establishing a close iconographic link between the decoration and the painting itself. The theme of the painting is reiterated in a medallion inside the vault of the pediment, depicting the Eternal Father sending a herald to the Virgin.[2] Work on the chapel was completed in 1629, when it was dedicated, according to the inscription on the medallion, 'in honorem gloriosae Deiparae Virginis'.[3] In the absence of documentary evidence, we can assume that the canvas was also finished in that year.

The painting remained on the altar until the mid-19th century. While it was at Santa Maria della Carità it was visited and admired by scholars ranging from Tullio Lazzari – who described it as 'supernatural and divine' – to Baldassarre Orsini, whose rambling description focuses on its shrewd use of light and harmony of colour.[4] In his 1853 guidebook, Giovanni Battista Carducci hailed it as 'the leading pictorial ornament in Ascoli'.[5] A few years later, when the painting was requisitioned by the State and transferred to the city's art gallery in 1861, it was replaced by a copy – now in the fourth chapel on the left – painted by Ferdinando Cicconi (1831–1886), a student of Tommaso Minardi (1787–1871).[6]

Reni's treatment of this theme proved remarkably successful. His early monumental version of 1609, painted for the Palazzo del Quirinale in Rome, brought him commissions from the provinces, including the altarpiece of San Pietro in Valle in Fano executed in 1620–21, the Ascoli painting discussed here, and the *Annunciation* now in the Louvre,[7] which was purchased by Marie de' Medici. Over time, Guido appears to have simplified the image: although the composition and luminosity of the Ascoli version echo those of the Louvre *Annunciation*, he has removed the table and the vase of flowers behind the figure of the Virgin and reduced the number of *putti* in the clouds above. In the resulting, more compact scene, the central figures have greater presence.[8]

Every time Guido meditated on this episode in the life of Mary he came up with a new and original result; here, there are echoes of a woodcut by Albrecht Dürer (1471–1528) on the same theme, part of a series of engravings entitled the *Life of the Virgin* executed from 1500 to 1511. Reni reinterprets Dürer's image with sentimental delicacy, removes certain details in the German master's busier version, and redistributes the space devoted to the Virgin and the archangel, who in the engraving appears as the central figure.[9]

The voluminous drapery is handled more gently in the Ascoli than in the Louvre painting, where the folds are more tightly gathered, producing an effect similar to that of the *Pallione del Voto* of 1630 [fig. 30]; this would suggest that – despite the short interval between the two – one version was produced shortly before, and the other shortly after, the *Pallione*.[10] The Ascoli *Annunciation* epitomises the light tones, porcelain-like modelling and delicate tenderness of Reni's silver period,

captured in that glimpse of an exterior where the light of dawn 'pearls the landscape', softening the whole setting like 'a breath of spring'.[11]

Two drawings have been associated with this painting, both executed in black pencil and both kept in the Uffizi. One is a study on azure paper for the two *putti*;[12] the other, depicting Gabriel, is regarded by Stephen Pepper as a preparatory study.[13] Although closely resembling the painting, the latter is not identical to the final version (A further sketch of the herald is generally thought to be copy of this latter study).[14] This second drawing in the Uffizi, linked to a study for an *Annunciation*[15] and dated between 1627 and 1630,[16] is thought to be a preparatory sketch for the version by Reni's pupil Giovanni Maria Tamburini (c. 1575–c. 1660) in the Vitali chapel of Santa Maria della Vita in Bologna, regarded as a contemporary variant of the Ascoli altarpiece.[17]

Countless copies over the next two centuries testify to the popularity of this treatment of the subject. Contemporary copies include one attributed to Ercole de Maria († 1640) in San Giovanni in Monte in Bologna,[18] and a smaller version – thought to be a workshop copy – which in 1922 belonged to Silvestro Baglioni in Rome.[19] There are a number of 18th-century copies in Umbria and the Marches, including one by Biagio Miniera (1697–1755), a student of Francesco Solimena (1657–1747), owned in 1850 by Candido Vecchi of Ascoli; and two by Nicola Monti (1736–1795), a student of Pompeo Batoni (1708–1787),

one dating from 1788–89 classed as a copy, but properly speaking a variant, destined for the Santissima Annunziata church in Porto Sant'Elpidio, now in a very poor state of repair; and the other painted for the oratory of the Annunziata in Perugia, at the request of Bishop Alessandro Maria Odoardi.[20]

Giulia Iseppi

1 Ferriani 1992, 156.
2 Semenza 1999, 11 and 18–19; Papetti 2007, 21.
3 Ferriani 1994, XI and 9; R. Morselli in Papetti 2012, 162.
4 Lazzari 1724, 67; Orsini 1790, 167–70.
5 Carducci 1853, 198.
6 *Guida della Galleria* 1919, 27; Ferriani 1994, 9; Ferriani 1995, 62.
7 Paris, Musée du Louvre, inv. 521.
8 Bertini and Ortenzi 1978, no. XXII; Pepper 1988, 268; R. Morselli in Papetti 2012, 162–65.
9 S. Papetti in Herrmann-Fiore 2007, 348, no. VII 20; Papetti 2007, 26–28; M. Francucci in Sgarbi 2015, 216.
10 S. Pepper in Perini Folesani 1986, 514.
11 Kurz 1937, 218; Cavalli 1954, 107, no. 44; R. Morselli in Papetti 2012, 165.
12 Florence, Gallerie degli Uffizi, Gabinetto dei Disegni e delle Stampe, inv. 12434 F; Jaffé 1954, fig. 7.
13 Florence, Gallerie degli Uffizi, Gabinetto dei Disegni e delle Stampe, inv. 1583 F; Pepper 1988, 268, no. 114, pl. 105; Bohn 2008, 64–65, no. 49.
14 Milan, Castello Sforzesco, Fondo Durini, inv. A 47, no. 2370.
15 Florence, Gallerie degli Uffizi, Gabinetto dei Disegni e delle Stampe, inv. 12467 F.
16 Johnston 1974, 1:183, no. 154.
17 Pepper 1988, 268.
18 Ibid.; Cellini 1992, 203.
19 Cantalamessa 1922–23, 165.
20 Orsini 1791, 128; Rossi 1850–51, 125; Ciociola 2014, 168–69, no. 49.

52 Guido Reni
The Virgin of the Chair

c. 1624–25
Oil on canvas, 213.8 × 137.5 cm
Madrid, Museo Nacional del Prado, P-210

Provenance: Mentioned in the prior's chapter room at the Real Monasterio de San Lorenzo de El Escorial on 21 September 1660, when the prior, Father Francisco del Castillo, wrote to inform King Philip IV that the redecoration of the room had been completed;[1] still at El Escorial in 1667, when Father Francisco de los Santos offered a laudatory description of the picture in his guide to the monastery; Palacio Real, Madrid, where it is listed in the 1811 inventory as hanging 'in a room of the Queen's chamber', having come from El Escorial;[2] Museo del Prado, Madrid, 1837.

Selected bibliography: Santos 1667, 75r-v; Andrés 1967, 118; Luna Fernández 1993, 108; Bassegoda i Hugas 2002, 166, no. CP12; Malvasia–Pericolo 2019, 1:73.

It is not known who commissioned this picture, nor is there any record of it entering the Spanish royal collection. In his *Felsina pittrice* (1678), Carlo Cesare Malvasia mentions in passing a Virgin by Guido Reni that was sent to the Spanish court when discussing royal patrons of the day who sought to embellish their residences with his work: 'as did the Queen of Spain, who decorated her regal apartments with a Madonna given to the king, which she requested from him and obtained forthwith'.[3] This rather laconic remark suggests that Malvasia never saw the work, for he offers no description of it, merely repeating what he had heard regarding a canvas of the Virgin sent to the king of Spain and placed in the queen's rooms at the Alcázar. It is by no means certain that Malvasia was referring to the *Virgin of the Chair*, as the 1636 inventory of the Alcázar lists no *Madonna* by Reni[4] and the painting is not mentioned in the 1647 inventory of the goods and jewellery of the queen consort, Elisabeth of France (1602–1644).[5] It probably entered the royal collection at a later date, then, perhaps in the 1650s together with other religious pictures by Guido sent by the king to the monastery of El Escorial as part of a redecoration programme then being undertaken by Diego Velázquez (1599–1660) in his role as royal chamberlain. Six canvases by Reni were hung in the monastery: two in the sacristy, *Saint Joseph and the Christ Child* [fig. 3] and a *Virgin and Child* [fig. 4]; three in the prior's chapter room, this *Virgin of the Chair* and two heads of *Saint Peter* and *Saint Paul* [cat. 33 and 34]; and one in the sacristy of the Pantheon, a *Virgin* – without Child, since the sources refer to it as a 'Virgin alone' – which disappeared without trace, perhaps owing to its small

format, during the French invasion.[6] We now know that the papal nuncio Camillo Massimo (1620–1677), on arriving at the Madrid court in May 1655, presented King Philip IV with two secular paintings of Cupid, one by Reni [cat. 64] and the other by Guercino (1591–1666) [cat. 65].[7] This diplomatic gift may well have included other larger, more important works; it would be surprising if it had not featured a single composition on religious themes.

As critics have noted, the position of the Child in Guido's painting – standing between his mother's legs – strongly resembles that of the *Madonna of Bruges* commissioned from Michelangelo (1475–1564) by the Flemish merchant Alexander Mouscron, sculpted around 1504 and placed shortly thereafter in the church of Our Lady in Bruges. Prints of the sculpture were not made at the time, so – as Elizabeth Cropper has noted[8] – Reni could only have been familiar with it through interpretations by Raphael (1483–1520), Parmigianino (1503–1540), and Annibale Carracci (1560–1609). Parmigianino's version – the well-known *Vision of Saint Jerome*, painted in 1526[9] – achieved considerable popularity thanks to a print by Giulio Bonasone (c. 1510–c. 1574).

In Guido's version the position of the Virgin's hands is reversed with regard to the prints – she holds the book in her left hand and caresses her son with her right – while the Child, standing directly on the ground, leans against his mother's right leg. He holds his right hand to his cheek in a coded gesture – associated with melancholy – also found in a marble relief by Michelangelo, the *Pitti Tondo*,[10] commissioned around 1503 by Bartolomeo Pitti, whose son – Friar Miniato Pitti – gave it to Luigi Guicciardini (1487–1551). Reni's *Virgin of the Chair* contains the two elements essential to this dual Michelangelesque sculptural tradition: the seated Virgin holding a book and the standing Child adopting a melancholy gesture. To these, he adds elements characteristic of his own painterly idiom: greater emphasis is given to the chair, which resembles those often found in papal portraits; and the Virgin is crowned by two cherubs, framed by a canopy of curtains. Mary's serious expression, the book she has been reading, the melancholy gesture of the Child, and the cloth that barely covers his nudity are all clear premonitory allusions to Christ's Passion, while the austere throne and the coronation allude to the *Sedes Sapientiae*, that is, to the Virgin as the seat of divine wisdom.

This elevated doctrinal content – exaltation of the Virgin as a necessary instrument for the redemption of mankind through the mystery of Christ's incarnation, death, and resurrection – is conveyed in Reni's interpretation through the solemnity of the Virgin's throne and the uncompromising frontality of both mother and child. A further key element for the meaning of this scene is the Virgin's gaze, directed not toward the viewer but downwards toward the Child, thus stressing the mediatory, subordinate nature of her role. In his description of the painting, Father Santos explained this idea with the following well-chosen words:

> The Queen and Mother looks upon her most Beloved Son, her eyes cast down with sovereign Majesty, as though saying through her gaze that this majestic grandeur is due to he who was made Man in her Virgin womb, who stripped himself of his greatness, becoming

a servant; this Painting inspires respect, and elicits love and tenderness, and the gentle manner of its Author in what he does is very much to the liking and pleasure of the viewer.[11]

Santos thus focuses on the pious meaning of the image, while recognising in the artist's 'gentle manner' one of Guido's essential skills and merits.

Bonaventura Bassegoda

1 Andrés 1967, 118.
2 Luna Fernández 1993, 108.
3 Malvasia–Pericolo 2019, 1:72: 'come fece la regina di Spagna che d'una Madonna donata al re, ed a lui chiesta instantemente ed ottenuta, arrichì il suo regio quarto'.
4 See Martínez Leiva and Rodríguez Rebollo 2007.
5 See Martínez Leiva and Rodríguez Rebollo 2015, 757–62.
6 On the decoration of El Escorial, see Bassegoda i Hugas 2002.
7 Beaven 2000.
8 Cropper 2017, 55–58.
9 London, The National Gallery, NG33.
10 Florence, Museo Nazionale del Bargello, inv. 93.
11 Santos 1667, 75v.

53 Guido Reni

The Virgin and Child with Saints Lucy and Mary Magdalene (Madonna della Neve)

c. 1623
Oil on canvas, 250 × 176 cm
Florence, Gallerie degli Uffizi, inv. 1890 n. 3088

Provenance: Santa Maria Corteorlandini, Lucca, by 1623; collection of Charles II, Duke of Bourbon-Parma, Lucca, by 1840; Christie's sale, London, 1877; collection of Dr Arthur de Noé Walker, London, 1877; gifted to the Gallerie degli Uffizi, Florence, 1893.

Selected bibliography: Marchiò 1721, 293; Trenta 1820, 112; Trenta–Mazzarosa 1829, 113; Baccheschi 1971, 116, VIII; Borea 1975, 137–41, no. 99; Pepper 1988, 345, A4; Nannini 2005, 129–30.

This painting and its pendant, a *Crucifixion with Saints Catherine and Julius*,[1] were originally placed symmetrically on the altars to either side of the main altar in the church of Santa Maria Corteorlandini in Lucca. They are only mentioned in contemporary sources from the eighteenth century onwards, by foreign travellers[2] and in local guidebooks.[3] In April 1840, Charles II, Duke of Parma (1799–1883) purchased both canvases and had them replaced by copies, still in the church today.[4] While the *Crucifixion* remained in Lucca, where it was placed on permanent loan to the Pinacoteca in 1871,[5] the *Madonna della Neve* was given to the Duke's steward, Count Enrico Cottrel, although it still appeared in the supplementary palace inventory drawn up in 1841.[6] After Cottrel's death, the painting was taken to London, where in 1877 it was sold by Christie's to Arthur de Noé Walker (1820–1900), who donated it to the Uffizi on 30 April 1893.[7] It was on show in the museum until 1940 and thereafter kept in temporary storage until 1974, when it was restored and again placed on display.

The canvas drew a mixed critical response from the authors of early Lucca guides: it was praised by Vincenzo Marchiò (1721); not included among Guido's 'best works' by Tommaso Trenta (1820); and clearly admired by Antonio Mazzarosa (1829), who stated: 'This is a painting of great value, in Guido's graceful style, with good use of colour and sober drapery'.[8] These views have raised doubts among modern critics regarding its full authorship. On the basis of a photograph of a nineteenth-century copy, Max von Boehn regarded it as a poor-quality autograph work, while Edi Baccheschi considered it a copy from the Neoclassical period; Stephen Pepper, who saw it before it was cleaned, concluded that it was a workshop copy. After its restoration in 1975, Evelina Borea once again attributed it to Guido Reni himself.[9]

A document in the church archives allegedly recording the payment, in 1623, of 132 scudi to Reni for the *Crucifixion*, published by Isa Belli Barsali[10] – on which the dating of this *Madonna della Neve* is also based – has not been confirmed by more recent research.[11] However, the date is supported by a later document examined by Borea: the record of a visit to the church on 16 May 1622, by Giuseppe Matraia, rector general of the Order of Clerics Regular of the Mother of God, notes the presence of a chapel devoted to Saints Julius and Catherine, founded 'de novo' by Giulio Franciotti and his brother Cesare, rector of the Mother House and a relative of the group's protector, Cesare Baronio; the brothers were close collaborators of Giovanni Leonardi, the founder of the Order.[12]

The Lucca merchant Giuliano Micotti was already patron of the *Madonna della Neve* altar by April 1625, when an annual mass in honour of Saint Lucy was instituted for its upkeep and maintenance.[13] The canvas must have been on the altar prior to 21 April 1623, when a new marble altar table was installed to replace the earlier wooden version: 'Una cum icona depicta eiusdem S.M.e ad nives'.[14] It is not known how Micotti came into contact with Reni: he may have had professional links with Bologna. In 1610, Micotti had married Lucrezia, the daughter of Federico Balbani.[15] The two families were involved in the silk trade between Lucca, France, and Bologna, and probably had close links with the Bologna Silk Guild, which in 1622 signed its first contract with Guido for the *Triumph of Job* [cat. 44].

The painting alludes to the legendary foundation of the Basilica of Santa Maria Maggiore in Rome, recognisable by the shadowy outlines of Trajan's Column and the Pantheon; in the foreground, the Virgin and Child, surrounded by angels, appear to Saints Lucy and Mary Magdalene, who are identifiable by their traditional attributes (eyes and a perfume flask, respectively). Above them, a cherub lying on a thick grey cloud scatters snow over the Esquiline Hill, where – after a miraculous vision – Pope Liberius is said to have marked out the boundaries of the new basilica. The choice of theme recalls the founding, in 1606, of the Congregazione della Neve in the church of Santa Maria Corteorlandini; the new order, founded by Giovanni Leonardi, was

devoted to the religious education of affluent young men, and was financed by frequent donations from the merchant families of Lucca.[16] The Order reflected Leonardi's own links with Pope Paul V, for whom he wrote a report on church reform in 1605.

The composition is similar in many respects to that of the *Virgin and Child with Saint Joseph and Saint Teresa of Avila* on the main altar of the Carmelite church of Santa Teresa in Caprarola, commissioned by Cardinal Odoardo Farnese (1573–1626). Since Reni was paid an advance of 100 ducats for this painting in June 1624, we may assume that the general design would have been completed not long after the *Madonna della Neve*.[17] In both pictures, the *sacra conversazione* is represented in a subdued pyramidal structure; the eye travels downwards from the Virgin and Child at the apex to the two saints, whose symmetrical position at the base echoes sixteenth-century compositions. The similarity between the two paintings is heightened, in the upper section, by Reni's almost identical treatment of the Virgin and Child, his hand raised in benediction. Borea saw in this gesture of blessing a modern re-reading of the ancient *Salus Populi Romani* icon, which in 1613 was placed in the new Borghese chapel at Santa Maria Maggiore, in whose decoration Guido had also taken part.[18] This would account for the discrepancy in style between the softness of the drapery and the tonal iridescence of the lower part and the more rigid forms in the upper section, perhaps intended as a deliberate allusion to the ancient image. The figure of the Virgin stands out against the golden oval formed by the surrounding cherubim, their faces transfigured by heavenly light, heightening the harmony of a celestial apparition amidst the clouds whose incorporeal consistency they seem to share. The angels on either side, in an attitude of adoring prayer, were to reappear in the late 1620s, in paintings whose structure was even more hieratic and tightly controlled, such as the *Immaculate Conception* of 1627 in New York,[19] in which Reni simplified the composition by removing the two half-length angels present in the *Madonna della Neve*. In both cases, the angels – engaging symmetrically with the Virgin – introduce a range of cold, shimmering colours that contrast with the background glow and the enamelled flesh, underlining the archaic aspect of the vision.

Giulia Iseppi

1 Lucca, Museo Nazionale di Villa Guinigi, inv. 20.
2 Dézallier D'Argenville 1762, 2:207; Cochin 1769, 3:XVI, 98; Lalande 1786, 3:444.
3 Grammatica 1741, 207–8; Marcello Oretti, *Notizie de' Professori del Disegno da Cimabue in qua*, manuscript, Bologna, Biblioteca comunale dell'Archiginnasio, Ms B 126, IV, 262; Mansi–Barsocchini 1836, 188.
4 Nannini 2005, 129–30.
5 S. Meloni Trkulja in Bertolini Campetti and Meloni Trkulja 1968, 211, no. 200; Nannini 2005, 132–33.
6 Nannini 2005, 129–30.
7 Borea 1975, 137–41, no. 99; Pepper 1988, 345, A4.
8 Marchiò 1721, 293; Trenta 1820, 112; Trenta–Mazzarosa 1829, 113.
9 Boehn 1910, 101; Baccheschi 1971, 116, VIII; Borea 1975, 139; Pepper 1988, 345, A4.
10 Belli Barsali 1953, 130 and 252; Belli Barsali 1970, 180–81.
11 Borea 1975, 138.
12 Ibid.: *Visitationes*. However, no documentary reference is provided regarding the visit; the data on Franciotti is erroneous; the information is to be found in the Biblioteca Statale di Lucca, Ms 1112, fols. 484–539; Del Gallo 1998.
13 Evelina Borea (1975, 138–39) transcribes the passage from a *Liber primus decretorum congregationium*, but provides no documentary reference; however, Giuseppe Valentino Baroni (18th century, fol. 535) states that on 16 June 1626 Clemenza, the widow of Dionigi Micotti, was buried in 'their' tomb facing the della Neve altar, belonging to the family.
14 Borea 1975, 138 (*Liber primus decretorum*, no documentary reference).
15 Giuseppe Valentino Baroni (18th century, fols. 533–35) transcribes part of the book entitled *Memorie di me Giuliano Micotti principiato in settembre 1608* which Borea (1975) regarded as lost, but which was subsequently located in the Archivio di Stato de Lucca, Fondi Speciali, S. Maria in Corteorlandini, no. 190.
16 Erra 1759–60 (1759), 1:134.
17 Carloni 2004.
18 Borea 1975, 140.
19 New York, The Metropolitan Museum of Art, Victor Wilbour Memorial Fund, 1959, 59.32.

Cat. 54 recto

Cat. 54 verso

54 Guido Reni

Study of Angel at Prayer (recto)
**Angel seated on a Cloud, holding a Piece
of Saint Catherine's Wheel** (verso)

1625–26
Black and white chalk on greenish-grey (faded blue) paper,
327 × 238 mm
Madrid, Museo de la Real Academia de Bellas Artes
de San Fernando, D-1659a and D-1659b

Provenance: Collection of Carlo Maratta; purchased from Rosalía O'Moore,
widow of the painter Andrea Procaccini, 1775.

Selected bibliography: Pérez Sánchez 1972a, 58, figs. 18 and 19; Johnston
1974, 1:166–68, no. 132; Birke 1981, 153, no. 108; V. Birke in Ebert-Schifferer,
Emiliani and Schleier 1988, 381–82, no. B55.

Like the *Study for Bust of Judith* in Madrid [cat. 77], this sheet
belonged to the collection of the painter Carlo Maratta
(1625– 1713). Together with a *Study of Bust of Angel from Right*,[1]
this *Study of Angel at Prayer* was identified by Alfonso E. Pérez
Sánchez as a preparatory drawing for the monumental *Trinity
adored by Angels* hanging in the church of the Santissima Trinità
dei Pellegrini in Rome [fig. 28].[2]

The Trinity altarpiece, commissioned from Guido Reni by
Cardinal Ludovico Ludovisi, the nephew of Pope Gregory XV,
to mark the jubilee of 1625,[3] was not sent to Rome until June
1626.[4] This was not Reni's first commission for the church; over
a decade earlier, between summer and December 1612, Guido
had painted a fresco for the lantern of the cupola showing a
foreshortened *God the Father*.[5]

In the *Trinity* canvas, the livid body of the dead Son hangs on a cross rising out of the globe, his face set in a display of anguish as if he were still alive. Above him, in the same vertical plane, the Father welcomes the faithful and pilgrims with arms outstretched as the dove of the Holy Spirit flutters before him. The horizontal beam of the cross divides the canvas into two contrasting areas of colour – empyrean gold above, earthly blue below – which symbolically complement the concept of the Trinity. The rounded upper part is bordered by flights of cherubim; two angels support the cross, and two young angels kneel in prayer on either side of Christ.

The iconographical element of the worshipping heavenly creatures was added later by Guido at the request of the Confraternità dei Pellegrini.[6] These are the figures represented in the two drawings at the Real Academia de San Fernando in Madrid commented here; specifically, the recto of the sheet on show depicts the angel to the right of Christ on the canvas.

Reni's study for this figure focuses on a meticulous rendering of the drapery wholly covering the angel's body, capturing only the final position of the clasped hands at his breast and omitting both the head and the wings. The artist's emphasis on these features recurs in the other conceptually similar drawing at the Real Academia, the abovementioned *Study of Bust of Angel from Right*. Using the same media – with occasional added highlights in red chalk[7] – it showcases Guido's careful attention when drawing from life. In this case, the generous bust suggests a female model, dressed in a fabric designed to remain stiff, with faceted folds which the artist captures graphically by thickening the black strokes and alternating them with traces in white chalk.

This *Angel at Prayer* shows a similar drawing concept and is a particularly significant example of a lively Neo-Renaissance taste in Reni, who dressed the angel in a costume fashionable at the time of the young Leonardo (1452–1519), from the last two decades of the fifteenth century onwards. Francesco Scannelli was the first to praise Guido's masterly rendering of *panneggiamento* (drapery);[8] subsequently Carlo Cesare Malvasia drew a parallel, in that sense, with Albrecht Dürer (1471–1528), whom he regarded as a key source of inspiration for the Bolognese artist.[9] The painting displays a number of variations in the execution of the drapery with respect to this preparatory study; the most noteworthy is the long furrow running down the angel's left thigh.

The drawing on the verso of the sheet, showing an angel seated on a cloud, holding a fragment of Saint Catherine of Alexandria's wheel, is generally considered an autograph work, but it is not of the same quality as the recto drawing and does not appear to be related to any known painted composition. However, the white patch at the centre and left of the sheet indicates that the paper must have been used in Reni's workshop.

Parenthetically, the Museo del Prado has a drawing[10] from the Pedro Fernández Durán bequest which shows the Santissima Trinità dei Pellegrini altarpiece in its entirety. Hitherto dismissed as an anonymous poor-quality copy of the painting,[11] its graphic style is reminiscent of Reni, suggesting that it might be the work of a pupil of his. Its alleged connection to the painting in Rome may even need to be reviewed. It should be noted, moreover, that the handwritten number '48[0?]' on the sheet signals that the drawing was originally in the so-called Double Numbering collection.[12]

Viviana Farina

1 Madrid, Real Academia de Bellas Artes de San Fernando, D-1658.
2 Pérez Sánchez 1972a, 58, figs. 17–19.
3 Pepper 1988, 256, no. 89.
4 Malvasia–Pericolo 2019, 1:282, note 185.
5 Pepper 1988, 232–33, no. 37 bis; Malvasia–Pericolo 2019, 1:281–82, note 185.
6 Malvasia–Pericolo 2019, 1:282, note 185.
7 V. Birke in Ebert-Schifferer, Emiliani and Schleier 1988, 379–89, no. B54.
8 Scannelli 1657, 85.
9 Malvasia–Pericolo 2019, 1:62, 1:64, and particularly 1:174.
10 Madrid, Museo Nacional del Prado, D-838.
11 Mena Marqués 1983, 138, fig. 580.
12 On this subject, see Prosperi Valenti Rodinò 2012.

55 Guido Reni

The Immaculate Conception

1627
Oil on canvas, 268 × 185.4 cm
New York, The Metropolitan Museum of Art, Victor Wilbour
Memorial Fund, 1959, 59.32

Provenance: Commissioned in Rome for Maria Anna, Infanta of Spain, 1627; Seville cathedral; Horace-François-Bastien Sebastiani de la Porta, Paris; Alexis Delahante, London; George Watson Taylor, Cavendish Square, London, and Erlestoke Mansion, Wiltshire, 1818–32; his sale at Christie's, London, 13 June 1823 (withdrawn); his sale George Robins, Erlestoke, 25 July 1832; with Smith, London, from 1832; Lord Francis Egerton, later 1st Earl of Ellesmere, Bridgewater House, by 1836; the Earls of Ellesmere, Bridgewater House, London, 1857–1944; John Sutherland Egerton, 5th Earl of Ellesmere, Bridgewater House, 1944–46; his sale at Christie's, London, 18 October 1946; David Reder, London, from 1946; with Oscar Klein, New York, 1956–58; with Acquavella, New York, 1958; sold to the Metropolitan Museum of Art, New York, 1959.

Selected bibliography: Malvasia 1678, 2:37; Blanc and Delaborde 1877, 16; Costantini 1928, 181; Friedlaender 1928–29, 222, no. 2; Kurz 1937, 218; Fiocco 1958; Pérez Sánchez 1965a, 169 and 175; Pepper 1968, 366; Hibbard 1969; Baccheschi 1971, 104; Angulo Íñiguez 1983, 161 and 163; Pepper 1984, 31, 256–57, and 261; S. Ebert-Schifferer in Ebert-Schifferer, Emiliani and Schleier 1988, 175–78, no. A-20; Colantuono 1997, 17–20, 22, 54, 109, and 248; Spear 1997, 18, 21, 111, 140–42, 293, 320, and 355; Bayer 2017, 131 and 152, note 11; Japón 2020b, 181–86; Eclercy 2022a, 102–3, no. 12; Eclercy 2022b, 30–34; Japón 2022b, 116.

This painting is the only recorded commission from the Spanish Crown that Guido Reni actually produced and delivered. In 1627, he agreed to paint an Immaculate Conception for the Infanta Maria Anna of Spain, the sister of Philip IV. The commission probably came to him through the Spanish ambassador to the Holy See, Íñigo Vélez de Guevara y Tassis, 5th Count of Oñate, though the intermediary could also have been Fernando Álvarez de Toledo y Beaumont, 7th Constable of Navarre.[1] In a letter to Antonio Galeazzo Fibbia dated August 1627, Reni wrote that he was in Rome, working on several pictures, among them this *Immaculate Conception*, a fresco on the same theme for an altar at St Peter's in the Vatican, and a smaller picture for the latter nobleman.[2] The sources suggest that the envoy, whoever he was, played a major role in the commission, almost triggering a diplomatic incident. In his *Felsina pittrice* (1678), Carlo Cesare Malvasia recounts that his over-frequent and somewhat impatient visits to Guido's studio eventually drove the artist to despair. Once the painting was completed, Reni was informed that payment might be delayed; in a fit of pique, he promptly sent the picture to Bologna, and also spread word around Rome of his quarrel with the Spanish envoy. He then returned to Bologna, leaving the fresco for St Peter's unfinished. In a bid to settle the dispute, Pope Urban VIII – who was familiar with, and tolerant of, Guido's idiosyncrasies – stepped in and arranged for the canvas to be returned to Rome.

Although it is not known how the picture was brought to Spain, it is widely thought to have reached Seville cathedral shortly after this episode.[3] The decision to place it there may have reflected the infanta's close ties with the then archbishop of Seville, Diego de Guzmán y Haro, who had acted as her tutor and accompanied her to Italy in 1631 on the occasion of her marriage to Ferdinand III, Holy Roman Emperor.[4] However, there is no record of the picture in any of the inventories either of the Spanish royal collection or of the cathedral itself, which does have a poor-quality copy sometimes adduced as proof that the original was once there. Given their close relationship, the painting may have been a personal gift from the infanta to the archbishop, rather than to the cathedral chapter; it could therefore have hung in his palace in Seville. The absence of records may signify that this large-format picture was used, in the manner of a *quadro riportato*, to decorate one of the ceilings in the palace, much like a canvas of the *Assumption of the Virgin* which has adorned the ceiling of the nuncio's ante-oratory in the same building since the 1660s.[5]

There is a further partial copy of this *Immaculate Conception* in the archbishop's palace, in which the Virgin's mantle features a kind of floral print, another attribute associated with this devotion.[6] These two are by no means the only copies recorded in and around Seville; many other reproductions and variants have survived, showing that this model was greatly admired both by the public and by local painters. In the seventeenth century, Seville spearheaded the defence of the doctrine of the Immaculate Conception, a fact which may also have influenced the infanta's decision.[7]

Though lacking in technical excellence, these reproductions help to explain the widespread popularity of Reni's model, on which Seville's leading artists – among them Francisco de

Zurbarán (1598–1664) and Bartolomé Esteban Murillo (1617–1682) – would later base their own compositions.[8] Murillo, in particular, made use of it in creating a hugely successful devotional image, though adopting a more naturalistic approach and introducing certain distinctive features that would more readily chime with the sensibilities of the Spanish public.[9]

Certain elements – including the strictly frontal depiction of the figure, the golden background glow, and the compositional simplicity – give the original an icon-like appearance. Guido may have been inspired by an *Assumption of the Virgin* painted by his first master, Denys Calvaert (c. 1540–1619),[10] in which the central figure is similarly flanked by two angels. Reni had used this device two years earlier in the *Trinity adored by Angels* for the church of Santissima Trinità dei Pellegrini in Rome [fig. 28][11] and in the *Virgin and Child with Saint Joseph and Saint Teresa of Avila* in the church of Santa Teresa in Caprarola, also painted around 1627.[12] In assimilating and streamlining his master's model, Guido reduced the background figures in order to increase the depth of the glory of angels and modified the direction of Mary's gaze, lightening her posture and enhancing the sense of ascent. He also changed the position of her hands: in Calvaert's painting they are folded on her breast, while here they are clasped in prayer. Reni was more faithful to Calvaert's composition in other works, as in the *Assumption* in the church of Gesù e dei Santi Ambrogio e Andrea in Genoa, and the *Immaculate Conception* in the church of San Biagio in Forlì, the latter painted around 1623. Although barely four years had passed since the Forlì picture, the evolution towards a more vibrant style is already apparent in the drapery, modelled in the New York painting with greater balance and a lightness of touch perhaps influenced by the sculptures of Gian Lorenzo Bernini (1598–1680).[13]

Rafael Japón

1 Pierguidi 2019b. The intermediary might also have been Fernando Afán Enríquez de Ribera, 3rd Duke of Alcalá; see S. Ebert-Schifferer in Ebert-Schifferer, Emiliani and Schleier 1988, 175, no. A-20. On this commission, see also Sefano Pierguidi's essay, 'Viceroys, Ambassadors, Agents, Theologians: Thirty Years of (Stormy) Relations between Guido Reni and Spain', in this catalogue.
2 Letter published in Bottari and Ticozzi 1822–25 (1822), 1:296–97; García Cueto 2016a, 284–88.
3 Its location is specified in the catalogue of paintings on sale at Christie's, London, in 1823, where it is confused with an *Assumption of the Virgin* (Catalogue 1823, 8, lot 65: 'The Assumption of The Virgin, with Two attendant Angels. A beautiful display of the clearness and brilliancy of Guido's tone, and the extreme delicacy of his pencil. This grand chef d'oeuvre is from the Cathedral at Seville').
4 Pierguidi 2019b, 85.
5 Japón 2020a, 1:566.
6 The painting was published by S. Ebert-Schifferer in Ebert-Schifferer, Emiliani and Schleier 1988, 176, no. A-20.
7 Maria Anna's decision to commission a painting displaying this iconography is thought to reflect the importance attached to the doctrine of the Immaculate Conception by Pope Urban VIII, who in 1626 had consecrated the church of Santa Maria della Concezione dei Cappuccini in Rome; see S. Ebert-Schifferer in Ebert-Schifferer, Emiliani and Schleier 1988, 176.
8 From the early twentieth century onwards, international critics have highlighted the direct influence of this painting on Sevillian painters' versions of the Immaculate Conception; see, for example, Friedlaender 1928–29, 222.
9 Angulo Íñiguez 1983, 161–63; Pérez Sánchez 1988, 700–2; Japón 2020b, 181–86.
10 Bologna, Pinacoteca Nazionale di Bologna, inv. 7616.
11 Hibbard 1969, 21.
12 Malvasia–Pericolo 2019, 1:293, note 211.
13 Schlegel 1985, 125.

56 Bartolomé Esteban Murillo
(Seville 1617–1682)

The Immaculate Conception of El Escorial

c. 1665
Oil on canvas, 206 × 144 cm
Madrid, Museo Nacional del Prado, P-972

Provenance: Spanish royal collection, Casita del Príncipe, El Escorial, 1778; Palacio de Aranjuez, 1809; Palacio Real, Madrid, 1814–18 (no. 1001?); Museo del Prado, Madrid, 1819.

Selected bibliography: Ceán Bermúdez 1800, 2:64; Madrazo 1884, 187; Mayer 1913, no. 74; Tormo 1914, 174; Mayer 1936, 46; Angulo Íñiguez 1981, 2:121; M. Mena Marqués in Mena Marqués 1982, 166–67, no. 31; Ayala Mallory 1983, 43, 46, and 65; *Museo del Prado* 1985, 449; *Museo del Prado* 1990, 1:79, no. 229; Brown 1998, 223; Valdivieso 2010, 372–73, no. 151; Checa Cremades 2016, 247–48; A. Aterido Fernández in Cano Rivero and Muñoz Rubio 2018, 221–23, no. 21.

Bartolomé Esteban Murillo's versions of the Immaculate Conception were among his greatest iconographic successes. His treatment of the subject met with public acclaim, not only for the tender beauty of his figures but also because his interpretations were perfectly in tune with the groundswell of popular devotion in the seventeenth century. In Seville, as elsewhere in Catholic Europe, the belief that Mary was free of original sin from the moment of her conception sparked lively debate, since it was not shared by all religious orders. While the Dominicans remained sceptical, Franciscans and Jesuits insisted that this belief should be elevated into a dogma, mobilising the people of Seville and turning their cause into a national issue. Copious use was made of cultural resources in a bid to convince the faithful by appealing to their senses: literary competitions led to catchy hymns, while countless images of the Immaculate Conception were commissioned.

While this theme first emerged in Italy and Spain in the sixteenth century, compositions became increasingly simplified over the following century, culminating in the approach adopted by Murillo. Complex allegories intended to account for Mary's purity by reference to the genealogy of Jesus Christ – as in some of the paintings by Giorgio Vasari (1511–1574) and Luis de Vargas (c. 1505–1567) – gave way to models in which Mary was associated with the Woman of the Apocalypse referred to by Saint John, and with the attributes mentioned in the Lauretan litanies. During the early seventeenth century, a number of artists developed a standard representation based on these features. Chief among them was Francisco Pacheco (1564–1644), whose *Arte de la pintura* (1649) laid down the canonical treatment of this subject. Murillo followed some of his recommendations – such as the colour of Mary's clothes and the moon beneath her feet – but gradually reduced the number of elements associated with her, relegating them to the gold-tinged celestial background.

Murillo's model indicates a familiarity not just with the iconographic tradition of the Seville school but also with the work of certain Italian masters, some of whose canvases he was able to examine. In his *Immaculate Conception* known as *La Colosal* painted for the now-demolished convent church of San Francisco in Seville,[1] echoes can be discerned of the version produced by Jusepe de Ribera (1591–1652) for the Augustinian church of La Purísima Concepción in Salamanca [figs. 3 Pierguidi and 22.1]. In addition, he also made use of an engraving by Simone Catarini (1612–1648) of the *Assumption and Coronation of the Virgin*.[2] Murillo thus displayed his admiration for the work of certain contemporary foreign artists, combining their compositions in new ways.

That said, the painting which most influenced his development of this theme was Guido Reni's *Immaculate Conception* now in the Metropolitan Museum, New York [cat. 55], which may well have hung in Seville cathedral in the seventeenth century.[3] Comparison of Reni's painting with this canvas by Murillo reveals similarities both in the positioning of the central figure – Mary stands, one knee advanced, on a crescent moon – and in her facial expression. An even stronger resemblance to Guido's painting is apparent in Murillo's *Immaculate Conception* in the oratory of San Felipe Neri in Cádiz, which includes the crown of stars against a very bright background, as well as the group of angels. However, Murillo went on to introduce a number of elements intended to engage more directly with the devotional surge in Spain, and perhaps even to ensure greater decorum; in all instances, for instance, he covered the Virgin's feet. Before the Sevillian provenance of Reni's painting was established, August L. Mayer pointed out that the upper section of Murillo's *Aranjuez Immaculate Conception*[4] was similar to Reni's *Assumption of the Virgin* then in the

Gemäldegalerie at the Vienna Kunsthistorisches Museum.[5] Later, Alfonso E. Pérez Sánchez once again noted the direct influence of a version by Reni in the church of San Biagio in Forlì on an *Immaculate Conception* by Murillo now in the Ishizuka collection, Tokyo.[6]

The *Immaculate Conception of El Escorial* is so called because it hung in the Casita de Príncipe (Prince's House), part of the El Escorial monastery complex, around 1787, following its acquisition – probably in Seville – by Charles IV. It is thought to have belonged previously either to the cabinetmaker Baltasar Angelo or to the naturalist Pedro Franco Dávila (1711–1786).[7] The painting can be reliably dated to around 1665, shortly after Pope Alexander VII issued two papal bulls in favour of the dogma, as a result of which Murillo received numerous commissions.

In order to meet demand and avoid repeating a single composition in the same city, the artist opted to produce a series of variations on a standard design.

Rafael Japón

1 Seville, Museo de Bellas Artes, CE0118P.
2 Japón 2020a, 1:613 and 1:618.
3 Hibbard 1969, 20–21.
4 Madrid, Museo Nacional del Prado, P-974.
5 Mayer 1936, 46. This painting was in fact a copy of a fragment of the *Assumption* in the church of Gesù e dei Santi Ambrogio e Andrea in Genoa.
6 A. E. Pérez Sánchez in Ebert-Schifferer, Emiliani and Schleier 1988, 718, no. D-62.
7 Juan Agustín Ceán Bermúdez (1800, 2:64) identified it as the painting purchased by the king in Seville, together with a *Saint Jerome* of the same size and a small *Saint Joseph*; Urriagli Serrano 2012, 197, no. 297.

VIII

BODIES AND DESIRE:
THE SENSUALITY OF THE NUDE

Guido Reni painted a number of male and female nudes in the course of his career, almost always within the framework of stories from classical mythology. In doing so, he made use both of life studies and of ancient statues. Some of the pupils at his studio would pose for him, and he occasionally used female models too. Nowhere is his masterly rendering of the beautiful naked body better displayed than in works like *Hippomenes and Atalanta* [cat. 61–62], where the superb anatomies of the young couple are captured at a moment of sensual interaction. Guido's more serene portrayal of *Bacchus and Ariadne* [cat. 58] contrasts sharply with the expressive force attained in *Apollo and Marsyas* [cat. 57], where his interpretation of the mythological account involves a violent confrontation between a beautiful male body and its coarser counterpart. Reni himself is widely assumed to have remained a virgin, having renounced all sexual relations. Although that renunciation might be viewed, from a modern perspective, as a symptom of repressed homosexuality, Guido was regarded in his day as an angelic being, a man who – like his art – was not entirely of this world.

57   Guido Reni

Apollo and Marsyas

c. 1621
Oil on canvas, 226 × 175 cm
Toulouse, Musée des Augustins, inv. 2004 1 45

Provenance: Bequeathed by Cardinal Alessandro d'Este to Cardinal Maurice of Savoy in 1624; mentioned in the Galleria Ducale of Turin in 1635; confiscated by the French and sent to Paris in 1799; sent to Toulouse as a state gift in 1803.

Selected bibliography: Cavalli 1955, 72, no. 47; Baccheschi 1971, 100, no. 103a; Pepper 1988, 244, no. 63; Malvasia–Pericolo 2019, 1:521, note 81, H. Aurenhammer in Eclercy 2022a, 242–43, no. 99.

In his testament of 11 May 1624, Cardinal Alessandro d'Este (1568–1624) expressed his wish to leave 'to Signor Prince Cardinal of Savoy the painting where Marsyas is depicted by Guido Reni'.[1] Reference is made here to Cardinal Maurice of Savoy (1593–1657). In the 1635 inventory of the paintings on display in the ducal gallery of Turin, there is already mention of

Fig. 84 Guido Reni, *Apollo and Marsyas*. Oil on canvas, 227 × 167 cm. Private collection

a 'Marsyas flayed by Apollo, full-length figures, by Guido Reni'.[2] During his visit to Turin of 1749, the French engraver Charles-Nicolas Cochin (1715–1790) saw Guido's painting in the gallery of the then Royal Palace, noting: 'The figure of Apollo is only sketched out in monochrome'.[3] Similarly, the French astronomer and writer Joseph-Jérôme Lefrançois de Lalande (1732–1807) observed during his visit to Turin in 1765 that the figure of Apollo was 'in monochrome' and 'unfinished'.[4] The painting stayed in the royal collection in Turin until it was confiscated by the French army and sent to Paris in 1799. From there, it was subsequently shipped to Toulouse.[5]

No doubt, the Toulouse painting is an original by Guido, although it is very difficult to assess its high quality for it needs urgent cleaning and perhaps restoration. It is also difficult to ascertain whether Cochin and Lalande were right in stressing that the figure of Apollo was only blocked out, and thus unfinished. Certainly, the Marsyas seems to be more 'achieved' than the Apollo, but this might have been deliberate on Guido's part. In fact, the figure of Apollo, despite the grime that obscures it, is a beautiful example of Guido's ability to play with the dark priming through layers of fluid and quasi-diaphanous pigments. This technique is already to be seen in works executed in 1619–20, such as the *Risen Christ embracing the Cross* now in the National Museum of Art MUŻA in Valletta [fig. 15], although the Apollo in the Toulouse painting bears a greater resemblance with the angel in Guido's 1621 *Annunciation*, now in the Pinacoteca e Museo Civico Malatestiano in Fano.[6] Not familiar with Guido's style as developed in these works, Cochin and Lalande might have misjudged the painting's degree of finish.

A second version of Guido's *Apollo and Marsyas* belonged to the collection of Diego Messía Felípez de Guzmán, 1st Marquis of Leganés (1580–1655), and is listed in the 1642 inventory of his paintings without the name of the author: 'Another [work] of two naked figures with their instruments, one flaying the other, three *varas* high and two *varas* wide'.[7] Although the measurements are slightly inaccurate – just an approximation – this painting can be identified with an *Apollo and Marsyas* that was for sale on the Madrid art market in 2005 [fig. 84]. Measuring 227 × 167 centimetres, this work is almost identical in size with the Toulouse painting. Further examination will be necessary to establish whether it is by Guido, his workshop, or both. Leganés certainly purchased it in Italy during his stay there between 1635 and 1641.

Sometime around 1630, Guido produced a completely different version of this subject. In his *Maraviglie dell'arte* (1648), the painter and art biographer Carlo Ridolfi (1594–1658) relates that the Flemish painter Nicolas Régnier (1591–1667) owned an

Fig. 85 Antonio Tempesta, *Apollo and Marsyas*, 1606. Etching on paper, 101 × 117 mm. New York, The Metropolitan Museum of Art, The Elisha Whittelsey Collection, The Elisha Whittelsey Fund, 1951, inv. 51.501.3909

'Apollo flaying Marsyas … life-size, of [Guido's] best manner'.[8] Because the painting does not appear in the list of works that Régnier intended to offer at a lottery in 1666, it is likely that it was already sold by that time. On 8 October 1677, Prince Karl Eusebius of Liechtenstein (1611–1684) purchased from the painter Johannes Spielberg (1619–1690) a most expensive work by Guido, a 'Marsyas flayed by Phoebus [Apollo], slightly smaller than life-size, original'.[9] This is likely to be the *Apollo and Marsyas* now in Munich.[10] Whether the painting in the Liechtenstein collection was the same as the one with Régnier remains unclear.

Apollo's act of flaying Marsyas alive was rarely represented in painting at the time Guido executed his Toulouse work. Commonly dated to 1616–20, Bartolomeo Manfredi's (1582–1622) *Apollo and Marsyas* now in Saint Louis[11] does evoke the moment when the Olympian god ruthlessly cuts into the satyr's skin, but the format (horizontal) and the tight framing of the figures – a little bit over half-length – differs substantially from Guido's invention.[12] Most likely, Guido drew inspiration from an etching (1606) by Antonio Tempesta (1555–1630) which illustrates this famous episode of Ovid's *Metamorphoses* [fig. 85]. In the print, Apollo stands to the left, an ample drapery encircling his torso and thighs, his shaded face bent in concentration even as he is about to plunge the blade into Marsyas' upper torso. With

ingenuity, Guido grants the satyr human figure, intensifying the impression of the pain dispensed by Apollo's almost surgical performance upon a stretched flap of skin: a detail that creates the equivalent of a bloody rip on the canvas. By interlacing the two figures in a single action – Apollo's left lower limb wedges itself between Marsyas' spread legs – Guido accentuates the sensual shocking contact between the god's poised body, delicately brushed and almost ethereal, and the defeated satyr's writhing figure, rendered with a thicker impasto as if to magnify his tactility. As usual in Guido, the action appears frozen in time, Apollo almost caught in contemplation in the midst of his cruel performance. The artist's insistence on representing male nudity is undoubtedly bold, and perhaps even provocative. The allusion, of course, is to ancient sculpture, and it is possible that, in conceiving the painting, he intentionally aimed to deliver the pictorial counterpart to a sculptural group. It is unclear whether such groups existed as early as the 1620s. It is known that Vincenzo Giustiniani paired an ancient statue of an Apollo that triumphantly wields a flayed skin with that of a skinless Marsyas attached to a trunk.[13] A similar group was on display later in the Chigi collection, Rome, and is reproduced in a print of 1808 by Christian Friedrich Stölzel (1751–1815) – the two statues were subsequently disassembled in Dresden (Antikensammlungen) and the seventeenth-century additions removed.[14] Although this group was created by Baldassare Mari only in 1663 by using fragments of ancient sculptures, it is not impossible that similar arrangements existed earlier.[15]

Lorenzo Pericolo

1 Cremonini 1998, 129: 'Al S[ign]or Prencipe Cardinal di Savoia il quadro sul quale è Martia fatto da Guido Reni'.
2 Baudi di Vesme 1897, 48, no. 335: 'Martia scorticato da Apollo, figure intere, di Guido Reni'.
3 Cochin 1769, 1:10: 'L'Apollon n'est qu'ébauché de grisaille'.
4 Lalande 1769, 1:81: 'L'Apollon est de grisaille et n'est point fini'.
5 Baudi di Vesme 1897, 22.
6 For these works, see Malvasia–Pericolo 2019, 1:428–29, note 636, and 1:339–40, note 338, respectively.
7 Pérez Preciado 2010, 619–20, no. 981: 'otra de dos figuras desnudas con sus ynstrumentos que esta desollando el uno al otro, tiene de alto tres varas y de ancho dos'.
8 Ridolfi 1648, 2:48: 'E Apollo, che scortica Marsia, pure al naturale, della stessa mano della miglior sua maniera'.
9 Fleischer 1910, 55, no. 2: 'ein Stuckh von Quido Reno, wie Marsias vom Phoebo geschunden wirdt, etwas Kleiner als das Leben, orig[inal]'.
10 Munich, Alte Pinakothek, inv. 513. On the painting, see Malvasia–Pericolo 2019, 1:521, note 81.
11 Saint Louis (Missouri), Saint Louis Art Museum, inv. 62:2004.
12 On Manfredi's *Apollo and Marsyas*, see Hartje 2004, 344–47, no. A25.
13 Fusconi 2001, 221–26, no. 14.
14 Becker 1804–11 (1808), 2:89–91, no. LVIII.
15 Sparti 1998b, 73.

58 Guido Reni

Bacchus and Ariadne

c. 1617–19
Oil on canvas, 222.5 × 147 cm
Private collection

Provenance: Luigi Zambeccari, Bologna, prior to 1630; inherited by his second son Francesco Maria Zambeccari, thence by descent to Giuseppe Luigi; sold, through the painter Marcantonio Franceschini, to Prince Johann Adam Andreas of Liechtenstein in January 1700; Stadtpalais Liechtenstein gallery, Vienna, until 1807; transferred to the Gartenpalais in Rossau, Vienna, until 1920; sold that year by Prince Johann II, with a further twenty-four pictures from the collection, to the Viennese antiquarian Glückselig; Switzerland, private collection.

Selected bibliography: C. Bentivoglio in Giacobbi 1632, 41; Fanti 1767, 82, no. 407; *Description des tableaux* 1780, 225–26, no. 680; *Catalogus* 1807, no. 43; Dallinger 1807, no. 292; Malvasia–Zanotti 1841, 2:33; Waagen 1866–67 (1866), 1:262; Falke 1873, no. 16; Falke 1885, no. 3.

In the life of Guido Reni in his *Felsina pittrice* (1678),[1] Carlo Cesare Malvasia identifies the Zambeccari family, hailing from the 'da Reno' district of Bologna,[2] as major clients of the leading Bolognese painter of the day. Through the good offices of Bartolomeo Belcollare[3] – who before entering Reni's service had been a 'domestic' in the Zambeccari household – Luigi Zambeccari (1570–1630) was able to acquire four half-length figures of saints from the master. This acquisition took place 'after having had him finish, again at a good price, the *Ariadne* and the *Samson*, both very famous paintings'.[4] Though not explicitly mentioned in the inventory of Luigi – who died of the plague in 1630[5] – the latter are clearly listed, side by side, in the 1649 inventory of his heir Francesco Maria (1607–1649): 'A painting by Signor Guido with an Ariana, in a gilt frame / A Samson by the same, over the chimney-breast'.[6] Thanks to Gian Piero Cammarota's painstaking transcription of the original documents for his comprehensive study for *Le origini della Pinacoteca Nazionale di Bologna*, we are now able to track the movements of both pictures by Reni which, on the untimely death of Francesco Maria, were inherited – together with the entire family estate – by the very young Giuseppe Luigi (1637–1699).[7] As early as 1664, the *Samson Victorious* [fig. 14] was put up for sale by Giuseppe Luigi (or his tutors), its place in the palace being taken by a copy made by Antonio Catalani, il Romano (c. 1590–1666).[8] But *Bacchus and Ariadne* remained in the collection until 1699 – the year Giuseppe Luigi died – when it was sold for 400 lire. According to the inventory: 'In the Great Hall upstairs', beside the copy of *Samson* occupying the place where

the original had hung over the chimney-breast, was 'An Ariana by the hand of Signor Guido Reni with its gilt frame, and canvas, and this was sold for L 400'.[9] Here again, before selling the original the family commissioned a reproduction, also recorded in the 1699 inventory ('In a Room adjoining that Hall …: A copy of the Ariadne, unframed, L. 12');[10] the copy was still in the Zambeccari palace in the eighteenth century,[11] when it was seen there by Charles-Nicolas Cochin.[12] This replacement copy may well be the painting donated – as part of the Corsi collection – to the city of Florence in 1938; the collection now occupies the upper floors of the Museo Bardini.[13]

According to Cammarota,[14] the sale of the Zambeccari *Bacchus and Ariadne* took place between March and August 1699. On 9 September 1699, the painter Marcantonio Franceschini (1648–1729), who from 1693 to 1702 acted as art dealer for Prince Johann Adam Andreas of Liechtenstein (1657–1712),[15] informed the prince that he had restored, on behalf of a certain Benedetto Donelli,[16]

a painting by Guido Reni, which had suffered some blistering, and with great diligence I sought to remedy it …, and since the painting is in the best style of the said master, and an authentic original, I thought it appropriate to persuade its owner to sell it, with the intention of having it purchased by Y[our] S[erene] H[ighness] …. In the painting are Arrianna [sic] and Bacchus, figures even larger than life-size, Ariadne is depicted full-length and nude; since Bacchus is shown in a lower plane, his legs are not visible; the painting is four feet wide, and six feet high in our measurements …. The style, as I have said, is that of the best Guido, and it may be said to be well preserved, for there is now no noticeable defect.[17]

Having obtained the Prince's agreement to purchase it for '160 doppie' (320 gold ducats), Franceschini personally packed and shipped the painting, safe in the conviction that he had satisfied his illustrious client by 'preserving the colour, the good taste and the strength' of the work.[18] Franceschini's restoration must have involved consolidating the paint surface (apparent here in the pressure to which the colour layers were subjected), stuccoing lacunae (especially near Ariadne's feet and Bacchus' hand and torso), and working on the colour intersections. Once the over-paint had been removed, during recent meticulous restorations the stucco was stripped and replaced prior to being reintegrated using tempera and watercolour.[19]

In Vienna, the painting was placed in the 'Seventh Room' in the Stadtpalais Liechtenstein gallery: 'Bacchus and Ariadne on the Island of Naxos, by the sea'[20] was flanked by two superb bronze reliefs by Massimiliano Soldani Benzi (1656–1740), today still in the Prince's collection.[21] In 1807, the canvas was transferred, along with the entire collection, to the Gartenpalais in Rossau, Vienna.[22] It remained there until 1920,[23] when Prince Johann II (1840–1929) – driven by a stern sense of moral rectitude – sold it, together with twenty-four other works he regarded as lewd or indecent, to the Viennese antiquarian Glückselig, who sold them on to collectors and other antique dealers.[24]

The picture depicts Ariadne, daughter of King Minos of Crete, on the rocky island of Naxos, where Theseus had abandoned her while she slept; beside her stands Bacchus (holding in one hand the thyrsus wrapped in vine leaves), drawn to the island by her lament. Unlike the famous painting by Titian (c. 1488–1576), in which Bacchus is accompanied by a group of satyrs and bacchantes,[25] here the essence of the myth is conveyed through the two isolated figures, captured at the start of a dialogue expressed through exchanged looks and opposing gestures. In the background, where the horizon line symmetrically separates the dark sky from the sea and the shadowy rocks, the sails of the fugitives' boats can be made out. The chromatic interplay between the light-bathed figures and the faint glow of dawn creeping over the horizon enhances the statuesque elegance of the two bodies, heightening the contrast not only in their poses, but also in their expressions and flesh tones: between Ariadne's pale, flawless complexion and the amber, lightly-modelled skin of Bacchus. In its compositional rigour, the painting reflects the sober account in Ovid's *Metamorphoses*;[26] at the same time, as a number of critics have suggested,[27] Reni's considerable interest in the theme[28] may also be linked to the success of Claudio Monteverdi's melodramatic opera *Lamento di Arianna*, composed in Mantua on 28 May 1608 for the wedding of Francesco Gonzaga and Margherita of Savoy, to which Guido adds his personal interpretation of the essential setting (the two main figures were placed 'on a steep cliff in the midst of the waves'[29]).

The finding of this major painting is a significant addition to Reni's oeuvre, dating from a stage in his career when the quest for a certain type of ideal beauty inspired by ancient sculpture was subordinate to the expressive requirements of the narrative. The exceptional balance of colour and composition accounts for

its success in Bolognese intellectual circles. Carlo Bentivoglio, 'accademico Ardito', dedicated a sonnet to the *Ariăna* [sic] *di Guido Reni in casa del Sig. Francesco Maria Zambeccari*, which effectively highlights the heroine's emotional conflict.[30] The rediscovery of this canvas also clears up certain misinterpretations of Carlo Cesare Malvasia's references to the painting.[31] Given the obvious similarities in style, composition, and colour range, this canvas must have been produced at around the same time as the *Samson Victorious* now in the Pinacoteca Nazionale di Bologna, the two versions of *Hippomenes and Atalanta* at the Museo di Capodimonte and the Prado [cat. 61 and 62] and the *Saint Sebastian* also at the Prado [cat. 19].[32] This places the execution of this *Bacchus and Ariadne* roughly between 1617 and 1619.

Mauro Natale

1 Malvasia–Zanotti 1841, 2:33; Malvasia–Pericolo 2019, 1:104.

2 Cammarota 2001, 26; see also Emiliani 1973; D'Amico 1979; Morselli 1997, 1998, and 2001; Clerici Bagozzi 2014.

3 Malvasia–Pericolo 2019, 1:332, note 310, and 1:318, note 279.

4 Malvasia–Zanotti 1841, 33; Malvasia–Pericolo 2019, 1:104–5: 'dopo avergli fatto lavorare prima a buon prezzo l'Arianna ed il Sansone, quadri tanto famosi'.

5 They were probably among a group of 'Nove quadri tra grandi e piccoli … di mano del Signor Guido Reni' ('Nine pictures, between large and small … by the hand of Signor Guido Reni') recorded en bloc in a room in the Palazzo on Via Santa Maria Maggiore: Cammarota 2001, 26.

6 Ibid., 119, notes 13 and 14: 'Un quadro del Signor Guido con un'Ariana cornisado d'oro / Un Sansone del detto sopra la Fuga'.

7 Ibid., 26.

8 Ibid., 138–45: Inventory of Giuseppe Luigi Zambeccari, 1699, Bologna, Palazzo on Santa Maria Maggiore (quoted in Morselli 1997, 142, note 884). On the famous painting in the Pinacoteca Nazionale, see the excellent catalogue entry by A. Stanzani in Bentini et al. 2008, 62–66, no. 33; Malvasia–Pericolo 2019, 1:318–19, note 279. On the breaking-up of the Bologna collections in the late seventeenth century, see Morselli 2001; on the copies of works by Guido Reni, see Morselli 1992; Bonfait 2000.

9 Cammarota 2001, 142, note 46; Malvasia–Pericolo 2019, 1:332–33, note 311: 'Nella Sala Grande di sopra … Un' Ariana mano del Signor Guido Reni con sua cornice dorata, e tela, e questa venduta per L 400'.

10 Cammarota 2001, 144, no. 64: 'In una Camera annessa a detta Sala …: Una copia dell'Ariana, senza cornice L.12'.

11 Ibid., 168–79: Inventory of Francesco Maria Zambeccari, 1752, 176, no. 106: 'Un quadro che rappresenta Ariana, e Bacco senza Cornice Scuola di Guido L. 25' ('A picture depicting Ariadne, and Bacchus unframed, School of Guido L. 25'). The painting does not appear in the subsequent inventory of the estate of Giacomo Zambeccari, who died on 7 April 1795: Cammarota 2001, 279–371.

12 Cochin 1759, 2:158: 'Un Bacchus et Ariane, de Gessi, retouché par le Guido'.

13 Florence, Museo Bardini, Donazione Corsi, inv. 1502. Slightly smaller than the original (184 × 151.5 cm), the Florence canvas is – as far as we know – the only version that faithfully reproduces the composition presented here. On the immense Corsi bequest, which has not yet been sufficiently studied as a whole, see Chiodo and Nesi 2011.

14 Cammarota 2001, 119, note 13.

15 Miller 1991, 62.

16 Presumably an invented name, intended to conceal the fact that the work belonged to a family facing financial difficulties.

17 Miller 1991, 243, no. 82: 'Un quadro di Guido Reni, che haveva patito qualche vessica, e con diligenza grande hò procurato farli un preservativo ..., e perché il quadro è della buona maniera di detto maestro, e vero originale, mi è parso bene l'indurre il padrone alla vendita, con pensiero di farlo acquistare a V.A.S. .... Nel quadro vi è Arrianna e Bacco, figure anche più grandi del naturale, l'Arianna figura intiera tutta e nuda, al Bacco, per essere figurato in un piano più basso, non si vedono le gambe; la larghezza del quadro è quattro piedi, e l'altezza sei piedi di nostra misura .... La maniera, come hò detto, è della buona di Guido, e puo dirsi ben conservato, perché adesso non vi si conosce difetto'.

18 Miller 1991, 248, no. 94: 'La conservazione del colore, il buon gusto, e forza', Bologna, 3 March 1770, Franceschini to Prince Hans-Adam I. The negotiations can be followed up in letters dated 3 December 1699 (Miller 1991, 245, no. 88), 6 January 1700 (ibid., 246, no. 89), 21 January 1700 (ibid., 247, no. 90), 17 February 1700 (ibid., 247, no. 92) and 27 February 1700 (ibid., 248, no. 93). The *Libro dei conti di Marcantonio Franceschini* (Miller and Chiodini 2014) makes no reference at all to this transaction.

19 An initial restoration was carried out by Marie Louise Sauerberger and Larry Keith in 2014; a second by Daniele Rossi in 2019.

20 Fanti 1767, 82, no. 407: 'Bacco e Arianna nell'Isola di Nasso, sulla riva del mare'.

21 Zikos 2005.

22 *Catalogus* 1807, no. 43; Dallinger 1807, no. 292.

23 Waagen 1866–67 (1866), 1:262; Falke 1873, no. 16; Falke 1885, no. 3.

24 I am deeply grateful to Dr Arthur Stögmann for providing me with the list of works sold, which is kept in the Liechtenstein archive; the list is headed: '11 VI 1920. Im allerhöchsten Auftrag Seiner Durchlaucht an Glückselig als verkauft übergeben'.

25 *Bacchus and Ariadne*, 1520–23, London, The National Gallery, NG35.

26 Ovid-Bernardini Marzolla 1979, 303 (VIII, 176–79).

27 Rudolph 1974; Morselli 2018a and 2020.

28 Four versions are mentioned by Malvasia and other sources; the identification of the canvas in the Los Angeles County Museum of Art as the painting owned by the Bolognese poet Cesare Rinaldi is entirely hypothetical: Pepper 1983 and 1984, 238–39, no. 66; Malvasia–Pericolo 2019, 1:332–33, note 311; on the *Ariadne* painted by Reni between 1639 and 1640 for Cardinal Francesco Barberini, see Guarino 2002b; Montanari 2004; Guarino and Seccaroni 2018; Morselli 2018c.

29 Federico (Follino 1608, 30) describes the setting of Monteverdi's scene as follows: 'su un alpestre scoglio in mezzo all'onde'.

30 The poem was published in Giacobbi 1632, 41; reproduced in Morselli 2018a, 256. On the composer Giacobbi, editor of the collection of poems in honour of Guido Reni, see Aceto 2000.

31 Pepper 1983, 68 and 74; Pepper 1984, 238–39, no. 66; S. Pepper in Emiliani et al. 1988, 58; Granata 2012, 274.

32 The attribution of the Prado *Saint Sebastian* to Reni is supported by Stephen Pepper (1984, 234, no. 54) and by Gabriele Finaldi (in Boccardo and Salomon 2007, 108–13, no. 5: c. 1617–19); Stéphane Loire has defended the attribution of the Louvre version (inv. 532) to Guido Reni (ibid., 144–47, no. 6). For other treatments of the same subject, see Boccardo and Salomon 2007.

59 Anonymous
Crouching Aphrodite

Mid-2nd century AD (head and body); 17th century (arms)
Marble, 128 × 56 × 54 cm
Madrid, Museo Nacional del Prado, E-33

Provenance: Collection of Cardinal Camillo Massimo, Rome, until 1677; collection of Queen Christina of Sweden, Rome, until 1689; Cardinal Azzolino; collection of Duke Livio Odescalchi, Rome, until 1713; purchased by King Philip V for the Palacio Real de La Granja de San Ildefonso, Segovia, in 1724; Spanish royal collection from then onwards.

Selected bibliography: Hübner [1862] 2008, 52–53, no. 28; Barrón 1908, 47, no. 33; Arslan 1968; Blanco and Lorente 1981, 28–29; B. Cacciotti in Borea and Gasparri 2000, 2:420–21, no. 17; Schröder 1993–2004 (2004), 2:267–70; D. Gasparotto in Settis, Anguissola and Gasparotto 2015, 240, no. 41.

In the fertile history of western art forms, a number of models gradually achieved canonical status; repeated over time, their endurance defied the passing centuries and fleeting fashions. We are not referring, here, to the standardisation of specific iconographical schemes as a means of conveying a given message, but rather to the lasting success of certain forms, certain gestural archetypes, certain compositions conveying an idea readily intelligible to the viewer, which – sanctioned by their use in classical antiquity – came to enjoy unchallenged primacy.

One such composition is the figure of the goddess Aphrodite crouching as she bathes; it is one of those clichés, endlessly re-iterated since it was first introduced in the third century BC, to be found decorating gardens, villas, and public baths, or adorning collectors' galleries. Albeit with certain variations, the piece at the Museo del Prado is based on a sculpture first mentioned in Pliny's *Natural History*, where it is attributed to Doidalsas of Bithynia (act. around 250 BC), but with borrowings from the Rhodes *Venus Anadyomene*, in which the goddess is depicted in a similar posture, though drying her hair as she emerges from the sea.

This sculpture, first recorded in the holdings of Cardinal Camillo Massimo (1620–1677), passed through the collections of Queen Christina of Sweden (1626–1689) and Duke Livio Odescalchi (1652–1713) in the seventeenth century before it was purchased in 1724 by King Philip V and moved to Spain. Interestingly, the earliest references to it date from the start of the sixteenth century, before the upper part of the sculpture was restored. A drawing of the fragment, made around 1514 and now attributed to Andrea Solario (c. 1465–1524), is preserved at the Galleria dell'Accademia in Venice.[1] Aphrodite's right knee rests on a tortoise, an unusual feature enabling the composition to be unmistakeably identified, even in a bronze recreation made for the Gonzaga family by Pier Jacopo Alari Bonacolsi, known as Antico (c. 1455–1528) around 1520.[2]

In representations of Aphrodite Urania, the image of heavenly or spiritual love, the goddess was shown standing, dressed, resting one foot on a tortoise; however, this animal symbol was not commonly used with the crouching Aphrodite. Its exceptional presence here may hint at an additional reading: for Plutarch, this detail in Phidias' *Aphrodite Urania* signified that a woman should look after her home – since the tortoise carries its house on its shoulders – and should preserve a decorous silence, tortoises then being thought to lack tongues; these features were taken up in later emblematic literature.[3]

The Prado *Aphrodite* offers a fascinating iconographic reinterpretation following restoration work carried out in the seventeenth century, which modified the original position of the right arm; now raised over her head, the right hand holds a perfume bottle, thus enhancing the bathing motif. The arm is similarly positioned in several other sculptures, including the *Crouching Aphrodite* at the Palazzo Altemps in Rome, which came from the Cesi–Ludovisi collection; it was restored *a posteriori* and later grouped with the *Boy with a Goose* to form an artificial *Leda*.[4]

The Leonardesque drawing of the incomplete sculpture, mentioned earlier, suggests that it had by then joined the select group of classical pieces regarded as suitable for study by budding sculptors; and this gives us an idea of its true importance.

Some years ago, reflecting on the success of this model, Selma Holo highlighted the marked influence of the Prado sculpture among Renaissance artists, noting that versions were to be found in frescoes painted by Francesco Salviati (1510–1563) for the Palazzo Vecchio in Florence and by Perino del Vaga (1501–1547) for the Palazzo Massimo alle Colonne in Rome.[5] The incomplete statue, the mutilated archaeological fragment – including such key pieces as the *Belvedere Torso*[6] – held a particular appeal for artists; these precious relics provided a conceptually solid basis on which they could construct their own imaginative recreation.

As his biographers stress, Guido Reni was fond of studying ancient statues, and devoted a great deal of time to 'the constant examination of the finest ancient heads and antique reliefs'.[7] A sculpture like this must have proved particularly attractive, since the specific posture held intriguing possibilities that he could explore in his own pictorial compositions; perhaps never literally copying them, but certainly drawing effective inspiration from them. And Reni was by no means alone in this. A self-portrait by Lavinia Fontana (1552–1614), commissioned in 1578 by Alfonso Chacón and now in the Galleria degli Uffizi,[8] features a number of small sculptures deemed worthy of study; among them is the Crouching Aphrodite that had inspired, and would continue to inspire, countless artists throughout history.

Manuel Arias Martínez

1 D. Gasparotto in Settis, Anguissola and Gasparotto 2015, 240.
2 Warren 2010; D. Gasparotto in Settis, Anguissola and Gasparotto 2015, 240.
3 Alciato–Sebastián 1985, 239–40.
4 Rome, Museo Nazionale Romano, Palazzo Altemps, inv. 8565 and 8565bis: see Palma and De Lachenal 1983, 72, no. 29.
5 Holo 1978–79.
6 Vatican City, Musei Vaticani, inv. 1192.
7 Bellori–Borea 2009, 2:490.
8 Florence, Gallerie degli Uffizi, Galleria delle statue e delle pitture, inv. 1890 n. 4013. D. Gasparotto in Settis, Anguissola and Gasparotto 2015, 242.

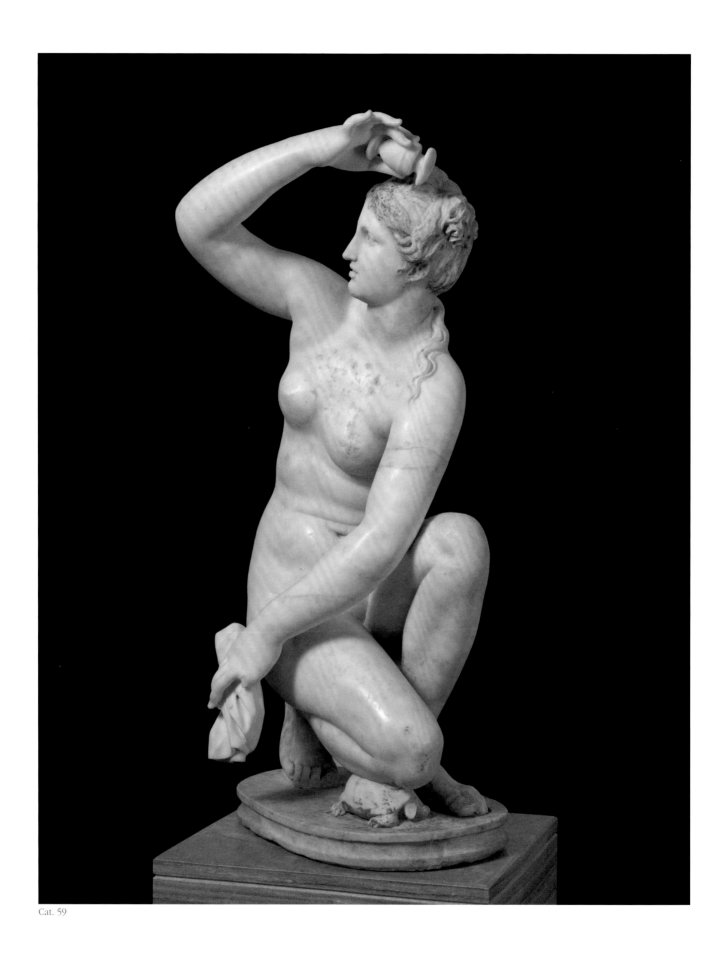

Cat. 59

60 Roman workshop
Hypnos

120–30 AD
Marble, 150 × 55 × 95 cm
Madrid, Museo Nacional del Prado, E-89

Provenance: Spanish royal collection; first listed in a Museo del Prado inventory in 1834.

Selected bibliography: Hübner [1862] 2008, 58–61, no. 39; Barrón 1908, 80–81, no. 89; Blanco and Lorente 1981, 62–63; Schröder 1993–2004 (2004), 2:231–36; Schröder 2008, 286–89; Becatti 2016; Carrasco Ferrer and Elvira Barba 2016.

In his essential 1862 survey of ancient sculpture in the Spanish capital, Emil Hübner praised this unique piece as 'the finest jewel in the Madrid Museum'. Yet despite its importance, very little information is available on its origins and its presence in the royal collection. Hübner himself notes that, according to an 'unreliable' oral source, it came from the palace of the Duke of Frías in Valladolid, but offered no certainty regarding this claim.

While the sculpture is unquestionably listed in the Prado inventories from 1834 onwards, its remote origin has prompted doubts as to its whereabouts prior to that date; Graziella Becatti recently suggested that it may even have entered the royal collection under Philip II. The fact that in 1557 Cardinal Montepulciano was granted papal permission to export two sculptures from Rome, a *Mercury* and 'a girl removing a thorn from her foot', led Becatti to speculate that the *Mercury* may in fact have been the Prado *Hypnos*.[1] In support of this hypothesis, she quotes from a contemporary account of Pope Leo X's ceremonial entry into Rome in 1513, according to which the remarkable ancient statues displayed to mark the pope's progress included a 'Mercury Running' – a pose not commonly associated with depictions of the messenger of the gods – belonging to the De' Rossi family.

The question of mistaken identity is compounded by the fact that the iconography itself was not correctly identified until 1851.[2] Prior to that date, the figure was classified as Mercury, because he was thought to be wearing a winged helmet, whereas in fact the wings are part of his head. Had his arms not been lost, the symbolism would have been much more readily apparent: he would have held two poppy stems in one hand, and in the other the horn from which he poured the drops of nectar that put mortals to sleep.

In any case, and despite the mutilations with which it has come down to us, there can be no doubting either the compositional importance or the unquestionable appeal of this piece, which stems from the precision with which it conveys the sense of movement, freezing the dynamic gesture in marble. The god of sleep is captured in mid-stride, intent upon his swift never-ending race to dispense, night after night, the numbing fluid that plunges mankind into restful sleep.

The telling eloquence of the gesture – above all, the capturing of an instant, the pent-up tension of the race, the lateral perspective – derives from the placing of the legs, using a kinetic approach that was to provide a model for artists throughout history, and which links this sculpture to other well-known compositions. In 1846, the German traveller De Quandt[3] compared it to the so-called *Borghese Gladiator*,[4] a classical sculpture reproduced ad infinitum in the most varied materials, an exquisite academy piece and a constant point of reference, without which it would be impossible to chart the modern history of sculpture and of painting too, such was its importance as a model for artists.

One could construct a whole corpus of works in which similar techniques were used, including the male figures adorning the famous Achilles sarcophagus from the same Borghese collection, now in the Louvre;[5] these, and others like them, formed part of the essential repertoire for art students in Baroque Rome, and were still being drawn, engraved, and examined in the days of Johann Joachim Winckelmann.[6] The three male figures around which the relief is structured, their movements frozen in space, are reinterpreted from an absolutely modern perspective in iconic figures such as Guido Reni's Hippomenes [cat. 61 and 62].

This interest in classical models, in sculptures and reliefs that offered reliable samples of carefully-studied anatomy and gestures in movement – sanctioned by the *auctoritas* of the classics – can be seen in Reni's paintings, as an example of the perfect re-working and constant re-interpreting of time-honoured codes.

Manuel Arias Martínez

1 Becatti 2016.
2 Emil Hübner ([1862] 2008, 59–61) provided a meticulous list of historiographical references to this piece under its new name, which was later updated by Stephan Schröder (1993–2004 [2004], 2:231–36). Archaeologists have unearthed similar pieces in bronze.
3 Hübner [1862] 2008, 60.
4 Paris, Musée du Louvre, Ma 527; Haskell and Penny 1990, 243–47.
5 Paris, Musée du Louvre, Ma 2120.
6 Raspi Serra 2002–5 (2002), 1:300–1.

61 Guido Reni

Hippomenes and Atalanta

c. 1618–19
Oil on canvas, 193 × 272 cm; 206 × 279 cm (with additions)
Madrid, Museo Nacional del Prado, P-3090

Provenance: Collection of Marquis Giovan Francesco Serra, Milan, 1656; Giuseppe Serra, Naples, 1664; acquired that year by the 3rd Count of Peñaranda for Philip IV; Galería del Cierzo at the Real Alcázar, Madrid, 1666 (no. 176); saved from the fire at the Real Alcázar, Madrid, 1734; Casas Arzobispales, Madrid, 1747; court painter's workshop at the Palacio Real Nuevo, Madrid, 1772 (no. 94); Casa de Rebeque, Madrid, 1794 (no. 94); Sala Reservada at the Real Academia de Bellas Artes de San Fernando, Madrid, 1817; Museo del Prado, Madrid, 1827; on long-term loan to the University of Granada by Royal Order of 12 November 1881, 1881–1964; Museo del Prado, Madrid, 1964.

Selected bibliography: Malvasia 1678, 1:116; Sánchez Rivero 1927, 36; Pérez Sánchez 1965a, 168–71; Pérez Sánchez 1970, 462; Schleier 1970, 345; Baccheschi 1971, 97–98, no. 84; Pepper 1984, 236, no. 59; Fumaroli 1987; S. Ebert-Schifferer in Ebert-Schifferer, Emiliani and Schleier 1988, 129–33; Pepper 1988, 242–43, no. 59; Vannugli 1988; Spear 1997, 62; Lleó Cañal 2005; Úbeda de los Cobos 2008; Cropper 2017, 60–71; Morselli 2020; L. Scanu in Cappelletti 2022a, 138–41, no. 11; H. Aurenhammer in Eclercy 2022a, 240–41, no. 98.

62 Guido Reni

Hippomenes and Atalanta

c. 1618–25
Oil on canvas, 192 × 264 cm
Naples, Museo e Real Bosco di Capodimonte, Q 349

Provenance: Collection of Francesco Pertusati, Milan, late 18th century; Capperoni collection, Rome, around 1800; acquired in Rome by Marquis Domenico Venuti, superintendent of excavations for the Kingdom of Naples and director of the Royal Factory of Capodimonte, for Ferdinand IV of Bourbon, King of Naples, 1802; Bourbon collections, Naples, 1803; Palazzo Reale, Naples, 1807; Real Museo Borbonico, Naples, 1854.

Selected bibliography: Malvasia 1678, 1:116; Braghirolli 1885, 98–99; Kurz 1937, 206 and 218; G. C. Cavalli in Cavalli 1954, 87–88, no. 23; Cavalli 1955, 71–74, no. 46; Pérez Sánchez 1965a, 168–71; Pérez Sánchez 1970, 462; Schleier 1970, 345; Baccheschi 1971, 97–98, no. 84; Pepper 1984, 236, no. 59; Fumaroli 1987; S. Ebert-Schifferer in Ebert-Schifferer, Emiliani and Schleier 1988, 129–33; Pepper 1988, 242–43, no. 59; Spear 1997, 62; Porzio 1999, 177; Emiliani 2000, 350–51, no. 12; M. Confalone in Utili 2002, 129; M. Tamajo Contarini in Bernardini, Bussagli and Anselmi 2015, 355, no. 8; Cropper 2017, 60–71; Morselli 2020; L. Scanu in Cappelletti 2022a, 138–41, no. 11.

The painting depicts a scene from the classical myth of Hippomenes and Atalanta as recounted in Ovid's *Metamorphoses* (Book X, verses 560–707). The episode had already been narrated by earlier writers – among them Hesiod, Sophocles, Euripides, and Apollodorus – whose accounts, though differing in minor details, were essentially the same.[1]

The young Atalanta, daughter of King Schoeneus, had been warned by an oracle that marriage would be her undoing. Her childhood had not been easy, having been abandoned in the woods by her own father, who refused to have a female heir. There, nursed by a she-bear sent by the goddess Diana, she survived until she was rescued by hunters. Having resolved to devote her virginity to Diana, she steadfastly refused to marry; at her father's insistence, however, she later agreed to receive suitors. But she established one harsh condition: as a swift runner herself, she would only marry the man that could beat her in a race, demanding that unsuccessful suitors be put to death. Young Hippomenes, great-grandson of the god Neptune, who had gone to watch the contest, fell in love with Atalanta at first sight. He therefore urged the maiden to race against him, arguing that – since he was descended from the gods – this would be a real challenge for her. Even so, aware of the difficulty and the risk involved, Hippomenes appealed for help to Venus, goddess of love and beauty, who devised a stratagem by which he could win the race. The goddess gave him three golden fruits, brought – depending on the version of the myth – either from the mythical Garden of the Hesperides or from Venus' own garden on Cyprus. Hippomenes should drop the fruits one by one in the course of the race to distract his beloved rival, thus enabling him to overtake her. For her own part, Atalanta had also felt some stirring of desire for the youth, and even as the race started was perhaps not unwilling to be outrun. Whenever Atalanta drew level with him, Hippomenes dropped one of the fruits at her feet, duly distracting her. Reni chooses to focus on the crucial moment just before Hippomenes drops the third apple (hidden behind his back), which Venus made much heavier than the rest. The youth thus gained the lead which would ensure his final victory, allowing him to claim Atalanta as his wife. The lovers'

Cat. 61

story, however, was to end in tragedy: as Hippomenes was taking Atalanta to his home, the couple was seized by a fit of passion and stopped to make love in a temple devoted to Cybele, thereby arousing the wrath of the goddess. In divine punishment, they were turned into lions, forever doomed to draw the chariot of the deity whom they had offended.

Studies of this painting have often highlighted its formal links with certain expressions of classical art, notably in the foregrounding of two large-scale human figures. This device was to be found in a number of classical pieces, including reliefs, painted vessels, and free-standing sculptures like that of Atalanta, familiar in early seventeenth-century Rome through copies.[2] Guido Reni may well have drawn on some earlier representation of the race between Hippomenes and Atalanta, perhaps the fresco by Giulio Romano (c. 1499–1546) decorating the Sala dei Venti (Hall of Winds) at the Palazzo Te in Mantua, a city Reni visited in July 1617. He may also have seen a print of Romano's drawing of Atalanta for the fresco.[3]

Cat. 62

Since Ovid's *Metamorphoses* was almost certainly the main literary source for Reni's interpretation of the myth, his composition may conceivably owe something to prints made for illustrated versions of that writer's famous account, including one by Antonio Tempesta (1555–1630) for an edition published in Amsterdam in 1606, which – like Guido's painting – is notable for its marked diagonals.[4] He may also have seen the title page of *Atalanta fugiens* (1618) – a complex book of emblems, alchemy, and music by the German physician Michael Maier – the lower portion of which depicts the race. This book, published at around the time Reni's painting is thought to have been produced, sparked such fierce controversy in Italy due to its heterodox message that it had to be republished immediately with a reinforced Christian reading.[5] In both prints, however, the position of the two figures is inverted with respect to the painting.

In opting to capture the high point of the race by means of an unusual foregrounding of the figures, Reni focused the viewers' attention on the tense, supple anatomies of Atalanta and

Hippomenes. Their bodies, flooded by a powerful white light, display all the beauty of youth, heightened by the sensual rippling vibrations of the colourful draperies that artfully conceal their private parts. A singular feature of both the Prado and the Capodimonte versions is Guido's painstaking treatment of the figures' faces, hands, and feet. This may to some extent reflect a deliberate self-imposed challenge, since – as Carlo Cesare Malvasia recalls in his *Felsina pittrice* (1678) – Reni found beautiful feet and hands very difficult to paint.[6] This anatomical exercise is also remarkable for the superb painterly handling of Hippomenes' torso, for which the artist's young apprentices were sometimes required to pose.[7]

In the coastal landscape stretching out behind Hippomenes and Atalanta, land and sky each occupy half the canvas. Groups of figures placed at either edge of the central area would appear to represent, respectively, the judges of the race and the spectators, including Atalanta's other suitors. The recent restoration of the Prado version[8] has shed new light on Reni's treatment of the horizon and shown how the deterioration of the pigment used for the sky – enamel blue – has irreversibly darkened the composition; restoration work has also confirmed that Guido applied subtle white glazes (now mostly lost) enveloping the clouds, giving them a much more fleecy appearance. Taking into account these alterations over time, we may conclude that this was not intended to be an artificially lit piece à la Caravaggio, but rather a much brighter painting, closer in that respect to the *Bacchus and Ariadne* in the Roland Römer collection featured in this exhibition [cat. 58]. This view is borne out by the only known early copy of the work, a small-format painting on copper, although it lightens the composition somewhat radically [fig. 86]. Two strips of canvas have been added to the left and lower edges of the Madrid version. Though not added by the artist himself, they were painted at an early stage. Both are now covered by the new frame that accompanies the painting, thus enabling the viewer to appreciate the master's original work.

Technical studies of the Madrid *Hippomenes and Atalanta* performed at the Museo del Prado on the occasion of this show have revealed that Reni's execution was, from the outset, both

Fig. 86 Anonymous, copy of Guido Reni, *Hippomenes and Atalanta*, 17th century. Oil on copper, 23 × 23 cm. Florence, Gallerie degli Uffizi, inv. 1890 n. 9983

Fig. 87. Infrared reflectogram of the Museo del Prado *Hippomenes and Atalanta* [cat. 61]

highly confident and precise. This is confirmed by the infrared reflectogram [fig. 87], which suggests that the artist may well have used a preparatory cartoon or 'veil'; if so, it must also have been used in the Capodimonte version, where only the figure of Hippomenes is apparently very slightly displaced with respect to its Prado counterpart.[9] Debate has long raged among Reni scholars as to which of the two is the 'original'. The technical research mentioned earlier, as well as a visual comparison with the Naples canvas, would appear to confirm Stephen Pepper's view that the Madrid version is the 'original',[10] though this does not rule out the possibility that the Capodimonte canvas is an autograph repetition by Reni himself, produced some time later. Pepper dates the Prado work to 1618–19, based on a comparison with contemporary pieces which he regards as closely related, such as the *Labours of Hercules* cycle in the Louvre,[11] while he believes that the Capodimonte version was painted in around 1625.[12]

Hippomenes' attitude towards his beloved rival is rather puzzling: in the painting he extends the palm of his right hand towards Atalanta in a gesture that, even in the seventeenth century, commonly indicated rejection,[13] although the position of his arm could also result from having thrown down the

apple that she is stooping to pick up. His distant, somewhat displeased expression seems inappropriate for the moment when, according to the myth, love was blossoming between the two. Guido's interpretation of the whole episode thus seems to reflect a Christian rereading common in the early modern period, in which Atalanta was associated with Eve, both women displaying a shared lack of principles. On that basis, Atalanta could be regarded in this new context as a temptress. The most elaborate theory in this sense was advanced by Marc Fumaroli, who argued that the painting was intended as an aid to Christian meditation and moral reflection, similar in that sense to the *compositio loci* of Saint Ignatius, and comparable in visual terms to the iconography of the *Noli me tangere*. Atalanta, in this reading, represents earthly instincts and the temptation to sin, while Hippomenes embodies celestial concerns and the conscious resistance of that temptation.[14]

It is therefore possible that the golden fruits were intended as an allusion to the apple with which Eve tempted Adam, and that the three fruits represent, in Vicente Lleó's words:

the three sins of concupiscence – of the flesh, of the eyes, and of pride – from which Hippomenes virtuously recoils and through which Atalanta's soul is lost. The competition between the two young people is thus the race of the Christian soul which, as it advances towards death, must make its own choice between salvation and perdition.[15]

This sense of warring elements, of the transition from the vile to the noble, may add yet another interpretation to the work, an alchemical reading within the context of the *Atalanta fugiens*, on whose controversial publication Reni may have wanted to make his own position clear.[16] Similar exegetical readings of the myth had appeared elsewhere in early modern Spain, for example in Juan Pérez de Moya's *Philosophia secreta* (1585),[17] and it had been the subject of numerous allusions in Spanish literature.[18]

We do not know who commissioned this singular yet undoubtedly beguiling picture from Reni, or for what purpose it was made, or where it was to be placed. Nor do we know what prompted the production of several replicas on the same theme. Guido's chief biographer, Malvasia, has nothing to say regarding this matter, merely mentioning the painting among those serving as the basis for engravings.[19] This lack of information may reflect the fact that the canvas was to be found, at the time, outside Bologna and probably in a place to which access was limited.

A plausible possibility, suggested by Sybille Ebert-Schifferer, is that it was commissioned by Ferdinando Gonzaga, Duke of Mantua (1587–1626), a collector particularly interested in Reni's work.[20] This hypothesis is supported by the mention of a painting by Guido depicting Hippomenes and Atalanta in a seventeenth-century inventory of the Gonzaga collections.[21] Since nothing is known of the subsequent destination of that composition or of the year in which the inventory was drawn up, the picture in question could have been either the Prado or the Capodimonte version, or even one of the two other works discussed below.

The Prado canvas definitely belonged to the collection of the Genoese nobleman Giovan Francesco Serra (1609–1656), who enjoyed a distinguished military career in the service of the Spanish monarchy. On his death, his collection was transferred by his heirs from Milan to Naples. There, the painting was among the pieces purchased in 1664 by Gaspar de Bracamonte y Guzmán, 3rd Count of Peñaranda – the Spanish viceroy – for Philip IV.[22] Once in Madrid, it was placed in the Galería del Cierzo (Hall of the North Wind) at the Real Alcázar, hanging alongside works such as *Venus, Adonis and Cupid* by Annibale Carracci (1560–1609),[23] also acquired from the Serra collection, and the *Feast of Bacchus* by Diego Velázquez (1599–1660).[24] There, it was seen in November 1668 by Prince Cosimo de' Medici, the future

Cosimo III, who remarked that it 'by no means deserves the fame it has attained', indicating that it had by then achieved a certain renown in Italy.[25] It remained in the Alcázar until the fire of 1734, from which it was saved, and thereafter spent a long time in the workshops of the court artists; in 1817, it entered the Real Academia de Bellas Artes de San Fernando, where it was placed in the restricted-access Sala Reservada owing to the nudity of the central figures. In 1827 it was finally moved to the Museo del Prado, where it hung for several years in a similarly restricted gallery in use at the time.[26] The Museum's 1872 catalogue dismissed it as a copy,[27] and in 1881 it was placed on long-term loan to the University of Granada, where it attracted little attention until the expiry of the loan in 1964, when it was returned to the Prado.

In the seventeenth century, apart from the picture in the royal collection, there was one more version of this painting in Madrid. It belonged to another great contemporary Spanish collector, the Diego Messía Felípez de Guzmán, 1st Marquis of Leganés (c. 1580–1655), and was recorded in 1655 in his Madrid residence. During his term as governor of Milan, Leganés had shown interest in Reni's work, purchasing several fine paintings by him, among them this replica or copy of *Hippomenes and Atalanta*.[28] From the Leganés collection it entered that of the Counts of Altamira, and was subsequently acquired by the painter José de Madrazo (1781–1859).[29] In 1861, the painting was purchased from the Madrazo family by José de Salamanca (1811–1883), who placed it in his country house in Vista Alegre. Following the sale of his collection in Paris in 1867, there is no news of its location.[30]

Another replica or copy of *Hippomenes and Atalanta* – whose current whereabouts is equally unknown – was seen in the 1850s by the German scholar Gustav Friedrich Waagen at Stafford House, then the London home of the Duke of Sutherland.[31]

The provenance of the Capodimonte painting can only be traced with any certainty to the period immediately before it entered the Museo Nazionale in Naples. By the late eighteenth century it was recorded in the collection of Francesco Pertusati in Milan,[32] whence it was acquired by the gem carver Gaspare Capperoni (1756–1808),[33] who took it to Rome. It was purchased from Capperoni by the agent Domenico Venuti, who had been commissioned by Ferdinand IV of Naples to buy major works for the royal gallery.[34] Once in Naples, the painting hung for several decades in different rooms in the Palazzo Reale, until it entered the Real Museo Borbonico in 1854.[35]

The presence of a version of *Hippomenes and Atalanta* in Milan at the end of the seventeenth century – either the Capodimonte canvas or the Sutherland version, since the other two were by then in Madrid – appears to be confirmed by an engraving made there by Giovanni Frederico Pesca, dedicated to Benedetto Cittadini, Cardinal Mazarin's agent in Milan.[36] In the late eighteenth century, the Milan engraver Giuseppe Benaglia (1766–1835) produced a new print of Reni's composition, probably after the painting that later entered the Museo Nazionale di Capodimonte.[37]

Although both the Naples and the Madrid versions were on show over much of the nineteenth century, and despite Benaglia's print, virtually no echoes of the painting are to be found in the art of that period, with the delightful exception of a canvas by Lord Frederic Leighton (1830–1896), *Greek Girls picking up Pebbles by the Sea* now in the Pérez Simón collection, in which one of the female figures clearly recalls Reni's Atalanta. It was not until the post-modern age that several artists drew inspiration from Guido's *Hippomenes and Atalanta* for their own creations, among them Renato Guttuso (1911–1987), Pamela Joseph (b. 1942), Carlo Adelio Galimberti (b. 1946), and Vik Muniz (b. 1961).[38]

David García Cueto

1 Rodríguez López 2018.

2 Morselli 2020.

3 Ibid. For earlier representations of the myth, see Quattrone 1993.

4 Rodríguez López 2018.

5 Maier 1618; S. Ebert-Schifferer in Ebert-Schifferer, Emiliani and Schleier 1988, 132; Hasler 2011.

6 Malvasia–Pericolo 2019, 1:72–73, note 164.

7 Ibid., 2:71.

8 Carried out by Almudena Sánchez Martín in 2020–21.

9 Technical studies by Ana González Mozo, Laura Alba Carcelén, Jaime García-Máiquez, Lola Gayo, and Maite Jover de Celis.

10 Pepper 1984, 236, no. 59: 'once one compares the Madrid painting to the work in Naples there can be no doubt that the Madrid painting is the original'.

11 Paris, Musée du Louvre, inv. 535–538.

12 Pepper 1984, 236, no. 59.

13 Spear 1997, 64–65.

14 Fumaroli 1987; Lleó Cañal 2005.

15 Lleó Cañal 2005, 145. Elizabeth Cropper (2017, 64), by contrast, argues that this moralisation of Ovid was not widespread in seventeenth-century Bologna.

16 S. Ebert-Schifferer in Ebert-Schifferer, Emiliani and Schleier 1988, 132.

17 Lleó Cañal 2005, 144.

18 Moncayo 1656; Franco Durán 1997; Roses Lozano 1998; Franco Durán 2001; Molina Huete 2018.

19 Malvasia 1678, 1:116. Luigi Crespi (1769, 79) notes that the engraving mentioned by Malvasia was the work of Giovanni Battista Bolognini (1611–1688). No print is currently known.

20 S. Ebert-Schifferer in Ebert-Schifferer, Emiliani and Schleier 1988, 132.

21 Braghirolli 1885, 97–98: 'In una nota di quadri posseduti dai Gonzaga ... senza data, ma del sec. XVII, si trova descritto così: Un quadro con la favola di Atalanta nel corso, che raccoglie i pomi d'oro, due figure del naturale, di mano di Guido Reni, alto p. 8 1/2 e largo 11'. Stephen Pepper (1984, 236, no. 59) claims that this inventory dates from the late seventeenth century, an error – prompted by a misreading of Braghirolli – repeated by others.

22 Vannugli 1988.

23 Madrid, Museo Nacional del Prado, P-2631.

24 Madrid, Museo Nacional del Prado, P-1170.

25 Sánchez Rivero 1927, 36.

26 Portús Pérez 1998, no. 43.

27 Madrazo 1872, 129–30, no. 273.

28 Pérez Preciado 2010, 706–7, no. 1110.

29 Ibid. The painting appears in the inventory drawn up by José de Madrazo (1856, no. 178), which records its measurements as 197 × 279 cm, making it slightly larger than the Capodimonte version. The Madrazo family claimed that their version was the original, regarding the Prado version – perhaps in their own interests – as a copy; see Pérez Sánchez 1965a, 71.

30 *Catalogue* 1867, 47–48; Pérez Preciado 2010, 707.

31 Waagen 1854, 2:64.

32 Bona Castellotti 1991, 68.

33 Visconti and Guattani 1820, 99–101.

34 Fiorillo 1991; L. Scanu in Cappelletti 2022a, 138–41, no. 11. Domenico Venuti himself owned a *Descent from the Cross* by Reni; see *Catalogue* 1857, 124.

35 Porzio 1999, 177.

36 London, British Museum, inv. 1874,0808.823. On Benedetto Cittadini, see Chéruel 1872–1906, VI (1890).

37 Milan, Civica Raccolta delle Stampe Achile Bertarelli, inv. 02036268.

38 Rodríguez López 2018.

IX

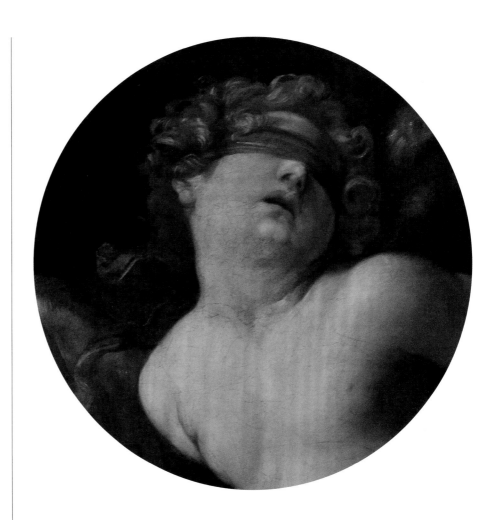

IN THE REALM OF CUPID:
PLAY, LOVE, AND TENDERNESS

Guido Reni shared with most Italian Renaissance and Baroque artists an interest in representing children's bodies, and striking examples are to be found in his work. Some paintings focus on playful *putti* or cherubs, while others feature Cupid, the pagan god and symbol of love. His models reflect a preference for what his biographer, Carlo Cesare Malvasia, described as 'tender and chubby' bodies. His portrayal of these infants was closely linked to representations by contemporary sculptors, including Alessandro Algardi – whose models were very similar to Reni's – and Giovanni Battista Morelli, a seventeenth-century Madrid-based Italian sculptor working mainly in stucco and terracotta.

Reni's iconography of love also assumed female form, for example in *Girl with a Rose* [cat. 72], which hung in Philip IV's summer study at the Alcázar in Madrid, beside a rather sensual Venetian lady by Domenico Tintoretto [cat. 71], in a unique pairing of contrasting yet complementary views of love.

63   Guido Reni

Landscape with Cupids playing

1601–3
Oil on canvas, 77 × 60 cm
Milan | Pesaro, Galleria Altomani & Sons

Provenance: Mentioned in the 1644 inventory of the Palazzo Farnese, Rome; listed in the Palazzo del Giardino, Parma, about 1680.

Selected bibliography: Gatta 2017; F. Gatta in Cappelletti 2022a, 156–59, no. 15; F. Gatta in Eclercy 2022a, 155–57, no. 41.

Guido Reni's *Landscape with Cupids playing* is first mentioned in an inventory of the Palazzo Farnese, Rome, drawn up in 1644: 'A painting on canvas with a large, gilded frame, where there is a landscape with Cupids playing, a work by Guido Reni, and within the painting a portrait of a lady is enclosed'.[1] The painting is described in greater detail in the 1653 inventory of the Farnese collection in Rome:

> A painting on canvas with a frame entirely gilded, the first cover is a landscape, and Cupids partly on earth and partly on a shell who play different games, and in the second cover a lady called the Serlupi with a large leaf ruff of gauze with a small plume on her head, a fan in her hand, the cover is by Guido Reni.[2]

By 1680, when Guido's painting is listed again – this time in the Palazzo del Giardino, Parma – it had already been separated from the portrait, which is now known to be a work by Scipione Pulzone (1544–1598), and whose sitter is described as holding 'a string that hangs from her neck' with her left hand, the right hand wielding a fan.[3] The lady portrayed by Pulzone can be identified with Marzia Massimo Serlupi (1569–1628).[4] While Pulzone's portrait remains untraced, and so any hypothesis about it cannot be confirmed, it was likely provided with a cover not necessarily to conceal the woman's identity, but to signal the treasured status of her painted likeness, displaying it as a 'portrait of love'.

In sixteenth-century Italy, portraits were occasionally supplied with a protective cover, an example in point being the 1505 *Portrait of Bishop Bernardo de' Rossi* by Lorenzo Lotto (c. 1480–1556) in the Museo di Capodimonte, Naples,[5] which was covered by an *Allegory of Virtue and Vice* in the National Gallery of Art, Washington, by the same painter.[6] This particular work is relevant here because it may have belonged to the Farnese in the seventeenth century, although it seems to have been kept in their palace in Parma. It was undoubtedly Cardinal Odoardo Farnese (1573–1626) who ordered the painting from Guido. Both the genre (landscape) and the subject (amorous) are known to have been dear to this prelate. If Lotto's *Allegory of Virtue and Vice* was meant to trigger moral reflection, Guido's *Cupids playing* created a light-hearted, almost parodic foil to the portrait it covered. On the one hand, there is the beautiful woman, the source of blissful sorrow in the lyrical tradition; on the other hand, there is an Arcadia inhabited by satyrs and nymphs – embodiments of lust – where carefree and reckless Cupids give themselves over to childish entertainment. Oblivious of their tasks, some pull a rope attached to a gigantic shell or shield turned into a boat, steering it along a river; two others, in the air, converse with one another, or deploy their attributes (a burning torch, an arrow, perhaps a whip) with no apparent use for them – for now, they are not inflicting wounds, inflaming hearts, or punishing lovers. Prominently, almost at the centre of the composition, one Cupid is directing his flow of piss over one of his companions, who touches his head as if unaware of the prank. By having a *scherzo* cover the portrait of the lady, Cardinal Farnese took distance from the staged drama of lyrical love, whose conventions are if not mocked, at least reduced to merry folly by Guido's painting.

From the 1644 inventory we learn that Cardinal Farnese commissioned other paintings from Guido: a *Saint Cecilia* and a *Wooded Landscape with Marauders*, both unidentified.[7] Because Guido ceased to execute landscapes very early in his career, it is fair to assume that these works date to the very early years of his stay in Rome. It is usually believed that Guido was introduced to Cardinal Farnese by one of his patrons in that city, Cardinal Paolo Emilio Sfondrato (1561–1618). In reality, there is evidence that Guido continued to gravitate around Annibale Carracci (1560–1609) after his arrival in Rome in 1601. In a letter to Cardinal Federico Borromeo (1564–1631) dated 13 February 1602, Guido explicitly complains about Annibale for having 'intercepted [his] own correspondence'.[8] In his *Felsina pittrice* (1678), Carlo Cesare Malvasia relates that when Annibale 'obtained commissions for Albani in Rome and assigned to him part of the decoration of the Herrera Chapel in San Giacomo degli Spagnoli', Annibale declined Guido's offer to work for him 'at no fee, which mortified Albani'.[9] This episode might also have occurred in 1602, when Annibale was contracted to execute the pictorial decoration of the Herrera Chapel. It is essential to place Guido's painting within this context, since works such as *Landscape with Cupids playing* cannot be fully understood outside an artistic dialogue about

landscape between Annibale Carracci and his three disciples in Rome: Guido, Francesco Albani (1578–1660), and Domenichino (1581–1641). Most importantly, the quality of Guido's painting demonstrates that, far from being a follower, he was a pioneer among his peers. In fact, *Landscape with Cupids playing* seems to prefigure much later works by Albani, and in the detail of the conversation between the naked nymph and the satyr at the left, there is almost a disconcerting premonition of Nicolas Poussin's (1594–1665) neo-Venetian production of the second half of the 1620s. Stylistically, Guido's painting bears affinity with works executed around 1601–3, such as the Borghese *Rest on the Flight into Egypt* (now in a private collection), *Saint Jerome with two Angels in a Landscape* (also in a private collection), and the *Assumption and Coronation of the Virgin* now at the Prado [cat. 8].[10]

Lorenzo Pericolo

1 Jestaz 1994, 167, no. 4270: 'Un quadro in tela con cornice grossa, dorata, dentro dipinto un Paese con un gioco d'Amorini, mano di Guido Reni, et dentro d'esso quadro è racchiuso un ritratto d'una dama'.

2 Bertini 1987, 210, no. 225: 'Un quadro in tela con cornice tutta dorata, la p[rim]a coperta con prospettiva de paesi, et amorini parte in terra e parte in una cocchiglia che fanno diversi giochi, e nella [second]a coperta una dama chiamata la Serlupi con collarone grande di velo a frappa, con pennacchino in testa, ventaglio in mano, la coperta di Guido Reni'.

3 Bertini 1987, 258–60, no. 571: 'Un quadro alto braccia uno, oncie una. Una femina vestita all'antica con grandissima frappa al collo, nella destra un ventaglio, la sinistra tiene un cordone che li pende al collo, del Gaetano'.

4 Gatta 2022, 75 and 82, note 19.

5 Naples, Museo e Real Bosco di Capodimonte, inv. Q 57.

6 Washington, National Gallery of Art, Samuel H. Kress Collection, inv. 1939.1.156. For a recent discussion of Lotto's portrait and its cover, see Villa and Villa 2011, 37–39.

7 For *Saint Cecilia*, see Jestaz 1994, 132, no. 3227 ('un quadro in tela, cornice dorata, S[anta] Cecilia con violino in mano, di Guido Reni') and Bertini 1987, 123–26, no. 125 ('quadro senza cornice, alto br[acci]a uno, once otto, largo bra[cci]a uno, once tre e mezza, S[an]ta Cecilia con gli occhi al cielo, un ornato di drappo bianco in capo, con violino alla spalla in atto di suonarlo'). For *Wooded Landscape with Marauders*, see Jestaz 1994, no. 4323 ('un quadro in tela con cornice dorata, dipintovi una prospettiva a paesi e bosco con malandrini, mano di Guido Reni') and Bertini 1987, 212, no. 277 ('un quadro in tela dorata con prospettiva a paesi e boscaglie con malandrini, mano di Guido Reno'). For another landscape attributed to Guido in the collection of Cardinal Odoardo Farnese, but apparently not by him, see Bertini 1987, 180, no. 273.

8 McGarry 2008, 431–33: 'M'ha intercette le l[ette]re part[icola]ri'.

9 Malvasia 1678, 2:16–17: 'Egli [Guido] … ben sapea per antica antipatia e per dispetto portargli contro l'Albani … ed avea addossato in parte la cappella Erera in San Giacomo de' Spagnuoli, escludendo affatto lui che se gli era fatto offrire al sudetto Croce senza mercede alcuna, e con dispiacere dell'Albani'. See further Malvasia–Pericolo 2019, 1:254–55, note 111.

10 For the *Rest on the Flight into Egypt* and *Saint Jerome with two Angels in a Landscape*, see Malvasia–Pericolo 2019, 1:374, note 436, and 1:452, note 680, respectively.

64 Guido Reni
Cupid with a Bow

c. 1637–38
Oil on canvas, 101 × 88 cm
Madrid, Museo Nacional del Prado, P-150

Provenance: Presented by Camillo Massimo to King Philip IV of Spain, 1655; Spanish royal collection at the Real Alcázar, Madrid, 1666; lower room, king's summer quarters at the Real Alcázar, Madrid, 1686 (no. 503) and 1700 (no. 281); listed among the paintings saved from the fire in the Alcázar in 1734; Palacio Real Nuevo, Madrid, 1747 and 1772; Infante don Carlos' quarters, sixth room at the Palacio Real, Madrid, 1814–18; Real Museo, Madrid, 1857 (no. 599); Museo del Prado, Madrid, 1849–58 (no. 599), 1872–1907 (no. 169), and 1910–20 (no. 150).

Selected bibliography: Pérez Sánchez 1965a, 142, no. 205, and 172, no. 150; Pepper 1984, no. 171, and 279, fig. 196; Spear 1997, 368, note 75; Beaven 2000; Colomer 2006, 237, note 44; González Martínez and Diéguez-Rodríguez 2008; Beaven 2014, 104–6; Cruz Yábar 2017–18; Greub 2019; Beaven and Colomer 2020; H. Aurenhammer in Eclercy 2022a, 272–75, no. 118.

In a letter to his friend Giovan Pietro Bellori (1613–1696) dated 30 August 1660, Cardinal Camillo Massimo (1620–1677), papal nuncio to Spain from 1654 to 1658, mentioned two paintings (*quadretti*) by Guido Reni and Guercino (1591–1666) which he had presented to King Philip IV as diplomatic gifts. In 2000 they were identified by Lisa Beaven as this painting and Guercino's *Cupid spurning Riches*, also at the Prado [cat. 65]. This finding was confirmed by a customs document dating to 16 February 1654 found by José Luis Colomer in Munich, which describes the goods that Massimo brought into Spain from Italy.[1]

Reni's painting is first mentioned in the 1666 inventory of the Madrid Alcázar as autograph, and is listed again as a secure work by Guido in the inventory of 1686.[2] From its first mention it was paired with Guercino's *Cupid spurning Riches*.[3] Its status as an original painting by the artist dating to 1637–38 has the consensus of scholars, and was only challenged in some Prado catalogues, most notably when it was re-attributed to Giovanni Francesco Gessi (1588–1649) in the catalogue of 1963.[4] The two paintings appear in the inventory of the Alcázar, six years after Massimo's letter, and are of similar dimensions. The Guercino measured 99 × 75 centimetres and the Reni, which had already been slightly enlarged on all sides, 105 × 80 centimetres.[5] In the 1686 inventory they were listed as hanging near Diego Velázquez's (1599–1660) *Las Meninas*[6] in a room in the summer quarters of the Alcázar reserved for the king's personal use ('pieza del despacho de verano'). The location of this study has been identified as the most northerly room in a suite of chambers on the ground floor of the

north side of the Alcázar.[7] There has been much discussion about how the paintings in this room might have originally been arranged, as the inventory only itemises them. The Reni is listed seventh, the Guercino eighth, and *Las Meninas* thirteenth. In the reconstructions of the display in this 'despacho de verano' by Thierry Greub and Juan María Cruz Yábar it is argued that the two Cupid paintings hung on the east wall among flower paintings, with *Las Meninas* on the opposite, west wall.

The iconography of this painting, entitled Cupid with a Bow from the outset, is unusual.[8] A young, blond Cupid stands in the foreground, his back to the sea. His left leg is bent, his foot awkwardly stepped up on a slab of rock, and his right hand grasps the tip of a large bow, its string loosened. A blue and gold quiver full of arrows lies at his feet. It is as if Cupid has ceased his activities, perhaps tamed. He reaches up with his left arm to receive a golden arrow from a dove suspended above him. The dove is a traditional attribute of Venus, and it conveys the arrow to Cupid as a sign from the goddess that he should recommence his activities. That he will do so is signalled by the presence of another Cupid in the distance, running along the seashore in the act of firing his bow. In his role as papal nuncio, Massimo was the representative in Spain of the Pamphilj pope, Innocent X, whose family arms included a dove with an olive branch. In such a combination the dove is a symbol of peace, a connotation here undermined by the presence of the arrow.

Reni's painting is reminiscent of several Dutch compositions that show Cupid standing and holding his bow, such as Jacob Huysman's (c. 1633–1696) *Cupid preparing his Bow* in Wimborne Minster, based on a lost original by Anthony van Dyck (1599–1641).[9] As Richard Spear noted, the Prado painting is also related iconographically to Guido's lost composition of *Cupid by the Sea*, now known only through copies.[10] The source of this current imagery may be traced to a version of the rape of Proserpina in Ovid's *Metamorphoses*, where Venus instructs Cupid on the seashore to fire a golden arrow at Pluto, a scene depicted by Hendrik Goltzius (1558–1617), among others.[11]

Lisa Beaven

1 See Colomer 2006, 237, note 44: 'Munich, Bayerische Staatsbibliothek, Cod. it. 699, fol. nn.: "En diez y seis de febrero de 1654 el Ill.mo Señor Nuncio de Su Santidad manifestó en el puerto de Requena para Madrid … dos pinturas de Cupido …"'. See also Beaven and Colomer 2020.

2 In 1666 the painting was described as: 'Vara de alto y tres quartas de ancho, de un cupido de mano del Guido Bolonés, marco tallado; 100 ducados'; see Pérez Sánchez 1965a, 172.

3 They were described respectively in the 1686 inventory as: 'Otra pintura de una vara de alto y tres quartas de ancho, de un cupido de mano de Guydo Boloñes y un cupido del mismo tamaño, de mano del Guarçhino'.

4 See Pepper 1984, 279, no. 171; Spear 1997, 368–69.

5 The Reni has been enlarged on all sides. It has an additional 1.5–2.5 cm added to the top and bottom, 3.5 cm on the left side and approximately 5.5 cm on the right (source: Prado painting file).

6 Madrid, Museo Nacional del Prado, P-1174.

7 Cruz Yábar 2017–18; Greub 2019.

8 See Pepper 1984, 279, no. 171.

9 National Trust, Wimborne Minster, Kingston Lacy, NT 1257118: oil on canvas, 132 × 101.5 cm.

10 Spear 1997, 369: 'Reni's lost *Cupid near the Sea* is an iconographic variant of the *Cupid with a Bow*'.

11 See for example the print by Jacob Matham (1571–1631) after Hendrik Goltzius, *Venus and Cupid* (c. 1590, engraving, 20.3 × 14.1 cm), which shows Cupid with his bow, holding an arrow in his left hand, while Venus points behind her to Pluto in his chariot in the distance. The same subject was engraved by Pieter de Jode I (1570–1634) after a composition by Bartholomeus Spranger (1546–1611), *Venus commanding Cupid to shoot his Arrow at Pluto* (c. 1590–92, 25.3 × 20.1 cm).

65 Guercino
(Cento 1591–1666 Bologna)
Cupid spurning Riches

c. 1653
Oil on canvas, 99 × 75 cm
Madrid, Museo Nacional del Prado, P-205

Provenance: Possibly commissioned by Camillo Massimo from the artist in 1653; presented by Camillo Massimo to King Philip IV of Spain, in 1655; Spanish royal collection at the Real Alcázar, Madrid, 1666; lower room, king's summer quarters at the Real Alcázar, 1686 (no. 504) and 1700 (no. 282); queen's new chambers at the Real Alcázar, Madrid, 1703; listed among the paintings saved from the fire in the Alcázar in 1734 (no. 994); antechamber of the infanta at the Palacio Real Nuevo, Madrid, 1772 (no. 993); Infante don Carlos' quarters, sixth room at the Palacio Real, Madrid, 1814–18 (no. 993?); Museo del Prado, Madrid, 1854–58 (no. 714), 1872–1907 (no. 253), 1910–20 (no. 205); deposited in the Museo de Pontevedra from 1933; Museo del Prado catalogue 1972 (no. 205); restored and exhibited in Melbourne in 2014; in the Museo del Prado, Madrid, since 2014.

Selected bibliography: Bottineau 1958, 322; Pérez Sánchez 1965a, 142, no. 205, and 172, no. 150; Salerno 1988, 372, no. 303; Mahon and Turner 1989, 72, no. 129; Stone 1991, 297, note 289; Ghelfi 1997, 165, no. 484; Spear 1997, 368–69, note 75; Pepper and Mahon 1999; Beaven 2000; Beaven 2014, 104–6; Martínez Leiva and Rodríguez Rebollo 2015, 279, no. 173; Beaven and Colomer 2020.

The papal nuncio to Spain, Camillo Massimo (1620–1677), presented Guercino's *Cupid spurning Riches* and Guido Reni's *Cupid with a Bow* [cat. 64] to King Philip IV as diplomatic gifts in 1655, and the pair are documented in the inventories of the Spanish royal collection from 1666. Guercino's painting depicts a youthful Cupid emptying a bag of gold coins, which are shown falling to the ground. More gold and silver coins are piled at his feet, and a bow with a loosened string and an abandoned quiver of arrows can be glimpsed behind him. A single arrow lies in the immediate foreground, while on the left is a large globe of the world. Behind his head a red silk curtain is drawn back, revealing a landscape beyond.

The painting has been variously entitled *Virtuous Cupid* and *Cupid spurning Riches*. This confusion points to its unusual iconography. Items such as the single arrow and the globe represent the universality of love and are often employed as attributes for Cupid, but the motif of emptying a bag of coins is not. The implication is that Cupid is so intent on spurning riches that he has abandoned his bow and arrows. Its iconography is related to Reni's *Allegory of Fortune* of about 1635-36, in which a naked Fortune is shown flying over a globe [fig. 54]. She holds a palm and sceptre in her left hand and upturns a purse in her right, from which coins and pearls

tumble. As Denis Mahon and Stephen Pepper argued, it is probable that Guercino was consulted with regard to the unfinished state of Reni's *Allegory of Fortune*, and so was familiar with its unusual iconography.[1] The upturned purse in Reni's painting can be interpreted as a representation of the transience of wealth; its message in the Guercino picture is more pointed, as Cupid appears to be openly contemptuous

of it. A preparatory figure study of Cupid by Guercino is in the Royal Collection at Windsor.[2]

Spear's observation that the two paintings are 'so complimentary in design and iconography that one wonders if Guercino made his picture as a pendant' to the Reni[3] is almost certainly correct. Massimo must have commissioned the painting from Guercino in order to match Guido's *Cupid*, painted several decades earlier, which he already owned, and so chose a complementary theme.

The Guercino painting has been linked to a payment recorded in the artist's account book (*libro dei conti*) on 19 June 1654:[4] this refers to the 10 Spanish dobles received for an 'Amore Virtuoso' from a certain Padre Don Salvatore of Piacenza, along with the crimson lake and lapis lazuli pigments charged for separately, as was Guercino's custom. This is the only entry in the account book of the artist from Cento which corresponds to this painting, and the choice of pigments is compatible with its vivid blue sky and red curtain. However, the 16 February 1654 document found by José Luis Colomer [see cat. 64], which lists both paintings in Massimo's possession as he crossed the border four months earlier, suggests that if the payment does refer to this picture, then it was only made some months after the canvas was received.

The painting was damaged, possibly in a fire at the Alcázar in 1734, when it was listed as among the items saved.[5] From 1933 to 2014 it was in deposit at Pontevedra; it was restored in 2014 and has been in the Prado ever since.

Lisa Beaven

1 Pepper and Mahon 1999, 158, note 21: 'It is very likely that Benadduci consulted Guercino concerning the unfinished state of the *Fortuna*, but it is safe to assume that Guercino would have expressed his disagreement at touching a work which was all but finished'. Benadduci is a reference to Benadduce Benadduci, whom Stephen Pepper and Denis Mahon conclude purchased the painting from its original owner, Abbot Giovanni Carlo Gavotti.

2 Windsor, Royal Collection, RCIN 902708: 25.5 × 17.1 cm (sheet).

3 Spear 1997, 368–69, note 75.

4 Luigi Salerno made this identification, acknowledging Denis Mahon as the first to suggest it (Salerno 1988, 372, no. 303). He noted that although there was another payment of 50 ducatons for an *Amor Virtuoso* itemised for 20 May 1654, this was for a half figure, and therefore ruled out the Prado painting. The *libro dei conti* was published by Malvasia in 1678 and Calvi in 1808; In 1841 the editors of the second edition of Malvasia's *Felsina pittrice* republished both Calvi's *Notizie* as well as the *Libro dei conti* in the second volume, see Malvasia–Zanotti 1841, 2:335. In 1997 Barbara Ghelfi published a new transcription of the *libro dei conti* and her entry states: '48v.: Adi 19 Giugno 1654 – 484 Dal P: D: Saluatore di Piazzenza, si è riceuto Doble n:º dieci, per la More Virtuoso, e questi fano L 150. In oltre si e riceuto 25 onze di Lacha e 21. Onza di Lappis Lazoli per far agiuro oltramarino, è questi fano Scudi 38 1/2'; Ghelfi 1997, 165.

5 See Pérez Sánchez 1965a, 142: 'Entre los cuadros salvados del incendio de 1734 se le cita sin atribución, cosa chocante, pero no cabe lugar a dudas: 994. Otro del mismo tamaño (más de vara por 3 cuartos) y marco, de otro cupido con un bolso en la mano bertiendo monedas, original de autor no conocido'.

---

66   Tommaso Fedele
(Fossombrone, Le Marche?, c. 1598–1658 Rome),
after François du Quesnoy
Sacred Love defeating Profane Love

c. 1630
Porphyry and bronze, 57 × 113 cm
Madrid, Museo Nacional del Prado, E-300

Provenance: Gifted by Cardinal Francesco Barberini to King Philip IV; Galería del Mediodía at the Real Alcázar, Madrid, 1686; Galería de Retratos at the Real Alcázar, Madrid, 1700 (no. 33); Palacio Real Nuevo, Madrid, 1747 (no. 13); Palacio Real, Madrid, 1794 (no. 825).

Selected bibliography: Bellori [1672] 1977, 271; Coppel 1998, 128–29; Muñoz González 1999; M. Boudon-Machuel in Borea and Gasparri 2000, 2:400; Boudon-Machuel 2005, 293–94; Colomer 2008, 17–18; Helmstutler Di Dio 2013, 62; García Cueto 2016b, 209–10; Pierguidi 2017, 62.

Nowhere is the fascinating world of diplomatic gifts and their language – the way an object can be turned into a persuasive instrument, able to dictate decisions and shape opinions – more intriguingly apparent than in this superb relief. There is a wealth of documentation on its production and origin, and on its entry into the Spanish royal collection as a gift from Cardinal Francesco Barberini (1597–1679) to King Philip IV. It is a copy, made by Tommaso Fedele, of a composition by the Flemish sculptor François du Quesnoy (1597–1643) that was to enjoy considerable success. The original patinated plaster model on which the Prado piece was directly based is now in the Fundação Calouste Gulbenkian in Lisbon,[1] while the Galleria Doria Pamphilj holds the marble version made by Du Quesnoy for the garden of the Villa Pamphilj or del Bel Respiro in Rome.

For this faithful reproduction of Du Quesnoy's composition, Fedele chose to use porphyry, an unusual rock which in the seventeenth century had regained the special symbolic dignity it had been accorded in the ancient world. Echoes of the imperial past are conveyed through its very materiality, its compact solidness, and above all its characteristic reddish-purple colour, associated with power.

The imperial purple turned any item into an exceptional, valuable piece of art in its own right; and its worth was enhanced when the workmanship was of the quality that a seasoned master like Fedele brought to his carving. The skilled artistry, that prodigious *tenerezza* so admired by Giovan Pietro Bellori[2] coupled with the subtle differentiation of textures – the rough ground, the interplay of polished facets to mark the shadows cast on other surfaces, thus achieving a

nuanced lighting that belies the uniformity of the stone – combine to make this piece a wonderful present; a gift fit for a prince.

François du Quesnoy's composition reflects his meticulous study of classical sources, reinterpreted here in a masterly manner. During their time in Rome, both he and Nicolas Poussin (1594–1665) examined the whole range of gestures displayed by those *putti*, whose representation – as the personification of innocent sentiments – was spared from moral constraints and censure. Close analysis of ancient statuary and of highly influential paintings such as the 1518 *Worship of Venus* by Titian (c. 1488–1576)[3] – which by the 1620s was in the Villa Ludovisi in Rome – provided the basis for a formal composition which achieved great success and was widely circulated.[4]

The theme of the struggle between Sacred Love and Profane Love is a classical *topos* which echoed down the centuries, highlighting the permanent relevance of that clash of opposites between which human nature is torn: the spiritual versus the carnal. We could trace the subject back to its earliest origins, highlighting numerous instances in western art; but here we need only focus on the period when this kind of relief was being produced to see how current the idea was in contemporary thought.

Illustrated publications aimed at an international readership – such as *Amoris divini et humani antipathia*, with verses in French, Spanish, and Flemish, first published in Antwerp in 1629 – clearly show that the notion of constantly-warring passions was topical at the time, and that cultured seventeenth-century society focused particularly on its development through love-related emblems. At the same time, though tackled with a less sophisticated rhetoric intended to convey a plainer message, the theme was popular in allegorical devotional prints, including an engraving by Hieronymus Wierix (1553–1619) – that served as a source for later reliefs and paintings – which shows Divine Love triumphing over Cupid, like a conventional Archangel Michael trampling the devil underfoot.[5]

Given this context, it is easy to see why the eternal battle between the spiritual and the earthly was a recurring motif in both literature and the fine arts. Guido Reni himself addressed the subject in a painting now at the Gallerie Nazionali di Palazzo Spinola in Genoa [cat. 67], while – again highlighting the significance of the context – Pope Urban VIII devoted verses to it in his poetry collection *Poemata*, which went through several editions from 1621 onwards. These links point to a shared community of interests, whose internal diversity thwarts any attempt to confine it to a single artistic discipline. Curiously enough, Pope Urban's verse collection included lines in praise of Reni, precisely likening his painterly skills to those of a sculptor, and highlighting the point at which the boundaries between the two disciplines become blurred, as they evidently do in a relief like this one.

Manuel Arias Martínez

---

1 Lisbon, Museu Calouste Gulbenkian, inv. 546.
2 Bellori 1672, 271: 'Tomaso Fedele Romano chiamato Tomaso del porfido, per la facilità sua nel lavorarlo, e condurlo con tenerezza in perfettione'.
3 Madrid, Museo Nacional del Prado, P-419.
4 Lingo 2007, 42–63; Pierguidi 2017.
5 Hollstein–Ruyven-Zeman, Stock and Leesberg 2004, 55, no. 1714.

67   Guido Reni

Sacred Love burning the Arrows of Profane Love

1622–23
Oil on canvas, 132 × 163 cm
Genoa, Gallerie Nazionali di Palazzo Spinola, GNPS 111

Provenance: Luigi Zambeccari, Bologna, 1630; Francesco Maria Zambeccari, Bologna, 1649; Giuseppe Luigi Zambeccari, Bologna, 1670; Paolo Francesco Spinola, Genoa, 1780.

Selected bibliography: G. Zanelli in Casazza and Gennaioli 2005, 130–31; E. Brachi in Swoboda and Scholten 2019, 131; A. Iommelli in Cappelletti and Gennari Santori 2021, 80; T. Gatarski in Eclercy 2022a, 244–45, no. 100.

The scene is set in an open space which is not readily identifiable: on the right, a chubby boy recognisable by his blindfold and wings as Eros, or Cupid, is immobilised, his hands tied behind his back. In the closer central foreground, a handsome young man – also winged – is busy casting arrows from a red quiver into a fire. This is Anteros who, by destroying Cupid's deadly darts, renders him wholly harmless. A theme addressed more widely in late-antique and medieval literature than in classical mythology, the battle between Eros and Anteros – that is, between earthly or profane love and heavenly or sacred love – was particularly popular during the Counter-Reformation, as it was held to represent the final triumph of virtue over vice, the latter identified with human passions. The score and musical instruments in the left background, possibly alluding to restored harmony, may be linked to that victory.[1]

Unlike the pictures produced in the early seventeenth century by painters such as Annibale Carracci (1560–1609) and Giovanni Baglione (c. 1566–1643), which focused on the clash between the two rivals, Guido Reni took as his source a well-known sixteenth-century work, Andrea Alciato's *Emblemata* (1531), a collection of moral motifs drawn mostly from classical mythology. Emblem 110 – or in later editions 111 – is entitled 'Anteros, Amor virtutis, alium Cupidinem superans',[2] and the illustration that accompanies the text in several of the subsequent editions of the book shows Anteros tying his opponent to a tree, while on the left Cupid's bow and arrows have been consigned to a bonfire.

Critics have long agreed that this canvas was painted in the early 1620s, a hypothesis borne out by stylistic comparisons with other paintings by Reni produced at around that time, among them the versions of *Saint Sebastian* in London, Paris,[3] and Madrid [cat. 19], whose pose exactly mirrors that of the little

Eros. But the most distinctive feature of a work like this is its focus on functional form as a means of achieving the ideal, classical beauty constantly pursued by the artist.

As for its provenance, most scholars – even in very recent studies – maintain that the first record of the painting in Bologna dates from 1670;[4] however, research carried out in past years into the Zambeccari collection in Bologna enables us to establish an earlier date.[5] It is clear that the owner at that time was Count Giuseppe Luigi Zambeccari (1637–1699), who hailed from a branch of the family – its prestige derived from several generations of army officers – known as 'da Reno' because it occupied a building behind the church of Santa Maria Maggiore in a complex overlooking the Reno canal. It is known that Giuseppe Luigi attempted to sell several masterpieces – among them Guido's *Samson Victorious* [fig. 14] – collected by his grandfather, Luigi (1570–1630), and by his father, Francesco Maria (1607–1649); the inventory drawn up after his father's death on 9 December 1649 includes an entry reading 'Two Loves by the aforementioned [Reni] in a painting',[6] which certainly refers to this canvas. However, given the chronology of the painting, and the information – albeit discovered somewhat later – that it was produced for the Zambeccari family,[7] we may conclude that it was commissioned by Luigi, and can therefore be identified as one of the 'nine paintings between large and small … by the hand of Signor Guido Reni'[8] mentioned in an inventory drawn up on 10 September 1630, just over a month after Luigi's death.[9]

Since the planned sale of 1670 proved unsuccessful, the painting must still have belonged to Giuseppe Luigi Zambeccari on that date, and although the inventory after his death also mentions 'a painting depicting Divine and Profane Love',[10] the lack of an attribution and the estimate of only 70 lire rules out any possibility that the canvas under study here still belonged to him.

The whereabouts of the painting between the time it belonged to Giuseppe Luigi and 1780 currently remains unknown. Thereafter, it is recorded as hanging continuously in the Palazzo Spinola in Genoa's Piazza Pellicceria[11] (where it is still located), which had been purchased around ten years earlier by Paolo

Francesco Spinola (1746–1824), who belonged to the San Luca branch of the family. Nor is it known when or how he acquired the painting. Paolo Francesco's uncle, Cardinal Girolamo Spinola (1713–1784), who in 1740 was living in Bologna in his capacity as papal vice-legate,[12] could have been a hypothetical intermediary.

Piero Boccardo

1 The meaning of these motifs remains unclear: Eva Brachi (in Swoboda and Scholten 2019, 131) regards them as of uncertain significance, though she refers to the study by Ziane 2011, 373–75; by contrast, Antonio Iommelli (in Cappelletti and Gennari Santori 2021, 80) reads them as emblems of vanity.

2 'Anteros, the love of virtue, defeating the other Cupid [that is, Eros]'. The first edition of the *Emblemata* was published in Augsburg in 1531, but over the following decades it was reprinted in Paris, Padua, Antwerp, Leiden, and elsewhere.

3 London, Dulwich Picture Gallery, DPG268; Paris, Musée du Louvre, inv. 532.

4 In his letter sent from Bologna on 18 January 1670 to the great Messina collector Antonio Ruffo, prince of Scaletta, the famous physiologist Marcello Malpighi – who was certainly well acquainted with the gentleman, having lived for many years in Messina – offered to sell him: 'Il quadro di Guido … quale è un amor divino, che avendo legato amor profano, abbrugia gl'istromenti di vanità, [e] oltre le due figure vi sono varij stromenti di musica et un paese' ('the painting by Guido … which is a divine love, which, having bound profane love, reduces to ashes the instruments of vanity, [and] beyond the two figures there are various musical instruments and a village'), cf. Ruffo 1916, 122–23. It should be noted, as confirming what follows in the text, that Malpighi – in the same letter – refers to the painting as 'Two Loves'.

5 Cammarota 2001.

6 'Due Amori del suddetto [Reni] in un quadro'.

7 This information also features in Marcello Malpighi's letter, quoted in note 4 above.

8 'Nove quadri tra grandi e piccoli … di mano del Signor Guido Reni'.

9 For the two inventory quotations, respectively, see Cammarota 2001, 120, no. 20, and 108. Gian Piero Cammarota had already suggested that the 'Two Loves' listed in 1649 was in fact one of the nine paintings cited in the 1630 inventory; although this suggests that it was sold after 1649 – indeed, it remained unsold until after 1670, as Malpighi's letter shows – Cammarota links the later entry to the painting in the Galleria Spinola.

10 'Un quadro di pittura rappresentante l'Amore Divino, e Profano'.

11 The long interval elapsing between these dates led Gianluca Zanelli (in Casazza and Gennaioli 2005, 130–31) – whom the reader can also consult for quotations from travellers' accounts and archival sources – to question whether the painting in the Palazzo Spinola can be unquestionably identified as the one that once belonged to the Zambeccari family. However, the fact that it is the best known painting on this subject, due in part – as argued here – to the prestige enjoyed by the gentleman who commissioned it, would appear to resolve this doubt.

12 After 1748, the cardinal settled in nearby Ferrara, as papal legate.

68 Alessandro Algardi

(Bologna 1595–1654 Rome)

Eros and Anteros

c. 1630
Marble, 82.5 cm
Vienna, Gartenpalais Liechtenstein, The Princely Collections,
SK 1481

Provenance: Palazzo Sampieri, Bologna, 1670; Eugène de Beauharnais, 1st Duke of Leuchtenberg, Milan; Leuchtenberg family, Munich and St Petersburg; on loan to the Academy of Arts, St Petersburg, 1884–97; art market, New York, 1980; private collection; Prince Hans-Adam II of Liechtenstein, 2006.

Selected bibliography: Montagu 1985, 2:397, L.112 (as disappeared); Boudon-Machuel 2005, 78–79; Pierguidi 2012a, 171–73; Mazza 2018, 283 and 307; F. Scholten in Swoboda and Scholten 2019, 127, no. 13.

This marble group representing Eros fighting with Anteros is one of the most exquisite pieces ever produced by Alessandro Algardi. The gentle gestures, the tender flesh, the meticulously rhythmic sculpting of each lock of the amoretti's hair, as though it had a life of its own, make this a uniquely refined contribution to Roman Baroque sculpture. The little brothers – sons of Venus and Mars (Aphrodite and Ares in Greek mythology) – are shown wrestling, after a model that Pausanias recalled seeing in a bas-relief in the gymnasium at Elis.[1] Echoes of the ancient dispute between the two Cupids resounded though the erudite literary and visual culture of the Renaissance and Baroque periods, from Andrea Alciato's well-known *Emblemata* (1531) to the gallery of the Palazzo Farnese, in whose corners Annibale Carracci (1560–1609) painted Eros and Anteros disputing the palm of victory, as described by Pausanias.[2] Although Annibale was probably Algardi's main and most authoritative visual source, this piece bears an even greater compositional affinity to the *Putti fighting* by Guido Reni at the Galleria Doria Pamphilj in Rome.[3] Algardi was apparently influenced by the postures of the *putti* in Reni's painting, almost like stills capturing different moments in the fight, and also included Cupid's standard attributes, the bow and quiver. Going further back, the *Eros and Anteros* group displays a striking resemblance to the foreshortened fresco of *Putti carrying a Mitre* painted by Guido around 1611 for the church of Santa Maria dei Servi in Bologna,

which Algardi must have seen before moving to Mantua and thence to Rome [fig. 88]. Nowhere is Malvasia's sobriquet for Algardi – 'a new Guido in marble' – better justified.[4]

The *Eros and Anteros* group is one of the major discoveries of the last twenty years in the field of Italian Baroque sculpture. It was first published in 2005 by Marion Boudon-Machuel, who based her attribution on Jennifer Montagu's exhaustive monograph on Algardi, in which she reconstructed the entire history of the piece, which she assumed was lost. Although nothing is known regarding either the timing or the circumstances of the original commission, there is evidence that Algardi's talent for carving *putti* – displayed from the moment he arrived in Rome in 1625 – earned him considerable contemporary acclaim.[5] His *Eros and Anteros* remained known throughout the seventeenth and eighteenth centuries; not in Rome, where it was probably sculpted, but in Bologna, where it was exhibited in the Palazzo Sampieri

Fig. 88 Guido Reni, *Putti carrying a Mitre*, c. 1611. Fresco removed from the former Cappella dell'Armi in Santa Maria dei Servi, Bologna (now in the sacristy)

on the Strada Maggiore. This is where it was presumably seen by Nicodemus Tessin the Younger (1654–1728) in the course of his travels around Italy between 1687 and 1688.[6] In the famous Sampieri collection, Algardi's *Amoretti* engaged with a number of highly prestigious paintings featuring similar figures, such as the *Dance of the Cupids* by Francesco Albani (1578–1660)[7] or the *Triumph of Venus* by Marcantorio Franceschini (1648–1729), now in a private collection.[8] In 1701, Luigi Sampieri even commissioned a marble pendant for the Algardi piece from the sculptor Giuseppe Maria Mazza (1653–1741), who before 1703 produced a *Sacred Love and Profane Love* identified as the piece auctioned by Trinity Fine Art, London, in 1990.[9] Luigi Sampieri's desire to pair Algardi's work with another piece on a similar theme highlights both the prestige enjoyed at the time by *Eros and Anteros* and the care with which the art patron was constructing a visual discourse on love through paintings and sculptures by local Bologna artists. In his inventory of the collection, drawn up in the early eighteenth century, Valerio Sampieri described *Eros and Anteros* as 'the work of Algardi's famous chisel, and in their naturalness, liveliness and softness they have nothing to envy Greek works'.[10] It is worth recalling, too, that an inventory of the Palazzo Sampieri compiled by the painter Galgano Perpignani (1694/95–1771) in 1743 included 'a terracotta model of Algardi's *putti*'.[11] His *Eros and Anteros* remained on display in the palace on the Strada Maggiore until its controversial sale by Francesco Sampieri to Eugène de Beauharnais in 1811.[12] It was probably in the Leuchtenberg collection in Munich in 1851, when it featured in a set of engravings by Johannes Nepomuk Muxel (1790–1870). After a somewhat eventful history, it was purchased in 2006 by the Prince of Liechtenstein, and is now in his collection.[13]

Fernando Loffredo

1 Merrill 1944.
2 Tervarent 1965; Dempsey 1995, 24–25 and 35–39; Comboni 2000, 9–12; Colonna 2007.
3 Rome, Galleria Doria Pamphilj, FC 257; Safarik and Torselli 1982, fig. 220; Pierguidi 2014.
4 Malvasia 1678, 2:35: 'Un nuovo Guido in marmo'. For the English translation, see Malvasia–Pericolo 2019, 1:83.
5 On Algardi and *putti* as an artistic genre in Baroque Rome, see Pierguidi 2012a, 166–67.
6 Montagu 1985, 2:397.
7 Milan, Pinacoteca di Brera, inv. 301.
8 Mazza 2018.
9 See Massari 2012–13, 643–46, no. 80; Mazza 2018, 298–99.
10 Mazza 2018, 298: 'Opera del famoso scarpello dell'Algardi, e per la sua naturalezza, vivacità e morbideza non hanno invidia alle opere greche'.
11 Ibid., 307: 'Un abbozzo de puttini dell'Algardi di terra cotta'.
12 Ibid., 282–83.
13 Ibid., fig. 16.

69   Giovanni Battista Morelli
(Rome, ?–1669 Madrid)

The Christ Child Asleep on a Heart

c. 1659–69
Polychrome terracotta, 44.5 × 56.5 × 31 cm
Valladolid, Museo Nacional de Escultura, CE1185

Provenance: Purchased from Eugenio Fontaneda in 1987.
Bibliography: Peña Martín 2011, 232; Coppel 2013, 191; Gil Saura 2018, 125–26.

In the wake of the Council of Trent, Counter-Reformation art encouraged a more humanised depiction of the childhood of Christ, combining a childlike tenderness and innocence with the premonition of his Passion and death. Guido Reni successfully tackled this theme in paintings such as the *Madonna adoring the Sleeping Christ Child* in the Galleria Doria Pamphilj[1] and the *Sleeping Christ Child* in the Princeton University Art Museum,[2] which achieved enormous renown through prints produced both in the master's workshop and by his followers.[3]

These compositions were known, copied, and reinterpreted in Spain, especially by painters sharing Reni's sensibility and his poetically *intimiste* approach, among them Bartolomé Esteban Murillo (1617–1682) [cat. 70]. They also arrived to the Iberian Peninsula by way of Italian artists such as the sculptor Giovanni Battista Morelli, who had trained in Rome under the classicist sculptor Alessandro Algardi (1595–1654). After a somewhat restless life, Morelli settled first in Valencia and later in Madrid, where he produced pieces for an aristocratic clientele with Italianate tastes in art and also worked on the decoration of Spanish palaces.

Like his master Algardi, Morelli was a skilled modeller in stucco, and even – as recent research has confirmed – cast some of his pieces in bronze.[4] In order to meet the demands of a devout clientele often interested in emotionally charged, polychrome terracotta images for their private oratories, he produced at least six sculptures of the sleeping Christ Child. Information on these pieces, now in private collections, has helped to expand knowledge of Morelli's oeuvre. All of these works contain allegorical elements characteristic of Baroque symbolism: in four, the Child's head rests on a skull,[5] while in two – including this one – it reclines on a heart.[6] Some also feature a decorative cartouche containing an inscription alluding to the subject matter depicted. The Christ Child under study here is the only one with a base made up of clouds and

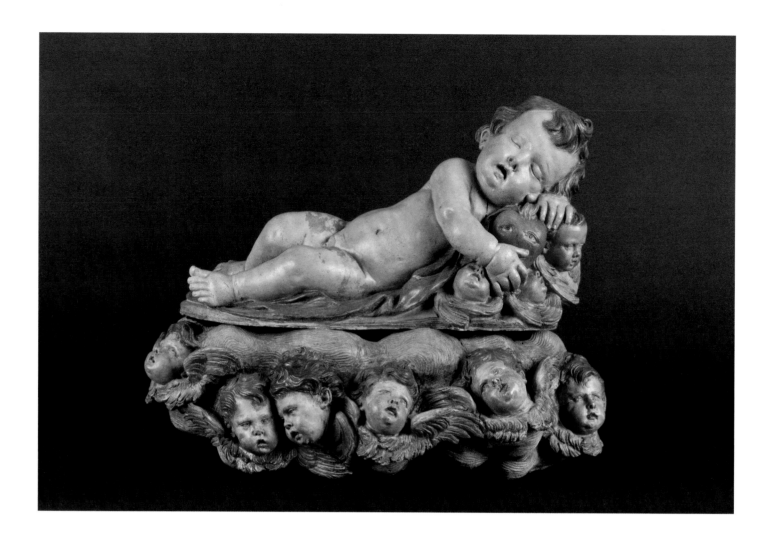

cherubim. Athough the figure does not sit seamlessly on the support, we assume that both parts were made by the same artist at the same date. Save for their attributes, all these pieces follow the same compositional pattern, have fairly similar dimensions, and share a style – characterised by a plump, chubby-cheeked figure with unruly, wavy hair – that is reminiscent of other documented works by Morelli, such as the *Infant Saint John the Baptist* in the Museo del Prado[7] and the stucco *putti* decorating Charles II's former study at the Palacio Real in Aranjuez. Royal records also contain references to other works sharing this iconography; in the inventory of Philip V (1747), Morelli is listed as the author of 'A Christ Child asleep on a world, resting on a cloth and a rock' and 'Another Christ Child holding the crown of thorns and a heart'.[8]

While drawing on these models, Morelli may also have been influenced by an interesting but little-known print now in the British Museum, whose graphic style closely resembles that of Guido [fig. 89]. It depicts a sleeping Cupid, his head resting on his right arm in a posture redolent of repose and sweet oblivion, while the left arm trails in front of his body. This overlapping of the Christ Child iconography with the classical representation of the sleeping Eros is hardly surprising, especially since Morelli's master Algardi is known to have taken ancient marbles on this theme as a reference for his *Allegory of Sleep* at the Galleria

Borghese.[9] Morelli may also have become familiar with Guido's work in an indirect manner, through paintings based on Reni prototypes well known in Rome, such as the *Holy Family* by Niccolò Tornioli (1606–1651) at the Galleria Spada,[10] sold in 1643 to Cardenal Bernardino Spada, whose family commissioned work from Morelli in 1646.[11] He might also have seen sculptural treatments of the theme, such as the *Christ Child Asleep on the Cross* – now in a private collection in Florence – attributed to Algardi.[12] Judging by the remarkable subsequent success of its profane variant, the *Cupid with a Bow*,[13] this must have been a favourite composition among contemporary Roman sculptors.

The iconography of the Christ Child asleep on a heart has its origin in a text from the *Song of Songs* (5:2) – 'I sleep, but my heart waketh' – often associated with the Child asleep on the cross, as a reflection on divine generosity and self-giving through redemption. But for its proper contextualisation we must take into account the increasingly popular cult of the heart spurred particularly by Benedictus van Haeften's *Schola cordis sive aversi a Deo cordis ad eumdem reductio et instructio* (Antwerp, 1629), an illustrated emblem book underpinned by the notion of the human soul in transit towards a path of spiritual perfection, guided by divine love.[14] The heart is the resting-place of the soul; in keeping with this, in the sculpture discussed here the heart's eyes are open – in allusion to the deity's watchful attitude – and aflame with divine love. Other contemporary texts, such as Herman Hugo's *Pia desideria emblematis...* (Antwerp, 1624), stressed the training of the soul through guiding love, which may account for the devotional efficacy and popularity of images of this kind, intended as an aid to pious meditation in private oratories.

Roberto Alonso Moral

1 Rome, Galleria Doria Pamphilj, FC 288.
2 Princeton (New Jersey), Princeton University Art Museum, Gift of J. Lionberger Davis, Class of 1900, y1952-33.
3 Candi 2016, 210–11.
4 Gil Saura 2018, 109–18; López Conde 2021.
5 Madrid, Alcalá Subastas, 6–7 May 2009, lot 135, more recently auctioned in New York at Sotheby's, *Master Sculpture and Works of Art, Part II*, 30 January 2021, lot 782; Munich, Neumeister, *Fine Art & Antiques*, 26 September 2018, lot 187, now in Jaime Eguiguren Art & Antiques; Barcelona, La Suite Subastas, 30 May 2019, lot 62; and New York, Sotheby's, *Master Painting & Sculpture Day Sale*, 31 January 2019, lot 224.
6 The other version was in Coll & Cortés in 2013, see Coppel 2013.
7 Madrid, Museo Nacional del Prado, E-632.
8 Coppel 2013, 190.
9 Rome, Galleria Borghese, CLX.
10 Weston 2016, 139–41, fig. 62.
11 Montagu 1985, 2:445 and 2:476.
12 Parronchi 1992, 19–20, pl. 16b. This work has also been attributed to Giovacchino Fortini (1670–1736), in Visonà 2011.
13 See Bellesi 2019.
14 Sebastián 1985, 322–27; Ruiz Gómez 1998, 182–84.

Fig. 89 Workshop of Guido Reni, *Cupid Asleep*, 1620–50. Etching, 42 × 80 mm. London, The British Museum, U,3.185

70 Bartolomé Esteban Murillo
(Seville 1617–1682)

The Christ Child Asleep on the Cross

c. 1660
Oil on canvas, 63 × 88 cm
Madrid, Museo Nacional del Prado, P-1003
[NOT ON DISPLAY IN THE EXHIBITION]

Provenance: Collection of Florencio and Juan Kelly, Amsterdam; Spanish royal collection, Madrid, 1764; Palacio Real, Madrid, 1772; dressing-room at the Palacio Real, Madrid, 1794; Infante Don Carlos' quarters, third room at the Palacio Real, Madrid, 1814–18.

Selected bibliography: Gaya Nuño 1978, 115, no. 336; Angulo Íñiguez 1981, 2:193–94; *Museo del Prado* 1990, 1:66, no. 179; Pérez Sánchez 1993, 136; Triadó 1999, 40; Orihuela and Pérez 2017, 123; Japón 2018b, 77–78.

Bartolomé Esteban Murillo created a series of images of the infancy of Jesus which, over time, became established in Spain's cultural consciousness through the diffusion of countless reproductions, right up to the present day. Good examples include the *Infant Christ and Saint John the Baptist with a Shell* [fig. 63] and the *Holy Family with a Little Bird*,[1] paintings which share a number of formal features that succeed in arousing devotion through endearing tenderness. In these everyday scenes, the common gestures of the holy figures elicit the empathy of the faithful. But Murillo also made use of children as a means of creating visual metaphors that prompted the viewer to reflect on theological matters. Such is the purpose of his depictions of the *Christ Child Asleep on the Cross*, in some cases surrounded by the attributes of his martyrdom, together with a skull that prefigures his Passion and death.

This iconography can be traced back to the early sixteenth century, and specifically to an engraving by Giacomo Francia (c. 1447–1517), in which the image of the infant Jesus asleep on the cross is accompanied by a verse from the *Song of Songs* (5:2), 'I sleep, but my heart waketh',[2] perhaps alluding to the contemplative soul, which remains watchful even though the body may sleep. Interpreted in Marian terms,[3] however, this verse might refer to the protective role assumed by Mary, aware of her son's destiny from the moment of his birth. Though not based on a biblical event – indeed, the composition was probably inspired by a Hellenistic sculpture representing the allegory of Sleep – this subject not only survived Church censorship following the Council of Trent, aimed at seeking authenticity in the visual arts, but also enjoyed widespread popularity as a theme for pious meditation. Guido Reni's various reworkings of the theme were highly successful, to judge by the numerous versions attributed to him, the engravings made of his compositions, and the influence they exerted on other painters.

Murillo was among the artists thus inspired, as is evident in this Prado canvas showing Jesus asleep on a cross, laying on the purple drapery beneath him, his right hand resting on a skull. In Seville, Murillo would have seen not only prints of Reni's work, but at least one painted copy that was on show in the archbishop's palace when Domingo Pimentel was the primate of Seville, around 1650, when this picture was painted.[4] At that time, moreover, the painter Alonso de Zamora y Toro had at his home in Seville an original painting on this theme by Reni.[5]

By contrast, Benito Navarrete Prieto suggests that Murillo may have been inspired by the figure in an engraving by Francesco Vanni (1563–1610) of the *Virgin adoring the Sleeping Christ Child*,[6] while Alfonso E. Pérez Sánchez had earlier discerned echoes of the *Christ Child Asleep on the Cross* by Bartolomeo Cavarozzi (c. 1587–1625) when he compared Murillo's canvas with a painting in the Museo del Prado[7] attributed at the time to Cavarozzi but now thought to be the work of Orazio Gentileschi (1563–1639).[8]

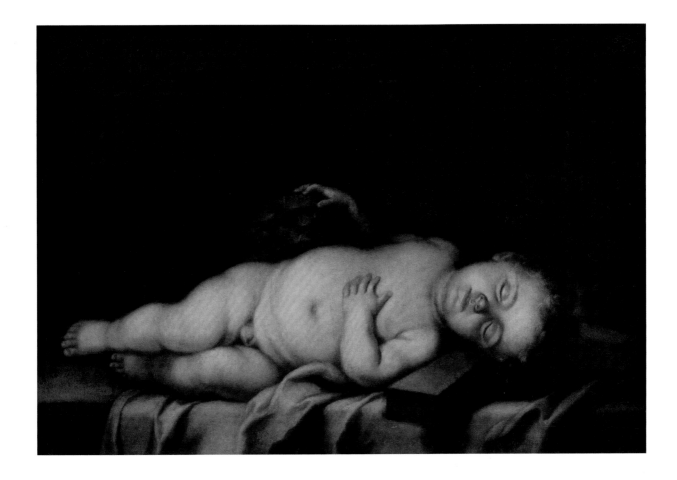

The authorship of this canvas has also sparked some debate. In the early twentieth century it was listed in the Museum's catalogues as a copy, a view rejected by a number of Murillo specialists, including August L. Mayer.[9] Later, Juan Antonio Gaya Nuño dismissed it as an unquestionable copy, but Diego Angulo Íñiguez hailed it as one of Murillo's finest originals on this subject, an attribution that has not since been challenged. Interestingly, a further *Sleeping Christ Child* by Murillo – once owned and exhibited at the palace of Boadilla del Monte by another member of the royal family, Luis Antonio Jaime de Borbón y Farnesio – was auctioned in 2018.[10]

Rafael Japón

1 Madrid, Museo Nacional del Prado, P-960.
2 Song of Songs 5:2: 'Ego dormio et cor meum vigilat'. Giacomo Francia is thought to have based his composition on a print – published by Barthel Beham (1502–1540) in Bologna in 1525 – showing a child asleep, resting on a skull, which has been interpreted as a kind of *vanitas* or allegory of the passage of time; see Pérez López 2015, 148.
3 Butiñá 1889, 435–36
4 Japón 2018b, 76.
5 It is listed in a 1651 inventory of his assets as an original by Reni, together with a *Christ carrying the Cross*; Kinkead 2009, 631; Japón 2020a, 1:488.
6 Navarrete Prieto 1998, 292.
7 Madrid, Museo Nacional del Prado, P-1240.
8 Pérez Sánchez 1993, 136.
9 Mayer 1913, 250.
10 Sotheby's, London, *Old Masters* sale, 5 December 2018, lot 22.

71 Domenico Tintoretto
(Venice 1560–1635)

Lady revealing her Breast

1580–90
Oil on canvas, 62 × 55.6 cm
Madrid, Museo Nacional del Prado, P-382

Provenance: Collection of Philip IV, 1636–66; Galería del Mediodía (South Gallery), Real Alcázar, Madrid, 1666; Real Alcázar, Madrid, 1686 and 1700; Real Museo, Madrid, 1834.

Selected bibliography: M. Falomir in Finaldi and Savvateev 2011, 80–81, no. 8; Ferino-Pagden 2022; Gazzola 2022, fig. 42.

A number of portraits of Venetian ladies entered the Spanish royal collection between 1636 and 1666.[1] One is known to have hung close to *Las Meninas*[2] and beside Guido Reni's *Girl with a Rose* [cat. 72] in Philip IV's summer study at the Alcázar in Madrid, as part of a decoration programme designed by Diego Velázquez (1599–1660).[3] Given the absence of detailed descriptions in the inventories, coupled with changes to the format of some of these works, it is difficult to identify the canvas in question with any certainty; however, the quality, gesture, and colour range make this picture a good candidate.

In iconographical terms, the portrait belongs to the 'Venetian beauty' type, whose precedents include busts sculpted by Tullio Lombardo (c. 1455–1532)[4] and the *Portrait of a Young Woman* painted by Giorgione (1477/78–1510) in 1506.[5] Although these pictures have traditionally been associated with courtesans – the lovers and mistresses of rich and influential men, women envied and despised for their freedom and power – some critics have also identified them as brides, wives, heroines, and saints, and have even termed them 'lyrical female portraits'.[6] The controversy over the status of these women stems from the narrow formal line separating them from Venetian noblewomen, highlighted in contemporary art and literature.[7] However, the identification of this lady as an 'honest and cultured courtesan'[8] is supported not only by two drawings in the *Mores Italiae* (1575)[9] – *Ritratto de la Ragusea in Venetia* and *Veronica Franco* – but also by a remark made by Veronica Franco, the famous Venetian poet and courtesan, in her *Lettere familiari a diversi*, addressed to a young woman about to enter the high-level prostitution business.[10] On the basis of these sources, some critics identify the sitter as Franco herself. The viewer cannot help being moved by her melancholy gaze, which seems to reflect the bitter thoughts expressed in one of her verses dedicated to women 'obliged to eat with another's mouth, sleep with another's eyes, and move according to another's will'.[11]

X-radiography has revealed that the young woman initially faced the viewer, but Domenico later placed her in profile. This marked a significant iconographical innovation, in that it suggests a comparison with the patrician women featured on Roman medals, thus interweaving the ancient world with Venetian society. Her static pose is countered by her movement in uncovering her breasts, a gesture described in *L'arte de' cenni* (1616), a contemporary treatise by Giovanni Bonifacio, as symbolising the desire to display oneself and attract the gaze, but also to receive and safeguard a lover's feelings.[12] Uncovering one's breast was thus an equivocal gesture, somewhere between virtuous and lascivious,[13] which makes it difficult to classify some of these portraits.

Whatever her status, the image of the bare-breasted lady achieved considerable success in the Venetian art world, and became a model for the painting of flesh in a lifelike manner,[14] this being a major concern of Venetian artists, inherited by Guido Reni. The young woman's alabaster skin is offset by her slight flush, her full lips, her copper-blond hair,[15] and the sensuality of her nipples. Whether or not she is Veronica Franco, she epitomises the archetypal eroticised beauty of the Venetian Renaissance – rooted in the Middle Ages – which is sufficiently lifelike to exert on the viewer an appeal both visual and tactile. Yet the rosy white complexion of these girls – much envied by European women – was not always natural. The large amount of lead white in these pictures, apart from being a painterly convention, recalls the widespread use of this toxic substance in make-up[16] – *trucco* – where it was tinged with mercury-based vermilion,[17] while veins were highlighted with lapis lazuli; these customs led to ageing, hair loss, and sometimes death.[18]

Ana González Mozo

1 M. Falomir in Finaldi and Savvateev 2011, 80–81.
2 Madrid, Museo Nacional del Prado, P-1174.
3 Palomino [1715–24] 1947, 920–22. Cruz Yábar 2017–18.
4 *Self-Portrait (?) with his Wife in Ancient Guise*, c. 1490, Venice, Galleria Giorgio Franchetti alla Ca' d'Oro; and *Bacchus and Ariadne*, c. 1505–10, Vienna, Kunsthistorisches Museum Wien, Kunstkammer, inv. 7471.
5 Vienna, Kunsthistorisches Museum Wien, Gemäldegalerie, inv. 31; Dal Pozzolo 2022.
6 Palacios Méndez 2021; Ferino-Pagden 2022.
7 Vecellio 1590, 137, 138, 143a, and 143; Villamont 1602, book I, 195–96; Montaigne–D'Ancona 1889, 133–36 and 301–2; Coryate [1611] 1978, 399.
8 Scarabello 2013, 14–35; and Masson 1975; Rosenthal 1992; Milani 1994, 87–102; S. F. Matthews-Grieco in Corbin, Courtine and Vigarello 2005, 202–4.
9 Rippa and Finucci 2007, 123 and 126.
10 Franco 1580, 46.
11 Ibid., 45.
12 Bonifacio 1616, 357–65.
13 Coryate [1611] 1978, 399.
14 *Sub voce* 'carnosità', in https://www.treccani.it/vocabolario/carnosita.
15 Vecellio 1590, 145; Cortese 1677, 71.
16 Vecellio 1590, 144; Cortese 1677, 138–39, 177, and 196–97.
17 Cortese 1677, 95–96.
18 Laguna [1554] 1968–69 (1969), 2:book V, ch. LXIX, 40, 51–52, and 67.

72 Guido Reni

Girl with a Rose

c. 1636–37
Oil on canvas, 81 × 62 cm (with additions)
Madrid, Museo Nacional del Prado, P-218

Provenance: First mentioned in an inventory of the Real Alcázar, Madrid, in 1666; listed in the Real Alcázar, Madrid, in 1686, 1701, 1703, and 1734 (no. 162); Casas Arzobispales, Madrid, in 1747; mentioned in the Palacio del Buen Retiro, Madrid, in 1772 (no. 86), 1787, 1794 (no. 376), and 1808–14; listed in the Palacio Real, Madrid, in 1814–18 (no. 376); first mentioned in the Museo del Prado in 1854–58.

Selected bibliography: Pérez Sanchez 1965a, 173; Ebert-Schifferer, Emiliani and Schleier 1988, 182–84, no. 182; Pepper 1988, 272, no. 122.

Recent technical examination carried out by the Museo del Prado has established that the original canvas on which *Girl with a Rose* was executed measured 67.5 × 53 centimetres, although the surface originally painted by Guido Reni was only 62.5 × 50 centimetres, with the remaining used as borders for the easel. This is confirmed by the first mention of the painting in the 1666 inventory of the Madrid Alcázar: 'Another painting three-quarters of a *vara* high and half a *vara* wide of a head by Guido from Bologna with a rose in the hand [prized] fifty ducats'.[1] According to this listing, *Girl with a Rose* thus measured 62.5 × 41.8 centimetres (a *vara* being 83.59 centimetres approximately). Prior to 1734, the canvas of the painting was re-stretched, relined, and enlarged through additions, as documented by the measurements recorded in the 1734 inventory of the Madrid Alcázar, 'una vara de alto y tres quartas de ancho', which corresponds to its current size.[2] In its original format, the outermost lower left corner tightly framed the hand holding the rose – the foreshortened arm, adjacent drape, and the parapet being absent.

It is unknown when and how the painting reached the Spanish royal collection. Because it was not recorded in the 1636 inventory of the Madrid Alcázar, it is certain that King Philip IV (1605–1665) received it after that date. He had it placed in his summer office, the 'despacho de verano', and it can be assumed that his choice of paintings for this space was consistent with his own taste. Since 1645, Diego Velázquez (1599–1660) had been tasked with refurbishing the king's summer quarters in the Alcázar. In 1658–59, Philip IV ordered the Bolognese *quadratura* painters Agostino Mitelli (1609–1660) and Angelo Michele Colonna (1604–1687) to decorate the vault of his summer office with a depiction of the *Fall of Phaethon*. In his *Felsina pittrice*

(1678), Carlo Cesare Malvasia describes Philip IV's satisfaction with Mitelli and Colonna's work in the Alcázar, adding, however, in connection with the decoration of the Salón de Espejos (Hall of Mirrors) in the same palace: 'They were to paint a Pandora in the centre [of the ceiling] and had produced a fine drawing of it, which, because it was disliked by Diego Velázquez, all the more so could not be to the liking of His Majesty, who trusted everything to him'.[3] Despite his reliance on Velázquez, the king was personally involved in the decoration of his summer quarters. In a letter of 6 February 1658 from Madrid, Cardinal Camillo Massimo (1620–1677), then the apostolic nuncio to the Spanish court, reported that the king had fallen sick 'for having spent a long time the previous day in his summer quarters to see some pictures be arranged'.[4] That the king was keen on the decoration of his summer office is above all suggested by the presence there of Velázquez's famous *Las Meninas* (1656),[5] which hung not far from a pair of allegories recently donated by Cardinal Massimo: Guido's *Cupid with a Bow* [cat. 64] and Guercino's (1591–1666) *Cupid spurning Riches* [cat. 65], both now at the Prado.[6] It is possible that *Girl with a Rose* served as a pendant to Domenico Tintoretto's (1560–1635) *Venetian Girl*, also listed in the summer office, although at the time the two paintings had differing sizes.[7] While the decoration of the summer office was characterised by a variety of pictorial genres and themes, the Massimo pair of Cupids along with the two female portraits by Guido and Tintoretto were clearly meant to introduce an amorous, gallant note, apparently dear to the king.

It bears remarking that the head of *Girl with a Rose* is substantially the reverse of the head of Helen in Guido's renowned *Abduction of Helen* at the Louvre [fig. 35], which was originally destined for Philip IV but ended up in the hands of Marie de' Medici, French queen regent (1575–1642) [see cat. 22 and 50].[8] This becomes evident by comparing *Girl with a Rose* with an untraced drawing by Guido of the *Head of Helen*.[9] Malvasia reports that the King of Spain, 'knowing full well what had happened with the Abduction of Helen, after complaining about it with his ambassadors', ordered from Guido a *Latona*, which remained unfinished upon the master's death in 1642.[10] Bearing this in mind, it is not completely unlikely that *Girl with a Rose*

was purchased or obtained for Philip IV as a 'reminder' of the lost *Abduction of Helen*, perhaps simultaneously to the *Latona* commission. In spite of its simplicity, *Girl with a Rose* epitomises Guido's exceptional dexterity in evoking female beauty with a palette restricted to a few pigments, the flesh tones almost imperceptibly different from the cream hues of the drooping chemise, the touch of pale red of the rose rhyming with the vermilion of the lips and the ruddiness of the cheeks. Similar chromatic effects are to be found in works executed in 1636–37, such as Guido's *Sibyl* at the Pinacoteca Nazionale di Bologna and *Circe* at the Birmingham City Art Gallery.[11]

Lorenzo Pericolo

1 Martínez Leiva and Rodríguez Rebollo 2015, 292, no. 191: 'Otra, de tres quartas de alto y media bara de ancho, de una caveza de mano de Guido Boloñés, con una rosa en la mano, en cinquenta ducados'.

2 Ibid.

3 Malvasia 1678, 2:408: 'Dovevano nel mezzo pingere una Pandora e n'avean fatto un compito disegno che, non piacendo a Diego Velasco, tanto meno poteva esser gradito a Sua Maestà, che tutto a lui differiva'.

4 Harris 1960, 166, note 12: 'Per essersi trattenuto lungamente il giorno antecedente nell'appartamento d'estate a veder collocare alcune pitture'.

5 Madrid, Museo Nacional del Prado, P-1174.

6 In this regard, see Beaven, 2000.

7 Madrid, Museo del Prado, P-383. See Cruz Yábar 2017–18, 182, and Greub 2019, 71, note 54, with erroneous identification of the Tintoretto painting.

8 Paris, Musée du Louvre, inv. 539. For an updated reconstruction of this commission, see Malvasia–Pericolo 2019, 1:295–97, note 218, and Stefano Pierguidi's essay, 'Viceroys, Ambassadors, Intendents, Theologians: Thirty Years of (Stormy) Relations between Guido Reni and Spain', in this catalogue.

9 The drawing, made in 'coloured chalks' and measuring 38 × 28.3 cm, appears as no. 174 (page 118) of the catalogue of the sale at Christie's, London, of 21 November 1958. See further Pepper 1988, 270. This drawing may correspond to a *Head of Helen* (which was accompanied by a *Head of Paris*) that, according to Malvasia 1678, 2:40, 'Guido made in pastel as a trial. Both drawings were in the "famous" gallery of the Ginetti' in Rome, and were 'even more beautiful than those depicted' in the *Abduction of Helen*. On works by Guido in the Ginetti collection, see Malvasia–Pericolo 2019, 1:317–18, note 275.

10 Malvasia 1678, 2:56: 'La favola di Latona pe'l re di Spagna, che risaputo il successo del Ratto di Elena, dolutosene co' gli ambasciadori, avea fatto ordinargli questo'. See further Malvasia–Pericolo 2019, 1:356–57, note 387.

11 *Sibyl*, Bologna, Pinacoteca Nazionale di Bologna, inv. 32532; *Circe* or *Lady with a Lapis Lazuli Bowl*, Birmingham, Birmingham City Art Gallery, inv. 1961P30, respectively. On these paintings, see Malvasia–Pericolo 2019, 1:429, note 637, and 1:403, note 558, respectively.

73   Guido Reni

Portrait of a Girl in Profile to the Right
(recto)
Female Figure raising a Veil
(verso; not by Reni)

c. 1625
Black and red chalk, traces of white chalk on light brown paper (recto); black and red chalk (verso); 342 × 233 mm
Florence, Gallerie degli Uffizi, Gabinetto dei Disegni e delle Stampe, inv. 1586 F

Provenance: Fondo Mediceo-Lorenese (?).

Selected bibliography: Pepper 1971b, 380, no. 33; Johnston 1973, 64, no. 65; Johnston 1974, 1:156–57, no. 123; Birke 1981, 57–58, note 10, in no. 26; Pepper 1988, 230, in no. 33; Petrioli Tofani 1991–2005 (2005), 2:270, no. 1586 F; Bohn 2008, 52–54, no. 40.

It is by no means certain that this study was one of the set of seventy-four generically listed in 1675 by Filippo Baldinucci, the expert appointed by Cardinal Leopoldo de' Medici (1617–1675) to reorganise his vast group of drawings, which provided the basis for the present-day collection of the Gabinetto dei Disegni e delle Stampe in the Uffizi; nor is it certain, thus, that it belonged at one stage to the Fondo Mediceo-Lorenese. The first reliable reference to it appears in an Uffizi inventory compiled in the late eighteenth century by Giuseppe Pelli Bencivenni.[1]

Even the title it was assigned, *Study for Bust of Young Woman*,[2] though formally impeccable, could be replaced by the more accurate *Portrait of a Girl in Profile to the Right*, which better highlights Guido Reni's purpose in drawing his model from life. Life studies were a common feature of the Bolognese master's working practice, but in the Uffizi drawing he achieved a quality unsurpassed in his surviving graphic oeuvre. Indeed, the Florentine work stands out for the complacency aroused in the viewer and the peculiar originality with which the image is presented. This uniqueness, which had never deserved a specific comment, is indirectly confirmed by the success of the sheet in exhibitions: it was included in the historic survey of Bolognese drawings at the Uffizi,[3] in the major retrospective at the Albertina in Vienna,[4] and in the exhibition of works on paper by Reni and his school, again in Florence.[5]

Stephen Pepper, in his second key contribution to the examination of Reni's *Libro dei conti*,[6] was among the first to focus on the drawing, regarding it – even in his later works – as a possible preparatory study for the kneeling maid to the right of the seated female figure holding the child Mary in the *Birth of the*

Virgin (1609–11), Guido's fresco for one of the lunettes in the Cappella dell'Annunziata at the Palazzo del Quirinale in Rome. Catherine Johnston questioned this connection shortly after, arguing that the graphic style was closer to that of the 1620s than the 1610s, and specifically linking the study to the figure of the Grace fastening the goddess' sandal in the *Toilet of Venus*, a canvas delivered to the Duke of Mantua in 1623 [cat. 74]. Veronika Birke also regarded Pepper's hypothesis as unconvincing. Finally, Babette Bohn has preferred to draw attention to a possible connection with the maid pouring water from a pitcher into a basin in the *Birth of Saint John the Baptist* at the John and Mable Ringling Museum of Art in Sarasota;[7] this painting was donated to the museum in 1936 by John Ringling, who believed it to be an autograph work by Reni, but Pepper later classified it as a possible copy of a lost original by the master.[8]

Bohn herself has noted that drawings of this kind must have provided a model as well as an inspiration for similar designs by Simone Cantarini (1612–1648), Flaminio Torri (1620–1661), and other artists within Guido's circle, and even beyond the city of Bologna. Here I want to add that the sensitive lines through which Reni brings the model's features to life on paper reflect not just his training in the workshop of the Carracci family, staunch advocates of drawing from life, but also an attention – far ahead of its time – to creating an icon symbolising a wholly new kind of fascination. Although her dress points to a humble background, the young woman has fine aristocratic facial features. Through his masterly use of red-chalk hatching, Reni captures the full youthful freshness of her face, her small heart-shaped mouth, the pink flesh of her earlobe. She is gazing downwards at a point in front of her but beyond the picture; it is as though she were pretending to concentrate or, perhaps, to be distracted. The viewer senses that she is discreetly aware not only of being observed but also of being admired for her beauty. This hint of the frivolous, of feigned modesty, heralds a new kind of feminine beauty – at once less classical and more coquettish – prefiguring eighteenth-century portraits by Gaetano Gandolfi (1734–1802).

The drawing on the verso – a female figure, her hair in a bun, looking down at the fringe of the veil she holds in her right hand – is not regarded by Johnston as an autograph work. Bohn has suggested a possible link to a lost work by Reni, which once hung in the church of Santa Maria Maggiore in Rome.[9] The inferior quality of the verso drawing compared to that of the recto, pointed out by both specialists, provides sufficient grounds for rejecting its attribution to the Bolognese master, and suggests that the sheet was reused in his workshop.

Viviana Farina

1 Petrioli Tofani 1991–2005 (2005), 2:270, no. 1586 F.
2 Bohn 2008, 52–54, no. 40.
3 Johnston 1973.
4 Birke 1981.
5 Bohn 2008.
6 Pepper 1971b, 380, no. 33.
7 Sarasota (Florida), John and Mable Ringling Museum of Art, Bequest of John Ringling, 1936, SN 118.
8 Pepper 1988, Appendix III (Rejected attributions), 351–52, no. B10. A good reproduction is available at https://emuseum.ringling.org/emuseum/objects/25234/presumed-copy-after-renis-lost-birth-of-saint-john-the-bapt?ctx=68a4cf50-8478-4520-9b3d-b20a12915097&idx=1. The drawing for the maid pouring water is in the Real Academia de Bellas Artes de San Fernando in Madrid (D-1660). Birke 1981, 133–34, no. 93.
9 See Pepper 1988, 265, no. 107; Malvasia–Pericolo 2019, 1:338, note 331.

FLESH AND DRAPERY

Guido Reni's paintings of goddesses, saints, and heroines of antiquity were
immensely successful in the Europe of his day. Most were depicted at half- or
three-quarter length, in the style of Caravaggio, thus encouraging a very direct
approach by the viewer. These portrayals of women from the past, handled with
consummate technical mastery and exceptional sensitivity, were not meant to
convey a direct sensory experience. Guido developed his own fascinating idiom
through the play of drapery, which envelops and largely conceals the figure
– thus defying Mannerist precepts – and contrasts with the smooth white skin.
The intense facial expressions are based on the heads of classical statues that
he studied in Rome, while the rich fabrics probably allude to Bologna as a major
silk-producing centre. All in all, an enigmatic sensuality – cold yet captivating –
emanates from these paintings, repeated by Reni himself with slight variations,
on numerous occasions, to meet the high market demand.

74   Guido Reni and assistants (?)

The Toilet of Venus

1622–23
Oil on canvas, 281.9 × 205.7 cm
London, The National Gallery, Presented by William IV, 1836,
NG90

Provenance: Commissioned by Ferdinando Gonzaga, Duke of Mantua, in 1621; finished and delivered to Mantua in 1623; sold to Charles I, King of England, in 1628; purchased by Luis Méndez de Haro y Guzmán, 6th Marquis of El Carpio, in 1651; by descent, Gaspar Méndez de Haro y Guzmán, 7th Marquis of El Carpio, by 1662; given to Pedro Rodríguez, 1692; bought by Ippolito de Mari and transported to Genoa in 1692–94; sold by Francesco de Mari to John Law prior to 1721; sold to George I, King of England; offered to the National Gallery, London, as a gift, by William IV, King of England, in 1836.

Selected bibliography: Baccheschi 1971, 98, no. 86; Pepper 1988, 248–49, no. 72; S. Lapenta in Morselli 2002, 191–92; K. Serres in Shawe-Taylor and Rumberg 2018, 247, no. 90; Malvasia–Pericolo 2019, 1:287–88, note 196.

The history of Guido Reni's *Toilet of Venus* is well documented. In a letter of 3 November 1621, Andrea Barbazza (1581/82–1656), a friend of Guido's and the agent of the Duke of Mantua, Ferdinando Gonzaga (1587–1626), urged the duke to provide the master with a down payment for the 'paintings' recently commissioned.[1] A few months later, on 10 August 1622, Barbazza informed the duke that

Guido was about to complete the *Toilet of Venus* and the *Judgement of Paris* at his request, thereby asking once again for a partial payment.[2] From other letters, it becomes evident that the duke had no intention of sending the money nor was Guido close to finishing his paintings. On 16 November 1622, Guido, through Barbazza, reiterated his request of money, arguing that the *Toilet of Venus* and the *Judgement of Paris* were much larger and comprised more figures than the four paintings with the *Labours of Hercules* he had previously executed for the duke (1617–21).[3] After further negotiation, Barbazza convinced the duke to disburse 300 ducatons to secure the *Toilet of Venus*, stressing that the work was being seen and admired by all Bologna.[4] Although Barbazza had managed to obtain 100 ducatons from the duke as down payment for the *Toilet of Venus*, the painting was still unfinished in January 1623. In a letter of 25 January 1623 to the duke, Barbazza noted:

> The negligence of Reni, and mine, in shipping the painting is not owing to lack of care but is a most opportune delay. The painting would have been finished by now, but Guido was at once seized by the whim to modify an entire figure in view of improvement, and this is what caused the delay.[5]

Only on 7 June 1623 did the duke receive confirmation that the *Toilet of Venus* was about to be shipped from Bologna to Mantua.[6] Guido's *Judgement of Paris* may have never been completed, for it appears in the inventory of Guido's estate drawn up in 1642.[7] The Duke of Mantua sold Guido's *Toilet of Venus* to King Charles I of England (1600–1649) in 1628. After the dispersal of the English royal collection in the aftermath of Charles I's execution, the painting was purchased by a private collector in 1651, then acquired by Alonso de Cárdenas, the Spanish ambassador to England (1650–55), on behalf of Luis Méndez de Haro y Guzmán, 6th Marquis of El Carpio (1598–1661).[8] Guido's *Toilet of Venus* is listed in the 1662 inventory of the paintings inherited by Gaspar Méndez de Haro y Guzmán (1629–1687), 7th Marquis of El Carpio.[9] In 1692, the painting was given to the Marquis of El Carpio's gardener, a certain Pedro Rodríguez, as settlement for reclaimed credits.[10] Sometime between 1692 and 1694, the Genoese Francesco de Mari (1656–1710) purchased the *Toilet of Venus* in Madrid and had it transported to Genoa.[11] Francesco's son, Ippolito de Mari (1681–after 1748), sold it to John Law

Fig. 90 Guido Reni, *The Flight into Egypt* (detail), c. 1622.
Oil on canvas, 157 × 131 cm. Naples, Biblioteca
e Complesso monumentale dei Girolamini, Quadreria

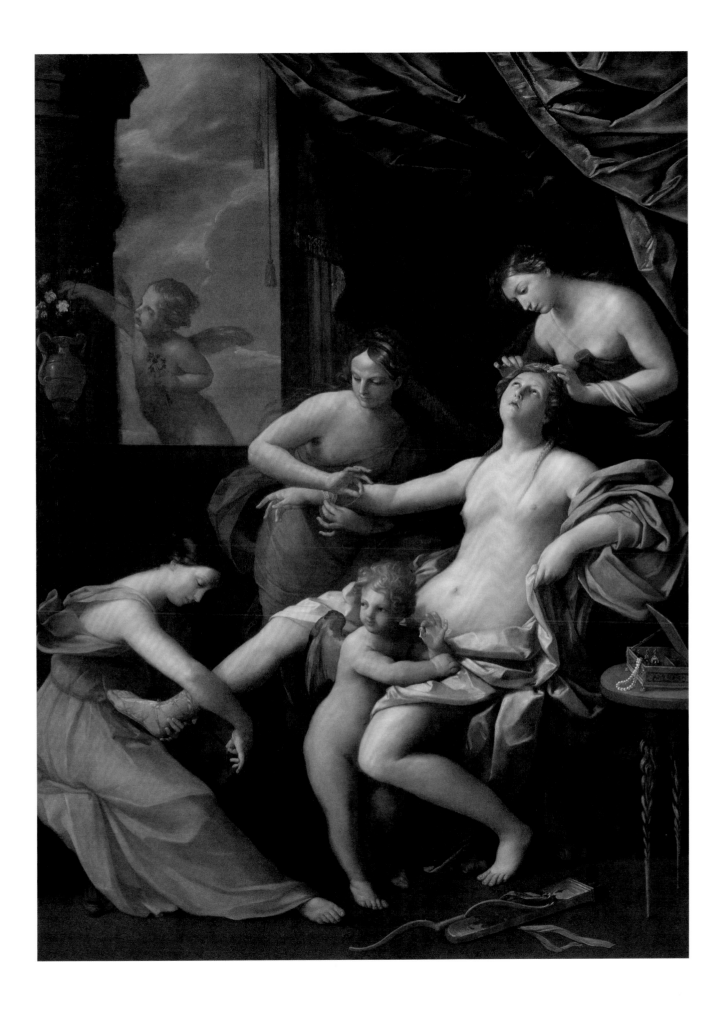

(1671–1729) prior to 1721. The painting was shipped to Paris, then to London in 1722. In a letter of 10 February 1723 to William Cavendish, 2nd Duke of Devonshire (1673–1729), the French art collector Pierre Crozat (1665–1740) remarked: 'Of the paintings purchased by Mr Law in Genoa I only remember a large work by Guido, which seemed beautiful to me but a little mended, and as if the ground had been remade'.[12] It is unlikely that Crozat was referring to a *Perseus and Andromeda* then attributed to Guido, which Law had also bought in Italy.[13] This painting, together with the *Toilet of Venus*, was then purchased by King George I of England (1660–1727). In 1836, William IV of England (1765–1837) donated both paintings to the National Gallery, London.

There is no doubt that the London painting is the *Toilet of Venus* made by Guido for Ferdinando Gonzaga in 1622–23. Besides the documentary evidence discussed here, X-ray analysis has revealed that Guido added the flying Cupid who fills the vase on the windowsill with flowers after finishing the painting, which arguably corresponds to Barbazza's observation about the modification of an 'entire figure'. Previous scholarship has proved particularly severe in assessing the *Toilet of Venus*. In 1988, after a recent cleaning of the painting, Stephen Pepper concluded that 'the work was executed mostly by Reni's workshop; ascribable to the master are the overall invention … and perhaps the execution of the figure of Venus'.[14] Cleaned and restored again in 2016, the painting is now exhibited in the National Gallery as 'Guido Reni and studio'.

Reasonable enough, this label is not unproblematic. In describing Guido's workshop practices, Carlo Cesare Malvasia distinguishes between two procedures that can be defined as 'covering' and 'retouching'.[15] Due to the sheer number of commissions Guido was used to receiving, it stands to reason that he would task his collaborators with transferring the figures of large compositions onto the canvas (through cartoons or otherwise), to block them out, and even to colour them. At that point, he would decide whether to 'cover' the work of his assistants thoroughly and consistently, or to leave it visible by making it even more noticeable through masterly 'retouching' in select spots. It is noteworthy that seventeenth-century Bolognese inventories seem to reflect Guido's practices by making distinctions between an original and a *ritocco*. Now, the *Toilet of Venus* presents obvious anomalies in this regard. On the one hand, one can still discern with the naked eye the traces of Guido's reworking of certain contours, in particular Venus' bent leg and right arm, or the Grace's hand that laces the goddess' sandals to the left, not to mention the entire lower body of the Cupid who holds the pearl. This is very unlikely the work of an assistant. On the other hand,

the figure of Venus together with the Cupid ensconced within her legs stand out on account of the specificity of their pictorial treatment. Whereas the rest of the composition is painted with great fluidity, through quasi-transparent layers of brighter pigments that play with the darker underground by creating an effect of opalescence, the group of Venus and the Cupid is characterised by a thicker impasto, which solidifies the flesh occasionally to an extreme degree and causes the draperies to flatten through chromatic saturation as if cast in metal. These stylistic discrepancies compromise the general high quality of the painting and are very difficult to explain, given the care Guido took in pondering every element of the composition, as confirmed by the series of head studies in red, black, and white chalk he executed in view of it, and which are of a most refined draughtsmanship.

Stylistically, most of the composition bears affinity with works executed prior to or after Guido's stay in Naples in 1621, such as the *Flight into Egypt* at the Quadreria dei Girolamini in Naples. It is interesting, for instance, to compare the Grace to the left in the *Toilet of Venus* with the veiled Virgin from the *Flight into Egypt* [fig. 90].[16] In light of these considerations, one might be led to conclude that Guido executed almost the entire composition by leaving an assistant to complete certain (crucial) parts of it, such as (most of) the group of Venus and the Cupid. If a collaborator did in fact finish the painting, then this can be Giovanni Giacomo Sementi (1583–1636), who at the time might have still been working with Guido.[17] Years after delivering the *Toilet of Venus*, Guido drew inspiration from the Grace who crowns Venus for an *Erigone* now in a private collection [cat. 75].

Lorenzo Pericolo

1 Furlotti 2000, 188, no. 328.
2 Ibid., 190, nos. 333–34.
3 Ibid., 191–92, no. 337. For Guido's *Labours of Hercules* now in Paris, Musée du Louvre, inv. 535–538, see Malvasia–Pericolo 2019, 1:285–86, note 193.
4 Furlotti 2000, 192, no. 338.
5 Ibid., 193, no. 342.
6 Ibid., 193, no. 343.
7 Spike and Di Zio 1988, 59.
8 Burke 1984, 3:167, doc. 3.4, no. 35.
9 Frutos Sastre 2009, 164, note 460.
10 Ibid., 164, notes 460 and 720.
11 See Boccardo 2002, 225 and 239, note 24.
12 Borean 2010, 443–44.
13 On this painting, see Pepper 1988, 283, no. 149.
14 Ibid., 248–49, note 72.
15 For 'covering', see Malvasia 1678, 2:19 and 2:74. On *ritocco*, see ibid., 2:32, 2:39, 2:44, 2:46, 2:60, 2:68, and 2:70–71. See further Malvasia–Pericolo 2019, 1:293–94, note 213.
16 On this painting, see Malvasia–Pericolo 2019, 1:445, note 671.
17 On this painting, see Malvasia–Cropper and Pericolo 2013, 136–37 and 219, note 369.

75 Guido Reni

Erigone

c. 1622–30
Tempera and oil over black chalk on two sheets partially
superimposed and joined, 45.9 × 58.8 cm
New York, private collection

Provenance: Kate Ganz Ltd, London; David Sylvester, private collection.
Selected bibliography: Ganz 1989, 40–41, no. 15; Bohn 2008, 66–68.

Identified by the art dealer Kate Ganz in the late 1980s as an original cartoon by Guido Reni, *Erigone* is an exceptional testimony to the master's range of working techniques, swiftness of execution, and inventiveness. It has been assumed correctly that the cartoon relates to and derives from the figure of the Grace on the right who crowns the Greek goddess of beauty in the London *Toilet of Venus* [cat. 74]. When superimposed upon the corresponding section of the *Toilet of Venus*, the two half-figures indeed overlap with one another quite well, with a few divergences especially in connection with the position of the hands – proportions are slightly fuller in the *Erigone*, particularly in the face and arms. While this may suggest that *Erigone* is the original cartoon employed by Guido in 1622–23 when painting the *Toilet of Venus*, this is belied by the material configuration of the work. Composed of two sheets of paper, the right border of the cartoon's left half is joined to the leftmost border of its right half, a strip of the latter being still visible under the join. A few centimetres wide, this section includes the uppermost contour of the bending shoulder grazed by cursive touches of fluttering hair, almost the entirety of the knot under the breast with a bit of drapery beneath, and a fragment of the yellow mantle enfolded around the wrist. The knot in the covered border is painted in oil as opposed to the knot on the left half of the cartoon, which is in tempera as is mostly the rest of the composition (the outlines being traced in black chalk). Although it is impossible to determine the reason for these differences between the overlapping sections, it is not impossible that Guido, dissatisfied with a previous version of the cartoon's left side, discarded it by replacing it with the one extant. This may explain the use of tempera as an alternative to oil: the former, on account of its opacity, was better suited to conceal the surface underneath, ensuring a greater degree of homogeneity across the two halves of the cartoon. This technical procedure makes sense only if Guido was working toward a new composition and not just reworking the cartoon previously used in his *Toilet of Venus*.

In fact, the red and yellow pigments employed in the cartoon, along with the presence of a white cloth instead of the tiara, find a clear correspondence in a painting by Guido of an identical composition, a much-documented *Erigone*, whose current whereabouts are unknown [fig. 91].[1] Measuring 59 × 66 centimetres, this work is almost exactly as large as the cartoon. First identified by Erwin Panofsky in 1960, the painting was published in 1986 as an original of about 1633 by Stephen Pepper after cleaning and restoration.[2] This *Erigone* is described in great detail in a 1727 inventory of the collection of Louis, Duke of Orléans (1703–1752), housed in the Palais-Royal, Paris:

> Almost a half-figure; Icarus's daughter [Erigone] is naked, her hair hovering over her shoulders with the exception of a braid on top of her head; a little piece of purple drapery passes between her arm and left breast. She is extremely enthralled in looking at grapes (Bacchus is hidden in this form) and she holds mid-air the cloth that covered them, seemingly unable to dare touch them, admiring them with a delectation that reveals what she feels; the ground of the painting is a sky.[3]

The inventory specifies that the painting came from the collection of Jean-Baptiste Colbert, Marquis de Seignelay (1651–1690), although an etching executed by Cornelis Vermeulen (c. 1644–c. 1708) where *Erigone* is reproduced (in reverse) belonged to a suite of prints that reproduced works of art in Pierre Crozat's (1665–1740) possession.[4] A further reproduction of Guido's *Erigone* appears in an etching by Bernard Picart (1673–1733) that was published in his posthumous *Impostures innocentes* (1734).[5] Guido's painting is once again reproduced in a print (etching and engraving) by François Hubert (1744–1809) in *Galerie du Palais-Royal* (1786): an illustrated catalogue of the Orléans collection.[6]

It is difficult to date Guido's *Erigone* with precision. It may have been produced about 1633 (as proposed by Stephen Pepper), that is, at the time of the *Penitent Magdalen* now in the Palazzo Barberini, Rome [cat. 86], or even earlier, about 1628–31, at the time of the Louvre *Abduction of Helen* [fig. 35] and the Ascoli Piceno *Annunciation* [cat. 51].[7] This can

be argued on the basis of a certain saturation of the colours and the almost crystalline palette specific to works executed in those years. How Guido came to depict a mythological episode as rare as the moment when Bacchus seduces *Erigone* in the guise of grapes (briefly evoked by Ovid in his *Metamorphoses*, VI, 125) is a mystery. As documented by Carlo Cesare Malvasia, Guido's erudition was almost non-existent – or so did the master himself claim – and he often resorted to literati for poetic motifs and assistance in visualising mythological subjects. Regardless of the person who proposed the subject, it is likely that Erigone's seduction by grapes was meant to symbolise the power of (false) images – the grapes are a fictive depiction of Bacchus – and hence the power of painting in deceiving and causing viewers to fall in love with the source of deception: the painted image. That Guido took his cue from a previous work, creating a cartoon ad hoc and colouring it to assess the general effect of the composition, reminds us of the playfulness that informed his painting sessions, when he was visited by patrons and admirers who enjoyed observing him at work while displaying his legendary bravura. Some of these sessions resulted in small paintings that Guido offered as gifts, which of course came with the tacit expectation of a counter-gift or remuneration. A breathtaking drawing in black, red, and white chalk preparatory for the head of the Grace in the *Toilet of Venus* (subsequently to be turned into the half-figure of Erigone) is to be found in the Museo Horne, Florence.[8]

Lorenzo Pericolo

1 See Pepper 1986; Ebert-Schifferer, Emiliani and Schleier 1988, 188–90, no. A24; Pepper 1988, 338, no. 34.
2 See Panofsky 1960, 31–34; Pepper 1986.
3 The Getty Provenance Index® Databases, F–12, no. 187: 'Presque demi-figure. La fille d'Icare est nue, ses cheveux flotant sur ses épaules à l'exception de ceux du haut de sa tête qui sont natés; un petit bout de draperie pourpre passe entre son bras et sa mamelle gauche. Elle est fort atachée à regarder des raisins (Bacchus étant caché sous cette forme) et elle tient en l'air la serviette qui les couvroit sans paroître oser y toucher, les admirant avec une délectation qui découvre ce qui se passe en elle. Le fond du tableau est un ciel'. (Accessible at https://www.getty.edu/research/tools/provenance/search.html)
4 Hollstein–Schuckman and Hoop Scheffer 1990, 25, no. 34.
5 Picart 1734, no. 30.
6 Fontenai 1786, École de Lombardie, no. xv.
7 On Guido's *Abduction of Helen*, Paris, Musée du Louvre, 539, see Malvasia–Pericolo 2019, 1:295–97, note 218. On his *Annunciation*, Ascoli Piceno, Pinacoteca Civica, see Pepper 1988, 268, no. 114.
8 See Bohn 2008, 55–56, no. 41.

Fig. 91 Guido Reni, *Erigone*, c. 1633. Oil on canvas, 59 × 66 cm. Private collection (whereabouts unknown)

76 Guido Reni

Head of Venus

c. 1621–22
Black and red chalk on faded blue paper, 319 × 255 mm
Oxford, Ashmolean Museum, Purchased, 1949, WA1949.210

Provenance: Richard Houlditch Jr., before 1760; Sir Frederick Ogilvie (1893–1949); Lady Ogilvie (1900–1990), until 1949, at which time it was purchased by the Ashmolean Museum.

Selected bibliography: Macandrew 1980, 140, no. 932; V. Birke in Ebert-Schifferer, Emiliani and Schleier 1988, 362, no. B47, fig. 64; Pepper 1988, 249, in no. 72; Bohn 2008, 55, note 143; Boyd 2021.

The drawing bears an inscription essential for its correct identification: 'The Head of Venus in the King's Picture att Kensington'; on the verso, the date '1736' and the name 'Guido Reni' have been added in handwriting attributable to the sheet's first known owner, Richard Houlditch Jr. († 1760).[1]

It is a study for the impressive *Toilet of Venus* in the National Gallery, London [cat. 74], a composition well known through multiple versions. Even the London canvas was traditionally regarded as a workshop copy.[2] After its recent restoration,[3] however, it appears that Reni's personal intervention was greater than hitherto supposed. Several *pentimenti* or revisions made while the painting was being executed are visible to the naked eye, while other more substantial changes have been revealed by infrared reflectography; together, these changes suggest that the composition was reworked by Guido with the aid of his studio assistants over a period of time. In view of these findings, it is now thought that the London work is the original composition on which the other versions were based. The painting, mentioned in letters written by Andrea Barbazza in 1621 and 1622, was commissioned by Ferdinando Gonzaga, Duke of Mantua (1587–1626), and delivered to him in 1623, prior to being sold in 1628 to King Charles I of England (1600–1649).[4]

In the canvas, the goddess of Love is attended by the three Graces, who carefully fasten her sandals and deck her with jewels. Cupid, crouching between his mother's legs, holds a pearl earring between his left forefinger and thumb. A *putto* leaning through the window arranges flowers in a classical vase.

This is one of the few paintings for which preparatory studies have survived for details – three, in this case – but not for the entire composition. The Oxford drawing exhibited here is a faithful first version of Venus' head, already fixed in the pose and in the distinctive 'sweet heavenward gaze'. Reni combined black and red chalks, using the latter to enliven the skin and lips. The paper support was originally blue, a colour derived from the tradition of the Carracci academy, common in Guido's repertoire, as remarked also in Count Malvasia's *Felsina pittrice* (1678), in which it states that 'blue paper' was Reni's 'most frequent way [i.e. support] of drawing'.[5]

This Ashmolean drawing is perhaps the most academic if compared to the other two drawing works considered as preparatory studies for the painting, one now in the Museo Horne in Florence[6] and the other in the Musée du Louvre,[7] both of which may well have been drawn on blue paper which has since faded to light brown. The Florentine design depicts a Grace crowning Aphrodite;[8] the Louvre study shows another daughter of Zeus fastening the goddess' embossed bracelet.[9] As noted earlier, these drawings are so remarkably lifelike, that scholars have often stressed, rightly, that Reni's figures were drawn *dal vero*, though any excessive resemblance to reality was later toned down to ensure a more idealised result. While the model in the Horne drawing is unquestionably female, the figure in the Louvre study is appealingly androgynous, its fine delicate features contrasting with its boyish, *à la garçon* hairstyle. It is among the master's drawings that most effectively prefigure the more frivolous sensibilities of the eighteenth century.

Examining the drawings related to the *Toilet of Venus*, Babette Bohn has focused on their immense value, when taken in conjunction, for our understanding of Guido's working practice from the 1620s onwards. He seems to have concentrated on making preparatory drawings of heads, leaving his assistants to transfer them to the painting, and possibly making rough sketches of the overall composition, which have not survived. He would then limit his work to retouching the painting, thus maintaining total control over the production process from beginning to end. This hypothesis, supported by suggestions to that effect by Carlo Cesare Malvasia, is also borne out by his reuse of sketched heads in later paintings, as in the case of the Horne design.[10] Though reasonable, this conjecture regarding Reni's working method must be viewed with caution since, of the vast number of drawings inventoried after his death, most have since been dispersed.[11]

Viviana Farina

1 I am grateful to the relevant staff at the Ashmolean Museum for granting
  me access to data not yet in the public domain. See Boyd 2021.

2 Pepper 1988, 248–49, no. 72.

3 Mandy et al. 2019.

4 See Malvasia–Pericolo 2019, 1:287–88, note 196.

5 Ibid., 158: 'Carta turchina … il suo modo più frequente di disegnare'; for
  the English translation, ibid., 1:159.

6 Florence, Museo Horne, inv. 5570.

7 Paris, Musée du Louvre, Départment des Arts graphiques, RF 90.

8 Bohn 2008, 55–56, no. 41.

9 Loisel 2013, 114, no. 84.

10 See note 8 above.

11 In this respect, see my essay, '"A man who perpetually observes Nature":
   Guido Reni and Drawing', in this catalogue.

77   Guido Reni

Study for the Bust of Judith

c. 1622–23
Black and white chalk on greenish-grey (faded blue) paper,
293 × 242 mm
Madrid, Real Academia de Bellas Artes de San Fernando, D-1657

Provenance: Collection of Carlo Maratta (1625–1713); purchased from Rosalía O'Moore, widow of the painter Andrea Procaccini (1671–1734), 1775.

Selected bibliography: Pérez Sánchez 1972a, 59, fig. 20; Johnston 1974, 1:166–68, no. 134; Birke 1981, 156–57, no. 111; V. Birke in Ebert-Schifferer, Emiliani and Schleier 1988, 375–76, no. B52; Azcárate Ristori 1994, 140–41.

This drawing was identified by Alfonso E. Pérez Sánchez as one of four known preparatory studies for the painting of *Judith and Holofernes* that formed part of the Sedlmayer collection, Geneva [fig. 92]. Two are in the Uffizi in Florence (nos. 12432 F and 17573 F); both are full-length sketches of the heroine, and there is some dispute regarding which of the two is an autograph

work.[1] The other is a magnificent study showing only Judith's head – in red and black chalk on originally blue paper now faded to light brown-grey – donated not long ago to the Metropolitan Museum of Art in New York[2] after being sold by Thomas Coke, 8th Earl of Leicester, of Holkham Hall.[3] The Metropolitan also has a first thought for the inclined torso and fallen arm of Holofernes, a sheet from the late seventeenth-century collection of Father Sebastiano Resta.[4]

This episode in the story of Judith – who in Guido Reni's depiction is shown standing full-length, her eyes raised towards God, holding with her left hand the body of the dead Assyrian general by the hair, and in her right a sword pointing downwards – proved highly popular, as attested by the numerous replicas and copies that have survived.[5]

According to Stephen Pepper's reconstruction, the life-size *Judith* by Reni listed in a 1623 inventory of the Ludovisi collection in Rome should be identified as the canvas on the same subject recorded in 1686 at the Alcázar in Madrid, where it was attributed to 'Guido' and described as being in a poor state of repair. It was subsequently damaged during the fire that destroyed the palace in 1734, and eventually lost. However, it was soon rediscovered and auctioned on several occasions until, after being purchased in Spain, it entered the Sedlmayer collection in Geneva.[6] The coat of arms on the verso of the painting is that of Cardinal Giulio Rospigliosi (1600–1669), the future Pope Clement IX, who may well have taken the canvas to the court of Philip IV on one of his trips to Madrid as papal legate from 1644 to 1653.[7] It is equally likely that the painting was commissioned directly by Cardinal Ludovico Ludovisi, who also ordered from Reni the *Trinity adored by Angels* altarpiece for the church of the Santissima Trinità dei Pellegrini in Rome [cat. 54 and fig. 28].[8]

Fig. 92 Guido Reni, *Judith and Holofernes*,
1625–26. Oil on canvas, 202 × 143 cm.
Geneva, former Sedlmayer Collection
(current whereabouts unknown)

Of all the designs for *Judith* recorded to date, this drawing in the Real Academia de Bellas Artes de San Fernando is perhaps the first study that best illustrates Guido's academic approach to painting. The full female figure is sketched using swift, loose strokes that give an idea of the first pose, eventually used in the painting. The superb study for the heroine's head – perhaps drawn from life, but later modified to conform to ideal parameters – should therefore be regarded as an independent, unrelated experiment in drawing, despite its effective link to the painted Judith. Finally, the study for the figure of Holofernes is a design so far removed from the end result that it seems closer to a painterly invention prompted by the mere coincidence of theme. By contrast, this sketch of the bust and part of the barely-outlined head of Judith is remarkable not only for its strong resemblance to the painted version but also for the meticulous close-up rendering of the drapery in the classical manner. In the area of the bust and right arm, the angular folds of the cloth are stressed by skilful white-chalk highlighting.

It should be pointed out that, in keeping with the rest of the preliminary drawings mentioned above, the faded greyish colour of the paper support of this sheet, shared by all the known preparatory studies for the painting, was originally blue.

This *Study for the Bust of Judith* is one of the few loose sheets correctly attributed to Reni in the Real Academia de Bellas Artes de San Fernando. The museum also holds other important drawings by the Bolognese artist which have not been selected for exhibition because they are still pasted into the volumes from the monastery of Valparaíso that entered the collections of the Real Academia in 1836. This is the case of the *Study for the Head of Saint Charles Borromeo*, inventoried as no. D-0146a in the second volume of that collection. Attributed to Reni by Pérez Sánchez,[9] it is a preparatory study for the three-quarter length figure of the saint at prayer in Guido's fresco of 1612–14, which was detached from the wall and cut back, and is now in the sacristy at the church of San Carlo ai Catinari in Rome.[10]

Viviana Farina

1 For a summary of the critical debate, see Bohn 2008, 56–57, no. 42, and 76, no. 59.
2 New York, The Metropolitan Museum of Art, Lila Acheson Wallace Gift, 1992, 1992.70.
3 Griswold 1992, with bibliography.
4 New York, The Metropolitan Museum of Art, Rogers Fund, 1962, 62.123.1; V. Birke in Ebert-Schifferer, Emiliani and Schleier 1988, 377–78, no. B53. The delicately drawn study of a half-draped female figure at lower left, also by Reni, is a separate sketch that has been pasted to the main sheet by a collector, most likely Sebastiano Resta, who also added the inscription legible at lower right (Warwick 2000, 30–31, fig. 11). The design relates to a different theme, possibly linked – according to Veronika Birke – to the lost canvas of *Bacchus and Ariadne* painted in the late 1630s, or to the central female figure in *Perseus and Andromeda*, of which two versions are documented, both painted in the mid-1630s (see the technical entry revised in 2014 by Carmen B. Bambach at https://www.metmuseum.org/art/collection/search/340614?what=Drawings&ft=Guido+Reni&offset=0&rpp=40&pos=4; on this painting, see Pepper 1988, 282–83, no. 149).
5 Pepper 1988, 258–59, no. 93.
6 Ibid.
7 S. Ebert-Schifferer in Ebert-Schifferer, Emiliani and Schleier 1988, 145–50, no. A11.
8 Lorenzo Pericolo (Malvasia–Pericolo 2019, 1:319–20, note 281) argues that the two commissions date from the same period.
9 Pérez Sánchez 1972a, 57–58, fig. 16.
10 Pepper 1988, 233, no. 38.

78   Guido Reni
Lucretia

1625–26
Oil on canvas, 128 × 99 cm
Private collection

Provenance: Collection of George Hayter prior to 1821; sold to Arthur Wellesley, 1st Duke of Wellington, 1821.

Selected bibliography: Whitfield 1973, no. 45; Ebert-Schifferer, Emiliani and Schleier 1988, 166, no. A17; Pepper 1988, 258, no. 52.

Very little is known about the early history of this impressive *Lucretia* by Guido Reni. According to Stephen Pepper, the work belonged to the English painter George Hayter (1792–1871).[1] It is possible, but far from certain, that Hayter purchased the painting during his sojourn in Italy in 1816–18 – while in Rome, he became acquainted with Antonio Canova (1757–1822), whose portrait (now in the British Embassy, Paris) he executed in 1817. In 1821, Hayter sold Guido's *Lucretia* to Arthur Wellesley, 1st Duke of Wellington (1769–1852). The painting remained in the Wellington collection until 1973.[2] Describing Guido's *Lucretia* in 1988, Sibylle Ebert-Schifferer felicitously remarked:

Here, Reni turns the curvilinear trace of the female shoulders into a grand, peaceful arc that comprises the contours from the temple to the hand that holds the dagger. Lucretia's left forearm is subordinated to this outline, which is reinforced by lighting … Reni here selects … the moment after the dagger strikes, when two precious drops of blood spring forth, tinged with a red that finds its counterpoint in the reflections of the rust-orange brocade. The painting … does not represent Lucretia's determination or heroism, but her silent suffering, of which the atmosphere, filled with elegiac pathos, is accentuated by the sumptuous greyish luminosity of the colours.[3]

Comparing this *Lucretia* with other versions by Guido of the same subject, Ebert-Schifferer concluded that the painting dated to 1626–27.

Guido's output in 1627 is relatively well known, and it is difficult to believe that this *Lucretia* was executed in the same year as his *Immaculate Conception*, now in the Metropolitan Museum, New York [cat. 55]. On the other hand, 'the free and angular brushstrokes' noticed by Ebert-Schifferer in *Lucretia*, along with the *cangiante* effects of the silky violet curtain, the green drapery, and the rust-orange brocade, present a strong affinity with those that characterise Guido's monumental *Trinity*

Fig. 93 Infrared reflectogram of *Lucretia* [cat. 78]

adored by Angels in the Santissima Trinità dei Pellegrini, Rome, produced in 1625 [fig. 28].[4] It is important to stress the novelty of Guido's chromatism as orchestrated in this *Lucretia*. It is no exaggeration to state that it was not only unprecedented, but also at odds with the tradition of lyrical poetry with which Guido's patrons, friends, and viewers were acquainted.

In his *Felsina pittrice* (1678), Carlo Cesare Malvasia evokes the affection of Cesare Rinaldi (1559–1636) for Guido. For this renowned Bolognese poet, Guido made a few paintings, among them a *Penitent Magdalen* with which Rinaldi was in love, which he praised in verse, and which was stolen to Rinaldi's desperation.[5] In Rinaldi's love poems, the beautiful woman is mostly celebrated on account of her white skin. In one of his madrigals, titled 'Fairness without comparison', Rinaldi writes:

'But your white hand's white ivory / Exceeds any mortal fairness'.[6] In another madrigal, the poet loses his senses (and his ability to distinguish whiteness) in admiring a pearl over the woman's breast:

A pure and bright pearl

Hangs from the neck over the breast

The fairest ever made by nature

And whiteness is

So equal among them

That the light of my sight, unused

To such shine, is thus blinded

That it cannot fully make out

Whether the breast is pearl or the pearl breast.[7]

Needless to say, fairness is not the only attribute of the beautiful woman. But even when it is commended in tandem with the red or the ruby of the woman's lips and cheeks, the contrast is made only to further exalt the mighty lure of fairness. In one of his sonnets, Rinaldi opposes the brightness of the hand to the blackness of a veil:

Shady veil, even if you shade and veil
Her fairness with your envious blackness
You cannot prevent it from shining
Forth, like a sun that hides its light in little cloud.[8]

Guido was undoubtedly aware of these lyrical conventions. There will be a moment when the artist will inflect and magnify the whiteness of flesh, blouses, pearls, and turbans as a token of female beauty. Much needs still to be said about the 'white manner' of his final output. Earlier works such as *Lucretia*, however, must have jolted contemporary viewers' expectations through chromatic shock. The fairness of the heroine's neck and breast is not heightened into dazzling incandescence but set off against a pale green underlayer that symbolically announces the onset of the heroine's death. This greenish undertone asserts its predominance in Lucretia's green drapery, where yellowy reflections anticipate the rusty-orange and vermilion triumph of the brocade, which grows darker, its intensity progressively dulled as it nears the violet curtain at the level of the left shoulder. Dusted with green highlights, the violet backdrop both contrasts and harmonises with the green drapery and greenish undertones of the flesh pigments on the face and breast, which are in turn embellished with pinkish glazes suffused on the surface, a prelude to the heroine's pink lips, nipple, and blood. Guido's chromatic experimentation goes beyond the feats of the Venetian broken colour technique, not only for his boldness in attempting chromatic combinations never tried before, but for his discreet disregard for naturalism, with lips, nipple, and blood tinged with the same 'precious' pink.

A reflectogram recently executed by the Prado Conservation Laboratory reveals Guido's prodigious ability to push to the limit the expressive potential of foreshortening. In the underlying version, Lucretia's face appears almost in profile, and Guido clearly adjusted the face's right outline and the modelling of the foreshortened forehead, right eye, and cheek freehand [fig. 93]. Perhaps, there is no better precedent to Guido's *Lucretia* than a painting of the same subject by Paolo Veronese (1528–1588), now in the Kunsthistorisches

Fig. 94 Paolo Veronese, *Lucretia*, c. 1580–83.
Oil on canvas, 109.5 × 90.5 cm. Vienna,
Kunsthistorisches Museum Wien,
Gemäldegalerie, inv. 1561

Museum in Vienna [fig. 94]. It is no coincidence that, according to Malvasia, Guido greatly esteemed Veronese, 'whom he called his Paolino'.[9]

Lorenzo Pericolo

1 Pepper 1988, 258, no. 52. This information is taken from Whitfield 1973, no. 45.
2 Ibid.
3 Ebert-Schifferer, Emiliani and Schleier 1988, 166, no. A17.
4 On this painting, see Malvasia–Pericolo 2019, 1:281–82, note 185.
5 On Rinaldi's *Penitent Magdalen*, see Malvasia–Pericolo 2019, 1:323, note 288; 1:324, note 289; 1:399, note 538; 1:417, note 604; and 2:84–86.
6 Rinaldi 1619, 315: 'Ma ogni mortal bianchezza / De la man bianca il bianco avorio eccede'.
7 Ibid., 266: 'Dal collo al seno pende / Bianco più che già mai fesse natura / Candida perla e pura / Et è fra loro equale / Così la candidezza / Ch'indi abbagliata la mia luce a tale / Candor non molto avvezza / Non può scorger a pieno / Se il seno perla o sia la perla seno'.
8 Ibid., 379: 'Ombroso vel, se ben tu adombri e veli / Col nero invido tuo l'altrui candore / Non però fai ch'ei non traluca fuore / Qual sol che 'n poca nube il lume celi'.
9 Malvasia 1678, 2:77.

79 Guido Reni
Cleopatra

1621–26
Oil on canvas, 110 × 94 cm
Madrid, Museo Nacional del Prado, P-209

Provenance: First mentioned as part of the Spanish royal collection at the Palacio Real, Madrid, in 1814–18; first listed in the Museo del Prado in 1854.

Selected bibliography: Pérez Sánchez 1965a, 172; Pepper 1988, 267, no. 111 (as a 'copy'); Malvasia–Pericolo 2019, 1:397–98, note 533.

80 Guido Reni
Cleopatra with the Asp

1627–28
Oil on canvas, 114.2 × 95 cm
The Royal Collection / HM King Charles III, RCIN 405338

Provenance: First recorded at Leicester House, London, in 1749, in the possession of Frederick Louis, Prince of Wales.

Selected bibliography: Baccheschi 1971, 103, no. 122; Pepper 1988, 266–67, no. 111; Malvasia–Pericolo 2019, 1:397–98, note 533.

In his *Maraviglie dell'arte* (1648), the Venetian painter and biographer Carlo Ridolfi (1594–1658) describes a *Cleopatra* by Guido Reni in the collection of the Flemish painter Nicolas Régnier (1591–1667): 'A life-size half-figure of Cleopatra who, wounded by a snake in the chest, fainting on account of the pain, seems to be expiring little by little'.[1] In his 1663 edition of Francesco Sansovino's *Venezia città nobilissima*, Giustiniano Martinioni singles out 'the beautiful Cleopatra by Guido Reni' in Régnier's house.[2] Carlo Cesare Malvasia equally mentions the painting, providing us with the precise circumstances of its production. In his *Felsina pittrice* (1678), he reports that the Venetian painter Palma Giovane (c. 1548/50–1628) convinced Guido 'to execute a Cleopatra in competition with three other half-figures, one by Palma himself, one by Régnier, salaried painter to the Venetian Republic, and one by Guercino, for a certain merchant Boselli'.[3] The identity of this Boselli remains unknown. In recounting the episode, Malvasia remarks: 'Guido later learned that the painting by Palma had been the most successful, since it was said that, even placed on top of Saint Mark's bell tower, it would have had an effect, whereas his own would have been wholly lost to view'.[4] With his usual witticism, Guido reportedly commented on this extravagant experiment: 'Didn't I tell you that in that place their Palma would have

won the palm? Besides, I wasn't told this Boselli used his campanile as a bedchamber, displaying the painting to the piazza from above'.[5] Despite the criticism of the Venetians, Guido's *Cleopatra* was cherished by Régnier, who had managed to purchase it, and who confessed to Malvasia (most probably during the latter's trip to Venice in 1664) that he 'lamented the disgrace suffered by that unrecognised divinity', keeping the picture in his collection 'like a diamond among other gems'.[6] Guido's *Cleopatra* is once again mentioned in the 1664 inventory of his paintings:

> A Cleopatra who has her breast bitten by the viper, half-figure, seated, life-size, and thereby there is a small table with a little basket of fruits, high six and a half *quarte*, wide more than five and a half *quarte*, the most beautiful painting and one of his best, with its carved and gilded frame.[7]

Guido's *Cleopatra* thus measured 111 × 94 centimetres approximately (the *quarta* being a quarter of a Venetian *braccio da lana*, which corresponds to 68.3 centimetres). The connoisseur and collector Paolo del Sera (1617–1672) defined Guido's *Cleopatra* as a copy when it sold in a public lottery held by Régnier on 4 December 1666.[8] Soon afterward, the painting ended up in the hands of the Venetian art dealer Francesco Fontana. In an inventory of his paintings drawn up in 1675, Guido's *Cleopatra* is described with almost the same words used in the Régnier inventory of 1664. Furthermore, the painting is listed there as a pendant to a *Poetry* by Guercino (1591–1666).[9] Further documentation informs us that Fontana tried to sell Guido's *Cleopatra* and Guercino's *Poetry* to Cardinal Leopoldo de' Medici (1617–1675).[10] In an attempt to raise the price of Guido's work, Fontana revealed to the prelate that the French ambassador in Venice, Jean-Antoine de Mesmes, Count d'Avaux (1640–1709), 'had truly fell in love with Guido's Cleopatra and its pendant by Guercino', offering 200 doubloons (400 scudi) for the two paintings and 'a portrait by Raphael', which was also part of the deal. In his letter to Leopoldo de' Medici, Fontana reports that he was in Paris in 1664 when a *Magdalen* by Guido, which 'was neither larger nor more beautiful than this Cleopatra of mine', sold for 800 scudi.[11] The prelate declined the offer.

The commission of Guido's *Cleopatra* in competition with paintings by Palma, Régnier, and Guercino, must have taken place between 1626 (when Régnier settled in Venice) and 1628 (the date of Palma's death). Which subjects were depicted by Palma and Régnier in their half-figures remains unknown. Guercino's *Poetry* is still to be traced. It might have resembled another *Poetry* he executed later, in 1640.[12] In light of the description and measurements of the Régnier *Cleopatra* as recorded in the 1664 inventory, the painting could be identified either with Guido's *Cleopatra* now in the English Royal Collection (114.2 × 95 centimetres) or with his painting of the same subject now in the Prado (110 × 94 centimetres). Regrettably, the provenance of both paintings is obscure. The Prado version is first mentioned in the Spanish royal collection in 1814–18.[13] The version in England is first listed in Leicester House, London, in 1749, and must thus have been purchased by Frederick Louis, Prince of Wales (1707–1751).[14] Unlike most of Guido's paintings, the Prado *Cleopatra* is executed on Venetian canvas, as evidenced by its herringbone weave. But so, too, is apparently the English version (more detailed technical examination is needed to corroborate this). It is unknown whether Guido ever visited Venice, although this might have occurred during his youth perhaps at the suggestion of the Carracci, who acknowledged the importance of study trips (*studioso corso*) to the most prominent Italian artistic centres. Were it not for Malvasia's testimony, Guido's acquaintance with Palma Giovane would not be known – Malvasia evokes an epistolary correspondence between the two.

Given the obscurity of the historical context, it is impossible to ascertain how or why Guido used a Venetian canvas for his two versions of the *Cleopatra*. Equally unclear is Guido's procedure in creating multiple versions of the same composition. If the two figures are superimposed, the left contour of the female heroine and most of the head can be said to coincide. It can therefore be assumed that Guido employed a cartoon (he might have traced the outlines with black chalk or oil pigment), or a *lucido* (an oiled paper or canvas that, on account of its transparency, was used for transfer), or, having the two canvases side by side, he might have reproduced the outlines from one to the other by relying on his confident draughtsmanship. It is

noteworthy that modifications between these two versions are much more extensive than it was usual to Guido in creating replicas. Even if in these cases Guido revelled in giving free rein to stylistic improvisation, he rarely varied a composition to the point where both replicas present elements of remarkable originality.

In the Prado picture, Cleopatra's left hand appears to pick a fruit (perhaps a fig) from a basket on a table nearby. As a result, her left shoulder recedes more into depth so that the contours of the upper right shoulder and neck are more distended. By changing the position of the left arm in the English painting, shifting the left hand to the foreground, and making it express acceptance and determination, Guido remedied the narrative anachronism present in the Prado version: there, the gesture of picking a fruit is absurdly synchronous with the biting of the serpent. The drapery in the Prado version is also more elaborate. The ruby mantle wrapped around the heroine's torso and deftly deployed across the foreground as a red parapet is marked by an angularity, discontinuity, and complexity absent in the English painting. The Royal Collection *Cleopatra* can indeed be considered the product of stylistic and compositional distillation, with a considerable reduction of the chromatism to two predominant tonalities – white and pink – where only a few touches of dark brown and blue (in the curtain), with the aid of the black hair of the heroine, counteract the brightness of the overall composition. In this sense, the English version presents itself as a chromatic feat: the whiteness of the chemise competes in sheen with, but also texturally detaches itself from, the ivory-like fairness of the heroine's flesh, while the white highlights of the pink mantle accentuate the luminosity of the painting, driving it into paroxysm. On the other hand, the Prado version better renders Cleopatra's emotional dilemma and ordeal, the pallor of her soon-to-be-bloodless chest exalted by the tortuous raggedness of her ruby mantle. Nothing is identical in these two versions: even the attitude and position of the hand that holds the snake, and the snake itself, differ in a perceptible measure. The increased whiteness and the recourse to thicker impasto characteristic of the English version better fits the style of works executed by

Cat. 79

Cat. 80

Guido in 1627–28, such as the 1627 *Immaculate Conception* in the Metropolitan Museum of Art, New York [cat. 55]. The chiaroscuro effect specific to the Prado version might instead relate to an earlier moment, between 1621 and 1626. In light of this, the English version is likely to be the one made for the Palma competition.

Lorenzo Pericolo

1 Ridolfi 1648, 2:48: 'Mezza figura quanto al vivo di Cleopatra che, ferita nel petto dal serpe, venendo meno per lo dolore, pare che a poco a poco esali lo spirito'.
2 Sansovino and Martinioni 1663, 378: 'La bella Cleopatra di Guido Reni'.
3 Malvasia 1678, 2:75: 'Forzato poi dalle preghiere del Palma giovane … ad una Cleopatra a concorrenza d'altre tre figure compagne, una del sudetto Palma, una del Renieri pittore salariato della Repubblica, ed una del Guercino per un tal mercante Boselli'.
4 Ibid.: 'Risaputo poi quella del Palma aver incontrato più di tutte, con dirsi che, posta anche sulla cima del campanile di San Marco, avria fatto il suo effetto, ove la sua si sarebbe perduta affatto'.
5 Ibid.: 'Non l'ho detto io, soggionse, che in quel paese il suo Palma avrebbe appunto la palma? Poi non m'han detto che questo Boselli si serva del campanile di San Marco per camera, e di là su faccia vedere le sue pitture alla piazza'.
6 Ibid.: 'Renieri … la tenea nel suo museo come un diamante fra l'altre gemme, esaggerando con me, quando lo visitai, la disgrazia d'una divinità non conosciuta'.
7 Campori 1870, 448; Lemoine 2007, 349, no. 60.
8 Lemoine 2007, 354.
9 Procacci and Procacci 1965, 98, doc. XXIV.
10 Ibid., 92, doc. ix.
11 Ibid., 97, doc. XXIII.
12 Salerno 1988, 272, no. 188; Ghelfi 1997, 104, no. 233; Turner 2017, 555, no. 264.
13 *Museo del Prado* 1996, 308, no. 209.
14 Levey 1991, 123–24, no. 576.

81   Guido Reni

Salome with the Head of Saint John the Baptist

c. 1635
Oil on canvas, 134 × 97 cm
Rome, Gallerie Nazionali d'Arte Antica, Galleria Corsini, inv. 191

Provenance: Cardinal Francesco Barberini, 1639; mentioned in the inventory of the estate of Cardinal Alessandro Bichi in 1658; in the collection of Cardinal Neri Maria Corsini in 1740; listed in the Corsini collection, Rome, until its donation to the Italian state in 1883.

Selected bibliography: Cavalli 1955, no. 79; Baccheschi 1971, no. 157; C. Casali Predielli in Emiliani et al. 1988, 300, no. 55; Pepper 1988, 292–93, no. 169; Malvasia–Pericolo 2019, 1:448, note 673.

A note of 13 December 1639 from the Barberini household account books reads: 'From the hands of Monsignor Fausto [we have] received a painting with gilded frame, high 6 *palmi* and 4 ¼, of Herodias, by Guido Reni'.[1] Marilyn Aronberg Lavin first identified this painting as Guido's *Salome with the Head of Saint John the Baptist* now in the Galleria Corsini. The Barberini painting measured approximately 134 × 95 centimetres (the Roman *palmo* being 22.34 centimetres), which corresponds to the dimensions of the Corsini *Salome*. Stephen Pepper supported this identification under the assumption that the Barberini painting had entered the Corsini collection by succession.[2] Misreading the 1639 note, Pepper believed that Cardinal Francesco Barberini (1597–1679), the nephew of the then reigning pope Urban VIII (1568–1644), had purchased the work from Monsignor 'Fausta'. Most likely, the note suggests that Cardinal Barberini had commissioned the painting from Guido, receiving it through the intermediary of Monsignor (later Cardinal) Fausto Poli (1581–1653), a close member of the Barberini circle. In fact, until now there has been no certainty that the Barberini *Salome* was the same as the Corsini one. In an inventory of the Corsini collection dated 1740, the painting is mentioned as a gift to Pope Clement XII (Lorenzo Corsini, 1652–1740) from or through the intermediary of Monsignor Bardi (to be identified with Girolamo Bardi, 1685–1761), who had obtained it from 'Bichi'.[3] This 'Bichi' is not to be identified with Cardinal Carlo Giacomo Bichi (1639–1718) but with his nephew, Francesco Bichi (b. 1676).[4] Francesco must have inherited the painting via his father, Metello (1633–c. 1685), from his grand-uncle, Cardinal Alessandro Bichi (1597–1657), who was a trusted member of the Barberini circle.[5] It can indeed be established that Cardinal Barberini either commissioned the painting on behalf of Bishop Bichi (during one of the

latter's stays in his bishopry at Carpentras) or for Cardinal Bichi as a gift – he was elevated to the cardinalate by the Barberini Pope Urban VIII in 1633. Guido's *Salome* (*Herodias* according to the inventories) is no doubt quoted in the inventory of Cardinal Bichi's estate drawn up on 22 June 1658: 'A painting representing a Herodias with the head of Saint John the Baptist in a basin'.[6]

Another *Herodias* by Guido identical in composition to the Corsini may have existed and, if so, remains untraced. An engraving executed in 1688 by Nicolas Bazin (1633–1710) and published by Pierre Mariette II (1634–1716) in Paris presents the same composition as the Corsini *Salome* (the print was issued twice, in reverse and in the sense of the painting).[7] In his *Abecedario*, Pierre-Jean Mariette (1694–1774) remarked that 'the painting of Herodias engraved by Bazin belonged to Monsieur de Crozat'.[8] On the basis of this annotation, Margret Stuffmann suggested that a *Herodias* attributed to Caravaggio (1571–1610) in the collection of Pierre Crozat (1665–1740) could be identified as the painting by Guido engraved by Bazin.[9] This is extremely unlikely, not only because the Crozat *Salome* inventoried in 1740 was a small painting (60.9 × 40.6 centimetres) on panel, but especially because a work by Guido of that calibre is unlikely to have been misattributed so blatantly.

If Crozat ever owned the *Salome* reproduced by Bazin – and there is no reason to doubt Mariette – then it is certain that by 1740 he had already dispensed with it, because it does not appear in the inventory of his estate drawn up in that year. Whether this painting was an original replica or a copy of Guido's *Salome* is impossible to ascertain. Even if the Corsini *Salome* was received by Cardinal Barberini in 1639, this does not necessarily imply, as proposed by Pepper, that the work was executed in 1638–39.

Stylistically, the painting bears a great affinity with Guido's *Saint Michael Archangel* for Santa Maria della Concezione, Rome, completed in 1635 (still in situ).[10]

Lorenzo Pericolo

1 Aronberg Lavin 1975, 34: 'P[er] le mani di Mon[si]g[no]r Fausto, hauto un quadro con cornice dorato alto p[al]mi 6 e 4 ¼, con Erodiade, mano di Guido Reni'.
2 Pepper 1988, 292–93, no. 169.
3 Magnanimi 1980a, issue no. 7, 101, no. B52; Borsellino 2017, 2:269, no. 41, and 2:282, no. 54.
4 Malvasia–Pericolo 2019, 1:448, note 673; Di Gioia 2007, 146–50.
5 Borsellino 2017, 1:183, note 489.
6 Maccherini 2007, 265: 'Un quadro rappresentante una Herodiade con la testa di San Giovanni Battista in un bacile'. Even if none of the paintings listed in this inventory bears the name of the author, the probability that this is the Corsini *Salome* (*Herodias*) by Guido is extremely high, not only in light of the circumstantial evidence adduced here, but also because it is known that Cardinal Francesco Barberini presented Cardinal Bichi with other paintings, such as a *Lot* by Domenichino (1581–1641) and a painting on copper of an unknown subject by Giovanni Francesco Romanelli (1610–1662). See Aronberg Lavin 1975, 14, doc. 113, and 36, doc. 286; Maccherini 2007, 247, note 21.
7 Weigert 1939, 323, no. 97.
8 Mariette 1851–60 (1858), 4:370: 'Le tableau de l'Hérodiade qu'a gravé Bazin appartenoît à M de Crozat'.
9 Stuffmann 1968, 81, no. 189.
10 On Guido's *Saint Michael Archangel*, see Malvasia–Pericolo 2019, 1:306–7, note 245.

82 Guido Reni

Salome receiving the Head of Saint John the Baptist

c. 1638–42
Oil on canvas, 248.5 × 174 cm
Chicago, The Art Institute of Chicago, Louise B. and Frank
H. Woods Purchase Fund, 1960.3

Provenance: Listed in 1642 among the paintings that were in Guido Reni's workshop upon his death; mentioned in the collection of Cardinal Girolamo Colonna in 1648; recorded in the Colonna collection on many occasions up until 1783; mentioned in the collection of John Blight, Earl of Darnley, in Cobham Hall (Kent), in 1851; purchased by the Art Institute of Chicago in 1957.

Selected bibliography: Zeri 1960; Baccheschi 1971, 110, no. 178; C. Casali Pedrielli in Emiliani et al. 1988, 308, no. 59; Pepper 1988, 297–98, no. 179; Malvasia–Pericolo 2019, 1:444, note 671; Pericolo 2019, 632–33; C. Puglisi in Eclercy 2022a, 298–99, no. 158.

In a letter to Cardinal Giulio Sacchetti (1587–1663) published in 1639, the Genoese writer Luca Assarino recorded that, among the paintings he had seen during a recent visit to Guido Reni's studio, he admired 'a Herodias to whom a page, bending, reverently offered the gift she had requested from the infatuated tyrant within a silver basin from which blood was still dripping'.[1] In the inventory of Guido's paintings compiled upon his death in 1642, there is mention of two

Fig. 95 Giovanni Andrea Sirani (?), *Salome receiving the Head of John the Baptist*, c. 1639–42. Oil on canvas, 190.5 × 152.4 cm. Sarasota (Florida), The John and Mable Ringling Museum of Art, Bequest of John Ringling, 1936, SN119

works certainly in relation with the *Herodias* described by Assarino: 'A Judith with her maidservants by Signor Guido' and 'another one said to be sketched out'.[2] The presence of two canvases with the same composition, one sketched out, the other in a more advanced state, is not surprising in light of Guido's working method. In his *Felsina pittrice* (1678), Carlo Cesare Malvasia singles out, among the paintings in the collection of Cardinal Girolamo Colonna (1604–1666) in Rome, 'a standing Judith, life-size, one hand on her side, the other placing the head of Holofernes on a salver presented to her by a kneeling little page, with maids in attendance'.[3] Malvasia was not the only one to misconstrue the action represented and, as a result, the painting's subject, as it appears in the 1648 inventory of Cardinal Colonna's estate, is listed as 'a large painting of a Judith, standing, the work of Guido Reni, with a gilded frame'.[4] This work is more accurately described in the 1667 inventory of the Colonna estate: 'A large painting of a Judith sketched out and not finished, standing, laying Holofernes' head in a large basin held by the hands of a page, with a gilded frame'.[5] The picture is still listed as being in the Colonna collection in 1783.[6] It is unknown when or how the Colonna sold the painting. In 1851, the art historian Gustav Friedrich Waagen saw it at Cobham Hall, in the collection of John Bligh, 6th Earl of Darnley (1827–1896), describing it in derogatory terms: 'The daughter of Herodias [Salome] with the head of Saint John, formerly in the Colonna palace in Rome; an insipid specimen of an often-repeated composition, grey in colouring and weak in modelling'.[7] This is the painting that was then purchased by the Art Institute of Chicago in 1957.

It is interesting that Waagen, in commenting upon a *Salome* then attributed to Guido in the collection of Charles Anderson Pelham, 2nd Earl of Yarborough (1809–1862), in Brocklesby (Lincolnshire), had nothing but praise: 'Dignified and tender in expression, and warm in colouring'.[8] This work, which is now in the Ringling Art Museum, Sarasota [fig. 95], may be defined as a copy in reverse of the group of Herodias (Salome) and the kneeling page in the Chicago painting, and could well have been produced by Guido's disciple, Giovanni Andrea Sirani (1610–1670). This perhaps explains why Waagen, bearing in mind the Yarborough painting, considered the composition of the Darnley *Salome* repetitious.

A superb painting, similar in composition to the Ringling version of Guido's Chicago *Salome*, was put up for sale at Sotheby's, New York, in 2013.[9] When presented at auction, the work was classified as an eighteenth-century anonymous. The picture would deserve much closer scrutiny given its unmistakable quality.

The existence of these two elaborations upon Guido's composition speaks volumes about the exceptional artistic feat represented by the Chicago painting. Even if unfinished, or specifically on this account, Guido's *Salome* is a manifesto of the master's unswerving search for perfection and dissatisfaction with the alleged limits of his own artistry during his final years. A palimpsest unravelling before the beholder, the painting presents itself in differing states of advancement, with a few *pentimenti* still visible, which, partially covered, seem to still be waiting for modification. The figure of the kneeling page is quickly scumbled, and the clothed part of his body is painted in green, a pigment Guido used as a chromatic underlayer to enliven and contrast the tints on the surface – something that can be verified in the pink mantle of Salome with its greenish undertones. What painting meant for the old Guido is perhaps epitomised in the love with which he modelled the rich impasto of the cruel protagonist's ochre gown, which swirls and dissolves into a colour blotch leaving the impression of instantaneous motion – a blotch that was most probably meant to be concealed upon the painting's completion. Having reached his sixties, Guido began to fear death's approach – as Malvasia, who knew the master personally, relates. Unfinished works such as this *Salome* are the master's ultimate challenge not against death, but against chance as an inherent factor in the game of painting. It is impossible to establish which of the two canvases listed as 'Judith' in Guido's 1642 inventory corresponds to the Chicago painting, but it is likely that it was the most advanced one.

Lorenzo Pericolo

1 Assarino 1639, 29: 'Un'Erudiade a cui inchinandosi un paggio porgeva riverente dentro un catino d'argento il dono ancora stillante di sangue ch'avea richiesto dell'innamorato tiranno'.
2 Spike and Di Zio 1988, 63: 'Una Giuditta con le sue damicelle del sig[no]r Guido' and 'un altro detto abbozzato'.
3 Malvasia 1678, 2:90: 'Giuditta in piedi grande del naturale che, con una mano sul fianco, con l'altra pone la testa di Oloferne s'un piatto presentatole da un paggetto genuflesso con damigelle'.
4 Safarik 1996, 70, no. 63: 'Un quadro grande di una Juditte in piedi, mano di Guido Reni, con cornice indorata'.
5 Ibid., 104, no. 21: 'Un quadro grande d'una Juditta sbozzata e non finita, in piedi, che pone la testa di Oloferne in un baccile grande, che lo tiene un paggio in mano, con cornice dorata'.
6 Ibid., 125, no. 75.
7 Waagen 1854, 3:21.
8 Ibid., 2:87.
9 Sotheby's, New York, *Old Master Paintings*, sale of 31 January 2013, lot 169.

83   Guido Reni

Saint Catherine of Alexandria

c. 1606
Oil on canvas, 98 × 75 cm
Madrid, Museo Nacional del Prado, P-230

Provenance: Collection of Ferdinand VII, Madrid; Real Museo, Madrid, 1834 (no. 691) and 1857 (no. 783).

Selected bibliography: Gaya Nuño 1954, 112; Pérez Sánchez 1962, 55–56; Pérez Sánchez 1965a, 131 and 180; Pepper 1984, 220; Espinós et al. 1986, 54; F. Valli in Emiliani et al. 1988, 46, no. 15; *Museo del Prado* 1990, 1:220, no. 783; Salvy 2001, 145; Aterido Fernández, Martínez Cuesta and Pérez Preciado 2004, 2:452; Ruiz Gómez 2009a, 214; Bernardini 2015, 36; L. Volk-Simon in Eclercy 2022a, 152–54, no. 39.

Saint Catherine, a third century martyr, belonged to a noble family in Alexandria. Driven by her Christian faith to disobey the Roman emperor, she was ordered to oppose him in a philosophical symposium. As a result of her debating skills, which led to the conversion of several highly placed figures at court including the empress herself, she was put to death. Given her social status and the fact that she was held to embody the virtues of wisdom, strength, and eloquence, she was hailed as a model for aristocratic ladies in early modern Spain. It is hardly surprising, therefore, that the Spanish royal collection should boast several works of art displaying this iconography, including the two paintings by Guido Reni in this exhibition [cat. 83 and 84].

In the late eighteenth century, Antonio Ponz and Antonio Conca both reported seeing one of these canvases – though mistakenly attributing it to Domenico Zampieri, Domenichino (1581–1641) – in the Casita del Príncipe at El Escorial.[1] The art historian Alfonso E. Pérez Sánchez assumed that they had also seen the other version in the royal palace of La Granja de San Ildefonso, though they made no specific reference to its iconography.[2] Pérez Sánchez based his hypothesis on a reference by Antonio Ponz to 'a half-length female martyr thought to be by Guido Reni',[3] whereas in fact the early editions of Ponz's *Viage* refer to a 'Holy Martyr' in the masculine.[4] Although Conca later noted that the painting in question was 'a half-length Female Martyr by Guido Reni',[5] it seems unlikely that Ponz – having recognised the Escorial canvas as a *Saint Catherine* by Domenichino – would be unable to correctly identify the theme, or that he would fail to link the two paintings. Indeed, Ponz noted that the same palace boasted a copy of Reni's *Saint Cecilia* made by Andrea Vaccaro (1604–1670);[6] it would therefore be surprising if he could not recognise the other with any certainty.

Comparison of this painting with the Escorial version [cat. 84], which was enlarged at some stage, suggests that the lower and right edges of the Prado canvas must have been cut off,[7] removing part of the saint's mantle. By contrast, the mantle is complete both in the Escorial canvas and in a seventeenth-century copy, mistakenly attributed to a follower of Caravaggio, sold at auction in 2016.[8] Given this possible reduction in size, and the fact that the inventory number matches that given by the Real Museo in 1857, it may well be that the picture was trimmed then, and that it had been in the Spanish royal collection for a long time. There is no reason why the painting seen by Ponz and Conca in El Escorial should not be the one now in the Prado; it could have been switched with the copy then at La Granja de San Ildefonso during the reorganisation and selection of works for the Museum. In compositional terms, the two canvases differ in just a few details: the martyr's wheel is placed lower down in the Escorial version, and the saint's right hand is more centrally positioned. However, recent X-ray examination has revealed that Reni traced the composition of the Prado picture, but made certain improvements to the position of the head and the fingers. These changes were replicated in the Escorial canvas, thus confirming that it was produced at a later date, using the Prado version as a model.[9] The technical quality of the Prado painting is much closer to that of other originals produced by Guido during his sojourn in Rome in the early seventeenth century, in which the influence of Caravaggio (1571–1610) and Raphael (1483–1520) is clearly discernible. Several elements in the Prado canvas – the precise flow of the ornamental motifs on the saint's mantle and the rendering of the folds in the upper part of the tunic and the sleeve – are missing from the Escorial version, suggesting the possible participation of a painter at Reni's workshop. Up until the nineteenth century, inventory compilers believed that the alleged original was at El Escorial, which may account for the unexpected shift in the perceived quality of the Prado canvas, from 'Reni original' through 'school of Reni' to 'copy'. In fact, the La Granja painting – which had come from the Maratta collection – had adorned important rooms in the royal residence, including the

king's private chapel, study, and bedchamber, suggesting that the monarchs held it in high esteem. After all, the composition depicts a member of the nobility whose martyrdom led to her canonisation, thus setting an edifying example to the royal family.

Rafael Japón

1 For the other *Saint Catherine* by Reni, in the care of Patrimonio Nacional, see cat. 84.

2 They may in fact have been referring to the *Saint Cecilia* by Reni which is identical in size to this canvas, and probably formed a pair with it. See cat. 87.

3 Pérez Sánchez 1965a, 180.

4 Ponz 1772–94 (1781), 10:140.

5 Conca 1793–97 (1793), 2:212: 'una Santa Martire in mezza figura di Guido Reni'.

6 Ponz 1772–94 (1781), 10:144.

7 This is confirmed in the report of the restoration work carried out by Laura Alba Carcelén in May 2022.

8 Doyle Auctions, *English & Continental Furniture & Decorative Arts/Old Master Paintings*, 18 May 2016, lot 8 (127 × 88 cm); https://doyle.com/auctions/16cn02-english-continental-furniture-decorative-artsold-master-paintings/catalogue/8 [accessed: 16 June 2022].

9 The X-ray examination was performed by Laura Alba Carcelén in May 2022.

84   Guido Reni and workshop
Saint Catherine of Alexandria

c. 1606
Oil on canvas, 103/108 × 79 cm (relined: 140 × 95.5 cm)
Patrimonio Nacional. Colecciones Reales. Real Sitio de La Granja de San Ildefonso, inv. 10033630

Provenance: Carlo Maratta, Rome, 1712; collection of Philip V, from 1723 (no. 157); Palacio Real de La Granja de San Ildefonso, Segovia, 1727; oratory at the Palacio Real de La Granja de San Ildefonso, Segovia, 1746; royal bedchamber at the Palacio Real de La Granja de San Ildefonso, 1794 (no. 238); king's study and bedchamber at the Palacio Real, Aranjuez, 1818 (no. 238); Casita del Príncipe, San Lorenzo de El Escorial, 1857 (no. 774).

Selected bibliography: Poleró 1857, 160; Zarco Cuevas 1926, 19; Pérez Sánchez 1962, 55; Pérez Sánchez 1965a, 179–80; Pepper 1984, 220; Aterido Fernández, Martínez Cuesta and Pérez Preciado 2004, 2:452, no. 878; G. Redín Michaus in Redín Michaus 2016a, 142–45, no. 12.

This depiction of *Saint Catherine of Alexandria* is currently regarded as an autograph replica of the painting in the Museo del Prado [cat. 83]. Although earlier historians confused the two on the basis of references in the royal inventories, it is now agreed that the canvas recorded in all these documents is in fact this version in the care of Patrimonio Nacional. It came from the collection of Carlo Maratta (1625–1713) who, knowing it to be by Guido Reni, placed it in a gallery beside the garden of his house in Rome, alongside works by other great masters.[1] In 1722 it was purchased for Philip V's collection and by 1727 it was already in the palace of La Granja de San Ildefonso.[2] There it hung in various important spaces, including the oratory and the royal bedchamber. Even though it was listed as an original by Reni in the inventories of the palace assets, in 1794 it was attributed to Domenichino (1581–1641);[3] in 1818 it figured as an anonymous copy after Guido,[4] and then as a workshop copy in the Museum catalogues from 1857 onwards; until in 1965 Alfonso E. Pérez Sánchez correctly identified it as an original dating from an early stage in Reni's career.[5]

While this canvas can be identified by the reference number 238 assigned to it in the inventories of the palaces of La Granja and Aranjuez, several contemporary chronicles refer to its presence in El Escorial at around the same time. In 1788, Antonio Ponz reported a *Saint Catherine* by Domenichino in the Casita del Príncipe, where it was also seen by Antonio Conca in 1793,[6] although only one year later it was recorded in Aranjuez – where it was still to be found in 1818 – and by 1857 it was back in El Escorial, where it has remained to this day. Although this toing and froing prompted a certain amount

of confusion, Gonzalo Redín Michaus concluded that all the above references were solely to the Escorial version, leaving the origins of the Prado picture open to question.[7] In this regard it should be stressed that the earliest record of the painting in the Museum has always been held to be the 1857 inventory, where it is identified as a work by the 'school of Reni' and entered under the reference number 783 – still visible on the canvas[8] – three years before Vicente Poleró located the other painting at El Escorial.[9] However, there is an earlier reference: an entry in the 1834 inventory of the Real Museo describes 'a female saint with a royal crown on her head', an original by Guido, which can only be identified as this version of *Saint Catherine*.[10]

This confirms that both pictures coexisted in the Spanish royal collection at least since the reign of Ferdinand VII, before being taken to El Escorial and the Museum, respectively. One of the most obvious physical differences between the two is their size, for although they originally had similar dimensions,[11] the Escorial canvas was relined before 1722, extending it to 140 × 95.5 centimetres. The composition was continued to the edges of the added strips, which appear to have been folded back in order to adapt the painting to a different frame when it entered the palace of La Granja.[12]

There is a third version of the painting in London, belonging to the Royal Collection Trust,[13] now regarded as a studio version. The saint's mantle is simpler though more richly decorated, with a border to the right not found in the Escorial canvas. Interestingly, the London painting shares the simpler rendering of the folds in the upper part of the tunic, which are more elaborate in the Prado version.[14] The London picture has been identified as the painting purchased by the painter Ciro Ferri (1634–1689) and later sent by Cardinal Francesco Barberini to the Duchess of York in 1674;[15] by contrast, nothing is known of the provenance of the two Spanish versions prior to 1712. Other historical documents mention works by

Reni on this subject, but they cannot be reliably linked to these two paintings. Of particular note is a large-format canvas recorded in the collection of Juan de Lezcano in 1633.[16] The existence of other treatments of this saint, depicted in various poses, makes it even more difficult to establish any accurate relationship between inventory references and the paintings themselves; a good example is the version in the Manchester Art Gallery [fig. 96].[17]

Rafael Japón

1 Galli 1928, 28.

2 G. Redín Michaus in Redín Michaus 2016a, 142–43, no. 12; Madrid, Museo Nacional del Prado [hereafter, MNP], Inventarios reales, vol. 7, *Real sitio de la Granja de San Ildefonso*, 1746, fol. 14, no. 12425 (238); MNP, Inventarios reales, vol. 9, *Palacio de San Ildefonso*, 1774, fol. 34, no. 17109 (238).

3 MNP, Inventarios reales, vol. 10, *Real Sitio de Aranjuez*, 1794, fol. 45, no. 19806 (238): 'Two feet and fourteen fingers long, and two feet and thirteen fingers high, Saint Catherine = Dominiquino [sic] = 3000'.

4 MNP, Inventarios reales, vol. 12, *Palacio del Real Sitio de Aranjuez*, 1818, fol. 17, no. 20742 (238): 'Ditto [seven *quartas* long and four high], Saint Catherine = copy after Guido [in the king's study and bedchamber]'.

5 Pérez Sánchez 1965a, 180.

6 Ponz 1787–93 (1788), 2:247; Conca 1793–97 (1793), 2:212. Conca identifies it as the work by Guido Reni.

7 G. Redín Michaus in Redín Michaus 2016a, 143, no. 12.

8 MNP, Inventario del Real Museo, 1857, no. 783.

9 Poleró 1857, 160, no. 774.

10 MNP, Inventarios reales, vol. 12, *Real Museo*, 1834, fol. 43, no. 691.

11 The Prado canvas measures 98 × 75 cm, and the El Escorial canvas 103/108 × 79 cm.

12 G. Redín Michaus in Redín Michaus 2016a, 142, no. 12.

13 Royal Collection Trust, RCIN 405547.

14 This was also attributed to Domenichino but, noting the quality of the work, Stephen Pepper (1984, 220) argued that it could be from Reni's studio.

15 Montanari 2004, 83–86.

16 Vannugli 2009, 354–55.

17 Identified by Stephen Pepper (1984, 282) as the painting from the Colonna collection. There are also a number of historical copies of this version, including one auctioned by Dorotheum (Vienna, *Old Master Paintings*, 23 October 2018, lot 194). Here, it was attributed to Reni's workshop.

85 Domenico Guidi

(Torano 1625–1701 Rome)

The Virgin Annunciate

1670
Marble, 89 × 76 cm (without base)
Vienna, Gartenpalais Liechtenstein, The Princely Collection,
SK 1494

Provenance: Charles Kinnaird, 8th Lord Kinnaird, 1822; library at Rossie Priory, Inchture (Perthshire); National Gallery of Scotland, Edinburgh, on loan from Graham Charles Kinnaird, 13th Lord Kinnaird of Inchture; Prince Hans-Adam II of Liechtenstein, 2007.

Selected bibliography: Bacchi 1996, 810–12, fig. 479; Giometti 2010, 269–70 and 351; M. Leithe-Jasper in Schröder 2019, 164–67, no. 40.

This half-length figure in white marble, in a large and rather unusual format, represents the Virgin Mary, interrupted in her reading; her left hand is pressed to her breast and she holds a book in her right. The sculpture has been identified by Andrea Bacchi as the 'half-length figure of the Holy Virgin Annunciate' by Domenico Guidi which – according to a biography of the artist in the so-called *Zibaldone Baldinucciano* (1691) – was to be found in his studio.[1] New evidence published by Cristiano Giometti has shown that on Guidi's death in 1701 there were two *Annunciates* of the same size in his studio, one unfinished, together with a half-length figure of an angel. The records make it clear that – as might be expected – the finished half-length Virgin was intended as a pendant to a matching figure of the archangel Gabriel, thus forming an Annunciation group. It is worth noting that the 1702 inventory of Guidi's estate describes the pair of sculptures as 'imperfect figures',[2] which would hardly seem to tally with the highly refined execution of this *Virgin Annunciate*. This minor inconsistency, however, does not suffice to undermine the very solid identification proposed by Bacchi and confirmed by renowned specialists such as Jennifer Montagu. It may be that the definition of 'imperfect' in the 1702 inventory was not wholly reliable, or that the piece was slightly retouched after Guidi's death. Whatever the case, this *Virgin*

Annunciate was purchased in Rome by Charles Kinnaird around 1822, probably as the work of Gian Lorenzo Bernini (1598–1680); it remained in the family collection at Rossie Priory (Perthshire) until it was loaned to the National Gallery of Scotland, Edinburgh, by Graham Charles Kinnaird, 13th Lord Kinnaird of Inchture (1912–1997). Subsequently, in 2007 it was acquired on the art market by Prince Hans-Adam II of Liechtenstein.[3] No trace has been found either of the second, unfinished *Annunziata* or of the angel, and there is no news of the whereabouts of the 'small, half-length models of an Angel and a Virgin' also listed in the 1702 inventory, which were very probably the *bozzetti* in terracotta, made by Guidi himself, for the *Annunciation* pair in marble.[4]

Fig. 96 Guido Reni, *Saint Catherine*, 1638–40. Oil on canvas, 102 × 83.6 cm. Manchester, Manchester Art Gallery, Purchased with the Assistance of the Victoria & Albert Museum Purchase Grant Fund and the Art Fund, 1974.88

The Virgin turns meekly aside, her gentle leftward movement giving Guidi the opportunity to capture the swirl of the opulent robe that completely surrounds her. Giometti associates this full, billowing drapery with sculptures produced in the late 1680s, and in particular with the marble half-length figure of the bookseller Zenobio Masotto in the church of Santa Barbara dei Librai in Rome. He also highlights stylistic affinities with the paintings of Carlo Maratta (1625–1713).[5] The close study of draperies (*panneggio*) was a major feature of an artist's training in seventeenth-century Rome, and served to showcase his technical skills.[6] Guidi boasted of having trained under the Bologna sculptor Alessandro Algardi (1595–1654) – whom Malvasia hailed as a 'new Guido in marble'[7] – and his lively drapery certainly derives, albeit indirectly, from models by Guido Reni. Indeed, in the delicate gestures of her hands, the inclination of her head, the shape of her face, and the gentle sway of her robe, Guidi's *Virgin Annunciate* engages perfectly with Reni's Manchester *Saint Catherine* [fig. 96] or the *Saint Margaret* now in a private collection, both of which had formerly belonged to the Naples collection of Lorenzo Onofrio Colonna, Prince of Paliano. This preoccupation with *panneggio* – almost as a genre in itself, independent of the figure – was a hallmark feature of Reni's later oeuvre. In Guidi's marble *Annunziata* we can clearly discern echoes of Reni's majestic *Salome* in the Galleria Corsini [cat. 81], and of his voluptuous *Cleopatras* in the Museo del Prado [cat. 79] and in the British Royal Collection [cat. 80]. Conversely, of course, the sculptural value of Reni's paintings had already been highlighted by Cardinal Maffeo Barberini when praising the frescoes for the Cappella Paolina in the church of Santa Maria Maggiore in Rome; 'Sculpta putas quae picta vides'.[8] There is no doubt that these figures by Guido, frescoed in the early 1610s, aroused considerable interest, and provided models for all future artists. It is perhaps no coincidence, then, that the position of Mary's hands in the Guidi marble recalls the gestures of Reni's *Saint Pulcheria* on one of the arches in the Pauline chapel.

Fernando Loffredo

1 Bacchi 1996, 810–12, fig. 479.
2 Giometti 2010, 269.
3 For the most recent reference, see M. Leithe-Jasper in Schröder 2019, 164–67, no. 40.
4 Giometti 2010, 351, no. 35.OP.
5 Ibid., 262.
6 Lingo 2011.
7 Malvasia 1678, 2:35: 'Un nuovo Guido in marmo'. For the English translation, see Malvasia–Pericolo 2019, 1:83.
8 Malvasia–Pericolo 2019, 1:50; Cappelletti 2022b, 53.

86 Guido Reni
The Penitent Magdalen

c. 1630
Oil on canvas, 234 × 151 cm
Rome, Gallerie Nazionali d'Arte Antica, Palazzo Barberini-Corsini, Palazzo Barberini, inv. 1437

Provenance: Believed to have been painted for Cardinal Antonio Santacroce, Bologna, before 1633; gifted to Cardinal Antonio Barberini by Valerio Santacroce, Rome, by 16 December 1641; passed by descent to the Sciarra collection, Rome, in 1812; sold from that collection around 1891–92 and then entered the Corsini collection, Florence; purchased by the Italian state in 1897.

Selected bibliography: Vizzani 1633; Richardson 1722, 163; *Descrizione di Roma moderna* 1739, 2:357 and 2:361; Rossini 1776, 2:186; Lalande 1786, 4:430; Vasi 1804, 1:219 and 1:222; Vasi 1812, 1:160; Vasi 1816, 1:19ff.; Michetti 1889, no. 10; Venturi 1897, 255; Cavalli 1954, 92–93, note 28; Gnudi and Cavalli 1955, no. 60, pl. 112; Mahon 1957, 241; Bardon 1968, 281–82; Garboli and Baccheschi 1971, no. 116; Spear 1972, no. 16; Aronberg Lavin 1975, doc. 269; Hibbard 1976, 227–31; Pepper 1984, 267, no. 137; Mosco 1986, no. 62; Emiliani et al. 1988, 142, no. 59 (Bologna), 279–80, no. 47 (Los Angeles–Fort Worth); Mochi Onori and Vodret Adamo 1989, 97; Spear 1997, 163, 174, 243, 363, and 388; Mochi Onori and Vodret Adamo 1998, 66; Borea and Gasparri 2000, 353, note 13; Strinati and Vodret Adamo 2000, 84–85, note 26; Marcenaro and Boragina 2001, 183–88, no. V.34; Algranti 2002, 140, no. 44; Mochi Onori and Vodret Adamo 2008, 324; Primarosa 2021, 134; Cristofori and Scanu 2022, 30; A. Rentzsch in Eclercy 2022a, 256–57, no. 109.

One of Guido Reni's most frequently repeated subjects was that of Mary Magdalene in penance. The artist's interpretation of the subject was apparently enormously popular: these paintings were coveted by seats of religious power, members of the aristocracy, and the wealthy middle class alike, and at least fifty-six individual single-figure variants portraying Mary Magdalene related to Reni's studio can be counted, among them a bust-length depiction in the collection of the Museo del Prado, attributed to the artist's workshop [fig. 97].[1] Many of these paintings of the Magdalen depict a reclined figure in a cave in the manner illustrated here, an arrangement that seems to have been particularly successful. Among the plethora of studio works and later copies that follow this format, two versions are generally accepted as autograph: one depicting the saint in three-quarter length that was once part of the Almagià collection and today is in private hands (whereabouts unknown), and the full-length work presently under discussion, which is thought to have originally been painted for Cardinal Antonio Santacroce (1599–1641), and later sent as a gift to Cardinal Antonio Barberini (1607–1671).

Fig. 97 Workshop of Guido Reni, *The Magdalen*,
c. 1600–1650. Oil on canvas, 75 × 62 cm.
Madrid, Museo Nacional del Prado, P000216

Reni's image of a reclined Mary Magdalene in the wilderness has become somewhat of a poster child of Italian Baroque art, famous for the manner in which it epitomises many facets of post-Tridentine ideology. A close follower of Christ, Mary Magdalene's identity has, over the course of the Church's history, been conflated with two other female figures mentioned in the Bible: Mary of Bethany and a sinful woman described in the Gospel of Luke (the repentant sinner who washes Jesus' feet at the home of Simon the Pharisee). This conflation led to the traditional belief that the Magdalen was a sinner, and though the Bible does not refer to the nature of this sin, it resulted in the widespread belief that she was a prostitute. According to legend, the Magdalen spent thirty years in solitude in a cave in the wilderness of the south of France atoning for these earlier transgressions. The sacrament of penance held important significance in Counter-Reformation theology, and penitent saints like the Magdalen were portrayed with frequency by seicento artists as examples for viewers to follow.[2]

During this period, numerous treatises were written advising artists on the appropriate manner in which to address religious subject matters. One such text, published during Guido's lifetime, offered instructions regarding the decorous presentation of the Magdalen, recommending that instead of being shown entirely naked, she was to be portrayed carefully with modest

gestures, and so that her arms raised in prayer covered as much of her body as possible, with her hair spread over her shoulders, chest and breasts.[3]

In this particular version of the Magdalen, Reni adheres carefully to this advice. While the ex-Almagià collection work illustrates the saint with her chest exposed, here her breasts have been covered with her hair as the treatise prescribes, as well as a billowing white shirt.

Despite the fact that the protagonist is depicted fully dressed, this image still reads as sensual, if not erotic. The contours of the saint's breasts are gently emphasised by the fabric of her undershirt and flowing blonde hair. She is depicted as a beautiful, healthy young woman with porcelain-white skin. Her iconic expression, with heavenward gaze, calls to mind the ancient *Niobe* sculptures upon which many of Reni's female heads are based. Though she is surrounded by symbols associated with her penance – a skull as a reminder of mortality, roots upon which to survive, and a crucifix to meditate on during her desert isolation – her voluptuous body has seemingly not yet been affected by this period of asceticism. Here, the Magdalen's physical beauty is a manifestation of divine grace, gifted by God and translated to an image intended to both move and educate the spectator. Her inviting form was intended to illustrate the dangers of temptation and bodily pleasure, and the importance of penance in the redemption of even the worst of sinners.[4]

Though not mentioned by Guido's primary biographer Carlo Cesare Malvasia, this version of the Penitent Magdalen closely matches the description of a composition celebrated in an encomium published in 1633 by Carlo Emanuele Vizzani, which provides a terminus ante quem for the execution of the work.[5] The precise date that should be ascribed to the painting is, however, disputed. In their respective studies of the work, Howard Hibbard noted that its date of origin had 'not proclaimed itself … by style or documentation', and Richard Spear cited a consensus that it was painted much earlier than 1633.[6] Suggested early dates for the painting have ranged from 1610 to 1624, but Hibbard points out that 'it would have been unusual to issue a booklet praising the acquisition of a picture that had not been painted for the patron, and on the face of it the booklet of 1633 would imply that Cardinal Santacroce had recently acquired a new painting', suggesting that the date of completion of the work was closer to 1633.[7] Stephen Pepper theorised that work on the painting may have commenced some years earlier, and that it was left unfinished for a period, before being completed in 1632 or 1633 and then delivered to Cardinal Antonio Santacroce, which explains 'the paradox of what looks like an

Flesh and Drapery

earlier figural composition' which also displays the 'light coloration [and] soft contours' associated with Reni's work in the 1630s.[8] The notion that work on this *Penitent Magdalen* might have commenced, been temporarily abandoned, and the remainder then completed in 1632 or 1633, and that the painting therefore rested, unfinished, in the artist's studio for much of the 1620s is an attractive one. Not only does it resolve the issues of style that make this painting difficult to date, but its presence in the studio would also have provided assistants ample opportunity to use the unfinished work (or parts of it) as a prototype in the production of new compositions during a busy and successful decade in Guido's workshop.[9]

Aoife Brady

1 Emiliani et al. 1988, 278; Brady 2017, 1:275–76.
2 Spear 1997, 164–65.
3 Lomazzo 1585, 365–66.
4 Spear 1997, 166.
5 Vizzani 1633.
6 Hibbard 1976, 227; Spear 1972, 39.
7 Hibbard 1976, 229.
8 Stephen Pepper, cited in Hibbard 1976, 230.
9 For more on the relationship of this painting to other works produced in Reni's studio, see Brady 2020.

87 Guido Reni
Saint Cecilia

c. 1605
Oil on canvas, 71.5 × 57 cm
Patrimonio Nacional. Colecciones Reales. Real Sitio de La Granja de San Ildefonso, inv. 10010037.

Provenance: Collection of Isabella Farnese, Palacio Real de La Granja de San Ildefonso, Segovia, 1746 (no. 1175); Palacio Real, Aranjuez, 1794 (no. 1175); Palacio Real, Madrid.

Selected bibliography: Pérez Sánchez 1965a, 179 and 181; Pepper 1984, 221; Aterido Fernández, Martínez Cuesta and Pérez Preciado 2004, 2:97; L. Volk-Simon in Eclercy 2022a, 152–54, no. 40.

This painting first appeared in the inventories of the royal collection in the mid-eighteenth century as one of a number of works belonging to Queen Isabella Farnese then hanging in the palace of La Granja de San Ildefonso. Although the records show that this *Saint Cecilia* was painted by Guido Reni, critics have not unanimously accepted this attribution. While Alfonso E. Pérez Sánchez not only hailed it as an original, but also

Fig. 98 Guido Reni, *Saint Margaret*, c. 1606–7. Oil on canvas, 92.5 × 76 cm. Münster, LWL–Museum für Kunst und Kultur, inv. 1222 BRD

ventured to date it to Reni's first sojourn in Rome,[1] Stephen Pepper dismissed it as a copy of the *Saint Cecilia* in the Norton Simon Museum in Pasadena [fig. 11].[2] One can only assume that he had not seen it, given the compositional differences between the two: in the Pasadena painting, Cecilia wears a turban and a red gown, and is playing the violin. In 2016, however, Carmen García-Frías Checa included it again among the autograph works by Guido purchased by the queen.[3]

In this half-length portrayal, Saint Cecilia turns slightly away from the viewer, gazing heavenwards, with one hand up against her breast and the other holding the martyr's palm. Noteworthy features include the fine veil falling from the beautiful garland of flowers in her hair, rendered with delicate glazes, and the cool tones of her garments. These elements, together with an organ barely visible in the left of the picture, stand out against a dark background lit only by golden rays, interpreted as the divine presence. By the late eighteenth century the canvas must have suffered severe blackening, for the compilers of the 1794 inventory of the royal palace at Aranjuez were unable to see the organ, and – in the absence of any other attribute – identified the figure as Saint Catherine.[4] Reni's *Saint Catherine* was already known at that time, since one of the two versions in the royal collection had hung, like this Saint Cecilia, at La Granja.[5]

The arrangement of the two figures is similar, although *Saint Catherine* is presented frontally to the viewer [cat. 83 and 84]. Reni used this model for many other depictions of holy martyrs, including the Prado *Martyrdom of Saint Apollonia* [cat. 13], the *Martyrdom of Saint Catherine of Alexandria* in the Museo Diocesano, Albenga, and the *Martyrdom of Saint Cecilia* in the convent of Santa Cecilia in Trastevere, Rome [fig. 21], to mention just a few examples painted between 1600 and 1606. Critics have pointed out that with this latter *Saint Cecilia* – commissioned by Cardinal Sfondrato for the Capella del Bagno – the young Guido created a new model that was wholly in keeping with the Early Christian paintings he discovered in Rome.[6] Reni based his composition mainly on a *Saint Cecilia* by Raphael (1483–1520),[7] with which he was very familiar, having copied it when it was in the church of San Giovanni in Monte in Bologna. The colour scheme is reminiscent of Mary Magdalene in Raphael's altarpiece, though here it is blended with some of the Caravaggesque innovations that Reni had encountered on arriving in Rome. A similar approach is apparent in another version of *Saint Cecilia*

in a private collection; though the composition is based on the Pasadena canvas – which may have been produced at the same time, around 1603 – the drapery more closely resembles that of the Patrimonio Nacional picture. This would account for the varying technical quality, the later *Saint Cecilia* being far sharper and brighter. Moreover, both the placing of the figure – turned slightly away from the viewer – and the use of blue-green tones against a dark background are found only in paintings from this period, such as the *Coronation of Saint Cecilia and Saint Valerian* in the church of Santa Cecilia in Trastevere, Rome, and another version of the *Martyrdom of Saint Cecilia* in the Museo della Certosa, Pavia. This is particularly apparent when comparing this canvas with the *Saint Margaret* at the LWL–Museum für Kunst und Kultur in Münster [fig. 98], which has been regarded as a kind of mirror-image pendant, due to similarities in both style and format.

The Spanish royal collection boasts other examples of this iconography, also associated with Reni. In the Casita del Príncipe at El Escorial, the *Saint Catherine* mentioned earlier was paired with a copy of the Pasadena *Saint Cecilia*, which – though now regarded as an autograph replica – was earlier attributed to Domenichino (1581–1641).[8] The Museo del Prado has a full-length version of Saint Cecilia, classified as being from Reni's workshop,[9] although it might better be attributed to the circle of Lorenzo Pasinelli (1629–1700).[10] The monarchy's taste for these paintings clearly spread to court officials: in 1662, another copy of Guido's *Saint Cecilia* was recorded – along with an *Immaculate Conception* by the same artist – at the home of Francisco Ocejo Rubalcaba, who was on the staff at Philip IV's War Office.[11]

Rafael Japón

1 Pérez Sánchez 1965a, 179.
2 Pepper 1984, 221.
3 García-Frías Checa 2016, 94.
4 Pérez Sánchez 1965a, 179.
5 For further information on this painting, see cat. 83 and 84.
6 Terzaghi 2022, 34–35.
7 Bologna, Pinacoteca Nazionale di Bologna, inv. 577.
8 Pérez Sánchez 1965a, 181.
9 Madrid, Museo Nacional del Prado, P-7469; *Museo del Prado* 1990, 1:511, no. 1922.
10 Japón 2022a, 60.
11 Agulló y Cobo 1981, 213; Pérez Sánchez 1993, 99.

XI

MONEY, MATTER, AND SPIRIT: RENI'S LAST YEARS AND THE *NON FINITO*

In his latter years, Guido Reni's art underwent a change so radical that even his most fervent admirers found it difficult to understand. In a burning quest for the essential in painting, his forms disintegrated, his drawing almost disappearing and his outlines becoming blurred. At the same time, his bright and varied palette was drastically pared back and muted until it closely resembled grisaille. This process of simplification largely reflected his deliberate decision to leave many paintings unfinished, perhaps for lack of time or energy, or possibly with the intention of keeping them in that state in his studio, until he found a potential buyer for whom he could complete them. This gave rise to Reni's *non finito* period, in which the weariness of old age, coupled with financial difficulties caused by his compulsive gambling, drove him to rush his work in order to pay off debts. But these paintings, while prompted by Guido's need for cash, also reflected a self-indulgent search for the beauty of the unfinished, conveying a sense of the spiritualisation of art, which was precisely what the artist sought. When Reni died in Bologna on 18 August 1642, his fellow citizens bade him a sincere and emotional farewell.

88 Guido Reni
Study for the Bust of Susannah

c. 1623–24
Red chalk on paper pasted onto turquoise mount of thick paper,
223 × 178 mm
Florence, Gallerie degli Uffizi, Gabinetto dei Disegni
e delle Stampe, inv. 3532 S

Provenance: Emilio Santarelli (L. 907); donated to the Uffizi in 1866.

Selected bibliography: Johnston 1974, 1:151–52, no. 116; Birke 1981, 127, no. 88; V. Birke in Ebert-Schifferer, Emiliani and Schleier 1988, 360–61, no. B46; Pepper 1988, 250, no. 75; Bohn 2008, 51–52, no. 39.

This drawing entered the Uffizi collection in 1866 as part of a donation by the *cavaliere* Emilio Santarelli (1801–1889). In the handwritten catalogue of 1870 it is listed as entry no. 41 – 'Half-length figure of seated, nude female' – among the works classed as 'School of Guido Reni'.[1]

Catherine Johnston was the first to attribute the sheet to Reni himself, proposing a link with *Susannah and the Elders,* a painting known through various copies, among which the most likely match was thought to be the canvas originally in the Palazzo Lancellotti in Rome (1640), which later entered the National Gallery in London [cat. 89]. After cleaning in 1984, the painting was confirmed as an autograph work.

The Uffizi drawing was later published as the work of Guido by Veronika Birke, first in 1981 and subsequently in 1988, on the occasion of a major Reni retrospective in Frankfurt, when she defended the attribution questioned by Stephen Pepper, who had earlier dismissed the Santarelli sheet as 'a studio drawing after the torso of Susannah'. More recently, Babette Bohn has called attention to the presence of Reni's hand in the study. In her view, the distinctive use of line in the Florence sketch rules out the possibility that this might be a copy based on the finished painting, while the partially completed figure and the evidence of *pentimenti* around the shoulders and arms confirm that it was a preparatory study.

Be that as it may, the visual power of the image weakens when it is compared with two differently striking studies of female nudes that can be related to *Bacchus and Ariadne*, the large-format painting commissioned from Guido by Cardinal Francesco Barberini for Henrietta Maria, Queen Consort of England.[2] The first of these studies, no. 12452 F in the Uffizi, was identified by Veronika Birke as an idea for the unsteady bacchante leaning on two *putti* in an early draft of Reni's composition.[3] In spite of the differing opinions mentioned above,

this drawing not only highlights the Bolognese master's tremendous ability to convey the sense of light flowing over a female body – a plump silhouette with imperfect breasts, nearly in the manner of Peter Paul Rubens (1577–1640) – but also reflects his preference for making initial sketches from life.[4] The second study, no. FC 125562 in the Istituto Nazionale per la Grafica in Rome, where it was classed with other works by 'Anonymous Bolognese artists', was identified by Johnston as a preparatory sketch for the figure of Ariadne.[5] This second drawing, superbly executed in red chalk, like this *Study for the Bust of Susannah*, provides a better point of comparison, in that the lines are looser than those shaping the anatomy of the Uffizi *Susannah*.

Babette Bohn, prompted by the objectively masculine appearance of the Bible heroine's torso, together with remarks and information provided by Carlo Cesare Malvasia in his biography of the master, focused yet again on the issue of Reni's alleged aversion to women – a mainstay of critical literature – arguing that using female models for his nudes might have caused him psychological distress.[6]

Opinions regarding the dating of the drawing have varied slightly over the years, ranging from Johnston's suggestion that it was produced around 1621, through Pepper's proposal of 1622–23, to Birke's rather more elaborate hypothesis – based on its similarity to a half-length study of Apollo for the famous *Aurora* fresco at the Casino Pallavicini-Rospigliosi in Rome (1612–14)[7] – which dates the Uffizi drawing to the mid-1610s.[8] Bohn, in turn, has chosen to lend her support to the original view that it was produced in the early 1620s.

Viviana Farina

1 'Mezza figura di donna nuda sedente': https://euploos.uffizi.it/donazione-santarelli/142/.
2 On this painting, datable to around 1637–40, cut into pieces for sale in 1650, and known through copies, prints, drawings, and an autograph fragment of the figure of *Ariadne* now on long-term loan to the Pinacoteca Nazionale di Bologna (inv. 10000), see Pepper 1988, 290–91, no. 166; S. Guarino in Bentini et al. 2008, 74–76, no. 36; Malvasia–Pericolo 2019, 1:341–46, notes 343–52. For the drawings linked to this composition, an

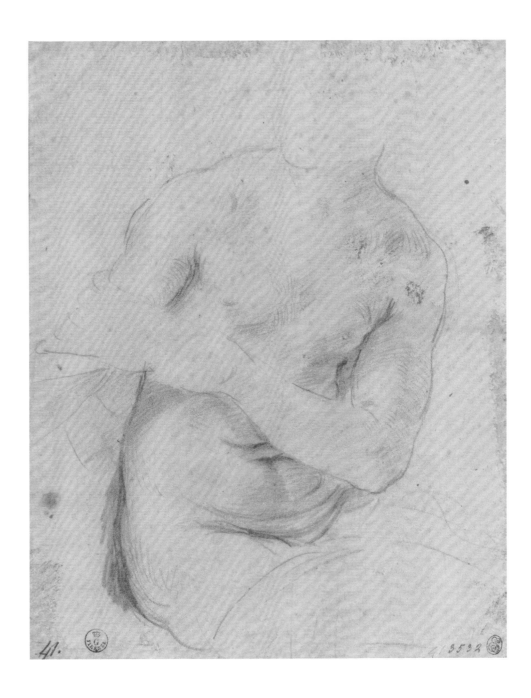

essential reconstruction can be found in Birke 1981, 177–80, no. 128, updated with new information in Bohn 2008, 69–71, no. 54.

3 Birke 1981, 177–80, no. 128. Though wholly plausible, its link to the first
draft of the painting, known through a drawing at Chatsworth House
attributed to Reni's circle (inv. 805; ibid., 179, fig. 67), was not accepted
by Pepper 1988, 290, in no. 166.

4 The opposite view is expressed in Bohn 2008, 71, no. 54.

5 Bohn 2008, 71, no. 55.

6 Ibid., 52.

7 Florence, Gallerie degli Uffizi, Gabinetto dei Disegni e delle Stampe,
inv. 11720 F.

8 Bohn 2008, 33–34, no. 22.

89   Guido Reni

Susannah and the Elders

c. 1623–24
Oil on canvas, 116.6 × 150.5 cm
London, The National Gallery, Purchased, 1844, NG196

Provenance: First mentioned in the Lancellotti collection, Rome, in 1644; in the collection of Captain John Penrice, Great Yarmouth, Norfolk, in 1824 as a purchase from James Irvine on behalf of Arthur Champernowne; purchased by the National Gallery, London, in 1844.

Selected bibliography: Baccheschi 1971, 100, no. 101; Ebert-Schifferer, Emiliani and Schleier 1988, 142–44, no. A10; Pepper 1988, 250–51, no. 75; Malvasia–Pericolo 2019, 1:514–15, note 31; L. Treves in Eclercy 2022a, 192–93, no. 66.

90   Guido Reni

Susannah and the Elders

c. 1640–42
Oil on canvas, 110 × 140 cm
Private collection

Provenance: Unknown.

Selected bibliography: Carofano 2017, 37–44; Pericolo 2019, 633–34.

The first mention of Guido Reni's *Susannah and the Elders* at the National Gallery in London [cat. 89] appears in the 1644 inventory of the pictures on display in the Palazzo Lancellotti: 'A painting of Saint Susanna in her bath, an original by Guido from Bologna'.[1] It is quite possible that the work was commissioned by the Roman nobleman Tiberio Lancellotti (1577–1629). Although less prominent as an art patron than his brother, Cardinal Orazio Lancellotti (1571–1620), Tiberio continued his sibling's ambitious project to decorate their family palace on Via dei Coronari, Rome. Around 1621, he contracted Guercino (1591–1666) to paint the ceilings of a few rooms in the palace. In a succinct biography of Guercino compiled by, among others, his brother, Paolo Antonio Barbieri (1603–1649), and published by Carlo Cesare Malvasia in his *Felsina pittrice* (1678), there is mention of a 'Madonna and Child with Saint Joseph and an angel playing music' executed in 1624 by Guercino for 'Signor Tiberio Lancellotti'.[2] That year or soon afterward, Guercino made a second painting for Lancellotti, a *Venus, Mars, Love, and Time*,[3] and it is most likely that Lancellotti commissioned other works from Guercino.[4] Because stylistically Guido's *Susannah and the Elders* bears some affinity with the *Trinity adored by Angels* in Santissima Trinità dei Pellegrini, Rome, executed in 1625 [fig. 28], it can be postulated that Tiberio, and not Orazio (whose death had occurred in 1620), ordered Guido's painting even as he was commissioning other works from Guercino around 1624. This is not the case of a second Lancellotti painting by Guido, *Lot and his Daughters leaving Sodom*, which was most likely produced in 1613–15,[5] and which, if originally commissioned by a Lancellotti, might have been purchased by Orazio rather than Tiberio.[6] It is unclear exactly when James Irvine (1757–1831), on behalf of Arthur Champernowne (1767–1819), purchased *Susannah and the Elders* (along with Guido's *Lot and his Daughters*) from the Falconieri family, who then owned the Palazzo Lancellotti.[7] After entering the collection of Captain John Penrice (1787–1844), the two Guido paintings were purchased by the National Gallery in 1844.[8]

A remarkable drawing in red chalk now in the Gallerie degli Uffizi, Florence, must be understood as preparatory for the torso of the figure of Susannah [cat. 88]. Similar to studies made by Guido in the early to mid-1610s – such as the *Study for Apollo in the Casino dell'Aurora* at the Uffizi[9] – this drawing may indicate that earlier versions of this composition were made before the London *Susannah and the Elders*.[10] In his manuscript notes (penned in the 1660s), Malvasia mentions a 'Susanna assaulted by the elders, life-size and almost full-length figure' in the possession of 'Quaranta Bianchetti', which he believed was then purchased by the Ratta.[11] This untraced work may be identified with the 'painting by Signor Guido of Susanna and two old men' listed in the 1635 inventory of the estate of Marcantonio Bianchetti.[12]

Another *Susannah and the Elders* by Guido belonged to the Dutch merchant Gerrit Reynst (1599–1658) and was most probably purchased in Italy by his brother, Jan (1601–1646), who settled in Venice around 1625.[13] The Reynst *Susannah* was reproduced in an engraving by Cornelis Visscher (c. 1629–1658).[14] Executed in brush, grey and black wash with highlights of white lead on prepared paper, the drawing by Visscher that served for his own print is now in the Rijksmuseum.[15] The Reynst version of Guido's painting is last mentioned in an auction sale in Amsterdam on 6 October 1801. In the auction catalogue (Schley sale), the painting is quoted as a work by Guido Cagnacci

(1601–1663), although it is clearly said that it had been reproduced in an engraving by Visscher.[16] In Visscher's drawing and print, a sea creature is represented supporting the basin of the fountain to the right of the composition. This is an essential detail that distinguishes this version from all the other known ones. A *Susannah and the Elders* in Shugborough Estate,[17] usually considered a copy after Guido but almost certainly a work by Guido with workshop assistance, presents this detail. This work is first mentioned in Shugborough in 1842 and may be the same as the Reynst painting.

Yet another version of Guido's *Susannah and the Elders* belonged to Archduke Leopold Wilhelm of Austria (1614–1662). Sometime around 1650–56, David Teniers the Younger (1610–1690) executed a reduced copy of this painting, then in Brussels and now in London.[18] The Flemish printmaker Peter van Liesebetten (1630–1678) relied on Teniers' copy in his engraving of Guido's composition.[19] This *Susannah and the Elders* is last mentioned in Vienna and has remained untraced since the eighteenth century.

Finally, Queen Christina of Sweden (1626–1689) owned another *Susannah and the Elders* attributed to Guido. The painting is first mentioned in 1688 by the Swedish architect Nicodemus Tessin the Younger (1654–1728), who saw it in Christina's palace in Rome.[20] Purchased by Duke Livio Odescalchi (1652–1713) in 1690, this work was sold to Louis d'Orléans (1703–1752) in 1721.[21] This picture is to be identified with a *Susannah and the Elders* now in the Uffizi, Florence,[22] and although its quality is difficult to assess since the painting is dirty and partially damaged, it is undoubtedly a workshop product, perhaps with some retouching by Guido.

It is noteworthy that among the many versions of Guido's *Susannah and the Elders*, only the one in London can be deemed entirely autograph. One of the master's most successful compositions, it was reproduced by his studio innumerable times. Of all the surviving variants, the most poignant is an unfinished canvas, now in a private collection, that must have been present in one of Guido's studios upon his death in 1642, even though it does not seem to appear in the inventory of the painter's estate compiled on that occasion.[23] In his biography of Guido, Malvasia explains how the old master, heavily pressed by creditors and disappointed by the hostile attitude of patrons, who now mistrusted him and criticised his paintings, 'had the great idea of beginning work on a multitude of canvases, and he put himself to sketching all of them with the intention of diverting himself and raising his spirits, just as he also set himself to finishing many of those he had started and that were scattered throughout his rooms'.[24] As a result, at the end of his life, he left 'an infinity of primed canvases' that were put up for sale, dispersed, and occasionally completed by his former disciples.[25] Guido's unfinished *Susannah and the Elders* [cat. 90], which has miraculously come down to us and is preserved pristinely, testifies to the master's feverish creation and relentless inventiveness at the end of his life. Executed free hand albeit perhaps based on tracing provided by one or more cartoons, this sketched-out *Susannah* allows us to glimpse into Guido's working technique, for it discloses not only his habit of covering the dark priming with grey, then white underlayers of pigment – the latter in connection with areas destined to be worked over with flesh tones – but also his playing with the roughed-out portions of the canvas through a 'chiselling' of minute hatching, coarse colour filaments, and thicker linear strokes, modelling bodies and draperies summarily, as if thinking of them three-dimensionally despite the flatness of the support. This technique is consistent with what X-rays and infrareds of later paintings by Guido reveal to us – for instance, his *Saint Peter* at the Prado [cat. 33] – and it is surprising to see how Guido did not care about the huge effort – useless, since it was meant to disappear under further covering – that he was lavishing upon his pictorial sketches. It is in works like this final *Susannah* that one can fathom the love for painting as a manual activity that animated Guido, his absorption into the material medium of the canvas, and his proud indifference to the demands of the art market and its taste for sellable 'finished' products. In a sense, this quasi-monochrome *Susannah* may qualify as one of Guido's most significant, beautiful works.

Lorenzo Pericolo

1 Cavazzini 1998, 151: 'Un quadro di Santa Susanna nel bagno, originale di Guido Bolognese'.
2 *Rest on the Flight into Egypt*, Cleveland (Ohio), Cleveland Museum of Art, Mr and Mrs William H. Marlatt Fund, inv. 1967.123. See Salerno 1988, 168, nos. 84–85 and 182, no. 100.
3 Cheshire, Dunham Massey, NT932333.
4 For the Dunham Massey painting, see Salerno 1988, 191, no. 109.
5 London, National Gallery, NG193.
6 For a recent assessment of Guido's *Lot and his Daughters*, see L. Calzona in Cappelletti 2022, 134–37, no. 10.
7 Buchanan 1824, 2:110.
8 Pepper 1988, 250, no. 75.
9 Florence, Gallerie degli Uffizi, Gabinetto dei Disegni e delle Stampe, inv. 11720 F.
10 For the Uffizi drawing of *Apollo*, see Bohn 2008, 33–34, no. 22. For a related drawing in the Royal Collection, Windsor Library, see V. Birke in Ebert-Schifferer, Emiliani and Schleier 1988, 291, B13.
11 See Malvasia–Pericolo 2019, 1:492: 'La Susanna tentata da' vecchi, grande del naturale e quasi intiera, credo quella ch'era in casa del Quaranta Bianchetti, oggi è presso i Signori Ratta'.
12 The Getty Provenance Index® Databases (hereafter GPI), I-1600: 'Un quadro di pittura del S[igno]r Guido Reni con Susanna e due vecchij' (Accessible at https://www.getty.edu/research/tools/provenance/search. html). See further Malvasia–Pericolo 2019, 1:514–15, note 31.
13 Logan 1979, 139–41, no. 23.
14 Hollstein–Schuckman and Hoop Scheffer 1992, 12, no. 3.
15 Amsterdam, Rijksmuseum, RP-T-00-745.
16 GPI, N–17, no. 13: 'Dit stuk gaat in Prent uit door C. de Visscher, in het werk van Reynst'.
17 Staffordshire, Shughborough Estate, NT1271039.
18 London, The Courtauld, Samuel Courtauld Trust, P.1978.PG.442.
19 Hollstein 1954, 85, no. 7.
20 Sirén 1914, 185: 'Die Susanne von Guido Rheni'.
21 GPI, I–629; Dubois de Saint-Gelais 1727, 190–91.
22 Florence, Gallerie degli Uffizi, inv. 1980 n. 3085.
23 On this painting, see Carofano 2017, 37–44; Pericolo 2019, 633–34.
24 Malvasia 1678, 2:48: 'Fece ben egli porre all'ordine quantità di tele, e si pose a sbozzarle tutte per divertirsi e farsi animo, come anche a finirne molte delle già cominciate ch'erano per le stanze'.
25 Ibid., 2:56: 'Restò parimente una infinità di tele imprimite solo'.

91   Guido Reni

Cleopatra

c. 1639–40
Oil on canvas, 77 × 65 cm
Dublin, National Gallery of Ireland, Presented by Sir Denis Mahon
to the British Fund for the National Gallery of Ireland, 2008,
NGI.4651

Provenance: British private collection from at least the early nineteenth century (based on the label on the painting's verso); purchased by Sir Denis Mahon from Christie's, London, 8 November 1957, lot 60; presented by Sir Denis Mahon to the British Fund for the National Gallery of Ireland, 2008.

Selected bibliography: Pepper 1984, 287, no. 189; Pepper 1988, 298, no. 181; Emiliani et al. 1988, no. 76; Ebert-Schifferer, Emiliani and Schleier 1988, 223, no. A 36; Finaldi and Kitson 1997, no. 64; Benedetti 1997, 20, no. 8; Ritschard and Morehead 2004, 112, no. 21; Benati and Paolucci 2008; A. Brady in Eclercy 2022a, 300–3, no. 160.

Guido Reni is perhaps best known today for his single-figure compositions depicting saints and mythological figures with their eyes thrown heavenward. This simplified format, in which protagonists are painted in isolation, half-length and set against a non-descript background, lent itself to the creation of studio replicas: it was a formula that Reni's assistants could follow with ease, and permitted the creation of high-quality copies and variants that could be executed rapidly and stayed true to the artist's brand. In his *Felsina pittrice* (1678), Carlo Cesare Malvasia praises the 'rapidity with which he knew how to unload those half-figures of his', and links them to the artist's financial success, noting that this ability 'could have amassed him an inestimable treasure'.[1] An inventory of the artist's belongings recorded post-mortem reveals that Guido maintained a selection of partially painted compositions in the form of *bozze* in his workshop, ready for completion at will, and notes, specifically, two half-figure *Magdalens* and two *Cleopatras*, among others.[2] Richard Spear determined that because a large proportion of the works depicting these subjects are 'relatively unambitious', many were painted for the open market, as opposed to being directly commissioned.[3] And indeed, Guido and his studio created innumerable paintings of this kind, responding to a burgeoning art market with a growing appetite for works that could be readily associated with celebrity artists of the day. Twenty-three Cleopatras associated with Reni's studio have been recorded by the present author, of which six are considered autograph.

Though the early provenance of the work under discussion is untraceable, the painting is universally accepted as an autograph iteration on these popular themes, executed by Reni himself late in his career. The artist portrays Cleopatra, Queen of Egypt, vulnerable and hopeless at the fatal moment that she is bitten by a poisonous snake – she and her husband Mark Antony committed suicide following their defeat at the Battle of Actium in 31 BC. The psychologically-charged composition displays the intuitive, dynamic handling of the artist's final years, when he was painting with a limited palette of light, pastel tonalities, and applying paint in sweeping, fluid brushstrokes. Reni imbues his subject with a statuesque elegance inspired by the antique and his Renaissance predecessors, as she gazes upward and meditates on her mortality.

While similar images of saints like the Magdalen were devotional in nature, and therefore easier to appreciate as a common subject in post-Tridentine Europe, the popularity of Reni's mythological women – particularly those dying women like Lucretia and Cleopatra – are less readily explanatory. The most obvious reason for the proliferation of such subjects is their sex appeal – like Titian's (c. 1488–1576) reclining nudes, these passive, partially naked figures were intended for the male viewer. There is some irony in the notion that these paintings might have been viewed as erotic, given reports of the artist's irrational fear of the female sex. Despite holding his mother and the Madonna in the greatest reverence, Reni is said to have been repulsed by other women, and terrified that, through witchcraft, they might steal his talents as a painter. Malvasia wrote that Reni 'was commonly held to be a virgin', and that while in the presence of the 'beautiful girls who served him as models' the artist appeared 'like marble', and he never wanted 'to be left alone' with them.[4] It has been observed that many of his female figures – including Dublin's *Cleopatra* – lack corporeality and appear as boneless, gelatinous, shapeless figures who are denied any definition in their collarbones, shoulders, or breasts – perhaps a result of the artist's reluctance to engage in the close observation of the female body.

Reni's simplification of forms in his final years was not always to the taste of his seicento critics. Malvasia described Guido's late works as lacking in invention and rich composition, and with less successful use of light and shadow and poor

expression of emotions.[5] Elsewhere the biographer caveats his statement with a description of a *Magdalen* painted for the artist's friend Cesare Rinaldi, saying that it and 'suchlike were among his most beautiful, if less vigorous, paintings'. He continues to say that 'every day one finds in them a deeper knowledge and an incomparable finish' that emerged in these mature works.[6] In this, the seicento writer captures the essence of Reni's late paintings, which in their simplicity offer the viewer a certain serenity, a meditative space: qualities that can still be appreciated today in this small canvas.

Aoife Brady

1 Malvasia–Pericolo 2019, 1:186: 'La prestezza con che sapeva scaricare quelle sue mezze figure, che si contano a migliaia, potevano ammassargli un erario inestimabile'. For the English translation, ibid., 1:187.

2 Spike and Di Zio 1988, 58–59 and 63: 'un altro quadro con una Madalena / meza figura; una Cleopatra meza figura; una Cleopatra meza figura del sig. Guido'.

3 Spear 1982, 84.

4 Malvasia–Pericolo 2019, 1:164: 'Fu comunemente tenuto per vergine, ... ed essendosi sempre mostrato un marmo alla presenza e contemplazione di tante belle giovani che gli servirono di modello, ed in ritrar le quali mai volle ridursi solo e rinserrarsi'. For the English translation, ibid., 1:165

5 Ibid., 1:114–15.

6 Ibid., 1:100: 'Queste, dico, e simili furono delle più belle, se non tanto vigorose, ... ancorché si scuoprano poi ogni dì d'un più profondo sapere, di una inarrivabile finitezza'. For the English translation, ibid., 101.

92   Guido Reni

The Virgin and Child with Saint John the Baptist and a Dove

c. 1638–42
Oil on canvas, 160 × 159 cm
Florence, Fondazione di Studi di Storia dell'Arte Roberto Longhi

Provenance: Perhaps Giovan Battista Ferri, 1642; perhaps Carlo Antonio Biagi, 1679.

Selected bibliography: Arcangeli 1946, 11; Cuppini 1952, 267; Cavalli 1955, 99, no. 110; Baccheschi 1971, 115, no. 207; Pepper 1979, 422; C. Casali Pedrielli in Emiliani 1988, 312, no. 61; Pepper 1988, 300, no. 189; Malvasia–Pericolo 2019, 1:349, note 366; B. Eclercy in Eclercy 2022a, 304–7, no. 161.

There is still uncertainty about the provenance of Guido Reni's *Virgin and Child with Saint John the Baptist and a Dove* now in the Fondazione Roberto Longhi. In his *Felsina pittrice* (1678), Carlo Cesare Malvasia evokes Guido's affection for the Bolognese merchant Giovan Battista Ferri.[1] In 1642, when Guido became seriously ill, Ferri hosted the master in his house on Via del Cane, Bologna, convincing him to make his last will and

witnessing his death on 18 August of that year. Malvasia informs us that Guido owed a large amount of money to Ferri, who had lent him 3000 doubloons to offset his gambling debts.[2] Narrating the fate of the many paintings that were found in Guido's house upon his death, Malvasia notes:

> Few were those who preferred to take the money instead of the sketched-out works, and this is why there are still so many of those pictures around, which are for the most part highly valued, such as the thirteen large history paintings retained by Ferri in settlement of the thousand doubloons Guido still owed him … These works belong now to Doctor Biagi, a great lecturer, who married a daughter of Ferri's.[3]

Malvasia refers here to the physician Carlo Antonio Biagi. Of the 'thirteen large history paintings retained by Ferri' only three seem to have remained in the Biagi collection, all three being 'unfinished'. In the 1679 inventory of Biagi's estate, there is mention of an untraced 'Venus with Love', a similarly unidentified 'Blessed Virgin with the Child in her Arms, Saint Joseph, Saint Anne, Saint Elizabeth, and Saint John the Baptist', and a 'Blessed Virgin who assists the Child presenting Saint John the Baptist with a dove'.[4] The latter painting is most probably to be identified with the work now in Florence.

Although this identification is compelling and almost certain, it must be said that the description of this third painting closely matches another unfinished late composition by Guido, the *Virgin and Child with Saint John the Baptist* now in the J. Paul Getty Museum, Los Angeles [fig. 99].[5] In the Getty painting, Saint Joseph appears sketched in the distant background, which may explain why the figure may have gone unnoticed in the 1679

Fig. 99 Guido Reni, *The Virgin and Child with Saint John the Baptist*, c. 1640–42. Oil on canvas, 165.7 × 142.9 cm. Los Angeles, Getty Foundation, 84.PA.122

inventory. Be that as it may, the Longhi painting belongs to a group of relatively large, unfinished works where Guido was exploring the theme of the holy family in a domestic setting. Malvasia himself possessed a *Holy Family with Saints Elizabeth, Anne, and John the Baptist* by Guido, which remains untraced, and was perhaps finished, but which was almost identical in composition with an unfinished *Holy Family with Saints Anne and John the Baptist* now in a private collection.[6]

Describing the Longhi painting in his 1955 catalogue of Guido's work, Gian Carlo Cavalli hardly contains his admiration:

> The ineffable charge of poetry of the sweetest, sensual poetic wave that almost overflows in the Naples *Adoration* [an unfinished painting now in Naples, Certosa di San Martino, fig. 31], comes soon afterward to assume – on the thread of a more intimate and domestic narrative – a measure that is still classically balanced, where the beauty of the forms, even if it dissolves in a sublime emotion of the senses, seems to contain and simplify itself through the broader spatial articulation typical of a fresco. It is almost a nostalgic return, in a marked degree, to the youthful works of the 1610s, a consolidation of the poetic trajectory that had emerged in the scene of the 'sewing maidservants' in the chapel of the Quirinal and that comes to an end here with the tones of a more archaic poetic essence.[7]

As a coda to his description, Cavalli quotes an observation on Guido by Francesco Arcangeli, which in turn includes a phrase by Roberto Longhi, the famous art historian owner of the painting: 'That long process of elaboration, as if submerged, is infused into a golden, silvery breath, into a "dust cloud of paradise"'.[8] Vigorously rhetorical in their formulation, both Cavalli's and Arcangeli's statements reveal an admiration for the 'modernity' embodied by Guido's unfinished works. In these critics' minds, Guido's final output is marked by a distillation and partial dissolution of forms, by a serene but relentless reminiscence of previously elaborated models – the allusion to Guido's 1609–10 *Virgin sewing in the Temple* in the Quirinal Palace, Rome – and by an inherent respect for classical symmetry and calibrated spatial rhythm. Insisting on the 'intimate' and the 'domestic' of Guido's unfinished painting, both Cavalli and, before him, Arcangeli might have been proposing a parallelism with another renowned Bolognese painter, Giorgio Morandi (1890–1964), still alive at the time of their comments. Not elements of a still life but the figural components of a mnemonic repertory, the sketched-out figures of Guido's *Virgin and Child with Saint John the Baptist and a Dove* become figments of a prolonged reflection upon familiar motifs, their forms almost disintegrating in a dust cloud of golden (flesh tones, brown, and yellow) and silvery (greyish blue) luminosity. It is touching to think of the old master in his final years moving from one composition to the next amid hundreds of unfinished canvases, obeying the whims of sudden inspiration, modelling figures with a restricted palette of tints, using the pictorial surface as a 'work in progress' sketch. It is a miracle that these 'palimpsests' have survived. They compellingly attest to Guido's unswerving commitment to experimenting with the limits of painting.

Lorenzo Pericolo

1 Malvasia 1678, 2:49, 2:54, and 2:57.

2 On these episodes, see Malvasia–Pericolo 2019, 1:337, note 328; 1:349, notes 365–66; 1:350, notes 367–68 and 370; 1:359, note 391.

3 Ibid., 1:130: 'Pochi si trovarono che più volentieri non prendessero anzi le bozze che la moneta. Onde tante se ne vedono anche oggidì e tanto si stimano presso molti, come que' tredici pezzi grandi ed istoriati rimasti al Ferri per le mille doppie, residuo del suo credito ascendente un giorno che fu a tre mila [...], ed oggi presso il signor dottore e bravo lettore Biagi, a cui toccò per moglie una figlia del detto Ferri'.

4 Morselli 1998, 103, nos. 42–43; Malvasia–Pericolo 2019, 1:359, note 391.

5 Pepper 1988, 343, no. 64.

6 For the painting, see Pepper 1988, 304, no. 208. For its identification, see Malvasia–Pericolo 2019, 1:359, note 391, and 2:112.

7 Cavalli 1955, 99, no. 110. For Guido's *Adoration of the Shepherds* in the Certosa di San Martino in Naples, see Pericolo Malvasia–2019, 1:329–30, note 299. For Guido's *Virgin sewing in the Temple* (*Madonna del cucito*), see Malvasia–Pericolo 2019, 1:259, note 123.

8 Arcangeli 1946; Longhi 1935, 133: 'Più spesso, da vero pittore e poeta, [Guido] escogita gamme paradisiache, contrappunti sempre più trepidi del tocco, digitazioni sempre più lievi; ed è allora che i suoi vecchi eremiti sembrano immaginazioni della valle di Giosafat; vecchie larve in aria d'argento, sotto gli angeli soffiati in rosa e biondo, entro un polverio di paradiso'.

93 Guido Reni

The Flagellation / Study for Saint Sebastian

c. 1640
Black and white chalk on light brown paper, 255 × 215 mm
Florence, Gabinetto dei Disegni e delle Stampe degli Uffizi,
inv. 3453 S

Provenance: Emilio Santarelli (L. 907); donated to the Uffizi in 1866.
Selected bibliography: Bohn 2008, 71–72, no. 56.

This drawing, listed in the inventory of the *cavaliere* Emilio Santarelli (1801–1889) and later in that of Pasquale Nerino Ferri (1851–1917), founder and first curator of the present Gabinetto dei Disegni e delle Stampe at the Uffizi, was largely overlooked until the recent Florence exhibition of drawings by Guido Reni and his school.[1]

Santarelli's turquoise passepartout, now preserved separately, bears the inscription 'Guido Reni / Studio per san Sebastiano della Pinacoteca di Bologna'. The reference – as Babette Bohn pointed out at the time – is to the *Saint Sebastian* of around 1640 in the Emilian Pinacoteca, which came from the sacristy of the church of the Santissimo Salvatore in Bologna[2] and is mentioned in Carlo Cesare Malvasia's *Felsina pittrice* (1678) as one of the artist's late works.[3] According to Bohn, the Santarelli drawing may additionally be related to the coeval *Flagellation* also housed in the Bolognese Pinacoteca [cat. 94], another of the series of *non finite* (left unfinished) works recorded by Malvasia among Reni's later paintings and identifiable as the canvas on the same theme which – according to an eighteenth-century report by Marcello Oretti – formed part of the collection of Marcantonio Ercolani in 1692.[4]

Indeed, the Florentine drawing represents an important testimony to one of the few late studies by Guido to have survived, as well as to the artist's new habit of adapting studies originally made for a given theme as models for a wholly different one. In this case, Reni evidently focused first on the full-length figure of Saint Sebastian – as the branches show, he is bound to a tree rather than a column, and an arrow pierces his stomach – and later on the scourging of Jesus. Another unique feature of the iconography is the attitude of the torturer seen face on, who almost seems to be resting his left hand on the arrow to better plunge it into the tortured body with an instrument gripped with his right hand. The chalk lines are confusing, so the conjecture is purely hypothetical, but some kind of violent fantasy on Guido's part – expressed solely in the drawing – cannot be ruled out. At the same time, it should be noted, particularly with reference to the torturers, that the Santarelli study in fact bears little resemblance to the picture in the Ercolani collection, which is better regarded as a late though shrewd tribute – especially in the paraphrasing of the kneeling torturer – to the *Flagellation* by Ludovico Carracci (1555–1619), now in the Musée de la Chartreuse, Douai.[5]

By contrast, the figure in the Uffizi drawing can be much more faithfully linked to the *Saint Sebastian* at the Pinacoteca Nazionale di Bologna, in which the viewer is offered an unusually peaceful view of the martyr, symbolised by the absence of arrows, perhaps alluding to the moment preceding his torture. The theme, apparently not particularly popular in the first half of the seventeenth century, had earlier been addressed in a similar manner by Jusepe de Ribera (1591–1652) in a set of drawings in which the saint – the former commander of a Roman legion – is already in a state of agony, his body sinking to the ground.[6]

Interestingly, the saint's pose, both in the Florence drawing and in the Bologna painting, differs from that of Guido's young *Saint Sebastian* in the Museo del Prado [cat. 19], in which the artist offers a personal reflection both on the ancient *Belvedere Torso*[7] and exercises deriving from it, and on the *Slaves* sculpted by Michelangelo (1475–1564) for the ill-starred *Tomb of Pope Julius II*. More specifically, the Prado painting seems to combine features of the *Bearded Slave* (1530–34)[8] with aspects of the *Rebellious Slave* (1513–15),[9] in a pose already used – and reminiscent of the bearded *prigione*, seen head-on – in the *Saint Sebastian bound to a Tree* (c. 1590) attributed first to Ludovico and later, with more general critical agreement, to Annibale Carracci (1560–1609).[10] By contrast, both the Santarelli drawing, dating from late in Reni's career, and the *Saint Sebastian* in the Pinacoteca in Bologna seem to pay tribute, primarily, to the *Rebellious Slave*. Such was the fame of this model – deliberately imitated by Titian (c. 1488–1576) in his early *Averoldi Polyptych* (1520–22) for the church of Santi Nazario e Celso in Brescia – and indeed of all Michelangelo's sculptures for the papal tomb, that they must also have circulated in the form of sketched copies. Guido seems to have examined the prototype from the left, retaining the position of the legs but eliminating the contrapposto by rotating and straightening the torso.

For an earlier study of *Saint Sebastian in a Landscape with Angels*, also in the Uffizi collection,[11] Reni drew freely on the *Rebellious Slave* for the lower part of the saint's body, but more particularly made use – though diluting Michelangelo's exploration of form – of the exhausted beauty of the head and torso of the *Dying Slave* (1513–15),[12] the other 'prisoner' in the second project for the papal tomb. Significantly, on examining the graphic style, Stephen Pepper tentatively attributed this earlier study – traditionally assigned to Reni in the core set of drawings *esposti* (on show) – to Agostino Carracci (1557–1602).[13] This is undoubtedly an early preparatory study by Guido, squarely in the Carracci tradition in terms of the extensive landscape, and should be regarded in itself as a devotional exercise, regardless of its later possible use for a painting. Comparing it with this *Flagellation / Study for Saint Sebastian,* it is clear that the two figures derive from a common compositional idea, though the legs are differently positioned. This early Uffizi drawing should also be viewed in the context of another *Saint Sebastian healed by Angels* in the Musée du Louvre,[14] previously assigned to Palma Giovane (c. 1548/50–1628) but brilliantly reattributed to Reni by Catherine Loisel. Discussing its possible dating to the early 1600s – in line with Bohn's chronological proposal for the Uffizi drawing on the same theme – Loisel has rightly stressed that Reni's pen drawings over this period are difficult to date, for the almost brutal strokes cannot usefully be compared either with the drawings made in the last five years of the 1590s or with the Borghese commissions on which Guido worked in Rome over the following decade.[15]

By contrast, as indicated earlier, this *Flagellation / Study for Saint Sebastian* is the work of a mature artist at the height of his powers, regardless of any possible link – however close or remote – to the paintings mentioned above. Nowhere is this more evident than in the loose, free line and the touches of white chalk, intended to facilitate the transfer to a painting made with a restrained palette, but enlivened by bright highlighting.

Viviana Farina

1 Bohn 2008.
2 Bologna, Pinacoteca Nazionale di Bologna, inv. 446.
3 Malvasia–Pericolo 2019, 1:198. Pepper 1988, 300, no. 188; G. P. Cammarota in Bentini et al. 2008, 79–83, no. 38; Malvasia–Pericolo 2019, 1:428, note 636.
4 Malvasia–Pericolo 2019, 1:200. In Marcello Oretti's eighteenth-century manuscript, *Le pitture che si ammirano nelli palazzi e case de' nobili nella città di Bologna e di altri edifici in detta città* (Bologna, Biblioteca Comunale dell'Archiginnasio, Ms B104, I, fol. 65), it is recorded in the Ercolani collection: 'altro quadro grande sul quale è dipinta la Flagellazione di N[ostro] S[ignore] con tre manigoldi; è un bozzo di figure come il naturale del S[ignor] Guido Reni' ('another large painting showing the Flagellation of Our Lord with three torturers; it is a sketch of life-size figures by Signor Guido Reni'). On this painting, see A. Stanzani in Bentini et al. 2008, 86–88, no. 40; Malvasia–Pericolo 2019, 1:436, note 655, and 2:427, fig. 293. There is an earlier reference in Pepper 1988, 300, no. 190.
5 Douai (France), Musée de la Chartreuse, inv. 2797; Brogi 2001, 1:119–21, no. 14.
6 See, among others, the drawings in Oxford, Ashmolean Museum, WA1936.213; Bloomington, Indiana University, Eskenazi Museum of Art, William Lowe Bryan Memorial, 57.7; San Francisco, Achenbach Foundation for Graphic Arts, 1963.24.612; Toronto, Art Gallery of Ontario, inv. 70/142.
7 Vatican City, Musei Vaticani, MV.1192.
8 Florence, Galleria dell'Academia, Inv. Scult. no. 1081.
9 Paris, Musée du Louvre, Département des Sculptures du Moyen Age, de la Renaissance et des temps modernes, MR 1589.
10 This composition, in a private collection in Modena, is also known through a replica – regarded as a copy – in the Museum der bildenden Künste Leipzig: Brogi 2001, 1:273–74, no. R53.
11 Florence, Gallerie degli Uffizi, Gabinetto dei Disegni e delle Stampe, inv. 1427 E.
12 Paris, Musée du Louvre, Département des Sculptures du Moyen Age, de la Renaissance et des temps modernes, MR 1590.
13 Bohn 2008, 19–20, no. 12. The comparison with sculptures by Michelangelo is my own.
14 Paris, Musée du Louvre, Départment des Arts graphiques, inv. 5252.
15 Loisel 2013, 102–3, no. 67. Reni may in this case have adapted a *Saint Sebastian* prototype by Ludovico Carracci, produced in 1599 (Gravina in Puglia, Museo Ettore Pomarici Santomasi: Brogi 2001, 1:175–76, no. 61).

The Flagellation

c. 1638–42
Oil on canvas, 278.5 × 180.5 cm
Bologna, Pinacoteca Nazionale di Bologna, inv. 6377

Provenance: Commissioned by the Beregani (Beregan) family of Vicenza and left unfinished upon Guido Reni's death in 1642; first mentioned in the Ercolani collection, Bologna, in 1692.

Selected bibliography: Cavalli 1955, 101, no. 114; Baccheschi 1971, 115, no. 212; C. Casali Pedrielli in Emiliani et al. 1988, 314, no. 62; Pepper 1988, 300, no. 190; A. Stanzani in Bentini et al. 2008, 86–88, no. 40; Malvasia–Pericolo 2019, 1:436, note 355.

In his *Felsina pittrice* (1678), Carlo Cesare Malvasia briefly evokes the 'great number of roughed-out works' left unfinished by Guido Reni upon his death in 1642, which, in his time, were on display in many Bolognese houses. Prominent among these unfinished paintings were the 'many possessed by Signor Marcantonio Ercolani'.[1] It is generally assumed, probably correctly, that it was Marcantonio Ercolani who purchased the works by Guido mentioned in the 1692 and 1694 inventories of the estate of his nephews, Astorre (1669–1718) and Filippo (1663–1722) Ercolani.[2] Guido's *Flagellation* now in the Pinacoteca Nazionale di Bologna is to be identified with a painting of the same subject quoted in the Ercolani inventory of 1692.[3] In the 1642 inventory of Guido's estate, the work is listed as 'a Flagellation that was said to belong to the Signori Beregani'.[4]

On 12 August 1644 – two years after Guido's death – Guercino (1591–1666) received from 'Signor Giovanni Locatelli on behalf of the Signori Beregani of Vicenza' 500 ducatons 'for the painting of the Flagellation made for the said Signori'.[5] Guercino's *Flagellation* now in Budapest [fig. 100] was destined for San Biagio, Vicenza.[6] In his *Gioielli pittoreschi* (1676), the Italian painter and art theorist Marco Boschini (1602–1681) mentions this 'flagellated Christ at the column' in the church.[7] An inscription on the altar, now lost, stated that Baldassare Beregani (or Beregan) had offered the painting.[8] It can thus be assumed that the Beregani first resorted to Guido in order to decorate their altar in San Biagio. Evidently, they refused the unfinished painting and contacted Guercino in order to have a new one executed. Marcello Oretti (1714–1787) describes the *Flagellation* in the Ercolani collection as 'another large painting where the Flagellation of Our Lord with three torturers is

Fig. 100 Guercino, *The Flagellation*, c. 1641–44.
Oil on canvas, 351 × 176.5 cm. Budapest,
Szépművészeti Múzeum, inv. 4225

depicted; it is a sketched composition of life-size figures by Signor Guido Reni'.[9] With great intelligence and audacity, Marcantonio Ercolani must have understood the extraordinary quality of Guido's unfinished canvases, such as the *Madonna and Child appearing to Saint Francis* in Bologna,[10] an untraced *Cupid and Psyche* (a copy of which is to be found in Rennes),[11] and a similarly untraced *Abel and Cain*.[12] This painting was donated by Count Filippo Ercolani as a gift to Prince Eugene of Savoy (1663–1736), although it does not appear in any of the inventories of Eugene's picture gallery at the Belvedere, Vienna.[13]

It is impossible to determine when and how Guido was contracted to execute the Beregani *Flagellation*. It is also unknown whether 'Signor Giovanni Locatelli' also acted as intermediary for the commission on behalf of the Beregani family. Documentary evidence indicates that some of the paintings left unfinished by Guido had been ordered as early as 1632. This is the case of a *Madonna and Child appearing to Saint Francis*. On 27 December 1632, the members of the Monte di Pietà of Reggio Emilia purchased a 'wheel of Piacenza cheese' to be sent to Guido as a gift by means of two delegates who were tasked with commissioning from him a brand-new altarpiece for the Brami Chapel in the Madonna della Giara, Reggio Emilia.[14] Letters exchanged between Guido and the members of the Monte di Pietà reveal that the painter was recontacted in 1635 and 1639 in hopes of obtaining the finished work. Upon Guido's death in 1642, the Monte di Pietà sent a delegation to Bologna to assess the painting's state of completion. In the end, they decided to sell the work.[15]

Guido's *Flagellation* may have been commissioned in 1636–40. The torturers in the painting are reminiscent of the figures in the left foreground of Guido's *Triumph of Saint Job* in Notre-Dame, Paris [cat. 44], especially in light of their bodily proportions, their heads and feet proportionally smaller by comparison with their broad chests and rather long limbs. These characteristics, however, may also have been found in the master's immense *Bacchus and Arianne* for Queen Henrietta Maria of England (1609–1669), finished in 1640, which was partially destroyed. A painting in relation with this work, *Two Bacchants,* now in a private collection, presents a dancing faun whose bodily proportions are close to those of the torturers in Guido's *Flagellation*.[16]

Lorenzo Pericolo

1 Malvasia 1678, 2:89.
2 On Astorre and Filippo Ercolani as collectors, see Ghelfi 2021, 24–31. It is extremely important that Astorre Ercolani had asked Giovanni Maria Viani (1636–1700) to complete Guido's *Flagellation* and *Cupid and Psyche*, which the painter declined to do, executing instead two 'completed' replicas of the unfinished compositions. See Marcello Oretti, *Le pitture che si ammirano nelli palazzi e case de' nobili nella città di Bologna e di altri edifici in detta città*, manuscript, Bologna, Biblioteca Comunale dell'Archiginnasio, Ms B 104, 1:65 (where there is a certain confusion about the name of the painter): 'Tutte le sudette pitture sono state fatte le copie e terminate da Domenico Maria Viani che fu ricercato dal principe Ercolani di terminare li sudetti pezzi del Signor Guido Reni, ma esso ricusò di metterli mano, e fece di pianta le copie sudette della medesima grandezza e le terminò'.
3 Ghelfi 2007, 465; Bianchi 2013, 87.
4 Spike and Di Zio 1988, 61: 'Una Flagellatione quale fu detta essere delli signori Beregani'.
5 Ghelfi 1997, 121, no. 313.
6 Salerno 1988, 290, no. 213; Stone 1991, 208, no. 194; Turner 2017, 587, no. 298.
7 Boschini 1676, 96: 'Cristo flagellato alla Colonna'.
8 Boschini–Boer 2008, 369.
9 Oretti, 1:65: 'Altro quadro grande su cui è dipinta la Flagellatione di N[ostro] S[ignore] con tre manigoldi; è un bozzo di figure come il naturale del Sig[nor] Guido Reni'.
10 Bologna, Pinacoteca Nazionale di Bologna, inv. 7190.
11 Rennes, Musée des Beaux-Arts, inv. 1794.1.37.
12 On these paintings, see Malvasia–Pericolo 2019, 1:435–36, no. 655. See further Ghelfi 2021, 26, note 28.
13 Bianchi 2013, 104–5.
14 A. Mazza in Benati and Mazza 2002, 57, note 48.
15 Balletti 1930, 84, note 3. See further Malvasia–Pericolo 2019, 1:435–36, note 655.
16 For these paintings, see Malvasia–Pericolo 2019, 1:341–42, no. 343.

95　Ionian workshop

Young Man

100–75 BC
Marble, 81 × 35 × 22.5 cm
Madrid, Museo Nacional del Prado, E-12

Provenance: Collection of Philip V, Palacio Real de La Granja de San Ildefonso, Segovia.

Selected bibliography: Hübner [1862] 2008, 73–74, no. 64; Barrón 1908, 32, no. 12; Blanco and Lorente 1981, 13, no. 12; Schröder 1993–2004 (2004), 2:274–77.

The history of the sculptures that graced the great galleries of European collectors is a living, moving chronicle. Objects unearthed by archaeologists – originally intended for some specific purpose, which they presumably fulfilled – tended to be mostly incomplete fragments. This was by no means a disadvantage: fragments were prized as proof of an antiquity that invested them with dignity and unquestionable prestige. The frontispiece to François Perrier's indispensable collection of engravings of great Roman sculptures, published in 1638, shows Saturn devouring the *Belvedere Torso*[1] in an explicit and highly-revealing allegory of the inexorable passage of time.

Moreover, at a time when restoration criteria differed from those in force today, the reconstruction of these works was regarded as both permissible and wholly natural. The great sculptors of sixteenth and seventeenth-century Rome, from Giovanni Angelo Montorsoli (1507–1563) to Gian Lorenzo Bernini (1598–1680), took part in the restoration of antique pieces which in some cases sought to challenge the teachings of the ancient masters. The well-known anecdote regarding the legs made by Guglielmo della Porta (c. 1500–1577) for the *Farnese Hercules*,[2] which Michelangelo (1475–1564) considered better than the originals discovered later, is further evidence that this concept was widespread.[3]

As a result, these sculptures went on to enjoy a second life, different from that for which they were first produced; henceforth, they were simply objects to be contemplated and enjoyed in their owners' galleries. This marble fragment of a young male body – which here helps to recreate the atmosphere of study and research with which classical statuary was associated in the work of Guido Reni – is a perfect example of the successive lives of ancient sculptures put to fresh uses.

Like other pieces in the Spanish royal collection, there is little certainty as to its provenance or when it was acquired. It is exhibited today stripped of certain earlier additions, which enabled it – at least in the eighteenth century – to be identified as Paris or Adonis, regardless of its original identity. The restored version was reproduced in the *Ajello Notebook*[4] as an example of those reconstructions based on historical fragments, often reusing old pieces that fitted the new design. At some point in the past – probably in the latter half of the nineteenth century, prompted by a more purist approach to restoration – these additions were removed, leaving the piece as it is today.

Stephan Schröder, noting its resemblance to a small winged youth from the island of Cos thought to represent Eros, suggested that this might be the identity of the Prado sculpture. If so, it would be a version of the *Eros of Parium*, one of the finest creations of the Athenian sculptor Praxiteles (c. 400–c. 330 BC), and just as important as his *Aphrodite of Cnidus*, to the extent that both – according to literary sources – were the victims of agalmatophilia: Pliny the Elder assures us that this Eros 'was a work that matches the Venus of Cnidus in its renown, as well as in the outrageous treatment which it suffered. For Alcetas, a man from Rhodes, fell in love with it and left upon it a similar mark of his passion'.[5]

The *Eros of Parium*, notable for the characteristically languid treatment of the human anatomy – the well-known 'Praxitelean curve' – was widely reproduced, even featuring on coins. In Rome, sculptors sought (some more faithfully than others) to duplicate the lost Greek original; a good example is the so-called *Borghese Genius* now in the Louvre.[6] Indeed, the composition proved so successful that in Roman times it was reused to represent the figure of the young Dionysus. Given the fragmentary nature of the Prado sculpture, and the resulting lack of attributes, it could be read in iconographic terms as either Eros or Dionysus; we cannot be absolutely sure which.

Manuel Arias Martínez

1 Perrier 1638.

2 Naples, Museo Archeologico Nazionale, inv. 6001.

3 Haskell and Penny 1990, 254–57.

4 Madrid, Museo Nacional del Prado, D003873 (*Cuaderno de Ajello*, dib. 44). The so-called *Ajello Notebook* contained the drawings made by Eutichio Ajello (1711–1793) of the sculptures in Philip V and Isabella Farnese's collection in the royal gallery of San Ildefonso. See Schröder and Elvira Barba 2006, 72.

5 Pliny the Elder, *Natural History*, Book 36, § 22. For more on agalmatophilia, see González García 2006.

6 Paris, Musée du Louvre, Ma 545; M. Minozzi, M.-L. Fábrega-Dubert, and J.-L. Martínez in Coliva et al. 2011, 368, no. 57.

Blessed Soul

c. 1638–42
Oil on canvas, 252 × 153 cm
Rome, Musei Capitolini, Pinacoteca Capitolina, PC106

Provenance: First mentioned in the 1642 inventory of Guido Reni's estate as destined for Alessandro Sacchetti; in the Sacchetti collection, Rome, until its donation to the Pinacoteca Capitolina in 1748.

Selected bibliography: Baccheschi 1971, 114, no. 203; Pepper 1988, 303, no. 201; P. Masini in Guarino and Masini 2006, 304–7, nos. 138–39; Guarino 2015, 126–28, no. 27; Malvasia–Pericolo 2019, 1:348, note 363.

Guido Reni's so-called *Blessed Soul* now in the Pinacoteca of the Musei Capitolini was destined for Alessandro Sacchetti (1589–1648), a friend of the master's in his final years. It is unclear when and how Guido became acquainted with Alessandro, but it is possible that the latter's brother, Cardinal Giulio Sacchetti (1587–1663), played a role in this friendship. In his *Felsina pittrice* (1678), Carlo Cesare Malvasia relates a few episodes in which Cardinal Sacchetti, as the papal legate to Bologna in 1637–40, expressed his admiration for and offered his protection to the artist.[1] In his life of Guido, Malvasia records that, while gravely ill in bed, Guido received the visits of 'two favourites', one of them being 'Alessandro, brother of Cardinal Sacchetti'.[2] Furthermore, Malvasia mentions a *Liberality and Modesty* by Guido for 'Signor Alessandro Sacchetti', which, unfinished upon the master's death in 1642, was completed 'so well' by Giovanni Andrea Sirani (1610–1670).[3] This painting is now in the Terruzzi collection, Milan.[4]

Despite the historical relevance of his family, very little is known about Alessandro Sacchetti. In 1623, Pope Urban VIII appointed him commander of the papal army in Valtellina and, in 1627, field marshal and commissary of the army in Romagna. In 1630, Alessandro was made commander of the army in Ferrara, but by 1631 he was already back in Rome. It is unknown exactly when and for what reason he found himself in Bologna during Guido's final years. In the 1642 inventory of Guido's paintings, there is mention of 'a large painting of a Divine Love, which was said to be for Signor Alessandro Sacchetti'.[5] A *bozzetto*, or reduced sketched version, of the same composition now in the Pinacoteca Capitolina, Rome, also seems to be listed in the 1642 inventory.[6] While there is no evidence that Cardinal Sacchetti collected works by Guido, it is very likely that many of Guido's unfinished paintings that entered the Sacchetti collection were purchased by Alessandro upon Guido's death: an unmistakable sign of his love and admiration for the master. Among these works, there are *Girl holding an Urn*, *Girl holding a Wreath* [fig. 48], *Cleopatra*, and *Lucretia*, all of them in the Pinacoteca Capitolina, Rome, where many works of the Sacchetti collection ended up in 1748.[7]

Guido's *Blessed Soul* may reflect the artist's obsession with his own death at the end of his life. 'Wearied of living longer among so many afflictions', Malvasia narrates, Guido 'seemed to prepare himself for death, foreseeing in a certain way that it was approaching and inadvertently predicting it'.[8] To his servant, Marco Bandinelli, who sought to convince him to put those ominous thoughts aside, Guido once responded: 'One cannot flee death, and I find myself so disposed that I do not fear it at all, nor does it frighten me'.[9] Despite its apparent simplicity, *Blessed Soul* combines different elements of the iconographical tradition, and on such account can be construed as an allegory about the spiritual bliss of the soul in its amorous contemplation of the divine. In this regard, the earlier documentary sources about the painting prove right in defining it as 'divine love' or 'love of God'. Without necessarily assuming that Guido relied on Cesare Ripa's *Iconologia* (first published in 1593) in devising the subject, it is useful to establish how *Blessed Soul* elaborates upon iconographical themes that circulated widely in the artist's time. That Guido thought of the figure in his painting as an allegory of Love is confirmed by a woodcut of *Love of Virtue* in Ripa's *Iconologia* [fig. 101]. Here, a nude young man, winged, poses in an antique contrapposto, his body mostly frontal, a fluttering veil covering his nudity.[10] Guido might have been familiar with Annibale Carracci's (1560–1609) so-called *Love of Virtue* of 1588–89 in Dresden, which partially draws on Ripa's example.[11] Of course, Guido did not intend to celebrate love of virtue, and indeed he adapted this iconography to his specific goals through conflation. In describing *Love of God*, Ripa proposes that it should be symbolised by 'a man standing in reverence, his face turned toward heaven'.[12] Ripa suggests a similar posture in his description of *Desire for God*, where a young man is gazing intently toward the sky 'to demonstrate that our works, eyes, heart, and everything in us must be turned toward God'.[13] Speaking about an allegory of 'the reasonable and blessed soul', Ripa depicts a very graceful woman, winged, with her face veiled, who in the woodcut appears with both arms raised upward in the traditional gesture of prayer.[14] In one of his allegories of *Prayer* [fig. 102], Ripa comments on the attitude of turning the head toward a celestial glory, which, as 'Saint Thomas says', implies that 'prayer is an act of elevating the mind and igniting the affects, through which man, speaking with God, prays to him, revealing the secrets and desires of his heart'.[15] Treading upon a sphere that symbolises the earth and human life, Guido's personification of the soul takes on the form of an ephebic and lithe body, its nudity standing for beauty, purity, truth, and detachment from earthly goods. Akin to an angel, the youth is solely focused on the contemplation of the divine, his stretched arms bespeaking both his desire to reach divinity and his heartfelt supplication to partake in celestial bliss.

Foreseeing the approach of death, Guido, in his *Blessed Soul*, summoned up his love and desire for God through the depiction of an angelic alter ego. It is significant that in embodying his vision of the virtuous soul, the master translates it into the pictorial equivalent of an antique, the delicacy of the torso's anatomical relief, its frontality with the slight asymmetry of the tilted hip, and the contrapposto reminding us of many a representation of ephebes as rendered in ancient sculpture, of which several examples existed in Roman collections at the time [cat. 95]. Summarising his views on Guido's art, Roberto Longhi noted that much remains to be said about Guido, in particular 'his desire, most acute within him, for an ancient beauty, but one that encloses a Christian soul'.[16] This phrase could easily apply to Guido's *Blessed Soul*.

Lorenzo Pericolo

1 Malvasia–Pericolo 2019, 1:297–98, note 219; 1:312–13, notes 261–62; 1:337, note 328; 1:341–43, notes 343–44; 1:346, note 353; 1:348 note 363; 1:364, note 407; 1:375, note 440; 1:376, note 449; 1:379–80, note 462; 1:382, note 466; 1:413, notes 591 and 593; 1:414, note 596; 1:442, note 671; 1:444, note 671.
2 Malvasia 1678, 2:53.
3 Ibid., 2:56.
4 Malvasia–Pericolo 2019, 1:353, note 379.
5 Spike and Di Zio 1988, 60.
6 Ibid.
7 Rome, Musei Capitolini, Pinacoteca, PC 182, PC 181, PC 217, and PC 211, respectively. For all these works, see Malvasia–Pericolo 2019, 1:442, note 670.
8 Malvasia 1678, 2:52: 'Stucco di più vivere fra tante angustie, parve andarsi accomodando al morire, prevedendolo in certo modo vicino, e inavedutamente presagendoselo'.
9 Ibid.: 'Ella non si può sfuggire la Morte, ed io mi ci trovo di gia così disposto, che punto non la temo, ne mi fa paura'.
10 Ripa 1603, 19.
11 Dresden, Gemäldegalerie Alte Meister, Gal.-Nr. 306. See Posner 1971, 2:22, no. 48.
12 Ripa 1603, 18.
13 Ibid., 101.
14 Ibid., 21–22.
15 Ibid., 372.
16 Longhi 1935, 132.

Fig. 101 *Love of Virtue*, in Cesare Ripa, *Iconologia*, Rome, Lepido Facii, 1603, page 19. Madrid, Biblioteca Nacional de España, ER/1363

Fig. 102 *Prayer*, in Cesare Ripa, *Iconologia*, Rome, Lepido Facii, 1603, page 372. Madrid, Biblioteca Nacional de España, ER/1363

BIBLIOGRAPHY

Aceto 2000. Marta Aceto, *sub voce* 'Giacobbi, Girolamo', in *Dizionario biografico degli italiani*, vol. 54, Rome, Istituto della Enciclopedia Italiana, 2000. Accessible at https://www.treccani.it/enciclopedia/girolamo-giacobbi_(Dizionario-Biografico).

Adamson and Musgrave 1954. Arthur Adamson and Ernest I. Musgrave, *Leeds City Art Gallery and Temple Newsam House: Catalogue of Paintings*, part 1: *Works by Artists Born before 1800*, Leeds, Leeds City Art Gallery and Temple Newsam House, 1954.

Agüero Carnerero 2018. Cristina Agüero Carnerero, 'Los almirantes de Castilla en el siglo XVII: políticas artísticas y coleccionismo nobiliario en la España de los Austrias', PhD diss., Universidad Nacional de Educación a Distancia, 2018.

Agulló y Cobo 1981. Mercedes Agulló y Cobo, *Más noticias sobre pintores madrileños de los siglos XVI al XVIII*, Madrid, Ayuntamiento de Madrid, Delegación de Cultura, 1981.

Ainaud de Lasarte 1947. Joan Ainaud de Lasarte, 'Ribalta y Caravaggio', *Anales y Boletín de los Museos de Arte de Barcelona* 5, 3–4 (1947), 345–413.

Alabern 1859. Camilo Alabern, *Galería de cuadros escogidos del Real Museo de Pinturas de Madrid*, Madrid, Imprenta de Tejado, 1859.

Albini 1934. Eugenio Albini, *Gli strumenti musicali nell'affresco di Guido Reni a S. Silvia*, Rocca S. Casciano, L. Cappelli, 1934.

Albl 2014. Stefan Albl, 'A Painting by Guido Reni for the Irish College in Rome', *The Burlington Magazine* 156, 1339 (2014), 650–52.

Alce 1997. Venturino Alce, 'La *Gloria di San Domenico* affrescata da Guido Reni (1615)', *Accademia Clementina, Atti e Memorie* 37 (1997), 9–18.

Alciato–Sebastián 1985. Andrea Alciato, *Emblemas*, ed. Santiago Sebastián, Madrid, Akal, 1985.

Algranti 2002. Gilberto Algranti, ed., *Titian to Tiepolo: Three Centuries of Italian Art* [exh. cat. Canberra, National Gallery of Australia, 28 March–16 June 2002; Melbourne, Melbourne Museum, 7 July–5 October 2002], Milan, Artificio–Skira, 2002.

Álvarez-Ossorio 1925. Francisco Álvarez-Ossorio, *Una visita al Museo Arqueológico Nacional*, Madrid, Tipografía de la Revista de Archivos, Bibliotecas y Museos, 1925.

Andrés 1967. Gregorio de Andrés, 'Nueve cartas inéditas del padre Francisco del Castillo a Felipe IV sobre diversas obras en el monasterio de El Escorial, años 1660–1663', *La Ciudad de Dios* 180 (1967), 116–27.

Andrés 1971. Gregorio de Andrés, 'Relación anónima del siglo XVII sobre los cuadros del Escorial', *Archivo Español de Arte* 44, 173 (1971), 49–64.

Andrews 1961. Keith Andrews, 'An Early Guido Reni Drawing', *The Burlington Magazine* 103, 704 (1961), 461–65.

Andrews 1968. Keith Andrews, *Catalogue of Italian Drawings: National Gallery of Scotland*, 2 vols, Cambridge, Cambridge University Press, 1968.

Andrews 1985. Keith Andrews, 'The Marriage at Cana: A Trio by Denys Calvaert', *The Burlington Magazine* 127, 992 (1985), 757.

Angulo Íñiguez 1964. Diego Angulo Íñiguez, 'La obra de Zurbarán', in Consuelo Sanz-Pastor, ed., *Zurbarán en el III centenario de su muerte* [exh. cat. Madrid, Casón del Buen Retiro, November 1964–February 1965], Madrid, Dirección General de Bellas Artes, 1964, 67–81.

Angulo Íñiguez 1981. Diego Angulo Íñiguez, *Murillo*, 3 vols, Madrid, Espasa-Calpe, 1981.

Angulo Íñiguez 1983. Diego Angulo Íñiguez, 'Varias pinturas sevillanas: *Asunción* de Tristán', *Archivo Español de Arte* 57, 222 (1983), 161–65.

Anselmi 2004. Alessandra Anselmi, *El diario del viaje a España del cardenal Francesco Barberini escrito por Cassiano dal Pozzo*, Aranjuez, Doce Calles (Visiones hispanas), 2004.

Anselmi 2014. Alessandra Anselmi, ed., *I rapporti tra Roma e Madrid nei secoli XVI e XVII: arte, diplomazia e politica*, Rome, Gangemi, 2014.

Arasse 2005. Daniel Arasse, 'La carne, la gracia, lo sublime', in Corbin, Courtine and Vigarello 2005, 395–456.

Arcangeli 1946. Francesco Arcangeli, 'Pittura bolognese alla mostra di Bologna', *Il Mondo* 2, 19 (5 January 1946), 10–11.

Aretino and Vasari–Zuffi 2008. Pietro Aretino and Giorgio Vasari, *Tiziano*, ed. Stefano Zuffi, Milan, Abscondita (Miniature, 64), 2008.

Ariuli 1999. Rossella Ariuli, 'Dipinti della chiesa di Santa Maria Maggiore di Pieve di Cento', in Campanini and Samaritani 1999, 113–64.

Armstrong 1897. Walter Armstrong, *Velázquez: A Study of His Life & Art*, London, Seeley, 1897.

Aronberg Lavin 1975. Marilyn Aronberg Lavin, *Seventeenth-Century Barberini Documents and Inventories of Art*, New York, New York University Press, 1975.

Arslan 1968. Ermanno A. Arslan, 'Un disegno rinascimentale della *Venere inginocchiata sulla tartaruga* al Museo del Prado', *Arte Lombarda* 13, 2 (1968), 51–54.

Askew 1978. Pamela Askew, 'Ferdinando Gonzaga's Patronage of the Pictorial Arts: The Villa Favorita', *The Art Bulletin* 60, 2 (1978), 274–96.

Assarino 1639. Luca Assarino, *Sensi d'humiltà e di stupore havuti da Luca Assarino intorno le grandezze dell'eminentissimo cardinal Sacchetti e le pitture di Guido Reni, e dedicati alla signora Geronima Assarini*, Bologna, Giacomo Monti & Carlo Zenero, 1639.

Assunta 2016. *L'Assunta di Castelfranco Emilia*, Modena, Sigem, 2016.

Aterido Fernández 2002. Ángel Aterido Fernández, ed., *Corpus Alonso Cano: documentos y textos*, Madrid, Ministerio de Educación, Cultura y Deporte, 2002.

Aterido Fernández 2015. Ángel Aterido Fernández, *El final del Siglo de Oro: la pintura en Madrid en el cambio dinástico, 1685–1726*, Madrid, Consejo Superior de Investigaciones Científicas and Coll & Cortés, 2015.

Aterido Fernández, Martínez Cuesta and Pérez Preciado 2004. Ángel Aterido Fernández, Juan Martínez Cuesta, and José Juan Pérez Preciado, *Inventarios reales: colecciones de pintura de Felipe V e Isabel de Farnesio*, 2 vols, Madrid, Fundación de Apoyo a la Historia del Arte Hispánico, 2004.

Auzas 1958. Pierre-Marie Auzas, 'L'influence du Guide et Lubin Baugin', *Gazette des Beaux-Arts* 100 (1958), 301–9.

Ayala Mallory 1983. Nina Ayala Mallory, *Bartolomé Esteban Murillo*, Madrid, Alianza (Alianza Forma, 38), 1983.

Azcárate Ristori 1994. José María Azcárate Ristori, *Obras maestras de la Real Academia de San Fernando: su primer siglo de historia* [exh. cat. Madrid, Real Academia de Bellas Artes de San Fernando, 31 May–28 August 1994], Madrid, Real Academia de Bellas Artes de San Fernando, 1994.

Baccheschi 1971. Edi Baccheschi, *L'opera completa di Guido Reni*, Milan, Rizzoli (Classici dell'arte, 48), 1971.

Baccheschi 1977. Edi Baccheschi, *La obra pictórica completa de Guido Reni*, Barcelona, Noguer, 1977.

Bacchi 1996. Andrea Bacchi, *Scultura del '600 a Roma*, Milan, Longanesi (Repertori fotografici Longanesi e C., 10), 1996.

Bacchi 2004. Andrea Bacchi, '"Fece di rilievo e se ne diportò bene": Guido Reni, la scultura e la "famosa testa detta del Seneca"', in Marina Cellini, ed., *Storie barocche: da Guercino a Serra e Savolini nella Romagna del Seicento* [exh. cat. Cesena, Biblioteca Malatestiana, 28 February–27 June 2004], Bologna, Abacus, 2004, 51–53.

Bacci 1939. Pèleo Bacci, 'L'elenco delle pitture, sculture e architetture di Siena, compilato nel 1625–26 da Mons. Fabio Chigi, poi Alessandro VII secondo il ms. Chigiano I.I.II', *Bullettino Senese di Storia Patria* 10, 4 (1939), 297–337.

Baglione 1642. Giovanni Baglione, *Le vite de' pittori, scultori et architetti: dal pontificato di Gregorio XIII del 1572 in fino a' tempi di Papa Urbano Ottavo nel 1642*, Rome, Andrea Fei, 1642.

Bailly–Engerand 1899. Nicolas Bailly, *Inventaire des tableaux du Roy, rédigé en 1709 et 1710 par Nicolas Bailly*, ed. Fernand Engerand, Paris, Ernest Leroux, 1899.

Baldassari 2007. Marco Baldassari, ed., *Capolavori da scoprire: Colonna, Pallavicini, Patrizi Montoro* [exh. cat. Rome, Galleria Pallavicini, 8–10 June 2007; Palazzo Patrizi Montoro, 15–17 June 2007; Galleria Colonna, 22–24 June 2007], Milan, Skira, 2007.

Baldi, Cibrario and Jatta 2015. Pio Baldi, Laura Cibrario, and Fabiola Jatta, eds, *Aperti per restauri: il restauro di* Venere e Amore *del Guercino e dell'*Allegoria della Fortuna *di Guido Reni* [exh. cat. Rome, Accademia Nazionale di San Luca, 7–29 November 2015], Rome, Gangemi, 2015.

Baldini 1598. Vittorio Baldini, *Felicissima entrata di N. S. PP. Clemente Ottavo nell'inclita città di Ferrara, con gli apparati publici fatti nelle città, terre, castelli, e luoghi, dove S. Santità è passata, dopò la sua partita di Roma*, Ferrara, Vittorio Baldini, 1598.

Baldinucci 1681a. Filippo Baldinucci, *Notizie de' professori del disegno da Cimabue in qua*, Florence, Santi Franchi, 1681.

Baldinucci 1681b. Filippo Baldinucci, *Vocabolario toscano dell'arte del disegno nel quale si esplicano i propri termini e voci, non solo della pittura, scultura, & architettura, ma ancora di altre arti a quelle subordinate, e che abbiano per fondamento il disegno*, Florence, Santi Franchi, 1681.

Baldinucci–Ranalli 1845–47. Filippo Baldinucci, *Notizie de' professori del disegno da Cimabue in qua … con nuove annotazioni e supplementi per cura di F. Ranalli*, 5 vols, Florence, Batelli e Compagni, 1845–47.

Baldinucci–Ranalli and Barocchi 1974–75. Filippo Baldinucci, *Notizie de' professori del disegno da Cimabue in qua … con nuove annotazioni e supplementi per cura di F. Ranalli*, with appendixes by Paola Barocchi, 7 vols, Florence, Studio per Edizione Scelte, 1974–75 (facsimile of the 1845–47 edition).

Balletti 1930. Andrea Balletti, *Il Santo Monte della Pietà di Reggio nell'Emilia: ricerche storiche*, Reggio Emilia, Anonima Poligrafica Emiliana, 1930.

Baños and Palacios 2022. Laura Baños and Alfonso Palacios, eds, *El factor Prado: los depósitos del Museo Nacional del Prado en el Museo de Bellas Artes de Asturias* [exh. cat. Oviedo, Museo de Bellas Artes de Asturias, 21 July–30 October 2022], Oviedo, Museo de Bellas Artes de Asturias, 2022.

Barbeito 2015. José Manuel Barbeito, 'De arte y arquitectura: el Salón de los Espejos en el Alcázar de Madrid', *Boletín del Museo del Prado* 33, 51 (2015), 24–43.

Barbieri 2012. Patrizio Barbieri, 'Caravaggio's *Denial of St Peter* acquired by Guido Reni in 1613', *The Burlington Magazine* 154, 1312 (2012), 487–89.

Barcia 1906. Ángel María de Barcia, *Catálogo de la colección de dibujos originales de la Biblioteca Nacional*, Madrid, Tipografía de la Revista de Archivos, Bibliotecas y Museos, 1906.

Barcia 1911. Ángel María de Barcia, *Catálogo de la colección de pinturas del Excmo. Sr. duque de Berwick y de Alba*, Madrid, Establecimiento Tipográfico de la Revista de Archivos, Bibliotecas y Museos, 1911.

Bardi 1837–42. Luigi Bardi, *L'imperiale e reale Galleria Pitti*, 4 vols, Florence, Tipografia della Galileiana, 1837–42.

Bardon 1968. Françoise Bardon, 'Le Thème de la Madeleine pénitente au XVIIeme siècle en France', *Journal of the Warburg and Courtauld Institutes* 31, 1 (1968), 274–306.

Baroni 18th c. Giuseppe Valentino Baroni, *Notizie genealogiche e stemmi delle famiglie lucchesi*, 18th c., manuscript, Lucca, Biblioteca Statale, Ms 1120.

Baroni 2014. Jean-Luc Baroni, *Paintings, Drawings, Sculptures* [exh. cat. New York, Carlton Hobbs LLC, 24 January–1 February 2014], London, Jean-Luc Baroni Ltd., 2014.

Barrio Moya 1979. José Luis Barrio Moya, 'La colección de pinturas de don Francisco de Oviedo, secretario del rey Felipe IV', *Revista de Archivos, Bibliotecas y Museos* 82 (1979), 163–71.

Barrón 1908. Eduardo Barrón, *Catálogo de la escultura: Museo Nacional de Pintura y Escultura*, Madrid, Imprenta y Fototipia J. Lacoste, 1908.

Bartolomé 1994. Belén Bartolomé, 'El conde de Castrillo y sus intereses artísticos', *Boletín del Museo del Prado* 15, 33 (1994), 15–28.

Bartsch 1803–21. Adam von Bartsch, *Le Peintre Graveur*, 21 vols, Vienna, J. V. Degen, 1803–21.

Bassegoda i Hugas 2002. Bonaventura Bassegoda i Hugas, *El Escorial como museo: la decoración pictórica mueble en el monasterio de El Escorial desde Diego Velázquez hasta Frédéric Quilliet (1809)*, Bellaterra, Universitat Autònoma de Barcelona; Barcelona, Edicions Universitat de Barcelona and Museu Nacional d'Art de Catalunya; Gerona, Universitat de Girona; Lérida, Universitat de Lleida (Memoria Artium, 2), 2002.

Baudi di Vesme 1897. Alessandro Baudi di Vesme, 'La regia pinacoteca di Torino', *Le Gallerie Nazionali Italiane: Notizie e Documenti* 3 (1897), 3–68.

Baxandall 1978. Michael Baxandall, *Pintura y vida cotidiana en el Renacimiento: arte y experiencia en el Quattrocento*, Barcelona, Gustavo Gili, 1978.

Bayer 2017. Andrea Bayer, 'Better Late than Never: Collecting Baroque Painting at The Metropolitan Museum of Art', in Edgar Peters Bowron, ed., *Buying Baroque: Italian Seventeenth-Century Paintings Come to America* [papers of the symposium, New York, Frick Collection, 20–21 September 2013], University Park, The Pennsylvania State University (The Frick Collection Studies in the History of Art Collecting in America, 3), 2017, 128–39.

Beaven 2000. Lisa Beaven, 'Reni's *Cupid with a Bow* and Guercino's *Cupid Spurning Riches* in the Prado: A Gift from Camillo Massimi to Philip IV of Spain?', *The Burlington Magazine* 142, 1168 (2000), 437–41.

Beaven 2014. Lisa Beaven, 'The Carracci and their Legacy', in *Italian Masterpieces* 2014, 94–119.

Beaven and Colomer 2020. Lisa Beaven and José Luis Colomer, '"Questo non basta a contentar una donna spagnola": Camillo Massimo as Papal Nuncio in Madrid and his Later Ties to Spain (1655–62)', in Jorge Fernández-Santos and José Luis Colomer, eds, *Ambassadors in Golden-Age Madrid: The Court of Philip IV through Foreign Eyes*, Madrid, Centro de Estudios Europa Hispánica, 2020, 201–43.

Becatti 2016. Graziella Becatti, 'Hipótesis para una contextualización del *Hypnos* del Prado', *Boletín del Museo del Prado* 34, 52 (2016), 6–9 and 104–6.

Becker 1804–11. Wilhelm Gottlieb Becker, *Augusteum: Dresden's antike Denkmäler enthaltend*, 3 vols, Leipzig, C. A. Hempel, 1804–11.

Becker 2022. Lilly Becker, 'Notes on the Painting Technique, Conservation and Restoration of the *Christ at the Column* at the Städel Museum', in Eclercy 2022a, 142–43.

Bellesi 2019. Sandro Bellesi, *Gioacchino Fortini: Cupido*, Pesaro, Altomani & Sons, 2019.

Belli 1632. Francesco Belli, *Osservazioni nel viaggio di D. Francesco Belli*, Venice, Gio. Pietro Pinelli, 1632.

Belli Barsali 1953. Isa Belli Barsali, *Guida di Lucca*, Lucca, Il Messaggero, 1953.

Belli Barsali 1970. Isa Belli Barsali, *Guida di Lucca*, Lucca, Pacini Fazzi, 1970 (2nd ed.).

Belloni 1973. Venanzio Belloni, *Penne, pennelli e quadrerie: cultura e pittura genovese del Seicento*, Genoa, Emme-Bi, 1973.

Bellori 1672. Giovanni Pietro Bellori, *Le vite de' pittori, scultori e architetti moderni*, Rome, Success. al Mascardi, 1672.

Bellori [1672] 1977. Giovan Pietro Bellori, *Le vite de' pittori scultori et architetti moderni* [1672], Rome, Arnaldo Forni (Italica gens, 86), 1977.

Bellori–Borea 1976. Giovan Pietro Bellori, *Le vite de' pittori, scultori e architetti moderni*, ed. Evelina Borea, Turin, Giulio Einaudi (I millenni), 1976.

Bellori–Borea 2009. Giovan Pietro Bellori, *Le vite de' pittori, scultori e architetti moderni* [1672], ed. Evelina Borea, 2 vols, Turin, Giulio Einaudi (Piccola Biblioteca Einaudi, nuova serie, 470, 1 and 2), 2009.

Bellori–Wohl 2005. Giovan Pietro Bellori, *The Lives of Modern Painters, Sculptors and Architects*, ed. Hellmut Wohl, trans. Alice Sedgwick Wohl, notes Hellmut Wohl, Cambridge, Cambridge University Press, 2005.

Belting 1994. Hans Belting, *Likeness and Presence: A History of the Image before the Era of Art*, Chicago, University of Chicago Press, 1994.

Benacci 1598. Vittorio Benacci, *Descrittione de gli apparati fatti in Bologna per la venuta di N. S. Papa Clemente VIII, con gli disegni de gli archi, statue, & pitture, dedicata a gli Ill.mi Sig. del Reggimento di Bologna*, Bologna, Vittorio Benacci, 1598.

Benati 1987. Daniele Benati, 'Antonio Giarola per Modena', *Paragone* 38, 447 (1987), 37–42.

Benati 1991. Daniele Benati, ed., *Disegni emiliani del Sei-Settecento*, 2 vols, Cinisello Balsamo, Silvana, 1991.

Benati 1998. Daniele Benati, 'Il Seicento: Emilia e Romagna', in Mina Gregori, ed., *Pittura murale in Italia*, vol. 3: *Il Seicento e il Settecento*, Bergamo, Gruppo Bancario San Paolo IMI, 1998, 8–21.

Benati 2000. Daniele Benati, 'Pier Francesco Cittadini, detto "il Milanese"', in Daniele Benati and Lucia Peruzzi, eds, *La natura morta in Emilia e in Romagna: pittori, centri di produzione e collezionismo fra XVII e XVIII secolo*, Milan, Skira, 2000, 84–97.

Benati 2001. Daniele Benati, *Alessandro Tiarini: l'opera pittorica completa e i disegni*, 2 vols, Milan, Motta, 2001.

Benati 2004–5. Daniele Benati, 'Per Guido Reni "incamminato" tra i Carracci e Caravaggio', *Nuovi Studi, Rivista di Arte Antica e Moderna* 9–10, 11 (2004–5), 231–47.

Benati 2013a. Daniele Benati, ed., *Quadri da collezione: dipinti emiliani dal XIV al XIX secolo* [exh. cat. Bologna, Galleria Fondantico, 9 November–21 December 2013], Bologna, Galleria Fondantico (Incontro con la pittura, 21), 2013.

Benati 2013b. Daniele Benati, '…sperando far cosa meglio della prima', in Diotallevi 2013, 23–31.

Benati 2015. Daniele Benati, ed., *Antichi maestri italiani: dipinti e disegni dal XVI al XIX secolo* [exh. cat. Bologna, Galleria Fondantico, 7 November–23 December 2015], Bologna, Fondantico, arte e antiquariato, 2015.

Benati 2018. Daniele Benati, 'Guido Reni per Henrietta Maria di Borbone: un nuovo frammento con due fauni danzanti', in Emiliani 2018, 59–63.

Benati 2022. Daniele Benati, 'Guido Reni: la strada per Roma', in Cappelletti 2022a, 14–27.

Benati and Frisoni 1986. Daniele Benati and Fiorella Frisoni, eds, *L'arte degli Estensi: la pittura del Seicento e del Settecento a Modena e Reggio* [exh. cat. Modena, Palazzo Comunale, Palazzo dei Musei, Galleria e Museo Estense and Galleria Civica, June–September 1986], Modena, Panini, 1986.

Benati and Mazza 2002. Daniele Benati and Angelo Mazza, eds, *Alessandro Tiarini: la grande stagione della pittura del '600 a Reggio* [exh. cat. Reggio Emilia, Palazzo Magnani and Chiostro di San Domenico, 23 March–16 June 2002], Milan, Motta, 2002.

Benati and Paolucci 2008. Daniele Benati and Antonio Paolucci, eds, *Guido Cagnacci: protagonista del Seicento tra Caravaggio e Reni* [exh. cat. Forli, Musei San Domenico, 20 January–22 June 2008], Cinisello Balsamo, Silvana, 2008.

Benati and Peruzzi 2006. Daniele Benati and Lucia Peruzzi, eds, *Banca Popolare dell'Emilia-Romagna: la collezione di dipinti antichi*, Milan, Skira, 2006.

Benati and Riccòmini 2006. Daniele Benati and Eugenio Riccòmini, eds, *Annibale Carracci* [exh. cat. Bologna, Museo Civico Archeologico, 22 September 2006–7 January 2007; Rome, Centro Culturale Internazionale Chiostro del Bramante, 25 January–6 May 2007], Milan, Electa, 2006.

Benedetti 1997. Sergio Benedetti, ed., *A Scholar's Eye: Paintings from the Sir Denis Mahon Collection* [exh. cat. Dublin, National Gallery of Ireland, 1997], Dublin, National Gallery of Ireland, 1997.

Benito Doménech 1991. Fernando Benito Doménech, *Ribera, 1591–1652*, Valencia, Bancaja, 1991.

Bentini et al. 2006. Jadranka Bentini et al., eds, *Pinacoteca Nazionale di Bologna: catalogo generale*, vol. 2: *Da Raffaello ai Carracci*, Venice, Marsilio, 2006.

Bentini et al. 2008. Jadranka Bentini et al., eds, *Pinacoteca Nazionale di Bologna: catalogo generale*, vol. 3: *Guido Reni e il Seicento*, Venice, Marsilio, 2008.

Bentini et al. 2011. Jadranka Bentini et al., eds, *Pinacoteca Nazionale di Bologna: catalogo generale*, vol. 4: *Seicento e Settecento*, Venice, Marsilio, 2011.

Bermejo 1820. Damián Bermejo, *Descripción artística del Real Monasterio de S. Lorenzo del Escorial, y sus preciosidades después de la invasión de los franceses*, Madrid, Imprenta de Doña Rosa Sanz, 1820.

Bernardini 2001. Maria Grazia Bernardini, *Caravaggio, Carracci, Maderno: la Cappella Cerasi in Santa Maria del Popolo a Roma*, Cinisello Balsamo, Silvana, 2001.

Bernardini 2004. Maria Grazia Bernardini, ed., *Studi sul Barocco romano: scritti in onore di Maurizio Fagiolo dell'Arco*, Milan, Skira (Biblioteca d'Arte Skira, 13), 2004.

Bernardini 2015. Maria Grazia Bernardini, 'Le radici del Barocco', in Bernardini, Bussagli and Anselmi 2015, 25–43.

Bernardini, Bussagli and Anselmi 2015. Maria Grazia Bernardini, Marco Bussagli, and Alessandra Anselmi, eds, *Barocco a Roma: la meraviglia delle arti* [exh. cat. Rome, Palazzo Cipolla, 1 April–26 July 2015], Milan, Skira, 2015.

Bernoulli 1901. Johann Jacob Bernoulli, *Griechische Ikonographie mit Ausschluss Alexanders und der Diadochen*, 2 vols, Munich, F. Bruckmann, 1901.

Bernstorff 2010. Marieke von Bernstorff, *Agent und Maler als Akteure im Kunstbetrieb des frühen 17. Jahrhunderts: Giovan Battista Crescenzi und Bartolomeo Cavarozzi*, Munich, Hirmer, 2010.

Bernstorff 2013. Marieke von Bernstorff, 'Doni eloquenti di un nobile romano: le nature morte presentate da Giovan Battista Crescenzi a Filippo III e Cassiano dal Pozzo', in Bernstorff and Kubersky-Piredda 2013, 161–81.

Bernstorff 2017. Marieke von Bernstorff, 'Da Roma a Genova e alla corte di Spagna: il viaggio di Crescenzi, Cavarozzi e Seghers come esempio del transfer artistico tra Anversa, Roma e Madrid', in Gianluca Zanelli, ed., *Bartolomeo Cavarozzi a Genova* [exh. cat. Genoa, Museo di Palazzo Reale e Galleria Nazionale di Palazzo Spinola, 6 December 2017–8 April 2018], Genoa, Sagep, 2017, 7–29.

Bernstorff and Kubersky-Piredda 2013. Marieke von Bernstorff and Susanne Kubersky-Piredda, eds, *L'arte del dono: scambi artistici e diplomazia tra Italia e Spagna, 1550–1650* [papers of the symposium, Rome, Bibliotheca Hertziana, 14–15 January 2008], Cinisello Balsamo, Silvana, 2013.

Bertini 1987. Giuseppe Bertini, *La galleria del duca di Parma: storia di una collezione*, Bologna, Nuova Alfa, 1987.

Bertini and Ortenzi 1978. Dante Bertini and Alfio Ortenzi, *La Pinacoteca Civica di Ascoli Piceno*, Rome, Autostrade, 1978.

Bertoli Barsotti 2014. Anna Maria Bertoli Barsotti, *Joannes Jacobs Bruxellensis 1575–1650: orefice a Bologna, fondatore del Collegio dei Fiamminghi*, Bologna, Bononia University Press, 2014.

Bertolini Campetti and Meloni Trkulja 1968. Licia Bertolini Campetti and Silvia Meloni Trkulja, eds, *Museo Nazionale di Villa Guinigi: la villa e le* *collezioni*, Lucca, Ente Provinciale per il Turismo di Lucca, 1968.

Beruete 1906. Aureliano de Beruete, *Velazquez*, London, Methuen & Co., 1906.

Berwick y Alba 1891. María del Rosario Falcó y Osorio, duquesa de Berwick y Alba, condesa de Siruela, *Documentos escogidos del archivo de la Casa de Alba*, Madrid, M. Tello, 1891.

Berzaghi 1995. Renato Berzaghi, 'La Galleria degli Specchi del Palazzo Ducale di Mantova: storia, iconografia, collezioni', *Quaderni di Palazzo Te* 2 (1995), 49–71.

Bianchi 2013. Ilaria Bianchi, 'La collezione di Filippo di Alfonso Hercolani, principe del Sacro Romano Impero (1663–1722)', in Frommel 2013, 85–108.

Biffis 2018. Mattia Biffis, '"Barberino gli volse donare un quadro": Francesco Barberini, Walter Leslie e una nuova traccia documentaria per il *Bacco e Arianna* di Guido Reni', *Studi Secenteschi* 59 (2018), 145–62.

Birke 1981. Veronika Birke, ed., *Guido Reni: Zeichnungen* [exh. cat. Vienna, Graphische Sammlung Albertina, 14 May–5 July 1981], Vienna, Freiburg, and Basel, Herder & Co., 1981.

Birke 1982. Veronika Birke, ed., *The Illustrated Bartsch*, vol. 40 (formerly vol. 18, part 2): *Italian Masters of the Sixteenth and Seventeenth Centuries*, New York, Abaris Books, 1982.

Birke 1987. Veronika Birke, ed., *The Illustrated Bartsch*, vol. 40.1 (formerly vol. 18, part 2): *Italian Masters of the Sixteenth and Seventeenth Centuries*, New York, Abaris Books, 1987.

Birke 1988a. Veronika Birke, 'I disegni di Guido Reni', in Ebert-Schifferer, Emiliani and Schleier 1988, 237–403.

Birke 1988b. Veronika Birke, *Guido Reni und der Reproduktionsstich* [exh. cat. Vienna, Graphische Sammlung Albertina, 15 September–13 November 1988], Vienna and Stuttgart, Albertina, 1988.

Bizzarri and Sainz de la Maza 1994. Hugo O. Bizzarri and Carlos N. Sainz de la Maza, 'La *Carta de Léntulo al Senado de Roma*: fortuna de un retrato de Cristo en la Baja Edad Media Castellana', *RILCE: Revista de Filología Hispánica* 10, 1 (1994), 43–58.

Bjurström, Loisel and Pilliod 2002. Per Bjurström, Catherine Loisel, and Elizabeth Pilliod, *Italian Drawings: Florence, Siena, Modena, Bologna*, Stockholm, Nationalmuseum (Drawings in Swedish Public Collections, 8), 2002.

Blanc and Delaborde 1877. Charles Blanc and Henri Delaborde, *Histoire des peintres de toutes les écoles: école bolonaise*, Paris, Librairie Renouard, 1877.

Blanco and Lorente 1981. Antonio Blanco and Manuel Lorente, *Catálogo de la escultura: Museo del Prado*, Madrid, Patronato Nacional de Museos, 1981.

Blanco Mozo 2015. Juan Luis Blanco Mozo, 'El sepulcro de la emperatriz María en las Descalzas Reales: ensayo e interpretación', *Reales Sitios* 203 (2015), 8–27.

Boccardo 2002. Piero Boccardo, 'Viceré e finanzieri: mercato artistico e collezioni tra Madrid e Genova (secoli XVII-XVIII)', in Piero Boccardo, José Luis Colomer, and Clario Di Fabio, eds, *Genova e la Spagna: opere, artisti, committenti, collezionisti*, Cinisello Balsamo, Silvana, 2002, 221–39.

Boccardo 2016. Piero Boccardo, 'Le rane del conte di Monterrey', in Anna Orlando, ed., *La Favola di Latona di Orazio de Ferrari: il ritorno di un capolavoro: con aggiunte al catalogo del pittore*, Genoa, Sagep, 2016, 31–39.

Boccardo and Salomon 2007. Piero Boccardo and Xavier F. Salomon, eds, *Guido Reni, il tormento e l'estasi: i San Sebastiano a confronto / The Agony and the Ecstasy: Guido Reni's Saint Sebastians* [exh. cat. Genoa, Musei di Strada Nuova, 6 October 2007–20 January 2008; London, Dulwich Picture Gallery, 5 February–11 May 2008], Cinisello Balsamo, Silvana, 2007.

Bodmer 1929. Heinrich Bodmer, 'Un capolavoro sconosciuto di Guido Reni', separata, *Rivista d'Arte* 11 (1929).

Boehn 1910. Max von Boehn, *Guido Reni, mit 105 Textabbildungen, darunter 4 mehrfarbige Einschaltbilder, nach Gemälden und Zeichnungen*, Bielefeld, Velhagen & Klasing, 1910.

Boesten-Stengel 2015. Albert Boesten-Stengel, 'Exégesis de *La rendición de Breda* por Carl Justi: hermenéutica e ironía según Schleiermacher y Schopenhauer', in Antonio Bonet Correa, Henrik Karge, and Jorge Maier Allende, eds, *Carl Justi y el arte español*, Madrid, Centro de Estudios Europa Hispánica, 2015, 155–74.

Bohn 2008. Babette Bohn, ed., *Le 'Stanze' di Guido Reni: disegni del maestro e della scuola* [exh. cat. Florence, Gallerie degli Uffizi, Gabinetto Disegni e Stampe, 15 March–1 June 2008], Florence, Olschki, 2008.

Bohn 2011. Babette Bohn, 'The Construction of Artistic Reputation in Seicento Bologna: Guido Reni and the Sirani', *Renaissance Studies* 25, 4 (2011), 511–37.

Bologna 1960. Ferdinando Bologna, 'Un documento napoletano per Guido Reni', *Paragone* 11, 129 (1960), 54–56.

***Bolognese Drawings* 1993.** *Bolognese Drawings in the National Gallery of Scotland* [Edinburgh, National Gallery of Scotland, 8 April–4 July 1993], Edinburgh, National Gallery of Scotland, 1993.

Bolognini Amorini 1839. Antonio Bolognini Amorini, *Vita del celebre pittore Guido Reni*, Bologna, Tipi della Volpe al Sassi, 1839.

Bona Castellotti 1991. Marco Bona Castellotti, *Collezionisti a Milano nel '700: Giovanni Battista Visconti, Gian Matteo Pertusati, Giuseppe Pozzobonelli*, Milan, Le Lettere (Fonti per la storia dell'arte, 3), 1991.

Bondi 2015. Fabrizio Bondi, *sub voce* 'Pona, Francesco', in *Dizionario biografico degli italiani*, vol. 84, Rome, Istituto della Enciclopedia Italiana, 2015. Accessible at https://www.treccani.it/enciclopedia/francesco-pona-%28Dizionario-Biografico%29/.

Bonfait 1994. Olivier Bonfait, ed., *Roma 1630: il trionfo del pennello* [exh. cat. Rome, Villa Medici, 25 October 1994–1 January 1995], Milan, Electa, 1994.

Bonfait 2000. Olivier Bonfait, *Les tableaux et les pinceaux: la naissance de l'école bolonaise (1680–1780)*, Rome, École Française de Rome (Collection de l'École Française de Rome, 266), 2000.

Bonifacio 1616. Giovanni Bonifacio, *L'arte de' cenni: con la quale formandosi favella visibile, si tratta della muta eloquenza, che non è altro che un facondo silentio: divisa in due parti...*, Vicenza, Francesco Grossi, 1616.

Borea 1975. Evelina Borea, *Pittori bolognesi del Seicento nelle gallerie di Firenze* [exh. cat. Florence, Gallerie degli Uffizi, February 1975–April 1975], Florence, Sansoni, 1975.

Borea and Gasparri 2000. Evelina Borea and Carlo Gasparri, eds, *L'idea del bello: viaggio per Roma nel Seicento con Giovan Pietro Bellori* [exh. cat. Rome, Palazzo delle Esposizioni, 29 March–26 June 2000], 2 vols, Rome, De Luca, 2000.

Borean 1998. Linda Borean, '"Ricchezze virtuose": il collezionismo privato a Venezia nel Seicento (1630–1700)', PhD diss., Università degli Studi di Udine, 1998.

Borean 2010. Linda Borean, 'Nuovi elementi e considerazioni sulla collezione di John Law', in Michel Hochmann, ed., *Venise & Paris, 1500–1700: la peinture vénitienne de la Renaissance et sa réception en France* [papers of the colloquium, Bordeaux and Caen, 24–25 February and 6 May 2006], Geneva, Droz, 2010, 441–62.

Borghi 2018. Fabio Borghi, 'La penna che dipinge: una raccolta di epistole in gloria di Guido Reni', *Lettere Italiane* 70, 3 (2018), 479–503.

Borghini 1584. Raffaello Borghini, *Il riposo di Raffaello Borghini in cui della pittura, e della scultura si fauella, de' più illustri pittori, e scultori, e delle più famose opere loro si fa mentione; e le cose principali appartenenti a' dette arti s'insegnano*, Florence, Giorgio Marescotti, 1584.

Borgo 1987. Ludovico Borgo, 'Fra Bartolomeo e Raffaello: l'incontro romano del 1513', in Micaela Sambucco Hamoud and Maria Letizia Strocchi, eds, *Studi su Raffaello* [proceedings of the international congress, Urbino–Florence, 6–14 April 1984], 2 vols, Urbino, QuattroVenti, 1987, 1:499–507.

Borrelli 1968. Mario Borrelli, *Contributo alla storia degli artefici maggiori e minori della mole Girolimiana, V*, Naples, Laurenziana, 1968.

Borsellino 2017. Enzo Borsellino, *La collezione Corsini di Roma dalle origini alla donazione allo Stato italiano: dipinti e sculture*, 2 vols, Rome, Efesto, 2017.

Boschini 1676. Marco Boschini, *I gioielli pittoreschi, virtuoso ornamento della città di Vicenza*, Venice, Francesco Nicolini, 1676.

Boschini–Boer 2008. Marco Boschini, *I gioielli pittoreschi, virtuoso ornamento della città di*

Vicenza, ed. Waldemar H. de Boer, Florence, Centro Di, 2008.

Bosio 1600. Antonio Bosio, *Historia passionis B. Caeciliae virginis…*, Rome, Stephanum Paulinum, 1600.

Bottari 1754–73. Giovanni Gaetano Bottari, *Raccolta di lettere sulla pittura, scultura ed architettura, scritte da' più celebri professori che in dette arti fiorirono dal secolo XV al XVII*, 7 vols, Bologna, Eredi di Giovanni Lorenzo Barbiellini, Carlo Barbielli, Niccolò Pagliarini, Marco Pagliarini & Stamperia di Pallade, 1754–73.

Bottari and Ticozzi 1822–25. Giovanni Gaetano Bottari and Stefano Ticozzi, *Raccolta di lettere sulla pittura, scultura ed architettura scritte da' più celebri personaggi dei secoli XV, XVI e XVII*, 8 vols, Milan, Giovanni Silvestri, 1822–25.

Bottineau 1958. Yves Bottineau, 'L'Alcázar de Madrid et l'inventaire de 1686: aspects de la cour d'Espagne au XVIIᵉ siècle', *Bulletin Hispanique* 60, 3 (1958), 289–326.

Boudon-Machuel 2005. Marion Boudon-Machuel, *François du Quesnoy, 1597–1643*, Paris, Arthena, 2005.

Bouza Álvarez 2012. Fernando J. Bouza Álvarez, 'Osuna a Napoli: feste, dipinti, sortilegi e buffoni (notizie dai libri contabili di Igún de la Lana)', in Encarnación Sánchez García, ed., *Cultura della guerra e arti della pace: il III duca di Osuna in Sicilia e a Napoli (1611–1620)*, Naples, Tullio Pironti (Materia hispánica, 1), 2012, 209–30.

Bowron 1999. Edgar Peters Bowron, 'A Brief History of European Oil Paintings on Copper, 1560–1775', in Komanecky 1999a, 9–30.

Boyd 2021. Rachel Boyd, 'Guido Reni, Head of Venus', entry (17 June 2021) in *Ashmolaen Museum: Italian Drawings online* (forthcoming).

Boyer and Volf 1988. Jean-Claude Boyer and Isabelle Volf, 'Rome à Paris: les tableaux du Maréchal de Créquy (1638)', *Revue de l'Art* 79 (1988), 22–41.

Brady 2017. Aoife Brady, 'The Painting Techniques and Workshop Practices of Guido Reni', PhD diss., 2 vols, Dublin, Trinity College, 2017.

Brady 2019. Aoife Brady, 'Durability and Disease: Guido Reni's Paintings on Silk', *Artibus et Historiae* 79 (2019), 151–66.

Brady 2020. Aoife Brady, 'The Studio of Guido Reni from 1620 to 1630: Formulating Compositions', *The Getty Research Journal* 12 (2020), 1–28.

Braghirolli 1885. Willemo Braghirolli, 'Guido Reni e Ferdinando Gonzaga', *Rivista Storica Mantovana* 1, 1–2 (1885), 88–104.

Brejon de Lavergnée 1987. Arnauld Brejon de Lavergnée, *L'inventaire Le Brun de 1683: la collection des tableaux de Louis XIV*, Paris, Réunion des Musées Nationaux, 1987.

Brigstocke and D'Albo 2020. Hugh Brigstocke and Odette D'Albo, *Giulio Cesare Procaccini: Life and Work, with a Catalogue of his Paintings*, Turin, Allemandi, 2020.

Brizzi 1969. Gian Paolo Brizzi, 'Inventario del fondo gesuitico conservato nell'archivio dell'ente comunale di assitenza di Bologna', *Atti e Memorie della Deputazione di Storia Patria per le Province di Romagna* 20 (1969), 343–408.

Brogi 2001. Alessandro Brogi, *Ludovico Carracci (1555–1619)*, 2 vols, Ozzano Emilia, Tipoarte, 2001.

Brogi 2017. Alessandro Brogi, 'Un Guido giovane, "tra i Carracci e Caravaggio", al Museo di Belle Arti di Budapest', in Marco Riccòmini, ed., *Scritti per Eugenio: 27 testi per Eugenio Riccòmini*, Modigliana, Tipografia Fabbri, 2017, 120–31.

Brogi 2018. Alessandro Brogi, 'Ludovico Carracci, effetti di un'invenzione: un caso di tramando di idee nella cerchia degli "incamminati"', *Prospettiva* 172 (2018), 78–93.

Brognara Salazzari 1974. Maddalena Brognara Salazzari, 'Antonio Giarola', in Licisco Magagnato, ed., *Cinquant'anni di pittura veronese 1580–1630* [exh. cat. Verona, Palazzo della Gran Guardia, 3 August–4 November 1974], Verona, Neri Pozza, 1974, 198–202.

Brown 1986. Jonathan Brown, *Velázquez: Painter and Courtier*, New Haven, Yale University Press, 1986.

Brown 1998. Jonathan Brown, *Painting in Spain 1500–1700*, New Haven, Yale University Press, 1998.

Brown 2001. Beverley L. Brown, ed., *The Genius of Rome: 1592–1623* [exh. cat. London, Royal Academy of Arts, 20 January–16 April 2001], London, Royal Academy, 2001.

Brown 2012. Jonathan Brown, *Murillo: Virtuoso Draftsman*, New Haven, Yale University Press, 2012.

Brown and Elliott 2002. Jonathan Brown and John Elliott, eds, *The Sale of the Century: Artistic Relations between Spain and Great Britain (1604–1655)* [exh. cat. Madrid, Museo Nacional del Prado, 13 March–2 June 2002], Madrid, Museo Nacional del Prado; New Haven, Yale University Press, 2002.

Brown and Elliott 2003. Jonathan Brown and John H. Elliott, *A Palace for a King: The Buen Retiro and the Court of Philip IV* [1980], New Haven, Yale University Press, 2003 (rev. and exp. ed.).

Brown and Kagan 1987. Jonathan Brown and Richard L. Kagan, 'The Duke of Alcalá: His Collection and its Evolution', *The Art Bulletin* 69, 2 (1987), 231–55.

Brunforte–Cesari 1860. Ugolino Brunforte, *Fioretti di S. Francesco* [1327–37], ed. Antonio Cesari, Livorno, Giovanni Mazzajoli Editore, 1860.

Buchanan 1824. William Buchanan, *Memoirs of Painting with a Chronological History of the Importation of Pictures by the Great Masters into England since the French Revolution*, 2 vols, London, R. Ackermann, 1824.

Buisseret 1875. Augustin de Buisseret, 'Au Louvre', *L'Art* 1, 1 (1875), 44.

Burke 1984. Marcus B. Burke, 'Private Collections of Italian Art in Seventeenth-Century Spain', 3 vols, PhD diss., University of New York, 1984.

Burke and Cherry 1997. Marcus B. Burke and Peter Cherry, *Collections of Paintings in Madrid, 1601–1755*, 2 vols, Los Angeles, Getty Institute (Documents for the History of Collecting, Spanish Inventories, 1), 1997.

Butiñá 1889. Francisco Butiñá, S. I., *Glorias de San José*, Barcelona, Imprenta y Librería de la Viuda e Hijos de J. Subirana, 1889.

Cabañas Bravo 2005. Miguel Cabañas Bravo, ed., *El arte foráneo en España: presencia e influencia*, Madrid, Consejo Superior de Investigaciones Científicas (Biblioteca de Historia del Arte, 9), 2005.

Cadoppi 2011a. Alberto Cadoppi, 'Il *Cristo Crocifisso* dell'Estense di Modena e un *Ecce Homo*: due quadri di Guido Reni per il nobiluomo reggiano Girolamo Resti', *Reggio Storia* 34, 131 (2011), 7–18.

Cadoppi 2011b. Alberto Cadoppi, '"…Desideroso per sua devotione far fare un ornamento d'altare di marmoro": Girolamo Resti e le vicende della committenza dell'ancona marmorea e del *Cristo crocifisso* di Guido Reni per l'oratorio del Santissimo Sacramento', in Casciu and Ghirelli 2011, 33–50.

Caldari Giovanelli 1992. Claudia Caldari Giovannelli, 'Il cardinale Antonio Maria Gallo a Loreto e Osimo', in Dal Poggetto 1992, 85–93.

Calvi 1808. Jacopo Alessandro Calvi, *Notizie della vita, e delle opere del cavaliere Gioan Francesco Barbieri detto il Guercino da Cento*, Bologna, Tipografia Marsigli, 1808.

Calvo Martín 2014. Rocío Calvo Martín, 'Nuevos datos acerca de la colección Valparaíso de la Real Academia de San Fernando', *Academia. Boletín de la Real Academia de Bellas Artes de San Fernando* 116 (2014), 99–107.

Cambrai–Meyer and Longnon 1882. Raoul de Cambrai, *Chanson de geste*, ed. Paul Meyer and Auguste Longnon, Paris, Librairie de Firmin Didot et Cie., 1882.

Cammarota 2001. Gian Piero Cammarota, *Le origini della Pinacoteca Nazionale di Bologna: una raccolta di fonti*, vol. 3: *La Collezione Zambeccari*, Bologna, Minerva (Fonti e studi, 3), 2001.

Campanini and Samaritani 1999. Graziano Campanini and Antonio Samaritani, eds, *La collegiata di S. Maria Maggiore di Pieve di Cento*, Bologna, Costa Editore, 1999.

Campori 1870. Giuseppe Campori, *Raccolta di cataloghi ed inventarii inediti di quadri, statue, disegni, bronzi, dorerie, smalti, medaglie, avorii, ecc., dal secolo XV al secolo XIX*, Modena, Carlo Vincenzi, 1870.

Candi 2016. Francesca Candi, *D'après le Guide: incisioni seicentesche da Guido Reni*, Bologna, Fondazione Federico Zeri (Nuovi diari di lavoro, 3), 2016.

Cano Rivero and Muñoz Rubio 2018. Ignacio Cano Rivero and María del Valme Muñoz Rubio, eds, *Murillo: IV centenario* [exh. cat. Seville, Museo de Bellas Artes, 29 November 2018–17 March 2019], Seville, Junta de Andalucía, Consejería de Cultura, 2018.

Cantalamessa 1922–23. Giulio Cantalamessa, 'Due Annunciazioni di Guido Reni', *Dedalo* 3, 1 (1922–23), 161–66.

Cappelletti 2009. Francesca Cappelletti, *Caravaggio: un ritratto somigliante*, Milan, Electa, 2009.

Cappelletti 2022a. Francesca Cappelletti, ed., *Guido Reni a Roma: il sacro e la natura / Guido Reni and Rome: Nature and Devotion* [exh. cat. Rome, Galleria Borghese, 1 March–22 May 2022], Venice, Marsilio, 2022.

Cappelletti 2022b. Francesca Cappelletti, 'Il pittore che sapeva troppo: Guido Reni a Roma, fra Aldobrandini e Borghese', in Cappelletti 2022a, 42–59.

Cappelletti and Gennari Santori 2021. Francesca Cappelletti and Flaminia Gennari Santori, eds, *Tempo Barocco* [exh. cat. Rome, Palazzo Barberini, 15 May–3 October 2021], Rome, Officina Libraria, 2021.

Carducci 1853. Giovanni Battista Carducci, *Su le memorie e i monumenti di Ascoli nel Piceno, discorso*, Fermo, Saverio Del Monte, 1853.

Carducho 1634. Vicente Carducho, *Dialogos de la pintura: su defensa, origen, esse[n]cia, definicion, modos y diferencias*, Madrid, Francisco Martínez, 1634.

Carloni 2004. Livia Carloni, 'Un quadro di Reni per i carmelitani di Caprarola', in Bernardini 2004, 69–76.

Carofano 2017. Pierluigi Carofano, ed., *Goya e Guido Reni: tesori d'arte al PALP* [exh. cat. Pontedera, Palazzo Pretorio, 15 June–10 August 2017], Pontedera, Bandecchi & Vivaldi, 2017.

Carrasco Ferrer and Elvira Barba 2016. Marta Carrasco Ferrer and Miguel Ángel Elvira Barba, '*Hipno*, El Sueño en el Museo del Prado: problemas iconográficos', *Eikón Imago* 5, 2 (2016), 27–38.

Carrillo 1616. Fray Juan Carrillo, *Relación histórica de la Real Fundación del Monasterio de las Descalças de S. Clara de la villa de Madrid*, Madrid, Luis Sánchez, 1616.

Carrió Invernizzi 2017. Diana Carrió Invernizzi, 'El convento de la Purísima Concepción de Toledo', in Ida Mauro, Milena Viceconte, and Joan Lluís Palos, eds, *Visiones cruzadas: los virreyes de Nápoles y la imagen de la Monarquía de España en el Barroco*, Barcelona, Universitat de Barcelona Edicions (Transferències 1400–1800, 1), 2017, 185–86.

Casazza and Gennaioli 2005. Ornella Casazza and Riccardo Gennaioli, eds, *Mythologica et Erotica* [exh. cat. Florence, Museo degli Argenti, 1 October 2005–15 January 2006], Livorno, Sillabe, 2005.

Casciu and Ghirelli 2011. Stefano Casciu and Tiziano Ghirelli, *Guido Reni per Reggio Emilia: il ritorno di due capolavori* [exh. cat. Reggio Emilia, Cattedrale e Museo Diocesano, 22 September–12 December 2011], Parma, Grafiche Step, 2011.

Casciu and Toffanello 2014. Stefano Casciu and Marcello Toffanello, eds, *Gli Este, Rinascimento e Barocco a Ferrara e Modena: splendori delle corti italiane* [exh. cat. Venaria Reale, Reggia, Sale delle Arti, 8 March–6 July 2014], Modena, Panini, 2014.

Castellanos de Losada 1847. Basilio Sebastián Castellanos de Losada, *Apuntes para un catálogo de los objetos que comprende la colección del Museo de Antigüedades de la Biblioteca Nacional de Madrid, con esclusión de las numismáticas*, Madrid, Imprenta de Sanchiz, 1847.

Catalogue 1823. *A Catalogue of the Very Distinguished Collection of Italian, French, Flemish, Dutch, and English Pictures of the Finest Class of George Watson Taylor, Esq.* [sale cat. Christie's, London, 13–14 June 1823], London, Christie's, 1823.

Catalogue 1857. *Catalogue of the New York State Library 1856: Maps, Manuscripts, Engravings, Coins, &c*, Albany, Van Benthuysen, 1857.

Catalogue 1867. *Catalogue des tableaux anciens des écoles espagnole, italienne, flamande & hollandaise composant la galerie de M. le M.⁵ de Salamanca, vente en son Hôtel, à Paris, rue de la Victoire, 50* [sale cat. Paris, 3–6 June 1867], Paris, 1867.

Catalogue of Pictures 1831. *Catalogue of Pictures by Italian, Spanish, Flemish, Dutch, and English Masters, with which the Proprietors Have Favoured the Institution*, London, British Institution, 1831.

Catalogus 1807. *Catalogus* [catalogue of the judicial appraisal of paintings found in the princely gallery of the palace on Bankgasse], 1807, manuscript, Vaduz–Vienna, Sammlungen des Fürsten von und zu Liechtenstein, Hausarchiv, Hofkanzleiregistratur 1793–1814, 28/18079.

Cattaneo Adorno et al. 1995. Carlotta Cattaneo Adorno et al., *Il Palazzo Durazzo Pallavicini*, Bologna, Nuova Alfa, 1995.

Caturla 1994. María Luisa Caturla, *Francisco de Zurbarán*, Paris, Wildenstein Institute, 1994.

Cavalli 1954. Gian Carlo Cavalli, ed., *Mostra di Guido Reni* [exh. cat. Bologna, Palazzo dell'Archiginnasio, 1 September–31 October 1954], Bologna, Alfa, 1954.

Cavalli 1955. Gian Carlo Cavalli, ed., *Guido Reni: cronologia della vita e delle opere, catalogo ragionato, antologia critica e bibliografia*, Florence, Vallecchi, 1955.

Cavazzini 1998. Patrizia Cavazzini, *Palazzo Lancellotti ai Coronari: cantiere di Agostino Tassi*, Rome, Istituto Poligrafico e Zecca dello Stato, Libreria dello Stato, 1998.

Cavazzoni 1603. Francesco Cavazzoni, *Pitture et sculture et altre cose notabili che sono in Bologna e dove si trovano*, Bologna, 1603, manuscript, Bologna, Biblioteca Comunale dell'Archiginnasio, Ms B 1343.

Cavazzoni Zanotti 1710. Giampietro Cavazzoni, *Dialogo di Gio. Pietro Cavazzoni Zanotti pittore bolognese in difesa di Guido Reni, stesa in una lettera al Sig. Dottor Girolamo Baruffaldi ferrarese*, Venice, Antonio Bortoli, 1710.

Caylus–Pons 1914. Anne-Claude-Philippe de Caylus, *Voyage d'Italie, 1714–1715*, ed. Amilda A. Pons, Paris, Fischbacher, 1914.

Ceán Bermúdez 1800. Juan Agustín Ceán Bermúdez, *Diccionario histórico de los más ilustres profesores de las Bellas Artes en España*, 6 vols, Madrid, Imprenta de la Viuda de Ibarra, 1800.

Cellini 1992. Marina Cellini, 'Ercole de Maria', in Negro and Pirondini 1992, 203–7.

Cennini–Thompson 1960. Cennino d'Andrea Cennini, *The Craftsman's Handbook: 'Il Libro dell'Arte'*, trans. Daniel V. Thompson Jr., New York, Dover, 1960.

Checa Cremades 2016. Fernando Checa Cremades, ed., *El arte de las naciones: el Barroco como arte global / Art of the Nations: The Baroque as Global Art* [exh. cat. Puebla, Museo Internacional del Barroco, October 2016–March 2017], Puebla, Consejo Estatal para la Cultura y las Artes de Puebla, 2016.

Cherry 2005. Peter Cherry, 'Las fuentes foráneas como impulso para la creación artística de la pintura española', in Cabañas Bravo 2005, 377–88.

Chéruel 1872–1906. Adolphe Chéruel, *Lettres du Cardinal Mazarin pendant son ministère*, 9 vols, Paris, Imprimerie Nationale, 1872–1906.

Chiappini Di Sorio 1983. Ileana Chiappini Di Sorio, 'Cristoforo Roncalli, detto il Pomarancio', in Dell'Acqua and Zampetti 1983.

Chiarini 2001. Marco Chiarini, '*L'Ercole al naturale … con l'Idra morta ai suoi piedi* di Guido Reni, appartenuto al cardinale de' Medici', in Michela Scolaro and Francesco Paolo Di Teodoro, eds, *L'intelligenza della passione: scritti per Andrea Emiliani*, Bologna, Minerva, 2001, 137–41.

Chiodo and Nesi 2011. Sonia Chiodo and Antonella Nesi, eds, *La Collezione Corsi: dipinti italiani dal XIV al XV secolo*, Florence, Centro Di, 2011.

Christiansen 1999. Keith Christiansen, 'Annibale Carracci's *Burial of Christ* Rediscovered', *The Burlington Magazine* 141, 1156 (1999), 414–18.

Ciammitti 2000. Luisa Ciammitti, '"Questo si costuma ora in Bologna": una lettera di Guido Reni, aprile 1628', *Prospettiva* 98–99 (2000), 194–203.

Ciatti, Martini and Torchio 1983. Marco Ciatti, Laura Martini, and Fabio Torchio, *Mostra di opere d'arte restaurate nelle province di Siena e Grosseto, III* [exh. cat. Siena, Pinacoteca Nazionale di Siena, 1983], Genoa, Sagep, 1983.

Cinotti 1983. Mia Cinotti, 'Michelangelo Merisi detto Caravaggio', in Dell'Acqua and Zampetti 1983, 203–641.

Ciociola 2014. Carolina Ciociola, *Nicola Monti (1736–1795)*, Ascoli Piceno, Fas, 2014.

Clark and Whitfield 2010. Edward Clark and Clovis Whitfield, eds, *Caravaggio's Friends & Foes* [exh. cat. London, Whitfield Fine Art, 27 May–23 July 2010], London, Whitfield Fine Art, 2010.

Clerici Bagozzi 2014. Nora Clerici Bagozzi, 'Gli Zambeccari nel palazzo di piazza Calderini: le decorazione del Settecento e dell'Ottocento', *Strenna Storica Bolognese* 64 (2014), 89–121.

Cochin 1759. Charles-Nicolas Cochin, *Voyage d'Italie, ou Recueil de notes sur les ouvrages de peinture & de sculptur, qu'on voit dans les principales villes d'Italie*, 3 vols, Paris, C.-A. Jombert, 1759.

Cochin 1769. Charles-Nicolas Cochin, *Voyage d'Italie, ou Recueil de notes sur les ouvrages de peinture & de sculpture qu'on voit dans les principales villes d'Italie*, 3 vols, Paris, C.-A. Jombert, 1769.

Coiro 2013. Luigi Coiro, 'Algardi e Napoli', in Mariangela Bruno and Daniele Sanguineti, eds, *La Cappella dei Signori Franzoni magnificamente architettata: Alessandro Algardi, Domenico Guidi e uno spazio del Seicento genovese* [papers of the study session, Genoa, Museo di Palazzo Reale, 26 September 2011], Genoa, Sagep, 2013, 157–81.

Colantuono 1997. Anthony Colantuono, *Guido Reni's* Abduction of Helen: *The Politics and Rhetoric of Painting in Seventeenth-Century Europe*, Cambridge, Cambridge University Press, 1997.

Colantuono 2008. Anthony Colantuono, 'Guido Reni's *Latona* for King Philip IV: An Unfinished Masterpiece Lost, Forgotten, Rediscovered and Restored', *Artibus et Historiae* 29, 58 (2008), 201–16.

Coliva et al. 2011. Anna Coliva et al., eds, *I Borghese e l'antico* [exh. cat. Rome, Museo e Galleria Borghese, 7 December 2011–9 April 2012], Milan, Skira, 2011.

Colomer 1990. José Luis Colomer, 'Un tableau "littéraire" et académique au XVIIᵉ siècle: l'*Enlèvement d'Hélène* de Guido Reni', *Revue de l'Art* 90 (1990), 74–87.

Colomer 1996. José Luis Colomer, 'Peinture, histoire antique et scienza nuova entre Rome et Bologne: Virgilio Malvezzi et Guido Reni', in Olivier Bonfait and Christoph Luitpold Frommel, eds, *Poussin et Rome* [papers of the colloquium, Rome, Académie de France and Bibliotheca Hertziana, 16–18 November 1994], Paris, Éditions de la Réunion des Musées Nationaux, 1996, 201–14.

Colomer 1999. José Luis Colomer, 'Roma 1630: *La túnica de José* y el estudio de las "pasiones"', *Reales Sitios* 36, 141 (1999), 39–49.

Colomer 2006. José Luis Colomer, 'Guido Reni en las colecciones reales españolas', in Colomer and Serra Desfilis 2006, 213–39.

Colomer 2008. José Luis Colomer, 'La *Adoración de los pastores* de Pietro da Cortona: regalos artísticos de Francesco Barberini a Felipe IV', *Boletín del Museo del Prado* 26, 44 (2008), 6–22.

Colomer and Serra Desfilis 2006. José Luis Colomer and Amadeo Serra Desfilis, eds, *España y Bolonia: siete siglos de relaciones artísticas y culturales*, Madrid, Centro de Estudios Europa Hispánica, Fundación Carolina and Villaverde, 2006.

Colonna 2007. Stefano Colonna, *La Galleria dei Carracci in Palazzo Farnese a Roma: Eros, Anteros, età dell'oro*, Rome, Gangemi, 2007.

Comboni 2000. Andrea Comboni, 'Eros e Anteros nella poesia italiana del Rinascimento: appunti per una ricerca', *Italique* 3 (2000), 7–21.

Conca 1793–97. Antonio Conca, *Descrizione odeporica della Spagna in cui specialmente si dà notizia delle cose spettanti alle belle arti degne dell'attenzione del curioso viaggiatore*, 4 vols, Parma, Stamperia Reale, 1793–97.

Condivi [1553] 1823. Ascanio Condivi, *Vita di Michelagnolo Buonarroti* [1553], Pisa, Capurro, 1823.

Coppel 1998. Rosario Coppel, *Catálogo de la escultura de época moderna: Museo del Prado, siglos XVI-XVIII*, Madrid, Museo del Prado; Santander, Fundación Marcelino Botín, 1998.

Coppel 2013. Rosario Coppel, 'Infant Christ Sleeping', in *Faces*, Madrid, Coll & Cortés, 2013, 182–93.

Corbin, Courtine and Vigarello 2005. Alain Corbin, Jean-Jacques Courtine, and Georges Vigarello, eds, *Historia del cuerpo*, vol. 1: *Del Renacimiento al Siglo de las Luces*, Madrid, Taurus, 2005.

Cortese 1677. Isabella Cortese, *Secreti varii, della signora Isabella Cortese, ne' quali si contengono cose minerali, medicinali, profumi, belletti, artifitij, & alchimia, con altre belle curiosità aggiunte*, Venice, Antonio Tivanni, 1677.

Coryate [1611] 1978. Thomas Coryate, *Coryats Crudities* [1611], intr. William M. Schutte, London, Scolar Press, 1978.

Cosnac 1884. Gabriel-Jules de Cosnac, *Les richesses du Palais Mazarin*, Paris, Renouard, 1884.

Costamagna, Härb and Prosperi Valenti Rodinò 2005. Philippe Costamagna, Florian Härb, and Simonetta Prosperi Valenti Rodinò, eds, *Disegno, giudizio e bella maniera: studi sul disegno italiano in onore di Catherine Monbeig Goguel*, Cinisello Balsamo, Silvana, 2005.

Costantini 1928. Vincenzo Costantini, *Guido Reni*, Milan, Alpes, 1928.

Cotté 1985. Sabine Cotté, 'Inventaire après décès de Louis Phélypeaux de La Vrillière', *Archives de l'Art Français* 27 (1985), 89–100.

Cottino 2001. Alberto Cottino, *Michele Desubleo*, Soncino, Edizioni del Soncino, 2001.

Cremonini 1998. Claudia Cremonini, 'Le raccolte d'arte del cardinale Alessandro d'Este: vicende collezionistiche tra Modena e Roma', in Jadranka Bentini, ed., *Sovrane passioni: studi sul collezionismo estense*, Milan, Federico Motta, 1998, 91–137.

Crespi 1769. Luigi Crespi, *Vite de' pittori bolognesi non descritte nella Felsina Pittrice*, Rome, Marco Pagliarini, 1769.

Crinò 1963. Anna Maria Crinò, 'A Letter Concerning Guido Reni', *The Burlington Magazine* 105, 726 (1963), 404 + 408.

Crispo 2018. Alberto Crispo, 'Il Maestro della morte di Didone alias Jan van Dalen: un artista italianizzante nei Paesi Bassi del Seicento', *Parma per l'Arte* 24 (2018), 257–83.

Cristofori and Scanu 2022. Romeo Pio Cristofori and Laura Scanu, *Guido Reni in Rome: A Guide*, Venice, Marsilio Arte, 2022.

Cropper 1984. Elizabeth Cropper, *The Ideal of Painting: Pietro Testa's Düsseldorf Notebook*, Princeton, Princeton University Press, 1984.

Cropper 1992. Elizabeth Cropper, 'Marino's *Strage degli innocenti*: Poussin, Rubens and Guido Reni', *Studi Secenteschi* 33 (1992), 137–64.

Cropper 2017. Elizabeth Cropper, *La pintura boloñesa en el Prado: tras las huellas de Malvasia como crítico de la pintura*, Madrid, Museo Nacional del Prado and Abada, 2017.

Cruz Yábar 2017–18. Juan María Cruz Yábar, 'El octavo espejo: *Las Meninas* en el despacho de verano del Alcázar de Madrid', *Anuario del Departamento de Historia y Teoría del Arte* 29–30 (2017–18), 169–90.

Cruzada Villaamil 1885. Gregorio Cruzada Villaamil, *Anales de la vida y de las obras de Diego de Silva Velázquez, escritos con ayuda de nuevos documentos*, Madrid, Miguel Guijarro, 1885.

Cuenca García, Hernández Pugh and Matilla 2019. María Luisa Cuenca García, Ana Hernández Pugh, and José Manuel Matilla, eds, *El maestro de papel: cartillas para aprender a dibujar de los siglos XVII al XIX* [exh. cat. Madrid, Museo Nacional del Prado, 15 October 2019–2 February 2020], Madrid, Museo Nacional del Prado and Centro de Estudios Europa Hispánica, 2019.

Cuppini 1952. Luciano Cuppini, 'L'ultima maniera di Guido Reni', *Commentari* 3 (1952), 265–73.

Cuppini and Matteucci 1969. Giampiero Cuppini and Anna Maria Matteucci Armandi, *Ville del Bolognese*, Bologna, Zanichelli, 1969 (2nd ed.).

Cuppini and Roversi 1974. Giampiero Cuppini and Giancarlo Roversi, *I palazzi senatorii a Bologna: architettura come immagine del potere*, Bologna, Zanichelli, 1974.

Curti 2007. Francesca Curti, *Committenza, collezionismo e mercato dell'arte tra Roma e Bologna nel Seicento: la quadreria di Cristiana Duglioli Angelelli*, Rome, Gangemi, 2007.

Dal Poggetto 1992. Paolo Dal Poggetto, ed., *Le arti nelle Marche al tempo di Sisto V* [exh. cat. Ascoli Piceno, Palazzo dei Capitani del Popolo and Palazzo Comunale-Sala dei Mercatori, 1992], Cinisiello Balsamo, Silvana, 1992.

Dal Pozzolo 2022. Enrico Maria Dal Pozzolo, 'Apri el cuore', in Ferino-Pagden, Del Torre Scheuch and Deiters 2022, 131–37.

D'Albo 2017. Odette D'Albo, 'Camillo y Giulio Cesare Procaccini al servicio de los gobernadores españoles en Milán', *Boletín del Museo del Prado* 35, 53 (2017), 66–75.

D'Albo 2018. Odette D'Albo, 'Giulio Cesare Procaccini "per Fiorenza": la destinazione del *San Carlo Borromeo* e *San Michele Arcangelo* di Dublino', *Paragone* 69, 815 (2018), 74–85.

Dallinger 1807. Johann Dallinger, *Inventaire manuscrit*, 1807, manuscript, Vaduz–Vienna, Sammlungen des Fürsten von und zu Liechtenstein, Hausarchiv.

D'Amico 1979. Rosa D'Amico, 'La Raccolta Zambeccari e il collezionismo bolognese del Settecento', in Jadranka Bentini and Rosa D'Amico, eds, *Biennale d'arte antica. L'arte del Settecento emiliano: l'arredo sacro e profano a Bologna e nelle Legazioni Pontificie* [exh. cat. Bologna, Palazzo Pepoli Campogrande–Pinacoteca Nazionale, 8 September–25 November 1979], Bologna, Alfa, 1979, 191–226.

Danesi Squarzina 1998. Silvia Danesi Squarzina, 'Natura morta e il collezionismo a Roma nella prima metà del Seicento: il terreno di elaborazione dei generi', *Storia dell'Arte* 93–94 (1998), 266–91.

Danieli 2010. Michele Danieli, 'Gli incisori fiamminghi di Dionisio Calvaert', in Sabine Frommel, ed., *Crocevia e capitale della migrazione artistica: forestieri a Bologna e bolognesi nel mondo (secoli XV–XVI)* [proceedings of the international congress, Bologna, May 2009], Bologna, Bononia University Press, 2010, 469–82.

De Dominici 1742–45. Bernardo De Dominici, *Vite de' pittori, scultori, ed architetti napoletani non mai date alla luce da autore alcuno,* 3 vols, Naples, Stamperia del Ricciardi, 1742–45.

Degli Esposti 1993. Carlo Degli Esposti, 'Un lungo viaggio verso la "magnificenza": il santuario prima della ricostruzione settecentesca', in Mario Fanti and Giancarlo Roversi, eds, *La Madonna di San Luca in Bologna: otto secoli di storia, di arte e di fede,* Cinisello Balsamo, Silvana, 1993, 137–45.

Degli Esposti 1998. Carlo Degli Esposti, 'Visita alla chiesa', in Mario Fanti and Carlo Degli Esposti, *La chiesa di San Giacomo Maggiore in Bologna,* Bologna, Inchiostri Associati, 1998, 91–107.

Del Gallo 1998. Elena Del Gallo, *sub voce* 'Franciotti, Cesare', in *Dizionario biografico degli italiani,* vol. 50, Rome, Istituto della Enciclopedia Italiana, 1998. Accessible at https://www.treccani.it/enciclopedia/cesare-franciotti_%28Dizionario-Biografico%29/.

Dell'Acqua and Zampetti 1983. Gian Alberto Dell'Acqua and Pietro Zampetti, eds, *I pittori bergamaschi dal XIII al XIX secolo,* vol 4: *Il Seicento,* Bergamo, Poligrafiche Bolis, 1983.

Dempsey 1995. Charles Dempsey, *Annibale Carracci: The Farnese Gallery, Rome,* New York, George Braziller, 1995.

Dempsey 2008. Charles Dempsey, 'Prefazione', in Bohn 2008, XI–XIV.

Denunzio 2000. Antonio E. Denunzio, 'Una nota di pagamento per Guido Reni e qualche aggiunta per Domenichino, Carlo Saraceni e Lanfranco al servizio del Cardinale Odoardo Farnese', *Aurea Parma* 84, 3 (2000), 365–86.

Denunzio 2004. Antonio E. Denunzio, 'Per Nicolò Radolovich e il conte-duca di Benavente: testimonianze e riflessioni su due committenti di Caravaggio', *Quaderni dell'Archivio Storico* (2004), 63–82.

Description des tableaux **1780.** *Description des tableaux, et des piéces de sculpture, que renferme la Gallerie de son altesse François Joseph chef et prince régnant de la maison de Liechtenstein,* Vienna, Jean Thomas Trattner, 1780.

Descrizione di Roma moderna **1739.** *Descrizione di Roma moderna,* 2 vols, Rome, Gregorio Roisecco, 1739.

Dézallier d'Argenville 1762. Antoine-Joseph Dézallier d'Argenville, *Abrégé de la vie des plus fameux peintres,* 4 vols, Paris, De Bure, 1762.

Di Gioia 2007. Elena Bianca Di Gioia, 'Il dono segreto di Francesco Bichi: Raffaello, Michelangelo e il fantasma di Bernini', in Elena Bianca Di Gioia, ed., *La Medusa di Gian Lorenzo Bernini: studi e restauri,* Rome, Campisano, 2007, 137–93.

Di Meola 2003. Barbara Di Meola, 'La collezione del Cardinale Girolamo I Colonna', in Francesca Cappelletti, ed., *Decorazione e collezionismo a Roma nel Seicento: vicende di artisti, committenti e mercanti,* Rome, Gangemi (Artisti, opere, committenti, 1) 2003, 113–25.

Diéguez-Rodríguez 2010. Ana Diéguez-Rodríguez, 'Dos pinturas de Denis Calvaert identificadas en los fondos del Museo del Prado', *Archivo Español de Arte* 83, 330 (2010), 173–78.

Diéguez-Rodríguez and González Martínez 2008. Ana Diéguez-Rodríguez and Eloy González Martínez, 'Dos imágenes del amor para Felipe IV: Guido Reni y Guercino', in César Chaparro et al., eds, *Paisajes emblemáticos: la construcción de la imagen simbólica en Europa y América* [proceedings of the international congress, Sociedad Española de Emblemática, Cáceres, March 2005], Mérida, Editorial Regional de Extremadura, 2008, 535–52.

Diotallevi 2013. Daniele Diotallevi, ed., *Guido Reni, 'La consegna delle chiavi': un capolavoro ritorna* [exh. cat. Fano, Pinacoteca San Domenico, 15 June–29 September 2013], Fano, Grapho5, 2013.

Dirani 1982. Maria Teresa Dirani, 'Mecenati, pittori e mercato dell'arte nel Seicento: il *Ratto di Elena* di Guido Reni e la *Morte di Didone* del Guercino nella corrispondenza del cardinale Bernardino Spada', *Ricerche di Storia dell'Arte* 16 (1982), 83–94.

Dolce 1557. Lodovico Dolce, *Dialogo della pittura intitolato l'Aretino,* Venice, Gabriel Giolito de' Ferrari, 1557.

D'Onofrio 1964. Cesare D'Onofrio, 'Inventario dei dipinti del cardinal Pietro Aldobrandini compilato da G. B. Agucchi nel 1603', *Palatino* 8 (1964), 15–20, 158–62, and 202–11.

Dossi 2008. Davide Dossi, 'La collezione di Agostino e Gian Giacomo Giusti', *Verona Illustrata* 21 (2008), 109–26.

Dossi and Marcorin 2020. Davide Dossi and Francesco Marcorin, *Le collezioni di Agostino e Giovan Giacomo Giusti a Verona: storia e dispersione,* Treviso, Zel Edizioni, 2020.

Dubois de Saint-Gelais 1727. Louis-François Dubois de Saint-Gelais, *Description des tableaux du Palais Royal avec la vie des peintres à la tête de leurs ouvrages,* Paris, D'Houry, 1727.

Ebert-Schiffer, Emiliani and Schleier 1988. Sybille Ebert-Schiffer, Andrea Emiliani, and Erich Schleier, eds, *Guido Reni e l'Europa: fama e fortuna / Guido Reni und Europa: Ruhm und Nachruhm* [exh. cat. Frankfurt, Schirn Kunsthalle Frankfurt, 1 December 1988–26 February 1989], Frankfurt, Schirn Kunsthalle Frankfurt; Bologna, Nuova Alfa, 1988.

Eclercy 2015. Bastian Eclercy, 'Kunststück no. 55. Guido Reni: Himmelfahrt Mariens, um 1596/97', *Weltkunst* 104 (2015), 106.

Eclercy 2022a. Bastian Eclercy, ed., *Guido Reni: The Divine* [exh. cat. Frankfurt, Städel Museum, 23 November 2022–5 March 2023], Berlin, Hatje Cantz, 2022.

Eclercy 2022b. Bastian Eclercy, 'Guido Reni and the Beauty of the Divine: The Assumption of the Virgin and its Metamorphoses', in Eclercy 2022a, 14–39.

Elliott 2002. John H. Elliott, 'Royal Patronage and Collecting in Seventeenth-Century Spain', in Simonetta Cavaciocchi, ed., *Economia e arte, secc. XIII–XVIII* [papers from the 33rd study week, Prato, 30 April–4 May 2000], Florence, Le Monnier (Istituto Internazionale di Storia Economica F. Datini, Prato, 2, 33), 2002, 551–66.

Emiliani 1973. Andrea Emiliani, ed., *La Collezione Zambeccari nella Pinacoteca Nazionale di Bologna: indagine di metodo per la realizzazione di un catalogo storico e critico delle raccolte statali bolognesi,* Bologna, Pinacoteca Nazionale di Bologna (Rapporto della Soprintendenza alle Gallerie di Bologna, 19), 1973.

Emiliani 1988. Andrea Emiliani, 'La vita, i simboli e la fortuna di Guido Reni' / 'The Life, Symbolism, and Fame of Guido Reni', in Emiliani et al. 1988, XVII–CIII (Italian); 17–99 (English).

Emiliani 1990. Andrea Emiliani, 'Per Guido Reni', *Accademia Clementina, Atti e Memorie* 25 (1990), 87–109.

Emiliani 1997. Andrea Emiliani, ed., *Simone Cantarini detto il Pesarese, 1612–1648* [exh. cat. Bologna, Accademia di Belle Arti and Pinacoteca Nazionale, 11 October 1997–6 January 1998], Milan, Electa, 1997.

Emiliani 2000. Andrea Emiliani, 'Guido Reni', in Borea and Gasparri 2000, 2:342–54.

Emiliani 2018. Andrea Emiliani, ed., *Bacco e Arianna di Guido Reni: singolari vicende e nuove proposte / Unusual Events and New Proposals* [exh. cat. Bologna, Pinacoteca Nazionale di Bologna, 11 October–15 November 2018], Rimini, NFC, 2018.

Emiliani et al. 1988. Andrea Emiliani et al., *Guido Reni, 1575–1642* [exh. cat. Bologna, Pinacoteca Nazionale, Accademia di Belle Arti, and Museo Civico Archeologico, 5 September–10 November 1988; Los Angeles, Los Angeles County Museum of Art, 11 December 1988–14 February 1989; Fort Worth, Kimbell Art Museum, 10 March–10 May 1989], Bologna, Nuova Alfa, 1988.

Erra 1759–60. Carlantonio Erra, *Memorie de' religiosi per pietà e dottrina insigni della Congregazione della Madre di Dio,* 2 vols, Rome, Giuseppe e Niccolò Grossi, 1759–60.

Espinós et al. 1986. Adela Espinós et al., '"El Prado disperso": cuadros depositados en Barcelona. I', *Boletín del Museo del Prado* 7, 19 (1986), 43–60.

Estenaga y Echevarría 1929–30. Narciso de Estenaga y Echevarría, *El Cardenal Aragón (1626–1677), estudio histórico,* 2 vols, Paris, Imp. E. Desfossés, 1929–30.

Evangelisti 1983. Gino Evangelisti, 'Bernardino Spada: legato (e collegato) di Bologna, 1627–1631', *Strenna Storica Bolognese* 33 (1983), 117–38.

Evans 1970. Joan Evans, *John Ruskin*, New York, Haskell, 1970.

Extermann 2011. Grégoire Extermann, '"Un talent digne de Périclès": Lorenzo Bartolini e la Grecia', in Franca Falletti, Silvestra Bietoletti, and Annarita Caputo, eds *Lorenzo Bartolini, scultore del bello naturale* [exh. cat. Florence, Galleria dell'Accademia, 31 May–6 November 2011], Florence, Giunti, 2011, 72–85.

Fagiolo and Madonna 1984. Marcello Fagiolo and Maria Luisa Madonna, eds, *Roma 1300–1875: l'arte degli anni santi* [exh. cat. Rome, Museo Nazionale del Palazzo di Venezia, 20 December 1984–5 April 1985], Rome, Mondadori, 1984.

Faietti 1988. Marzia Faietti, 'Conoscenza critica e restauro: *Elia e l'Angelo* di Guido Reni a Ravenna', *Accademia Clementina, Atti e Memorie* 22 (1988), 67–81.

Faietti 2015. Marzia Faietti, '"Una certa facilità e disinvoltura parmigianesca": Guido Reni e l'acquaforte', in Susanne Meurer, Anna Schreurs-Morét, and Lucia Simonato, eds., *Aus aller Herren Länder*, Turnhout, Brepols (Collection Théorie de l'Art, 8), 2015, 110–23.

Faietti, Oberhuber and Rosenauer 1990. Marzia Faietti, Konrad Oberhuber, and Artur Rosenauer, 'Nuove proposte su Guido Reni a seguito della rassegna bolognese', *Accademia Clementina, Atti e Memorie* 25 (1990), 59–79.

Falke 1873. Jacob von Falke, *Katalog der Fürstlich Liechtensteinischen Bilder-Galerie im Gartenpalais der Rossau zu Wien*, Vienna, Verlag von H. O. Miethke, 1873.

Falke 1885. Jacob von Falke, *Katalog der Fürstlich Liechtensteinischen Bilder-Galerie im Gartenpalais der Rossau zu Wien*, Vienna, Verlag der Fürstlichen Galerie, 1885.

Falomir 2003. Miguel Falomir, ed., *Tiziano* [exh. cat. Madrid, Museo Nacional del Prado, 10 June–7 September 2003], Madrid, Museo Nacional del Prado, 2003.

Falomir 2007. Miguel Falomir, '*Christ Mocked*, a Late "invenzione" by Titian', *Artibus et Historiae* 28, 55 (2007), 53–61.

Faluschi 1784. Giovacchino Faluschi, *Breve relazione delle cose notabili della città di Siena*, Siena, Roffi, 1784.

Faluschi 1815. Giovacchino Faluschi, *Breve relazione delle cose notabili della città di Siena*, Siena, Mucci, 1815 (2nd ed.).

Fanti 1767. Vincenzo Fanti, *Descrizzione completa di tutto ciò che ritrovasi nella Galleria di Pittura e Scultura di Sua Altezza Giuseppe Wenceslao del S. R. I., Principe Regnante della casa di Liechtenstein*, Vienna, Trattner, 1767.

Farina 2002. Viviana Farina, *Giovan Carlo Doria: promotore delle arti a Genova nel primo Seicento*, Florence, Edifir (Le voci del museo, 8), 2002.

Farina 2014. Viviana Farina, *Al sole e all'ombra di Ribera: questioni di pittura e disegno a Napoli nella prima metà del Seicento*, Castellammare di Stabia, Longobardi, 2014.

Farina 2018. Viviana Farina, 'El arte en Nápoles en la época del gobierno del III duque de Osuna

(1616–1621)', in Pedro Jaime Moreno de Soto, ed., *Italia en Osuna* [exh. cat. Osuna, Colegiata de Nuestra Señora de la Asunción and Monasterio de la Encarnación y Nuestra Señora de Trápana, 26 October 2018–4 April 2019], Osuna, Patronato de Arte de Osuna y Amigos de los Museos de Osuna, 2018, 45–91.

Felton 1991. Craig Felton, 'Ribera's Early Years in Italy: The *Martyrdom of St Lawrence* and the *Five Senses*', *The Burlington Magazine* 133, 1055 (1991), 71–81.

Ferino-Pagden 2022. Sylvia Ferino-Pagden, 'Le "Belle veneziane": spose poetizzate?', in Ferino-Pagden, Del Torre Scheuch and Deiters 2022, 147–79.

Ferino-Pagden, Del Torre Scheuch and Deiters 2022. Sylvia Ferino-Pagden, Francesca Del Torre Scheuch, and Wencke Deiters, eds, *Tiziano e l'immagine della donna nel Cinquecento veneziano* [exh. cat. Milan, Palazzo Reale, 23 February–5 June 2022], Milan, Skira, 2022.

Fernández Bayton 1975–85. Gloria Fernández Bayton, *Inventarios reales: testamentaría del Rey Carlos II: 1701–1703*, Madrid, Museo del Prado, 1975–85.

Fernández Gasalla 1992. Leopoldo Fernández Gasalla, 'Las obras de Guido Reni en la colección del arzobispo de Santiago, don Pedro Carillo (1656–1667)', *Boletín del Seminario de Estudios de Arte y Arqueología* 58 (1992), 431–35.

Fernández Gracia 2002. Ricardo Fernández Gracia, *Arte, devoción y política: la promoción de las artes en torno a sor María de Ágreda*, Soria, Diputación Provincial de Soria, 2002.

Fernández-Miranda 1988–91. Fernando Fernández-Miranda, *Inventarios Reales: Carlos III, 1789–1790*, 3 vols, Madrid, Patrimonio Nacional, 1988–91.

Fernández Pardo 1996. Francisco Fernández Pardo, ed., *Pintura flamenca barroca (cobres, siglo XVII)* [exh. cat. Vitoria-Gasteiz, Sala Fundación Caja Vital Kutxa, 7 March–20 April 1997], San Sebastián, Diócesis de Calahorra y La Calzada-Logroño, 1996.

Ferretti 2019. Massimo Ferretti, 'Da Guido Reni a Guercino: le mostre bolognesi dal 1954 al 1968', in Michela di Macco and Giuseppe Dardanello, eds, *Fortuna del Barocco in Italia: le grandi mostre del Novecento*, Genoa, Sagep (Quaderni di ricerca, 2), 2019, 177–95.

Ferri 1832. Marco Ferri, *Guida della città di Siena per gli amatori delle belle-arti*, Siena, Marco Ferri e Figlio, 1832 (2nd ed.).

Ferriani 1992. Daniela Ferriani, 'La chiesa di Santa Maria della Carità ad Ascoli Piceno', in Dal Poggetto 1992, 153–56.

Ferriani 1994. Daniela Ferriani, ed., *Ascoli Piceno: Pinacoteca Civica*, Bologna, Calderini (Musei d'Italia, Meraviglie d'Italia, 29), 1994.

Ferriani 1995. Daniela Ferriani, ed., *Pinacoteca civica: Ascoli Piceno*, Florence, Octavo, 1995.

Ferriani 2011. Daniela Ferriani, 'Il *Crocifisso* del *Santissimo Sacramento*: a zonzo per la vicenda critica vecchia e nuova', in Casciu and Ghirelli 2011, 67–81.

Fidanza and Serafinelli 2022. Giovan Battista Fidanza and Guendalina Serafinelli, *Patronage and Devotion: A Focus on Six Roman Baroque Paintings*, London, Paul Holberton, 2022.

Finaldi 1991. Gabriele Finaldi, 'The Patron and Date of Ribera's *Crucifixion* at Osuna', *The Burlington Magazine* 133, 1060 (1991), 445–46.

Finaldi 2007. Gabriele Finaldi, 'Works by Alessandro Turchi for Spain and an Unexpected Velázquez Connection', *The Burlington Magazine* 149, 1256 (2007), 749–58.

Finaldi 2009. Gabriele Finaldi, 'Sobre Maíno e Italia', in Ruiz Gómez 2009a, 41–55.

Finaldi 2011. Gabriele Finaldi, '"Se è quello che dipinse un S. Martino in Parma…": ancora sull'attività del giovane Ribera a Parma', in Spinosa 2011, 16–29.

Finaldi 2013. Gabriele Finaldi, 'Zurbarán, il "Caravaggio spagnolo" e la pittura italiana', in Ignacio Cano Rivero, ed., *Zurbarán (1598–1664)* [exh. cat. Ferrara, Palazzo dei Diamanti, 14 September 2013–6 January 2014], Ferrara, Fondazione Ferrara Arte, 2013, 49–59.

Finaldi 2014. Gabriele Finaldi, 'Francisco Zurbarán, "le Caravage espagnol" et la peinture italienne', in Ignacio Cano Rivero, ed., *Francisco de Zurbarán (1598–1664)* [exh. cat. Brussels, Palais des Beaux-Arts, 29 January–25 May 2014], Brussels, Bozar Books and Fonds Mercator, 2014, 43–53.

Finaldi and Kitson 1997. Gabriele Finaldi and Michael Kitson, *Discovering the Italian Baroque: The Denis Mahon Collection* [exh. cat. London, The National Gallery, 26 February–18 May 1997], London, National Gallery Publications, 1997.

Finaldi and Savvateev 2011. Gabriele Finaldi and Svjatoslav Savvateev, eds, *El Prado en el Hermitage* [exh. cat. St Petersburg, State Hermitage Museum, 25 February–29 May 2011], St Petersburg, State Hermitage Museum and Museo Nacional del Prado, 2011.

Fiocco 1958. Giuseppe Fiocco, 'Una pala ritrovata di Guido Reni', *Arte Antica e Moderna* 1, 4 (1958), 388–89.

Fiorillo 1991. Ciro Fiorillo, 'Una vendita all'asta nel Real Museo Borbonico (II)', *Napoli Nobilissima* 4, 30 (1991), 135–44.

Fleischer 1910. Victor Fleischer, *Fürst Karl Eusebius von Liechtenstein als Bauherr und Kunstsammler (1611–1684)*, Vienna and Leipzig, C.W. Stern, 1910.

Follino 1608. Federico Follino, *Compendio delle sontuose feste fatte l'anno MDCVIII nella città di Mantova, per le reali nozze del Serenissimo Prencipe D. Francesco Gonzaga, con la Serenissima Infante Margherita di Savoia*, Mantua, Aurelio & Lodovico Osanna Stampatori Ducali, 1608.

Fontenai 1786. L'Abbé de Fontenai, *Galerie du Palais-royal, gravée d'après les tableaux des différentes écoles qui la composent, avec un abrégé de la vie des peintres et une description historique de chaque tableau*, Paris, J. Couché and J. Bouillard, 1786.

Forgione 2020. Gianluca Forgione, *I Girolamini: storie di artisti e committenti a Napoli nel Seicento*, Rome, Paparo, 2020.

Forgione and Saracino 2019. Gianluca Forgione and Francesco Saracino, 'Per una ricostruzione dell'*Apostolado* del Duca d'Alcalá', *Napoli Nobilissima* 7, 5, 3 (2019), 5–19.

Fortini 1999. Paola Fortini, 'Confraternite e iniziativa privata dal Rinascimento al Barocco', in Campanini and Samaritani 1999, 39–46.

Franck and Malgouyres 2015. Louis Franck and Philippe Malgouyres, eds, *La fabrique des saintes images: Rome–Paris 1580–1660* [exh. cat. Paris, Musée du Louvre, 2 April–29 June 2015], Paris, Louvre Éditions and Somogy, 2015.

Franco 1580. Veronica Franco, *Lettere familiari a diversi della S. Veronica Franca*, [Venice], 1580.

Franco Durán 1997. María Jesús Franco Durán, 'El mito de Atalanta e Hipómenes: fuentes grecolatinas y su pervivencia en la literatura española', PhD diss., Universidad Complutense de Madrid, 1997.

Franco Durán 2001. María Jesús Franco Durán, ed., *Gaspar de Ovando, 'La Atalanta'*, Kassel, Reichenberger (Ediciones críticas, 117), 2001.

Francucci 2013. Massimo Francucci, 'Tra Guido Reni e il Pomarancio: la committenza del cardinale Antonio Maria Gallo a Osimo e Loreto', in Sgarbi and Papetti 2013, 39–45.

Francucci 2014. Massimo Francucci, *Giuseppe Puglia, il Bastaro: il naturalismo classicizzato nella Roma di Urbano VIII*, San Casciano Val di Pesa, Libro Co., 2014.

Francucci 2015. Massimo Francucci, 'Giovanni Giacomo Sementi tra Bologna e Roma', *Paragone* 66, 787–89 (2015), 21–35.

Francucci 2017. Massimo Francucci, 'Guido Reni, Antonio Giarola', in Vittorio Sgarbi, ed., *Da Raffaello a Balla: capolavori dell'Accademia Nazionale di San Luca* [exh. cat. Forte di Bard, 1 July 2017–7 January 2018], Bard, Forte di Bard editore, 2017, 76–77.

Francucci 2020. Massimo Francucci, 'Il cardinale Antonio Maria Gallo tra Rinascimento e Modernità', *The Art Master* 3 (2020), 152–61.

Francucci 2021. Massimo Francucci, 'Precisazioni e nuove proposte sul passaggio di Guido Reni a Roma', *About Art online* (19 December 2021). Accessible at https://www.aboutartonline.com/precisazioni-e-nuove-proposte-sul-passaggio-di-guido-reni-a-roma/.

Fréart de Chantelou–Lalanne 1986. Paul Fréart de Chantelou, *Diario del viaje del caballero Bernini a Francia*, ed. Ludovic Lalanne, intr. Valeriano Bozal, Madrid, Consejo General de Colegios Oficiales de Aparejadores y Arquitectos Técnicos, 1986.

Friedlaender 1928–29. Walter Friedlaender, 'Der antimanieristische Stil um 1590 und sein Verhältnis zum Übersinnlichen', *Vorträge der Bibliothek Warburg* 2 (1928–29), 214–43.

Friedlaender 1945. Walter Friedlaender, 'The *Crucifixion of St Peter*: Caravaggio and Reni', *Journal of the Warburg and Courtauld Institutes* 8 (1945), 152–60.

Frommel 2013. Sabine Frommel, ed., *Crocevia e capitale della migrazione artistica: forestieri a Bologna e bolognesi nel mondo (secolo XVIII)* [proceedings of the international congress, Bologna, 22–24 May 2012], Bologna, Bononia University Press, 2013.

Frutos Sastre 2006. Leticia M. Frutos Sastre, 'Las colecciones del Marqués del Carpio', in José Manuel Pita Andrade and Ángel Rodríguez Rebollo, eds, *Tras el centenario de Felipe IV: jornadas de iconografía y coleccionismo dedicadas al profesor Alfonso E. Pérez Sánchez* [proceedings, Madrid, 5–7 April 2006], Madrid, Fundación Universitaria Española, 2006, 207–70.

Frutos Sastre 2009. Leticia M. Frutos Sastre, *El Templo de la Fama: alegoría del Marqués del Carpio*, Madrid, Fundación Caja Madrid and Fundación Arte Hispánico, 2009.

Frutos Sastre 2016. Leticia M. Frutos Sastre, 'El retrato de un valido: las colecciones artísticas de don Luis de Haro', in Rafael Valladares Ramírez, ed., *El mundo de un valido: don Luis de Haro y su entorno, 1643–1661*, Madrid, Marcial Pons, 2016, 347–76.

Fumagalli 1990. Elena Fumagalli, 'Guido Reni (e altri) a San Gregorio al Celio e a San Sebastiano fuori le Mura', *Paragone* 41, 483 (1990), 67–94.

Fumagalli 1994. Elena Fumagalli, 'Guido Reni e il cardinale Carlo de' Medici', *Paragone* 45, 529–33 (1994), 240–46.

Fumaroli 1987. Marc Fumaroli, 'Une peinture de méditation: à propos de l'*Hippomène et Atalante* du Guide', in *'Il se rendit en Italie': études offertes à André Chastel*, Rome, Edizioni dell'Elefante; Paris, Flammarion, 1987, 337–58.

Fumaroli 1997. Marc Fumaroli, 'El abrazo de *Las Lanzas*', in Javier Portús Pérez, ed., *El Museo del Prado: fragmentos y detalles* [conference cycle, Madrid, October 1996–March 1997], Madrid, Fundación Amigos del Museo del Prado, 1997, 39–61.

Furlotti 2000. Barbara Furlotti, *Le collezioni Gonzaga: il carteggio tra Bologna, Parma, Piacenza e Mantova (1563–1634)*, Cinisello Balsamo, Silvana, 2000.

Furlotti 2003. Barbara Furlotti, *Le collezioni Gonzaga: il carteggio tra Roma e Mantova (1587–1612)*, Cinisello Balsamo, Silvana, 2003.

Fusconi 2001. Giulia Fusconi, ed., *I Giustiniani e l'antico* [exh. cat. Rome, Palazzo Fontana di Trevi, 26 October 2001–27 January 2002], Rome, L'Erma di Bretschneider, 2001.

Gállego 2011. Julián Gállego, *La realidad trascendida y otros estudios sobre Velázquez*, Madrid, Centro de Estudios Europa Hispánica, 2011.

Galli 1928. Romeo Galli, *La collezione d'arte di Carlo Maratti: inventario e notizie*, Bologna, Azzoguidi, 1928.

Gallo 1992. Marco Gallo, 'Orazio Borgianni, l'Accademia di S. Luca e l'Accademia degli Humoristi: documenti e nuove datazioni', *Storia dell'Arte* 76 (1992), 296–345.

Gallo 1997. Marco Gallo, *Orazio Borgianni: pittore romano (1574–1616) e Francisco de Castro, Conte di Castro*, Rome, UNI, 1997.

Galvani 1864. Giovanni Galvani, *Cenni storici relativi alla B. V. Assunta in Cielo dipinta da Guido Reni per la venerabile confraternita di Santa Maria degli Angioli in Spilamberto*, Modena, Vincenzi, 1864.

Gambassi 1989. Osvaldo Gambassi, *Il concerto palatino della Signoria di Bologna: cinque secoli di vita musicale a corte (1250–1797)*, Florence, Olschki (Historiae musicae cultores, 55), 1989.

Gandolfi 2021. Riccardo Gandolfi, *Le vite degli artisti di Gaspare Celio: compendio delle Vite di Vasari con alcune altre aggiunte*, Florence, Olschki (Biblioteca dell'Archivum Romanicum. Serie 1, Storia, letteratura, paleografia, 504), 2021.

Ganz 1989. Kate Ganz, *Master Drawings 1500–1900* [exh. cat. London, Douwes Fine Art, 28 June–8 July 1989], London, Kate Ganz Ltd, 1989.

Garas 1967a. Klára Garas, 'The Ludovisi Collection of Pictures in 1633. I', *The Burlington Magazine* 109, 770 (1967), 287–89.

Garas 1967b. Klára Garas, 'The Ludovisi Collection of Pictures in 1633. II', *The Burlington Magazine* 109, 771 (1967), 339–49.

Garboli and Baccheschi 1971. Cesare Garboli and Edi Baccheschi, *L'opera completa di Guido Reni*, Milan, Rizzoli (Classici dell'arte 48), 1971.

García Boiza 1945. Antonio García Boiza, *Una fundación de Monterrey: la iglesia y convento de MM. Agustinas de Salamanca*, Salamanca, Universidad de Salamanca, 1945.

García Cueto 2006. David García Cueto, *Seicento boloñés y Siglo de Oro español: el arte, la época, los protagonistas*, Madrid, Centro de Estudios Europa Hispánica, 2006.

García Cueto 2010a. David García Cueto, 'Diplomacia española e historia artística romana: la embajada en Roma de don Rodrigo Díaz de Vivar y Mendoza, VII duque del Infantado (1649–1651), y su colección de pinturas', *Storia dell'Arte* 127 (2010), 93–152.

García Cueto 2010b. David García Cueto, 'Los nuncios en la corte de Felipe IV como agentes del arte y la cultura', in José Martínez Millán and Manuel Rivero Rodríguez, eds, *Centros de poder italianos en la Monarquía Hispánica (siglos XV-XVIII)*, 3 vols, Madrid, Polifemo, Fundación Lázaro Galdiano, and Universidad Rey Juan Carlos, 2010, 3:1823–90.

García Cueto 2011. David García Cueto, 'The Contract for Domenico Guidi and Ercole Ferrata's Firedogs for the King of Spain', *The Sculpture Journal* 20, 1 (2011), 43–53.

García Cueto 2014. David García Cueto, 'La pintura italiana en la Granada del Barroco: artistas y coleccionistas, originales y copias', in José Policarpo Cruz Cabrera, ed., *Arte y cultura en la Granada renacentista y barroca: relaciones e influencias*, Granada, Universidad de Granada, 2014, 363–92.

García Cueto 2016a. David García Cueto, 'La embajada extraordinaria del Condestable de Navarra ante Urbano VIII en 1627 y Guido Reni', in Diana Carrió-Invernizzi, ed., *Embajadores culturales: transferencias y lealtades de la diplomacia española de la Edad Moderna*, Madrid, Universidad Nacional de Educación a Distancia, 2016, 263–88.

García Cueto 2016b. David García Cueto, 'Potere e distinzione: i marmi policromi italiani nella Spagna del Seicento', in Grégoire Extermann and Ariane Varela Braga, eds, *Splendor marmoris: i colori del marmo, tra Roma e l'Europa, da Paolo III a Napoleone III*, Rome, De Luca, 2016, 197–218.

García Cueto 2016c. David García Cueto, 'La llegada de pintura y escultura del Seicento a las Colecciones Reales españolas durante el reinado de Felipe IV: adquisiciones y regalos de la aristocracia', in Redín Michaus 2016a, 47–66.

García Cueto 2019. David García Cueto, ed., *La pintura italiana en Granada: artistas y coleccionistas, originales y copias*, Granada, Universidad de Granada, 2019.

García Cueto 2021a. David García Cueto, ed., *Las copias de obras maestras de la pintura en las colecciones de los Austrias y el Museo del Prado* [proceedings of the international congress, Madrid, Museo Nacional del Prado, June 2017], Madrid, Museo Nacional del Prado, 2021.

García Cueto 2021b. David García Cueto, 'La Colección Real española en los siglos XVI y XVII y el copiado pictórico: una aproximación contextual', in García Cueto 2021a, 8–16.

García Cueto and Japón 2019. David García Cueto and Rafael Japón, 'Otras copias de obras italianas y algunos originales en el patrimonio artístico granadino', in García Cueto 2019, 513–52.

García Felguera 1989. María de los Santos García Felguera, *La fortuna de Murillo*, Seville, Diputación Provincial de Sevilla (Publicaciones de la Excma. Diputación Provincial de Sevilla, Sección Historia, 1, 24), 1989.

García Hidalgo [1693] 1965. José García Hidalgo, *Principios para estudiar el nobilísimo y real arte de la pintura* [1693], Madrid, Instituto de España, 1965.

García Sanz 1992. Ana García Sanz, 'Una *Oración en el Huerto* sobre el sepulcro de la Emperatriz María', *Reales Sitios* 29, 113 (1992), 58–59.

García-Frías Checa 2001. Carmen García-Frías Checa, 'Dos dibujos inéditos de los Aposentos Reales de San Lorenzo de 1755', *Reales Sitios* 38, 150 (2001), 16–25.

García-Frías Checa 2016. Carmen García-Frías Checa, 'Los Borbones españoles y sus colecciones pictóricas del Seicento italiano', in Redín Michaus 2016a, 87–105.

García-Frías Checa (in press). Carmen García-Frías Checa, 'Sor Margarita de Austria y el Monasterio de las Descalzas Reales de Madrid: entre devoción y coleccionismo', in Fernando Checa, ed., *Espacios del coleccionismo en la casa de Austria (siglos XVI y XVII)*, Madrid, Universidad Complutense de Madrid, (in press), 333–62.

García-Hidalgo Villena 2022. Cipriano García-Hidalgo Villena, 'Un *Ecce Homo* de Francisco Camilo en el Museo de Segovia', *Cipripedia* (8 April 2022). Accessible at https://cipripedia.com/2022/04/08/un-ecce-homo-de-francisco-camilo-en-el-museo-dc-segovia/.

Gardini 1876. Pietro Gardini, *Cenni biografici di Saulo ed Alessandro Guidotti, illustri patrizi bolognesi*, Bologna, Regia Tipografia, 1876.

Gash 1986. John Gash, 'Success and Failure of Classicism', *Art History* 9, 4 (1986), 516–29.

Gasnier 1992. Marie-Dominique Gasnier, 'Trouver un corps: éléments pour une pensée chrétienne du corps', in Jean-Christophe Goddard and Monique Labrune, eds, *Le Corps*, Paris, Vrin, 1992, 71–90.

Gatta 2017. Francesco Gatta, 'Guido Reni e Domenichino: il ritrovamento degli *Scherzi di amorini* dai camerini di Odoardo e novità su due paesaggisti al servizio dei Farnese', *Bollettino d'Arte* 7, 102, 33–34 (2017), 157–70.

Gatta 2022. Francesco Gatta, 'Odoardo Farnese e Guido Reni: una vicenda collezionistica nella Roma di primo Seicento tra mistero e sfortuna critica' / 'Odoardo Farnese and Guido Reni: A Tale of Collecting in Early Seventeenth-Century Rome between Mystery and Critical Misfortune', in Cappelletti 2022a, 72–83.

Gatta (in press). Francesco Gatta, 'Guido Reni paesaggista: bilancio critico e nuove proposte', in Francesca Cappelletti, ed., *Atti della giornata di studi su Guido Reni* [Rome, Galleria Borghese, 15 May 2022], Genoa, Sagep, (in press).

Gauna 1998. Chiara Gauna, 'Giudizi e polemiche intorno a Caravaggio e Tiziano nei trattati d'arte spagnoli del XVII secolo: Carducho, Pacheco e la tradizione artistica italiana', *Ricerche di Storia dell'Arte* 64 (1998), 57–78.

Gaya Nuño 1954. Juan Antonio Gaya Nuño, 'Notas al catálogo del Museo del Prado (El Prado disperso e inédito)', *Boletín de la Sociedad Española de Excursiones* 58 (1954), 101–42.

Gaya Nuño 1964. Juan Antonio Gaya Nuño, *Pintura europea perdida por España: de Van Dyck a Tiépolo*, Madrid, Espasa-Calpe, 1964.

Gaya Nuño 1969. Juan Antonio Gaya Nuño, *Historia del Museo del Prado (1819–1969)*, León, Everest, 1969.

Gaya Nuño 1978. Juan Antonio Gaya Nuño, *La obra pictórica completa de Murillo*, Barcelona, Noguer, 1978.

Gaye 1839–40. Johann Wilhelm Gaye, *Carteggio inedito d'artisti dei secoli XIV, XV, XVI, pubblicato ed illustrato con documenti pure inediti*, 3 vols, Florence, Giuseppe Molini, 1839–40.

Gazzola 2022. Silvia Gazzola, 'Con Tiziano e Bonifacio all'ombra di un gesto', in Ferino-Pagden, Del Torre Scheuch and Deiters 2022, 87–102.

Ghelfi 1997. Barbara Ghelfi, ed., *Il libro dei conti del Guercino, 1629–1666*, Bologna, Nuova Alfa, 1997.

Ghelfi 2002. Barbara Ghelfi, 'Vicende collezionistiche di casa Hercolani: la quadreria di Maria

Malvezzi Hercolani nelle carte dell'archivio di famiglia', in Daniele Benati and Massimo Medica, eds, *La quadreria di Gioachino Rossini: il ritorno della Collezione Hercolani a Bologna* [exh. cat. Bologna, Palazzo di Re Enzo e del Podestà, 24 November 2002–23 February 2003], Cinisello Balsamo, Silvana, 2002, 15–24.

Ghelfi 2007. Barbara Ghelfi, 'Un nuovo inventario della Galleria Hercolani nella Biblioteca dell'Archiginnasio', *L'Archiginnasio* 102 (2007), 405–69.

Ghelfi 2021. Barbara Ghelfi, *La nascita di una collezione: gli Hercolani di Bologna (1718–1773)*, Bologna, Bononia University Press (Studi sul patrimonio culturale, 9), 2021.

Giacobbi 1632. Girolamo Giacobbi, *Lodi al Signor Guido Reni: raccolte dall'Imperfetto Accademico Confuso*, Bologna, Nicolò Tebaldini, 1632.

Gigli 1723. Girolamo Gigli, *Diario sanese in cui si veggono alla giornata tutti gli avvenimenti più ragguardevoli spettanti sì allo spirituale, sì al temporale della città, e stato di Siena; con la notizia di molte nobili famiglie di essa, delle quali è caduto in acconcio il parlarne*, 2 vols, Lucca, Leonardo Venturini, 1723.

Gil Saura 2018. Yolanda Gil Saura, 'Giovanni Battista Morelli y el Duque de Montalto, entre Roma, Valencia y la corte española', in Mercedes Gómez-Ferrer Lozano and Yolanda Gil Saura, eds, *Ecos culturales, artísticos y arquitectónicos entre Valencia y el Mediterráneo en Época Moderna*, Valencia, Universitat de València (Cuadernos Ars Longa, 8), 2018, 109–28.

Gilet and Moinet 1996. Annie Gilet and Éric Moinet, eds, *Italies: peintures des musées de la région Centre* [exh. cat. Chartres, Musée des Beaux-Arts; Orléans, Musée des Beaux-Arts; Tours, Musée des Beaux-Arts, 23 November 1996–3 March 1997], Paris, Somogy, 1996.

Giometti 2010. Cristiano Giometti, *Domenico Guidi 1625–1701: uno scultore barocco di fama europea*, Rome, L'Erma di Bretschneider (LermArte, 5), 2010.

Giometti 2011. Cristiano Giometti, *Museo Nazionale del Palazzo di Venezia: sculture in terracotta*, Rome, Gangemi, 2011.

Giongo 1953. Guido Giongo, 'La critica su Guido Reni e la fortuna della sua fama', *Rivista dell'Istituto Nazionale d'Archeologia e Storia dell'Arte* 2 (1953), 353–67.

Giordani 1840. Gaetano Giordani, *Cenni sopra diverse pitture staccate dal muro e trasportate su tela e specialmente di una grandiosa con maestria eseguita da Guido Reni ed ammirata entro nobile palazzo in Bologna*, Bologna, Tipografia della Volpe, 1840.

Girometti 2022. Stefania Girometti, *In Italien Karriere machen: der flämische Maler Michele Desubleo zwischen Rom, Bologna und Venedig (ca. 1624–1664)*, Heidelberg, arthistoricum.net, 2022.

Giustiniani–Banti 1981. Vincenzo Giustiniani, 'Discorso sopra la Pittura', in *Discorsi sulle arti e sui mestieri*, ed. Anna Banti, Florence, Sansoni, 1981, 41–45.

Glanville 1995. Helen Glanville, 'Varnish, Grounds, Viewing Distance, and Lighting: Some Notes of Seventeenth-Century Italian Painting Technique', in Arie Wallert, Erma Hermens, and Marja F. J. Peek, eds, *Historical Painting Techniques, Materials, and Studio Practice* [papers of the symposium, University of Leiden, 26–29 June 1995], Los Angeles, Getty Conservation Institute, 1995, 12–19.

Glendinning 2010. Nigel Glendinning, 'Reception of Zurbarán in Britain and Ireland', in Nigel Glendinning and Hilary Macartney, eds, *Spanish Art in Britain and Ireland, 1750–1920: Studies in Reception in Memory of Enriqueta Harris Frankfort*, Woodbridge, Tamesis, 2010, 198–207.

Gnudi 1954. Cesare Gnudi, 'Introduzione', in Cavalli 1954, 15–44.

Gnudi and Cavalli 1955. Cesare Gnudi and Giancarlo Cavalli, *Guido Reni*, Florence, Vallecchi, 1955.

Gómez-Moreno 1967. Manuel Gómez-Moreno, *Catálogo monumental de España: provincia de Salamanca*, Madrid, Ministerio de Educación y Ciencia, 1967.

González García 2006. Juan Luis González García, 'Por amor al arte: notas sobre la agalmatofilia y la *Imitatio Creatoris*, de Platón a Winckelmann', *Anales de Historia del Arte* 16 (2006), 131–50.

González Martínez 2004. Eloy González Martínez, 'Un regalo de Felipe IV en el Museo de Pontevedra: el *Amor desinteresado* de Guercino', *El Museo de Pontevedra* 58 (2004), 201–6.

González Martínez and Diéguez-Rodríguez 2008. Eloy González Martínez and Ana Diéguez-Rodríguez, 'Dos imágenes del amor para Felipe IV: Guido Reni y Guercino', in César Chaparro Gómez et al., eds, *Paisajes emblemáticos: la construcción de la imagen simbólica en Europa y América* [proceedings of the 5th international congress, Sociedad Española de Emblemática, Cáceres, March 2005], 2 vols, Mérida, Editorial Regional de Extremadura, 2008, 2:535–552.

González Mozo 2018. Ana González Mozo, ed., *In lapide depictum: pintura italiana sobre piedra, 1530–1555* [exh. cat. Madrid, Museo Nacional del Prado, 17 April–5 August 2018], Madrid, Museo Nacional del Prado, 2018.

Gracia Rivas 2010. Manuel Gracia Rivas, 'Otra obra sobre San Francisco de Borja y nuevos datos en torno a la familia García Condoy', *Boletín Informativo del Centro de Estudios Borjanos* 129–30 (2010), 11.

Grammatica 1741. Gabriele Grammatica, *Guida sacra alle chiese di Lucca per tutti gli anni del Signore, nella quale si contengono le feste stabili e mobili di tutto l'anno, processioni, indulgenze, corpi santi, reliquie insigni, fondazioni, e pitture delle chiese*, Lucca, Salvatore & Gian Domenico Marescandoli, 1741 (2nd ed.).

Granata 2012. Belinda Granata, 'Note sui pittori bolognesi nella collezione del cardinale Alessandro Peretti Montalto', in Vodret Adamo 2011–12 (2012), 2:273–83.

Greco 1598. Vincenzo Greco, *La reale entrata del serenissimo duca di Parma et Piacenza &c. in Ferrara*, Ferrara, Vittorio Baldini, 1598.

Gregori 1985. Mina Gregori, ed., *The Age of Caravaggio* [exh. cat. New York, The Metropolitan Museum of Art, 5 February–14 April 1985; Naples, Museo Nazionale di Capodimonte, 12 May–30 June 1985], New York, The Metropolitan Museum of Art and Electa International, 1985.

Gregori 1989. Mina Gregori, 'Il *Sacrificio di Isacco*: un inedito e considerazioni su una fase savoldesca del Caravaggio', *Artibus et Historiae* 10, 20 (1989), 99–142.

Gregori 1991. Mina Gregori, 'Come dipingeva il Caravaggio', in Mina Gregori, ed., *Michelangelo Merisi da Caravaggio: come nascono i capolavori* [exh. cat. Florence, Palazzo Pitti, 12 December 1991–15 March 1992; Rome, Palazzo Ruspoli, 26 March–24 May 1992], Milan, Electa, 1991, 13–29.

Gregori and Maffeis 2007. Mina Gregori and Rodolfo Maffeis, *Un'altra bellezza: Francesco Furini* [exh. cat. Florence, Palazzo Pitti, Museo degli Argenti, 22 December 2007–27 April 2008], Florence, Mandragora, 2007.

Greub 2019. Thierry Greub, 'Reconstructing *la Pieza del Despacho de Verano* at the Alcázar in Madrid, the Room of *Las Meninas*: Problems and Possibilities', *Philostrato* 5 (2019), 56–78.

Grimaldi and Sordi 1988. Floriano Grimaldi and Katy Sordi, *Pittori a Loreto: committenze tra '500 e '600: documenti*, Ancona, Soprintendenza per i Beni Ambientali e Architettonici delle Marche, 1988.

Griswold 1992. William M. Griswold, 'Guido Reni, *The Head of a Woman Looking Up*', *The Metropolitan Museum of Art Bulletin* 50, 2 (1992), 29.

Gualandi 1840–45. Michelangelo Gualandi, *Memorie originali risguardanti le belle arti*, 6 vols, Bologna, Tipografia Sassi nelle Spaderie, 1840–45.

Guarino 2002a. Sergio Guarino, ed., *L'Arianna di Guido Reni* [exh. cat. Rome, Musei Capitolini, 18 September–27 October 2002; Bologna, Pinacoteca Nazionale di Bologna, 9 November 2002–12 January 2003], Milan, Electa, 2002.

Guarino 2002b. Sergio Guarino, '"Il quadro della Regina": la storia delle *Nozze di Bacco e Arianna* di Guido Reni', in Guarino 2002a, 15–44.

Guarino 2015. Sergio Guarino, ed., *Guido Reni e i Carracci, un atteso ritorno: capolavori bolognesi dai Musei Capitolini*, Bologna, Bononia University Press, 2015.

Guarino and Masini 2006. Sergio Guarino and Patrizia Masini, eds, *Pinacoteca Capitolina: catalogo generale*, Milan, Electa, 2006.

Guarino and Seccaroni 2018. Sergio Guarino and Claudio Seccaroni, 'Il *Bacco e Arianna* di Guido Reni: uno sfortunato originale ma un fortunato prototipo', in Emiliani 2018, 39–57.

Guida della Galleria 1919. *Guida della Galleria Comunale di Ascoli Piceno*, Ascoli Piceno, Tipografia Giuseppe Cesari, 1919.

Guidicini 1868–73. Giuseppe Guidicini, *Cose notabili della città di Bologna, ossia Storia cronologica dei suoi stabili sacri, pubblici e privati*, 5 vols, Bologna, Tipografia G. Vitali, 1868–73.

Guzzo 2004. Enrico Maria Guzzo, 'Per la storia del collezionismo a Verona: nuovi documenti sulle quadrerie India, Giusti, Museli, Canossa e Gherardini', *Studi Storici Luigi Simeoni* 54 (2004), 393–425.

Haffner 1988. Christel Haffner, 'La Vrillière, collectionneur et mécène', in Arnauld Brejon de Lavergnée and Nathalie Volle, eds, *Seicento: le siècle de Caravage dans le collections françaises* [exh. cat. Paris, Galeries Nationales d'Exposition du Grand Palais, 11 October 1988–2 January 1989], Paris, Réunion des Musées Nationaux, 1988, 29–38.

Harris 1960. Enriqueta Harris, 'A Letter from Velázquez to Camillo Massimi', *The Burlington Magazine* 102, 685 (1960), 162–66.

Harris 1980. Enriqueta Harris, 'G. B. Crescenzi, Velázquez and the "Italian" Landscapes for the Buen Retiro', *The Burlington Magazine* 122, 929 (1980), 562–64.

Hartje 2004. Nicole Hartje, *Bartolomeo Manfredi (1582–1622): ein Nachfolger Caravaggios und seine europäische Wirkung*, Weimar, VDG, 2004.

Haskell 1988. Francis Haskell, 'Guido Reni e il mecenatismo artistico del suo tempo', in Ebert-Schifferer, Emiliani and Schleier 1988, 32–43.

Haskell and Penny 1981. Francis Haskell and Nicholas Penny, *Taste and the Antique: Lure of Classical Sculpture (1500–1900)*, New Haven, Yale University Press, 1981.

Hasler 2011. Johann F. W. Hasler, 'Performative and Multimedia Aspects of Late-Renaissance Meditative Alchemy: The Case of Michael Maier's *Atalanta Fugiens* (1617)', *Revista de Estudios Sociales* 39 (2011), 135–44.

Helmstutler Di Dio 2013. Kelley Helmstutler Di Dio, 'Sculpted Diplomacy: State Gifts of Sculpture from Italy to Spain in the Sixteenth and Seventeenth Centuries', in Bernstorff and Kubersky-Piredda 2013, 51–65.

Hendler 2013. Sefy Hendler, *La Guerre des arts: le Paragone peinture-sculpture en Italie XVᵉ–XVIIᵉ siècle*, Rome, L'Erma di Bretschneider, 2013.

Henning 2008. Andreas Henning, 'The New Technique of Painting on Copper', in Henning and Schaefer 2008, 25–35.

Henning and Schaefer 2008. Andreas Henning and Scott Schaefer, eds, *Captured Emotions: Baroque Painting in Bologna, 1575–1725* [exh. cat. Los Angeles, J. Paul Getty Museum, 16 December 2008–3 May 2009], Los Angeles, J. Paul Getty Museum, 2008.

Henning and Weber 1998. Andreas Henning and Gregor J. M. Weber, eds, *'Der himmelnde Blick': zur Geschichte eines Bildmotivs von Raffael bis Rotari* [exh. cat. Dresden, Semperbau, 3 November 1998–10 January 1999], Emsdetten, Imorde, 1998.

Hereza 2019. Pablo Hereza, *Corpus Murillo: pinturas y dibujos, encargos*, Seville, Ayuntamiento de Sevilla, 2019.

Herrmann-Fiore 2007. Kristina Herrmann-Fiore, ed., *Dürer e l'Italia* [exh. cat. Rome, Scuderie del Quirinale, 10 March–10 June 2007], Milan, Electa 2007.

Hess 1934a. Jacob Hess, 'Le fonti dell'arte di Guido Reni', *Il Comune di Bologna* 21, 3 (1934), 25–33.

Hess 1934b. Jacob Hess, ed., *Die Künstler-biographien von Giovanni Battista Passeri*, Leipzig and Vienna, Heinrich Keller and Anton Schroll & Co., 1934.

Hess 1967. Jacob Hess, *Kunstgeschichtliche studien zu Renaissance und Barock*, 2 vols, Rome, Edizioni di Storia e Letteratura, 1967.

Hibbard 1965. Howard Hibbard, 'Notes on Reni's Chronology', *The Burlington Magazine* 107, 751 (1965), 502–10.

Hibbard 1969. Howard Hibbard, 'Guido Reni's Painting of the Immaculate Conception', *The Metropolitan Museum of Art Bulletin* 28, 1 (1969), 18–32.

Hibbard 1976. Howard Hibbard, 'Guido Reni's Corsini Magdalen: Its Date and Influence', in Larissa Bonfante and Helga von Heintze, eds, *In Memoriam Otto J. Brendel: Essays in Archaeology and the Humanities*, Mainz, Philipp von Zabern, 1976, 227–31.

Hillary and Kisler 2009. Sarah Hillary and Mary Kisler, 'Auckland's *St Sebastian* by Guido Reni', *Journal of the Institute of Conservation* 32, 2 (2009), 205–18.

Hollstein 1954. Friedrich W. Hollstein, *Dutch and Flemish Etchings, Engravings and Woodcuts ca. 1450–1700*, vol. 11: *Leyster–Matteus*, Amsterdam, Menno Hertzberger, 1954.

Hollstein–Ruyven-Zeman, Stock and Leesberg 2004. Zsuzsanna van Ruyven-Zeman, comp., and Jan van der Stock and Marjolein Leesberg, eds, *F. W. Hollstein: Dutch and Flemish Etchings, Engravings and Woodcuts 1450–1700*, vol. 66: *The Wierix Family, VIII*, Rotterdam, Sound & Vision, 2004.

Hollstein–Schuckman and Hoop Scheffer 1990. Christiaan Schuckman, comp., and Dieuwke de Hoop Scheffer, ed., *F. W. Hollstein: Dutch and Flemish Etchings, Engravings and Woodcuts ca. 1450–1700*, vol. 36: *Claudius Vermeulen to Paulus Willemsz van Vianen*, Roosendaal, Koninklijke Van Poll, 1990.

Hollstein–Schuckman and Hoop Scheffer 1992. Christiaan Schuckman, comp., and Dieuwke de Hoop Scheffer, ed., *F. W. Hollstein: Dutch and Flemish Etchings, Engravings and Woodcuts 1450–1700*, vol. 40: *Cornelis de Visscher, Cornelis Visscher, Hendrick Jansz Visscher, Lambert Visscher*, Roosendaal, Koninklijke Van Poll, 1992.

Holo 1978–79. Selma Holo, 'A Note on the Afterlife of the *Crouching Aphrodite* in the Renaissance', *The J. Paul Getty Museum Journal* 6–7 (1978–79), 23–36.

Horovitz 1999. Isabel Horovitz, 'The Materials and Techniques of European Paintings on Copper Supports', in Komanecky 1999a, 63–92.

Hübner [1862] 2008. Emil Hübner, *Las colecciones de arte antiguo en Madrid, con un apéndice sobre otras colecciones existentes en España y Portugal* [1862], Madrid, Instituto Arqueológico Alemán de Madrid, 2008.

Iseppi 2020. Giulia Iseppi, 'Oltre Guido Reni: norma e arbitrio della bottega a Roma, 1620–1640', PhD diss., Rome, Università di Roma 'La Sapienza', 2020.

Iseppi (in press). Giulia Iseppi, *Le stanze di Guido Reni: Francesco Gessi (1588–1649) e Giacomo Sementi (1583–1636)* (in press).

***Italian Masterpieces* 2014.** *Italian Masterpieces from Spain's Royal Court, Museo del Prado* [exh. cat. Melbourne, National Gallery of Victoria, 16 May–31 August 2014], Melbourne, National Gallery of Victoria, 2014.

Jaffé 1954. Michael Jaffé, 'Some Figure Drawings in Chalk by Guido Reni', *Paragone* 5, 59 (1954), 3–6.

Jähnig 1929. Karl Wilhelm Jähnig, *Die Staatliche gemäldegalerie zu Dresden: Vollständiges beschreibendes verzeichnis der älteren gemälde*, vol. 1: *Die Romanischen Länder*, prol. Hans Posse, Dresden, Baensch-Stiftung, 1929.

Japón 2018a. Rafael Japón, ed., *Bartolomé Esteban Murillo y la copia pictórica* [papers of the international study day, Granada, 14 December 2017], Granada, Universidad de Granada, 2018.

Japón 2018b. Rafael Japón, 'Murillo copista de copias italianas en la Sevilla del siglo XVII: la colección del arzobispo fray Domingo Pimentel', in Japón 2018a, 55–118.

Japón 2018c. Rafael Japón, 'La presenza della pittura bolognese a Siviglia: collezionismo e influssi', in Marinella Pigozzi, ed., *Dialogo artistico tra Italia e Spagna: arte e musica* [papers of the conference, Bologna, Reale Collegio di Spagna, 2017], Bologna, Bononia University Press, 2018, 27–38 and 169–76.

Japón 2019. Rafael Japón, 'El Apostolado de la Catedral de Granada: entre el naturalismo y el clasicismo italianos', in García Cueto 2019, 345–72.

Japón 2020a. Rafael Japón, 'La influencia de la pintura italiana en la escuela barroca sevillana', PhD diss., 2 vols, Universidad de Granada and Universitá di Bologna, 2020.

Japón 2020b. Rafael Japón, 'Guido Reni's Influence in Seville through Originals, Copies and Prints', in Kelley Helmstutler Di Dio and Tommaso Mozzati, eds, *Artistic Circulation between Early Modern Spain and Italy*, London and New York, Routledge, 2020, 173–91.

Japón 2022a. Rafael Japón, 'Las copias y el copiado de Guido Reni en el Prado', *Boletín del Museo del Prado* 38, 58 (2022), 52–67.

Japón 2022b. Rafael Japón, *The Influence of Italian Culture on the Sevillian Golden Age of Painting*, London and New York, Routledge, 2022.

Jestaz 1994. Bertrand Jestaz, ed., *Le Palais Farnèse*, vol. 3.3: *L'inventaire du palais et des propriétés Farnèse à Rome en 1644*, Rome, École Française de Rome, 1994.

Johnston 1966. Catherine Johnston, 'A New Drawing by Guido Reni', *The Burlington Magazine* 108, 758 (1966), 251–53.

Johnston 1969. Catherine Johnston, 'Reni Landscape Drawings in Mariette's Collection', *The Burlington Magazine* 111, 795 (1969), 377–80.

Johnston 1973. Catherine Johnston, *Mostra di disegni bolognesi dal XVI al XVIII secolo* [exh. cat. Florence, Gabinetto Disegni e Stampe degli Uffizi], Florence, Olschki (Gabinetto Disegni e Stampe degli Uffizi, Cataloghi, 40), 1973.

Johnston 1974. Catherine Johnston, 'The Drawings of Guido Reni', PhD diss., 3 vols, Courtauld Institute of Art, University of London, 1974.

Johnston 1993. Catherine Johnston, 'A Visual Source for an Early Fresco by Guido Reni and Speculations on its Meaning', *Art Bulletin of Nationalmuseum* 17, 2 (1993), 11–20.

Johnston 2009. Catherine Johnston, 'Review of Babette Bohn, *Le "Stanze" di Guido Reni, Disegni del maestro e della scuola*', *The Burlington Magazine* 151, 1281 (2009), 847.

Jones 1993. Pamela M. Jones, *Federico Borromeo and the Ambrosiana: Art Patronage and Reform in Seventeenth-Century Milan*, Cambridge, Cambridge University Press, 1993.

Justi 1953. Carl Justi, *Velázquez y su siglo*, Madrid, Espasa-Calpe, 1953.

Keazor 2001. Henry Keazor, '"Il beneficio delle statue": Antikenrezeption in Guido Renis Herkules-Zyklus', *Artibus et Historiae* 22, 43 (2001), 137–60.

Kinkead 2009. Duncan T. Kinkead, *Pintores y doradores en Sevilla, 1650–1699: documentos*, Bloomington, AuthorHouse, 2009 (2nd rev. ed.).

Kirby 1999. Jo Kirby, 'The Painter's Trade in the Seventeenth Century: Theory and Practice', *National Gallery Technical Bulletin* 20 (1999), 5–49.

Klinka-Ballesteros 2009. Isabelle Klinka-Ballesteros, ed., *Guide des collections: Musée des Beaux-Arts de Orléans*, Clermont-Ferrand, Le Musée des Beaux-Arts de Orléans and Un, Deux, Quatre, 2009.

Kloek 1993. Wouter T. Kloek, 'Calvaerts oefeningen met spiegelbeeldigheid', *Oud Holland* 107 (1993), 59–74.

Komanecky 1999a. Michael K. Komanecky, ed., *Copper as Canvas: Two Centuries of Masterpiece Paintings on Copper, 1575–1775* [exh. cat. Phoenix, Phoenix Art Museum, 19 December 1998–28 February 1999; Kansas City, Nelson-Atkins Museum of Art, 28 March–13 June 1999; The Hague, Mauritshuis, 26 June–22 August 1999], New York, Oxford University Press, 1999.

Komanecky 1999b. Michael K. Komanecky, 'Introduction', in Komanecky 1999a, 3–8.

Krüger 2017. Klaus Krüger, 'Visions of Inaudible Sounds: Heavenly Music and its Pictorial Representations', in Andreas Beyer et al., eds, *Voir l'au-delà: l'expérience visionnaire et sa représentation dans l'art italien de la Renaissance* [papers of the international colloquium, Paris, 3–5 June 2013], Turnhout, Brepols, 2017, 77–93.

Kugler 1850. Franz Kugler, 'Lithographie', *Deutsches Kunstblatt* 1 (1850), 277–78.

Kugler–Burckhardt 1847. Franz Kugler, *Handbuch der Geschichte der Malerei seit Constantin dem Grossen, zweite auflage unter Mitwirkung des Verfassers umgearbeitet und vermehrt von Dr. Jacob Burckhardt*, 2 vols, Berlin, Duncker und Humblot, 1847 (2nd rev. ed.).

Kühn-Hattenhauer 1979. Dorothee Kühn-Hattenhauer, 'Das graphische Oeuvre des Francesco Villamena', PhD diss., Berlin, Freie Universität, 1979.

Kurz 1935–36. Otto Kurz, 'Guido Reni (1575–1642): the *Fall of Phaethon*; collection of Sir Archibald Campbell, Bart., of Garscube; inscribed below to L. Lelio da Novolara', *Old Master Drawings* 10 (1935–36), 14–16.

Kurz 1937. Otto Kurz, 'Guido Reni', *Jahrbuch der Kunsthistorischen Sammlungen in Wien* 11 (1937), 189–220.

Kurz 1942. Otto Kurz, 'A Sculpture by Guido Reni', *The Burlington Magazine* 81, 474 (1942), 222–26.

Kurz 1955. Otto Kurz, *Bolognese Drawings of the XVII and XVIII Centuries in the Collection of Her Majesty the Queen at Windsor Castle*, London, Phaidon Press (The Italian Drawings at Windsor Castle, 6), 1955.

Kurz and McBurney 1988. Otto Kurz, *Bolognese Drawings of the XVII and XVIII Centuries in the Collection of Her Majesty the Queen at Windsor Castle, with a New Appendix to the Catalogue by Henrietta McBurney*, Bologna, Nuova Alfa, 1988.

Labrot 1992. Gérard Labrot, *Collections of Paintings in Naples, 1600–1780*, Munich, London, and New York, K. G. Saur (Documents for the History of Collecting, Italian Inventories, 1), 1992.

Laguna [1554] 1968–69. Andrés Laguna, *Pedacio Dioscorides Anazarbeo* [Lyon, 1554], 2 vols, Madrid, Instituto de España, 1968–69.

Lalande 1769. Joseph-Jerôme Lefrançois de Lalande, *Voyage d'un françois en Italie fait dans les années 1765 & 1766*, 9 vols, Paris, Desaint, 1769.

Lalande 1786. Joseph-Jerôme Lefrançois de Lalande, *Voyage d'un françois en Italie fait dans les années 1765 & 1766*, 9 vols, Paris, Veuve Desaint, 1786 (2nd ed.).

Landolfi 1992. Francesco Landolfi, 'Per la *Strage degli innocenti* di Guido Reni: un inedito documento d'archivio', *Accademia Clementina, Atti e Memorie* 30–31 (1992), 181–83.

Landrus 1995. Matt Landrus, 'Caravaggism in the Work of Guido Reni', *Athanor* 13 (1995), 23–29.

Lange 2004. Justus Lange, 'Jusepe de Riberas *Kreuzigung* für die Herzogin von Osuna – Zur Typologie des "Cristo vivo en la cruz"', in Jutta Held, ed., *Kirchliche Kultur und Kunst des 17. Jahrhunderts in Spanien*, Frankfurt, Vervuert (Ars Iberica et Americana, 9), 2004, 123–43.

Lanzi 1823. Luigi Lanzi, *Storia pittorica della Italia dal risorgimento delle belle arti fin presso al fine del XVIII secolo*, 6 vols, Milan, Giovanni Silvestri, 1823 (6th ed.).

Lapuerta Montoya 2002. Magdalena de Lapuerta Montoya, *Los pintores de la Corte de Felipe III: la Casa Real de El Pardo*, Madrid, Comunidad de Madrid, Consejería de las Artes, 2002.

Lazzari 1724. Tullio Lazzari, *Ascoli in prospettiva colle sue più singolari pitture, sculture, e architetture*, Ascoli, Morganti & Picciotti, 1724.

Legati 1677. Lorenzo Legati, *Museo Cospiano, annesso a quello del famoso Ulisse Aldrovandi e donato alla sua patria dall'illustrissimo signor Ferdinando Cospi, patrizio di Bologna e senatore cavaliere commendatore di S. Stefano, Bali d'Arezzo, e march. di Petriolo, fra' gli accademici Gelati Il Fedele, e principe al presente de' medesimi*, Bologna, Giacomo Monti, 1677.

Lemoine 2007. Annick Lemoine, *Nicolas Régnier (alias Niccolò Renieri), ca. 1588–1667: peintre, collectionneur et marchand d'art*, Paris, Arthena, 2007.

Leslie and Taylor 1865. Charles Robert Leslie and Tom Taylor, *Life and Times of Sir Joshua Reynolds: With Notices of Some of his Contemporaries*, 2 vols, London, John Murray, 1865.

Levey 1991. Michael Levy, *The Later Italian Pictures in the Collection of Her Majesty the Queen*, Cambridge, Cambridge University Press, 1991 (2nd ed.).

Lingo 2007. Estelle Lingo, *François Duquesnoy and the Greek Ideal*, New Haven and London, Yale University Press, 2007.

Lingo 2008. Stuart Lingo, *Federico Barocci: Allure and Devotion in Late Renaissance Painting*, New Haven, Yale University Press, 2008.

Lingo 2011. Estelle Lingo, 'Beyond the Fold: Drapery in Seventeenth-Century Sculptural Practice and Criticism', in Tristan Weddigen, ed., *Unfolding the Textile Medium in Early Modern Art and Literature*, Berlin, Imorde (Textile Studies, 3), 2011, 121–29.

Ljaljević Grbić et al. 2014. Milica Ljaljević Grbić et al., 'Implementation of ATP Bioluminescence Method in the Study of the Fungal Deterioration of Textile Artefacts', *Fibres and Textiles in Eastern Europe* 22, 6 (2014), 132–36.

Lleó Cañal 2005. Vicente Lleó Cañal, '*Atalanta e Hipómenes* de Guido Reni', *Atrio. Revista de Historia del Arte* 10–11 (2005), 141–46.

Lo Bianco 2016. Anna Lo Bianco, ed., *Rubens e la nascita del Barocco* [exh. cat. Milan, Palazzo Reale, 26 October 2016–26 February 2017], Venice, Marsilio, 2016.

L'Occaso 2003. Stefano L'Occaso, 'Pitture dell'epoca del duca Ferdinando', *Atti e Memorie. Accademia Nazionale Virgiliana di Scienze Lettere ed Arti* 71 (2003), 53–68.

Loffredo 2012. Fernardo Loffredo, 'La vasca del *Sansone* del Giambologna e il *Tritone* di Battista Lorenzi in un'inedita storia di duplicati (con una nota sul *Miseno* di Stoldo per la villa dei Corsi)', *Saggi e Memorie* 36 (2012), 57–114.

Logan 1979. Anne-Marie S. Logan, *The 'Cabinet' of the Brothers Gerard and Jan Reynst*, Amsterdam, Oxford, and New York, North-Holland, 1979.

Loire 1990. Stéphane Loire, 'Guido Reni dopo la mostra di Bologna: qualche aggiunta', *Accademia Clementina, Atti e Memorie* 25 (1990), 9–30.

Loire 1994. Stéphane Loire, 'Guido Reni', in Emilio Negro and Massimo Pirondini, eds., *La scuola dei Carracci: dall'Accademia alla bottega di Ludovico*, Modena, Artioli, 1994, 225–34.

Loire 1996. Stéphane Loire, *Musée du Louvre, Département des peintures: école italienne, XVIIe siècle*, vol. 1: *Bologne*, Paris, Réunion des Musées Nationaux, 1996.

Loire 2017. Stéphane Loire, '*Dejanira rapita dal centauro Nesso* del Museo del Louvre', in Mario Scalini and Elena Rossoni, eds, *Nesso e Dejanira di Guido Reni, dal Louvre di Parigi alla Pinacoteca di Bologna* [exh. cat. Bologna, Pinacoteca Nazionale di Bologna, 6 September 2017–7 January 2018], Rimini, Polo Museale Emilia-Romagna, 2017, 17–38.

Loisel 2013. Catherine Loisel, *Dessins italiens du Museé du Louvre*, vol. 10: *Dessins bolonais du XVII siècle. Tome II*, Paris, Officina Libraria, 2013.

Loisel 2022. Catherine Loisel, 'L'empreinte de Ludovico Carracci sur Guido Reni dessinateur et quelques hypothèses sur ses relations avec Agostino et Annibale', *About Art online* (2 October 2022). Accessible at https://www.about-artonline.com/lempreinte-de-ludovico-carracci-sur-guido-reni-dessinateur-et-quelques-hypotheses-sur-ses-relations-avec-agostino-et-annibale/.

Lomazzo 1585. Giovanni Paolo Lomazzo, *Trattato dell'arte della pittura, scoltura, et architettura*, Milan, Paolo Gottardo Pontio, 1585.

Longhi 1916. Roberto Longhi, 'Gentileschi padre e figlia', *L'Arte* 19 (1916), 245–314.

Longhi 1935. Roberto Longhi, 'Momenti della pittura bolognese', *L'Archiginnasio* 30, 1–3 (1935), 111–35.

Longhi 1943. Roberto Longhi, 'Ultimi studi sul Caravaggio e la sua cerchia', *Proporzioni* 1 (1943), 5–63.

Longhi 1973. Roberto Longhi, 'Momenti della pittura bolognese' (introduction to the Università di Bologna courses for the academic year 1934–35), in *Edizione delle opere complete di Roberto Longhi*, vol. 6: *Lavori in Valpadana*, Florence, Sansoni, 1973, 189–205.

López Conde 2021. Rubén López Conde, 'Retratos de una obsession: las genealogías del duque de Montalto y la llegada de Morelli a España', *Goya* 375 (2021), 138–53.

Luna Fernández 1993. Juan José Luna Fernández, *Las pinturas y esculturas del Palacio Real de Madrid en 1811*, Madrid, Fundación Rich, 1993.

Maaz, Koch and Diederen 2014. Bernhard Maaz, Ute Christina Koch, and Roger Diederen, eds, *Rembrandt, Tizian, Bellotto: Geist und Glanz der Dresdner Gemäldegalerie* [exh. cat. Munich, Kunsthalle der Hypo-Kulturstiftung, 22 August–23 November 2014; Groningen, Groninger Museum, 13 December 2014–25 May 2015; Vienna, Österreichische Galerie Belvedere, 11 June–26 October 2015], Munich, Hirmer, 2014.

Macandrew 1980. Hugh Macandrew, ed., *Ashmolean Musem, Oxford: Catalogue of the Collection of Drawings*, vol. 3: *Italian Schools: Supplement*, Oxford, Clarendon Press, 1980.

Macandrew 1990. Hugh Macandrew, ed., *Old Master Drawings from the National Gallery of Scotland* [exh. cat. Washington, National Gallery of Art, 24 June–23 September 1990; Fort Worth, Kimbell Art Museum, 3 November 1990–13 January 1991], Washington, National Gallery of Art, 1990.

Maccherini 1995. Michele Maccherini, 'Annibale Carracci e i "bolognesi" nel carteggio familiare di Giulio Mancini', PhD diss., Università degli Studi di Siena, 1995.

Maccherini 2007. Michele Maccherini, 'Alexandris cardinalis Bichij: arte e mecenatismo tra Italia e Francia', in M. Raffaella de Gramatica, Enzo Mecacci, and Carla Zarrilli, eds, *Archivi, carriere, committenze: contributi per la storia del patriziato senese in età moderna* [proceedings of the congress, Siena, 8–9 June 2006], Siena, Il Leccio, 2007, 240–67.

Madero López 2019. José Carlos Madero López, 'La pintura italiana del convento del Santo Ángel Custodio de Granada', in García Cueto 2019, 405–32.

Madocks 1984. Susan Madocks, '"Trop de beautez découvertes": New Light on Guido Reni's Late *Bacchus and Ariadne*', *The Burlington Magazine* 126, 978 (1984), 544–47.

Madrazo 1843. Pedro de Madrazo, *Catálogo de los cuadros del Real Museo de Pintura y Escultura de S. M.*, Madrid, Oficina de Aguado, 1843.

Madrazo 1845. Pedro de Madrazo, *Catálogo de los cuadros del Real Museo de Pintura y Escultura de S. M.*, Madrid, Viuda de Jordán e hijos, 1845 (2nd ed.).

Madrazo 1856. José de Madrazo, *Catálogo de la galería de cuadros del Excmo. D. José de Madrazo*, Madrid, Imprenta de Cipriano López, 1856.

Madrazo 1858. Pedro de Madrazo, *Catálogo de los cuadros del Real Museo de Pintura y Escultura de S. M.*, Madrid, Antonio Aoiz, 1858 (5th ed.).

Madrazo 1872. Pedro de Madrazo, *Catálogo descriptivo e histórico del Museo del Prado de Madrid, seguido de una sinópsis de las várias escuelas … Parte primera: escuelas italianas y españolas*, Madrid, M. Rivadeneyra, 1872.

Madrazo 1884. Pedro de Madrazo, *Viaje artístico de tres siglos por las colecciones de cuadros de los reyes de España desde Isabel la Católica hasta la formación del Real Museo del Prado de Madrid*, Barcelona, Daniel Cortezo y Cª, 1884.

Madruga Real 1983. Ángela Madruga Real, *Arquitectura barroca salmantina: las Agustinas de Monterrey*, Salamanca, Centro de Estudios Salmantinos, 1983.

Magalotti 2018. Lorenzo Magalotti, *Viaje de Cosme III de Médici por España y Portugal (1668–1669)*, trans. David Fermosel Jiménez, intro. José María Sánchez Molledo, Madrid, Miraguano, 2018.

Magnanimi 1980a. Giuseppina Magnanimi, 'Inventari della collezione romana dei principi Corsini (I)', *Bollettino d'Arte* 6, 65, 7 (1980), 91–126.

Magnanimi 1980b. Giuseppina Magnanimi, 'Inventari della collezione romana dei principi Corsini (II)', *Bollettino d'Arte* 6, 65, 8 (1980), 73–114.

Mahon 1947a. Denis Mahon, *Studies in Seicento Art and Theory*, London, Warburg Institute (Studies of the Warburg Institute, 16), 1947.

Mahon 1947b. Denis Mahon, 'The Construction of a Legend: The Origins of the Classic and Eclectic Misinterpretations of the Carracci', in Mahon 1947a, 193–229, Appendix I.

Mahon 1957. Denis Mahon, 'Some Suggestions for Reni's Chronology', *The Burlington Magazine* 99, 652 (1957), 238–41.

Mahon and Turner 1989. Denis Mahon and Nicholas Turner, *The Drawings of Guercino in the Collection of Her Majesty the Queen at Windsor Castle*, Cambridge and New York, Cambridge University Press, 1989.

Maier 1618. Michael Maier, *Atalanta fugiens hoc est emblemata nova de secretis naturae chymica*, Oppenheim, Hieronymus Galleri, 1618.

Malaguzzi Valeri 1895. Francesco Malaguzzi Valeri, *La chiesa e il convento di S. Michele in Bosco*, Bologna, Fava e Garagnani, 1895.

Malaguzzi Valeri 1897. Francesco Malaguzzi Valeri, 'L'arte dei pittori a Bologna nel secolo XVI', *Archivio Storico dell'Arte* 2, 3 (1897), 309–14.

Malaguzzi Valeri 1926. Francesco Malaguzzi Valeri, 'Due statue di Guido Reni', *Cronache d'Arte* 3 (1926), 227–30.

Malaguzzi Valeri 1929. Francesco Malaguzzi Valeri, *Guido Reni*, Florence, Le Monnier, 1929.

Malpezzi 2008. Pietro Malpezzi, *I bandi di Bernardino Spada durante la peste del 1630 in Bologna*, Faenza, Casanova, 2008.

Malvasia 1678. Carlo Cesare Malvasia, *Felsina pittrice: vite de pittori bolognesi*, 2 vols, Bologna, Erede di Domenico Barbieri, 1678.

Malvasia 1686. Carlo Cesare Malvasia, *Le pitture di Bologna che nella pretesa, e rimostrata fin hora da altri maggiore antichità, & impareggiabile eccellenza nella pittura, con manifesta evidenza di fatto, rendono il passeggiere disingannato ed instrvtto*, Bologna, Giacomo Monti, 1686.

Malvasia–Arfelli 1961. Carlo Cesare Malvasia, *Vite di pittori bolognesi: appunti inediti*, ed. Adriana Arfelli, Bologna, Commissione per i testi di lingua, 1961.

Malvasia–Brascaglia 1971. Carlo Cesare Malvasia, *Felsina pittrice: vite dei pittori bolognesi* [1678], ed. Marcella Brascaglia, Bologna, Alfa (Fonti e studi per la storia di Bologna e delle province emiliane e romagnole, 3), 1971.

Malvasia–Cropper and Pericolo 2013. Carlo Cesare Malvasia, *Felsina Pittrice: Lives of the Bolognese Painters*, vol. 13: *Lives of Domenichino and Francesco Gessi*, ed. Elizabeth Cropper and Lorenzo Pericolo, London, Harvey Miller, 2013.

Malvasia–Cropper and Pericolo 2017. Carlo Cesare Malvasia, *Felsina Pittrice: Lives of the Bolognese Painters*, vol. 13: *Lives of Domenichino and Francesco Gessi*, ed. Elizabeth Cropper and

Lorenzo Pericolo, London, Harvey Miller, 2017 (2nd ed.).

Malvasia–Emiliani 1969. Carlo Cesare Malvasia, *Le pitture di Bologna, 1686*, ed. Andrea Emiliani, Bologna, Alfa (Fonti e studi per la storia di Bologna e delle province emiliane e romagnole, 1), 1969.

Malvasia–Marzocchi 1983. Carlo Cesare Malvasia, *Scritti originali del conte Carlo Cesare Malvasia spettanti alla sua Felsina pittrice*, ed. Lea Marzocchi, Bologna, Alfa, 1983.

Malvasia–Pericolo 2019. Carlo Cesare Malvasia, *Felsina Pittrice: Lives of the Bolognese Painters*, vol. 9: *Life of Guido Reni*, ed. Lorenzo Pericolo, 2 vols, London, Harvey Miller, 2019.

Malvasia–Takahatake and Pericolo 2017. Carlo Cesare Malvasia, *Felsina Pittrice: Lives of the Bolognese Painters*, ed. Naoko Takahatake and Lorenzo Pericolo, vol. 2, 2.1: *Life of Marcantonio Raimondi and Critical Catalogue of Prints by or after Bolognese Masters*, London, Harvey Miller, 2017.

Malvasia–Zanotti 1841. Carlo Cesare Malvasia, *Felsina pittrice: vite de' pittori bolognesi, con aggiunte, correzioni e note inedite del medesimo autore di Giampietro Zanotti, e di altri scrittori viventi*, ed. Giampietro Zanotti, 2 vols, Bologna, Tipografia Guidi all'Ancora, 1841.

Malvezzi 1651. Virgilio Malvezzi, *Introduttione al racconto de' principali successi accaduti sotto il comando del potentissimo rè Filippo IV*, Rome, Heredi del Corbelletti, 1651.

Mancini 2004. Matteo Mancini, 'Partecipare con le parole: partecipare con le immagini. Antichi e moderni, un dibattito geografico?', in Fernando Checa Cremades, ed., *Velázquez, Bernini, Luca Giordano: le corti del Barocco* [exh. cat. Rome, Scuderie del Quirinale, 12 February–2 May 2004], Milan, Skira, 2004, 209–23.

Mancini–Marucchi 1956–57. Giulio Mancini, *Considerazioni sulla pittura*, ed. Adriana Marucchi, 2 vols, Rome, Accademia Nazionale dei Lincei, 1956–57.

Mandy et al. 2019. Kristina Mandy et al., 'Rediscovering Reni: The Technical Investigation, Treatment, and Reattribution of *The Toilet of Venus*', *National Gallery Technical Bulletin* 40 (2019), 18–41.

Mann 1993. Judith W. Mann, 'The Annunciation Chapel in the Quirinal Palace, Rome: Paul V, Guido Reni, and the Virgin Mary', *The Art Bulletin* 75, 1 (1993), 113–34.

Mann 2017. Judith W. Mann, 'Deciphering Artemisia: Three New Narratives and How They Expand Our Understanding', in Sheila Barker, ed., *Artemisia Gentileschi in a Changing Light*, London and Turnhout, Harvey Miller, 2017, 167–86.

Manrique Ara 2001. María Elena Manrique Ara, *Jusepe Martínez, un pintor zaragozano en la Roma del Seicento*, Zaragoza, Institución 'Fernando el Católico', 2001.

Mansi–Barsocchini 1836. Giovan Domenico Mansi, *Diario sacro delle chiese di Lucca di monsignore*

Giovan Domenico Mansi accomodato all'uso del tempi presenti ed accresciuto di molte notizie storiche del nostro paese dall'ab. Dom. Barsocchini, Lucca, Tipografia Giusti, 1836.

Manzini 1633. Giovanni Battista Manzini, ed., *Il trionfo del pennello: raccolta d'alcune composi-tioni nate a gloria d'un Ratto d'Helena di Guido Reni*, Bologna, Niccolò Tebaldini & Paolo Veli, 1633.

Marcenaro and Boragina 2001. Giuseppe Marcenaro and Piero Boragina, eds, *Viaggio in Italia: un corteo magico dal Cinquecento al Novecento* [exh. cat. Genoa, Palazzo Ducale, 31 March–29 July 2001], Milan, Electa, 2001.

Marchiò 1721. Vincenzo Marchiò, *Il forestiere informato delle cose di Lucca*, Lucca, Salvatore & Giandomenico Marescandoli, 1721.

Marco García 2021. Víctor Marco García, *Pintura barroca en Valencia, 1600–1737*, Madrid, Centro de Estudios Europa Hispánica, 2021.

Marías 2014. Fernando Marías, 'Pintura, diplomacia y censura en la Cappella Paolina: desde Toledo y Madrid hasta Roma', in Anselmi 2014, 58–86.

Marías and De Carlos 2009. Fernando Marías and María Cruz de Carlos Varona, 'El arte de las "acciones que las figuras mueven": Maíno, un pintor dominico entre Toledo y Madrid', in Ruiz Gómez 2009a, 57–75.

Mariette 1741. Pierre-Jean Mariette, *Description sommaire des desseins des grands maistres d'Italie, des Pays-Bas et de France, du cabinet de feu M. Crozat*, Paris, Mariette, 1741.

Mariette 1753. Pierre-Jean Mariette, *Catalogue des tableaux, desseins, marbres, bronzes, modeles, estampes, et planches gravées; ainsi que des bijoux, porcelaines, et autres curiosités de prix, du cabinet de feu M. Coypel, premier peintre du roi et de monseigneur le duc d'Orléans, & directeur de l'Académie Royale de Peinture & Sculpture*, Paris, 1753.

Mariette 1851–60. Pierre-Jean Mariette, *Abecedario*, ed. Philippe de Chennevières and Anatole de Montaiglon, 6 vols, Paris, J. B. Dumoulin, 1851–60.

Marin 2015. Chiara Marin, *Girolamo Forabosco*, Verona, Cierre Edizioni (Venezia barocca, 4), 2015.

Marinas 1981. Cristina Marinas, 'La Galerie espagnole', in Jeannine Baticle and Cristina Marinas, eds, *La Galerie espagnole de Louis-Philippe au Louvre 1838–1848*, Paris, Réunion des Musées Nationaux, 1981, 13–26.

Marinelli 1982. Sergio Marinelli, 'Su Antonio Giarola e altri fatti veronesi del suo tempo', *Paragone* 33, 387 (1982), 33–43.

Marini 1974. Maurizio Marini, *Io Michelangelo da Caravaggio*, Rome, Studio B–Bestetti e Bozzi Editori, 1974.

Marini 1996. Maurizio Marini, 'Un contributo all'iconografia del *David e Golia* del Prado', in Mina Gregori and Elisa Acanfora, eds, *Come dipingeva il Caravaggio* [papers of the study day, Florence, 28 January 1992], Milan, Electa, 1996, 135–42.

Marini 2001. Maurizio Marini, *Caravaggio 'pictor praestantissimus': l'iter artistico completo di uno dei massimi rivoluzionari dell'arte di tutti i tempi*, Rome, Newton & Compton (Quest'Italia, 117), 2001 (3rd ed.).

Marini 2005. Maurizio Marini, *Caravaggio 'pictor praestantissimus': l'iter artistico completo di uno dei massimi rivoluzionari dell'arte di tutti i tempi*, Rome, Newton & Compton, 2005 (4th ed.).

Marino 1620. Giambattista Marino, *La galeria del cavalier Marino: distinta in pitture, & sculture*, Ancona, Cesare Scaccioppa, 1620.

Marino–Borzelli and Nicolini 1911–12. Giambattista Marino, *Epistolario: seguito da lettere di altri scrittori del Seicento*, ed. Angelo Borzelli and Fausto Nicolini, 2 vols, Bari, Laterza, 1911–12.

Marino–Pieri 1979. Giambattista Marino, *La Galeria*, ed. Marzio Pieri, 2 vols, Padua, Liviana, 1979.

Martin 2008. Elisabeth Martin, 'Grounds on Canvas 1600–1640 in Various European Artistic Centres', in Joyce Townsend et al., eds, *Preparation for Painting: The Artist's Choice and its Consequences*, London, Archetype, 2008, 59–67.

Martín González 1958. Juan José Martín González, 'Sobre las relaciones entre Nardi, Carducho y Velázquez', *Archivo Español de Arte* 31, 121 (1958), 59–66.

Martínez–Carderera 1866. Jusepe Martínez, *Discursos practicables del nobilísimo arte de la pintura, sus rudimentos, medios y fines que enseña la experiencia, con los ejemplares de obras insignes de artífices ilustres*, ed. Valentín Carderera y Solano, Madrid, Real Academia de San Fernando, 1866.

Martínez–Manrique Ara 2006. Jusepe Martínez, *Discursos practicables del nobilísimo arte de la pintura*, ed. María Elena Manrique Ara, Madrid, Cátedra, 2006.

Martínez Leiva and Rodríguez Rebollo 2007. Gloria Martínez Leiva and Ángel Rodríguez Rebollo, eds, *Quadros y otras cosas que tiene Su Magestad Felipe IV en este Alcázar de Madrid. Año de 1636*, Madrid, Fundación Universitaria Española (Inventarios Reales con cuadros del Museo del Prado, 1), 2007.

Martínez Leiva and Rodríguez Rebollo 2015. Gloria Martínez Leiva and Ángel Rodríguez Rebollo, *El inventario del Alcázar de Madrid de 1666: Felipe IV y su colección artística*, Madrid, Consejo Superior de Investigaciones Científicas y Polifemo, 2015.

Martorelli 1705. Luigi Martorelli, *Memorie historiche dell'antichissima, e nobile città d'Osimo*, Venice, Andrea Poletti, 1705.

Marzullo 2019. Giacomo Marzullo, 'La raccolta di lettere di Ottavio Rossi', in Clizia Carminati, ed., *'Testimoni dell'ingegno': reti epistolari e libri di lettere nel Cinquecento e nel Seicento*, Sarnico, Edizioni di Archilet, 2019, 325–56.

Masini 1666. Antonio di Paolo Masini, *Bologna perlustrata*, 3 vols, Bologna, Erede di Vittorio Benacci, 1666 (3rd ed.).

Massari 2012–13. Silvia Massari, '"Il nostro moderno Algardi": Giuseppe Maria Mazza scultore bolognese tra Sei e Settecento', PhD diss., 2 vols, Università degli Studi di Trento, 2012–13.

Masson 1975. Georgina Masson, *Courtesans of the Italian Renaissance*, London, Secker & Warburg, 1975.

Matthiesen 2017. Patrick Matthiesen, 'A Genre Scene with a Country Dance or Fête Champêtre', in Patrick Matthiesen, ed., *Guido Reni, The 'Divine' Guido: A Trio* [exh. cat.], London, Matthiesen Gallery, 2017, 25–43.

Matthiesen and Pepper 1970. Patrick Matthiesen and Stephen Pepper, 'Guido Reni: An Early Masterpiece Discovered in Liguria', *Apollo* 91 (1970), 452–62.

Mayer 1913. August L. Mayer, *Murillo: l'oeuvre du maître*, Paris, Hachette, 1913.

Mayer 1934. August L. Mayer, 'Anotaciones a algunos cuadros del Museo del Prado', *Boletín de la Sociedad Española de Excursiones* 42 (1934), 291–99.

Mayer 1936. August L. Mayer, 'Anotaciones al arte y a las obras de Murillo', *Revista Española de Arte* 5 (1936), 46–48.

Mayer 1938. August L. Mayer, 'Murillo und seine italienischen Barockvorbilder', *Critica d'Arte* 3 (1938), 120.

Mayer 1947. August L. Mayer, *Historia de la pintura española*, Madrid, Espasa-Calpe, 1947 (3rd ed.).

Mazza 1996. Angelo Mazza, 'La conversione emiliana di Antonio Giarola', in Jadranka Bentini, Angelo Mazza, and Sergio Marinelli, eds, *La pittura veneta negli stati estensi*, Verona, Banco Popolare di Verona, Banco S. Geminiano e S. Prospero, 1996, 235–58.

Mazza 2018. Angelo Mazza, 'La galleria Sampieri "superbissimo Museo", da Bologna a Milano sulle tracce del *Ballo degli amorini* di Francesco Albani', *L'Archiginnasio* 105–12 (2018), 281–327.

Mazzarelli 2016. Carla Mazzarelli, 'L'occhio del conoscitore e la questione della "ripetizione" tra copie e repliche: alcune note intorno al caso de *La Fortuna* di Guido Reni nella storia critica', in Stefan Albl, ed., *Il metodo del conoscitore: approcci, limiti, prospettive*, Rome, Artemide, 2016, 273–89.

McGarry 2007. Rachel L. McGarry, 'The Young Guido Reni: The Artist in Bologna and Rome, 1575–1605', PhD diss., Institute of Fine Arts, New York University, 2007.

McGarry 2008. Rachel L. McGarry, 'Guido Reni, Cardinal Federico Borromeo's Reluctant Copyist', *Studia Borromaica* 22 (2008), 431–48.

McTighe 2008. Sheila McTighe, 'The Old Woman as Art Critic: Speech and Silence in Response to the Passions, from Annibale Carracci to Denis Diderot', *Journal of the Warburg and Courtauld Institutes* 71 (2008), 239–60.

Meijer 1992. Bert W. Meijer, 'L'Emilia e il Nord: alcune aggiunte (Baburen, Bramer, Renieri ed altri)', in Giovanna Perini Folesani, ed., *Il luogo ed il ruolo della città di Bologna tra Europa continentale e mediterranea* [papers of the colloquium, Bologna, C.I.H.A., 1990], Bologna, Nuova Alfa, 1992, 279–95.

Melasecchi and Pepper 1998. Olga Melasecchi and D. Stephen Pepper, 'Guido Reni, Luca Ciamberlano and the Oratorians: Their Relationship Clarified', *The Burlington Magazine* 140, 1146 (1998), 596–603.

Mélida 1895. José Ramón Mélida, 'La cabeza de Séneca, bronce del Museo Arqueológico Nacional', *Historia y Arte* 1, 8 (1895), 149–51.

Mena Marqués 1982. Manuela Mena Marqués, ed., *Bartolomé Esteban Murillo (1617–1682)* [exh. cat. Madrid, Museo del Prado, 8 October–12 December 1982; London, Royal Academy of Arts, 15 January–27 March 1983], Madrid, Ministerio de Cultura, Dirección General de Bellas Artes, 1982.

Mena Marqués 1983. Manuela Mena Marqués, *Museo del Prado: catálogo de dibujos*, vol. 4: *Dibujos italianos del siglo XVII*, Madrid, Museo del Prado, 1983.

Mena Marqués 1988. Manuela Mena Marqués, *Disegni italiani dei secoli XVII e XVIII della Biblioteca Nazionale di Madrid* [exh. cat. Milan, Palazzo Reale, October–November 1988; Bologna, Museo Civico Archeologico, November 1988–January 1989; Rome, Academia de España, January–February 1989], Madrid, Ministerio de Asuntos Exteriores, 1988.

Mena Marqués 1996. Manuela Mena Marqués, 'Velázquez e Italia: las metamorfosis del arte de la pintura', in Trinidad de Antonio, ed., *Velázquez: El Papa Inocencio X de la Galleria Doria Pamphilj, Roma* [exh. cat. Madrid, Museo del Prado, 8 January–15 February 1996], Madrid, Museo del Prado, 1996, 61–94.

Mendelsohn 1982. Leatrice Mendelsohn, *Paragoni: Benedetto Varchi's Due Lezzioni and Cinquecento Art Theory*, Ann Arbor, Michigan, UMI Research Press (Studies in the Fine Arts, Art Theory, 6), 1982.

Merrill 1944. Robert V. Merrill, 'Eros and Anteros', *Speculum* 19, 3 (1944), 265–84.

Mesonero 2002. Enrique Mesonero, ed., *Tramo segundo, el pincel y la palabra* [exh. cat.], Salamanca, Diputación de Salamanca and Fundación Germán Sánchez Ruipérez, 2002.

Michel 2007. Patrick Michel, *Le commerce du tableau à Paris dans la seconde moitié du XVIIIe siècle: acteurs et pratiques*, Villeneuve d'Ascq, Presses Universitaires du Septentrion (Histoire de l'Art, 1046), 2007.

Michetti 1889. Francesco Paolo Michetti, *Dieci quadri della Galleria Sciarra*, Rome, Tipografia Tribuna, 1889.

Michiel–Morelli 1800. Marcantonio Michiel, *Notizia d'opere di disegno nella prima metà del secolo XVI esistenti in Padova, Cremona, Milano, Pavia, Bergamo, Crema e Venezia*, ed. Jacopo Morelli, Bassano, Giuseppe Remondini e figli, 1800.

Milani 1994. Marisa Milani, ed., *Contro le puttane: rime venete del XVI secolo*, Bassano del Grappa, Ghedina e Tassotti, 1994.

Milicua 1952. José Milicua, 'En el centenario de Ribera: Ribera en Roma. El manuscrito de Mancini', *Archivo Español de Arte* 25, 100 (1952), 309–22.

Milicua [1952] 2016. José Milicua, 'En el centenario de Ribera: Ribera en Roma. El manuscrito de Mancini' [1952], in José Milicua, *Ojo crítico y memoria visual: escritos de arte*, ed. Artur Ramon, Madrid, Centro de Estudios Europa Hispánica, 2016, 153–64.

Milicua 2005. José Milicua, ed., *Caravaggio y la pintura realista europea* [exh. cat. Barcelona, Museu Nacional d'Art de Catalunya, 10 October 2005–15 January 2006], Barcelona, Museu Nacional d'Art de Catalunya, 2005, 56–59.

Milicua and Portús Pérez 2011. José Milicua and Javier Portús Pérez, eds, *El joven Ribera* [exh. cat. Madrid, Museo del Prado, 5 April–31 July 2011], Madrid, Museo del Prado, 2011.

Miller 1991. Dwight C. Miller, *Marcantonio Franceschini and the Liechtensteins: Prince Johann Adam Andreas and the Decoration of the Liechtenstein Garden Palace at Rossau-Vienna*, Cambridge, Cambridge University Press, 1991.

Miller and Chiodini 2014. Dwight C. Miller and Fabio Chiodini, *Il libro dei conti di Marcantonio Franceschini*, Bologna, Grafiche dell'Artiere, 2014.

Minozzi 1641. Pier Francesco Minozzi, *Sfogamenti d'ingegno*, Venice, Turrini, 1641.

Mocante 1598. Giovanni Paolo Mocante, *Relatione dell'entrata solenne fatta in Ferrara a dì 13. di novembre 1598. Per la Serenis. D. Margarita d'Austria Regina di Spagna: et del Concistoro publico con tutti li preparamenti fatti dall Santità di N. S. Clemente Papa VIII. per tal'effetto*, Rome, Nicolò Mutii, 1598.

Mochi Onori and Vodret Adamo 1989. Lorenza Mochi Onori and Rossella Vodret Adamo, *La Galleria Nazionale d'Arte Antica: regesto delle didascalie*, Rome, Palombi, 1989.

Mochi Onori and Vodret Adamo 1998. Lorenza Mochi Onori and Rossella Vodret Adamo, *Capolavori della Galleria Nazionale d'Arte Antica: Palazzo Barberini*, Rome, De Luca, 1998.

Mochi Onori and Vodret Adamo 2008. Lorenza Mochi Onori and Rossella Vodret Adamo, *Galleria Nazionale d'Arte Antica: Palazzo Barberini, i dipinti: catalogo sistematico*, Rome, L'Erma di Bretschneider, 2008.

Moir 1976. Alfred Moir, *Caravaggio and His Copyists*, New York, New York University Press (Monographs on Archaeology and Fine Arts, 31), 1976.

Molina Huete 2018. Belén Molina Huete, 'Sobre recepción y canon de la fábula mitológica del Siglo de Oro: *La Atalanta* de Juan de Matos Fragoso (1662)', *Criticón* 134 (2018), 159–93.

Moncayo 1656. Juan de Moncayo y Gurrea, marqués de San Felices, *Poema trágico de Atalanta, y Hipómenes*, Zaragoza, Diego Dormer, 1656.

Montagu 1967. Jennifer Montagu, 'A Flagellation Group: Algardi or Du Quesnoy?', *Bulletin des Musées Royaux d'Art et d'Histoire* 4, 38–39 (1967), 153–93.

Montagu 1985. Jennifer Montagu, *Alessandro Algardi*, 2 vols, New Haven, Yale University Press, 1985.

Montaigne–D'Ancona 1889. Michel de Montaigne, *Journal de voyage de Michel de Montaigne en Italie, par la Suisse et l'Allemagne en 1580 et 1581*, ed. Alexandre D'Ancona, Città di Castello, S. Lapi, 1889.

Montanari 2004. Tomaso Montanari, 'Francesco Barberini, l'*Arianna* di Guido Reni e altri doni per la corona d'Inghilterra: l'ultimo atto', in Bernardini 2004, 77–88.

Montanari 2009. Tomaso Montanari, 'Barocci in barocco: indizi di una persistenza', in Alessandra Giannotti and Claudio Pizzorusso, eds, *Federico Barocci 1535–1612, l'incanto del colore: una lezione per due secoli* [exh. cat. Siena, Santa Maria della Scala, 11 October 2009–10 January 2010], Cinisello Balsamo, Silvana, 2009, 216–25.

Morello 1603. Benedetto Morello, *Il funerale d'Agostin Carraccio fatto in Bologna sua patria da gl'Incaminati Academici del Disegno, scritto all'Ill.ᵐᵒ e R.ᵐᵒ Sig.ʳ Cardinal Farnese*, Bologna, Vittorio Benacci, 1603.

Morello, Francia and Fusco 2005. Giovanni Morello, Vincenzo Francia, and Roberto Fusco, eds, *Una donna vestita di sole: l'Immacolata Concezione nelle opere dei grandi maestri* [exh. cat. Vatican City, Braccio di Carlo Magno, 11 February–13 May 2005], Milan, Motta, 2005.

Moretti 2005. Massimo Moretti, 'La "Concezione" di Maria in Spagna: profili storici e iconografici', in Morello, Francia and Fusco 2005, 79–89.

Moretti 2014. Massimo Moretti, 'Influssi spagnoli nell'arte e nella spiritualità caracciolina del Seicento: Madrid, Roma e il ducato di Urbino', in Anselmi 2014, 508–36.

Mormando 1999. Franco Mormando, ed., *Saints & Sinners: Caravaggio & the Baroque Image* [exh. cat. Boston, McMullen Museum of Art, Boston College, 1 February–24 May 1999], Boston, McMullen Museum of Art, 1999.

Morselli 1992. Raffaella Morselli, 'Guido Reni: i collezionisti, gli allievi, le copie', in Negro and Pirondini 1992, 17–25.

Morselli 1997. Raffaella Morselli, *Repertorio per lo studio del collezionismo bolognese del Seicento*, Bologna, Pàtron, 1997.

Morselli 1998. Raffaella Morselli, *Collezioni e quadrerie nella Bologna del Seicento: inventari 1640–1707*, ed. Anna Cera Sones, Los Angeles, The J. Paul Getty Trust (Documents for the History of Collecting, Italian Inventories, 3), 1998.

Morselli 2001. Raffaella Morselli, 'Tendenze e aspetti del collezionismo bolognese del Seicento', in Olivier Bonfait et al., *Geografia del collezionismo: Italia e Francia tra il XVI e il XVIII secolo* [Giuliano Briganti study day, Rome, 19–21 September 1996], Rome, École Française de Rome (Collection de l'École Française de Rome, 287), 2001, 61–81.

Morselli 2002. Raffaella Morselli, *Gonzaga: la celeste galeria, le raccolte* [exh. cat. Mantua, Palazzo Te and Palazzo Ducale, 2 September–8 December 2002], Milan, Skira, 2002.

Morselli 2007. Raffaella Morselli, '"Io Guido Reni Bologna": profitti e sperperi nella carriera di un pittore "un poco straordinario"', in Raffaella Morselli, ed., *Vivere d'arte: carriere e finanze nell'Italia moderna*, Rome, Carocci (Annali del Dipartimento di Scienze della Comunicazione dell'Università degli Studi di Teramo, 2), 2007, 71–134.

Morselli 2008. Raffaella Morselli, '"Io Guido Reni Bologna": profitti e sperperi nella carriera di un pittore "un poco straordinario"', in Raffaella Morselli, ed., *Vivere d'arte: carriere e finanze nell'Italia moderna*, Rome, Carocci (Annali del Dipartimento di Scienze della Comunicazione dell'Università degli Studi di Teramo, 2), 2008 (2nd ed.), 71–134.

Morselli 2012a. Raffaella Morselli, 'Da Guido Reni a Cantarini: l'arte di ben copiare e ritoccare al servizio del mercato felsineo', in Anna Maria Ambrosini Massari, ed., *Fano per Simone Cantarini: genio ribelle 1612–2012* [exh. cat. Fano, 30 June–30 September 2012], Fano, Fondazione Cassa di Risparmio di Fano, 2012, 140–51.

Morselli 2012b. Raffaella Morselli, 'Guido Reni da Bologna a Roma e ritorno', in Vodret Adamo 2011–12 (2012), 2:285–93.

Morselli 2013. Raffaella Morselli, '"La colleganza di un gran nobile e di un gran virtuoso": Saulo Guidotti e Guido Reni', in Frommel 2013, 55–84.

Morselli 2016. Raffaella Morselli, 'La pala di San Giobbe di Guido Reni: commissione, cronologia, fortuna', *Paragone* 129–130, 799–801 (2016), 3–29.

Morselli 2018a. Raffaella Morselli, 'Il *Lamento di Arianna* di Guido Reni', *Storia della Critica d'Arte* 2 (2018), 239–75.

Morselli 2018b. Raffaella Morselli, 'Jan Meyseens' 1649 Portfolio of Artists: The Conception and Composition of the Book *Image de diverse hommes d'esprit sublime* (and the Inclusion of Three Italian Painters)', in Paolo Coen, ed., *The Art Market in Rome in the Eighteenth Century: A Study in the Social History of Art*, Leiden and Boston, Brill (Studies in the History of Collecting & Art Markets, 5), 2018, 87–114.

Morselli 2018c. Raffaella Morselli, 'Sotto il segno di Arianna: dal Lamento all'Incontro con Bacco sull'Isola di Nasso. Reni 1620–1640', in Emiliani 2018, 65–73.

Morselli 2020. Raffaella Morselli, 'Una gemma antica e un disegno di Giulio Romano: rimembranze iconografiche mantovane nell'*Arianna* e nell'*Atalanta* di Guido Reni', in Adriano Amendola, Loredana Lorizzo, and Donato Salvatore, eds, *Lo sguardo di Orione: studi di storia dell'arte per Mario Alberto Pavone*, Rome, De Luca, 2020, 253–58.

Morselli 2022a. Raffaella Morselli, 'I Ludovisi e il "bizzarro Barbieri" tra Bologna e Roma', in Daniele Benati, Barbara Ghelfi, and Raffaella Morselli, eds., *Guercino nel Casino Ludovisi 1621–1623*, Rome, De Luca (*Storia dell'Arte* special issue), 2022, 33–50.

Morselli 2022b. Raffaella Morselli, '"Torcimanni e barattieri": agenti, intermediari, periti, mallevadori e mercanti nella Bologna di primo Seicento',

in *Nuove scenografie del collezionismo europeo tra Seicento e Ottocento: attori, pratiche, riflessioni di metodo*, Berlin, De Gruyter, 2022, 63–82.

Morselli 2022c. Raffaella Morselli, 'Tre anni da salariato (1609–1612): il registro della contabilità di Guido in casa Borghese', in Cappelletti 2022, 60–71.

Morselli 2022d. Raffaella Morselli, *Professione pittore: il caso di Bologna tra Cinque e Seicento*, Venice, Marsilio, 2022.

Morselli 2022e. Raffaella Morselli, 'Guido Reni e lo studio della statuaria classica: metamorfosi dei modelli antichi', in Sonia Antonelli et al., eds, *Archaeologiae: una storia al plurale. Studi in memoria di Sara Santoro*, Oxford, Università degli Studi G. d'Anunzio and Archaeopress (Reports, Excavations and Studies of the Archaeological Unit of the University G. d'Anunzio of Chieti-Pescara, II), 2022, 89–92.

Morselli and Iseppi 2021. Raffaella Morselli and Giulia Iseppi, 'Un poeta tra i pittori: Cesare Rinaldi nell'ecfrastica Bologna tra Cinque e Seicento', in Emilio Russo, Patrizia Tosini, and Andrea Zezza, eds, *Marino e l'arte tra Cinque e Seicento*, Rome, L'Erma di Bretschneider (L'Ellisse, XIV, 2), 2021, 227–52 and 276–78.

Mosco 1986. Marilena Mosco, ed., *La Maddalena tra sacro e profano, da Giotto a De Chirico* [exh. cat. Florence, Palazzo Pitti, 24 May–7 September 1986], Milan, Mondadori; Florence, Casa Usher, 1986.

Mosco 2007. Marilena Mosco, *Cornici dei Medici: la fantasia barocca al servizio del potere / Medici Frames: Baroque Caprice for the Medici Princes*, Florence, Mauro Pagliai, 2007.

***Mostra del Caravaggio* 1951.** *Mostra del Caravaggio e dei caravaggeschi* [exh. cat. Milan, Palazzo Reale, 21 April–June 1951], intr. Roberto Longhi, Florence, Sansoni, 1951.

Moya Valgañón 2011. José Gabriel Moya Valgañón, ed., *Skarby Korony Hiszpańskiej / Treasures of the Spanish Crown* [exh. cat. Krakow, Muzeum Narodowe w Krakowi, 13 June–9 October 2011], Madrid, Patrimonio Nacional, 2011.

Muñoz González 1999. María Jesús Muñoz González, 'Los relieves de Bacanales que decoraban el Alcázar', *Archivo Español de Arte* 72, 288 (1999), 576–82.

***Museo del Prado* 1945.** *Museo del Prado: catálogo de los cuadros*, intr. Francisco Javier Sánchez Cantón, Madrid, Museo del Prado, 1945.

***Museo del Prado* 1972.** *Museo del Prado: catálogo de las pinturas*, intr. Xavier de Salas, Madrid, Museo del Prado, 1972.

***Museo del Prado* 1985.** *Museo del Prado: catálogo de las pinturas*, Madrid, Museo del Prado, 1985.

***Museo del Prado* 1990.** *Museo del Prado: inventario general de pinturas*, 3 vols, Madrid, Museo del Prado and Espasa-Calpe, 1990.

***Museo del Prado* 1996.** *Museo del Prado: catálogo de las pinturas*, rev. ed. Javier Portús and Montserrat Sabán, Madrid, Ministerio de Educación y Cultura, 1996.

Muti 2006. Laura Muti, '*Cristo in preghiera nell'orto* di Guido Reni: tema per una riflessione ed una presentazione', in Laura Muti and Daniele De

Sarno Prignano, *Capolavori in proscenio: dipinti del Cinque, Sei e Settecento*, Faenza, Edit Faenza, 2006, 52–65.

Nannini 2005. Alessandra Nannini, *La Quadreria di Carlo Lodovico di Borbone, Duca di Lucca*, Lucca, Pacini Fazzi, 2005.

Nava Cellini 1969. Antonia Nava Cellini, 'Stefano Maderno, Francesco Vanni e Guido Reni a Santa Cecilia in Trastevere', *Paragone* 20, 227 (1969), 18–41.

Navarrete Prieto 1998. Benito Navarrete Prieto, *La pintura andaluza del siglo XVII y sus fuentes grabadas*, Madrid, Fundación de Apoyo a la Historia del Arte Hispánico, 1998.

Navarrete Prieto 2005. Benito Navarrete Prieto, 'Pinturas y pintores en la catedral de Granada', in Lázaro Gila Medina, ed., *El libro de la Catedral de Granada*, 2 vols, Granada, Cabildo Metropolitano de la Catedral de Granada, 2005, 1:316–74.

Negro 2007. Angela Negro, *La Collezione Rospigliosi: la quadreria e la committenza artistica di una famiglia patrizia a Roma nel Sei e Settecento*, Rome, Campisano, 2007.

Negro and Pirondini 1992. Emilio Negro and Massimo Pirondini, eds, *La scuola di Guido Reni*, Modena, Artioli, 1992.

Nicolaci and Gandolfi 2011. Michele Nicolaci and Riccardo Gandolfi, 'Il Caravaggio di Guido Reni: *La Negazione di Pietro* tra relazioni artistiche e operazioni finanziarie', *Storia dell'Arte* 130 (2011), 41–64 and 147–50.

Nicolau Castro 1990. Juan Nicolau Castro, 'Unos bronces de Alejandro Algardi en el monasterio toledano de Madres Capuchinas', *Archivo Español de Arte* 63, 249 (1990), 1–13.

Nicolau Castro 1991. Juan Nicolau Castro, 'La correspondencia del cardenal D. Pascual de Aragón a las madres capuchinas', *Toletum, Boletín de la Real Academia de Bellas Artes y Ciencias históricas de Toledo* 26 (1991), 9–23.

Nicolau Castro 2007. Juan Nicolau Castro, 'Sobre una pintura de San Ildefonso en la Capilla Paulina de la Basílica de Santa María la Mayor de Roma', *Toletum, Boletín de la Real Academia de Bellas Artes y Ciencias históricas de Toledo* 54 (2007), 191–97.

Nicolau Castro 2014. Juan Nicolau Castro, *El Cardenal Aragón y el Convento de Capuchinas de Toledo*, Toledo, Cuarto Centenario, 2014.

Nicolson 1954. Benedict Nicolson, 'The Rediscovery of Guido', *The Burlington Magazine* 96, 619 (1954), 301–2.

Nugent 1925–30. Margherita Nugent, *Alla mostra della pittura italiana del '600 e '700: note e impressioni*, 2 vols, San Casciano, Società Editrice Toscana, 1925–30.

Olin 2016. Martin Olin, 'A Portrait Drawing of Pope Paul V Attributed to Guido Reni', *Art Bulletin of Nationalmuseum Stockholm* 23 (2016), 107–10.

Orbaan 1920. Johannes Albertus Franciscus Orbaan, *Documenti sul barocco in Roma*, 2 vols, Rome, Società Romana di Storia Patria, 1920.

Orihuela and Pérez 2017. Mercedes Orihuela and Luz Pérez, 'El "Prado disperso": obras depositadas en la embajada de España en Buenos Aires', *Boletín del Museo del Prado* 35, 53 (2017), 121–26.

Orsini 1790. Baldassarre Orsini, *Descrizione delle pitture, sculture, architetture ed altre cose rare della insigne città di Ascoli nella Marca*, Perugia, Stamperia Baduelliana, 1790.

Orsini 1791. Baldassarre Orsini, *Risposta alle lettere pittoriche del signore Annibale Mariotti*, Perugia, Carlo Baduel, 1791.

Orso 1986. Steven N. Orso, *Philip IV and the Decoration of the Alcázar of Madrid*, Princeton, Princeton University Press, 1986.

Ossorio y Bernard 1883–84. Manuel Ossorio y Bernard, *Galería biográfica de artistas españoles del siglo XIX*, Madrid, Moreno y Rojas, 1883–84.

Ostrow 1996a. Steven F. Ostrow, *Art and Spirituality in Counter-Reformation Rome: The Sistine and Pauline Chapels in S. Maria Maggiore*, Cambridge, Cambridge University Press, 1996.

Ostrow 1996b. Steven F. Ostrow, 'Cigoli's Immacolata and Galileo's Moon: Astronomy and the Virgin in Early Seicento Rome', *The Art Bulletin* 78, 2 (1996), 218–35.

Ovid–Bernardini Marzolla 1979. Ovid, *Ovidio Metamorfosi*, ed. Piero Bernardini Marzolla, with a text by Italo Calvino, Turin, Einaudi, 1979.

Oy-Marra 2000. Elisabeth Oy-Marra, 'Paintings and Hangings for a Catholic Queen: Giovan Francesco Romanelli and Francesco Barberini's Gift to Henrietta Maria of England', in Elizabeth Cropper, *The Diplomacy of Art: Artistic Creation and Politics in Seicento Italy* [papers of the colloquium, Florence, Villa Spelman, 1998], Bologna, Nuova Alfa, 2000, 177–93.

Pacheco–Bassegoda 1990. Francisco Pacheco, *El arte de la pintura*, ed. Bonaventura Bassegoda i Hugas, Madrid, Cátedra, 1990.

Padovani 2009. Serena Padovani, 'In margine alla mostra di Furini: l'*Ercole* di Guido Reni', *Paragone* 87–88 (2009), 113–17.

Pagliani 1990. Maria Luisa Pagliani, 'Guido Reni (1575–1642): percorsi nell'antico', *Accademia Clementina, Atti e Memorie* 25 (1990), 155–63.

Palacios Méndez 2021. Laura María Palacios Méndez, '¿*Flora?* de Tiziano: virtudes y verdadera amistad en el retrato de una reciente esposa', *Mitteilungen des Kunsthistorischen Institutes in Florenz* 63, 3 (2021), 325–57.

Pallucchini and Rossi 1982. Rodolfo Pallucchini and Paola Rossi, eds, *Tintoretto: le opere sacre e profane*, 2 vols, Milan, Electa, 1982.

Palma 1636. Fray Juan de Palma, *Vida de la serenissima infanta Sor Margarita de la Cruz, religiosa descalça de S. Clara*, Madrid, Imprenta Real, 1636.

Palma and De Lachenal 1983. Beatrice Palma and Lucilla De Lachenal, *Museo Nazionale Romano*, vol. 1.5: *Le Sculture: i marmi Ludovisi nel Museo Nazionale Romano*, Rome, De Luca, 1983.

Palomino [1715–24] 1947. Antonio Palomino de Castro y Velasco, *El museo pictórico y escala óptica* [1715–24], Madrid, Aguilar, 1947.

Palos 2016. Joan-Lluís Palos, *L'impero di Spagna allo specchio: storia e propaganda nei dipinti del Palazzo reale di Napoli*, Naples, Arte'm, 2016.

Palude 1784. Giacomo della Palude, *Descrizione de' quadri del ducale appartamento di Modena*, Modena, Eredi Bartolomeo Soliani, 1784.

Pampalone and Barchiesi 2017. Antonella Pampalone and Sofia Barchiesi, *Iconografia di un santo: nuovi studi sull'immagine di san Filippo Neri*, Rome, Edizioni Oratoriane, 2017.

Pancaldi 1637. Giovanni Pellegrino Pancaldi, *Il trionfo di Giobbe dipinto da Guido Reni*, Bologna, Giacomo Monti, 1637.

Panofsky 1960. Erwin Panofsky, *A Mythological Painting by Poussin in the Nationalmuseum Stockholm*, Stockholm, Kungl. Boktryckeriet P.A. Norstedt & Söner (Nationalmusei skriftserie, 5), 1960.

Paoluzzi 2014. Maria Cristina Paoluzzi, *La collezione Colonna nell'allestimento settecentesco: la Galleria negli acquerelli di Salvatore Colonnelli Sciarra*, Rome, Campisano (Saggi di storia dell'arte, 28), 2014.

Papetti 2007. Stefano Papetti, *Guido Reni*: l'Annunciazione *di Ascoli Piceno* [exh. cat.], New York, Istituto Italiano di Cultura, 2007.

Papetti 2012. Stefano Papetti, ed., *Opere d'arte dalle collezioni di Ascoli Piceno: la Pinacoteca Civica e il Museo Diocesano. Scoperte, ricerche e nuove proposte*, Rome, Ugo Bozzi, 2012.

Papetti 2013. Stefano Papetti, '*L'Annunciazione* di Ascoli Piceno', in Diotallevi 2013, 69–71.

Papi 1990. Gianni Papi, 'Un'apertura sul soggiorno italiano di Jacob van Oost il Vecchio', *Studi di Storia dell'Arte* 1 (1990), 171–201.

Papi 2021. Gianni Papi, 'Lanfranco per il duca di Alcalà', in Pietro di Loreto, ed., *L'archivio di Caravaggio: scritti in onore di don Sandro Corradini*, Rome, Etgraphiae (I Quaderni di AboutArtonline, 1), 2021, 255–64.

Papi and Zicarelli 1988. Federica Papi and Emanuela Zicarelli, 'Nuove testimonianze sui rapporti fra Guido Reni e i padri dell'oratorio', *Accademia Clementina, Atti e Memorie* 22 (1988), 105–17.

Parma Armani 1978–79. Elena Parma Armani, 'I "quadretti" di San Filippo Neri e un'ipotesi per Bartolomeo Cavarozzi disegnatore', *Studi di Storia delle Arti* 2 (1978–79), 131–48.

Parronchi 1980. Alessandro Parronchi, 'Sculture e progetti di Michelangelo Nacherino', *Prospettiva* 20 (1980), 34–46.

Parronchi 1992. Alessandro Parronchi, *Opere giovanili di Michelangelo*, vol. 4: *Palinodia michelangiolesca*, Florence, Olschki (Accademia Toscana di Scienze e Lettere La Colombaria: Studi, 125), 1992.

Passeri 1772. Giovanni Battista Passeri, *Vite de' pittori, scultori ed architetti che anno lavorato in Roma, morti dal 1641 fino al 1673*, Roma, Gregorio Settari, 1772.

Pastor 1891–1953. Ludwig Freiherr von Pastor, *The History of the Popes, from the Close of the Middle Ages*, 40 vols, ed. Ralph Francis Kerr, London, Routledge and Kegan Paul, 1891–1953.

Pecci 1752. Giovanni Antonio Pecci, *Relazione delle cose più notabili della città di Siena si antiche, come moderne, descritta in compendio*, Siena, Francesco Quinza & Agostino Bindi, 1752.

Pecci 1759. Giovanni Antonio Pecci, *Ristretto delle cose più notabili della città di Siena a uso de' forestieri*, Siena, Francesco Rossi, 1759.

Pecci 1761. Giovanni Antonio Pecci, *Ristretto delle cose più notabili della città di Siena a uso de' forestieri*, Siena, Francesco Rossi, 1761 (2nd ed.).

Pedrocchi 2000. Anna Maria Pedrocchi, *Le stanze del tesoriere: la quadreria Patrizi: cultura senese nella storia del collezionismo romano del Seicento*, Milan, Alcon, 2000.

Pellicciari 1984. Armanda Pellicciari, 'Giovan Giacomo Sementi, allievo di Guido Reni', *Bollettino d'Arte* 6, 69, 24 (1984), 25–40.

Peña Martín 2011. Ángel Peña Martín, 'Yo duermo, pero mi corazón vela: el Niño Jesús dormido sobre el corazón', in Ricardo de la Fuente Ballesteros and Jesús Pérez Magallón, eds, *Del Barroco al Neobarroco: realidades y transferencias culturales* [proceedings of the international congress, Valladolid, September 2010], Valladolid, Universitas Castellae, 2011, 229–50.

Pepper 1968. D. Stephen Pepper, 'Guido Reni's Early Drawing Style', *Master Drawings* 6, 4 (1968), 364–82 and 424–31.

Pepper 1969a. D. Stephen Pepper, 'Guido Reni's Early Style: His Activity in Bologna, 1595–1601', *The Burlington Magazine* 111, 797 (1969), 472–83.

Pepper 1969b. D. Stephen Pepper, '*The Angel Appearing to Saint Jerome* by Guido Reni, a New Acquisition', *Bulletin of the Detroit Institute of Arts* 48, 2 (1969), 28–35.

Pepper 1971a. D. Stephen Pepper, 'Guido Reni's Roman Account Book. I: The Account Book', *The Burlington Magazine* 113, 819 (1971), 309–17.

Pepper 1971b. D. Stephen Pepper, 'Guido Reni's Roman Account Book. II: The Commissions', *The Burlington Magazine* 113, 820 (1971), 372–86.

Pepper 1971c. D. Stephen Pepper, 'Caravaggio and Guido Reni: Contrasts in Attitudes', *Art Quarterly* 34, 3 (1971), 325–44.

Pepper 1979. D. Stephen Pepper, 'A New Late Work by Guido Reni for Edinburgh and His Late Manner Re-Evaluated', *The Burlington Magazine* 121, 916 (1979), 418–25.

Pepper 1983. D. Stephen Pepper, '*Bacchus and Ariadne* in the Los Angeles County Museum: The "Scherzo" as Artistic Mode', *The Burlington Magazine* 125, 959 (1983), 68–75.

Pepper 1984. D. Stephen Pepper, *Guido Reni: A Complete Catalogue of His Works with an Introductory Text*, New York, New York University Press; Oxford, Phaidon, 1984.

Pepper 1986. D. Stephen Pepper, 'Guido Reni's *Erigone*: A Work Restored and a Mystery Resolved', *The Burlington Magazine* 128, 996 (1986), 208–9.

Pepper 1988. D. Stephen Pepper, *Guido Reni: l'opera completa*, Novara, De Agostini, 1988.

Pepper 1990. D. Stephen Pepper, 'Afterthoughts on the Guido Reni Exhibition', *Accademia Clementina, Atti e Memorie* 25 (1990), 31–58.

Pepper 1991. D. Stephen Pepper, 'Guido Reni: Additions to the Catalogue', *Accademia Clementina, Atti e Memorie* 28–29 (1991), 81–89.

Pepper 1992. D. Stephen Pepper, 'Guido Reni's *Davids*: The Triumph of Illumination', *Artibus et Historiae* 13, 25 (1992), 129–44.

Pepper 1998. D. Stephen Pepper, 'Da Reni a Masoch', *Quadri & Sculture* 6 (1998), 43–45.

Pepper 1999a. D. Stephen Pepper, 'La storia del *Ratto di Elena* di Guido Reni: la conferma del resoconto di Sandrart del 1632', in Denis Mahon and Maria Elisa Tittoni, eds, *Nicolas Poussin: i primi anni romani* [exh. cat. Rome, Palazzo delle Esposizioni, 26 November 1998–1 March 1999], Milan, Electa, 1998, 129–43 / *Nicolas Poussin: Works from His First Years in Rome*, Rome, Quadri e Sculture; Jerusalem, The Israel Museum, 1999.

Pepper 1999b. D. Stephen Pepper, 'Guido Reni's Practice of Repeating Compositions', *Artibus et Historiae* 20, 39 (1999), 27–54.

Pepper and Mahon 1999. D. Stephen Pepper and Denis Mahon, 'Guido Reni's *Fortuna with a Purse* Rediscovered', *The Burlington Magazine* 141, 1152 (1999), 156–63.

Pepper and Morselli 1993. D. Stephen Pepper and Raffaella Morselli, 'Guido Reni's Hercules Series: New Considerations and Conclusions', *Studi di Storia dell'Arte* 4 (1993), 129–47.

Pérez López 2015. Nerea Virginia Pérez López, 'Murillo y los orígenes de la iconografía del Niño Jesús dormido sobre la cruz', *Boletín de Arte* 36 (2015), 145–54.

Pérez Preciado 2010. José Juan Pérez Preciado, 'El marqués de Leganés y las artes', PhD diss., Universidad Complutense de Madrid, 2010.

Pérez Sánchez 1962. Alfonso E. Pérez Sánchez, 'Algunos pintores italianos del siglo XVII en el Museo del Prado', *Archivo Español de Arte* 35, 137 (1962), 51–60.

Pérez Sánchez 1965a. Alfonso E. Pérez Sánchez, *Pintura italiana del s. XVII en España*, Madrid, Universidad de Madrid and Fundación Valdecilla, 1965.

Pérez Sánchez 1965b. Alfonso E. Pérez Sánchez, 'Torpeza y humildad de Zurbarán', *Goya* 64–65 (1965), 266–75.

Pérez Sánchez 1970. Alfonso E. Pérez Sánchez, *Pintura italiana del siglo XVII: exposición conmemorativa del ciento cincuenta aniversario de la fundación del Museo del Prado* [exh. cat. Madrid, Casón del Buen Retiro, April–May 1970], Madrid, Ministerio de Educación y Ciencia, 1970.

Pérez Sánchez 1972a. Alfonso E. Pérez Sánchez, 'Dessins de Lanfranco et de Reni a l'Académie San Fernando de Madrid', *Revue de l'Art* 15 (1972), 53–61.

Pérez Sánchez 1972b. Alfonso E. Pérez Sánchez, *Museo del Prado: catálogo de dibujos*, vol. 1: *Dibujos españoles siglos XV-XVII*, Madrid, Museo del Prado, 1972.

Pérez Sánchez 1973. Alfonso E. Pérez Sánchez, *Caravaggio y el naturalismo español* [exh. cat. Seville, Sala de Armas de los Reales Alcazares, September–October 1973], Madrid, Ministerio de Educación y Ciencia, 1973.

Pérez Sánchez 1977. Alfonso E. Pérez Sánchez, 'Las colecciones de pintura del conde de Monterrey (1653)', *Boletín de la Real Academia de la Historia* 174 (1977), 417–59.

Pérez Sánchez 1988. Alfonso E. Pérez Sánchez, 'Reni e la Spagna', in Ebert-Schifferer, Emiliani and Schleier 1988, 690–708.

Pérez Sánchez 1993. Alfonso E. Pérez Sánchez, *De pintura y pintores: la configuración de los modelos visuales en la pintura española*, Madrid, Alianza, 1993.

Pérez Sánchez and Spinosa 1992. Alfonso E. Pérez Sánchez and Nicola Spinosa, eds, *Jusepe de Ribera, 1591–1652* [exh. cat. New York, The Metropolitan Museum of Art, 18 September–29 November 1992], New York, The Metropolitan Museum of Art, 1992.

Pericolo 2011. Lorenzo Pericolo, *Caravaggio and Pictorial Narrative: Dislocating the* Istoria *in Early Modern Painting*, 2 vols, London, Harvey Miller, 2011.

Pericolo 2015. Lorenzo Pericolo, '*Statuino*: An Undercurrent of Anticlassicism in Italian Baroque Art Theory', *Art History* 38, 5 (2015), 862–89.

Pericolo 2017. Lorenzo Pericolo, '"Donna bella e crudele": Michelangelo's Divine Heads in Light of the *Rime*', *Mitteilungen des Kunsthistorischen Institutes Florenz* 59, 2 (2017), 203–33.

Pericolo 2019. Lorenzo Pericolo, 'Whiteout: Self-Identity and Self-Awareness in Guido Reni's *Non-Finito*', in Shao Dazhen, Fan Di'an, and LaoZhu, eds, *Proceedings of the 34th International Congress of Art History*, 3 vols, Beijing, Commercial Press, 2019, 1:625–36.

Pericolo (in press). Lorenzo Pericolo, '1582: The Beginnings of the Carracci Academy between Bologna and Rome', in Vita Segreto, ed., *The Dawning of the Drawing Academy: Rome, Florence, Bologna*, Turnhout, Brepols, (in press).

Perini Folesani 1984. Giovanna Perini Folesani, 'L'epistolario del Malvasia, primi frammenti: le lettere all'Aprosio', *Studi Secenteschi* 25 (1984), 183–230.

Perini Folesani 1986. Giovanna Perini Folesani, ed., *Nell'età di Correggio e dei Carracci: pittura in Emilia dei secoli XVI e XVII / The Age of Correggio and the Carracci: Emilian Painting of the Sixteenth and Seventeenth Centuries* [exh. cat. Bologna, Pinacoteca Nazionale, Accademia di Belle Arti and Museo Civico Archeologico, 10 September–10 November 1986; Washington, National Gallery of Art, 19 December 1986–16 February 1987; New York, The Metropolitan Museum of Art, 26 March–24 May 1987], Bologna, Nuova Alfa; Washington, National Gallery of Art, 1986.

Perini Folesani 1990. Giovanna Perini Folesani, ed., *Gli scritti dei Carracci: Ludovico, Annibale, Agostino, Antonio, Giovanni Antonio*, Bologna, Nuova Alfa, 1990.

Perrier 1638. François Perrier, *Segmenta nobilium signorum et statuarum*, Rome, 1638.

Peruzzi 1986. Lucia Peruzzi, 'Per Michele Desubleo, fiammingo', *Paragone* 37, 431–33 (1986), 85–92.

Pestilli 1993. Livio Pestilli, '"The Burner of the Midnight Oil", a Caravaggesque Rendition of a Classic *Exemplum*: An Unrecognized Self-Portrait by Michael Sweerts?', *Zeitschrift für Kunstgeschichte* 56 (1993), 119–33.

Petrioli Tofani 1991–2005. Annamaria Petrioli Tofani, *Inventario: Gabinetto disegni e stampe degli Uffizi. Disegni di figura*, 2 vols, Florence, Olschki, 1991–2005.

Petrucci 2008. Francesco Petrucci, *Pittura di ritratto a Roma: il Seicento*, 3 vols, Rome, Andreina & Valneo Budai, 2008.

Picarelli 1904. Torquato Picarelli, *Basilica e casa romana di Santa Cecilia in Trastevere*, Rome, Tipografia Romana, 1904.

Picart 1734. Bernard Picart, *Impostures innocentes ou Recueil d'estampes d'après divers peintres illustres*, Amsterdam, Veuve de Bernard Picart, 1734.

Piergiovanni 2018. Patrizia Piergiovanni, ed., *Galleria Colonna: catalogo dei dipinti*, Rome, De Luca, 2018.

Pierguidi 2010. Stefano Pierguidi, 'Il ciclo dei costumi de' Romani antichi del Buen Retiro di Madrid', *Storia dell'Arte* 125–26 (2010), 79–93.

Pierguidi 2012a. Stefano Pierguidi, 'Bellori e i putti nella scultura del Seicento: Bernini, Duquesnoy, Algardi', *Marburger Jahrbuch für Kunstwissenschaft* 39 (2012), 155–80.

Pierguidi 2012b. Stefano Pierguidi, *Il capolavoro e il suo doppio: il Ratto di Elena di Guido Reni e la sua replica tra Madrid, Roma e Parigi*, Rome, Artemide, 2012.

Pierguidi 2014. Stefano Pierguidi, 'La *Lotta di amorini e baccarini* di Guido Reni', *Bollettino della Società Piemontese di Archeologia e Belle Arti* 63–64 (2014), 161–77.

Pierguidi 2015. Stefano Pierguidi, 'Il *Seneca* di Guido Reni e il dibattito sul primato tra Naturale e Antico', *Strenna Storica Bolognese* 65 (2015), 363–77.

Pierguidi 2016a. Stefano Pierguidi, 'Napoli, Madrid e Salamanca: tre casi di antologie delle scuole pittoriche tra Spagna e Viceregno', *Ricerche sull'Arte a Napoli in Età Moderna* 3 (2016), 21–29.

Pierguidi 2016b. Stefano Pierguidi, '*Ordinando varie favole ad un fine*: sulle *ekphrasis* di Giovanni Pietro Bellori degli affreschi di Annibale Carracci e Raffaello', *Barockberichte* 64 (2016), 7–15.

Pierguidi 2017. Stefano Pierguidi, 'La nascita di un genere: i putti', in Andrea Bacchi and Anna

Coliva, eds, *Bernini* [exh. cat. Rome, Galleria Borghese, 1 November 2017–4 February 2018], Milan, Officina Libraria, 2017, 54–73.

Pierguidi 2018. Stefano Pierguidi, ed., *Guido Reni, i Barberini e i Corsini: storia e fortuna di un capolavoro* [exh. cat. Rome, Galleria Nazionale di Arte Antica and Galleria Corsini, 16 November 2018–17 February 2019], Milan, Officina Libraria, 2018.

Pierguidi 2019a. Stefano Pierguidi, 'Guido Reni nella basilica di San Pietro: il soggetto della pala incompiuta', *Arte Cristiana* 107, 911 (2019), 148–53.

Pierguidi 2019b. Stefano Pierguidi, 'Sull'*Immacolata Concezione* di Guido Reni per l'Infanta di Spagna: una committenza del conestabile di Navarra, viceré di Napoli', *Strenna Storica Bolognese* 69 (2019), 79–85.

Pierguidi 2020. Stefano Pierguidi, *Gloriose gare: la coscienza storica delle scuole pittoriche italiane*, Trento, Temi, 2020.

Pierguidi 2022a. Stefano Pierguidi, 'Ancora sulla lettera di Annibale del 1608: l'uso delle fonti in Malvasia e una nota sul cantiere del Quirinale', *Mitteilungen des Kunsthistorischen Institutes in Florenz* 64, 2 (2022), 241–49.

Pierguidi 2022b. Stefano Pierguidi, '*La Crocifissione di San Pietro* di Guido Reni: stile, iconografia e fortuna', *Intrecci d'Arte* 64, 2 (2022), 53–75.

Pierguidi 2022c. Stefano Pierguidi, 'Guido Reni, Siena e i pittori di Giulio Mancini: il rapporto con Bartolomeo Manfredi e Rutilio Manetti', *Accademia dei Rozzi* 29/1, 56 (2022), 65–73.

Pierleoni 1991. Paolo Pierleoni, *Denti e santi, il mito di Apollonia: la 'rappresentazione' di Apollonia in una raccolta iconografica di artisti italiani*, Milan, Asclepio, 1991.

Piles 1715. Roger de Piles, *Abregé de la vie des peintres*, Paris, Jacques Estienne, 1715.

Pirovano 1985. Carlo Pirovano, ed., *Caravaggio e il suo tempo* [exh. cat. Naples, Museo Nazionale di Capodimonte, 14 May–30 June 1985], Naples, Electa, 1985.

Pita Andrade 1960. José Manuel Pita Andrade, *Colecciones artísticas de la Casa de Alba: catálogo de pinturas, por José Manuel Pita Andrade con inclusión de los datos aprovechables del de D. Ángel M. Barcia*, 3 vols, Madrid, Casa de Alba, 1960.

Ploegaert 2018. Mireille Ploegaert, 'Nicolaes Sohier (1588–1642): From Merchant to Member of the Cultural Elite in Seventeenth-Century Amsterdam', Master thesis, Universiteit Leiden, 2018.

Poleró 1857. Vicente Poleró y Toledo, *Catálogo de los cuadros del Real Monasterio de San Lorenzo, llamado del Escorial, en el que se comprenden los del Real Palacio, Casino del Principe y Capilla de la Fresneda*, Madrid, Imprenta de Tejado, 1857.

Polvillo 2009–10. Antonio González Polvillo, 'La Congregación de la Granada, el Inmaculismo sevillano y los retratos realizados por Francisco Pacheco de tres de sus principales protagonistas:

Miguel del Cid, Bernardo de Toro y Mateo Vázquez de Leca', *Atrio. Revista de Historia del Arte* 15–16 (2009–10), 47–72.

Pona 1620. Francesco Pona, *Sileno, overo Delle bellezze del luogo dell'Ill. Sig. Co. Gio. Giacomo Giusti*, Verona, Angelo Tamo, 1620.

Ponce Cárdenas 2018. Jesús Ponce Cárdenas, 'Pintura y panegírico: usos de la écfrasis en Manoel de Galhegos', *Versants* 65, 3 (2018), 97–123.

Poncet 2020. Olivier Poncet, *sub voce* 'Ubaldini, Roberto', in *Dizionario biografico degli italiani*, vol. 97, Rome, Istituto della Enciclopedia Italiana, 2020. Accessible at https://www.treccani.it/enciclopedia/roberto-ubaldini_%28Dizionario-Biografico%29/.

Ponz 1772–94. Antonio Ponz, *Viage de España, o Cartas, en que se da noticia de las cosas mas apreciables, y dignas de saberse que hay en ella*, 18 vols, Madrid, Joachin Ibarra, 1772–94 (1st ed.).

Ponz 1787–93. Antonio Ponz, *Viage de España en que se da noticia de las cosas mas apreciables, y dignas de saberse, que hay en ella*, 6 vols, Madrid, Viuda de Ibarra, Hijos y Compañía, 1787–93 (3rd rev. and exp. ed.).

Ponz 1988–89. Antonio Ponz, *Viaje de España seguido del Viaje fuera de España*, 5 vols, Madrid, Aguilar, 1988–89.

Portús Pérez 1998. Javier Portús Pérez, *La sala reservada del Museo del Prado y el coleccionismo de pintura de desnudo en la corte española, 1554–1838*, Madrid, Museo del Prado, 1998.

Portús Pérez 2004. Javier Portús Pérez, 'El Conde de Sandwich en Aranjuez (las fuentes del Jardín de la Isla en 1668)', *Reales Sitios* 41, 159 (2004), 46–59.

Portús Pérez 2017. Javier Portús Pérez, *Velázquez: La túnica de José*, Madrid, Patrimonio Nacional (Colección Palatina, 3), 2017.

Porzio 1999. Annalisa Porzio, *La quadreria di Palazzo Reale nell'Ottocento: inventari e museografia*, Naples, Arte Tipografica Napoli, 1999.

Posner 1963. Donald Posner, 'Spada, Reni and Roncalli at Loreto', *Arte Antica e Moderna* 23 (1963), 254–57.

Posner 1971. Donald Posner, *Annibale Carracci: A Study in the Reform of Italian Painting around 1590*, 2 vols, London, Phaidon (Kress Foundation Studies in the History of European Art, 5), 1971.

'Prado disperso' 1994. 'El "Prado disperso": cuadros depositados en Huesca', *Boletín del Museo del Prado* 15, 33 (1994), 85–88.

Prasad 2003. Shilpa Prasad, 'Guercino's "Theatricality" between Italy and Spain', in José Luis Colomer, ed., *Arte y diplomacia de la Monarquía Hispánica en el siglo XVII*, Madrid, Centro de Estudios Europa Hispánica and Villaverde, 2003, 389–402.

Primarosa 2017. Yuri Primarosa, *Ottavio Leoni (1578–1630): eccellente miniator di ritratti. Catalogo ragionato dei disegni e dei dipinti*, Rome, Ugo Bozzi, 2017.

Primarosa 2021. Yuri Primarosa, ed., *100 capolavori: Palazzo Barberini, Galleria Corsini*, Milan, Officina Libraria, 2021.

Procacci and Procacci 1965. Lucia Procacci and Ugo Procacci, 'Il carteggio di Marco Boschini con il cardinale Leopoldo de' Medici', *Saggi e Memorie di Storia dell'Arte* 4 (1965), 85–114.

Profili 2011. Francesca Profili, 'Alcune considerazioni su due dipinti della collezione Sfondrato: il *San Francesco in estasi* del Cavalier d'Arpino e l'*Estasi di Santa Cecilia* di Guido Reni', in Maria Giulia Aurigemma, ed., *Dal Razionalismo al Rinascimento: per i quaranta anni di studi di Silvia Danesi Squarzina*, Rome, Campisano, 2011, 136–43.

Prohaska 1988. Wolfgang Prohaska, 'Guido Reni e la pittura napoletana del Seicento', in Ebert-Schifferer, Emiliani and Schleier 1988, 644–51.

Prosperi Valenti Rodinò 2012. Simonetta Prosperi Valenti Rodinò, 'Il collezionista della doppia numerazione: un mistero ancora da svelare nella Roma del tardo Seicento', *Les Cahiers d'Histoire de l'Art* 10 (2012), 51–59.

Prota Giurleo 1957. Ulisse Prota Giurleo, 'Fanzago ignorato', *Il Fuidoro* 4 (1957), 146–49.

Puente [1605] 1935. Luis de la Puente (S.I.), *Meditaciones de los misterios de nuestra santa Fe con la práctica de la oración mental sobre ellos* [1605], 2 vols, Madrid, Apostolado de la Prensa, 1935 (5th ed.).

Puglisi 1999. Catherine R. Puglisi, *Francesco Albani*, New Haven, Yale University Press, 1999.

Puglisi 2020. Catherine R. Puglisi, '"Certe palliole da processione": Guido Reni, Silk, Civic Piety and Ceremony', *Artibus et Historiae* 81 (2020), 253–79.

Puglisi 2021. Catherine R. Puglisi, '"Bisognare pensarvi un'anno intero": Guido Reni's Second Manner and "Bianchezza"', *Artibus et Historiae* 83 (2021), 173–204.

Pulini 2002. Massimo Pulini, *Il secondo sguardo: la copia e la replica tra invenzione, emulazione e agone; il caso di Simone Cantarini*, Milan, Medusa (Le porte regali, 11), 2002.

Pulini 2012. Massimo Pulini, ed., *Rimini per Simone Cantarini 1612–2012: opere da raccolte private* [exh. cat. Rimini, Museo della Città, 15 December 2012–17 February 2013], Rimini, Museo della Città, 2012.

Pulini 2018. Massimo Pulini, 'Copia e replica nelle industrie pittoriche bolognesi del Seicento: La bottega di Guido Reni', in Pietro di Loreto, ed., *Originali, repliche, copie: uno sguardo diverso sui grandi maestri*, Rome, Ugo Bozzi, 2018, 160–65.

Pulini 2019. Massimo Pulini, *Guido Reni e i suoi Amori in gioco*, Maastricht, Altomani & Sons, 2019.

Pulini 2020. Massimo Pulini, 'Capolavori a Salamanca: novità e inedite attribuzioni per importanti artisti italiani del Seicento', *About Art online* (6 September 2020). Accessible at https://www.aboutartonline.com/capolavori-a-salamanca-novita-e-inedite-attribuzioni-per-importanti-artisti-italiani-del-seicento/.

Puncuh 1984. Dino Puncuh, 'Collezionismo e commercio di quadri nella Genova Sei-Settecentesca:

note archivistiche dai registri contabili dei Durazzo', *Rassegna degli Archivi di Stato* 44, 1 (1984), 164–218.

Pupillo 1996. Marco Pupillo, 'I Crescenzi, Francesco Contarelli e Michelangelo da Caravaggio: contesti e documenti per la commissione in S. Luigi dei Francesi', in Stefania Macioce, ed., *Michelangelo Merisi da Caravaggio: la vita e le opere attraverso i documenti* [proceedings of the international congress, Rome, 5–6 October 1995], Rome, Logart Press, 1996, 148–66.

Pupillo 1998. Marco Pupillo, 'Il "Virtuoso tradito": una società tra Orazio Borgianni, Gaspare Celio e Francesco Nappi e i rapporti con Giovan Battista Crescenzi', *Storia dell'Arte* 93–94 (1998), 303–11.

Quattrone 1993. Stefania Quattrone, 'Iconografia e iconologia del mito di Atalanta dall'antichità classica all'età barocca', *Arte Lombarda*, 2–4, 105–107 (1993), 148–52.

Quazza 1950. Romolo Quazza, *Preponderanza spagnuola (1559–1700)*, Milan, Vallardi, 1950.

Rada y Delgado 1883. Juan de Dios de la Rada y Delgado, *Catálogo del Museo Arqueológico Nacional*, Madrid, Imprenta de Fortanet, 1883.

Rasmussen 2000. Beth L. Rasmussen, 'The Antithetical Mary Magdalene: Grace, Guido Reni, and Early Italian Baroque Art', PhD diss., Long Beach, California State University, 2000.

Raspi Serra 2002–5. Joselita Raspi Serra, *Il primo incontro di Winckelmann con le collezioni romane: ville e palazzi di Roma, 1756*, 4 vols, Rome, Quasar (Eutopia. Quaderni, 6), 2002–5.

Ratti 1766. Carlo Giuseppe Ratti, *Istruzione di quanto può vedersi di più bello in Genova in pittura, scultura ed architettura*, Genoa, Paolo & Adamo Scionico, 1766.

Redín Michaus 2013. Gonzalo Redín Michaus, 'Guido Reni's *Conversion of Saul*: A Newly Attributed Painting in the Escorial', *The Burlington Magazine* 155, 1327 (2013), 677–82.

Redín Michaus 2016a. Gonzalo Redín Michaus, ed., *De Caravaggio a Bernini: obras maestras del Seicento italiano en las colecciones reales de Patrimonio Nacional* [exh. cat. Madrid, Palacio Real, 7 June–16 October 2016], Madrid, Patrimonio Nacional, 2016.

Redín Michaus 2016b. Gonzalo Redín Michaus, 'De Caravaggio a Bernini: pintura y escultura del Seicento en las Colecciones Reales de Patrimonio Nacional', in Redín Michaus 2016a, 13–45.

Redín Michaus 2017. Gonzalo Redín Michaus, 'El XIV duque de Alba, Carlos Miguel Fitz-James Stuart, y la pintura napolitana', in Elisa Acanfora and Mauro Vincenzo Fontana, eds, *Camillo d'Errico (1821–1897) e le rotte mediterranee del collezionismo ottocentesco*, Foggia, Claudio Grenzi, 2017, 171–83.

Reggio 2000. Sonia Reggio, 'Le vicende costruttive e decorative di palazzo Zani: alcune precisazioni sugli affreschi di Guido Reni', *Accademia Clementina, Atti e Memorie* 40 (2000), 17–46.

Respaldiza Lama 2002. Pedro José Respaldiza Lama, *San Isidoro del Campo (1301–2002): fortaleza de la espiritualidad y santuario del poder* [exh. cat. Santiponce, Monasterio de San Isidoro del Campo, 10 July–8 December 2002], Seville, Junta de Andalucía, 2002.

Restellini 2001. Marc Restellini, ed., *Meisterwerke von Fra Angelico bis Bonnard: fünf Jahrhunderte Malerei: die Sammlung des Dr. Rau* [exh. cat. Cologne, Wallraf-Richartz Museum in der Josef-Haubrich-Kunsthalle, 26 May–26 August 2001; Munich, Haus der Kunst, 5 October 2001–13 January 2002], Milan, Skira, 2001.

Rice 1997. Louise Rice, *The Altars and Altarpieces of New St Peter's: Outfitting the Basilica, 1621–1666*, Cambridge, Cambridge University Press, 1997.

Richardson 1722. Jonathan Richardson, *An Account of Some of the Statues, Bas-Reliefs, Drawings and Pictures in Italy*, London, J. Knapton, 1722.

Ridolfi 1648. Carlo Ridolfi, *Le maraviglie dell'arte, overo Le vite de gli'illustri pittori veneti e dello Stato*, 2 vols, Venice, Gio. Battista Sgava, 1648.

Riedl 1976. Peter Anselm Riedl, *Disegni dei baroccheschi senesi: Francesco Vanni e Ventura Salimbeni*, Florence, Olschki (Gabinetto Disegni e Stampe degli Uffizi, 46), 1976.

Riedl 1978. Peter Anselm Riedl, 'Zu Francesco Vannis Tätigkeit für römische Auftraggeber', *Mitteilungen des Kunsthistorischen Institutes in Florenz* 22, 3 (1978), 313–54.

Rinaldi 1617. Cesare Rinaldi, *Lettere di Cesare Rinaldi, il Neghittoso Academico Spensierato*, Venice, Tomaso Baglioni, 1617.

Rinaldi 1619. Cesare Rinaldi, *Rime*, Bologna, Gieronimo Mascheroni, 1619 (3rd ed.).

Rinaldi 1620. Cesare Rinaldi, *Lettere*, 2 vols, Bologna, Bartolomeo Cochi, 1620.

Ripa 1603. Cesare Ripa, *Iconologia, ovvero Descrittione di diverse imagini cavate dall'antichità & di propria inventione*, Rome, Lepido Facij, 1603.

Rippa and Finucci 2007. Maurizio Rippa Bonati and Valeria Finucci, eds, *Mores Italiae: costumi e scene di vita del Rinascimento / Mores Italia: Costume and Life in the Renaissance*, Yale University, Beinecke Library, MS. 457, Cittadella (Padua), Biblos, 2007.

Ritrovato 2002. Salvatore Ritrovato, '"Ciò che chiudo nel cor dipingo in carte": la poesia di Cesare Rinaldi nell'ambiente artistico bolognese di fine Cinquecento', *Schifanoia* 22–23 (2002), 145–55.

Ritschard and Morehead 2004. Claude Ritschard and Allison Morehead, eds, *Cléopâtre dans le miroir de l'art occidental* [exh. cat. Geneva, Musée Rath, 25 March–1 August 2004], Geneva, Musée d'art et d'histoire; Milan, 5 Continents, 2004.

Rivas Albaladejo 2014a. Ángel Rivas Albaladejo, 'La embajada extraordinaria del VI conde de Monterrey en Roma (1628–1631): instrumentos de delegación del poder real y líneas generales de su actuación política', in Daniel Aznar, Guillaume Hanotin, and Niels F. May, eds, *À la place du roi: vice-rois, gouverneurs et ambassadeurs dans les monarchies française et espagnole (XVIᵉ-XVIIIᵉ siècles)*, Madrid, Casa de Velázquez, 2014, 87–110.

Rivas Albaladejo 2014b. Ángel Rivas Albaladejo, 'Viaje, casa, secretaría, celebraciones y algunos aspectos culturales de la embajada del VI conde de Monterrey en Roma (1628–1631)', in Anselmi 2014, 310–39.

Rivas Albaladejo 2015. Ángel Rivas Albadalejo, 'Entre Madrid, Roma y Nápoles: el VI conde de Monterrey y el gobierno de la Monarquía Hispánica (1621–1653)', PhD diss., Universitat de Barcelona, 2015.

Rivera de las Heras 2013. José Ángel Rivera de las Heras, *Catálogo de pinturas de la Catedral de Zamora*, Zamora, Imprenta Jambrina, 2013.

Robertson 2008. Clare Robertson, *The Invention of Annibale Carracci*, Cinisello Balsamo, Silvana (Studi della Bibliotheca Hertziana, 4), 2008.

Rodríguez López 2018. María Isabel Rodríguez López, 'Atalanta e Hipomenes': recreación iconográfica de un mito', *Eikón Imago* 13 (2018), 167–96.

Rodríguez-Buzón Calle 1982. Manuel Rodríguez-Buzón Calle, *La Colegiata de Osuna*, Seville, Diputación Provincial (Arte Hispalense, 28), 1982.

Romagnoli 1822. Ettore Romagnoli, *Nuova guida della città di Siena per gli amatori delle belle arti*, Siena, Stamperia Mucci, 1822.

Romagnoli before 1835. Ettore Romagnoli, *Biografia cronologica de' bell'artisti senesi dal secolo XII a tutto il XVIII*, before 1835, manuscript, 13 vols, Siena, Biblioteca Comunale, Ms L.II.1-13.

Romagnoli 1836. Ettore Romagnoli, *Cenni storico-artistici di Siena e suoi suburbii*, Siena, Onorato Porri, 1836.

Romagnoli 1840. Ettore Romagnoli, *Cenni storico-artistici di Siena e suoi suburbii, riveduti e nuovamente pubblicati con un breve discorso sulla vita e gli scritti dell'autore*, Siena, Onorato Porri, 1840.

Rombouts and Lerius 1961. Philippe Rombouts and Théodore van Lerius, *De Liggeren en andere historische archieven der Antwerpsche Sint Lucasgilde*, vol. 1: *Liggere van 1453–1615*, Amsterdam, Israel, 1961.

Rose-de Viejo 1983. Isadora Rose-de Viejo, 'Manuel Godoy: patrón de las artes y coleccionista', PhD diss., 2 vols, Universidad Complutense de Madrid, 1983.

Rose-de Viejo 2021. Isadora Rose-de Viejo, *Catálogo actualizado de la colección de Manuel Godoy*, 2021. Accessible at https://www.isadaroseviejo.eu.

Rosenberg et al. 2019. Pierre Rosenberg et al., *Les dessins de la collection Mariette: écoles italienne et espagnole*, 4 vols, Paris, Somogy and Association Mariette, 2019.

Rosenberg and Choueiry 2022. Pierre Rosenberg and Marie-Liesse Choueiry, *Les dessins de la collection Mariette : écoles flamande, hollandaise et allemande*, 2 vols, Madrid, El Viso; Paris, Association Mariette, 2022.

Rosenthal 1992. Margaret F. Rosenthal, *The Honest Courtesan: Veronica Franco, Citizen and Writer in Sixteenth-Century Venice*, Chicago and London, University of Chicago Press, 1992.

Roses Lozano 1998. Joaquín Roses Lozano, 'La *Fábula de Adonis, Hipómenes y Atalanta* de Diego Hurtado de Mendoza: grados de la imitación renacentista', in *Congreso internacional sobre Humanismo y Renacimiento*, 2 vols, León, Universidad de León, 1998, 2:123–50.

Roskill 1968. Mark W. Roskill, *Dolce's* Aretino *and Venetian Art Theory of the Cinquecento*, New York, New York University Press (Monographs on Archaelogy and the Fine Arts, 15), 1968.

Rossi 1850–51. Stefano Rossi, '*L'Annunciat*a di Guido Reni in Ascoli', *L'Album. Giornale Letterario e di Belle Arti* 17, 16 (1850–51), 121–25.

Rossini 1776. Pietro Rossini, *Il Mercurio errante delle grandezze di Roma, tanto antiche, che moderne*, 2 vols, Rome, Gaetano Quojani, 1776 (10th ed.).

Rotatori 2020. Francesco Rotatori, 'Paintings by Andrea Sacchi and Andrea Camassei for the Count of Monterrey', *The Burlington Magazine* 162, 1413 (2020), 1072–75.

Röttgen 2002. Herwarth Röttgen, *Il cavalier Giuseppe Cesari d'Arpino: un grande pittore nello splendore della fama e nell'incostanza della fortuna*, Rome, Ugo Bozzi, 2002.

Rudolph 1974. Stella Rudolph, 'Il *Bacco e Arianna* di Guido Reni a Villa Albani', *Arte Illustrata* 7, 57 (1974), 36–42.

Ruffo 1916. Vincenzo Ruffo, 'Galleria Ruffo nel secolo XVII in Messina (con lettere di pittori ed altri documenti inediti), II', *Bollettino d'Arte del Ministero della Pubblica Istruzione* 10, 3–4 (1916), 95–128.

Ruiz Gómez 1998. Leticia Ruiz Gómez, *La colección de estampas devocionales de las Descalzas Reales de Madrid*, Madrid, Fundación Universitaria Española, 1998.

Ruiz Gómez 2009a. Leticia Ruiz Gómez, ed., *Juan Bautista Maíno: 1581–1649* [exh. cat. Madrid, Museo Nacional del Prado, 20 October 2009–17 January 2010], Madrid, Museo Nacional del Prado, 2009.

Ruiz Gómez 2009b. Leticia Ruiz Gómez, 'Juan Bautista Maíno: la construcción de un pintor', in Ruiz Gómez 2009a, 17–29.

Safarik 1981. Eduard A. Safarik, with the collaboration of Gabriello Milantoni, *Catalogo sommario della Galleria Colonna in Roma: dipinti*, Rome, Bramante Editrice, 1981.

Safarik 1996. Eduard A. Safarik, *Collezione dei dipinti Colonna: inventari 1611–1795*, ed. Anna Cera Sones, Los Angeles, The J. Paul Getty Trust (Documents for the History of Collecting, Italian Inventories, 2), Munich, K. G. Saur, 1996.

Safarik 1999. Eduard A. Safarik, *Palazzo Colonna*, Rome, De Luca, 1999.

Safarik and Torselli 1982. Eduard A. Safarik and Giorgio Torselli, *La Galleria Doria Pamphilj a Roma*, Rome, Palombi, 1982.

Sajonia–Dadreo 1853. Ludolfo de Sajonia, *Vida de nuestro adorable Redentor Jesucristo*, ed. Juan Dadreo, Mexico City, Juan Navarro, 1853.

Salerno 1960. Luigi Salerno, 'The Picture Gallery of Vincenzo Giustiniani, II: The Inventory, Part I', *The Burlington Magazine* 102, 684 (1960), 93–104.

Salerno 1988. Luigi Salerno, *I dipinti del Guercino*, Rome, Ugo Bozzi, 1988.

Salort Pons 2002. Salvador Salort Pons, *Velázquez en Italia*, Madrid, Fundación de Apoyo a la Historia del Arte Hispánico, 2002.

Salort Pons 2012. Salvador Salort Pons, 'A Letter of Introduction for Velázquez in Bologna', *The Burlington Magazine* 154, 1314 (2012), 616–19.

Salvy 2001. Gérard-Julien Salvy, *Reni*, Milan, Electa (I Maestri, 17), 2001.

Sánchez Rivero 1927. Ángel Sánchez Rivero, *Viaje de Cosme III por España (1668–1669): Madrid y su provincia*, Madrid, Imprenta Municipal, 1927.

Sandri 2005. Serena Sandri, 'Il funerale di Agostino Carracci e il ruolo degli artisti nei cerimoniali funebri bolognesi del Seicento', *Annuario della Scuola di Specializzazione in Storia dell'Arte* 6 (2005), 6–35.

Sani 1998. Bernardina Sani, 'The Sixteenth and Seventeenth Centuries', in Giulietta Chelazzi Dini, Alessandro Angelini, and Bernardina Sani, *Sienese Painting from Duccio to the Birth of the Baroque*, New York, Harry N. Abrams, 1998, 323–461.

Sansovino and Martinioni 1663. Francesco Sansovino, *Venetia città nobilissima et singolare, con aggiunta di tutte le cose notabili della stessa città, fatte, et occorse dall'anno 1580 fino al presente 1663 da D. Giustiniano Martinioni*, Venice, Steffano Curti, 1663.

Santi 1980–81. Bruno Santi, ed., *Zibaldone Baldinucciano: scritti di Filippo Baldinucci, Francesco Saverio Baldinucci, Luca Berrettini, Bernardo De Dominici, Giovanni Camillo Sagrestani e altri*, 2 vols, Florence, SPES, 1980–81.

Santos 1657. Francisco de los Santos, *Descripción breve del Monasterio de S. Lorenzo el Real del Escorial*, Madrid, Imprenta Real, 1657.

Santos 1667. Francisco de los Santos, *Descripción breve del Monasterio de S. Lorenzo el Real del Escorial*, Madrid, Ioseph Fernandez de Buendia, 1667 (2nd ed.).

Santos 1680. Francisco de los Santos, *Quarta parte de la Historia de la Orden de San Gerónimo*, Madrid, Imprenta de Bernardo de Villa Diego, 1680.

Santos 1681. Francisco de los Santos, *Descripción del Real Monasterio de S. Lorenzo del Escorial*, Madrid, Imprenta de Bernardo de Villa Diego, 1681 (3rd ed.).

Santos 1698. Francisco de los Santos, *Descripción del Real Monasterio de S. Lorenzo del Escorial*, Madrid, Imprenta de Bernardo de Villa Diego, 1698 (4th ed.).

Saracini 1629. Gherardo Saracini, *Oratione per l'esequie della serenissima Madama Caterina de'*

Medici duchessa di Mantova, Siena, Bonetti, 1629.

Saxony [1470s] 2019–22. Ludolph of Saxony, *The Life of Jesus Christ* [1470s], trans. Milton T. Walsh, 4 vols, Collegeville (MN), Liturgical Press, 2019–22.

Scannelli 1657. Francesco Scannelli, *Il microcosmo della pittura, overo Trattato diviso in due libri*, Cesena, Neri, 1657.

Scannelli [1657] 1989. Francesco Scannelli, *Il microcosmo della pittura* [1657], 2 vols, Bologna, Nuova Alfa, 1989.

Scarabello 2013. Giovanni Scarabello, *Venezia, tre figlie della Repubblica: Bianca Cappello, Veronica Franco, Arcangela Tarabotti*, Venice, Supernova, 2013.

Scaramuccia 1674. Luigi P. Scaramuccia, *Le finezze de' pennelli italiani, ammirate e studiate da Girupeno sotto la scorta e disciplina del genio di Raffaello d'Urbino*, Pavia, Gio. Andrea Magri, 1674.

Scaramuccia–Giubbini 1965. Luigi P. Scaramuccia, *Le finezze de' pennelli italiani, ammirate, e studiate da Girupeno sotto la scorta e disciplina del genio di Raffaello d'Urbino* [1674], ed. Guido Giubbini, Milan, Labor, 1965.

Schaefer 1988. Scott Schaefer, 'Io Guido Reni Bologna: "l'uomo e l'artista"' / 'Io Guido Reni Bologna, Man and Artist', in Emiliani et al. 1988, CV-CXXI (Italian) / 1–16 (English).

Schilling and Blunt 1971. Edmund Schilling, *The German Drawings in the Collection of Her Majesty the Queen at Windsor Castle, and Supplements to the Catalogues of Italian and French Drawings with a History of the Royal Collection of Drawings by Anthony Blunt*, London and New York, Phaidon, 1971.

Schlegel 1985. Ursula Schlegel, 'Bernini und Guido Reni', *Jahrbuch der Berliner Museen* 27 (1985), 101–45.

Schleier 1970. Erich Schleier, 'Pintura italiana del siglo XVII: zur Jubiläumsausstellung des Prado im Casón del Buen Retiro in Madrid', *Kunstchronik* 23, 12 (1970), 341–49.

Schleier 1983. Erich Schleier, ed., *Disegni di Giovanni Lanfranco (1582–1647)* [exh. cat. Florence, Gallerie degli Uffizi, Gabinetto dei Disegni e delle Stampe], Florence, Olschki, 1983.

Schleier 1986. Erich Schleier, 'Una proposta per Guido Reni giovane', *Arte Cristiana* 74 (1986), 106–12.

Schmidt-Linsenhoff 1988. Viktoria Schmidt-Linsenhoff, 'La grazia di Guido: storia ed estetica della fortuna critica', in Ebert-Schifferer, Emiliani and Schleier 1988, 62–69.

Schröder 1993–2004. Stephan F. Schröder, *Catálogo de la escultura clásica: Museo del Prado*, 2 vols, Madrid, Museo Nacional del Prado, 1993–2004.

Schröder 2008. Stephan F. Schröder, ed., *Entre dioses y hombres: esculturas clásicas del Albertinum de Dresde y el Museo del Prado* [exh. cat. Madrid, Museo Nacional del Prado, 4 November 2008–12 April 2009; Dresden, Staatliche Kunstsammlungen, 20 May–27

September 2009], Madrid, Museo Nacional del Prado, 2008.

Schröder 2019. Klaus Albrecht Schröder, ed., *From Rubens to Makart: Liechtenstein, The Princely Collections* [exh. cat. Vienna, Albertina, 16 February–10 June 2019], Cologne, Wienand, 2019.

Schröder and Elvira Barba 2006. Stephan F. Schröder and Miguel Ángel Elvira Barba, 'Eutichio Ajello (1711–1793) y su *Descripción de la célebre Real Galería de San Ildefonso*', *Boletín de Museo del Prado* 24, 42 (2006), 40–88.

Sebastián 1985. Santiago Sebastián, *Contrarreforma y barroco: lecturas iconográficas e iconológicas*, Madrid, Alianza (Alianza Forma, 21), 1985 (2nd ed.).

Semenza 1999. Giulia Semenza, 'Sebastiano Ghezzi', in Giulia De Marchi, *Sebastiano e Giuseppe Ghezzi: protagonisti del barocco* [exh. cat. Comunanza, Palazzo Pascali, 8 May–22 August 1999], Venice, Marsilio 1999, 7–19.

Senkevitch 2008. Tatiana Senkevitch, 'The Critical Reception of the Bolognese School', in Henning and Schaefer 2008, 94–99.

Serafinelli 2015. Guendalina Serafinelli, 'L'ultimo soggiorno romano di Gian Giacomo Sementi, collaboratore di Guido Reni: alcune novità e una conferma documentaria sulla sua data di morte', *Valori Tattili* 5–6 (2015), 298–307.

Serrera 1982. Juan Miguel Serrera, 'Murillo y la pintura italiana de los siglos XVI y XVII: nuevas relaciones y concomitancias', *Goya* 169–71 (1982), 126–32.

Serrera 1988. Juan Miguel Serrera, ed., *Zurbarán* [exh. cat. Madrid, Museo del Prado, 3 May–30 July 1988], Madrid, Ministerio de Cultura, 1988.

Settis, Anguissola and Gasparotto 2015. Salvatore Settis, Anna Anguissola, and Davide Gasparotto, eds, *Serial/Portable Classic: The Greek Canon and Its Mutations* [exh. cat. Venice, Fondazione Prada, 9 May–24 August 2015], Milan, Fondazione Prada, 2015.

Sgarbi 2015. Vittorio Sgarbi, ed., *Da Cimabue a Morandi: Felsina pittrice* [exh. cat. Bologna, Palazzo Fava and Pinacoteca Nazionale, 14 February–17 May 2015], Bologna, Bononia University Press, 2015.

Sgarbi and Papetti 2013. Vittorio Sgarbi and Stefano Papetti, eds, *Da Rubens a Maratta: le meraviglie del Barocco nelle Marche*, vol. 2: *Osimo e la Marca di Ancona* [exh. cat. Osimo, Palazzo Campana, 29 June–15 December 2013], Cinisello Balsamo, Silvana, 2013.

Shawe-Taylor and Rumberg 2018. Desmond Shawe-Taylor and Per Rumberg, eds, *Charles I: King and Collector* [exh. cat. London, Royal Academy of Arts, 27 January–15 April 2018], London, Royal Academy of Arts, 2018.

Sickel 2001. Lothar Sickel, 'Künstlerrivalität im Schatten der Peterskuppel: Giuseppe Cesari d'Arpino und das Attentat auf Cristoforo Roncalli', *Marburger Jahrbuch für Kunstwissenschaft* 28 (2001), 159–89.

Simal López 2011. Mercedes Simal López, 'Nuevas noticias sobre las pinturas para el Real Palacio del Buen Retiro realizadas en Italia (1633–1642)', *Archivo Español de Arte* 84, 335 (2011), 245–60.

Sirén 1914. Osvald Sirén, *Nicodemus Tessin d.y:s, studieresor i Danmark, Tyskland, Holland, Frankrike och Italien: anteckningar, bref och ritningar*, Stockholm, Norstedt, 1914.

Sirocchi 2018. Simone Sirocchi, *Parigi e Modena nel Grand Siècle: gli artisti francesi alla corte di Francesco I e Alfonso IV d'Este*, Trieste, Edizioni Università di Trieste (Ricerche e documenti d'arte, 3), 2018.

Soria 1955. Martin S. Soria, *The Paintings of Zurbaran*, London, Phaidon, 1955 (2nd ed.).

Sparkes 1876. John C. L. Sparkes, *A Descriptive Catalogue of the Pictures in the Dulwich College Gallery with Biographical Notices of the Painters*, London, William Clowes and Sons, 1876.

Sparti 1998a. Donatella Livia Sparti, 'Il *Musaeum Romanum* di Francesco Angeloni: formazione e dispersione', *Paragone* 49, 585 (1998), 47–80.

Sparti 1998b. Donatella Livia Sparti, 'Tecnica e teoria del restauro scultoreo a Roma nel Seicento, con una verifica sulla collezione di Flavio Chigi', *Storia dell'Arte* 92 (1998), 60–131.

Spear 1972. Richard E. Spear, *Renaissance and Baroque Paintings from the Sciarra and Fiano Collections*, Rome, Ugo Bozzi, 1972.

Spear 1982. Richard E. Spear, *Domenichino*, 2 vols, New Haven and London, Yale University Press, 1982.

Spear 1989. Richard E. Spear, 'Re-viewing the "Divine" Guido', *The Burlington Magazine* 131, 1034 (1989), 367–72.

Spear 1994. Richard E. Spear, 'Guercino's "prix-fixe": Observations on Studio Practices and Art Marketing in Emilia', *The Burlington Magazine* 136, 1098 (1994), 592–602.

Spear 1997. Richard E. Spear, *The 'Divine' Guido: Religion, Sex, Money and Art in the World of Guido Reni*, New Haven and London, Yale University Press, 1997.

Spear 2007. Richard E. Spear, 'San Sebastiano e le repliche di Reni', in Boccardo and Salomon 2007, 33–50.

Spenlé 2008. Virginie Spenlé, *Die Dresdner Gemäldegalerie und Frankreich: Der 'bon goût' im Sachsen des 18. Jahrhunderts*, Beucha (Germany), Sax-Verlag, 2008.

Spezzaferro 1985. Luigi Spezzaferro, 'Un imprenditore del primo Seicento: Giovanni Battista Crescenzi', *Ricerche di Storia dell'Arte* 26 (1985), 50–74.

Spike and Di Zio 1988. John T. Spike and Tiziana Di Zio, 'L'inventario dello studio di Guido Reni (11 Ottobre 1642)', *Accademia Clementina, Atti e Memorie* 22 (1988), 43–65.

Spinosa 2003. Nicola Spinosa, *Ribera: l'opera completa*, Naples, Electa Napoli, 2003.

Spinosa 2008. Nicola Spinosa, *Ribera: la obra completa*, Madrid, Fundación Arte Hispánico, 2008.

Spinosa 2011. Nicola Spinosa, ed., *Il giovane Ribera tra Roma, Parma e Napoli, 1608–1624* [exh. cat. Naples, Museo di Capodimonte, 23 September 2011–8 January 2012], Naples, Arte'm, 2011.

Stanzani 1992. Anna Stanzani, 'Vent'anni di pittura nelle chiese di Bologna 1600–1620', in Andrea Emiliani, ed., *La pittura in Emilia e in Romagna*, vol. 5.1: *Il Seicento*, Milan, Nuova Alfa, 1992, 113–56.

Stirling-Maxwell 1848. William Stirling-Maxwell, *Annals of the Artists of Spain*, 3 vols, London, John Ollivier, 1848.

Stoichiţă 1997. Victor I. Stoichiţă, *Das mystische Auge: Vision und Malerei im Spanien des Goldenen Zeitalters*, Munich, Wilhelm Fink, 1997.

Stone 1991. David M. Stone, *Guercino: catalogo completo dei dipinti*, Florence, Cantini (I gigli dell'arte, 21), 1991.

Stratton 1994. Suzanne L. Stratton, *The Immaculate Conception in Spanish Art*, Cambridge, Cambridge University Press, 1994.

Strazzullo 1978. Franco Strazzullo, *La real cappella del Tesoro di S. Gennaro: documenti inediti*, Naples, Società Editrice Napoletana (Studi e testi di storia e critica dell'arte, 5), 1978.

Strazzullo 1994. Franco Strazzullo, *La Cappella di San Gennaro nel Duomo di Napoli: documenti inediti*, Naples, Istituto Grafico Editoriale Italiano (Le chiese di Napoli, 1), 1994.

Strinati and Mignosi Tantillo 1996. Claudio Strinati and Almamaria Mignosi Tantillo, eds, *Domenichino 1581–1641* [exh. cat. Rome, Museo Nazionale del Palazzo di Venezia, 10 October 1996–14 January 1997], Milan, Electa, 1996.

Strinati and Vodret Adamo 2000. Claudio Strinati and Rossella Vodret Adamo, eds, *Guercino e la pittura emiliana del '600 dalle collezioni della Galleria Nazionale d'Arte Antica di Palazzo Barberini* [exh. cat. Padua, Fondazione Zabarella, 7 October 2000–28 January 2001], Venice, Marsilio, 2000.

Stuffmann 1968. Margret Stuffmann, 'Les tableaux de la collection de Pierre Crozat: historique et destinée d'un ensemble célèbre, établis en partant d'un inventaire après décès inédit (1740)', *Gazette des Beaux-Arts* 72 (1968), 11–144.

Summerscale 2000. Anne Summerscale, *Malvasia's Life of the Carracci: Commentary and Translation*, University Park, Pennsylvania State University Press, 2000.

Sutherland Harris 1999. Ann Sutherland Harris, 'Guido Reni First Thoughts', *Master Drawings* 37, 1 (1999), 3–34.

Sutherland Harris 2009. Anne Sutherland Harris, 'Guido Reni's Royal Patrons: A Drawing and a Proposal', *The Burlington Magazine* 151, 1272 (2009), 156–59.

Swoboda and Scholten 2019. Gudrun Swoboda and Frits Scholten, eds, *Caravaggio & Bernini: Early Baroque in Rome* [exh. cat. Vienna, Kunsthistorisches Museum, 15 October 2019–19 January 2020; Amsterdam, Rijksmuseum, 14 February–7 June 2020], Vienna, Kunsthistorisches Museum; Amsterdam, Rijksmuseum, 2019.

Szanto 2011. Mickaël Szanto, 'Venise, Reni et la romanité: la collection de tableaux de Michel Particelli d'Hémery', in Michel Hochmann, *Venise & Paris, 1500–1700: la peinture vénitienne de la Renaissance et sa réception en France* [papers of the congress, Bordeaux and Caen, 24–25 February and 6 May 2006], Geneva, Droz, 2011, 221–81.

Takahashi 2001. Kenichi Takahashi, 'La memoria di Papa Clemente VIII: una nuova proposta per *La caduta di Fetonte* e *La separazione della Luce dalle Tenebre* di Guido Reni', *Carrobbio* 27 (2001), 79–87.

Takahashi 2002. Kenichi Takahashi, 'Mazenta e Guido Reni: il *San Carlo* per la chiesa dei Catinari a Roma', *Arte Lombarda* 134, 1 (2002), 174–79.

Tarchiani 1922. Nello Tarchiani, *Mostra della pittura italiana del Seicento e del Settecento in Palazzo Pitti* [exh. cat. Florence, Palazzo Pitti, 1922], Rome, Bestetti & Tuminelli, 1922.

Taylor 2015. Paul Taylor, *Condition: The Ageing of Art*, London, Paul Holberton, 2015.

Temple Newsam 1951. *Temple Newsam House*, Leeds, The Libraries and Arts Committee of the Leeds Corporation, 1951.

Tervarent 1965. Guy de Tervarent, 'Eros and Anteros or Reciprocal Love in Ancient and Renaissance Art', *Journal of the Warburg and Courtauld Institutes* 28 (1965), 205–8.

Terzaghi 2007. Maria Cristina Terzaghi, *Caravaggio, Annibale Carracci, Guido Reni: tra le ricevute del Banco Herrera & Costa*, Rome, L'Erma Di Bretschneider, 2007.

Terzaghi 2021. Maria Cristina Terzaghi, 'Alle origini del naturalismo spagnolo: la *Santa Caterina* del Prado nel contesto delle prime copie da Caravaggio in Spagna (1610–20 ca.)', in García Cueto 2021, 89–105.

Terzaghi 2022. Maria Cristina Terzaghi, 'Roma 1600–1605: le occasioni di Guido' / 'Rome 1600–1605: the Opportunities of Guido', in Cappelletti 2022a, 28–41.

Toajas Roger 2016. María Ángeles Toajas Roger, 'Palacios ocultos: las Descalzas Reales de Madrid', in Bernardo García García, ed., *Felix Austria: lazos familiares, cultura política y mecenazgo artístico en las cortes de los Habsburgo*, Madrid, Fundación Carlos de Amberes, 2016, 327–74.

Tomory 1976. Peter A. Tomory, *The John and Mable Ringling Museum of Art, Sarasota: Catalogue of the Italian Paintings before 1800*, Sarasota (Florida), Stinehour Press, 1976.

Tormo 1914. Elías Tormo, 'La Inmaculada y el arte español', *Boletín de la Sociedad Española de Excursiones* 22 (1914), 108–32 and 173–218.

Tormo 1985. Elías Tormo, *Las iglesias del antiguo Madrid*, reed. with notes by María Elena Gómez-Moreno, Madrid, Instituto de España, 1985.

Toscano 2009. Bruno Toscano, 'Una nota sugli "straordinari talenti" del giovane Reni', in Frédéric Elsig, Noémie Étienne, and Grégoire Extermann, *Il più dolce lavorare che sia: mélanges en l'honneur de Mauro Natale*, Cinisello Balsamo, Silvana (Biblioteca d'arte, 23), 2009, 365–71.

Tóth and Falvay 2014. Peter Tóth and Dávid Falvay, 'New Light on the Date and Authorship of the *Meditationes vitae Christi*', in Stephen Kelly and Ryan Perry, eds, *Devotional Culture in Late Medieval England and Europe: Diverse Imaginations of Christ's Life*, Turnhout, Brepols, 2014, 17–105.

Totti 1638. Pompilio Totti, *Ritratto di Roma moderna*, Rome, Mascardi, 1638.

Tovar Martín 1979. Virginia Tovar Martín, *La arquitectura olvidada madrileña de la primera mitad del siglo XVIII*, Madrid, Instituto de Estudios Madrileños del Consejo Superior de Investigaciones Científicas, 1979.

Trapier 1952. Elizabeth du Gué Trapier, *Ribera*, New York, The Hispanic Society of America, 1952.

Trenta 1820. Tommaso Felice Trenta, *Guida del forestiere per la città e il contado di Lucca*, Lucca, Tipografia di Francesco Baroni, 1820.

Trenta–Mazzarosa 1829. Tommaso Felice Trenta, *Guida del forestiere per la città e il contado di Lucca di Tommaso Trenta, rifata dal Marchese Antonio Mazzarosa*, Lucca, Jacopo Balatresi, 1829.

Triadó 1999. Juan Ramon Triadó, *La pintura española*, vol. 2: *El Siglo de Oro*, Barcelona, Carroggio, 1999.

Turner 2004. Nicholas Turner, 'Pedro Fernández Durán, coleccionista de dibujos', in Nicholas Turner with the collaboration of José Manuel Matilla, *Museo del Prado: catálogo de dibujos*, vol. V: *Dibujos italianos del siglo XVI*, Madrid, Museo del Prado, 2004, 23–30.

Turner 2017. Nicholas Turner, *The Paintings of Guercino: A Revised and Expanded Catalogue Raisonné*, Rome, Ugo Bozzi, 2017.

Twiehaus 2002. Simone Twiehaus, *Dionisio Calvaert (um 1540–1619): Die Altarwerke*, Berlin, Dietrich Reimer, 2002.

Úbeda de los Cobos 2005. Andrés Úbeda de los Cobos, ed., *El palacio del Rey Planeta: Felipe IV y el Buen Retiro* [exh. cat. Madrid, Museo Nacional del Prado, 6 July–27 November 2005], Madrid, Museo Nacional del Prado, 2005 / *Paintings for the Planet King: Philip IV and the Buen Retiro Palace*, London, Paul Holberton, 2005.

Úbeda de los Cobos 2006. Andrés Úbeda de los Cobos, 'España y la fortuna crítica de los pintores boloñeses', in José Luis Colomer and Amadeo Serra Desfilis, eds, *España y Bolonia: siete siglos de relaciones artísticas y culturales*, Madrid, Centro de Estudios Europa Hispánica, 2006, 197–212.

Úbeda de los Cobos 2008. Andrés Úbeda de los Cobos, 'Guido Reni: *Hipómenes y Atalanta*', in *100 Obras Maestras del Museo del Prado*, Madrid, Museo Nacional del Prado, 2008, 102.

Uginet 1980. Francois-Charles Uginet, *Le Palais Farnèse*, vol. 3.1: *Le Palais Farnèse à travers les documents financiers (1535–1612)*, Rome, École Française de Rome, 1980.

Ugurgieri Azzolini 1649. Isodoro Ugurgieri Azzolini, *Le pompe sanesi, o'vero Relazione delli huomini, e donne illustri di Siena, e suo stato*, 2 vols, Pistoia, Pier'Antonio Fortunati, 1649.

Unglaub 1999. Jonathan Unglaub, 'Bolognese Painting and Barberini Aspirations: Giovanni Battista Manzini in the Archivio del Pozzo', *Accademia Clementina, Atti e Memorie* 38–39 (1999), 31–75.

Urriagli Serrano 2012. Diana Urriagli Serrano, *Las colecciones de pintura de Carlos IV en España*, Madrid, Fundación Universitaria Española, 2012.

Utili 2002. Mariella Utili, ed., *Museo di Capodimonte*, Milan, Touring Club, 2002.

Val Moreno 2016. Gloria del Val Moreno, 'Giovanni Battista Crescenzi (Roma, 1577–Madrid, 1635) y la renovación de las artes durante el reinado de Felipe IV', PhD diss., Universidad Complutense de Madrid, 2016.

Valdivieso 2005. Enrique Valdivieso, 'Presencia e influencia de las obras foráneas en el devenir del barroco pictórico sevillano', in Cabañas Bravo 2005, 199–206.

Valdivieso 2010. Enrique Valdivieso, *Murillo: catálogo razonado de pinturas*, Madrid, Ediciones El Viso, 2010.

Valli 1988. Francesca Valli, 'La *Strage degli innocenti* di Guido Reni', *Accademia Clementina, Atti e Memorie* 22 (1988), 97–103.

Van Hout 2001. Nico Van Hout, 'Reconsidering Rubens's Flesh Colour', *Boletín del Museo del Prado* 19, 37 (2001), 7–20.

Van der Sman 2016. Gert Jan van der Sman, ed., *Caravaggio and the Painters of the North* [exh. cat. Madrid, Museo Thyssen-Bornemisza, 21 June–18 September 2016], Madrid, Fundación Colección Thyssen-Bornemisza, 2016.

Vannugli 1988. Antonio Vannugli, 'La colección del marqués Giovan Francesco Serra', *Boletín del Museo del Prado* 9, 25–27 (1988), 33–43.

Vannugli 2000. Antonio Vannugli, 'Enigmi caravaggeschi: i quadri di Ottavio Costa', *Storia dell'Arte* 99 (2000), 55–83.

Vannugli 2009. Antonio Vannugli, 'La collezione del segretario Juan de Lezcano: Borgianni, Caravaggio, Reni e altri nella quadreria di un funzionario spagnolo nell'Italia del primo Seicento', *Memorie. Accademia Nazionale dei Lincei. Classe di Scienze Morali, Storiche e Filologiche* 9, 24, 3 (2009), 322–539.

Vasari–Bettarini and Barocchi 1966–97. Giorgio Vasari, *Le vite de' più eccellenti pittori, scultori e architettori nelle redazioni del 1550 e 1568*, ed. Rosanna Bettarini and Paola Barocchi, Florence, Studio per Edizioni Scelte, 1966–97.

Vasco Rocca 1979. Sandra Vasco Rocca, *Ss. Trinità dei Pellegrini*, Rome, Istituto di Studi Romani (Le Chiese di Roma illustrate, 133), 1979.

Vasi 1804. Mariano Vasi, *Itinerario istruttivo di Roma antica e moderna, ovvero Descrizione generale dei monumenti antichi e moderni, e* delle opere le più insigni di pittura, scultura ed architettura di questa alma città e delle sue adjacenze, 2 vols, Rome, Lazzarini, 1804.

Vasi 1812. Mariano Vasi, *Itinerario istruttivo di Roma antica e moderna ovvero Descrizione generale dei monumenti antichi e moderni, e delle opere le più insigni di pittura, scultura ed architettura di questa alma città e delle sue adjacenze*, 2 vols, Rome, Autore, 1812.

Vasi 1816. Mariano Vasi, *Itinerario istruttivo di Roma antica e moderna ovvero Descrizione generale dei monumenti antichi e moderni, e delle opere le più insigni di pittura, scultura ed architettura di questa alma città e delle sue vicinanze*, 2 vols, Rome, Autore, 1816.

Vecellio 1590. Cesare Vecellio, *De gli habiti antichi et moderni di diverse parti del mondo*, Venice, Damiano Zenaro, 1590.

Vega Loeches 2016. José Luis Vega Loeches, 'Idea e imagen de El Escorial en el siglo XVII: Francisco de los Santos', PhD diss., Universidad Complutense de Madrid, 2016.

Velázquez y lo velazqueño 1960. *Velázquez y lo velazqueño* [exh. cat. Madrid, Museo del Prado, 10 December 1960–23 February 1961], Madrid, Dirección General de Bellas Artes, 1960.

Venturi 1882. Adolfo Venturi, *La Regia Galleria Estense*, Modena, Paolo Toschi, 1882.

Venturi 1897. Adolfo Venturi, 'La Galleria Nazionale in Roma: nuovi acquisti', *Le Gallerie Nazionali Italiane* 3 (1897), 250–57.

Venturi 1927. Adolfo Venturi, *Studi dal vero attraverso le raccolte artistiche d'Europa*, Milan, Hoepli, 1927.

Vergara 1999. Alejandro Vergara, *Rubens and his Spanish Patrons*, Cambridge, Cambridge University Press, 1999.

Verità 1631. Domenico Verità, *Vera relatione di quanto è occorso nella città di Bologna in occasione che l'Illustrissimo Reggimento soddisfece al voto fatto alla Beatiss. Verg. del Santiss. Rosario, per la liberatione del contagio nella chiesa di S. Domenico il giorno di S. Gio. Evangelista dell'anno 1630*, Bologna, Clemente Ferroni, 1631.

Vignau 1903. Vicente Vignau, 'Manuel Napoli y la colección de cuadros del exconvento del Rosario', *Revista de Archivos, Bibliotecas y Museos* 9, 11 (1903), 372–76.

Villa and Villa 2011. Renzo Villa and Giovanni C. F. Villa, *Lorenzo Lotto*, Ciniselo Balsamo, Silvana, 2011.

Villaamil y Castro 1876. José Villaamil y Castro, 'La cabeza de Séneca: escultura en bronce que se conserva en el Museo Arqueológico Nacional', *Museo Español de Antigüedades* 7 (1876), 433–40.

Villamont 1602. Jacques de Villamont, *Les voyages du seigneur de Villamont, Chevalier de l'ordre de Hierusalem, gentilhomme ordinaire de la chambre du Roy divisez en trois livres*, Paris, Claude de Montr'oeil & Iean Richer, 1602.

Villar y Macías 1887. Manuel Villar y Macías, *Historia de Salamanca*, 3 vols, Salamanca, Imprenta de Francisco Núñez Izquierdo, 1887.

Villarreal y Águila 1686. Francisco Villarreal y Águila, *La Thebayda en poblado, el convento de la Concepción Capuchina en la imperial Toledo: su fundación y progresos, y las vidas de sus anacoretas religiosas, que con su santidad le han ilustrado*, Madrid, Imprenta de Antonio Román, 1686.

Visconti and Guattani 1820. Filippo Aurelio Visconti and Giuseppe Antonio Guattani, *Il Museo Chiaramonti descritto e illustrato*, Milan, Editori, 1820.

Visonà 2011. Mara Visonà, 'Un'opera di Giovacchino Fortini nuova e chiarificatrice', *Paragone* 100, 741 (2011), 45–48.

Vizzani 1633. Carlo Emanuele Vizzani, *La Maddalena dell'Em.mo e Reverendiss. Sig. Card. Santacroce dipinta da Guido Reni*, Bologna, Clemente Ferroni, 1633.

Vodret Adamo 2011–12. Rossella Vodret Adamo, ed., *Roma al tempo di Caravaggio, 1600–1630* [exh. cat. Rome, Museo Nazionale di Palazzo Venezia, 16 November 2011–5 February 2012], 2 vols, Milan, Skira, 2011–12.

Vodret Adamo 2021. Rossella Vodret Adamo, *Caravaggio, 1571–1610*, Cinisello Balsamo, Silvana, 2021.

Vsevoložskaja 2010. Svetlana N. Vsevoložskaja, *Museo Statale Ermitage: la pittura italiana del Seicento*, Milan, Skira, 2010.

Waagen 1854. Gustav Friedrich Waagen, *Treasures of Art in Great Britain, Being an Account of the Chief Collections of Paintings, Drawings, Sculptures, Illuminated Mss., &c.*, 3 vols, London, John Murray, 1854.

Waagen 1857. Gustav Friedrich Waagen, *Galleries and Cabinets of Art in Great Britain*, London, John Murray, 1857.

Waagen 1866–67. Gustav Friedrich Waagen, *Die vornehmsten Kunstdenkmäler in Wien*, 2 vols, Vienna, Wilhelm Braumüller, 1866–67.

Ward-Jackson 1979. Peter Ward-Jackson, *Italian Drawings*, vol. II: *17th–18th Century*, London, Her Majesty's Stationary Office, 1979.

Warren 2010. Jeremy Warren, 'Antico's *Nude of the Tortoise*', *Nuovi Studi* 15, 16 (2010), 27–31.

Warren 2016. Jeremy Warren, *The Wallace Collection: Catalogue of Italian Sculpture*, 2 vols, London, The Trustees of the Wallace Collection, 2016.

Warwick 2000. Genevieve Warwick, *The Arts of Collecting: Padre Sebastiano Resta and the Market for Drawings in Early Modern Europe*, Cambridge, Cambridge University Press, 2000.

Weber 1994. Christoph Weber, *Legati e governatori dello Stato pontificio (1550–1809)*, Rome, Istituto Poligrafico e Zecca dello Stato (Pubblicazioni degli Archivi di Stato. Sussidi, 7), 1994.

Weigert 1939. Roger-Armand Weigert, *Inventaire du fonds français: graveurs du XVIIe siècle. Bibliothèque nationale. Tome 1*, Paris, Bibliothèque nationale de France, 1939.

Weizsäcker 1900. Heinrich Weizsäcker, ed., *Catalog der Gemälde-Gallerie des Städelschen Kustinstituts in Frankfurt am Main*, vol. 1: *Die Werke der Älteren Meister vom 14. bis zum 18. Jahrhundert*, Frankfurt, A. Osterrieth, 1900.

Westheider and Philipp 2019. Ortrud Westheider and Michael Philipp, eds, *Wege des Barock: Die Nationalgalerien Barberini Corsini in Rom / Baroque Pathways: The National Galleries Barberini Corsini in Rome* [exh. cat. Potsdam, Palais Barberini, 13 July–6 October 2019], Munich, Prestel, 2019.

Weston 2016. Giulia Martina Weston, *Niccolò Tornioli (1606–1651): Art and Patronage in Baroque Rome*, Rome, Artemide, 2016.

Whitaker and Clayton 2007. Lucy Whitaker and Martin Clayton, *The Art of Italy in the Royal Collection: Renaissance and Baroque* [exh. cat. London, Buckingham Palace, The Queen's Gallery, 29 May 2007–19 January 2008], London, Royal Collection Publications, 2007.

Whitfield 1973. Clovis Whitfield, *England and the Seicento: A Loan Exhibition of Bolognese Paintings from British Collections* [exh. cat. London, Agnew and Sons, 6 November–7 December 1973], London, Lund Humphries, 1973.

Whitfield 2008. Clovis Whitfield, ed., *Exhibition at Partridge Fine Art Ltd.* [exh. cat. London, Whitfield Fine Art at Partridge Fine Arts, 4 June–18 July 2008], London, 2008.

Wimböck 2002. Gabriele Wimböck, *Guido Reni (1575–1642): Funktion und Wirkung des religiösen Bildes*, Regensburg, Schnell & Steiner (Studien zur christlichen Kunst, 3), 2002.

Wisch and Newbigin 2013. Barbara Wisch and Nerida Newbigin, *Acting on Faith: The Confraternity of the Gonfalone in Renaissance Rome*, Philadelphia, Saint Joseph's University Press, 2013.

Witte 2008. Arnold A. Witte, *The Artful Hermitage: The Palazzetto Farnese as a Counter-Reformation Diaeta*, Rome, L'Erma di Bretschneider, 2008.

Wood 1992. Carolyn H. Wood, 'The Ludovisi Collection of Paintings in 1623', *The Burlington Magazine* 134, 1073 (1992), 515–23.

Wouk 2018. Edward H. Wouk, *Frans Floris (1519/20–1570): Imagining a Northern Renaissance*, Leiden and Boston, Brill, 2018.

Ximénez 1764. Andrés Ximénez, *Descripción del Real Monasterio de San Lorenzo del Escorial: su magnífico templo, panteón y palacio, compendiada de la descripción antigua y exornada con nuevas vistosas láminas de su planta y montea, aumentada con la noticia de varias grandezas y alhajas … y coronada con un tratado apendice de los insignes profesores de las bellas artes estatuaria, arquitectura y pintura…*, Madrid, Imprenta de Antonio Marín, 1764.

Zanti–Banchieri 1712. Giovanni Zanti, *Origine delle porte, strade, borghi contrade, vie, viazzoli, piazzole, salicate, piazze, e trebbi dell'illustris. città di Bologna* [1635], ed. Adriano Banchieri, Bologna, Costantino Pisarri, 1712.

Zarco Cuevas 1926. Julián Zarco Cuevas, *El monasterio de San Lorenzo el Real de El Escorial y la*

Casita del Príncipe, Madrid, Imprenta Helénica, 1926.

Zavatta and Bigi Iotti 2004. Giulio Zavatta and Alessandra Bigi Iotti, 'Precisazioni sui dipinti di Alessandro Tiarini e Guido Reni della distrutta chiesa di San Tommaso di Strada Maggiore', *Il Carrobbio* 30 (2004), 145–64.

Zen Benetti 1972. Francesca Zen Benetti, 'Adriaan van den Spieghel: relazioni di parentela e di cultura, testamento, fortuna delle opere', *Quaderni per la Storia dell'Università di Padova* 5 (1972), 45–73.

Zeri 1954. Federico Zeri, *La Galleria Spada in Roma: catalogo dei dipinti*, Florence, Sansoni, 1954.

Zeri 1960. Federico Zeri, 'La *Salomè* di Guido già in casa Colonna', *Paragone* 11, 121 (1960), 50–60.

Zeri 1984. Federico Zeri, *Il Ratto di Europa di Guido Reni e 'Un gran personaggio in Ispagna'*, Milan, Leasarte (I cornici, 1), [1984].

Zeri 1991. Federico Zeri, ed., *Pinacoteca di Brera: scuola emiliana*, Milan, Electa, 1991.

Zezza 2010a. Andrea Zezza, ed., *Napoli e l'Emilia: studi sulle relazioni artistiche* [papers of the study days, Santa Maria Capua Vetere, 28–29 May 2008], Naples, Luciano, 2010.

Zezza 2010b. Andrea Zezza, 'Appunti su Guido Reni e i napoletani', in Zezza 2010a, 87–104 and 244–51.

Ziane 2011. Alexandra Ziane, *Amor divino, Amor profano: Liebe in geistlicher Musik und bildender Kunst in Rom um 1600*, Munich, Schöningh, 2011.

Zikos 2005. Dimitrios Zikos, 'Fürst Johann Adam Andreas I. von Liechtenstein und Massimiliano Soldani Benzi: die florentinische Bronzeplastik des Spätbarock', in Johann Kräftner, Claudia Lehner-Jobst, and Andreina D'Agliano, eds, *Barocker Luxus Porzellan: die Manufakturen Du Paquier in Wien und Carlo Ginori in Florenz* [exh. cat. Vienna, Liechtenstein Museum, 10 November 2005–29 January 2006], Munich, Prestel, 2005, 157–77.

Zucchini 1943. Guido Zucchini, 'San Michele in Bosco di Bologna', *L'Archiginnasio* 38 (1943), 18–70.

Zucchini 1953. Guido Zucchini, 'Comunicazione dell'Accademico Guido Zucchini su quadri e disegni inediti di Gaetano Gandolfi', *Accademia Clementina, Atti e Memorie* 5 (1953), 49–60.

INDEX

EXHIBITION

CURATOR
David García Cueto
Head of the Department of Italian
and French Painting up to 1800
at the Museo Nacional del Prado

with the assistance of
Gloria Antoni

COORDINATION
Silvia Villanueva Beltramini
Área de Exposiciones Temporales
del Museo Nacional del Prado

RESTORATION
Área de Restauración del Museo Nacional
del Prado [cat. 3, 8, 19, 22, 52, 61, 72, 78,
83, 95]
External workshop: Ana Isabel Ortega Díaz
[cat. 35]

INSTALLATION DESIGN AND DIRECTION
Desirée González García. Estudio GD
Gestión de Diseño

GRAPHIC DESIGN
This Side Up

INSTALLATION PRODUCTION
Intervento

TRANSPORTATION
Tti, Bovis Group

INSURANCE
Howden Artai Arte
Government Indemnity Scheme

CATALOGUE

COORDINATION
Luis Zolle
Área de Edición del Museo Nacional del Prado

EDITION
Erica Witschey

PRODUCTION
Gonzalo Saavedra
Lucía Varela
Ediciones El Viso

DESIGN
Subiela Bernat

TRANSLATION
Jenny Dodman (essays – Spanish to English)
Paul Edson (entries – Spanish to English)

INDEX
Teresa Prieto Palomo

PHOTOGRAPHIC DOCUMENTATION
Teresa Prieto Palomo

COLOUR SUPERVISION
Ana González Mozo
Gabinete Técnico de Documentación
del Museo Nacional del Prado

PREPRESS
Lucam

PRINTING AND BINDING
Impresos Izquierdo

Printed on H-UV presses with a low CO_2 emission
and energy-efficient system, using EMAS certified
paper made from sustainably managed forests

Cover: 350 g Invercote G
Interiors: 150 g Gardamatt ultra

© this edition: 2023, Museo Nacional del Prado

ISBN: 978-84-8480-591-5
NIPO: 829-23-019-X
D. L.: M-6325-2023

Cover: Guido Reni, *Hippomenes and Atalanta*,
c. 1618–19 (detail of cat. 61)

Page 2: Guido Reni, *Bacchus and Ariadne*,
c. 1617–19 (detail of cat. 58)

Pages 12–13: Guido Reni, *The Triumph of Job*,
1636 (detail of cat. 44)

ILLUSTRATION CREDITS

Album / Oronoz: fig. 64

Amsterdam, Rijksmuseum: fig. 66

Ascoli Piceno, Domenico Oddi: cat. 51

Astorga, Imagen M.A.S.: fig. 71

Berlin, bpk / Staatliche Kunstsammlungen Dresden / Elke Estel / Hans-Peter Klut: fig. 72

Bologna, Arcidiocesi di Bologna: fig. 20

Bologna, Palazzo Bentivoglio, photo: Carlo Favero: p. 203; cat. 24

Bologna, Pinacoteca Nazionale di Bologna: figs. 47, 74

Budapest, Szépművészeti Múzeum / Museum of Fine Arts: figs. 36, 38, 100

Cambridge, © Fitzwilliam Museum, Cambridge: cat. 29

Chicago, The Art Institute of Chicago: cat. 82

Courtesy Daniele Benati: figs. 50, 52-55, 57

Courtesy Aoife Brady: figs. 46, 48

Courtesy Rachel McGarry: figs. 21, 22

Courtesy Lorenzo Pericolo: fig. 84

Courtesy private collections: fig. 18; cat. 58

Courtesy Sotheby's: fig. 77

Courtesy Städel Museum, Frankfurt: cat. 7, 25

Detroit, Detroit Institute of Arts: p. 235; cat. 41

DRAC Île de France, David Bordes: p. 62; cat. 44

Dresden, © Gemäldegalerie Alte Meister, Staatliche Kunstsammlungen Dresden, photo: Elke Estel / Hans-Peter Klut: cat. 27

Dublin, photo © National Gallery of Ireland: fig. 78; cat. 91

Edinburgh, National Galleries of Scotland: p. 92; cat. 10, 47

Florence, Alinari Archives, fig. 88

Florence, Mario Bonotto / Photo Scala, Florence: fig. 1; Photo Scala, Florence: figs. 14, 28, 29, 34, 49, 59; White Images / Scala, Florence: fig. 24; Photo Scala, Florence – courtesy Ministero Beni e Att. Culturali e del Turismo: fig. 31; Cameraphoto / Scala: fig. 69; DeAgostini Picture Library / Scala, Florence: figs. 91, 98; Photo Austrian Archives / Scala Florence: fig. 94; Photo Scala Florence / Heritage Images: cat. 96; Liechtenstein, The Princely Collections, Vaduz-Vienna / Scala, Florence: cat. 68, 85

Florence, Fondazione di Studi di Storia dell'Arte Roberto Longhi, photo: Giusti Claudio: cat. 92

Florence, Gabinetto Fotografico delle Gallerie degli Uffizi: p. 267; figs. 39, 42, 83, 86; cat. 48, 53, 73, 88, 93

Florence, © Foto Giusti Claudio: pp. 30, 385; figs. 16, 25, 30, 60; cat. 20, 21, 94

Florence, Su concessione del Ministero della Cultura, Biblioteca Centrale Nazionale di Firenze: cat. 50

Genoa, © MIC, Galleria Nazionale di Palazzo Spinola: p. 321, cat. 67

Houston, © The Museum of Fine Arts, Houston; Thomas R. DuBrock: cat. 39

Liverpool, Courtesy National Museums Liverpool, Walker Art Gallery: fig. 73

London, Courtesy private collection: cat. 1

London, Dulwich Picture Gallery, Post-conservation image: p. 102, cat. 23

London, © The National Gallery, London: p. 149; fig. 6; cat. 9, 74, 89

London, Royal Collection Trust / © His Majesty King Charles III 2022: cat. 30, 31, 80

London, © The Trustees of the British Museum. All rights reserved: fig. 89

London, © Victoria and Albert Museum, London: fig. 9

Los Angeles, The J. Paul Getty Museum: fig. 99

Madrid, Agefotostock: Universal Images Group / Agefotostock: fig. 15; Giuseppe Schiavinotto / Mondadori / Agefotostock: figs. 32, 79; Jozef Sedmak / Alamy / Agefotostock: fig. 75; Artokoloro / Agefotostock: fig. 90

Madrid, Biblioteca Nacional de España: figs. 33, 101, 102; cat. 43

Madrid, Fundación Casa de Alba, Palacio de Liria, photo: Joaquín Cortés: cat. 35

Madrid, © Cuauhtli Gutiérrez: fig. 8

Madrid, Museo Arqueológico Nacional, photo: José Luis Municio García: cat. 36

Madrid, Museo de la Real Academia de Bellas Artes de San Fernando, photo: Pablo Linés: cat. 54, 77

Madrid, Museo Nacional del Prado (Gabinete Técnico): figs. 44, 45, 70, 76, 80, 87, 93

Madrid, Museo Nacional del Prado, photos: José Baztán and Alberto Otero: pp. 114, 179, 281, 288, 317, 347; figs. 2, 3, 58, 62, 63, 81, 97; cat. 3–6, 8, 13–15, 19, 22, 28, 33, 34, 37, 38, 49, 52, 56, 59–61, 64–66, 70–72, 78, 79, 83, 95

Madrid, Patrimonio Nacional, photo: Real Monasterio de San Lorenzo de El Escorial, p. 14; fig. 61; cat. 40; Patrimonio Nacional, Palacio Real de La Granja de San Ildefonso (Segovia): fig. 56, cat. 84, 87; photo: Mario Sedeño. Monasterio de las Descalzas Reales, Madrid, cat. 12

Mairie de Toulouse, Musée des Augustins, photo: Daniel Marti: cat. 57

Manchester, © Manchester Art Gallery / Bridgeman Images: fig. 96

Manvers © National Trust Images / John Hammond: fig. 19

Marseille, Claude Almodovar: cat. 46

Milan, Courtesy Porro & C.: fig. 65

Modena, Su concessione del Ministero della Cultura, Archivio fotografico delle Gallerie Estensi, photo: Carlo Vannini: cat. 32

Montecatini Terme, Studio Fotografico Rosellini: cat. 90

Naples, Per gentile concessione del MIC – Museo e Real Bosco di Capodimonte: cat. 62

New York, photo: Jerry L. Thompson: cat. 75

New York, The Metropolitan Museum of Art: p. 126; figs. 82, 85; cat. 55

Orléans, musée des Beaux-arts © M. Lombard Mathieu: p. 46; cat. 16

Ottawa, photo: NGC: fig. 7

Oxford, © Ashmolean Museum, University of Oxford: cat. 76

Paris, Photo © RMN-Grand Palais (musée du Louvre) / Gérard Blot: fig. 27; Photo © RMN-Grand Palais (musée du Louvre) / Hervé Lewandowski: p. 77; fig. 35; RMN-Grand Palais (musée du Louvre) / Tony Querrec: figs. 37, 40; RMN-Grand Palais (musée du Louvre) / Michèle Bellot: fig. 43; RMN-Grand Palais (musée du Louvre) / Franck Raux: p. 141; cat. 2; RMN-Grand Palais (musée du Louvre) / Mathieu Rabeau: fig. 67; RMN-Grand Palais (musée du Louvre) / Michel Urtado: fig. 68; RMN-Grand Palais (musée du Louvre) / Philipp Bernard: cat. 11

Pasadena, © The Norton Simon Foundation: fig. 11

Pesaro, Su gentile concessione del Comune di Pesaro / U.O. Beni e Attività Culturali: cat. 45

Potsdam, Prussian Palaces and Gardens Foundation Berlin-Brandenburg / Wolfgang Pfauder: fig. 13

Providence (RI), Courtesy of the RISD Museum: fig. 12

Raleigh, North Carolina Museum of Art: fig. 4

Remagen, © Arp Museum Bahnhof Rolandseck / Collection Rau für UNICEF, inv. no. GR 1.261: cat. 17

Rome, Galleria Borghese / photo: Mauro Coen: fig. 23

Rome, Galleria Colonna: cat. 42

Rome, Gallerie Nazionali di Arte Antica (MiC) – Bibliotheca Hertziana, Istituto Max Planck per la storia dell'arte / Enrico Fontolan: cat. 81, 86

St Petersburg, © The State Hermitage Museum / photo: Pavel Demidov: fig. 5

Sarasota, photo © The John and Mable Ringling Museum of Art, State Art Museum of Florida: fig. 95

Seville, Martín García Pérez: cat. 18

Stockholm, photo: Cecilia Heisser / Nationalmuseum: fig. 17; Nationalmuseum: fig. 41

Toledo, David Blázquez: cat. 26

© Gilberto Urbinati: cat. 63

Valladolid, Museo Nacional de Escultura, photo: Javier Muñoz and Paz Pastor: cat. 69

Vatican City, © Governorate of the Vatican City State – Directorate of the Vatican Museums: figs. 10, 51

Vienna, KHM-Museumsverband: fig. 26